1997-98

EVANGELICAL
SUNDAY SCHOOL
LESSON
COMMENTARY

FORTY-SIXTH ANNUAL VOLUME

Based on the

Evangelical Bible Lesson Series

Editorial Staff

James E. Humbertson—*EDITORIAL DIRECTOR*

Homer G. Rhea—*EDITOR IN CHIEF*

Kenneth T. Harvell—*GENERAL DIRECTOR OF
PUBLICATIONS*

Lesson Exposition Writers

J. Don Amison   Eugene C. Christenbury

Rodney Hodge   Oliver McMahan

Published by
PATHWAY PRESS
Cleveland, Tennessee

Lesson treatments in the *Evangelical Sunday School Lesson Commentary* for 1997-98 are based upon the outlines of the Evangelical Bible Lesson Series prepared by the Evangelical Curriculum Commission (formerly the Curriculum Commission of the National Sunday School Association).

Copyright 1997

PATHWAY PRESS, Cleveland, Tennessee
ISBN: 0-87148-976-7

Printed in the United States of America

TABLE OF CONTENTS

INTRODUCING THE 1997-98 COMMENTARY

The *Evangelical Sunday School Lesson Commentary* contains in a single volume a full study of the Sunday school lessons for the months beginning with September 1997 and running through August 1998. The 12 months of lessons draw from both the Old Testament and the New Testament in an effort to provide balance and establish relationship between these distinct but inspired writings. The lessons in this 1997-98 volume are drawn from the fifth year of a seven-year cycle, which will be completed in August 1999. (The cycle is printed in full on page 16 of this volume.)

The lessons for the *Evangelical Commentary* are based on the Evangelical Bible Lesson Series Outlines, prepared by the Evangelical Curriculum Commission. (The Evangelical Curriculum Commission is a member of the National Association of Evangelicals.) The lessons in this volume are drawn from the Old and New Testaments; and taken together with the other annual volumes of lessons in the cycle, they provide a valuable commentary on a wide range of Biblical subjects. Each quarter is divided into two or more units of study.

The 1997-98 commentary is the work of a team of Christian scholars and writers who have developed the volume under the supervision of Pathway Press. All the major writers, introduced on the following pages, represent a team of ministers committed to a strictly Evangelical interpretation of the Scriptures. The guiding theological principles of this commentary are expressed in the following statement of faith:

1. WE BELIEVE the Bible to be the inspired, the only infallible, authoritative Word of God.

2. WE BELIEVE that there is one God, eternally existing in three persons: Father, Son, and Holy Spirit.

3. WE BELIEVE in the deity of our Lord Jesus Christ, in His virgin birth, in His sinless life, in His miracles, in His vicarious and atoning death through His shed blood, in His bodily resurrection, in His ascension to the right hand of the Father, and in His personal return in power and glory.

4. WE BELIEVE that for the salvation of lost and sinful men, personal reception of the Lord Jesus Christ and regeneration by the Holy Spirit are absolutely essential.

5. WE BELIEVE in the present ministry of the Holy Spirit by whose cleansing and indwelling the Christian is enabled to live a godly life.

6. WE BELIEVE in the personal return of the Lord Jesus Christ.

7. WE BELIEVE in the resurrection of both the saved and the lost—they that are saved, unto the resurrection of life; and they that are lost, unto the resurrection of damnation.

8. WE BELIEVE in the spiritual unity of believers in our Lord Jesus Christ.

USING THE 1997-98 COMMENTARY

The *Evangelical Sunday School Lesson Commentary* for 1997-98 is presented to the reader with the hope that it will become his weekly companion through the months ahead.

The fall quarter 1997 continues a seven-year cycle of lessons which will be completed with the summer quarter 1999. The 28 quarters of studies, divided into two or more units each, draw from both the Old and New Testaments. Also a number of studies will be topical in nature as attention is focused on contemporary issues. A complete listing of the themes that will be included in the seven-year cycle is printed on page 16 of this volume.

Quarterly unit themes for the 1997-98 volume are as follows:

Fall Quarter—Unit One: "James and 1 and 2 Peter"; Unit Two: "Work of the Holy Spirit"

Winter Quarter—Unit One: "Celebrating Advent"; Unit Two: "Let's Study the Bible"; Unit Three: "God's Word in Psalm 119"

Spring Quarter—Unit One: "Book of Hebrews"; Unit Two: "Lessons From the Patriarchs"

Summer Quarter—Unit One: "Messages of Minor Prophets"; Unit Two: "Bible Answers to Current Issues."

The lesson sequence used in this volume is prepared by the Evangelical Curriculum Commission. (The Evangelical Curriculum Commission is a member of the National Association of Evangelicals.)

The specific material used in developing each lesson is written and edited under the guidance of the editorial staff of Pathway Press.

STUDY TEXT: At the opening of each week's lesson, you will see printed the study text. These ref- erences point out passages of Scripture that are directly related to the lesson, and it is advisable for you to read each one carefully before beginning the lesson study.

TIME and PLACE: A time and place is given for each lesson. Where there is a wide range of opinions regarding the exact time or place, the printed New Testament works of Merrill C. Tenney and Old Testament works of Samuel J. Schultz are used to provide the information.

PRINTED TEXT and CENTRAL TRUTH: The printed text is the body of Scripture designated each week for verse-by-verse study in the classroom. Drawing on the study text the teacher delves into this printed text, expounding its content to the students. Although the printed text contains different insights for each teacher, the central truth states the single unifying principle that the expositors attempted to clarify in each lesson.

DICTIONARY: A dictionary, which attempts to bring pronunciation and clarification to difficult words or phrases, is included with most lessons. Pronunciations are based on the phonetic system used by Field Enterprises Educational Corporation of Chicago and New York in *The World Book Encyclopedia.* Definitions are generally based on *The Pictorial Bible Dictionary,* published by Zondervan Publishing Company, Grand Rapids, Michigan.

EXPOSITION and LESSON OUT- LINE: The heart of this commentary—and probably the heart of the teacher's instruction each week—is the exposition of the printed text. This exposition material is preceded by a lesson outline, which indicates how the material is to be divided for study. These lesson outlines are not exhaustive but, rather, provide a skeleton for the teacher to amplify upon and to build around.

REVIEW and DISCUSSION QUESTIONS: Immediately following the expository material in each lesson are five review questions. These questions are designed as discussion starters, along with the discussion questions appearing throughout the expository material. The review questions also serve to restate the major bits of information in the text and may be supplemented by questions of your own drawn from the expository material.

GOLDEN TEXT HOMILY: The golden text homily for each week is a brief reflection on that single verse. As the word *homily* implies, it is a discourse or sermon on a particular point. The homily may often be used effectively to give the lesson a life-related slant.

SENTENCE SERMONS: Two or more sentence sermons—popular and pithy single-line thoughts on the central truth of the lesson—are included each week.

EVANGELISM APPLICATION: The evangelism application relates the general theme of the week's lesson to the ongoing task of evangelism. The theme of the lesson (but not necessarily of the lesson text) is used to make this application. At times the emphasis of the section bears on direct evangelism of class members who may not be Christians; at other times the emphasis bears upon exhorting the class members to become more involved in evangelizing others.

ILLUMINATING THE LESSON: In this section, illustrative material is provided for the teacher to use to support the lesson at whatever point seems most appropriate.

DAILY BIBLE READINGS: The daily Bible readings are included for the teacher to use in his own devotions throughout the week, as well as to share with members of his class.

EXPOSITION WRITERS

Writers for the expository materials for the 1997-98 volume are as follows:

The lesson expositions for the fall quarter (September, October, November) were prepared by the Reverend Dr. Eugene C. Christenbury (B.A., M.A., M.S., Ed.D.).

Dr. Christenbury earned his bachelor of arts and master of arts degrees at George Peabody College for Teachers and his doctorate of education from the University of Tennessee. He also earned the M.S. degree in religion from the Church of God School of Theology, Cleveland, Tennessee. An ordained minister in the Church of God, Dr. Christenbury has served as state youth and Christian education director, pastor, and assistant superintendent at the Home for Children in Sevierville, Tennessee. He is retired after serving as senior adjunct professor of education at Lee College, Cleveland, Tennessee.

Dr. Christenbury is a member of Phi Delta Kappa and the Council on Public Education of Religious Studies. Recognized for his academic and religious knowledge, he is a popular speaker on the Lee College campus and in the broader church community.

Lesson expositions for the winter quarter (December, January, February) were written by the Reverend J. Don Amison (A.S., M.Div.). Reverend Amison is an ordained minister of the Church of God who has served in numerous pastoral and leadership roles both in the United States and in foreign countries. He is a graduate of DeKalb College and the Church of God School of Theology.

Reverend Amison is best known for pioneering the Ministry to Military in Europe—a work that was the foundation and model for the Church of God's vast Ministry to the Military worldwide. He is founding editor of *On Guard* magazine, a periodical that has shared Christ with America's military men and women for more than 35 years. He is also a recognized wordsmith throughout the Pentecostal community.

Lesson expositions for the spring quarter (March, April, May) were written by the Reverend Dr. Oliver McMahan (B.A., M.Div., D.Min.).

The Reverend Dr. McMahan is former dean of students and associate professor at Northwest Bible College, Minot, North Dakota. Presently, he is associate professor of pastoral studies and director of external studies at the School of Theology, Cleveland, Tennessee. He is a graduate of West Coast Bible College and of Brite Divinity School at Texas Christian University.

An ordained minister in the Church of God, Dr. McMahan has served his denomination as pastor, educator, and personal counselor. From 1976-1981 he served as minister of youth and outreach at the Oak Cliff Church of God in Dallas, Texas.

Dr. McMahan has written a number of articles for the *Church of God Evangel* and is a contributor of definitions and articles for the *Complete Biblical Library*.

Dr. McMahan is a member of the Evangelical Theological Society and the Association for Clinical Pastoral Education.

Lesson expositions for the summer quarter (June, July, August) were written by the Reverend Rodney Hodge, an ordained minister who has served as minister of music for 24 years at Northwood Temple Pentecostal Holiness Church in Fayetteville, North Carolina. He holds degrees from Emmanuel College and the University of Georgia and did graduate studies in history at the University of Georgia.

Reverend Hodge has written numerous Bible study programs, as well as dramas and music productions, and has produced an entire series of theater productions for church use.

The Reverend Hodge presently writes adult Sunday school literature for the International Pentecostal Holiness Church.

GOLDEN TEXT HOMILY WRITERS
1997-98

French L. Arrington, Ph.D.
Professor of New Testament Greek and
  Exegesis
Church of God School of Theology
Cleveland, Tennessee

Richard Y. Bershon, Ph.D.
Chaplain, State Veterans Home
Hot Springs, South Dakota

Noel Brooks, D.D. (Retired)
Writer, *Adult Sunday School Teacher
  Quarterly*
International Pentecostal Holiness Church
Oklahoma City, Oklahoma

Karl W. Bunkley, D.D. (Retired)
Former General Sunday School President
International Pentecostal Holiness Church
Oklahoma City, Oklahoma

Eugene C. Christenbury, Ed.D. (Retired)
Former Faculty Member at Lee College
Cleveland, Tennessee

Jerald Daffe, D.Min.
Associate Professor/Pastorial Studies and
  Chairman/Department of Bible and
  Christian Ministries
Lee College
Cleveland, Tennessee

Harvey L. Davis
Retired Consultant
Jackson, Mississippi

James L. Durel, Captain
The Salvation Army
Vacaville, California

Thomas Griffith, Jr., D.Min.
Pastor, Church of God
Porterville, California

Joel Harris
Pastor, Church of God
Mobile, Alabama

Willie F. Lawrence, D.D.
Pastor, Church of God
Danville, Illinois

F.J. May, D.Min., Professor
Church of God School of Theology
Cleveland, Tennessee

William R. McCall
Missionary, Church of God
Cleveland, Tennessee

Aaron D. Mize, Clinical Chaplain
Alcohol and Drug Treatment Center
Parchman, Mississippi

Levy E. Moore, Mayor
City of Franklin Springs
Franklin Springs, Georgia

Richard L. Pace, Chaplain (MAJ)
Command and Staff College
Fort Leavenworth, Kansas

Ronald M. Padgett
Director of Chaplaincy Services
Mississippi Department of Corrections
Parchman, Mississippi

Luther E. Painter, D.Min.
Assistant Professor of Religion
Lee College
Cleveland, Tennessee

O.W. Polen, D.D.
Coordinator of Special Projects
Pathway Press
Cleveland, Tennessee

Wayne S. Proctor
Former Pastor
Harrisburg, Illinois

Jerry Puckett
Customer Service Representative
Pathway Press
Cleveland, Tennessee

John J. Secret (Major)
Senior Protestant Chaplain
Grissom Air Force Bace
Grissom, Indiana

Marion H. Starr, Pastor
Church of God
Marion, South Carolina

Michael S. Stewart, Senior Pastor
First Assembly of God
Raleigh, North Carolina

Robert B. Thomas, Vice President
Church of God School of Theology
Cleveland, Tennessee

Dennis W. Watkins
Director of Legal Services
Church of God International Offices
Cleveland, Tennessee

Fred H. Whisman (Lt. Col.)
Group II Chaplain
Civil Air Patrol
Chattanooga, Tennessee

Charles G. Wiley, Pastor
Church of God
Graham, Texas

Eugene Wigelsworth, M.S.W., M.Div.
Senior Chaplain, Pasquotank Corr. Inst.
Elizabeth City, North Carolina

Florie Brown Wigelsworth, M.Div.
Elizabeth City, North Carolina

Sabord Woods, Ph.D.
Professor of English
Lee College
Cleveland, Tennessee

SCRIPTURE TEXTS USED IN LESSON EXPOSITION

Genesis

1:	27	August 9
2:	7	August 16
2:	21-24	August 9
3:	15	December 7
5:	1, 2	August 30
9:	5, 6	August 16
10:	1, 31, 32	August 30
12:	4-7	April 19
13:	8-17	April 19
14:	14-16	May 3
15:	1-6	April 26
17:	1, 7-10	April 26
18:	17-25, 32, 33	May 3
21:	1-5	April 26
25:	27-34	May 10
27:	34, 35, 41	May 10
33:	4, 8-11	May 10
39:	7-12, 20-23	May 17
41:	38, 41-43	May 17
45:	1, 8-14	May 24
50:	15-21	May 24

Exodus

1:	15-17, 20	August 16
20:	13	August 16
20:	14	August 9

Deuteronomy

4:	2	January 25
6:	4-9	January 18
18:	15	December 7

Joshua

1:	8	January 11

Job

23:	12	January 11
27:	4-6	August 2
33:	4	August 16

Psalm

1:	1, 2	January 11
18:	30	January 25
19:	7-14	January 4
24:	3-5	August 2
119:	1-16	February 1
119:	25-40	February 8
119:	49, 50, 57-64, 73-80, 89-94	February 15
119:	105-112	February 8
119:	113-120, 161-176	February 22
139:	13-16	August 16

Proverbs

4:	23-27	August 2
30:	5, 6	January 25

Isaiah

5:	20-23	July 26
7:	14	December 7
9:	6, 7	December 7
53:	3-6	December 7

Jeremiah

15:	16	January 11

Hosea

4:	1-6, 15-19	June 7
6:	1-3	June 7

Joel

1:	11, 12, 14	June 14
2:	12, 13, 18-21, 23, 27-29	June 14

Amos

8:	4-7, 9-11	June 21

Obadiah

1:	17, 18, 21	June 28

Jonah

3:	1-5, 10	June 28

Micah

2:	1-3	July 5
3:	9-11	July 5
5:	2	December 7
6:	9-15	July 5
7:	18, 19	July 5

Nahum

1:	2, 3, 7-9	June 28

Habbakuk

1:	1-4	July 12
2:	1-4, 20	July 12
3:	16-19	July 12

Haggai

1:	2-9	July 19

2 Peter (Cont)
1: 19-21   January 4
3: 1-14   October 26

1 John
2: 9-11   August 30

3: 6, 7   November 16
4: 20, 21   August 30

Revelation
20: 10   November 2

SCRIPTURE TEXTS USED IN GOLDEN TEXT HOMILIES

Genesis
18: 19   May 3
50: 20   May 24

Exodus
20: 3   July 19
20: 13   August 16

Psalm
86: 7   July 12
107: 19, 20   May 10
119: 9   February 1
119: 50   February 15
119: 105   February 8
119: 117   February 22

Proverbs
3: 7   July 26
11: 3   August 2

Isaiah
7: 14   December 7

Lamentations
3: 22   July 5

Hosea
6: 1   June 7
Joel
2: 13   June 14

Nahum
1: 3   June 28

Zechariah
7: 9   June 21

Matthew
1: 23   December 14

Luke
2: 20   December 28
12: 15   August 23

John
1: 14   December 21
3: 6   November 9
16: 8   November 2
16: 13   November 23

Acts
1: 8   November 30
2: 39   May 31

Romans
4: 20   April 26
8: 28   May 17

1 Corinthians
15: 20   April 12

Ephesians
5: 3   August 9

1 Thessalonians
5: 23   November 16

2 Timothy
2: 15   January 11
3: 16   January 4
4: 2   January 25

Hebrews
3: 1   March 1
4: 16   March 8
7: 25   March 15
10: 16   March 22
11: 6   March 29
11: 8   April 19
12: 14   April 5

James
1: 12   September 7
1: 22   January 18
2: 26   September 14
3: 13   September 21
4: 8   September 28

1 Peter
1: 13   October 5
2: 9   October 12

2 Peter
1: 3   October 19
3: 11   October 26

1 John
4: 20   August 30

ACKNOWLEDGMENTS

Many books, magazines, and newspapers have been used in the research that has gone into this 1997-98 *Evangelical Commentary*. A few of the major books that have been used are listed below.

Bibles

King James Version, Oxford University Press, Oxford, England
New American Standard Bible (NASB), A.J. Holman Co., Publishers, New York, New York
New Century Bible, Word Publishing, Dallas Texas
New English Bible (NEB), Oxford University Press, Oxford, England
New International Version (NIV), Zondervan Publishing House, Grand Rapids, Michigan
New King James Version, *(NKJV)* Thomas Nelson Publisher, Nashville, Tennessee
The Berkeley Version, Zondervan Publishing House, Grand Rapids, Michigan

Commentaries

Clarke's Commentary, Abingdon-Cokesbury, Nashville, Tennessee
Commentaries on the Old Testament (Keil & Delitzsch), Eerdmans Publishing Co., Grand Rapids, Michigan
Ellicott's Bible Commentary, Zondervan Publishing House, Grand Rapids, Michigan
Expositions of Holy Scriptures (Alexander MacLaren), Eerdmans Publishing Co., Grand Rapids, Michigan
The Broadman Bible Commentary, Volumes 10 and 11, Broadman Press, Nashville, Tennessee
The Expositor's Greek Testament, Eerdmans Publishing Co., Grand Rapids, Michigan
The Interpreter's Bible, Abingdon Press, New York, New York
The Letters to the Corinthians, William Barclay, Westminster Press, Philadelphia, Pennsylvania
The Pulpit Commentary, Eerdmans Publishing Co., Grand Rapids, Michigan
The Wesleyan Commentary, Eerdmans Publishing Co., Grand Rapids, Michigan

Illustrations

Dictionary of Illustrations for Pulpit and Platform, Moody Press, Chicago, Illinois
I Quote, George W. Stewart Publishers, Inc., New York, New York
Knight's Master Book of New Illustrations, Eerdmans Publishing Co., Grand Rapids, Michigan
Notes and Quotes, The Warner Press, Anderson, Indiana
1,000 New Illustrations, Al Bryant, Zondervan Publishing Co., Grand Rapids, Michigan
Quotable Quotations, Scripture Press Publications, Wheaton, Illinois
The Encyclopedia of Religious Quotations, Fleming H. Revell Co., Old Tappan, New Jersey
The Pointed Pen, Pathway Press, Cleveland, Tennessee
The Speaker's Sourcebook, Zondervan Publishing House, Grand Rapids, Michigan
3,000 Illustrations for Christian Service, Eerdmans Publishing Co., Grand Rapids, Michigan

General Reference Books

Harper's Bible Dictionary, Harper and Brothers Publishers, New York, New York
Pictorial Dictionary of the Bible, Zondervan Publishing House, Grand Rapids, Michigan
The International Standard Bible Encyclopedia, Eerdmans Publishing Co., Grand Rapids, Michigan
The Interpreter's Dictionary of the Bible, Abingdon Press, Nashville, Tennessee
The World Book Encyclopedia, Field Enterprises Education Corp., Chicago, Illinois
Word Pictures in the New Testament (Robertson), Broadman Press, Nashville, Tennessee

Evangelical Bible Lesson Series (1992-1999)

Fall Quarter September, October, November	Winter Quarter December, January, February	Spring Quarter March, April, May	Summer Quarter June, July, August
1992 Unit One—Personalities in Genesis Unit Two—Psalms, Proverbs and Ecclesiastes	**1992-93** Unit One—Following Jesus Unit Two—Evangelism	**1993** Unit One—Building Positive Relationships Unit Two—Life and Teachings of Moses	**1993** Unit One—The Church Is Launched Unit Two—Ministry in the Church
1993 Unit One—Learning From Israel's Experiences Unit Two—Living in Today's World	**1993-94** Unit One—The Gospel According to John Unit Two—Christian Growth	**1994** Unit One—Covenants in the Bible Unit Two—Joshua and Ruth	**1994** Unit One—Understanding Cultism Unit Two—Spiritual Revival and Renewal Unit Three—Ezra, Nehemiah, Ruth
1994 Unit One—Truths From Romans Unit Two—Spiritual Warfare	**1994-95** Unit One—Mosaic Law and New Testament Counterparts Unit Two—Worship in the OT and NT	**1995** Unit One—1 & 2 Corinthians Unit Two—Strengthening Marriage and Family Ties	**1995** Unit One—Principles of Godly Leadership Unit Two—Christian Values
1995 Unit One—Galatians and Ephesians Unit Two—Christian Fellowship	**1995-96** Unit One—Wisdom Literature Unit Two—Building a Consistent Devotional Life	**1996** Unit One—Triumphing Over Life's Crises Unit Two—Philippians and Colossians	**1996** Unit One—Isaiah Unit Two—God's Providential Care
1996 Unit One—Insights from 1 & 2 Timothy, Titus Unit Two—Ministering to One Another	**1996-97** Unit One—Christ in Prophecy Unit Two—Teachings from Ezekiel and Daniel	**1997** Unit One—Teachings of Jesus Unit Two—Basic Christian Truths	**1997** Unit One—God's Word for Difficult Times Unit Two—Servanthood
1997 Unit One—James, 1 & 2 Peter Unit Two—Work of the Spirit	**1997-98** Unit One—Celebrating Advent Unit Two—God's Word in Psalm 119	**1998** Unit One—The Book of Hebrews Unit Two—Lessons From the Patriarchs	**1998** Unit One—Messages of Minor Prophets Unit Two—Bible Answers to Current Issues
1998 Unit One—Life and Teachings of Paul Unit Two—Help for Life's Journey	**1998-99** Unit One—God's Plan of Redemption Unit Two—Truths From the Tabernacle	**1999** Unit One—People Who Met Jesus Unit Two—Personal Evangelism	**1999** Unit One—Understanding Revelation Unit Two—The Mission of the Church

September marks the fall quarter and the beginning of a series of lessons divided into two distinct units of study. Unit One (lessons 1-8) is presented under the theme "James, 1 and 2 Peter." The Book of James, like Proverbs in the Old Testament, deals with practical application of truth to everyday situations. In vivid language it sets forth the ethical requirements of the Christian life. First Peter shows Christians how to live out their redemption even in a hostile world. Salvation may involve suffering, but it brings a hope also, as the grace of God is amplified in the individual's life. In 2 Peter, the emphasis is on the merits of true knowledge given by God.

Unit Two (lessons 9-13) is presented under the theme "Work of the Holy Spirit." As the title implies, the lessons remind and challenge us to be thankful and submissive to what the Holy Spirit is leading us into. Both units of study are certain to draw the honest Bible scholar to a closer relationship with Christ.

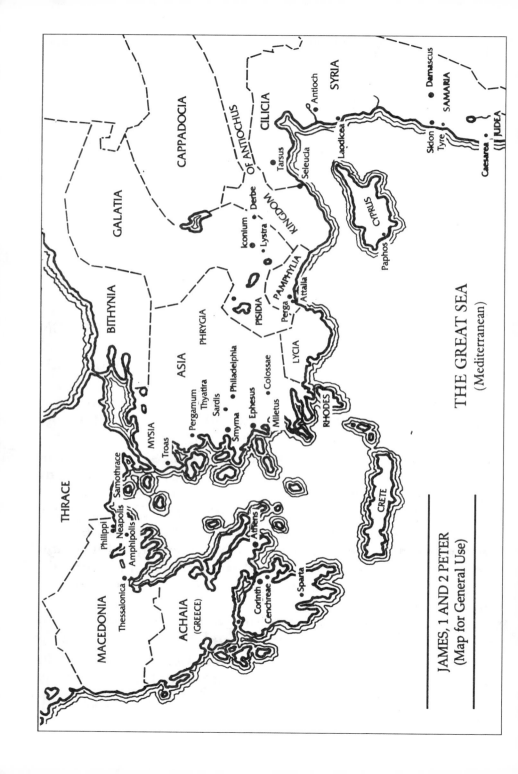

THE GREAT SEA
(Mediterranean)

JAMES, 1 AND 2 PETER
(Map for General Use)

Victory Over Temptation

Study Text: James 1:1-27

Objective: To recognize that all Christians experience temptation and overcome sin by obeying God's Word.

Time: The Book of James was probably written between A.D. 48 and 50.

Place: The Book of James was probably written at Jerusalem.

Golden Text: Blessed is the man that endureth temptation: for when he is tried, he shall receive the crown of life, which the Lord hath promised to them that love him" (James 1:12).

Central Truth: The believer has victory over temptation through obedience to God's Word.

Evangelism Emphasis: Accepting Christ as Savior is the first step to overcoming sin.

PRINTED TEXT

James 1:2. My brethren, count it all joy when ye fall into divers temptations;

3. Knowing this, that the trying of your faith worketh patience.

4. But let patience have her perfect work, that ye may be perfect and entire, wanting nothing.

5. If any of you lack wisdom, let him ask of God, that giveth to all men liberally, and upbraideth not; and it shall be given him.

6. But let him ask in faith, nothing wavering. For he that wavereth is like a wave of the sea driven with the wind and tossed.

7. For let not that man think that he shall receive any thing of the Lord.

8. A double minded man is unstable in all his ways.

12. Blessed is the man that endureth temptation: for when he is tried, he shall receive the crown of life, which the Lord hath promised to them that love him.

13. Let no man say when he is tempted, I am tempted of God: for God cannot be tempted with evil, neither tempteth he any man:

14. But every man is tempted, when he is drawn away of his own lust, and enticed.

15. Then when lust hath conceived, it bringeth forth sin: and sin, when it is finished, bringeth forth death.

19. Wherefore, my beloved brethren, let every man be swift to hear, slow to speak, slow to wrath:

20. For the wrath of man worketh not the righteousness of God.

21. Wherefore lay apart all filthiness and superfluity of

naughtiness, and receive with meekness the engrafted word, which is able to save your souls.

22. But be ye doers of the word, and not hearers only, deceiving your own selves.

23. **For if any be a hearer of the word, and not a doer, he is like unto a man beholding his natural face in a glass:**

24. For he beholdeth himself, and goeth his way, and straightway forgetteth what manner of man he was.

25. **But whose looketh into the perfect law of liberty, and continueth therein, he being not a forgetful hearer, but a doer of the work, this man shall be blessed in his deed.**

LESSON OUTLINE

I. ENDURE TEMPTATION
   A. Author
   B. Resources
   C. Reward

II. UNDERSTAND TEMPTA-TION
   A. Facts
   B. Focus

III. OVERCOME TEMPTATION
   A. Preparation
   B. Response

LESSON EXPOSITION

INTRODUCTION

The Book of James was slow in gaining canonical recognition, but there can be no doubt that it is inspired Scripture. Eastern church Fathers (Origen, Cyril of Jerusalem, Athanasius, Jerome, and Augustine) accepted its authenticity well before Western church leaders did. It did not gain general recognition as a genuine canonical book until the Council of Carthage (A.D. 397). Among the possible reasons given for the delay in acceptance is its apparent contradiction of Paul's writings concerning the relation-ship of faith to works. Also, since James was not well known outside Palestine, the fact that he wrote an early book to Jewish Christians might have caused some Gentile churches to be opposed to it.

In the contemporary setting, both liberals and Evangelicals have tended to neglect the Book of James. The Pauline writings have received much emphasis (and rightly so), but James and other New Testament epistles also have much to say to modern Christians. In fact, the Book of James speaks to a current need which is the focus of our lesson today—victory over temptation.

I. ENDURE TEMPTATION
(James 1:1-12)

A. Author (v. 1)

(James 1:1 is not included in the printed text.)

Verse 1 presents a simple, unimposing introduction to the author of the book. He could perhaps have boosted his ego by saying, "I am James, the brother of Jesus Christ, the founder of the church, and the first Bishop." That would undoubtedly have made people stand up and take notice. But instead, he simply said in essence, "I am James, a servant of God and of the Lord Jesus Christ."

Who was James? Paul called him "the Lord's brother" (Galatians 1:19), the son of Joseph and Mary, and thus, according to the flesh, a half brother of Jesus. Matthew listed him first in a group of four brothers of Jesus (13:55). Apparently he was the oldest son of Joseph and Mary after the virgin birth of Jesus.

Many think that James was not a believer in Jesus before His death. This is based on the fact that John said, "Neither did his brethren believe in him" (John 7:5). However, after seeing the death and resurrection of Jesus, James, along with other brothers, became a firm believer and was a participant in the prayer meeting which took place between the Ascension and Pentecost (Acts 1:13, 14). According to the Book of Acts, James soon rose to a position of leadership in the Jerusalem church. At the time of the great council of Acts 15, James was the recognized leader of the body of believers. In fact, Paul spoke of James as one of the "pillars" of the church (Galatians 2:9).

James' letter is addressed to "the twelve tribes which are scattered abroad." These were primarily, but not altogether, Jewish Christians. Many who came from Jerusalem had been members of the mother church and had fled from Jerusalem because of Saul's persecution. Since so many of them knew James personally, they felt close to the Jerusalem church.

B. Resources (vv. 2-11)

(James 1:9-11 is not included in the printed text.)

2. My brethren, count it all joy when ye fall into divers temptations.

All human beings are beset by adversity. Battered and depressed Job sighed, "Man . . . is short-lived and full of turmoil" (Job 14:1, NASB). David, who enjoyed an enviable closeness with God, confessed, "Many are the afflictions of the righteous" (Psalm 34:19). And Paul explained, "We are afflicted in every way . . . perplexed . . . persecuted . . . struck down" (2 Corinthians 4:8, 9, NASB). It has been said that to trace Paul's journeys in the first century would be like tracking the path of a wounded deer running from a hunter, leaving one bloody trail after another.

According to James the believer is to expect trials. He did not say, "If you fall into various trials" but "when you fall into various trials" (NKJV). The new believer is in for a shock if he expects the Christian life to be easy. Even Jesus gave His followers a strange promise, "In the world ye shall have tribulation" (John 16:33). And Paul said, "Yea, and all that live godly in Christ Jesus shall suffer persecution" (2 Timothy 3:12). Paul also said, "We must through much tribulation enter into the kingdom of God" (Acts 14:22). Christians have found this to be true. We are surrounded by many and varied trials. How then should we react to them? James said to "count it all joy." In the verses that follow he tells us how and why we can do this.

3. Knowing this, that the trying of your faith worketh patience.

4. But let patience have her perfect work, that ye may be perfect and entire, wanting nothing.

Through trials faith is developed

into constancy and brave perseverance. Faith produces strong character as it is tested and impurities are removed. Christians can therefore rejoice because of this and not feel sorry for themselves. Christians should regard trials as tests of faith. The New Testament compares the suffering of trials to the process of testing gold. However, faith is not cold metal to be weighed and subjected to strong acids; it is living, vital. The testing of faith produces patience.

Patience has been called a noble word which always has a background of manliness. The patient man is one who, under siege of trials, bears up and does not lose heart. His faith is genuine and, because it is living, grows with every test. The patient man is one who, encountering difficult individuals, does not allow himself to be easily provoked or to blaze in anger.

The phrase "lacking in nothing" (*NASB*) means neither coming short of the goal nor having one or the other part still missing in us. Trials do something necessary and blessed for our faith. When viewed in this way, it is a joy to see that trials test our faith for possible weak spots in order to make us genuine and to mature us in our relationship to God.

5. If any of you lack wisdom, let him ask of God, that giveth to all men liberally, and upbraideth not; and it shall be given him.

6. But let him ask in faith, nothing wavering. For he that wavereth is like a wave of the sea driven with the wind and tossed.

7. For let not that man think that he shall receive any thing of the Lord.

8. A double minded man is unstable in all his ways.

Three things are listed by James as necessary for coping with trials: wisdom, prayer, and faith. These are not only needed, but they are also available through God's generous provision.

James did not say, "If any of you lack knowledge, let him ask of God." God does not offer knowledge—He expects us to obtain that through work and study—but He does offer wisdom. The Christian needs to see his trials in a true light and make appropriate use of them.

James was not referring to worldly astuteness but to divine wisdom. He described it as "pure, then peaceable, gentle, and easy to be intreated, full of mercy and good fruits, without partiality" (3:17). He also described worldly wisdom as "earthly, sensual, and devilish" (v. 15). Divine wisdom is indispensable if we are to triumph over trials. How do we obtain this wisdom? Simply ask God.

James underscored the generosity of God. He gives to all men liberally; it is His disposition to give. He gives unconditionally, without bargaining, without any of the imperfections which mar human giving.

James emphasized in verses 7 and 8 that if faith is lacking and the heart wavers in unbelief, it is useless to ask of God. The person lacking faith must not expect to receive anything from the Lord. A doubting, wavering attitude is fatal to effectiveness in prayer. Faith unlocks the divine storehouse; unbelief bars the door. The double-minded person dishonors God and insults Him by wavering and doubting the truth of His Word, treating Him as unworthy of confidence.

The believer who is subjected to

trials learns to appreciate true values. Appearances are often deceptive. The Christian who is poor can nevertheless be spiritually rich, and he should rejoice in his spiritual wealth. And the Christian who is rich should rejoice to learn of the riches of humility in Christ's service. Earthly riches fade like flowers, but spiritual riches abide forever. Appreciation of true values will enable the Christian to endure physical hardship with spiritual intelligence and joy.

C. Reward (v. 12)

12. Blessed is the man that endureth temptation: for when he is tried, he shall receive the crown of life, which the Lord hath promised to them that love him.

The man who successfully endures invitations to evil is pronounced "blessed" or "happy." By turning from such temptation, he demonstrates his purity of heart and that he really loves God; therefore he is promised "the crown of life," with which God will some day reward all those who have truly loved Him.

Why do trials overwhelm us?

II. UNDERSTAND TEMPTATION (James 1:13-18)

A. Facts (vv. 13-16)

(James 1:16 is not included in the printed text.)

13. Let no man say when he is tempted, I am tempted of God: for God cannot be tempted with evil, neither tempteth he any man.

The temptations the apostle dealt with in verses 2-12 have the sense of outward trials. This includes troubles and afflictions of every kind. In verses 13-15 he dealt with temptation as inward enticement to evil. A close connection exists between the two. Outward testings are often the occasion for inward temptations to evil. This seems especially true when one fails outward testing. The result may be a stirring up of evil impulses and desires and the committing of open sin against God.

Who is responsible when temptation comes? Is God implicated in any way? The New Testament teaches that there is a natural history in the moral world as well as in the physical world—"the law of the Spirit of life in Christ Jesus" and "the law of sin and death" (Romans 8:2).

Some assign the origin of temptation to God. This theory has roots as far back as the Garden of Eden. Our first parents blamed God for the first sin. The world has adopted the same excuse, in various forms, ever since. Some believe that their misdeeds are necessitated by divine decrees. Some blame their human nature for their sins; they say God is responsible for the origin of their corrupt nature. Others trace their sins to their circumstances, blaming God for surrounding them with evil influences which place them under what they feel is the inevitable necessity to sin.

James used reason and logic against those who would blame God for temptation and sin. Think, he said, of the purity and perfection of God's nature. Moral evil has no place in God. There is nothing in Him that sin can take hold of. And if He is not Himself open to the seductions of sin, then it is impossible for Him to be a tempter of others. God is the infinite light. In contrast, sin is darkness. God is the eternal righteousness; sin is crookedness. God is undiminished, unchangeable beauty; sin is deformity.

14. But every man is tempted, when he is drawn away of his own lust, and enticed.

According to James, temptation originates within the heart of man himself. His attempts to blame his Creator are in vain. A person sins only when he is enticed by the bait and drawn away by the hook of his own lust. This means the power which seduces toward evil is the corrupt nature within us. The world and the devil can tempt effectually only when they stir up the filthy pool of depraved personal desire. Besides the appetites of the body, lust includes the evil dispositions of the mind, such as pride, malice, envy, vanity, and love of ease. Any appeal made from without to these vile principles and affections can be successful only with the consent of the will. Every man is personally responsible for his own sin, for each man's sin is the result of his own lust.

15. Then when lust hath conceived, it bringeth forth sin: and sin, when it is finished, bringeth forth death.

Within all of us are evil desires, ready to express themselves in action. The evil desire, vitalized by the will, produces sin. Thomas á Kempis put it this way: "First comes to mind a simple thought, then a strong imagination, afterwards delight and an evil movement and assent." Thus, evil is the product of desire. Furthermore, this evil becomes the producer of death. Here is a double birth: lust brings forth sin and sin brings forth death. Desire, sin, death. Man alone is to blame for yielding to desire and sin, which brings death. This is the truth about the origin of sin and its results—death.

"Do not be deceived, my beloved brethren" (v. 16, *NKJV*). James gave a specific warning. He did not want his "beloved brethren" in the Lord to be deceived. Whatever you do, do not become so warped in your thinking that you accuse the God who sent His Son to die for us of originating temptation and sin and death. This is the exact opposite of the truth.

B. Focus (vv. 17, 18)

(James 1:17, 18 is not included in the printed text.)

Instead of attributing evil to God, let us realize that our heavenly Father sends only good things to us. Everything good proceeds from Him. "Every good gift and every perfect gift is from above, and cometh down from the Father of lights, with whom is no variableness, neither shadow of turning" (v. 17).

James once again calls our attention to the giving God. He is called "the Father of lights," perhaps an allusion to God as creator of the marvelous heavenly lights. Light speaks of purity and holiness, and these heavenly bodies, brilliant and wonderful as they are, but feebly represent the glorious light of the great Creator himself.

But these physical lights are subject to variations of light and darkness. Even the shining sun has its spots. But there are no spots—no variableness—within the perfect light of the great Creator. "Shadow of turning" could be understood as the shadow mark cast from a heavenly body in its turning or revolution, such as when the moon is eclipsed by the earth, and the sun by the moon. Even the greatest of created things may change—but God never!

In verse 18, James points us to the greatest gift of all: this sovereign and omnipotent God, of His own free will, chose us to be heirs of eternal life through faith in His Son. He confirmed this choice by sending His Son—"the word of truth." And when we believed the Word, He regenerated us—we were born again.

Why did God deal this way with us? "That we should be a kind of firstfruits of his creatures" (v. 18). Paul said we are "created in Christ Jesus unto good works, which God hath before ordained that we should walk in them" (Ephesians 2:10).

In speaking of our being firstfruits, James was referring to the Old Testament practice of bringing the first sheaf of the new crop of grain harvested, together with a sacrifice, for presentation in the Levitical ceremony in the Temple on the day after the Passover Sabbath. By this act, acknowledgment was made that all came from God and belonged to Him. None of the harvest was to be used for food until this ceremony of gratitude had been performed.

The firstfruits were also a representative sample of the bounteous harvest of golden grain which would follow. Firstfruits imply "afterfruits." They give assurance that the harvest is coming. In similar fashion, Paul referred to Christ as "the firstfruits of them that slept" (1 Corinthians 15:20). In His resurrection we see what God will eventually do for all believers.

How can believers better understand temptation?

III. OVERCOME TEMPTATION
(James 1:19-27)

A. Preparation (vv. 19-21)

19. Wherefore, my beloved brethren, let every man be swift to hear, slow to speak, slow to wrath:

20. For the wrath of man worketh not the righteousness of God.

21. Wherefore lay apart all filthiness and superfluity of naughtiness, and receive with meekness the engrafted word, which is able to save your souls.

As one matures in the Christian life and in the Word, he is more able to cope with trials and temptations. The Word is a dominant factor in maintaining, disciplining, and maturing the life which it originates.

It is important that we develop attitudes and actions favorable to the realization of the saving power that is made known to us through the Word of truth. With this in view, these verses contain four admonitions, each touching a deeper part of our nature than the one preceding. We must have a quick ear (swift to hear), a cautious tongue (slow to speak), a calm temper (slow to wrath), and a pure heart. Further, we are to receive and obey the Word of God. It is to be engrafted, or implanted, in our hearts, that it may save our souls.

B. Response (vv. 22-27)

(James 1:26, 27 is not included in the printed text.)

22. But be ye doers of the word, and not hearers only, deceiving your own selves.

23. For if any be a hearer of the word, and not a doer, he is like unto a man beholding his natural face in a glass:

24. For he beholdeth himself, and goeth his way, and straightway forgetteth what manner of man he was.

25. But whoso looketh into the perfect law of liberty, and continueth therein, he being not a forgetful hearer, but a doer of the work, this man shall be blessed in his deed.

Hearing the Word is not enough. The hearing must be converted into action, lest we deceive ourselves. The mere hearer is like the man who glances in the mirror only to soon forget what he saw. But the doer is like the one who looks carefully into the mirror of revelation, which has become his freely accepted law of life; sees what needs to be done; and does it. It is a law of liberty to him, which he gladly obeys, not because of legal requirements, but from a compulsion of love for his Savior and Lord (*Proclaiming the New Testament*).

What are some of the best ways to prepare yourself to overcome temptation?

REVIEW QUESTIONS

1. How did James describe himself?

2. To whom did James write his letter?

3. How did James say a Christian should accept trials?

4. How did James describe the man who doubts?

5. According to James, what are the steps in the downward spiral of succumbing to temptation?

GOLDEN TEXT HOMILY

"BLESSED IS THE MAN THAT ENDURETH TEMPTATION: FOR WHEN HE IS TRIED, HE SHALL RECEIVE THE CROWN OF LIFE, WHICH THE LORD HATH PROMISED TO THEM THAT LOVE HIM" (James 1:12).

It is clear that James considered trials and testings as norms for the Christian life. He had already stated that "the trying of your faith worketh patience [perseverance]" (James 1:3). The word *endure* is most often used to indicate an ongoing experience rather than a onetime test. Jesus said, "He that endureth to the end shall be saved" (Matthew 10:22). The word *endureth* is the same one James used and the same one Paul used in Romans 12:12, "patient in tribulation"—*patient* and *endure* being the same word. We as Christians tend to think of our trials in terms of episodes or incidents, and it is true that sometimes there are specific testing periods. But actually, we are in a continuous state of trial, for to live where Satan is "the prince of the power of the air" (Ephesians 2:2) is to be surrounded by the potential to do evil. To regard the Christian life in this way may seem negative, but this is one of those unique paradoxes found in the Christian experience where even testing produces joy (James 1:2; 2 Corinthians 7:4) and is of inestimable value. The promise of the eternal reward ought to help us endure the temporal trials, as is so beautifully expressed in 1 Peter 1:6, 7.—**Thomas Griffith, Jr., D.Min., Pastor, Lindsay, California**

SENTENCE SERMONS

THE BELIEVER has victory over temptation through obedience to God's Word.

—Selected

WHAT YOU DO in the hour of temptation will depend upon what you were the day before.

—Bob Jones

PATIENCE IS a bitter plant that produces sweet fruit.

—*Inspiring Quotations*

TEMPTATIONS are never so dangerous as when they come to us in religious garb.

—Dwight L. Moody

EVANGELISM APPLICATION

ACCEPTING CHRIST AS SAVIOR IS THE FIRST STEP TO OVERCOMING SIN.

There is hardly any power in the mechanical world greater than that of the wedge. Once the thin edge is in, it is only a question of time and force as to how far the remainder can be driven. The hardest stone or the toughest wood is not able to resist its power for separation.

Sin has the same power. Beware of its thin edge. Resist it in faith.

ILLUMINATING THE LESSON

There are times for the Christian when retreat is the way to victory. Sometimes the Christian is confronted with situations in which the bravest and most sensible thing to do is to retreat—to run away. Many times the way to deal with a strong temptation is to take to our heels and run for our lives.

There is the amusing story of the storekeeper who asked a boy who had been lingering too long near a tempting display of candy, "What are you doing? Trying to steal some candy?"

"No," replied the boy, "trying not to."

In such a case, it is a good thing for a boy or a man to remove the temptation by removing himself.

Any person who finds his standards lowered, his ideals suffering, or his character deteriorating by reason of the business or social situation in which he finds himself may find it wise to change things by simply withdrawing from that business or environment.

The sensible thing in some battles is retreat. One way of winning is not to be defeated, and the way not to be defeated is resolutely to depart from the place and the situation where defeat will naturally result.

DAILY BIBLE READINGS

M. Flee Immorality.
    Genesis 39:9-12, 19-21
T. Do Not Forget God.
    Deuteronomy 8:11-20
W. Resist Idol Worship.
    Daniel 3:13-18
T. Pray for Deliverance.
    Matthew 6:9-13
F. Look for a Way Out.
    1 Corinthians 10:11-13
S. Seek God's Grace.
    Hebrews 4:14-16

Prove Your Faith

Study Text: James 2:1-26

Objective: To understand that faith must include action and express our faith by loving others.

Time: The Book of James was probably written between A.D. 48 and 50.

Place: The Book of James was probably written at Jerusalem.

Golden Text: "As the body without the spirit is dead, so faith without works is dead also" (James 2:26).

Central Truth: Genuine faith is always accompanied by godly works.

Evangelism Emphasis: Faith in Christ is necessary for salvation.

PRINTED TEXT

James 2:5. Hearken, my beloved brethren, Hath not God chosen the poor of this world rich in faith, and heirs of the kingdom which he hath promised to them that love him?

6. But ye have despised the poor. Do not rich men oppress you, and draw you before the judgment seats?

7. Do not they blaspheme that worthy name by the which ye are called?

8. If ye fulfil the royal law according to the scripture, Thou shalt love thy neighbour as thyself, ye do well:

9. But if ye have respect to persons, ye commit sin, and are convinced of the law as transgressors.

10. For whosoever shall keep the whole law, and yet offend in one point, he is guilty of all.

14. What doth it profit, my brethren, though a man say he hath faith, and have not works? can faith save him?

15. If a brother or sister be naked, and destitute of daily food,

16. And one of you say unto them, Depart in peace, be ye warmed and filled; notwithstanding ye give them not those things which are needful to the body; what doth it profit?

17. Even so faith, if it hath not works, is dead, being alone.

18. Yea, a man may say, Thou hast faith, and I have works: shew me thy faith without thy works, and I will shew thee my faith by my works.

19. Thou believest that there is one God; thou doest well: the devils also believe, and tremble.

20. But wilt thou know, O vain man, that faith without works is dead?

21. Was not Abraham our father justified by works, when

he had offered Isaac his son upon the altar?

22. Seest thou how faith wrought with his works, and by works was faith made perfect?

23. And the scripture was fulfilled which saith, Abraham believed God, and it was imputed unto him for righteousness: and he was called the Friend of God.

24. Ye see then how that by works a man is justified, and not by faith only.

25. Likewise also was not Rahab the harlot justified by works, when she had received the messengers, and had sent them out another way?

26. For as the body without the spirit is dead, so faith without works is dead also.

LESSON OUTLINE

I.   AVOID FAVORITISM
  A. Principle
  B. Illustration
  C. Motive
  D. Explanation

II. FULFILL THE LAW OF LOVE
  A. The Royal Law
  B. Application

III. DEMONSTRATE YOUR FAITH
  A. Question
  B. Genuine Faith
  C. Examples of Genuine Faith

LESSON EXPOSITION

INTRODUCTION

The Book of James is often looked at as an exposition of practical religious experience. And it is that. Its primary concern is not creed but conduct, not belief but behavior, not doctrine but deeds. However, in addition, there are important doctrinal concepts in the book. For example, the doctrine of faith is prominent in chapter 2.

The word *faith* is found frequently in James. In the New Testament only Romans, Galatians, 1 Timothy, and Hebrews have more occurrences of the noun for *faith* than James. In only six of the New Testament Epistles is the verb for *believe* found more than in James. The Book of James speaks of the testing of faith, the prayer of faith, the works of faith, the perfection of faith, being rich in faith, a dead faith, an idle faith, and more. Some scholars see the theme of James to be the tests of faith.

Many consider chapter 2 to be the heart of James' message. In it he talked about faith in relation to avoiding favoritism (vv. 1-7), faith in relation to fulfilling the law of love (vv. 8-13), and faith as being important in demonstrating good works (vv. 14-26).

I. AVOID FAVORITISM
(James 2:1-7)

A. Principle (v. 1)

(James 2:1 is not included in the printed text.)

The second chapter of James opens with a command: "My brethren, have not the faith of our Lord Jesus Christ, the Lord of glory, with respect of persons." It should be noted that Christian faith in this verse is faith in the Lord Jesus Christ. The One to whom we owe allegiance in the faith is our Lord, Jesus the Savior. He is Christ, the Anointed One of God. James was saying that Christian faith is faith in a person who is both human and divine, a Savior who is Prophet, Priest, and King and "God with us." Faith of any less quality does not deserve the name Christian.

B. Illustration (vv. 2, 3)

(James 2:2, 3 is not included in the printed text.)

These verses in James illustrate the fact that people who have faith in Christ—who loved all and gave Himself for all—must not practice favoritism. One function of the early church was to create a sphere in which there should be neither Jew nor Gentile, Greek nor barbarian, bond nor free. The statement "All are equal within the church's gate" is true. To be like Christ, the divine Head, the church must show no favoritism. The equality of Christians, indicated by the title "brethren," is the foundation of the admonition with which chapter 2 begins.

James cited an example of the kind of favoritism that is forbidden—the respect shown to the rich in Christian assemblies. The two contrasted visitors are outsiders. One is rich, important socially, and ostentatious. The expensive ring on his finger and his costly clothing, probably a flowing robe of pure white silk or of the finest wool, attract the attention of the congregation. Then there comes in a poor man in a shabby garment. The eyes of all observe his poverty. He

too has heard of these Christians and comes to see what their religion and worship are like.

The behavior of the church members shows their bias. Their favoritism is obvious. The one wearing the gold ring and expensive clothing is invited to sit in a prominent seat. Everyone is delighted that he has condescended to visit them. He is shown every consideration. No consideration whatever is shown to the poor man. He is told to stand by the wall or wherever he can be wedged in. Or he is asked by someone to sit on the floor, close to the other person's footstool, where there is just enough room for a man to stoop.

It should be remembered that most people sat cross-legged on the floor; only important people had elevated seats, chairs, or benches. No one would think of asking the rich visitor to sit on the floor. Absolutely not! And this is just the point that James was making. His readers were guilty of showing favoritism. They thought like the world in relation to social status.

How do we treat our poor??

C. Motive (v. 4)

(James 2:4 is not included in the printed text.)

The apostle used a double question to drive his point home in verse 4. He was asking, "Aren't you being partial? Aren't you evil-thinking judges?" Their faith should have taught them to show the same consideration to all their visitors and not to make distinctions that are wrong and wicked. He said in effect, "Since when does faith in the Lord Jesus Christ justify attitudes which treat the man with a fine garment as superior and the man with a shabby garment as inferior?" Is the

✱ soul of the one worth more than the soul of the other? Are not all men, rich and poor, equal in the house of God? Something is wrong with our faith if we have not learned from Christ to treat all people with love and respect, without regard to their social or economic status in this world. *Are we guilty of this*

D. Explanation (vv. 5-7)

5. Hearken, my beloved brethren, Hath not God chosen the poor of this world rich in faith, and heirs of the kingdom which he hath promised to them that love him?

Favoritism can result in snobbery, which is contrary to the purpose of God. James said that the poor are the special objects of God's concern. Discrimination against them is therefore an affront to God; it defies His will. The apostle did not mean that God's choice has been limited to the poor. Neither did he mean that all the poor will be saved. But the poor have often been more ready to hear the gospel and accept its blessings than those who are rich in this world's goods. Preaching the gospel is not left to chance but is the deliberate strategy of God. Jesus said that part of His divine mission was to preach the gospel to the poor. That mission has been delegated to the church.

✗ James was referring to people who were poor in one respect, namely, in regard to the riches of the world. They had little money. But in another respect, they were rich. They possessed faith. James mentioned this in verse 5. Their wealth consisted of the heavenly kingdom of which they were joint heirs with Christ.

6. But ye have despised the poor. Do not rich men oppress you, and draw you before the judgment seats?

James now dealt with the rich. He spoke primarily of the rich Jews who were for the most part Sadducees. At this time they were the tyrannous oppressors of poorer Jews. They also made a special effort to harass Jewish Christians. This abuse of the poor and of Jewish Christians was possible because the Roman government allowed the Jews of the Diaspora a great deal of legal control over their own people.

James said the rich oppressed the Christians and dragged them into court. According to one translation, "It is the rich who grind you down" (Weymouth). The Greek word used here for "oppress," meaning "to exploit, oppress, or dominate someone," is used in the Septuagint (Greek version of the Old Testament) in referring to the mistreatment of widows, orphans, and the poor. In the only other place where this same Greek word occurs in the New Testament, it is used of the tyrannical rule of the devil (Acts 10:38). The class of individuals to whom favoritism was being shown was the very class that was violently mistreating the Christians.

7. Do not they blaspheme that worthy name by the which ye are called?

James stated it was even more inappropriate for Christians to show favoritism to the rich because it was the rich who were blaspheming the worthy name by which Christians were called. The rich were content to oppress the poor and spoke with contempt of the honorable name of Christ, their Lord.

I may not be rich - but in the end - IF I remain Faithful - I'll be the son of A King + live in a mansion

Why are so many Christians inclined to look with disdain on the poor?

II. FULFILL THE LAW OF LOVE (James 2:8-13)

A. The Royal Law (vv. 8-11)

(James 2:11 is not included in the printed text.)

8. If ye fulfil the royal law according to the scripture, Thou shalt love thy neighbour as thyself, ye do well:

The royal law is the law of love, expressed in the command "Thou shalt love thy neighbour as thyself" (Leviticus 19:18). Christ taught that all who need our help in any way are to be thought of as neighbors. The command to love our neighbor may then be seen as a summary of the horizontal dimension of the law.

This command may be called "the royal law" because it is thought of as supreme, that is, "the king of all laws." It can also be considered the royal law because Christ, the true King, is its promulgator. Love is the law of His kingdom. To fulfill the royal law is to carry it out, that is, to put it into practice.

9. But if ye have respect to persons, ye commit sin, and are convinced of the law as transgressors.

James argued that the obedience his readers claimed to be giving the law was only a partial obedience and actually contrary to the meaning of the law. The poor man, no less than the rich, is neighbor, and to show respect to one while dishonoring the other can in no wise be called a fulfilling of the law. "If ye have respect to persons, ye commit sin"—literally, "you work sin." The readers were not showing love but favoritism, and their actions were not acts of obedience (as they pretended) but acts of sin.

"'And are convinced . . . as transgressors' means to stand convicted as lawbreakers. The word here translated 'transgressors' denotes one who steps over a line. Thus it is fittingly used of those who violate a law. In the phrase 'of [by] the *law*,' law is personified and thought of as judge" (Curtis Vaughn, *James: A Study Guide*).

10. For whosoever shall keep the whole law, and yet offend in one point, he is guilty of all.

James pinpointed the showing of favoritism as a transgression of the law by which we are to be judged, and one which, like every other, involves the guilt of breaking the whole law. In verse 8, the apostle cites the words of Leviticus 19:18 as the precept which forbids showing partiality: "Thou shalt love thy neighbour as thyself." This was the same precept Jesus had used as His summary of the principle underlying the last six commandments. We are to love our neighbor—that is, anyone to whom we have it within our power to become helpful, even though he may be a stranger. Those who discharge this duty appropriately do well. We may not limit the precept to either our wealthy neighbor or our poor neighbor. Those who practice partiality are guilty of sin against both the Old Testament law and the law of the Spirit of life in Christ Jesus.

James warned us that transgression in one point of the law is transgression of the whole law. No one should accept the idea that "respect of persons" in the church is a trivial matter to be overlooked in view of the social and financial benefits which may result from it. James distinctly tells us that partiality is sin and that he who indulges in it disobeys the whole moral law.

B. Application (vv. 12, 13)

In verse 12, James dealt with the subject of judgment. "So speak ye, and so do." This standard will be applied to our words and to our behavior. The apostle's words here echo the words of Jesus in Matthew 7:21-23; 12:34-37. A person's habits of speech and action are always an index of his moral state. If we compare human character to a tree, words correspond to its leaves, deeds to its fruit, and thoughts to its roots underground. Words and actions will be judged in connection with the counsels of the hearts of which they are the products.

James continued his treatment of judgment in verse 13. The doctrine of judgment to the unmerciful is emphasized in many parts of Scripture. It receives special prominence in the teaching of our Lord in the Gospel of Matthew. We can never, of course, merit eternal life by cherishing a compassionate spirit. But since mercy and love are supreme elements in the character of God, it is clear that those who do not manifest active compassion toward others have not themselves been renewed into His image. The purpose of the gospel is to restore man's likeness to God, who is love; so, then, the man who exhibits no love shows that he has not permitted the gospel to exercise its sanctifying power within him, and he shall therefore be condemned for rejecting it.

There is another side. The apostle added, "Mercy rejoiceth against [triumphs over] judgment." This means that the tenderhearted and actively compassionate follower of Christ need not fear the final judgment. His mercifulness is an evidence that he is himself a partaker of the mercy of God in Christ. *God looks upon the heart*

In what ways can a Christian show mercy?

III. DEMONSTRATE YOUR FAITH (James 2:14-26)

A. Question (v. 14)

14. What doth it profit, my brethren, though a man say he hath faith, and have not works? can faith save him?

The insufficiency of barren faith is the subject of verse 14. The case James cited is not that of a hypocrite but of a self-deceiver. The man has faith, of a sort, but it is only the cold assent of the mind. It does not purify his heart, or renew his will, or change his moral nature, as saving faith always does. Its weakness is seen in the fact that it is unproductive. It does not motivate its possessor to any acts of self-denial or compassionate benevolence. This defective faith coexists with showing favoritism, or an unbridled tongue, or a passionate temper, or a disposition to decline accepting the blame for one's own sins.

B. Genuine Faith (vv. 15-20)

15. If a brother or sister be naked, and destitute of daily food,

16. And one of you say unto them, Depart in peace, be ye

warmed and filled; notwithstanding ye give them not those things
which are needful to the body;
what doth it profit?

**17. Even so faith, if it hath
not works, is dead, being alone.**

To illustrate what he was talking
about in these verses, James said it
is the bitterest mockery for a man
who is himself living in ease and
comfort to say to his shivering,
starving brother, "Depart in peace.
Do not be discouraged; God has
said He will never forsake His people. He shall give His angels charge
concerning you, and I myself will
pray for you." Sentimental profes-
sions of concern which offer no
practical help do not profit either
person. They tempt the destitute
man to give up, and they ruin the
moral health of the false symapthiz-
er. Mere lip compassion is not true
compassion, and a professed faith
that is barren of good works is dead
in itself.

**18. Yea, a man may say, Thou
hast faith, and I have works:
shew me thy faith without thy
works, and I will shew thee my
faith by my works.**

**19. Thou believest that there
is one God; thou doest well: the
devils also believe, and tremble.**

**20. But wilt thou know, O vain
man, that faith without works is
dead?**

James issued a direct challenge
to those who claim to be true and
consistent believers. He defied professing Christians who divorce faith
from practice to exhibit their faith
apart from works. He said in effect,
"A believer is to let his light shine.
Well, I point to the new life I am
now living as the appropriate example of my faith; but since you
neglect good works, I challenge you
to indicate how you can manifest

your faith otherwise." A faith which
produces no works is unable to
show itself; therefore it is not true
faith at all.

James cited an example of what
he was talking about in verse 19. If
any professing Christian prided
himself upon the correctness of his
beliefs, here was a warning to him.
If he was satisfied with the thought
that he was holding fast to the doctrine of the unity of one God, then
in spite of the fact that he was living in the midst of idol worshipers,
this verse was to remind him of the
uselessness of such a conviction
unless it produced the fruit of holiness. The demons believe, and yet
they remain demons—and condemned. The unclean spirits whom
Jesus cast out had plenty of knowledge and belief regarding God and
Christ. But their believing was a
kind that made them shudder with
terror when they realized the purpose of Jesus' mission and message. A mere assenting intellectual
belief cannot cleanse from sin; it
can only produce the fear of coming
torment. *Are we a fruit-
producing Christian?*

C. Examples of Genuine Faith
   (vv. 21-26)

**21. Was not Abraham our
father justified by works, when
he had offered Isaac his son upon
the altar?**

**22. Seest thou how faith
wrought with his works, and by
works was faith made perfect?**

**23. And the scripture was ful-
filled which saith, Abraham
believed God, and it was imputed
unto him for righteousness: and
he was called the Friend of God.**

**24. Ye see then how that by
works a man is justified, and not
by faith only.**

Contrast between Abraham + Rahab

Paul said that Abraham was justified by faith before Isaac was born. James said that he was justified by works, because he offered up Isaac his son upon the altar. But, James was careful to add, in this crowning manifestation of his piety, the patriarch's faith cooperated with his works. The confidence that he had had in God for so many years enabled him to be willing to obey the dreadful command to kill his only son. Only a strong faith in God's dependability could have given Abraham victorious passage through such an awful ordeal.

God surely knew Abraham well to ask him to do such a deed, knowing full well He would never allow Abraham to complete the job. On Abraham's part, he had to trust God's wisdom and purpose, as well as the final outcome, to attempt to carry out the command. After all, God had promised that Abraham's descendants would become a great nation through Isaac. So Abraham must have told God in essence, "OK, Lord, You've promised a great nation would spring from Isaac, and that can't happen if he's dead. So the only possible solution I see for this dilemma is for You to raise him back to life after I've obeyed You." (See Genesis 21:12.) Abraham had no doubts that he and Isaac would return home together (22:5). And he put his faith into action through his obedience.

25. Likewise also was not Rahab the harlot justified by works, when she had received the messengers, and had sent them out another way?

26. For as the body without the spirit is dead, so faith without works is dead also.

James gave Rahab as his second example. Her case seems to have been chosen because it was so unlike that of Abraham. Abraham was a Jew and the father of the chosen nation; Rahab was a pagan woman. Abraham had for many years received special training in the school of faith; Rahab had received no training at all. Abraham was a good and pure man; Rahab had lived a sinful and sensual life. Yet this degraded Canaanite obtained like precious faith with the illustrious patriarch Abraham. These same two Old Testament examples are also cited in Hebrews 11. The contrast between Abraham and Rahab is useful to show that invariably good works flow from a living faith. Rahab's belief was expressed in her own words (Joshua 2:9-11), and her diligent attempts to guarantee the safety of the two spies at the risk of her life brought her faith into prominence through her works.

Ask:
Discuss ways Christians should demonstrate their faith in our day.

REVIEW QUESTIONS

1. What principle did James exemplify in 2:1?
2. How did he illustrate this principle?
3. What is the royal law?
4. How did James explain the royal law?
5. What two examples of faith and works did James use?

GOLDEN TEXT HOMILY

"AS THE BODY WITHOUT THE SPIRIT IS DEAD, SO FAITH WITHOUT WORKS IS DEAD ALSO" (James 2:26).

Paul's writings emphasize faith; Peter's hope; John's love. James stressed that all these graces are to be synthesized in the life of the believer in a ministry of good works.

Paul taught, "By grace are ye saved through faith . . . not of works" (Ephesians 2:8, 9). James taught, "Faith without works is dead." Paul was not saying the life of faith should not include good works; he was saying that man is not saved through his own good works. James was not saying that salvation comes by works; he was saying that the life of the person who has experienced salvation is to be filled with good deeds. There is no disagreement of doctrine. Paul taught against self-righteous pharisaism; James taught against dead formalism and antinomianism.

The words of James 2:18 can be read, "You say you have faith. . . ." Saying you have faith is quite different from having faith. James' teaching is that faith cannot truly subsist without producing works. Proof of faith, James said, is faithfully carrying out merciful kindness and charity taught by the Lord Jesus (Matthew 25:34-36). The living principle that animates faith is love for God and obedience to His commands, accompanied by love for humankind which results in good works. Faith must control the whole man: his intellect, his attitudes, his actions. Belief that there is a God is not sufficient; devils believe and tremble. True faith, saving faith, is manifested in actions. Adam Clarke comments: "There can be no more a genuine faith without good works than there can be a living human being without a soul."

James believed in faith; he illustrated his belief by the examples of the faith of Abraham and Rahab. Paul believed in works—works done not only for God but also with God (1 Corinthians 3:9; 2 Corinthians 6:1), even as Jesus taught the necessity of abiding in Him— "Without me ye can do nothing" (John 15:5).

A marriage of faith and works is God's plan for spreading the gospel and building the family of God. Therefore what God has joined together, let not man even attempt to put asunder!—**Karl W. Bunkley, (Retired), Former General Sunday School President, International Pentecostal Holiness Church, Oklahoma City, Oklahoma**

SENTENCE SERMONS

GENUINE FAITH is always accompanied by godly works.
                                    —Selected

TRUE FAITH commits us to obedience.
                                —A.W. Tozer

HE WHO feeds his faith will starve his doubts to death.
            —Draper's Quotations for the Christian World

FAITH IS dead to doubt, dumb to discouragement, and blind to impossibilities.
                        —The Defender

EVANGELISM APPLICATION

FAITH IN CHRIST IS NECESSARY FOR SALVATION.

Faith is the very cornerstone of salvation and personal relationship with Jesus Christ. Paul declared in Ephesians 2:8, "For by grace are ye saved through faith." It is because God is gracious that sinful men are forgiven, converted, purified, and saved. We are saved through faith, but salvation is by grace. Faith is the channel or conduit that brings grace to our hearts. Grace is the foundation and the stream; faith is the channel along which the flood of mercy flows to refresh the weary souls of men.

ILLUMINATING THE LESSON

The story is told of a Christian woman who had a beautiful flower garden in which she took great pride. It was her custom to give away large quantities of flowers. Two large baskets were fastened by the gate, and these were filled every morning with freshly cut flowers, to which passersby were invited to help themselves. The children on their way to school, men on their way to work, and tramps as they passed—all alike blessed the thoughtful kindness of this woman. When asked, "Are you not afraid you will rob yourself?" she replied, "The more I cut, the more I have."

This is the way it is with faith. The more we give, the more we have, but what we withhold escapes us.

DAILY BIBLE READINGS

M. Faith to Build.
   Genesis 6:11-22
T. Faith to Obey.
   Genesis 22:1-12
W. Faith for Protection.
   Exodus 2:1-10
T. Faith for Healing.
   Mark 5:25-34
F. Faith Replaces Doubt.
   John 20:24-29
S. Faith Pleases God.
   Hebrews 11:1-6

Seek Wisdom

Study Text: James 3:1-18

Objective: To discover that God's wisdom is necessary for righteous behavior and apply that wisdom in daily living.

Time: The Book of James was probably written between A.D. 48 and 50.

Place: The Book of James was probably written at Jerusalem.

Golden Text: "Who is a wise man and endued with knowledge among you? let him shew out of a good conversation his works with meekness of wisdom" (James 3:13).

Central Truth: A truly wise person lives to please God.

Evangelism Emphasis: Effective witnessing requires God's wisdom.

PRINTED TEXT

James 3:1. My brethren, be not many masters, knowing that we shall receive the greater condemnation.

2. For in many things we offend all. If any man offend not in word, the same is a perfect man, and able also to bridle the whole body.

3. Behold, we put bits in the horses' mouths, that they may obey us; and we turn about their whole body.

4. Behold also the ships, which though they be so great, and are driven of fierce winds, yet are they turned about with a very small helm, whithersoever the governor listeth.

5. Even so the tongue is a little member, and boasteth great things. Behold, how great a matter a little fire kindleth!

6. And the tongue is a fire, a world of iniquity: so is the tongue among our members, that it defileth the whole body, and setteth on fire the course of nature; and it is set on fire of hell.

7. For every kind of beasts, and of birds, and of serpents, and of things in the sea, is tamed, and hath been tamed of mankind:

8. But the tongue can no man tame; it is an unruly evil, full of deadly poison.

9. Therewith bless we God, even the Father; and therewith curse we men, which are made after the similitude of God.

10. Out of the same mouth proceedeth blessing and cursing. My brethren, these things ought not so to be.

11. Doth a fountain send forth at the same place sweet water and bitter?

12. Can the fig tree, my brethren, bear olive berries? either a vine, figs? so can no fountain both yield salt water and fresh.

13. Who is a wise man and endued with knowledge among you? let him shew out of a good conversation his works with meekness of wisdom.

14. But if ye have bitter envying and strife in your hearts, glory not, and lie not against the truth.

15. This wisdom descendeth not from above, but is earthly, sensual, devilish.

16. For where envying and strife is, there is confusion and every evil work.

17. But the wisdom that is from above is first pure, then peaceable, gentle, and easy to be intreated, full of mercy and good fruits, without partiality, and without hypocrisy.

18. And the fruit of righteousness is sown in peace of them that make peace.

LESSON OUTLINE

I. CONTROL YOUR TONGUE
   A. Small but Powerful
   B. Necessary but Dangerous
   C. Helpful but Inconsistent

II. SHUN EVIL ATTITUDES
   A. The Proof of Wisdom
   B. False Wisdom

III. EMBRACE GOD'S WISDOM
   A. The Characteristics of True Wisdom
   B. The Effect of True Wisdom

LESSON EXPOSITION

INTRODUCTION *Read*

Some of history's greatest discoveries were made by keen observation. Many men before Galileo had seen a hanging weight swing with a measured beat. But Galileo saw and applied the principle to the measurement of time. He invented the pendulum, one of the world's most important inventions.

Many men before Samuel Brown had seen spiderwebs suspended across a path. But Brown saw a web in his garden one dewy morning and perceived that a bridge of iron might be built in the same way. He invented the suspension bridge.

Many men before James Watt had idly watched the bouncing lid of a teakettle. However, when Watt observed this, he built the first steam engine.

Many other inventions have been developed thus, apparently by chance. Why have the inventors been so fortunate? Louis Pasteur answered this question: "Chance favors only the minds which are prepared."

Those who discover the best way to live are like that. They don't blunder into the way of wisdom accidentally. Their minds are prepared. They are searching. They are sensitive to God's leadership. They can distinguish wise ways from foolish ways.

They have learned that wisdom is more than knowledge. Man may have extensive and accurate knowledge but be sadly lacking in wisdom. The wisdom so often and so highly commended in the Bible is a spiritual perception, a right understanding of what is best and right, and the application of it to life.

Today there is too much dependence on the ability of human wisdom, human ingenuity, scientific research, the study of statistics, and the theories of learned men to show us what to do and how to be delivered from the vast problems which confront modern life. God's promise of His wisdom is an antidote for this dangerous contemporary self-sufficiency.

I. CONTROL YOUR TONGUE (James 3:1-12)

A. Small but Powerful (vv. 1-5)

1. My brethren, be not many masters, knowing that we shall receive the greater condemnation.

John Calvin may have been correct when he wrote of this verse: "The common and almost universal interpretation of this passage is that the apostle discourages the desire for the office of teaching, and for this reason, because it is dangerous, and exposes one to a heavier judgment in case he transgresses. . . . But I take masters not to be those who performed a public duty in the church, but such as took upon them the right of passing judgment upon others, for such reprovers sought to be accounted as masters of morals."

The apostle's warning is against having censorious or critical tongues that are always seeking to set other people straight. To be always criticizing others is not a manifestation of godly wisdom but reveals instead our own imperfection in relation to God.

The apostle Paul declared, "Therefore thou art inexcusable, O man, whosoever thou art that judgest: for wherein thou judgest another, thou condemnest thyself; for thou that judgest doest the same things" (Romans 2:1).

2. For in many things we offend all. If any man offend not in word, the same is a perfect man, and able also to bridle the whole body.

James specifically addressed the problem of the unruly tongue. The unruly tongue is a universal plague to mankind; it continually frustrates human efforts to control it. So difficult is it to control the tongue that James ascribes perfection to the man who does not offend with his words. We reveal the state of our inner lives by what we say. Jesus said to the Pharisees, "How can ye, being evil, speak good things? for out of the abundance of the heart the mouth speaketh" (Matthew 12:34).

3. Behold, we put bits in the horses' mouths, that they may obey us; and we turn about their whole body.

The apostle began to talk about the mastery of the tongue in verse 3. Without a bit in the horse's mouth it is impossible for the rider to have control over him. Likewise, without a bridle on the tongue, no man can govern himself appropriately. David recognized this truth: "I will take heed to my ways, that I sin not with my tongue: I will keep my mouth with a bridle" (Psalm 39:1). Moses, the meekest of men, was forbidden by God to enter the Land of Promise because "he spake unadvisedly with his lips" (Psalm 106:33). It has been said, "We rule irrational animals with a bit; how much more ought we to be able to govern ourselves?"

4. Behold also the ships, which though they be so great, and are driven of fierce winds, yet are they turned about with a very small helm, whithersoever the governor listeth.

5. Even so the tongue is a little member, and boasteth great things. Behold, how great a matter a little fire kindleth!

In these verses the author referred to little things. The bridle is a very little thing, but the rider can control the whole body of the horse with it. The rudder (helm) is very small, but it enables the steersman to guide a large boat. A tiny spark may set a huge forest on fire. Likewise, the tongue is a very little member of the body, but a victory over it can save the whole man from many evils.

The evil tongue is a tormentor. It is a dagger that can stab the hearts of loved ones. It can be a scourge that tortures the lives of others. But the tongue disciplined by the grace and Spirit of God and governed by godly wisdom ministers healing and strength and blessing to others. *PRAY DAILY*

B. Necessary but Dangerous
   (vv. 6-8)

6. And the tongue is a fire, a world of iniquity: so is the tongue among our members, that it defileth the whole body, and setteth on fire the course of nature; and it is set on fire of hell.

James used the term *fire* to represent all iniquity, saying that it finds its expression in the tongue. It is almost impossible to seethe with anger or bitterness, burn with pride or selfishness, or lust for power without expressing it some-how with the tongue. James added that the tongue is "set on fire of hell." The Greek word for *hell* in this verse is not *hades* (the abode of the dead) but *gehenna*. In James' day the word *gehenna* (hell) was used to describe the torments of hell as a place of burning or punishment for the wicked. The garbage dump south of Jerusalem where the refuse of the city burned with a stench day and night was referred to as "the Valley of Gehenna." The tongue set on fire by hell evokes images of torment and filth associated with the evil tongue.

As a spark can set a forest on fire, as one lighted match can start a conflagration, so the tongue can kindle the whole course of nature (the whole life) into a flame.

7. For every kind of beasts, and of birds, and of serpents, and of things in the sea, is tamed, and hath been tamed of mankind:

8. But the tongue can no man tame; it is an unruly evil, full of deadly poison.

The apostle characterized the tongue as an untamed beast. We marvel at man's success in calming the wild nature of various animals known for their ability to hunt and kill, yet man fails to tame the muscle in his mouth. In fact, James stressed man's inability to tame the tongue. Behind the teeth lies a deadly weapon; it can dispense death-dealing poisonous words.

C. Helpful but Inconsistent
   (vv. 9-12)

9. Therewith bless we God, even the Father; and therewith curse we men, which are made after the similitude of God.

10. Out of the same mouth

proceedeth blessing and cursing. My brethren, these things ought not so to be.

11. Doth a fountain send forth at the same place sweet water and bitter?

12. Can the fig tree, my brethren, bear olive berries? either a vine, figs? so can no fountain both yield salt water and fresh.

A person may put the faculty of speech to its highest use and then almost immediately afterward wickedly abuse it. The tongue has been given us that we might bless God the Father. To utter praise of the Divine is the most ennobling exercise of human speech. The Christian calls God "Lord" and adores Him for His eternal glory; he also calls Him "Father" and blesses Him for His redeeming grace. Then with absolute inconsistency, the same mouth which praised God may be heard invoking evil upon men. How often do those who profess godliness speak passionate and spiteful words? Do not Christians who belong to the same congregation sometimes backbite one another? Do not believers of different fellowships often, out of mere sectarian rivalry, denounce one another's churches?

God is the Creator of all men, for men are made after the likeness of God. God and man are closely related to each other by creation and through Christ's incarnation and mission. Real reverence for God requires that we respect all men as creatures of God. How inconsistent, then, for the same mouth to bless the Father but curse His children.

The inconsistency found in man is not found in the world of nature.

A spring of water cannot transgress the law of its nature. A fruit tree can only produce fruit according to its kind. How unnatural, then, that in the moral world the same fountain of speech should emit just now a rill of clear, sweet praise and soon afterward a torrent of bitter slander or evil utterances. In the case of a person who has experienced the renewing grace of the Holy Spirit, this unnatural inconsistency of speech ought not to be; but neither does it need to be.

Why are gossip and slander so fascinating to some believers?

II. SHUN EVIL ATTITUDES
   (James 3:13-16)

A. The Proof of Wisdom (v. 13)

13. Who is a wise man and endued with knowledge among you? let him shew out of a good conversation his works with meekness of wisdom.

Some among the early Christians desired to appear wise because they had knowledge. Having knowledge does not mean that one is automatically wise. A person may possess a large library, or even amass vast stores of knowledge, and yet be a fool. In fact, no fool is so great as a knowing fool. The wise man is the one who can use his knowledge for the greatest moral and spiritual good. And true wisdom is bound up with the life of faith in the Lord Jesus Christ—the will of God its rule and His glory its end. So the man who lives without trust in God is unwise indeed.

A wise man's wisdom will be seen in his good life. The quiet flow of one's daily behavior will furnish ample evidence of it. Character is perceived not only by its subtle attitudes, but in connection with individual actions. Wisdom shows itself in acts of holiness. And these acts are done in meekness, which is one of wisdom's attributes. True wisdom is mild, calm, patient, and self-restraining. A meek spirit is not a mean spirit. The meekness of wisdom is possessed with great courage and ardent zeal. As one writer said, "Moses was very meek in his own cause, but as hot as fire in the cause of God." And the man Christ Jesus was mild, just because He was strong and brave. There was no fierceness, no fanaticism, and no sourness about Him. He is our perfect pattern of the meekness of wisdom.

B. False Wisdom (vv. 14-16)

14. But if ye have bitter envying and strife in your hearts, glory not, and lie not against the truth.

False, or worldly, wisdom carries with it not Christian zeal but bitter zeal. Its spirit is divisive, arrogant, bigoted. Its roots lie in the angry passions of the heart. Its aim is personal victory rather than the triumph of the truth. While it may be sometimes necessary to contend earnestly in defense of the gospel, the love of controversy for its own sake or the cherishing of a contentious spirit toward fellow Christians is always sinful—and is certainly not ground for glorying. A professing Christian who lives only to foster doctrinal disputes or social quarrels presents to the world a false image of Christianity and is himself a living contradiction of the truth he professes to believe.

15. This wisdom descendeth not from above, but is earthly, sensual, devilish.

James identified the origin of false wisdom as earthly. Every good gift and every perfect gift is from above, but this so-called wisdom that is occupied with earthly things is of earthly origin. Those who cultivate it are those whose souls are completely immersed in worldly pursuits. It is sensual—that is, of the nature of the senses as opposed to spirituality.

16. For where envying and strife is, there is confusion and every evil work.

Where ill will and division exist in the heart, strife and wretchedness may be expected in society. Look at what misery the spirit of strife and self-seeking have caused in families and even in churches. It is a source of sorrows and of lifelong alienations. It sows tares among the wheat. And the harvest of this devilish wisdom is jealousy, selfish ambition, disharmony, chaos, and antagonism.

What is the effect of one's influence if one pretends before others to be very spiritual and to possess great knowledge of the Word of God but is, at the same time, known as a person of bitter or impure speech?

III. EMBRACE GOD'S WISDOM (James 3:17, 18)

A. The Characteristics of True Wisdom (v. 17)

17. But the wisdom that is from above is first pure, then peaceable, gentle, and easy to be intreated, full of mercy and good fruits, without partiality, and without hypocrisy.

The characteristics of true wisdom are presented here with terseness and beauty. The qualities of true and godly wisdom are produced by a sincere reception of the truth. This picture of true wisdom given by James is in direct contrast to what he has said about false or earthly wisdom.

The origin of true wisdom is from above. It is not the product of human culture but is supernatural and gracious. And being a gift of God, it is good and perfect in all its characteristics. James represents the heavenly wisdom as distinguished by seven attributes. Seven was the symbolic number for perfection among the Jews. There are, so to speak, seven notes in the harmony of Christian character; or seven colors in the rainbow of the Christian life, which, when blended, form its pure white sunlight. Purity, the first of these seven, is marked off from the others, because it refers to what a person is within his own heart. The other six deal with qualities shown by true wisdom in one's behavior toward others.

According to James, true wisdom is first of all *pure*. This word means "chaste, unsullied, holy." Purity is the fundamental characteristic of everything that is from above. Righteousness lies at the foundation of all that is beautiful in character. Christian wisdom leads a man to keep himself unspotted from the world and to cleanse himself from all defilements of the flesh and spirit. Every person, therefore, who lives a sensual, selfish, or openly sinful life shows himself to be destitute of the heavenly wisdom—for its chief element is holiness, that purity obtained through the blood of Christ and by the

indwelling of the Spirit.

The expressions *first* and *then* do not imply that the wise man must first be perfectly pure before he begins to be peaceable. These words indicate rather the logical order and not necessarily the sequence. The phrase "first pure, then peaceable" has been abused in the interest of those with the jealousy and factionalism that belong to false wisdom. We are to be peaceable with a view to purity, as well as pure for the sake of peace. *Peaceable* means being indisposed to conflict or dissension. Rivalry and division are characteristic of earthly wisdom. The heavenly wisdom seeks peace.

True wisdom is *gentle*. This means it is forbearing, courteous, and considerate. Gentleness is just the outward aspect of the grace of peaceableness, the garment in which the peaceable spirit should be clothed.

True wisdom is *easy to be intreated*. This means it is accessible, open to conviction, and willing to listen to reason. The wise man thinks more about his duties and responsibilities than his rights and privileges.

True wisdom is *full of mercy and good fruits*. This means it is overflowing with feelings of kindness and compassion. It finds an outlet for these in good works.

True wisdom is *without variance*. It is steady, persistent, unmistakable, never divided in its purpose, and therefore never halting in the fulfillment of its mission.

True wisdom is *without hypocrisy*. It is sincere, always being what it appears and professes to be. Wisdom's ways are not devious; it knows that a straight line is the shortest distance between two points.

B. The Effect of True Wisdom (v. 18)

18. And the fruit of righteousness is sown in peace of them that make peace.

It is interesting to observe that the traits of heavenly wisdom listed by James are without exception qualities which were embodied in Christ during His earthly life. He was in the fullest sense the embodiment of the wisdom of God.

James affirmed that the seed which produces the fruit of righteousness is "sown in peace of them that make peace." Righteousness, indeed, cannot be promoted either in ourselves or in others except as we are men of peace. And men of peace are those who not only love peace but promote it by every means in their power. Such people are those who possess the true heavenly wisdom.

What did James mean when he said that true wisdom is without hypocrisy?

REVIEW QUESTIONS

1. What little things did James compare the tongue to?
2. How is the tongue helpful but inconsistent?
3. List some of the sins of the tongue.
4. How may the tongue be used to bless people?
5. List the characteristics of true wisdom.

GOLDEN TEXT HOMILY

"WHO IS A WISE MAN AND ENDUED WITH KNOWLEDGE AMONG YOU? LET HIM SHEW OUT OF A GOOD CONVERSATION HIS WORKS WITH MEEKNESS OF WISDOM" (James 3:13).

The Golden Text begins with the question "Who is a wise man and endued with knowledge among you?" It ends with the challenge "Let him shew out of a good conversation his works with meekness of wisdom." The essential point that James makes is this: A man may profess to be wise and endued with knowledge, but mere profession is not proof enough. Instead, let him demonstrate the reality of his wisdom and knowledge by living out a good life. He continues by saying that out of a man's good life will flow works wrought in the Spirit of meekness. And when you observe these things in a man's life, you can conclude that he is indeed wise and endued with knowledge. This same logic is used by James concerning faith. He said that the proof of the reality of man's faith will be seen in the works that are its outcome (James 2:17, 18); and so it is with wisdom, which if a man has will be seen in the way he lives, the things he does, and the attitude in which he does them.—**Excerpts from the** ***Evangelical Commentary*, Vol. 32**

SENTENCE SERMONS

A TRULY WISE PERSON lives to please God.
—Selected

THE WISE MAN learns from tragedy; the foolish merely repeat it.
—Michael Novak

BEING IN THE RIGHT does not depend on having a loud voice.
—Chinese Proverb

KNOWLEDGE IS horizontal. Wisdom is vertical—it comes down from above.

—Billy Graham

EVANGELISM APPLICATION

EFFECTIVE WITNESSING RE-QUIRES GOD'S WISDOM.

When it is remembered that a person in regular occupations, or on any ordinary day, will speak approximately 30,000 words, one begins to realize the tremendous importance of making our words count for good. The tragedy is that once a word is spoken, it cannot be recalled. Even an apology, or a retraction of what one has said, cannot completely heal the wound that the sharp thrust of a bitter statement has made.

There is no finer admonition in all the New Testament concerning words than that of the apostle Paul to the Ephesians: "Let no corrupt communication proceed out of your mouth, but that which is good to the use of edifying, that it may minister grace unto the hearers" (4:29).

To be an effective witness the believer must walk his talk.

ILLUMINATING THE LESSON

The believer is to be a fruit grower rather than a fruit inspector. To do this he needs the wisdom of God. The prayer of Saint Francis of Assisi can help in watering the seeds of God's wisdom:

Lord, make me an instrument of Your peace.
Where there is hatred, let me sow love;
Where there is injury, pardon;
Where there is doubt, faith;
Where there is despair, hope;
Where there is darkness, light;
Where there is sadness, joy.
O Divine Master, grant that I may not so much seek
To be consoled as to console;
To be understood as to understand;
To be loved as to love.
For it is in giving that we receive;
It is in pardoning that we are pardoned;
It is in dying that we are born to eternal life.

DAILY BIBLE READINGS

M. Available Wisdom.
    1 Kings 3:3-14
T. Excellence of Wisdom.
    Proverbs 2:1-7
W. Wisdom From God.
    Daniel 2:19-23
T. Wise Worshipers.
    Matthew 2:1-12
F. Christ's Wisdom.
    Matthew 13:53-58
S. The Wisdom of God.
    1 Corinthians 1:18-25

Depend on God

Study Text: James 4:1-10; 5:7-18

Objective: To acknowledge our need of God's help and depend on Him in all circumstances.

Time: The Book of James was probably written between A.D. 48 and 50.

Place: The Book of James was probably written at Jerusalem.

Golden Text: "Draw nigh to God, and he will draw nigh to you" (James 4:8).

Central Truth: God will never fail those who rely on Him.

Evangelism Emphasis: God will save all who call on Him.

PRINTED TEXT

James 4:6. But he giveth more grace. Wherefore he saith, God resisteth the proud, but giveth grace unto the humble.

7. Submit yourselves therefore to God. Resist the devil, and he will flee from you.

8. Draw nigh to God, and he will draw nigh to you. Cleanse your hands, ye sinners; and purify your hearts, ye double minded.

9. Be afflicted, and mourn, and weep: let your laughter be turned to mourning, and your joy to heaviness.

10. Humble yourselves in the sight of the Lord, and he shall lift you up.

5:7. Be patient therefore, brethren, unto the coming of the Lord. Behold, the husbandman waiteth for the precious fruit of the earth, and hath long patience for it, until he receive the early and latter rain.

8. Be ye also patient; stablish your hearts: for the coming of the Lord draweth nigh.

9. Grudge not one against another, brethren, lest ye be condemned: behold, the judge standeth before the door.

10. Take, my brethren, the prophets, who have spoken in the name of the Lord, for an example of suffering affliction, and of patience.

11. Behold, we count them happy which endure. Ye have heard of the patience of Job, and have seen the end of the Lord; that the Lord is very pitiful, and of tender mercy.

12. But above all things, my brethren, swear not, neither by heaven, neither by the earth, neither by any other oath: but let your yea be yea; and your nay, nay; lest ye fall into condemnation.

13. Is any among you afflicted? let him pray. Is any merry? let him sing psalms.

14. Is any sick among you? let him call for the elders of the church; and let them pray over

him, anointing him with oil in the name of the Lord:

15. And the prayer of faith shall save the sick, and the Lord shall raise him up; and if he have committed sins, they shall be forgiven him.

16. Confess your faults one to another, and pray one for another, that ye may be healed. The effectual fervent prayer of a righteous man availeth much.

LESSON OUTLINE

I. DRAW NEAR TO GOD

    A. The Problem

    B. The Solution

    C. Practical Advice

II. BE PATIENT IN SUFFERING

    A. The Appeal

    B. Reverence for God's Name

III. PRAY IN ALL SITUATIONS

    A. The Place of Prayer and Praise

    B. The Power of Prayer

LESSON EXPOSITION

INTRODUCTION

The Christian always lives between the times: between the time of his conversion and the time of his consummation, which comes at death or the second coming of Christ. He lives between the time of his justification and the moment of his glorification. He has to decide how he will live between these times. He soon discovers that life is full of mirages—people following their cravings for earthly satisfaction. It is a tragic, pathetic moment of abject disillusionment when a tired, weary, hungry, thirsty traveler in a hot, sandy desert comes to the terrible realization that he has been following a mirage and not reaching an oasis.

It will be even more tragic and more pathetic for an immortal soul to come to life's end, never having found a refreshing, soul-satisfying oasis but having slavishly followed one illusory mirage after another and to end up empty, disillusioned, and lost. Souls that are needy, hungry, thirsty, tired, and weary strive for knowledge, money, position, power, social prestige, and pleasure and finally discover they have followed a will-o'-the-wisp— never having found rest, security, peace, or happiness. The Bible pictures this distressing futility: "There is a way which seemeth right unto a man, but the end thereof are the ways of death" (Proverbs 14:12).

The spirit of this age, even among Christians, is one that so frequently revolves around self and caters to one's own feelings. So how should a Christian act in this world until Jesus comes again? The answer is really simple when you realize that he faces three foes—the world, the flesh, and the devil. He must depend on God. He must put his faith in God.

Dependence on God is the very cornerstone of salvation and personal relationship with Jesus Christ. Paul declared, "For by grace are ye saved through faith" (Ephesians 2:8). It is because God is gracious that sinful men are forgiven, converted, purified, and saved.

I. DRAW NEAR TO GOD
(James 4:1-10)

A. The Problem (vv. 1-4)

(James 4:1-4 is not included in the printed text.)

The quality of life portrayed by James in chapter 4 is appallingly low. The readers are charged with wars and fightings, self-indulgence, prayerlessness, lust, adultery, envy, pride, slander, and murder. In fact, James painted such a depressing picture that many Bible scholars question whether he was addressing Christian Jews or unbelieving Jews. For example, Alfred Plummer says there are places in this letter where James "seems to go beyond the precise circle of readers addressed in the opening words, and to glance at the Jewish nation, whether outside Palestine or not, and whether Christian or not." He therefore feels that James was thinking here, in part at least, of the bitter contentions which divided Pharisees, Sadducees, Herodians, Essenes, Zealots, and Samaritans from one another (*The Expositor's Bible*).

Curtis Vaughn writes: "We must not exclude the Jewish Christians entirely from these charges. The situation described must to some extent have been applicable to them. Though believers, they were still endued with the spirit of their unconverted neighbors and had some of the same evil passions at work within them.

"The whole passage, then, is an in-depth treatment of the havoc wrought when worldly wisdom rather than heavenly wisdom dominates the life. This worldly-mindedness expresses itself in choosing pleasure (the passion for self-gratification) as the chief end of life, in harsh criticism of fellow Christians, and in arrogant disregard of God" (*James: A Study Guide*).

In verse 4, James said the problem is really the incompatibility of worldliness and godliness. The two simply will not mix. The Christian has been called to renounce the world and submit to God. This is the way to peace and victory.

In the words of Russel B. Jones: "The desires of the worldly-minded man are stimulated by his depraved nature and the world's temptations. The result: strife, whether the big strife called war or the little strife that merits no greater designation than feud. The friend of the world is out for pleasure. The end is always the opposite of pleasure— conflict and frustration.

"The worldly man either neglects or abuses prayer, the key to God's storehouse of satisfaction. When prayer is neglected, when God as the source of all is ignored, we fail to get what the deeper self desires. 'Ye have not, because ye ask not.' Frustration is the result of not going to God for our needs. If we attempt to use prayer selfishly, we fail again. God cannot give us the things that will build up our sinful self. To do so would be contrary to His deity. 'Ye ask, and receive not, because ye ask amiss, that ye may consume it upon your lusts'" (*Preacher's Homiletic Library*).

B. The Solution (vv. 5, 6)

(James 4:5 is not included in the printed text.)

6. But he giveth more grace. Wherefore he saith, God resisteth the proud, but giveth grace unto the humble.

Verse 5 is a confirmation of the fact that friendship with the world and friendship with God are incompatible. God has put His Holy Spirit within the Christian and regards with intense concern the Christian's harboring of any rival spirit in his heart. God claims us entirely for Himself. No alien relationship, such as friendship with the world, will be tolerated by Him. He wants the undivided devotion of every human heart.

Verse 6 emphasizes that although God makes great demands on His people, He also makes great provision for them: "He giveth more grace." The word *grace* is used here to describe God's generous and effective help. "More grace" means that He gives abundant grace, all the help that mankind needs. The difficulties of living a separated life for God in a wicked world are many and formidable, but God's grace is more than adequate for all our needs. God is indeed a jealous God and makes exacting demands of us, but He provides what is necessary to enable us to resist those influences and forces that would draw us away to the world. The greater our needs, the greater is God's supply of grace. *No problem is so Big that God cannot handle it—*

C. Practical Advice (vv. 7-10)

7. Submit yourselves therefore to God. Resist the devil, and he will flee from you.

A literal rendering of "Submit yourselves . . . to God" is "Set yourselves under God." To set ourselves under God is to subordinate ourselves to Him, to bring our will under His control, to yield sincere obedience to His commands.

The call for submission is followed by a command to resist the devil. Actually this is involved in our submission to God. To be a loyal subject of God's, one must, of necessity, resist God's archfoe. The Greek word used here for "resist" means "take your stand against." It is used by Paul in Ephesians 6:13, where we are charged to "withstand" the assaulting forces of evil. The word is also used by Peter in 1 Peter 5:9 in another command to "resist" the devil. We resist him when we refuse to yield to him, when we fearlessly defy him.

8. Draw nigh to God, and he will draw nigh to you. Cleanse your hands, ye sinners; and purify your hearts, ye double minded.

We are to earnestly seek for God, and the assurance is given that if we do so, He will unfailingly respond. No one has ever really sought Him in vain. Since God is omnipresent, He is always near. This reference has to do with fellowship and communion.

How are we to draw near to God? We cannot walk in harmony with God and with the world; we cannot live in sin and have fellowship with God. So we have to cleanse our hands if we want to hold the hand of God. The double-minded man—the man whose heart is divided between God and the world—is called upon to purify his heart, to set it completely on God.

It should be noted that in Old Testament times the washing of the hands was a ritual required especially of the priests as a part of the process that qualified them to perform their ceremonial duties (Exodus 30:20). By adding "purify your hearts," James further accentuated the symbolism of cleansing he had already employed in this verse.

9. Be afflicted, and mourn, and weep: let your laughter be turned

to mourning, and your joy to heaviness.

10. Humble yourselves in the sight of the Lord, and he shall lift you up.

There is nothing wrong with joy and laughter in themselves. The Lord wants our mouths to be filled with laughter and our hearts with joy. But if we are not right with Him, if sin has come between us and God, if we are out of fellowship with Him, if our hands are soiled with sin and our hearts are divided, we ought to "be afflicted [grieve], mourn, and weep." Only through sorrow for our sins, through repentance in true humility, will God lift us up to sit with Him in "heavenly places." Then we can experience joy everlasting in His presence.

Why are our prayers not answered at times? Explain.

II. BE PATIENT IN SUFFERING
   (James 5:7-12)

A. The Appeal (vv. 7-11)

7. Be patient therefore, brethren, unto the coming of the Lord. Behold, the husbandman waiteth for the precious fruit of the earth, and hath long patience for it, until he receive the early and latter rain.

8. Be ye also patient; stablish your hearts: for the coming of the Lord draweth nigh.

9. Grudge not one against another, brethren, lest ye be condemned: behold, the judge standeth before the door.

James exhorted his readers to wait. Waiting constitutes a large part of the Christian life. Patience is not merely an aspect of Christian character; it is a virtue which

should pervade the whole life. In all ages, spiritual desires and trials are much the same; all believers, therefore, have the same need of patience. A frequent exhortation of Scripture is that we wait on the Lord.

Christian patience coexists with suffering. Inherent in the word *long-suffering* is the meaning of suffering patiently for a long time. Sometimes it involves enduring personal offenses; at other times, it may require patience while suffering through unpleasant circumstances. But the Christian receives comfort as a result of waiting upon God and trusting His good will in the face of life's difficulties.

How long should this patient endurance continue? "Unto the coming of the Lord!" What exactly does this mean? It could mean any intervention of the Lord to deliver us from trouble, including our deliverance through death. But the ultimate reference is to the Lord's final advent at the close of the age, when the Savior will appear as the judge of all; at that time He will put an end forever to tyranny and wrong. The thought of that great event is surely well designed to "stablish" our hearts, to strengthen us for patient endurance. James used the illustration of the farmer to encourage patience. The next morning after the farmer has planted seed, the ground looks the same as before the planting. But he knows that with the right conditions and care, the seed will slowly become a plant and the plant will produce a crop.

It is not difficult to be patient when we know our sufferings are just for a time, that a glorious tomorrow lies ahead. We are to establish our hearts, to rest calmly upon God's promises, even though for a time the wicked seem to prosper and the righteous suffer. Some day, perhaps soon, all that will be changed, "for the coming of the Lord draweth nigh." We are to live in continual expectancy of the Lord's coming. Nothing can more establish the heart amid troubles than the realization that His coming is drawing ever nearer.

The word *grudge* used in verse 9 means sighing or groaning with ill will toward another, or to complain against another brother or sister in Christ. It is altogether too easy to blame others for our troubles. In the midst of hardship, especially when we may feel helpless to change the circumstances, frustration against the oppressor may find an outlet in grumbling and complaining against those closest to us—in our own families or in the church family. James was clear in his declaration: this should not be!

Don't Blame Anyone else For your Troubles

10. Take, my brethren, the prophets, who have spoken in the name of the Lord, for an example of suffering affliction, and of patience.

11. Behold, we count them happy which endure. Ye have heard of the patience of Job, and have seen the end of the Lord; that the Lord is very pitiful, and of tender mercy.

The example of the prophets should encourage us. It should cheer us in every trial to remember how the prophets and saints of old endured their afflictions. One lesson we should learn from Job's experience is that "the Lord is very pitiful [compassionate], and of tender mercy." He is compassionate in allowing the trial, in the intensity of

it, in the grace which He gives to bear it, in the unraveling of its merciful purpose, and in the happy results with which He rewards His people when they have been approved.

B. Reverence for God's Name, (v. 12) *Do Not Take His Name in Vain*

12. But above all things, my brethren, swear not, neither by heaven, neither by the earth, neither by any other oath: but let your yea be yea; and your nay, nay; lest ye fall into condemnation.

James referred often in this letter to sins of speech. Verse 12 is an appeal for reverence and honesty in everyday conversation.

"But above all things, my brethren, swear not" had no reference to courtroom procedure. The prohibition was against the flippant use of God's name to guarantee the truth of one's statements. Among Jews and other people of the first century, ordinary standards of truthfulness had sunk so low that a statement was thought to be without value unless it was supported by an oath. But James was saying here, just as Jesus did in His Sermon on the Mount, let your basic honesty be such that "your word is your bond." The honest man's yes and no can be trusted completely; but even with an oath, who could trust the word of an otherwise dishonest one?

Ask: *How is it possible for a Christian to be patient in a hostile world?*

III. PRAY IN ALL SITUATIONS
(James 5:13-18)

A. The Place of Prayer and Praise (vv. 13-16)

13. Is any among you afflicted? let him pray. Is any merry? let him sing psalms.

14. Is any sick among you? let him call for the elders of the church; and let them pray over him, anointing him with oil in the name of the Lord:

15. And the prayer of faith shall save the sick, and the Lord shall raise him up; and if he have committed sins, they shall be forgiven him.

In verse 12 swearing was forbidden as unbecoming of Christians; but in verses 13-15, James identified the kind of language that is becoming to Christians. Strong emotions should not be expressed in irreverent oaths but in an act of worship. James made an earnest appeal to let prayer and praise hallow every aspect of life. He did this by mentioning three classes of people: the suffering, the cheerful, and the sick. This prayer is to be both personal and intercessory. It grows out of a sense of need or gratitude, is to be offered in faith, and must be joined with confession of sin.

The afflicted would be those with any kind of trouble, whether physical or mental; personal or domestic; or arising from ordinary trials, spiritual battles, or religious persecution. The Greek word means "to suffer misfortune; to have hard experiences."

How should the Christian react when in these situations? "Let him pray."

Trouble does not last always. There are periods of joy. During those times the believer is exhorted to sing psalms.

These verses teach that in sickness our faith should be in God. All healing is of God, but during Jesus' ministry He employed certain physical symbols in His miracles. For example, in Mark's record of Jesus' healing of the deaf man with a speech impediment, He took the man aside and put His fingers into his ears, spat and touched the man's tongue, looked up toward heaven, and commanded the healing to take place (7:33, 34). So also in the practice prescribed by James is recognition of the fact that only God can heal, but there is also the fact that God often uses human means for effecting His healing work—prayer and the anointing with oil, which was perhaps the great symbol of medical remedies (Mark 6:13; Luke 10:34).

James mentioned three specific results of prayer in verse 15: restoration, raising up (healing), and forgiveness.

16a. Confess your faults one to another, and pray one for another, that ye may be healed.

In dealing with the first part of this verse, Charles Swindoll writes: "Remember, James has just dealt with those who were bedridden. According to the context of verses 13-16, these people were ill as a result of unconfessed sin in their lives. Beginning in verse 16, however, James turns a corner, as evidenced by his use of 'therefore' and his switch from 'him' to 'you.' *Therefore* lets us know that James is about to make an important point, and *you* takes this point out of the theoretical and into the personal. In short, James is advising that, to keep sin from making us ill, we need to confess our sins to one another regularly and pray continuously" (*James: Practical and Authentic Living*).

16b. The effectual fervent prayer of a righteous man availeth much.

These words summarize the importance of the preceding verses with a statement concerning the remarkable power of prayer. The *Twentieth Century New Testament* reads: "Great is the power of a good man's fervent prayer." The word translated "prayer" here emphasizes the idea of petition or supplication.

Two conditions of effectual prayer are stressed: One concerns the character of the petitioner—he is to be a righteous man. By this, James meant a man who is genuinely pious, who has a living faith manifested by the deeds of his life. The other condition of effectual prayer has to do with earnestness. The basic idea in the Greek text is that of a petition "having energy."

B. The Power of Prayer (vv. 17, 18)

(James 5:17, 18 is not included in the printed text.)

With many examples from the Old Testament to select from, James chose Elijah. Although he had an extraordinary personality and was an eminent prophet, Elijah was by no means divine. He was a man of "like passions" with us. He had the same human nature that we have—the same susceptibilities, dispositions, and infirmities. He too had his faults. But being a righteous man, he was a man of prayer; and his success in prayer should be an example to us.

James cited two special petitions of Elijah as examples. One was a prayer for judgment and then a prayer for mercy. Both of these vividly illustrate the power in the prayer of faith.

Discuss other Old Testament people who excelled in prayer.

REVIEW QUESTIONS

1. What reason does James give for prayers not being answered?
2. How may prayers be offered "amiss"?
3. What is involved in submitting to God?
4. How does James say a believer should react in times of difficulty?
5. What are the two conditions of effectual prayer stressed by James?

GOLDEN TEXT HOMILY

"DRAW NIGH TO GOD, AND HE WILL DRAW NIGH TO YOU" (James 4:8).

The majority of people desire to have the good things of God—to know the truth, to find true purpose for life, and to know the bliss of eternity in heaven. But this verse teaches us that in order for God to draw close to us, we must draw close to Him. Scripture teaches us how to draw near to God.

The latter part of verse 8 instructs, "Cleanse your hands . . . and purify your hearts." If we sincerely desire to do His will, our hands must be helping, worshiping, serving hands that do those things which glorify Him. Furthermore, our hearts are made pure when we accept Christ as our Savior. Then our sins are forgiven, and our deeds and thoughts will be guided by the Holy Spirit.

The Holy Spirit exhorts us to pray, to be burdened for the unsaved and the hurting of our society. He also teaches us to serve God with humility. Such a life will create a desire to do the will of God. And we are to love one another, as this is a commandment of God (John 15:12).

Although many desire spiritual blessings from God, there is only one way to obtain them: "Draw nigh to [Him]." We can only accomplish such a lofty goal by a life of faith, commitment, prayer, humility, and love. Then He will draw nigh to us.—**Jerry Puckett, Customer Service Representative, Pathway Press, Cleveland, Tennessee**

SENTENCE SERMONS

GOD WILL NEVER FAIL those who rely on Him.

—Selected

BELIEVERS HAVE access to God's abundant resources through prayer and faith.

—Selected

WHAT ISN'T won in prayer first is never won at all.

—Malcolm Cronk

WHEN GOD intends to bless His people, the first thing He does is set them to praying.

—Matthew Henry

EVANGELISM APPLICATION

GOD WILL SAVE ALL WHO CALL ON HIM.

D.L. Moody used to say that God has put the offer of salvation in such a way that the whole world can lay hold of it. All men can believe. A lame man might not perhaps be able to visit the sick, but he can believe. A blind man, by reason of his infirmity, cannot do many things; but he can believe. A deaf man can believe. A dying man can believe. God has put salvation so simply that young and old, wise and foolish, rich and poor, can all believe if they will. *How about you? What are your beliefs ??*

ILLUMINATING THE LESSON

Throughout the Book of James we are encouraged not to leave God out but rather to acknowledge Him in our speech, in our plans, and in our deeds. A Christian, Dorothea Day, has beautifully answered the poem "Invitus" in one which she titled "My Captain":

Out of the light that dazzles me,
   Bright as the sun from pole to pole,
   I thank the God I know to be
   For Christ the conqueror of my soul.
   I have no fear, though strait the gate,
   He cleared from punishment the scroll.
   Christ is the Master of my fate,
   Christ is the Captain of my soul.

DAILY BIBLE READINGS

M. Divine Leadership.
   Exodus 33:12-16
T. God's Healing Power.
   2 Kings 20:1-7
W. Miraculous Victory.
   2 Chronicles 14:9-15
T. Live in the Spirit.
   Romans 8:6-14
F. The Lord Is Near.
   Philippians 4:4-9
S. Focus on Christ.
   Hebrews 12:1-3

Hope Inspires Holy Living

Study Text: 1 Peter 1:3 through 2:3

Objective: To appreciate the believer's hope and commit to holy living.

Time: The Book of 1 Peter was probably written between A.D. 63 and 65

Place: The Book of 1 Peter was probably written at Rome.

Golden Text: "Be sober, and hope to the end for the grace that is to be brought unto you at the revelation of Jesus Christ" (1 Peter 1:13).

Central Truth: The Christian's hope is a daily incentive to holy living.

Evangelism Emphasis: God gives the hope of eternal life to all who believe in His Son.

PRINTED TEXT

1 Peter 1:3. Blessed be the God and Father of our Lord Jesus Christ, which according to his abundant mercy hath begotten us again unto a lively hope by the resurrection of Jesus Christ from the dead,

4. To an inheritance incorruptible, and undefiled, and that fadeth not away, reserved in heaven for you,

5. Who are kept by the power of God through faith unto salvation ready to be revealed in the last time.

6. Wherein ye greatly rejoice, though now for a season, if need be, ye are in heaviness through manifold temptations:

7. That the trial of your faith, being much more precious than of gold that perisheth, though it be tried with fire, might be found unto praise and honour and glory at the appearing of Jesus Christ:

13. Wherefore gird up the loins of your mind, be sober, and hope to the end for the grace that is to be brought unto you at the revelation of Jesus Christ;

14. As obedient children, not fashioning yourselves according to the former lusts in your ignorance:

15. But as he which hath called you is holy, so be ye holy in all manner of conversation;

16. Because it is written, Be ye holy; for I am holy.

18. Forasmuch as ye know that ye were not redeemed with corruptible things, as silver and gold, from your vain conversation received by tradition from your fathers;

19. But with the precious blood of Christ, as of a lamb without blemish and without spot:

22. Seeing ye have purified

your souls in obeying the truth through the Spirit unto unfeigned love of the brethren, see that ye love one another with a pure heart fervently:

23. Being born again, not of corruptible seed, but of incorruptible, by the word of God, which liveth and abideth for ever.

2:1. Wherefore laying aside all malice, and all guile, and hypocrisies, and envies, and all evil speakings,

2. As newborn babes, desire the sincere milk of the word, that ye may grow thereby:

3. If so be ye have tasted that the Lord is gracious.

LESSON OUTLINE

I. THE CHRISTIAN'S HOPE
   A. A Living Hope
   B. A Glorious Faith

II. CALL TO HOLINESS
   A. Called to Be Different
   B. Called to Unity

III. CHANGED BY GOD'S WORD
   A. Called to Love
   B. Called to Progress

LESSON EXPOSITION

INTRODUCTION

The name Simon Peter is well known. It is mentioned 210 times in the New Testament, whereas the name of Paul is recorded 162 times and the combined names of all the other apostles are found only 142 times.

Peter was a native of Bethsaida, a village on the northeastern tip of the sea of Galilee (John 1:44). He made his living as a fisherman along with his father, Jonas, and his brother, Andrew (Matthew 16:17; John 1:40). After his marriage, he and his wife apparently moved to a nearby town, Capernaum (see Matthew 8:5; 8:14). The record does not show whether they ever had any children. Andrew became convinced that Jesus was the Messiah. He then introduced Simon personally to Jesus (John 1:41, 42). On this occasion, Simon was given the additional name of Cephas (Aramaic), or Peter (Greek), both meaning "a rock" (John 1:42). Shortly after this event Christ called Peter to become a full-time follower or disciple (Matthew 4:18-20). Peter was selected to be a member of the Twelve from the multitude of Christ's followers. He became a prominent member of this select group during the remaining years of Christ's earthly ministry. He also became the leading apostle during the early days of the church.

Peter wrote his letter to "the strangers scattered throughout Pontus, Galatia, Cappadocia, Asia, and Bithynia." The letter has several purposes: to explain the relationship of trials to God's purpose in salvation (1:1-12); to provoke the readers to lives of holiness, love, growth, and testimony (1:13-2:12); to call for submission of believers to civil authorities (2:13-17), of servants to masters (2:18-25), and of wives to husbands (3:1-8); to discuss the proper attitude of believers to suffering (3:9-4:19); to give guidelines to the elders for the proper performance of their ministry (5:1-4); to call them to humility (5:5-7); to warn them against the tactics of Satan (5:8-11); and to send greetings (5:12-14).

I.   THE CHRISTIAN'S HOPE
     (1 Peter 1:3-12)

A. A Living Hope (vv. 3-5)

3. Blessed be the God and Father of our Lord Jesus Christ, which according to his abundant mercy hath begotten us again unto a lively hope by the resurrection of Jesus Christ from the dead,

4. To an inheritance incorruptible, and undefiled, and that fadeth not away, reserved in heaven for you,

5. Who are kept by the power of God through faith unto salvation ready to be revealed in the last time.

The people to whom Peter wrote were entering a period of severe trial. The apostle wanted to send them encouragement and support. So in this letter he burst forth with praise. The reason for such gratitude is the believer's hope. Paul was preeminently the apostle of faith, John the apostle of love, Peter the apostle of hope.

What is there about this lively hope that caused Peter to rejoice and bless God? He says "God . . . hath begotten us again unto a lively hope." God has made us His children by regeneration and heirs to an incorruptible inheritance in heaven. This means something follows our earthly life. Life does not explode into nothingness at death, leaving no trace of its glory. "I am the resurrection, and the life," Jesus said; "he that believeth in me, though he were dead, yet shall he live." Then He asked, "Believest thou this?" (John 11:25, 26). So in

the midst of the troubles we face, we may confidently believe that beyond this life there is the hope of more life, abundant life; and beyond the kingdom of this world is a kingdom forever with the Father.

This inheritance is permanent. "Incorruptible, and undefiled, and that fadeth not away" (v. 4). These three descriptions all imply permanence, but they treat it in different ways. "Incorruptible" means spiritual, not material. The blessedness of that state will not depend on anything that can decay. The blessedness of heaven will be in the development of our spiritual nature. "Undefiled" means untainted, unblemished by earthly defects and human infirmities. "That fadeth not away," means all of this is to be everlasting—eternal.

Peter also said this inheritance is certain—"reserved in heaven for you, who are kept by the power of God" (vv. 4, 5). No earthly heritage is sure, but this one is! "Reserved in heaven" means it is safe. That we are "kept by the power of God" means we are safe in God's love.

Our inheritance is made sure to us by the resurrection of Jesus Christ from the dead. Jesus Christ, our brother (see Hebrews 2:11, 12, 17), representative, and Lord, identified Himself with us in life and death, and made us one with Himself in resurrection, which is God's seal—the *amen*—to all Jesus said and did.

B. A Glorious Faith (vv. 6-12)

(1 Peter 1:8-12 is not included in the printed text.)

6. Wherein ye greatly rejoice, though now for a season, if need be, ye are in heaviness through manifold temptations:

7. That the trial of your faith, being much more precious than of gold that perisheth, though it be tried with fire, might be found unto praise and honour and glory at the appearing of Jesus Christ.

First Peter reflects for us, as in a mirror, the dark shadows that were gathering over the scattered saints—partakers of Christ's suffering—buffeted for doing well, reviled and suffering, exposed to railing and terror, evilly spoken of, tried in fiery trial, reproached for the name of Christ, and experiencing the same afflictions as brethren throughout the world. Such sorrows were some sources of their manifold trials. To suffer as Christians sometimes meant the loss of business, reputation, and home; desertion by parents, children, and friends; misrepresentation; hatred; and even death.

For ourselves, trials generally come from three sources: those brought on us by others; those caused by our own sins, mistakes, and indiscretions; and those permitted as tests from God, our Father. No wonder that at times the heart is bowed down beneath such pressures.

According to the apostle, the saints' joy can grow out of manifold trials—joy experienced even during times of sorrow (v. 7). The believer ought to always rejoice. The idea that a believer ought to rejoice *only* is as foolish as it is false. But it is possible *always* to rejoice; "as sorrowful, yet always rejoicing" (2 Corinthians 6:10). In Peter's words, we have grounds for joy; they are faith, hope, and love.

The heaviness—grief, suffering—that we have to endure through the trials of life is for the purpose of proving and purifying our faith. "Trial" (1 Peter 1:7) is equivalent to trying, testing, proving. Is it not in darkness that our faith is tested? "Heaviness" (v. 6) is the time when we discover who we are. It is the time when we show what we are. Just as gold is tested by fire and the impurities removed so that after the refining process all that remains is pure gold, when we are tried by fire, our pure faith will prove its genuineness—with the result of bringing praise, honor, and glory to God. Heaven and earth are gathered around us as we are being tried and refined—God and Satan looking— the divine honor and joy at stake. What a sublime and sobering thought!

The heaviness of our trials contributes to the enlargment of our hope. In every aspect of life we are cheered on through difficulties by the hope of eternal life. We need hope beyond this life. And we have it! Hope points us to the blessed end and whispers, "Be of good cheer." We shall not only survive the storms of life, but we shall also be stronger because of them.

Our present life becomes unbearable if we live as though this life is all there is. But Peter concluded this part of his letter by saying that salvation awaits individual believers. The end result of our faith is our eternal salvation, brought to us by God's grace (vv. 9, 10). It is to us that the things revealed by the Spirit to the prophets are ministered. If the gifted prophets and holy angels found sacred joy in pondering the provisions of God's love and mercy, how urgent it becomes for us to heed the gospel which offers gracious pardon, a spiritual cleansing, and a dauntless life.

What should be the Christian's attitude toward trials?

II. CALL TO HOLINESS
   (1 Peter 1:13-21)

A. Called to Be Different
   (vv. 13-16)

13. Wherefore gird up the loins of your mind, be sober, and hope to the end for the grace that is to be brought unto you at the revelation of Jesus Christ;

When Peter used the phrase "gird up your loins," he was referring to the type of clothing worn in the East. The hot climate dictated the wearing of long, loose, flowing robes. That was fine as long as the movement of the body was deliberate. But if there had to be movement in a hurry, then the clothing could be hampering. Therefore, they must take up their garments so as not to impede their progress. When the Israelites were expecting the summons to leave Egypt, they stood around the tables on which the paschal lamb was smoking. They were ready for the journey with their loins girded. Elijah, the prophet of fire, girded himself for the swift run before Ahab's chariot from Carmel to Jezreel (1 Kings 18:46).

Peter urged his readers to guard their tastes, appetites, affections, and inclinations. "Gird up the loins of your mind" is an appropriate imagery, because sin begins in the thought life. Here the idea is entertained before the behavior emerges. We must not let our thoughts stream as they will; to do so puts us at great peril.

One of the ancient preachers said, "We must 'gird up' the habits of our souls, and trim ourselves, so as to pass as quickly and easily as possible through the thorny jungle of the world." Elders, deacons, women, aged men, young men, and maidens are all exhorted in the New Testament to be sober.

Peter urged believers to hope to the end. Hope motivates the believer onward. It strengthens him through the discomforts of the journey. It provides an inward joy that keeps things bright within his heart.

The object of the believer's hope is grace. Grace comes from God. It is His favor. He gave the first gift of grace. It is never deserved by any merits of men. Someone has very aptly said that grace is glory begun and glory is grace completed. So it is for the one who surrenders to Jesus Christ.

14. As obedient children, not fashioning yourselves according to the former lusts in your ignorance.

Those who are fashioned "according to the former lusts" have allowed their natural inclinations to run wild, overthrowing wholesome restraints and asserting their own arrogant will. Those in darkness, unillumined by grace, allow their lusts to dominate their lives. They become molded or fashioned by their lusts, as a potter molds clay. Being ignorant of how abominable sin is, of its disastrous results and its insidious growth, unbelievers yield to it, allowing it to rule them until it becomes a tyrant and eventually ruins their lives.

15. But as he which hath called you is holy, so be ye holy in all manner of conversation;

16. Because it is written, Be ye holy; for I am holy.

The model for holiness is the all-holy God himself. One of the early theologians said that the essence of religion consists in imitating the One we worship.

"In the Old Testament, heathen gods were represented as actuated by human passions and stained with hateful sins; their character must have reacted upon their ignorant worshipers; their worship was degrading. Our God is the most holy One, awful in holiness. He has not called us unto uncleanness, but unto holiness; He has set us apart for Himself, that we should be holy to Him. Holiness unto the Lord was written upon the miter of the high priest; it should be written in the hearts of Christians who are a holy priesthood, dedicated to the service of God. Holiness lies in the imitation of God. 'Be ye followers of God as dear children,' writes Paul. The word *followers* literally means 'imitators'" (*Pulpit Commentary*).

Obviously, Christians cannot perfectly imitate God's holiness, because holiness in God is inherent; in believers it is acquired. In God, holiness is infinite and unchangeable; it allows no increase and no diminution; it is an immutable attribute of His divine nature. Holiness in believers admits degrees and can only be maintained by perpetual increase. Saints on earth and saints in heaven will become more intelligently holy, beautiful in worship, and exact in obedience as the ages roll on.

Holiness in men is conditional and may be lost, at least while our probationary life on earth continues; in God it is integral and substantive and can no more be lost than God can cease to be. In God, holiness is commensurate with infinite capacity; in man, it is measured by finite and fallen capabilities—capabilities limited and weak.

B. Called to Unity (vv. 17-21)

(1 Peter 1:17, 20, 21 is not included in the printed text.)

18. Forasmuch as ye know that ye were not redeemed with corruptible things, as silver and gold, from your vain conversation received by tradition from your fathers;

19. But with the precious blood of Christ, as of a lamb without blemish and without spot.

The recognition of God's fatherhood gives true character to the Christian's fear. Men would say, "If God is our Father, and not our judge, then He need not be feared." To the contrary, Peter's view refutes this sentiment. Holy fear, which is befitting for all Christians, is made gracious and purifying by our knowledge that the Father's eye is upon us and the Father's heart never ceases to cherish us.

Verses 17-21 contain one long reason why we who have salvation through Christ should live in reverence. The apostle spoke strongly of the certainty of our salvation: he called us elect; he blessed God that we have an inheritance reserved for us and that we are kept for it. He said that loving Christ, we now have the salvation of our souls. Then he added that the revelation of this salvation, being given through the Holy Spirit, is infallibly true. But after all that, he bids us pass the time of our sojourning here in fear, an emphatic contradiction of the idea that the doctrine of grace fosters a spirit of carelessness. A reverent concern about the salvation of our souls is the natural result of God's free salvation.

Is there any difference between "fearing God" and having reverence for Him? Explain.

III. CHANGED BY GOD'S WORD
(1 Peter 1:22—2:3)

A. Called to Love (vv. 22-25)

(1 Peter 1:24, 25 is not included in the printed text.)

22. Seeing ye have purified your souls in obeying the truth through the Spirit unto unfeigned love of the brethren, see that ye love one another with a pure heart fervently:

23. Being born again, not of corruptible seed, but of incorruptible, by the word of God, which liveth and abideth for ever.

"Love one another" is the major theme of these verses. Many other duties are imposed in the words that surround these, but loving one another is the basic emphasis. The meaning of verse 22 is that only after we have become pure through our acceptance of and obedience to the gospel truth are we able in the highest sense to love, or to live a life of love. This is real love—love from the heart. It is intense, sincere, genuine, and fervent. Peter commanded, "See that ye love one another." Jesus himself had told His disciples, "By this shall all men know that ye are my disciples, if ye have love one to another" (John 13:35). This becomes possible because we have been changed. We have been born again by the Word of God.

B. Called to Progress
(1 Peter 2:1-3)

1. Wherefore laying aside all malice, and all guile, and hypocrisies, and envies, and all evil speakings,

2. As newborn babes, desire the sincere milk of the word, that ye may grow thereby:

3. If so be ye have tasted that the Lord is gracious.

Peter identified a representative selection of the evils that are harmful to the spiritual life. Probably these are mentioned here rather than others because, judging from Peter's frequent exhortations to love and to be subject to one another, they represent a class of sins to which the Christians to whom he wrote were especially prone. These were the sins which most easily beset them.

The term "newborn babes" (v. 2) emphasizes that the new life Peter was talking about was immature. These words teach us that there is Christian character not yet perfected in all Christians and especially in newborn babes in Christ. As we cannot see what a baby can become, neither can we see in the newborn child of God the perfected saint bowing in the eternal glory before His throne. Spiritual maturity comes through growth. The nourishment of God's Word provides for the balanced growth of all our spiritual faculties, so that we become more and more like Christ our Lord.

The graciousness of our Lord is a delight to our spiritual appetite (v. 3). We who have tasted His love have developed a desire to be fed by His Word and to grow in His grace. We must come again and again to the Word to satisfy our appetite which, though always being fed, is ever increasing.

How does the believer develop a spiritual appetite?

REVIEW QUESTIONS

1. What is the Christian's hope?
2. What is the basis of the believer's hope?
3. What did Peter say about the believer's inheritance?
4. Where is the believer's inheritance?
5. Why should we be holy?

GOLDEN TEXT HOMILY

"BE SOBER, AND HOPE TO THE END FOR THE GRACE THAT IS TO BE BROUGHT UNTO YOU AT THE REVELATION OF JESUS CHRIST" (1 Peter 1:13).

Preparing for the glorious revelation of the Lord at His second advent is a sobering thought. To get ready and stay ready for eternity is something to be taken seriously.

God has given us all things necessary for life and godliness. Let us accept His gifts with thankfulness and then faithfully use them. We should always remember that the highest gift of all is to be made partakers of the divine nature.

Peter's admonition is to be sober and hope to the end. We should remember that our life on earth is short and we should live godly, daily, in order to be ready for eternity.

The Christian who desires to be ready at the revelation of Jesus Christ must seek to love God with all his heart, soul, and mind. One's goal to the end should be to have and never lose a full, unwavering, constant hope.

The Christian's hope must be directed to, set toward, continued growth in grace. James 4:6 tells us, "He giveth more grace."

Sometimes our hope is mixed with doubts and fears. At those times we must lift up our eyes to the hills from whence comes our help. And thank God for the glorious help that is always available to us: "[Our] help cometh from the Lord" (Psalm 121:2).

God's grace comes in a continually increasing measure as the Lord reveals Himself more and more to the believing soul. What a glorious time it will be when His saints shall see Him, as He is, in His kingdom.—**O.W. Polen, D.D., Coordinator of Special Projects, Church of God Publishing House, Cleveland, Tennessee**

SENTENCE SERMONS

THE CHRISTIAN'S HOPE is a daily incentive to holy living.
—Selected

HOPE NOT ONLY bears up the mind under suffering, but makes her rejoice in them.
—Joseph Addison

A HOLY LIFE will produce the deepest impression. Lighthouses blow no horns; they only shine.
—Dwight L. Moody

IN THE BIBLE there is no twilight, but intense light and intense darkness.
—Oswald Chambers

EVANGELISM APPLICATION

GOD GIVES THE HOPE OF ETERNAL LIFE TO ALL WHO BELIEVE IN HIS SON.

Jesus appealed to men just to come to Him. To many of them He had to say, "Ye will not come to me, that ye might have life" (John 5:40). He is still appealing, saying, "Come unto me, all ye that labour and are heavy laden, and I will give you rest" (Matthew 11:28). But one has to respond to His call and believe in His Son.

ILLUMINATING THE LESSON

The Christian's hope is a daily incentive to holy living. Clouds may come, but they do not intervene between God and his soul. He may pass a whole life of conflict, trial, and suffering, like Daniel, Paul, Luther, and thousands more whose sufferings never gained notoriety, and yet in the midst of all, and continuously, in spite of all, he sings a song of victory. It is not victory in the sense of putting an end to his warfare. It is often the best-equipped soldiers who fight the greatest battles. The victory which he celebrates is that of a succession of triumphs. He comes out of every engagement shouting, "Thanks be unto God, which always causeth us to triumph in Christ, and maketh manifest the savour of his knowledge by us in every place" (2 Corinthians 2:14).

DAILY BIBLE READINGS

M. Blessings of Holiness.
    Deuteronomy 28:1-12
T. Hope in God's Presence.
    Psalm 16:1-11
W. Stand in God's Holy Place.
    Psalm 24:1-10
T. Hope for the Future.
    1 Thessalonians 4:13-18
F. Say "No" to Ungodliness.
    Titus 2:11-14
S. Holiness Required.
    Hebrews 12:11-17

Christians in Today's World

Study Text: 1 Peter 2:4-10, 13-17; 3:13-18; 4:1, 2, 12-19; 5:5-7

Objective: To understand that believers are God's chosen people and respond to society in a godly manner.

Time: The Book of 1 Peter was probably written between A.D. 63 and 65.

Place: The Book of 1 Peter was probably written at Rome.

Golden Text: "Ye are a chosen generation, a royal priesthood, an holy nation, a peculiar people; that ye should shew forth the praises of him who hath called you out of darkness into his marvellous light" (1 Peter 2:9).

Central Truth: Believers are Christ's representatives to a lost world.

Evangelism Emphasis: Believers are Christ's representatives to a lost world.

PRINTED TEXT

1 Peter 2:9. But ye are a chosen generation, a royal priesthood, an holy nation, a peculiar people; that ye should shew forth the praises of him who hath called you out of darkness into his marvellous light:

10. Which in time past were not a people, but are now the people of God: which had not obtained mercy, but now have obtained mercy.

13. Submit yourselves to every ordinance of man for the Lord's sake: whether it be to the king, as supreme;

14. Or unto governors, as unto them that are sent by him for the punishment of evildoers, and for the praise of them that do well.

5:5. Likewise, ye younger, submit yourselves unto the elder. Yea, all of you be subject one to another, and be clothed with humility: for God resisteth the proud, and giveth grace to the humble.

6. Humble yourselves therefore under the mighty hand of God, that he may exalt you in due time:

7. Casting all your care upon him; for he careth for you.

3:14. But and if ye suffer for righteousness' sake, happy are ye: and be not afraid of their terror, neither be troubled;

15. But sanctify the Lord God in your hearts: and be ready always to give an answer to every man that asketh you a reason of the hope that is in you with meekness and fear:

16. Having a good conscience; that, whereas they speak evil of you, as of evildoers, they may be ashamed that falsely accuse your good conversation in Christ.

17. For it is better, if the will of God be so, that ye suffer for well doing, than for evil doing.

18. For Christ also hath once suffered for sins, the just for the unjust, that he might bring us to God, being put to death in the flesh, but quickened by the Spirit.

4:1. Forasmuch then as Christ hath suffered for us in the flesh, arm yourselves likewise with the same mind: for he that hath suffered in the flesh hath ceased from sin;

2. That he no longer should live the rest of his time in the flesh to the lusts of men, but to the will of God.

LESSON OUTLINE

I.   CHOSEN BY GOD
  A. Living Stones
  B. The Cornerstone
  C. A Royal Priesthood

II. CALLED TO RESPECT AUTHORITY
  A. Submission to Authority
  B. Concern for Humility

III. CHRISTIAN RESPONSE TO PERSECUTION
  A. Be Prepared
  B. Militant Attitude Toward Sin
  C. Learn the Facts

LESSON EXPOSITION

INTRODUCTION

The Christian is a pilgrim; but he should never forget that while his true citizenship is in heaven, he also retains citizenship on earth (see 1 Peter 2:11; Philippians 3:20). As a citizen of two kingdoms, the kingdom of God and the kingdom of Caesar (Matthew 22:21), he is called to live by the principles of God's kingdom while existing physically for a time in the kingdom of Caesar (John 14:15). This unusual-sounding life is not as bad as it might first appear, for there are laws of life that are common to both kingdoms. Problems arise, however, when men deny the existence of God's laws of life or if when they acknowledge them, they refuse to abide by them. Even Christians can thwart God's plan when they, like men of the world, fail to obey God's law.

How is the Christian different from the non-Christian? He is different because he has experienced a second, or new, birth (1 Peter 1:23) and has been redeemed by the blood of Christ. Subsequent to regeneration the believer starts his new life. He is not yet perfect and will not be glorified until the end of the age. Meanwhile he enters into that period of his new life between justification and glorification.

The Christian is different from the non-Christian because he experiences a new and different estrangement. Prior to becoming a Christian, he was the enemy of God; he loved the world and the world loved him. But once he became a child of God, he became estranged from the world. Formerly the world loved him, whereas now it hates him (John 15:18, 19). So man, whether saved or lost, experiences alienation in this life—either from God or from the world.

I. CHOSEN BY GOD
  (1 Peter 2:4-10)

A. Living Stones (vv. 4, 5)

(1 Peter 2:4, 5 is not included in the printed text.)

Christ was considered by Peter to be the Jehovah (Lord) of the Old Testament. There was no hesitation on his part to identify Him as the gracious "Lord" of the Psalms (v. 3; Psalm 34:8). This indicates that the doctrine of the divinity of Jesus was familiar to the people to whom Peter was writing. Verses 4 and 5 reveal to us the office Christ occupies, the highest gift He bestows, and the conditions on which we receive it from Him.

According to Peter, Christ's office is the foundation stone for all men's lives and hopes. Many Old Testament references are united in Peter's metaphor. The Shepherd, the Stone of Israel, had been celebrated in ancient poetry. Isaiah spoke of the tried foundation laid by God's own hand in Zion, which yet should be a stone of stumbling to those who refused to build on it (28:16).

Jesus Christ is the foundation stone for the Christian's life. He is "the firstborn of every creature," the agent of creation, the mediator between God and man through whom all things came to be and in whom all things continue to exist. He is the supreme example for humanity, the head of the church, which is His body (Colossians 1:15-19). He is the foundation on which the individual soul must build all hope, joy, and goodness. He is the foundation of the highest and purest form of social life. He is the source of all true thoughts about God, man, immortality, and duty.

In coming to Christ, we become living stones. How? The condition is expressed in the words "to whom coming." The original word implies a close approach. We must be so near Him as to touch Him if His transforming power is to flow into our hearts. We come in faith. The form of expression in the Greek shows that the coming is not an act done once for all time but one continually repeated.

B. The Cornerstone (vv. 6-8)

(1 Peter 2:6-8 is not included in the printed text.)

In verse 5, Peter said the household of God is like a spiritual temple. What kind of materials are used in this spiritual temple, and how is it built? The foundation is of prime importance. Jesus Christ is called the "chief corner stone" (v. 6). He is also a living stone whom God, not man, has established as the rock on which to build. This is in fulfillment of God's promise.

This spiritual house (v. 5) included all believers throughout the Roman provinces referred to in the first chapter of this letter. This indicates that Peter understood Jesus' mention of the church in Matthew 16:18 to be not merely the local church but the universal church. All believers, as "living stones" (v. 5, NKJV), are built upon the Living Stone, who is the foundation. They partake of the life of the Living Stone, evidencing corporate growth as other new stones are bonded in by the Holy Spirit.

C. A Royal Priesthood (vv. 9, 10)

9. But ye are a chosen generation, a royal priesthood, an holy nation, a peculiar people; that ye should shew forth the praises of

him who hath called you out of darkness into his marvellous light.

10. Which in time past were not a people, but are now the people of God: which had not obtained mercy, but now have obtained mercy.

Peter listed in this verse what Christians are to Christ. They are "a chosen generation," or an "elect race." The greater the privilege, the greater the responsibility. The elect position of the nation of Israel, to whom pertained "the adoption, and the glory, and the covenants" (Romans 9:4), was expressly entrusted to them that through them God might bless all the nations of the earth. But during the present period of Israel's rejection of Christ, the church has been summoned to this glorious work of being the channel for the divine blessings to mankind.

Peter also said Christians are to be "a royal priesthood." The offices of royalty and priesthood were carefully kept apart in Israel. When King Uzziah attempted to combine them, he was driven from the Temple, branded with leprosy (2 Chronicles 26:16-20). But in Christ they blend. He is a priest upon His throne. His followers are constituted as kings and priests. As priests we worship. As kings we rule over men with love that blesses and saves.

The apostle calls Christians a "holy nation." This expression, like the former, comes from the ancient covenant which God made with Israel at Sinai. Israel, as a nation, failed to keep the covenant. But individuals, whether Jews or Gentiles, who accept Christ constitute a holy nation, an innumerable

multitude obeying a higher morality, and they are citizens of the city which can never pass away.

Believers are also identified as "a peculiar people." This means we are God's own possession. The word *peculiar* comes from the Latin word *peculium*, meaning "private property," especially the private treasure of a king or wealthy person. Peter regarded the church as God's private treasure on earth.

The message of divine love had touched their hearts. By God's mercy they were numbered among His people—pardoned and cleansed. It was only fitting, then, that they should offer their highest tribute of praise to the excellence of that mercy that had found them in their forlorn condition. And do we not all have reason to praise the God of mercy who has changed our circumstances, has broken down the hardness of our hearts, and has admitted us to such a glorious privilege of being called children of God?

Is every believer chosen by God? Explain.

II. CALLED TO RESPECT AUTHORITY (1 Peter 2:13-17; 5:5-7)

A. Submission to Authority (2:13-17)

(1 Peter 2:15-17 is not included in the printed text.)

13. Submit yourselves to every ordinance of man for the Lord's sake: whether it be to the king, as supreme;

14. Or unto governors, as unto them that are sent by him for the punishment of evildoers, and for the praise of them that do well.

In New Testament times Christianity was considered revolutionary in character. But it was spiritual rather than social or political. Perhaps this is why Peter gave the advice to "submit yourselves to every ordinance of man."

We might be disposed to hesitate in our submission to every ordinance of man. But the command continued, "Submit . . . for the Lord's sake." Why should we go on patiently doing right amid the detraction of the ignorant opposition of foolish men? "For so is the will of God, that with well doing ye may put to silence the ignorance of foolish men" (v. 15). Though we are free, we must not use our liberty as a veil for evil living (v. 16). We are the servants of God, and therefore His representatives to the world. We are to submit, not through fear of punishment, but to follow Christ's example, to carry out Christ's will, and for the best interests of Christ's church.

It is no secret that from the beginning the world hated the principles for which Christ died. The world professed to suspect His followers of being an evil threat. A charge against the early Christians was that they were plotting the overthrow of the Roman Empire and the dethronement of Caesar in favor of Jesus. The private worship services of early Christians were said to be held for unlawful purposes. Therefore, it was important to eliminate from the thinking of men the idea that Christians were subversive and were intent on destroying the established government and social order.

Both Paul and Peter especially exhorted early Christians to conform, as far as they could, to the just demands of government. They were to render to Caesar the things that were Caesar's. Accepting the order, safety, and privileges of civil and national life, they were to bear their share of its cost and submit to the government, agreeing to modify or alter it only by orderly and peaceful methods.

Christians were therefore called upon to "render . . . to all their dues: tribute to whom tribute is due; custom to whom custom; fear to whom fear; honour to whom honour" (Romans 13:7). Their goal was to lead a quiet and peaceful life, submitting to laws, and doing good. Thus, in time, they would disarm prejudice and conciliate their foes.

Peter gave four commands for Christians in verse 17. First, "Honour all men." Perhaps "value" or "esteem" would be a more appropriate translation than *honor*. Christians should manifest a genuine interest in all men.

But what if the men are not honorable? Actually every man, however wicked or degraded, has been created in the image of God. That image may be defaced, but it is still to be honored. God had taught Peter this in a wonderful way on a housetop in Joppa when He had told Peter in essence, "Do not call any man common or unclean" (Acts 10:15). And Peter had not forgotten the lesson.

Christians are to recognize the worth of all men. There is some worth in the most degraded of men. In each human being there is something which, in the sight of God, is of infinite value. Christ died for the sins of every person. Let us try to see every individual as God does—a person for whom Christ died.

The second injunction of Peter is "Love the brotherhood." There is to be respect for all outside the body of believers, but warm affection should be manifest for all Christians because they are bound together more closely through mutual love for Christ. This love is not mere sentiment but self-sacrifice; not just liking others but making others instead of oneself the pivot of living. This is the spirit in which Christians should conduct themselves toward all who belong to the brotherhood of the saints in Christ.

"Fear God" is the third command from the apostle. This is not a cringing dread but a worshipful awe. It is the profound reverence due to His infinite holiness, His perfect wisdom, and His majestic and incomprehensible power. True love expels the fear that brings torment; it begets godly fear instead. Love persuades, for the goodness and loveliness of God, to fear Him.

"Honour the king" is the fourth injunction of Peter. Though the emperor might be a Nero, Christians were to honor his office and show respect to him as representing authority and orderly government. The Roman emperors claimed the right to be worshiped as deities, but by plain implication, Peter denies them this. The king is rightfully to be honored, but to God only belong reverential awe and worship. Worship God ONLY But Honor those in office

B. Concern for Humility (5:5-7)

5. Likewise, ye younger, submit yourselves unto the elder. Yea, all of you be subject one to another, and be clothed with humility: for God resisteth the proud, and giveth grace to the humble.

6. Humble yourselves therefore under the mighty hand of God, that he may exalt you in due time:

7. Casting all your care upon him; for he careth for you.

Respect for experience is graceful and becoming in the young and has the sanction of Scripture. They must submit themselves to their elders, for "the hoary head is a crown of glory, if it be found in the way of righteousness" (Proverbs 16:31).

Peter said all believers, young and old, should submit to each other; and all should submit to God. How do we do this? "Be clothed with humility" is the answer. Just as Jesus laid aside His outer garment and put on a towel to become a servant, so each of us should have a servant's attitude and minister to each other. Humility is not demeaning ourselves and thinking poorly of ourselves. It is simply not thinking of ourselves at all.

It takes grace to submit to another believer, but God can give that grace if we humble ourselves before Him.

God resists the proud because He hates the sin of pride. The only antidote to pride is the grace of God, and we receive that grace when we yield ourselves to Him. The evidence of that grace is that we yield to one another.

God does not promise to exalt those who have been humbled, but he will exalt all who humble themselves—"in due time" (v. 6). Let us seek the grace of Him who is meek and lowly in heart. "He humbled himself, and became obedient unto death, even the death of the cross," and He is now exalted in heaven (Philippians 2:8, 9). God will exalt those who learn of Him the grace of humility, who take up their cross, thereby denying themselves. He will exalt them in His own good time, when He sees it is best.

Life is full of anxieties. They vary with our position in life, our circumstances, and our characters; but no one escapes them. They push in upon our thoughts and disturb our rest with their distracting presence. The Lord said, "Take no thought . . ." (Matthew 6:25, 31, 34; 10:19). Paul echoed His words, "Be careful for nothing" (Philippians 4:6). Peter, quoting the ancient Scriptures (see Psalm 55:22), bids us to cast all our care upon the Lord (1 Peter 5:7). It is not thoughtfulness which our Lord and His apostles forbids; it is not carelessness and improvidence which the Holy Scripture commends. The original word in each passage means "anxiety or distracting care." We must do our duty; we must provide, as best we can, for ourselves and for those dependent upon us; and then we must trust in God—casting our anxiety upon Him. If we have learned to humble ourselves under the mighty hand of God, we shall know that His fatherly hand is ever over His people, that we are in His hand always. Humility increases trustfulness; the sense of our own weakness deepens our confidence in God.

The grounds for our trustfulness are, in Peter's words, "He careth for you." He knows all our needs, difficulties, dangers, and temptations, with the same fullness of knowledge and depth of sympathy as if there were no others in the world besides ourselves and God.

Why do believers have so much difficulty with respecting authority?

III. CHRISTIAN RESPONSE TO PERSECUTION (1 Peter 3:13-18; 4:1, 2, 12-19)

A. Be Prepared (1 Peter 3:13-18)

(1 Peter 3:13 is not included in the printed text.)

14. But and if ye suffer for righteousness' sake, happy are ye: and be not afraid of their terror, neither be troubled;

15. But sanctify the Lord God in your hearts: and be ready always to give an answer to every man that asketh you a reason of the hope that is in you with meekness and fear:

16. Having a good conscience; that, whereas they speak evil of you, as of evildoers, they may be ashamed that falsely accuse your good conversation in Christ.

17. For it is better, if the will of God be so, that ye suffer for well doing, than for evil doing.

18. For Christ also hath once suffered for sins, the just for the unjust, that he might bring us to God, being put to death in the flesh, but quickened by the Spirit.

Peter did not say that if a man lives blamelessly, he will always be free from cruel treatment. The Christian is, by his very appearance, a moving conscience to excuse or condemn the people of the world. In verse 14 Peter echoed the Lord's message concerning persecution: They are blessed who suffer for the testimony of Christ because theirs is the kingdom of heaven (Matthew 5:11, 12).

Patient preparation means permanent overcoming power.

Do we Have it?

A good conscience is one that has been purged from dead works (Hebrews 9:14); is sprinkled with the blood of Christ (Hebrews 10:22); is witnessed by the Holy Spirit (Romans 9:1); is full of joy and has glory, welling up within it (2 Corinthians 1:12); and, as a calm, unruffled lake of peace, reflects the cloudless heaven of God's good pleasure. Detractors will be ashamed at the triumphant answer made to their accusations by the unblemished beauty of a Christian life, while those who love God will be encouraged.

John Calvin said, "If we suffer unjustly, it is not by chance, but according to the divine will. God wills nothing or appoints nothing but for the best reason. . . . They are led by Him to the contest . . . under His protection to give proof of their faith."

Jesus was "the Holy One and the Just" (Acts 3:14), and yet He was treated unjustly. Why? That He might die, "the just for the unjust," and bring them to God! (1 Peter 3:18). He died as our substitute (2:24), and He died only once (Hebrews 9:24-28). In other words, Jesus suffered for doing good; He did not die because of His own sins, for He had none (1 Peter 2:22).

B. Militant Attitude Toward Sin (4:1, 2)

1. Forasmuch then as Christ hath suffered for us in the flesh, arm yourselves likewise with the same mind: for he that hath suffered in the flesh hath ceased from sin;

2. That he no longer should live the rest of his time in the flesh to the lusts of men, but to the will of God.

In the words of F.B. Meyer, "When strong desires come through our bodies, and strive to send evil thoughts and passions through the heart and the will, they will find the fire-proof iron door slammed suddenly in their face, so that the dread contagion will not spread. The flesh may have its desires; but the cleansed heart will refuse to yield to them" (*Tried by Fire*).

Thanks Be to God

C. Learn the Facts (4:12-19)

(1 Peter 4:12-19 is not included in the printed text.)

Peter showed a deep sympathy with his suffering brethren; he spoke to them in the language of tenderness; he called them "beloved." He did not minimize the severity of the coming persecution; he called it a "fiery trial." By his example, we learn how to deal with the afflicted. He encouraged them.

We suffer thus to prove our faith; it is a time of testing. We must not think it strange. Indeed, this bitterness of persecution must be considered a partaking in Christ's suffering. And suffering is the portion of Christians, so we must regard it as belonging to our profession and accustom ourselves to patient endurance.

REVIEW QUESTIONS

1. What did Peter mean when he referred to Christ as the chief cornerstone?

2. How do Christians serve as "royal priests"?

3. Why, according to 1 Peter 2:13-15, are Christians to "submit . . . to every ordinance of man"?

4. What four admonitions did Peter give in verse 17 regarding the Christians' behavior toward others?

5. What encouragement did Peter give regarding the merits of humility?

GOLDEN TEXT HOMILY [Read]

"YE ARE A CHOSEN GENERATION, A ROYAL PRIESTHOOD, AN HOLY NATION, A PECULIAR PEOPLE; THAT YE SHOULD SHEW FORTH THE PRAISES OF HIM WHO HATH CALLED YOU OUT OF DARKNESS INTO HIS MARVELLOUS LIGHT" (1 Peter 2:9).

Christians are a chosen people. The Christian is called out of insignificance into significance. A man's greatness lies not in himself but in what he has been given to do and how well he does it.

The Christian's greatness lies not in himself but in the fact that God, through Christ, has chosen him to do His work in this world. A Christian is chosen for three things:

1. *Obedience.* The Christian is not chosen to do as he likes but to do as God likes.

2. *Privilege.* This means a new and intimate relationship and fellowship with God through Christ will exist.

3. *Service.* A Christian's honor is that he is a servant of God, and this privilege is that he will be used for the purpose of God.

Christians are a royal priesthood. Every Christian has the right of access and approach to God, and every Christian must offer his work, his worship, and himself to God. As a priest, he speaks to God in behalf of fellow believers and the unrighteous.

Christians are a holy nation. The basic meaning of the word *holy* in Greek means "different." When God chose us, He chose us to be different from other people. That difference lies in the fact that the Christian is dedicated to God's will and to God's service. Other people may follow the standards of this world, but for the Christian the only law is the standard of God and the will of God. God's standard of holiness and the law of love is seen in Jesus Christ.

Christians are God's special possession. It frequently happens that the value of a thing lies in the fact that someone has possessed it. A very ordinary thing often acquires a new value according to the importance or fame of the person who possessed it. In any museum you will find ordinary things which are of value only because they were once possessed and used by some great person. It is the ownership which gives them worth. This is also true of the Christian. You may have been a very ordinary person; but when Christ came into your life, you acquired a new value, dignity, and greatness because you belong to God. The greatness of the Christian lies in the fact that he is owned and used of God.—**Excerpts from the *Evangelical Commentary*, Vol. 32** Praise God "OUR Father"

SENTENCE SERMONS

BELIEVERS ARE CHRIST'S representatives to a lost world.
—Selected

IN GOD'S WILL every believer has a ministry to others.
—Anonymous

THE WAY of the world is to praise dead saints and persecute living ones.
—*Draper's Quotations for the Christian World*

HE PROFITS most who serves best.

—Motto of Rotary International

EVANGELISM APPLICATION

BELIEVERS ARE CHRIST'S REPRESENTATIVES TO A LOST WORLD.

Christians, by the command of the Lord, are to be witnesses, testimony bearers. We are to witness to the world that Jesus Christ is abundantly and superabundantly able to save "to the uttermost [all those who] that come unto God by him, seeing he ever liveth to make intercession for them" (Hebrews 7:25). We are to witness by our courageous, heroic, challenging, lofty living that this Jesus not only saves but keeps. With the brightness of God on our faces, with the joy of salvation bubbling up in our hearts, with the songs of the redeemed on our lips, with springing step and head held high—let us march on to Zion. Why? Because we are Christ's representatives to a lost world.

ILLUMINATING THE LESSON

In the Old Testament, David refused to touch Saul's life when Saul was at his mercy, because he was the Lord's anointed. The Roman government could not make the Christians of the early church worship the emperor or offer sacrifices to idols or even eat meat offered to idols. They preferred death to disobedience to God, and the blood of martyrs was the seed of the church.

The Christian will be a good citizen; he will obey his country's laws and respect the authorities. But he will put God first and Caesar second. No nation has ever failed to prosper when its people put God first and their country second. The best way for any citizen to love his country and to serve it well is to do this very thing. *God First In All Things.*

DAILY BIBLE READINGS

M. Chosen for Leadership.
    1 Samuel 16:4-13
T. Respecting Authority.
    1 Samuel 24:1-10
W. Loving Your Enemies.
    Matthew 5:43-48
T. Chosen by Christ.
    John 15:16-19
F. Submitting to Authorities.
    Romans 13:1-7
S. Promise to Overcomers.
    Revelation 2:8-11

Growing in Christian Character

Study Text: 2 Peter 1:1-21

Objective: To consider key aspects of Christian growth and pursue godly character.

Time: The Book of 2 Peter was written between A.D. 66 and 67.

Place: The Book of 2 Peter according to many Bible scholars, was written at Rome shortly before Peter's martyrdom.

Golden Text: "[God's] divine power hath given unto us all things that pertain unto life and godliness, through the knowledge of him that hath called us to glory and virtue" (2 Peter 1:3).

Central Truth: Knowing Jesus Christ and applying God's Word to daily living results in Christian growth.

Evangelism Emphasis: A maturing believer will be involved with winning the lost to Christ.

PRINTED TEXT

2 Peter 1:3. According as his divine power hath given unto us all things that pertain unto life and godliness, through the knowledge of him that hath called us to glory and virtue:

4. **Whereby are given unto us exceeding great and precious promises: that by these ye might be partakers of the divine nature, having escaped the corruption that is in the world through lust.**

5. And beside this, giving all diligence, add to your faith virtue; and to virtue knowledge;

6. **And to knowledge temperance; and to temperance patience; and to patience godliness;**

7. And to godliness brotherly kindness; and to brotherly kindness charity.

8. **For if these things be in you, and abound, they make you that ye shall neither be barren nor unfruitful in the knowledge of our Lord Jesus Christ.**

9. But he that lacketh these things is blind, and cannot see afar off, and hath forgotten that he was purged from his old sins.

10. **Wherefore the rather, brethren, give diligence to make your calling and election sure: for if ye do these things, ye shall never fall:**

11. For so an entrance shall be ministered unto you abundantly into the everlasting kingdom of our Lord and Saviour Jesus Christ.

16. **For we have not followed cunningly devised fables, when we made known unto you the power and coming of our Lord Jesus Christ, but were eyewitnesses of his majesty.**

17. For he received from God the Father honour and glory,

when there came such a voice to him from the excellent glory, This is my beloved Son, in whom I am well pleased.

18. And this voice which came from heaven we heard, when we were with him in the holy mount.

19. We have also a more sure word of prophecy; whereunto ye do well that ye take heed, as unto a light that shineth in a dark place, until the day dawn, and the day star arise in your hearts:

20. Knowing this first, that no prophecy of the scripture is of any private interpretation.

21. For the prophecy came not in old time by the will of man: but holy men of God spake as they were moved by the Holy Ghost.

LESSON OUTLINE

I. INCREASE IN CHRISTIAN QUALITIES

    A. Provision

    B. Diligence

    C. Victory

II. REMEMBER THE ESSENTIALS

    A. Concern

    B. Responsibility

III. HEAR AND OBEY GOD'S WORD

    A. Corroboration

    B. Assurance

LESSON EXPOSITION

INTRODUCTION

Peter knew that it was his responsibility to remind his readers of proper Christian doctrine and ethics (1:12, 13). However, he also knew that he was about to die (1:14). In order for his readers to have a permanent written record of his teaching after his death, he purposed to write (1:15; 3:1). In this Epistle, therefore he wanted to encourage his readers to grow into Christian maturity (1:3-11), to explain the imminence of his death (1:12-15), to show how the transfiguration of Christ guaranteed His second advent (1:16-18), to inform them that the truth of the second coming was not a concept originated by humans (1:19-21), to describe the moral and doctrinal characteristics of the false teachers (2:1-22), to explain the delay in Christ's return (3:1-9), to describe the destruction of the universe in the Day of the Lord (3:12,13), and to motivate them to vigilance and growth.

I. INCREASE IN CHRISTIAN QUALITIES (2 Peter 1:3-11)

A. Provisions (vv. 1-4)

(2 Peter 1:1, 2 is not included in the printed text.)

3. According as his divine power hath given unto us all things that pertain unto life and godliness, through the knowledge of him that hath called us to glory and virtue;

4. Whereby are given unto us exceeding great and precious promises: that by these ye might be partakers of the divine nature, having escaped the corruption that is in the world through lust.

Peter described himself in his first letter as "an apostle of Jesus Christ (1:1)." In this letter he again claimed that lofty title, but here he added the lowlier title of "servant" (2 Peter 1:1). Christ's servants must learn of their Master and remember that they are the bondservants of Jesus Christ.

Who were the readers of Peter's epistle? They were believers. They had listened to the preaching of the gospel. They had "obtained like precious faith" (v. 1) with those who had preached the faith to them. Now faith was also their possession and their inheritance.

The apostle invoked a blessing upon his readers in verse 2. It is the same form of salutation he used in his first letter—the prayer that grace and peace be multiplied to them. He could express no holier wishes for them. What more could they need than God's all-sufficient grace and the peace of God that surpasses understanding.

God's blessings of grace and peace are above what we can ask or think. We shrink from asking for blessings so far above what we deserve. But God has called us. The invitation comes from Him; freely of His own sovereign bounty He bids us come to Him. He attracts us by His own glory and virtue, manifesting His love and power in the ceaseless activity of His providence and grace. Thus He kindles in the Christian the strong desire for the knowledge of God and satisfies that desire by the revelation of Himself. Through that full and holy knowledge, granted to those who hunger and thirst after righteousness, He gives all things necessary for life and godliness. These are within our grasp, weak and helpless as we are, because God has given them.

In keeping with the worthiness of the giver, the gifts of God are of necessity great and precious. Peter mentioned two in verse 4: an escape from corruption and the privilege of partaking of the divine nature. The sinful corruption of the world is all around us. We see the results of its workings every day. Its miserable defilement is everywhere, so it is hard to escape from it. As God's angels once laid hold of the hand of Lot, brought him out of the doomed city, and said to him, "Escape for thy life . . . escape to the mountain, lest thou be consumed" (Genesis 19:17), so now the Holy Spirit alone can give us strength to escape the many sins which would so easily ensnare us.

To be kept safe from sin we need the abiding presence of the Holy Spirit. We need to be made partakers of the divine nature. This lofty state seems to be above our reach. The promise of the Spirit is a precious and exceedingly great promise. Will God indeed dwell with man? Can these poor bodies of ours become the temples of the Holy Spirit? Yes. We have His promise, and we know that God is true to His word. By the gift of the Holy Spirit we can partake of the divine nature.

B. Diligence (vv. 5-7)

5. And beside this, giving all diligence, add to your faith virtue; and to virtue knowledge;

6. And to knowledge temperance; and to temperance patience; and to patience godliness;

7. And to godliness brotherly kindness; and to brotherly kindness charity.

Verse 5 is an exhortation to earnest effort. It is a call to duty. We are enjoined to be diligent in our living for Christ. Peter had already said that God's divine power is with us. God has granted us all necessary help. But this, says the apostle, is the very reason we should be all the more diligent. It would be heartless work if we did not have the power of God to assist us. But this gift of power is the very ground on which the apostle based his exhortation to persevering, self-denying labor. God's power is fighting for us. We are told to bring to the side of that mighty aid all our earnestness. It may seem strange to be told to put our weak, trembling endeavors beside the strength of God, but the infinite and finite work together. The work is God's work. He began it and He "will perform it until the day of Jesus Christ" (Philippians 1:6). It is on that very ground that we must also work—in trusting faith, love, and gratitude.

Faith is the first of God's gifts for Christian living. This is the precious faith of which Peter spoke so warmly throughout his first letter. Faith, the first gift of God, cannot remain alone, however. As it works, *virtue* issues out of its active energies.

Virtue is the holy courage which enables Christians to act with boldness in the service of Christ. In the midst of temptations we need a resolute determination to do what is right in the sight of God, a steadfast strength of will to choose always what is good. This is the virtue of the Christian, and this is the result of faith.

With virtue comes *knowledge*. Courage and firmness may do harm unless they are directed by knowledge. Christian virtue leads to knowledge. Irresolute men, double-minded and undecided men, waver between right and wrong. They do not develop that keen perception of good and evil which can only be developed in conjunction with Christlike virtue. Holy discretion grows from Christian virtue.

The next grace on Peter's list is *temperance* (v. 6). The union of virtue and knowledge will produce temperance, or self-control, which enables the Christian to govern his appetites and to keep them under the rule of a Christian conscience. Without self-control there is no unity of purpose. The Christian must strive to devote his energies to the service of Christ.

Side by side with self-control comes *patient endurance*. He who controls his appetites will learn to endure hardness. Some of God's people have to wait in patient endurance; others labor in active service. Both may serve with equal faithfulness. It is not work itself, but inner faithfulness of spirit, that wins praise from God.

Godliness is next on Peter's list. Godliness is the spirit of reverence, the holy fear of God. The godly man sets God always before him; the thought of God controls his whole life. His effort is to do all things in the name of the Lord Jesus, to live for the Lord, to seek His glory only. This holy reverence for God can only be maintained through faith and self-control. It cannot flourish in an atmosphere of worldly pleasure and business.

Brotherly kindness (v 7.) naturally follows godliness. Out of godliness must flow the love of the brethren. John tells us, "If a man say, I love God, and hateth his brother, he is a liar: for he that loveth not his brother whom he hath seen, how can he love God whom he hath not seen?" (1 John 4:20). God's people are knit together in one family and fellowship. As we all love the same Father in heaven, we must for love's sake love all who by the new birth are made the children of God.

The last grace in Peter's list is *charity*. Christian love must not be confined within the limits of the church. It is especially due to those who are of the household of faith, but it cannot stop there. Love comes from God, who is love and whose love is without limits. The love we learn from God will be like His love. It must continually increase in depth and extent.

C. Victory (vv. 8-11)

8. For if these things, be you, and abound, they make you that ye shall neither be barren nor unfruitful in the knowledge of our Lord Jesus Christ.

9. But he that lacketh these things is blind, and cannot see afar off, and hath forgotten that he was purged from his old sins.

10. Wherefore the rather, brethren, give diligence to make your calling and election sure: for if ye do these things, ye shall never fall:

11. For so an entrance shall be ministered unto you abundantly into the everlasting kingdom of our Lord and Saviour Jesus Christ.

When we possess all these qualities, we will be effective and productive "in the knowledge of our Lord Jesus Christ," for the divine power of God is with us. When, by the help of that power working in and with us, the precious graces of Christ are made our own, they will not let us be unfruitful. Love, the crown of all graces of Christian character, is not mere sentiment; it is active spiritual energy. It will not allow the Christian to be idle; it must work, and in its working it will bring us nearer to the full knowledge of Christ.

Men are spiritually blind without these graces of Christian character. They cannot discern the cross of the Lord Jesus Christ. They cannot see the blessed realities of the eternal world. Nor can they discern the spiritual powers that are working in the church. Through spiritual blindness they incur forgetfulness of cleansing from their old sins.

In verse 10, Peter again urged his readers to be diligent. He used the language of entreaty. "Brethren," he said, in tones of affectionate appeal. He knew how hard it is to persevere and how much we all need encouragement.

Working with that divine power which alone is the source of our salvation, we can make our calling and election sure. While we are diligent in working out our own salvation, we feel God working in us. Doubts arise if we relax our efforts. If we put ourselves into perilous situations to which He has not called us, our doubts increase and our souls are vexed. On the other hand, earnest work for God deepens our assurance of God's love and our election to eternal life.

What is the responsibility of the church in helping believers develop Christian character?

II. REMEMBER THE ESSENTIALS (2 Peter 1:12-15)

A. Concern (vv. 12, 13)

(2 Peter 1:12, 13 is not included in the printed text.)

Peter was aware that most of his life was behind him. He knew there was a need for a continuing witness for Christ after his death. This weighed heavily upon his heart. Because of this burden, he not only determined to continue a personal ministry while living but also to write an account of his experiences so that his readers and those who would come after them would have an account and a defense of the faith.

B. Responsibility (vv. 14, 15)

(2 Peter 1:14, 15 is not included in the printed text.)

Those to whom Peter wrote had knowledge of the gospel. They had heard it from Paul and his companions. Peter gladly acknowledged this, but he also had a duty to perform. He felt, like Paul, that he was a debtor both to Jews and Gentiles. He felt that he must do his utmost to preach the gospel of Christ and to keep alive the holy flame of love in those who knew the truth. Therefore, he took advantage of every opportunity to stir his readers. He refused to relax his efforts so long as he lived.

Peter looked forward to his death with holy and peaceful calmness. He felt it was near at hand, for he was now an old man and the hour of which the Lord had spoken could not be delayed long (see John 21:18, 19). He called death the putting off of his tabernacle. His earthly body was regarded as a tent. The tent was old, worn out; it could not last long. He knew, like Paul, that he had "a building of God, an house not made with hands, eternal in the heavens" (2 Corinthians 5:1). Knowing this, he calmly awaited the dissolution of his earthly tabernacle. The approach of death, however, was also a reason for more earnest work while there was time.

The thought of our approaching death should be kept before us. It will help us to calmly and thoughtfully reflect upon it. Such meditation throws a clear light upon the meaning of our earthly life and impresses upon us the importance of finishing the work God has given us to do. Sometimes men do that work better when the shadow of approaching death is falling upon them. Testimony seems often to be deeper and more convincing from individuals on the point of departure, whose immediate future is in the world beyond the grave.

The thought of coming death will make true Christians more eager to work for God and more earnest to pray that Christ may be magnified in them, whether it be by life or death.

Pulpit Commentary has some interesting thoughts on this section of Peter's second letter. "To Christians, death is a departure, an exodus, out of a life of sorrows into the Land of Promise, the heavenly Canaan. The Lord who died for them is with them when they die. He accomplished His death for them at Jerusalem. His death has destroyed the power of the king of terrors, and taken away the sting of death. His death was a departure out of humiliation into glory. He told Peter once that he could not follow where He was going, but that he should follow Him afterward.

And so now it is His will that all those whom the Father has given Him should be with Him where He is."

Why do believers need to be continually reminded of spiritual matters?

III. HEAR AND OBEY GOD'S WORD (2 Peter 1:16-21)

A. Corroboration (vv. 16-18)

16. For we have not followed cunningly devised fables, when we made known unto you the power and coming of our Lord Jesus Christ, but were eyewitnesses of his majesty.

17. For he received from God the Father honour and glory, when there came such a voice to him from the excellent glory, This is my beloved Son, in whom I am well pleased.

18. And this voice which came from heaven we heard, when we were with him in the holy mount.

Peter proclaimed the certainty of the truths of the gospel. He stated first that these truths are not fables (v. 16). There were many legends and religious myths circulating among the people at that time in history—some among the Jews and some among the Gentiles. However, the gospel of Christ stands apart from them all in its unimpeachable truthfulness. The story of Jesus contains wonderful works of power and wonders of grace, but all of these are related with a simplicity that bears the stamp of truth.

The gospel truths which Peter presented were verified by eyewitnesses. But even more convincing is that Peter himself was a witness of the things about which he wrote. Likewise, John wrote concerning the Christ, the Son of God, "We beheld his glory" (1:14). There were also many other eyewitnesses of the Lord's life and works. Five hundred brethren at one time saw Him after He had risen from the dead (1 Corinthians 15:6). But there were three who had been eyewitnesses of His majesty when He was transfigured on the mountain and declared by God to be the Son of God (Matthew 17:1-5). Peter was one of those who had seen Jesus in His majesty on the Mount of Transfiguration.

Compelling evidence of the Savior's divine majesty was granted to the eyes and ears of Peter, James, and John on the day of His transfiguration. That radiant glory came from God the Father. The highly favored three had a preview of the glorious Christ the redeemed will behold in heaven. That blessed vision was to prepare them for and sustain them through the terrible events of crucifixion that would soon follow.

From time to time God gives to His saints glimpses of the blessings of heaven. The Savior manifests Himself to His chosen as He does not to the world. Sometimes those who are most highly favored with the vision of His love are called in a special manner to be partakers of His sufferings, to bear in their body the marks of the dying Lord Jesus (see Galatians 6:17).

The Lord Jesus was despised and rejected of men, but He belonged to the Lord God omnipotent—He was the most holy Son of God. Surely, as God was well pleased with His Son, who humbled Himself and became obedient unto death, so He is well pleased now with those to whom the only begotten Son has given power to become the children of God.

Peter, James, and John heard that august voice as it spoke from heaven. They heard God speak. They heard it with their own ears, and there was no way to mistake it. There was no room for doubt, no possibility of error. The voice came from heaven, and it spoke to Christ. The three chosen witnesses heard it, as they were with Him in the holy mount. We have their testimony, the testimony of eyewitnesses, who declared to us what they saw and heard.

B. Assurance (vv. 19-21)

19. We have also a more sure word of prophecy; whereunto ye do well that ye take heed, as unto a light that shineth in a dark place, until the day dawn, and the day star arise in your hearts.

Many to whom the apostle wrote had experienced the knowledge of the day star in their hearts. But what about those of whom this was not true? What could they do? For them there was the "sure word of prophecy"—the holy Scriptures—to confirm the gospel proclaimed by the apostles. Let them take heed to that, and it would bring them to the dawn. Many of the predictions about the Messiah in the Old Testament had seemed vague and mysterious; but now that they had been fulfilled in Jesus of Nazareth, their meaning and truth were apparent. They could be read and pondered with a confidence not possible before.

20. Knowing this first, that no prophecy of the scripture is of any private interpretation.

21. For the prophecy came not in old time by the will of man: but holy men of God spake as they were moved by the Holy Ghost.

No testimony could be more explicit to the inspiration of the Scriptures than these verses. It is the testimony of the New Testament to the Old. As such, it is the Old Testament which needs the testimony. Christians have no difficulty accepting the New Testament. We understand that the Savior spoke the words of God by a direct and self-evident inspiration. We understand, on the strength of Christ's own promise, that the apostles were inspired by a direct gift of the Holy Spirit. For the inspiration of the Old Testament we look to the New. The treatment of the Old Testament by our Lord, His frequent appeals to it in controversy, His many references to it as fulfilled in Himself, and the express assertion of its inspiration by Paul and Peter are the grounds on which we believe the Old Testament is the inspired Word of God.

How can the church enforce the need for spiritual truth?

REVIEW QUESTIONS

1. What Christian qualities did Peter list in verses 3-11?

2. What responsibility did Peter say he had to his readers in verses 12-15?

3. What did Peter say about his death in this chapter?

4. What evidence did Peter give that what he preached was true?

5. How did prophecy come about according to Peter?

GOLDEN TEXT HOMILY

"[GOD'S] DIVINE POWER HATH GIVEN UNTO US ALL THINGS THAT PERTAIN UNTO LIFE AND GODLINESS" (2 Peter 1:3).

Things get old. Everything that we know or have in the natural wears out, breaks down, depreciates, or doesn't work. Think about your house, car, clothes, appliances, bank account. Even our bodies deteriorate as they get older, and for many of us that means we are just not able to do the things we could do a few years ago!

His divine power is different. It is truly a renewable source from God the Father, God the Son, and God the Holy Spirit. The divine resource is not from a supply that can be depleted; it is inherently creative power with the ability to reproduce itself. The word power here means "ability and strength that is miraculous, abundant, and inexhaustible."

"His divine power hath given unto us". . . . Think about the practical aspect of what this means. God's gifts to us go beyond any human resources and abilities we may have. God loves us, cares about us, and gives to us out of an absolutely inexhaustible supply!

His divine power has given us life. Here is what people since the beginning of the human race have searched for and worked so hard to find. Many people would give everything they have for just a little more time to live. But God is offering to give everyone eternal life. What an opportunity—what a gift!

His divine power has given us life and godliness. Godliness is not a negative element. God gives His people His positive characteristics, like life, love, peace, and contentment!

Would you rather have a god who would give to you if he could but he can't or a god who could give to you if he would but he won't? Fortunately for us, our Lord is not like either of those. He can give, He does give, and He will continue to give to His people from His inexhaustible resources!—**Excerpts from the** *Evangelical Commentary,* **Vol. 38**

SENTENCE SERMONS

KNOWING JESUS CHRIST and applying God's Word to daily living results in Christian growth.

—Selected

THE CHRISTIAN LIFE is like riding a bicycle, if you don't go on, you go off.

—W.H. Griffith Thomas

GET NEXT TO GOD when it is calm if you want Him next to you in the storm.

—Robert Shaffer

GOD CALLS every believer to grow in the grace and knowledge of Jesus Christ.

—Selected

EVANGELISM APPLICATION

A MATURING BELIEVER WILL BE INVOLVED WITH WINNING THE LOST TO CHRIST.

The Christian who goes out to win the lost and glows with genuine testimony for his Lord is invariably one who grows in grace and in the knowledge of his Lord and Savior Jesus Christ. A barren believer is good for nothing. A Christian is like a tree planted in the earth to reproduce his own kind. As an apple tree produces apples and a pear tree pears, so a Christian should yield Christians. The one who finds

Christ and then follows Christ must inevitably become a fisher of men.

ILLUMINATING THE LESSON

The best defense is a strong offense. Peter illustrated that axiom by calling his readers to a life of maturity as the best safeguard against the inroads of apostasy. Maturity reflects a proper knowledge of Christ. All believers positionally have obtained like precious faith, have been given all things that pertain to life and godliness, and have been given exceedingly great and precious promises. Practically, however, they need to develop these graces: faith, virtue, knowledge, temperance, patience, godliness, brotherly kindness, and love. A maturing Christian will not only produce positive spiritual fruit but will also protect himself from falling from his positive steadfastness. Such maturity and vigilance will be rewarded and later manifested in the millennial kingdom.

DAILY BIBLE READINGS

M. Honor God. Exodus 20:1-8
T. Respect Others.
    Exodus 20:9-17
W. Obey the Lord.
    Psalm 119:33-40
T. Join With God's People.
    Acts 2:41-47
F. Keep Yourself Pure.
    1 John 2:28 through 3:3
S. Overcome Satan.
    Revelation 12:7-11

Christ's Promised Return

Study Text: 2 Peter 3:1-18

Objective: To believe that Christ will return and to live righteously in anticipation of His coming.

Time: The Book of 2 Peter was written between A.D. 66 and 67.

Place: The Book of 2 Peter, according to many Bible scholars, was written at Rome shortly before Peter's martyrdom.

Golden Text: "Seeing then that all these things shall be dissolved, what manner of persons ought ye to be in all holy conversation and godliness?" (2 Peter 3:11).

Central Truth: The Christian lives a godly life in anticipation of Christ's return.

Evangelism Emphasis: Only those who know Jesus Christ as Savior will be ready for His return.

PRINTED TEXT

2 Peter 3:1. This second epistle, beloved, I now write unto you; in both which I stir up your pure minds by way of remembrance:

2. That ye may be mindful of the words which were spoken before by the holy prophets, and of the commandment of us the apostles of the Lord and Saviour:

3. Knowing this first, that there shall come in the last days scoffers, walking after their own lusts,

4. And saying, Where is the promise of his coming? for since the fathers fell asleep, all things continue as they were from the beginning of the creation.

5. For this they willingly are ignorant of, that by the word of God the heavens were of old, and the earth standing out of the water and in the water:

6. Whereby the world that then was, being overflowed with water, perished:

7. But the heavens and the earth, which are now, by the same word are kept in store, reserved unto fire against the day of judgment and perdition of ungodly men.

8. But, beloved, be not ignorant of this one thing, that one day is with the Lord as a thousand years, and a thousand years as one day.

9. The Lord is not slack concerning his promise, as some men count slackness; but is longsuffering to us-ward, not willing that any should perish, but that all should come to repentance.

10. But the day of the Lord will come as a thief in the night; in the which the heavens shall pass away with a great noise, and the elements shall melt with fervent heat, the earth also and the works that are therein shall be burned up.

11. Seeing then that all these

things shall be dissolved, what manner of persons ought ye to be in all holy conversation and godliness,

12. Looking for and hasting unto the coming of the day of God, wherein the heavens being on fire shall be dissolved, and the elements shall melt with fervent heat?

13. Nevertheless we, according to his promise, look for new heavens and a new earth, wherein dwelleth righteousness.

14. Wherefore, beloved, seeing that ye look for such things, be diligent that ye may be found of him in peace, without spot, and blameless.

LESSON OUTLINE

I. REMEMBER CHRIST'S PROMISE

    A. Reflection

    B. Reaction

    C. Recount

II. RECOGNIZE GOD'S PATIENCE

    A. Patience

    B. Warning

III. PREPARE FOR CHRIST'S RETURN

    A. Provision

    B. Attitude

    C. Attainment

LESSON EXPOSITION

INTRODUCTION

Scoffers speak with derision of the second advent of Christ. They say nothing has changed for centuries; everything goes on the same as it always has. Where, then, they ask, is the fulfillment of the promise of His coming? But they have failed to take into consideration that with the Lord one day is as a thousand years and a thousand years as one day.

The apostle Peter had no such doubts that Christ would keep His promise to return. He had been a witness of Christ's transfiguration on the holy mount and thus had experienced a foretaste of the future glory.

The purpose of this epistle is twofold: (1) that believers should not be seduced by the teachers of false doctrine, especially their disbelief in the Second Coming; (2) that believers might grow in grace and in the knowledge of their Lord and Savior and thereby be found blameless in the day of the Lord's return.

I. REMEMBER CHRIST'S PROMISE (2 Peter 3:1-7)

A. Reflection (vv. 1, 2)

1. This second epistle, beloved, I now write unto you; in both which I stir up your pure minds by way of remembrance:

2. That ye may be mindful of the words which were spoken before by the holy prophets, and of the commandment of us the apostles of the Lord and Saviour.

The apostle took a personal interest in the spiritual welfare of the Christians of Asia Minor. He felt a great affection for them. He called them "beloved" four times in this chapter. We do not know whether he had seen them face-to-face. Some believe that Silas told him about their circumstances, their dangers, their temptations. So he wrote to them. In his first letter he comforted them in the presence of persecution. In the second he warned them about the seductions of false teachers.

Peter wrote to "stir up [their] pure minds" (v. 1). Their minds were pure. They were single-minded Christians. Their commitment to Christ was genuine. Nevertheless, it was appropriate to stir them up. We all need to be aroused from time to time.

We ought to continually ask God to stir up the wills of His faithful people. It is only He who, by the power of His Spirit, can really arouse us. He used Peter as His agent to stir up the minds of the Christians in Asia Minor.

Peter wanted the Christians in Asia Minor to be mindful of, or remember, the words of the prophets and apostles (v. 2). He urged the study of prophecy in both letters. Christians ought to study the prophets and give heed to the word of prophecy. We should also be mindful of the Lord's commandments given through His apostles. The writings of the prophets and apostles both have a message for us. It is important that we recognize that message. To neglect it shows a lack of reverence and gratitude to Him from whom the message comes. The commandments delivered to us by the apostles are in truth the commandments of our Lord.

B. Reaction (vv. 3, 4)

3. Knowing this first, that there shall come in the last days scoffers, walking after their own lusts,

4. And saying, Where is the promise of his coming? for since the fathers fell asleep, all things continue as they were from the beginning of the creation.

The apostle warned that scoffers would come (v. 3). It has always been so. There have always been men who mocked those who trusted in God. It was so with Lot in Sodom, with Isaac the heir of promise, with the psalmist David, with the Lord Jesus himself. Those mockers of whom Peter spoke were men of sensual habits, walking after their own lusts. There is such a thing as honest doubt, such as that of Thomas. As it has been in all ages, however, many of those who profess skepticism are using the claim to cover up an ungodly life—men who reject the faith because they are unwilling to believe. The pure morality of the gospel offends their self-judgment; it is a reproach to them. The teaching of Scripture concerning judgment is repulsive to them; therefore, they try to keep such thoughts from their minds. Besides this, sin hardens their hearts. A sensual life blinds the eye of the soul and makes men incapable of appreciating spiritual truth.

The scoffers will say, "Where is the promise of his coming?" (v. 4). The fathers have fallen asleep; generation after generation has passed. Christians have lived in expectation of the Lord's coming, but still He has not come. Are we to spend our lives waiting for an advent which seems to be continually delayed? Yes, we are to wait for and expect the Lord to come. The scoffers are wrong. The Lord will come again as He promised.

C. Recount (vv. 5-7)

5. For this they willingly are ignorant of, that by the word of

God the heavens were of old, and the earth standing out of the water and in the water:

6. Whereby the world that then was, being overflowed with water, perished:

7. But the heavens and the earth, which are now, by the same word are kept in store, reserved unto fire against the day of judgment and perdition of ungodly men.

Peter began to answer the scoffers with verse 5. He says that all things have not always continued as they were. Creation itself was the introduction of a vast change, a mighty interposition of divine power. "In the beginning God created the heaven and the earth" (Genesis 1:1). "Through faith we understand that the worlds were framed by the word of God, so that things which are seen were not made of things which do appear" (Hebrews 11:3). This truth is also revealed in the Old Testament: "By the word of the Lord were the heavens made; and all the host of them by the breath of his mouth" (Psalm 33:6). It was God himself who said, "Let the waters under the heaven be gathered together unto one place, and let the dry land appear" (Genesis 1:9).

Scoffers willfully ignore this. They shut their eyes to this unalterable, eternal truth and forget that He who made the world can also destroy it. They disregard the fact that the great God of Creation has the power to make other great changes in the future.

Verse 6 is a reference to the Deluge. The earth, which God had pronounced to be "very good," became corrupt and was filled with violence. Then God brought the Flood upon the world of the ungodly. By His word "were all the fountains of the great deep broken up, and the windows of heaven were opened. . . . And all flesh died that moved upon the earth" (Genesis 7:11, 21). That awful judgment was a warning of coming judgments. All things did not go on in the same unvarying course as the scoffers said. When the earth was corrupted by sin, God interposed His justice; and the earth, by a baptism of water, was restored and purified, prepared for a new beginning.

The time that Peter referred to in verse 7 will be a day of destruction to the ungodly. It will sweep them into eternal death. A state of separation from the life of God—separation from light and joy and love—will be felt in all its blank and utter misery. Then all things will not continue as they are. He who made the world in the beginning, He who swept away the wicked with the waters of the Flood, will visit the earth "in flaming fire taking vengeance on them that know not God, and that obey not the gospel of our Lord Jesus Christ" (2 Thessalonians 1:8).

Do you think the second advent of Christ gets enough attention in the church today? Explain.

II. RECOGNIZE GOD'S PATIENCE (2 Peter 3:8-10)

A. Patience (vv. 8, 9)

8. But, beloved, be not ignorant of this one thing, that one day is with the Lord as a thousand years, and a thousand years as one day.

9. The Lord is not slack concerning his promise, as some

men count slackness; but is long-suffering to us-ward, not willing that any should perish, but that all should come to repentance.

Peter borrowed a concept from Psalm 90:4, a prayer of Moses, to impress upon his readers the reason for God's patient dealings with man in his sin and unbelief: "A thousand years in thy sight are but as yesterday when it is past." The apostle not only adopted the concept, but he also adapted the words for his own purpose.

George Cramer says, "This cannot be construed as a standard by which God works in time, nor can it be used as a key for interpreting all temporal references in prophecy. Because Peter equates a thousand years as one day and one day as a thousand years, it is quite obvious he is clearly saying that God recognizes no temporal measure for the working out of His purposes.

"The apostles expected Christ to return in their lifetime and shared this hope with the early church. His longsuffering with man in his sinful ways has spanned more than 1900 years, although the door of grace could have been closed at any time" (First and Second Peter).

The apparent delay in Christ's coming does not mean indifference (v. 9). It does not mean that the Lord is unaware of the conduct of men. The ungodly say, "God has forgotten; He hides His face; He will never see" (Psalm 10:11, NKJV). It is not so. The delay of judgment comes from a far different reason. The Lord is "not willing that any should perish, but that all should come to repentance."

The power to choose good or evil has been given to men by God. Without that power there could be no moral action, no responsibility, no obedience, no holiness, no love. Life without power of choice would be the working of a machine, not the energy of a creature made after the likeness of God. Man has often abused his freedom and turned that which should have led to holiness into an occasion to sin. But God has no pleasure in the death of the wicked. His desire is that all should come to repentance.

Pulpit Commentary states: "Therefore He gives us time. The delay comes from the longsuffering of God. How sad that men should scoff at that which should be the basis of deep gratitude."

B. Warning (v. 10)

10. But the day of the Lord will come as a thief in the night; in the which the heavens shall pass away with a great noise, and the elements shall melt with fervent heat, the earth also and the works that are therein shall be burned up.

The apostle sounded a warning when he said, "But the day of the Lord will come." It must be so, for it is so decreed in the counsels of God. The scoffers may mock and ask in bitter sarcasm, "Where is the promise of his coming?" The Christian knows the answer; it is hidden in the secret purposes of God. But the Day of the Lord will come; that we know, though we do not know the time. Its coming is certain, as sure as the Word of God. It will come suddenly, as the thief comes unexpectedly. Men will carry on with the daily round of activities—"eating and drinking, marrying and giving in marriage" (Matthew 24:38)—without a thought of God and the future. But the coming of Christ and the Day of the Lord should not take us unawares. We must live daily in anticipation of the Lord's coming.

The Day of the Lord will be terrible for the ungodly. Peter's words bring vividly before our minds the awful scenes: the crash of falling mountains, the roar of destroying flames, the dissolution of the elements into chaos, the conflagration that will burn up the earth. All the works of the earth will be swept away in one tremendous ruin. This is the apostle's answer and warning to scoffers.

Why do unbelievers accuse God of being slack concerning His promises?

III. PREPARE FOR CHRIST'S RETURN (2 Peter 3:11-18)

A. Provision (vv. 11-13)

11. Seeing then that all these things shall be dissolved, what manner of persons ought ye to be in all holy conversation and godliness,

12. Looking for and hasting unto the coming of the day of God, wherein the heavens being on fire shall be dissolved, and the elements shall melt with fervent heat?

13. Nevertheless we, according to his promise, look for new heavens and a new earth, wherein dwelleth righteousness.

The catastrophe of judgment that is to follow the second coming of Christ is here spoken of with such certainty it is almost as though it was already accomplished. In view of this, we are to live holy and godly lives.

The picture so vividly presented

is given as a reason for being concerned about our behavior. Peter exclaimed, "What manner of persons ought ye to be in all holy conversation and godliness?" (v. 11). Holy living is the lifestyle of those who are set apart to the service of a holy God. Godliness points to this living as based on our relationship to God. Godly living includes a dependence on God and reverence toward Him, a desire for the blessings of God and a trust in Him for those blessings, ardent love for God because of who He is and gratitude toward Him for His mercies, and a knowledge of God's will and a resolve to do His will. All of these are part of a holy and godly life.

Peter referred to the believer's attitude toward the second coming of Christ in these words: "Looking for and hasting unto the coming of the day of God" (v. 12). This reference to the end of the age as "the day of God" has the same meaning as the more usual wording—"day of the Lord." Both refer, of course, to Christ's second coming. Our attitude toward that day is to be one of expectancy. We are to look for His coming. The first Christians longingly looked for it to come in their day; we should desire it no less eagerly.

Some Bible scholars say that the proper translation in verse 12 is not "hasting unto" but "hasten on." The idea of hastening the coming of the Lord is expressed elsewhere by Peter. He preached, "Repent therefore and be converted . . . so that times of refreshing may come from the presence of the Lord, and that He may send Jesus Christ" (Acts 3:19, 20, *NKJV*). It is thus scriptural to think of the coming of Christ as an event which may be hastened

hastened on by repentance and prayers and the spread of the gospel.

The apostle continued his description of the end of the age: "The heavens being on fire shall be dissolved, and the elements shall melt with fervent heat." The Bible says the heavens are not clean in God's sight. Even the heavens have been defiled by those who live under them. Once, Christ did not shrink from living on the earth; but when He comes again in judgment, the material universe will shrink from the glory of His presence. Revelation 20:11 says that earth and heaven will flee from the face of Him who sits upon the throne. Even the heavens which envelope the earth will be dissolved by fire and the elements of the material world will melt with fervent heat.

Verse 13 identifies the Christian's hope for the future. Peter's writing agrees with John's in Revelation 21:1: "And I saw a new heaven and a new earth: for the first heaven and the first earth were passed away." The promise cited by Peter is recorded in Isaiah 65:17: "For, behold, I create new heavens and a new earth: and the former shall not be remembered, nor come into mind."

Some scholars say that we cannot be certain from the original languages of the Bible (Hebrew and Greek), whether the "new" heaven(s) and earth will be an absolutely new creation or a renovated (re-created, made-over) heaven(s) and earth.

Some scholars believe the present heaven and earth will be destroyed into nonexistence by the judgment of God. Then God will create a new heaven and earth. Other scholars believe the fiery judgment will merely cleanse the heaven and earth of evil, and the new heaven and earth will be the same which now exist, only renovated or regenerated by God so as to be a new creation. (Compare the new creation of the believer in Christ as recorded in 2 Corinthians 5:17.)

B. Attitude (v. 14)

14. Wherefore, beloved, seeing that ye look for such things, be diligent that ye may be found of him in peace, without spot, and blameless.

The catastrophe at the end of the age will introduce the new heavens and earth. Our concern must be to be found in peace with God—to be friends of God so that trouble will not reach us and so that the new heavens and new earth shall be our blessed and eternal abode. We can expect this only if we are without spot and blameless. The spots and blemishes of sin attract the fire of divine judgment. We must give diligence to have all spots and blemishes of sin removed by the cleansing blood of Christ.

C. Attainment (vv. 15-18)

(2 Peter 3:15-18 is not included in the printed text.)

Peter encouraged his readers to remember the long-suffering of our Lord and to be steadfast in the truths they knew even before he wrote his letters to them. What they knew beforehand was the gospel preached by Paul and Peter. The apostle also warned against being swayed by the errors of false teachers. These were condemned by their lawless behavior. Having a firm footing in the gospel, Christians are not to be moved from that; instead they are to "grow in grace, and in the knowledge of our Lord and Saviour Jesus Christ" (v. 18).

How are you preparing for the coming of Christ? Explain.

REVIEW QUESTIONS

1. What was the question of the scoffers?

2. What did Peter want his readers to remember?

3. How did Peter explain the delay of the Lord's coming?

4. What is God's will for all men?

5. What should be the attitude of the believer toward the Lord's coming?

GOLDEN TEXT HOMILY

"SEEING THEN THAT ALL THESE THINGS SHALL BE DIS-SOLVED, WHAT MANNER OF PER-SONS OUGHT YE TO BE IN ALL HOLY CONVERSATION AND GOD-LINESS" (2 Peter 3:11).

This entire chapter is so closely tied together it is difficult to separately deal with one verse and not with the whole.

Science affirms there will come a day when all of this earth and the heavens, because of its own daily workings, will become so worn out it will pass into nothingness. Although this is not the scriptural implication here, we see that even unbelievers realize the system of the universe cannot last forever.

In all ages man has been prone to unbelief, as seen initially in the Garden of Eden by Adam and Eve. But God keeps His promises; He does not lie.

Mankind, from Abraham through the prophets, looked in faith for the coming of the Savior. When that day came, Simeon was so excited—knowing in his spirit, through the Holy Spirit, that the promise of the coming of Messiah had been fulfilled—he asked to depart this life in peace. God had kept His word!

Because Christ has not yet returned a second time is no reason for His church to give up hope. This seeming delay reveals God's mercy to all—yet more time for the sinner to repent and more time for His own to be about their mission and personal preparation.

The special measures to be taken for this day are found not only in verse 11 but also in verse 14.

Our preparation must include holy conversation (holy living, or holy conduct, as noted in some versions) and godliness, but also to live in peace with God and man, spotless, and blameless.

Inasmuch as God keeps His promises, let us work out our own salvation with fear and trembling (Philippians 2:12), then look up, realizing our redemption is drawing near (Luke 21:28).—**Fred H. Whisman, Cost Analyst, Church of God Publishing House, Cleveland, Tennessee**

SENTENCE SERMONS

THE CHRISTIAN lives a godly life in anticipation of Christ's return.

—Selected

THE CHURCH of Jesus Christ is bidden to look forward to Christ's second coming as its great hope.

—William Evans

THE TEST which the church should apply to all questions of practice: Would I like to have Christ find me doing this when He comes?

—William Evans

I NEVER BEGIN my work in the morning without thinking that perhaps He may interrupt my work and begin His own. I am not looking for death; I am looking for Him.

—**G. Campbell Morgan**

EVANGELISM APPLICATION

ONLY THOSE WHO KNOW JESUS CHRIST AS SAVIOR WILL BE READY FOR HIS RETURN.

The glorious certainty of Christ's return shines like a star through all the darkness of these gloomy times. The eternal state will be even more glorious than all that is promised in connection with the millennial kingdom. God has stamped the eternal on all His work; therefore in the resurrection state there is no decay. This hope, which is indeed blessed, will one day become a fact in the lives of the righteous, when the Lord and lover of our hearts shall Himself appear. Then He will give rewards to those who have been faithful. The last word from the throne in heaven is "Surely I come quickly" (Revelation 22:20). The next will be the shout of triumph when He comes again.

ILLUMINATING THE LESSON

Are we sure that Christ is coming back again? Christ himself declared that if He went away, He would come again. Death is not the coming of Christ, for we are told to look forward to His coming. We are never told to look forward to death. Our Lord is a friend, not an enemy. Death is called "the last enemy" (1 Corinthians 15:26). Then follows the angelic confirmation (Acts 1:11) and last the apostolic revelation. The apostles Peter and John tell of His return; Jude also alludes to a special manifestation of the return of our Lord to the earth to rule and reign.

DAILY BIBLE READINGS

M. God's Deliverance.
   Isaiah 52:1-10
T. New Heavens and Earth.
   Isaiah 65:17-25
W. Zion Established. Micah 4:1-7
T. Christ's Coming in Glory.
   Matthew 24:29-35
F. Assurance of Christ's Coming.
   Acts 1:6-11
S. Marriage of the Lamb.
   Revelation 19:5-9

The Spirit Brings Conviction

Study Text: Matthew 25:31-33, 41; John 3:18-21; 16:5-11; Romans 8:1-11; Hebrews 9:27, 28; Revelation 20:10

Objective: To understand ways in which the Holy Spirit convicts people and respond to God in faith.

Golden Text: "When [the Holy Spirit] is come, he will reprove the world of sin, and of righteousness, and of judgment" (John 16:8).

Central Truth: The Holy Spirit exposes sin and draws people into a right relationship with God.

Evangelism Emphasis: The Holy Spirit exposes sin and draws people into a right relationship with God.

PRINTED TEXT

John 16:7. Nevertheless I tell you the truth; It is expedient for you that I go away: for if I go not away, the Comforter will not come unto you; but if I depart, I will send him unto you.

8. And when he is come, he will reprove the world of sin, and of righteousness, and of judgment:

3:18. He that believeth on him is not condemned: but he that believeth not is condemned already, because he hath not believed in the name of the only begotten Son of God.

19. And this is the condemnation, that light is come into the world, and men loved darkness rather than light, because their deeds were evil.

20. For every one that doeth evil hateth the light, neither cometh to the light, lest his deeds should be reproved.

21. But he that doeth truth cometh to the light, that his deeds may be made manifest, that they are wrought in God.

Romans 8:6. For to be carnally minded is death; but to be spiritually minded is life and peace.

7. Because the carnal mind is enmity against God: for it is not subject to the law of God, neither indeed can be.

8. So then they that are in the flesh cannot please God.

9. But ye are not in the flesh, but in the Spirit, if so be that the Spirit of God dwell in you. Now if any man have not the Spirit of Christ, he is none of his.

10. And if Christ be in you, the body is dead because of sin; but the Spirit is life because of righteousness.

Matthew 25:41. Then shall he say also unto them on the left hand, Depart from me, ye cursed, into everlasting fire, prepared for the devil and his angels.

Revelation 20:10. And the devil that deceived them was

cast into the lake of fire and brimstone, where the beast and the false prophet are, and shall be tormented day and night for ever and ever.

Hebrews 9:27. And as it is appointed unto men once to die, but after this the judgment:

28. So Christ was once offered to bear the sins of many; and unto them that look for him shall he appear the second time without sin unto salvation.

LESSON OUTLINE

I. CONVICTS OF SIN
   A. The Spirit and Christ
   B. The Spirit and the World
   C. Life Is by Faith
II. CONVINCES OF RIGHTEOUSNESS
   A. The Righteousness of Jesus
   B. The Spirit-Led Life
   C. The Spirit-Filled Life
III. CONVINCES OF JUDGMENT
   A. The Great Punishment
   B. Judgment of Satan

LESSON EXPOSITION

INTRODUCTION

One of the most distinctive aspects in the life of Christ is the perfect calmness He manifested in regard to the future course of the disciples He had gathered around Him and the future advancement of the work He had begun. He set his face forward. He did not permit any amount of disappointment concerning the people's response to His own work to dull His understanding of what lay beyond the time of His departure. He discerned the relationship between His departure from His disciples and the future, divine visitations the disciples would know. He could see that for their perfection in grace, it was expedient that He should go away.

Christ called His disciples from their contemplation of their own impending loss to the great gift that would follow His going away. The disciples did not understand it, and they were grief-stricken and bewildered. All they knew was that they were going to lose Jesus. But Jesus told them that in the end this was all for the best, because when He went away, the Holy Spirit, the Helper, would come.

"These things I have spoken unto you that ye should not be offended" (John 16:1). Well did Jesus know that nothing is so dangerous to our comfort as to indulge false expectations. He therefore prepared His disciples for what they must expect to encounter in His service. They must not look for a smooth course and a peaceful journey. They must make up their minds to face battles, conflicts, opposition, persecutions, perhaps even death. Like a wise army officer, He did not conceal from His soldiers the nature of the battle they were beginning. He told them all that was before them.

Jesus promised to send the Holy Spirit to assist the apostles and all Christians in all areas of life. True to His word, Christ has sent the Holy Spirit to work in and through the believer.

I. CONVICTS OF SIN
(John 16:5-9; 3:18-21)

A. The Spirit and Christ (16:5-7)

(John 16:5, 6 is not included in the printed text.)

7. Nevertheless I tell you the truth; It is expedient for you that I go away: for if I go not away, the Comforter will not come unto you; but if I depart, I will send him unto you.

The Lord Jesus knew that the disciples were crushed at the thought of His leaving them. They did not realize the full meaning of what He had told them. They had but a vague idea that they were about to be left like orphans in a cold and unkind world, and their hearts were sad at the thought. Jesus cheered them with words of deep and mysterious meaning. He told them that His departure, however painful it might seem, was not an evil but was, instead, for their good. They would actually find it a gain, not a loss.

As difficult as it may seem at first to understand how in any sense Christ's going away could have been good for the disciples, it was. A little reflection will show us that this, like all our Lord's sayings, was wise, right, and true.

As mysterious as it is to us, there was a connection between the ascension of Christ and the outpouring of the Holy Spirit. If Christ had not died, risen again, and ascended up into heaven, it is clear that the Holy Spirit would not have come down with special power on the Day of Pentecost.

If Christ had remained on the earth and had not gone up into heaven, He could not have become the High Priest for His people in the same full and perfect manner that He became after His ascension. He went away to sit at the right hand of God to serve as our Great High Priest and advocate with the Father.

It was after the Lord Jesus went back to the Father and the Holy Spirit came down on the Day of Pentecost that the outlook and conduct of the disciples became a new thing altogether. The growth of their knowledge, faith, hope, zeal, and courage was so remarkable that they were twice the men they were before. They did far more for Christ when He was absent than they had done when He was present. What stronger proof do we need than that it was necessary for them and for us that Christ go away?

B. The Spirit and the World (16:8, 9)

(John 16:9 is not included in the printed text.)

8. And when he is come, he will reprove the world of sin, and of righteousness, and of judgment.

Jesus said the Holy Spirit would convict the world of sin. The world really knows nothing about sin, even though sin is the cause of all its problems. The explanation for all the damage and deterioration of human character is sin. All the ills of human life and society come from sin. Many terms are used by the world to describe the manifestations and results of sin. The world is well aware, for example, of the defects of human character, and it can describe them in detail. It says of one man that he is unjust, of another that he is cruel, or proud, or covetous. Yet these are but minor terms to describe the deep, central, fundamental evil that prompts such attitudes and actions. It is lamentable that even though the world has had an immense experience of sin, it has had little or no sense of sin.

The first outstanding characteristic of the gospel message is the gravity which it attaches to the fact of sin. Apart from the conviction of sin by the Holy Spirit, using the Word of God proclaimed by the disciples, the world knows little of the power of sin—its universality and the fact that it affects man's whole being and all his relations to God. All these concepts are the result of the work of the Holy Spirit.

The first sin of which the world has to be convinced is the sin of unbelief. The Spirit convinces men of sin "because they believe not on me." The Holy Spirit shows men that unbelief is sin. It is the very root of sin. The greatest sin that man can commit is the rejection of Christ. The message of the gospel is so framed that no excuse will be able to extenuate the act of refusing it. Wherever Christ is preached, hearers who do not believe on Him will be condemned.

C. Life Is by Faith (John 3:18-21)

18. He that believeth on him is not condemned: but he that believeth not is condemned already, because he hath not believed in the name of the only begotten Son of God.
19. And this is the condemnation, that light is come into the world, and men loved darkness rather than light, because their deeds were evil.

20. For every one that doeth evil hateth the light, neither cometh to the light, lest his deeds should be reproved.
21. But he that doeth truth cometh to the light, that his deeds may be made manifest, that they are wrought in God.

In commenting on these verses, Roy L. Laurin writes, "As great as are the facts of Christ's death and God's love, they are not enough until we believe them and receive them in personal faith and experience. Faith is a choice—man's choice of Jesus Christ as God's way to life. Salvation is not forcibly or automatically thrust upon us, nor is it arbitrarily demanded of us. It is offered to us in the realm of our consciousness. The medium of participation in this life is faith, for salvation is to him 'that believeth.'"

Laurin continues, "The alternative to faith is unbelief, which may be either passive or active, negative or positive. It can be either the positive unbelief of skepticism or agnosticism, with their rejection of Jesus Christ, or it can be the negative unbelief of neglect and indifference in which a person may agree with all the facts of the gospel, yet never take the active step of faith that embraces Christ.

"Condemnation as the alternative to salvation is the natural state of all life. He who believes escapes being condemned, while he who does not believe is 'condemned already.' This already is the condition of life into which we were born, just as the state of physical life into which we were born is death.

"A person need do nothing in order to die—just be negative to life and not eat, drink, or breathe. Similarly, a person need do nothing to be lost—just be what he already is and not act upon the gospel" (*John: Life Eternal*).

How does the Holy Spirit convict one of sin?

II. CONVINCES OF RIGHTEOUS-NESS (John 16:10; Romans 8:1-11)

A. The Righteousness of Jesus (John 16:10)

(John 16:10 is not included in the printed text.)

Christ said of the Holy Spirit that He would convict the world of right-eousness. What does this mean? The meaning becomes clear when we see that it is Jesus Christ's righteousness of which men will be convinced. Jesus was crucified as a criminal. He was tried. He was found guilty. He was regarded by the Jews as an evil heretic and by the Romans as a dangerous char-acter. He was given the punish-ment that the worst criminals had to suffer; He was branded as a felon and an enemy of God. What changed that? What made man see in this crucified Jew the Son of God, as the centurion saw at the cross and as Paul saw on the Damascus road? It is an amazing thing that men should put their trust for all eternity in a crucified Jewish criminal. What convinces men that this crucified criminal is the Son of God? It is the work of the Holy Spirit. It is the Holy Spirit who convinces men of the sheer righteousness of Christ, backed by the fact that Jesus rose again and went to His Father (William Barclay, *The Gospel of John*).

B. The Spirit-Led Life (Romans 8:1-7)

(Romans 8:1-5 is not included in the printed text.)

6. For to be carnally minded is death; but to be spiritually minded is life and peace.

7. Because the carnal mind is enmity against God: for it is not subject to the law of God, neither indeed can be.

When we believe in Christ, a new and spiritual principle is infused into us by the Holy Spirit. And where that principle exists, it, of necessity, manifests itself by its appropriate operations. Therefore, our carnal nature and our spiritual nature are clearly distinguished. The carnal nature follows after car-nal things. Whatever our feelings or our pursuits we are influenced by that principle which we have in common with all men. We seek nothing beyond the things of time and sense. Pleasure, riches, and honor are the source of our happi-ness. They alone are considered worthy of our attention.

There is another side to the coin. Our spiritual nature follows after the things of the Spirit. In following such, a spiritual principle is infused into us by the Spirit of God, and it operates to produce a new spiritual life. We seek those things suited to spiritual life. Acceptance with God is the primary pursuit of our life. In comparison to the spiri-tual life, nothing is of value. The care of our soul is the one thing necessary. We therefore devote much time to prayer and to the reading of the Scriptures. The great work of salvation now occu-pies our mind; and the Lord Jesus Christ is endeared to us as the Savior of the world. Even in our earthly pursuits we keep in mind but one objective—"that [we] may know him" (Philippians 3:10)—and this makes all else subservient.

C. The Spirit-Filled Life
(Romans 8:8-11)

(Romans 8:11 is not included in the printed text.)

8. So then they that are in the flesh cannot please God.

9. But ye are not in the flesh, but in the Spirit, if so be that the Spirit of God dwell in you. Now if any man have not the Spirit of Christ, he is none of his.

10. And if Christ be in you, the body is dead because of sin; but the Spirit is life because of righteousness.

The carnal mind is enmity against God. There is not one divine attribute to which it is not averse. It considers His holiness too strict, His justice too severe, and His truth too inflexible.

A person under the influence of the carnal mind is incapable of rendering acceptable service to God (v. 8). This is the disposition that rules in the heart of every man who has not accepted Christ as Savior.

After God created man in His own image, He communed with him as a friend. But this harmony was broken when man sinned and God in righteous judgment departed from him (see Genesis 1-3). Not willing, however, that His apostate creatures should irrecoverably perish, God sent His Son to make atonement for their sins, and His Spirit to renew their natures, that they might be restored to His favor and made ready for the inheritance they had forfeited. It was this Spirit of which the apostle was speaking when he declared that we must have the Spirit of God dwelling in us if we would belong to Christ (v. 9).

The work of God's Spirit is necessary for us to know Christ. By nature we are completely blind to spiritual things; the natural man thinks the things of the Spirit are foolishness. He not only does not receive them, but he cannot even know them, "because they are spiritually discerned" (1 Corinthians 2:14). As "no man knoweth the Son, but the Father; neither knoweth any man the Father, save the Son, and he to whomsoever the Son will reveal him" (Matthew 11:27). The Spirit of God must take the things that are Christ's and show them to us (John 16:14). He must open our spiritual understanding to divine things. Unless He guides us into all truth (John 16:13), we will wander in the mazes of ignorance and error until we perish.

We have lost the image of God, and we cannot recover it by any power of our own. That image consists of righteousness and true holiness (Ephesians 4:24), not the smallest part of which we can obtain without the Spirit. If we would cease to fulfill the lusts of the flesh, it must be through the Spirit. If we would mortify the deeds of the body, it must be through the Spirit. If we would have our trials sanctified, it must be through the Spirit. If we would wait for the hope of righteousness by faith, it must be through the Spirit. There is no aspect of grace that can be produced by any other means.

The Spirit of God dwells within the believer's spirit, and in the proportion to which this dwelling is allowed to possess every part of one's being, individual holiness becomes possible.

Why does man need to be convinced of righteousness?

III. CONVINCES OF JUDGMENT
(John 16:11; Matthew 25:31-33, 41; Revelation 20:10; Hebrews 9:27, 28)

A. The Great Punishment (John 16:11; Matthew 25:31-33, 41)

(Matthew 25:31-33 and John 16:11 are not included in the printed text.)

41. Then shall he say also unto them on the left hand, Depart from me, ye cursed, into everlasting fire, prepared for the devil and his angels.

In the sentencing of the wicked we have some of the most terrible words ever spoken by Christ. The sentence is eternal fire. This is a vivid picture of the endless consequences of unrepented and unforgiven sin. Often in this world sin brings punishment, but it is not always in proportion to the sin.

We cannot escape the biblical picture that the man who sins with impunity is reserving for himself a moral ruin. What awaits him is more than he is expecting. The human mind cannot imagine the consequences of spending eternity in everlasting fire.

B. The Judgment of Satan
(Revelation 20:10)

10. And the devil that deceived them was cast into the lake of fire and brimstone, where the beast and the false prophet are, and shall be tormented day and night for ever and ever.

Jesus tells us that the prince of this world is Satan. God condemns the world's prince by and in the cross of Christ, for through His death Christ destroyed the power of the devil in the heart of all believers. The Holy Spirit reveals to us this divine condemnation, so that Satan is now for us a judged and condemned being.

By the Cross evil stands condemned, judged, and defeated. What confronts a man with the certainty of judgment? Why should a man not do what he likes? What makes him feel certain that judgment lies ahead? It is the work of the Holy Spirit. It is the Holy Spirit who gives us the inner and unmistakable conviction that we shall all stand before the judgment seat of God.

C. Judgment of Man
(Hebrews 9:27, 28)

27. And as it is appointed unto men once to die, but after this judgment:

28. So Christ was once offered to bear the sins of many; and unto them that look for him shall he appear the second time without sin unto salvation.

Men die once, and they will be judged once. Christ died once, and His sacrificial death dealt conclusively with the problem of sin. Since Christ was perfect, He was not judged after His death as man will be judged; but there is what we might call a second phase to Christ's departure from this earth—His return to it. "I will come again," Jesus said to His disciples, "and receive you unto myself; that where I am, there ye may be also" (John 14:3). "Unto them that look for Him will he appear the second time without sin unto salvation." He will come again, not to deal with sin, for

He dealt with it the first time He came. He will come to deliver the bodies of believers from the empire of death, to reunite them to their purified souls and bring both into eternal glory. He will come to catch up the living saints to meet Him in the air. "Even so, come, Lord Jesus" (Revelation 22:20).

Why does man want to deny the fact of judgment?

REVIEW QUESTIONS

1. Why did Jesus say it was necessary for Him to depart?
2. How does the Holy Spirit convict of sin?
3. Why does the Holy Spirit convict of righteousness?
4. Why is it important to live a Spirit-filled life?
5. What kind of judgment does Satan receive?

GOLDEN TEXT HOMILY

"WHEN [THE HOLY SPIRIT] IS COME, HE WILL REPROVE THE WORLD OF SIN, AND OF RIGHTEOUSNESS, AND OF JUDGMENT" (John 16:8).

William Barclay tells the story of a missionary who was telling the story of Christ in an Indian village. He used lantern slides flashed on the white-washed wall of a village house. When the picture of the cross was shown, an Indian stepped forward, as if he could not help it: "Come down!" he cried. "I should be hanging there—not you." He recognized his sense of sin. This is the work of the Holy Spirit that John refers to in this verse.

The work of the Holy Spirit in convincing and indicating the unregenerate is referred to by the older theologians as "prevenient grace," the effect of the Spirit on the heart prior to surrender and obedience. An example of this is the reaction of the crowd to Peter's sermon at Pentecost. After hearing Peter's description of Jesus' life and death and realizing that they did not believe in Him or accept Him, many were convinced by the Spirit that their judgment had been wrong, that they had made a tragic mistake in their attitude toward Jesus. They were convicted by the Spirit, and they felt guilty. This prepared the way for their reaction to Peter's sermon.

It is the Holy Spirit who convinces men of sin. He convicts them of the absolute righteousness of Christ, backed by the fact that Jesus rose again and went to His Father. He gives us the inner and unshakable conviction that we shall all stand before the judgment seat of God.—**Eugene C. Christenbury, Ed.D., Senior Adjunct Professor of Education, Lee College, Cleveland, Tennessee**

SENTENCE SERMONS

THE HOLY SPIRIT exposes sin and draws people into a right relationship with God.

—Selected

THE HOLY SPIRIT does not obliterate a person's personality; He lifts it to its highest use.

—Oswald Chambers

THE SPIRIT'S CONTROL will replace sin's control. His power is greater than the power of all your sins.

—Erwin W. Lutzer

THERE IS ONE THING we cannot imitate; we cannot imitate being full of the Holy Spirit.

—Oswald Chambers

EVANGELISM APPLICATION

THE HOLY SPIRIT EXPOSES SIN AND DRAWS PEOPLE INTO A RIGHT RELATIONSHIP WITH GOD.

In many ways the Holy Spirit is the unique and ultimate fact and force in Christianity. Everything in the revelation of divine redemption is culminated in him. Other religions have their founders, their sacred books, and their ethics, but not one of them has anything resembling the person of the Holy Spirit as found in the New Testament. The Holy Spirit is the mediator who makes real to the soul of man the divine revelation given historically in Jesus Christ. This is unique to Christianity.

ILLUMINATING THE LESSON

One of the early church fathers emphasized that the grace of the Spirit brings the machinery of redemption into vital connection with the individual soul. Apart from the Spirit, the Cross stands inert, a vast machine at rest, and about it lie the stones of the building. Until the rope has been attached, the lifting of the individual life—through faith and love—to the place prepared for it in God's church cannot proceed.

DAILY BIBLE READINGS

M. Chastisement for Sin.
    Psalm 28:1-9
T. Acknowledge Sin.
    Psalm 32:1-5
W. Confess Sin. Psalm 51:3-12
T. Convicted by the Miraculous.
    Luke 5:4-8
F. Convicted by the Master.
    Acts 9:1-6
S. Conviction Brings Salvation.
    Acts 16:25-34

The Spirit Imparts New Life

Study Text: John 3:5-8; Romans 8:15-17; 2 Corinthians 1:21, 22; 5:5; Galatians 4:4-7; Ephesians 1:13, 14; 4:30; Titus 3:3-7

Objective: To examine the role of the Holy Spirit in salvation and praise God for new life in Christ.

Golden Text: "That which is born of the flesh is flesh; and that which is born of the Spirit is spirit" (John 3:6).

Central Truth: The Holy Spirit transforms lives at salvation and assures believers of their place in the body of Christ.

Evangelism Emphasis: The Holy Spirit gives new life to those who accept Christ as Savior.

PRINTED TEXT

John 3:5. Jesus answered, Verily, verily, I say unto thee, Except a man be born of water and of the Spirit, he cannot enter into the kingdom of God.

6. That which is born of the flesh is flesh; and that which is born of the Spirit is spirit.

7. Marvel not that I said unto thee, Ye must be born again.

8. The wind bloweth where it listeth, and thou hearest the sound thereof, but canst not tell whence it cometh, and whither it goeth: so is every one that is born of the Spirit.

Titus 3:5. Not by works of righteousness which we have done, but according to his mercy he saved us, by the washing of regeneration, and renewing of the Holy Ghost;

6. Which he shed on us abundantly through Jesus Christ our Saviour.

Romans 8:15. For ye have not received the spirit of bondage again to fear; but ye have received the Spirit of adoption, whereby we cry, Abba, Father.

16. The Spirit itself beareth witness with our spirit, that we are the children of God:

17. And if children, then heirs; heirs of God, and joint-heirs with Christ; if so be that we suffer with him, that we may be also glorified together.

Galatians 4:4. But when the fulness of the time was come, God sent forth his Son, made of a woman, made under the law,

5. To redeem them that were under the law, that we might receive the adoption of sons.

6. And because ye are sons, God hath sent forth the Spirit of his Son into your hearts, crying, Abba, Father.

7. Wherefore thou art no more a servant, but a son; and if a son, then an heir of God through Christ.

2 Corinthians 1:21. Now he which stablisheth us with you in Christ, and hath anointed us, is God;

22. Who hath also sealed us, and given the earnest of the Spirit in our hearts.

Ephesians 1:14. Which is the earnest of our inheritance until the redemption of the purchased possession, unto the praise of his glory.

4:30. And grieve not the holy Spirit of God, whereby ye are sealed unto the day of redemption.

LESSON OUTLINE

I. BORN OF THE SPIRIT

   A. Nature of the New Birth

   B. Results of New Birth

II. ADOPTED AS CHILDREN

   A. Basis of Sonship

   B. Assurance of Sonship

III. SEALED BY THE SPIRIT

   A. The Earnest

   B. The Sealing

LESSON EXPOSITION

INTRODUCTION

The books of the New Testament are new birth books, since they came directly from the new life in Christ which pervaded the Christian fellowship during the period in which it was written. Out of their new experience with Jesus, regenerated men wrote to others who were realizing the same transformation of life.

When we use the term *new birth* today we think immediately of Christian conversion. It suggests revival meetings, gospel choruses, altar calls, praying through, the assurance of salvation, and public testimony. This is the setting and the content of the experience as it was preached by our fathers, experienced in our youth, and indeed is still expressed in some places in the church today.

The sincerity of the heart, the depth of the conviction, the thoroughness of the repentance, and the fullness of the faith—these mark the conditions for the new birth as they did centuries ago. In the case of Peter, conversion seems to have been gradual, while for Paul it was sudden and dramatic. In the case of Nicodemus, it was somewhat comparable to an interview in the pastor's study today.

It is not our prerogative to choose the type of conversion we experience, although our individual temperament has much to do with the way we experience the new birth. In any event, when God's work of conversion has been completed in us, we find the experience satisfying, for God knows each of us individually better than we know ourselves.

I. BORN OF THE SPIRIT
(John 3:5-8; Titus 3:3-7)

A. Nature of the New Birth
(John 3:5-8)

5. Jesus answered, Verily, verily, I say unto thee, Except a man be born of water and of the Spirit, he cannot enter into the kingdom of God.

6. That which is born of the flesh is flesh; and that which is born of the Spirit is spirit.

7. Marvel not that I said unto thee, Ye must be born again.

8. The wind bloweth where it listeth, and thou hearest the sound thereof, but canst not tell

whence it cometh, and whither it goeth: so is every one that is born of the Spirit.

The new birth was defined by John Wesley as "that great change which God works in the soul when He brings it into life, when He raises it from the death of sin to the life of righteousness. It is the change wrought in the whole soul by the almighty Spirit of God when it is created anew in Christ Jesus, when it is renewed after the image of God in righteousness and true holiness" *(Sermon on the New Birth).*

Nicodemus was an exponent of the Pharisaic beliefs and teachings which placed great emphasis on outward conformity to the law, but Jesus said, in essence, "Outward conformity to either ceremonial or moral requirement is insufficient. Religion alone cannot meet the need of man or the requirement of God."

Jesus revealed both the nature and the manner of this new birth when He said, "That which is born of the flesh is flesh; and that which is born of the Spirit is spirit" (v. 6). Here are two realms of life: the realm of the flesh and the realm of the spirit. We enter the realm of the flesh by the first birth, which was a natural birth; we enter the realm of the Spirit by the new birth, which is a spiritual birth.

But how does it take place? This is what Nicodemus asked. He was concerned with the mystery of it. Jesus answered, "The wind bloweth where it listeth, and thou hearest the sound thereof, but canst not tell whence it cometh, and wither it goeth: so is every one that is born of the Spirit" (v. 8). This is a mystery our small minds cannot really understand.

When Nicodemus came to Jesus, instead of being confirmed in his righteousness or perhaps being told what omissions he had to make good in order that his obedience to the law might be perfect, he was told that the whole framework of his life was wrong. His relation had been to the law, not to the person of God. He had obeyed God as a servant. The whole structure of righteousness which he had built up by rigid observance of the precepts of the law had, therefore, to be taken down. He had to begin again; or, to use the words of Jesus, he had to "be born again."

B. Results of the New Birth (Titus 3:3-7)

(Titus 3:3, 4, 7 is not included in the printed text.)

5. Not by works of righteousness which we have done, but according to his mercy he saved us, by the washing of regeneration, and renewing of the Holy Ghost;

6. Which he shed on us abundantly through Jesus Christ our Saviour.

What we have become in contrast to what we once were furnishes a powerful motive for Christian living. What we are is no ground for self-exaltation, for the change is due entirely to God's salvation freely bestowed on us. Our salvation had its historical starting point in the kindness of God our Savior, and his love toward man. Although God hates the sinner's sin, He loves the sinner and yearns to save him.

The words "He saved us" (v. 5) state the saving act as a past fact; "us" refers to all those who have accepted Christ as Savior. Although salvation is still incomplete and awaits its consummation at the return of our Savior, it is the present possession of all those who by faith have been united to Christ.

God, in the gift of the Spirit, has made ample provision for the carrying out of renewal within us. "Through Jesus Christ our Saviour" (v. 6) gives the medium through which the Spirit's presence is brought to us. It speaks of the Incarnation as the condition essential to and preparatory for the coming of the Spirit. The application of the term *Saviour* to both the Father (v. 4) and the Son (v. 6) provides eloquent testimony to Paul's conviction concerning the deity of Christ. The confessional "our" emphasizes the personal appropriation of Him as Savior on our part.

In these verses, all three persons of the Trinity are present and cooperative in the work of grace, each having His special function in the salvation of our soul.

How does believing prove what Jesus said about the new birth?

II. ADOPTED AS CHILDREN (Romans 8:15-17; Galatians 4:4-7)

A. Basis of Sonship (Romans 8:15-17)

15. For ye have not received the spirit of bondage again to fear, but ye have received the Spirit of adoption, whereby we cry, Abba, Father.

16. The Spirit itself beareth witness with our spirit, that we are the children of God:

17. And if children, then heirs; heirs of God, and joint-heirs with Christ; if so be that we suffer with him, that we may be also glorified together.

Christian sonship involves both justification and regeneration. There are, however, real points of difference between them. The necessity for justification lies in the fact of guilt and penalty, while that of regeneration is due to the moral depravity of human nature after the fall. The former cancels guilt and removes penalty; the latter renews the moral nature and reestablishes the privileges of sonship. The two, however, coincide in time, for they are accomplished in answer to the same act of faith. We may say, then, that Christian righteousness and Christian sonship—involving justification, regeneration, adoption and cleansing from sin—are offered as inseparable blessings and occur at the same time. The regenerate man is justified, and the justified man is regenerated.

The two tables of the Law, which were given to Moses, were so holy, that though in the letter they might be observed, in the spirit they could not be kept by any human being. Yet they were enforced by awful sanctions. The smallest violation of any one command subjected the offender to death, even eternal death. Could anything but fear result from such an economy as this?

The very sacrifices prescribed for the relief of those consciences which were oppressed with guilt tended, in fact, to confirm rather than relieve the bondage of their minds. For how could they imagine that the blood of bulls and goats should take away sin? Hence, the offerings were never made perfect, because the sacrifices could not, in fact, remove sin. The annual repetition of the same sacrifices confirmed their apprehensions that their sins, so imperfectly atoned for, were not effectually removed.

In contrast to the Law, the Christian economy tends to produce in the believer a happy, child-like disposition. The New Covenant, which is given to us, offers life and salvation on far different terms than those prescribed by the Old Covenant. The Old Covenant says, "Do this and live." The New Covenant says, "Believe and be saved." The gospel reveals to us a sacrifice; that is, "the propitiation . . . for the sins of the whole world" (1 John 2:2). The gospel offers to us a Savior who is able to save to the uttermost all that come to God by Him (Hebrews 7:25). Under this covenant everyone is privileged to enjoy the most intimate access to God (Ephesians 2:18; 3:12), to come with boldness into the Holiest by the blood of Jesus, to "draw near with a [pure] heart in full assurance of faith" (Hebrews 10:22), having his heart altogether sprinkled and purged from an evil conscience.

But besides this clearer revelation of God's grace and mercy, there is a manifestation of it made to the souls of the faithful by the Spirit of God, who sheds abroad in our hearts the love of God the Father (Romans 5:5) and takes the things of Christ and shows them unto us (John 16:15). The Spirit by His own sanctifying operations delivers us from the bondage of corruption into the glorious liberty of the children of God.

Paul added the expression "joint-heirs with Christ." Christ is the Lord and heir of all things (Hebrews 1:2). But He is not ashamed to call us brethren (Hebrews 2:11). By virtue of this relationship to Him, we are partakers of all that He inherits (Colossians 1:12). Has His Father appointed Him a kingdom? Such is appointed to us also (Colossians 1:13; Hebrews 12:28). Has His Father called Him to a throne? We also are seated together with Him (Ephesians 2:6). Does He possess a glory infinitely surpassing our highest conceptions? The same is also given to us for an everlasting portion. Our right and title to this arises wholly from our relationship to God the Father as His children: "If children, then heirs."

B. Assurance of Sonship
(Galatians 4:4-7)

4. But when the fulness of the time was come, God sent forth his Son, made of a woman, made under the law,
5. To redeem them that were under the law, that we might receive the adoption of sons.
6. And because ye are sons, God hath sent forth the Spirit of his Son into your hearts, crying, Abba, Father.

The words "but when" (v. 4) mark the beginning of a change in the existing circumstances. "The fulness of the time" (v. 4) occurred when world conditions were most ready for the coming of Christ and at a time appointed by the Father. Perhaps at no other point in the history of the world could Christ and the church so effectively have entered the human drama.

The Greeks had prepared the way for the coming of Christ and the church by providing a culture and a language that were adopted by Rome and had spread throughout the Mediterranean world. Rome had prepared the way politically by uniting the Mediterranean world under one government and one citizenship. The Jews had prepared the way religiously by preaching monotheism in some 150 synagogues scattered throughout the empire and by anticipating a

Messiah who could solve the world's problems. Philosophers also had made a religious contribution in a negative way. They had doubts about the established pagan systems of religion and had looked for a unifying power behind all of the old polytheistic beliefs. At the most opportune time, God sent forth His Son. He took the initiative, according to His divine plan, and sent His Son on the divine mission of providing salvation. The fact that He "sent forth his Son" (v. 4) reveals that the Son was preincarnate. Taking on human flesh so He could identify with fallen humanity, the Son was born "of a woman, made under the law, to redeem them that were under the law" (vv. 4, 5).

It is one thing for God to assert that we are adopted to sonship in the family of God; it is another to give evidence of the fact. The evidence that God gives is the inner testimony of the Holy Spirit. The Holy Spirit is the witness of our sonship.

Because we are sons, God has sent into our hearts "the Spirit of his Son" (v. 6). This is another name for the Holy Spirit, who is also sometimes called the Spirit of Christ or the Spirit of Jesus. The indwelling Spirit prompts the cry "Abba, Father."

A sure sign of adoption is the unerring leading of the Holy Spirit in all matters (Romans 8:14). Having the Spirit as the seal of adoption, we take on a likeness to God that marks us as His in this present evil world. As His children we are God-directed and godlike.

Whom God adopts, He anoints; whom He makes sons, He makes saints. When a man adopts another for a son and heir, he may give him his name, but he cannot give him his own disposition and characteristics. But when God adopts us, He sanctifies us. He not only gives us a new name, but He also gives us a new nature. He turns the lion into a lamb. He works such a change that it is as if a different soul is dwelling in the old body.

7. Wherefore thou art no more a servant, but a son; and if a son, then an heir of God through Christ.

The termination of enslaving fear and the advent of a sense of sonship are the results of what we call conversion. But we hardly realize at once the meaning of our inheritance. How magnificent it is! How glorious it is to realize that God is no longer angry with us but that He looks at us with ineffable tenderness as our heavenly Father! How marvelous it is to realize that although we have nothing of ourselves, we have become heirs of all things (Romans 8:17); to find that all things are being made to work together for our good (Romans 8:28); and to realize that we are heirs of God through Christ! Who would want to live as servants when we have been given instead the privilege of becoming children of God?

Describe the relationship of adopted sons to God.

III. SEALED BY THE SPIRIT
(2 Corinthians 1:21, 22; 5:5; Ephesians 1:13, 14; 4:30)

A. The Earnest (2 Corinthians 1:21, 22; 5:5; Ephesians 1:14)

(2 Corinthians 5:5 is not included in the printed text.)

21. Now he which stablisheth us with you in Christ, and hath anointed us, is God;

22. Who hath also sealed us, and given the earnest of the

Spirit in our hearts.

Ephesians 1:14. Which is the earnest of our inheritance until the redemption of the purchased possession, unto the praise of his glory.

The word *stablished* was a business term and referred to the guarantee of the fulfilling of a contract. It was the assurance that the seller gave to the buyer that the product was as advertised or that the service would be provided as promised.

The word *earnest* is also a business term and means a kind of down payment. The buyer pays the earnest money to show that he intends to complete the contract.

The Holy Spirit is God's guarantee that He is dependable and will accomplish all that He has promised.

B. The Sealing

(Ephesians 1:13; 4:30)

(Ephesians 1:13 is not included in the printed text.)

30. And grieve not the holy Spirit of God, whereby ye are sealed unto the day of redemption.

A seal is used to denote several different things: a finished transaction, a mark of ownership, a guarantee of safe delivery. All these things are true of Christians. The Holy Spirit has also sealed us so that we belong to Christ and are claimed by Him. The witness of the Spirit within guarantees that we are authentic children of God and not counterfeit. The Spirit also assures us that He will protect us, because we are His property. Paul was careful not to grieve the Holy Spirit; and because the Holy Spirit was not convicting him, he knew that his motives were pure and his conscience was clear.

REVIEW QUESTIONS

1. What did Nicodemus want to know about the new birth?

2. How did Jesus answer Nicodemus' question?

3. What is the basis of sonship for the believer?

4. What assurance does God give that believers are His sons?

5. What is the meaning of the term *earnest*?

GOLDEN TEXT HOMILY

"THAT WHICH IS BORN OF THE FLESH IS FLESH; AND THAT WHICH IS BORN OF THE SPIRIT IS SPIRIT" (John 3:6).

The material and the spiritual: two realms created by God for human habitation. The material realm is the physical universe. The spiritual realm is unseen, approached through divinely initiated faith. God made human beings for both realms. As physical organisms we are motivated by physical impulses to satisfy God-given hungers—for food, sleep, sex, new experience. As fallen creatures we are driven to satisfy physical needs at the expense of the spiritual.

Some human beings, in their fallen state, are so intent on satisfaction of physical desires that they deny the very existence of the spiritual. They function as if the physical were the sum total of existence. They prefer to believe in an always-existent material universe in which life accidentally evolved from lifeless matter.

Christian revelation presents a spiritual realm coexistent with the physical yet extending beyond it, interacting with it, preserving it, and making claims on it. This is Jesus' word to Nicodemus: You must acknowledge the spiritual realm and accept its claims on you, and you must be born into that realm, an experience which will affect you profoundly. You will then behave in ways which seem strange to those around you who have never experienced being "born from above." An unseen force, in some ways like the wind, will motivate you, make claims on you, and cause you to do, say, and believe things at odds with the bent of the "once born." In fact, being "twice born" will make a temporal and an eternal difference.—**Sabord Woods, Ph.D., Professor of English, Lee College, Cleveland, Tennessee**

SENTENCE SERMONS

THE HOLY SPIRIT transforms lives at salvation and assures believers of their place in the body of Christ.

—Selected

ADOPTION into the family of God reflects our position in relationship to Him.

—William Evans

ADOPTION TAKES PLACE the moment one believes in Jesus Christ.

—William Evans

THE HOLY SPIRIT gives new life to those who accept Christ as Savior.

—Selected

EVANGELISM APPLICATION

THE HOLY SPIRIT GIVES NEW LIFE TO THOSE WHO ACCEPT CHRIST AS SAVIOR.

The natural world is not full of life; it is full of death. It is not natural for a flower or an animal or a man to live. These forms of life are kept from dying only by a temporary endowment of life which gives them a day-by-day dominion over the elements. Withdraw the temporary endowment and death results.

The biblical view of life is the same as the scientific view. The natural condition into which he is born is death. To counteract this natural condition, God introduces a new principle of life which reverses the process of death and results in eternal life. This is salvation.

Jesus said to Nicodemus, "You seek eternal life. The only way you can have it is by believing on Me." This is the unchangeable condition for entrance into the kingdom of God—then and now.

DAILY BIBLE READINGS

M. New Covenant.
    Jeremiah 31:27-34
T. New Heart. Ezekiel 36:22-30
W. New Life. Ezekiel 37:3-14
T. New Commandment.
    John 13:31-35
F. New Creation.
    2 Corinthians 5:16-21
S. All Things New.
    Revelation 21:1-5

The Spirit Sanctifies Believers

Study Text: Romans 8:12-14; 1 Corinthians 6:11; Galatians 5:16-25; 2 Thessalonians 2:13; 1 Peter 1:2; 1 John 3:6, 7

Objective: To acknowledge the Holy Spirit's sanctifying ministry and seek His power for personal and corporate holiness.

Golden Text: "The very God of peace sanctify you wholly; and I pray your whole spirit and soul and body be preserved blameless unto the coming of our Lord Jesus Christ" (1 Thessalonians 5:23).

Central Truth: The Holy Spirit sets apart believers from sin for holy living.

Evangelism Emphasis: Living a holy life is a powerful testimony to the unsaved.

PRINTED TEXT

2 Thessalonians 2:13. But we are bound to give thanks alway to God for you, brethren beloved of the Lord, because God hath from the beginning chosen you to salvation through sanctification of the Spirit and belief of the truth.

1 Corinthians 6:11. And such were some of you: but ye are washed, but ye are sanctified, but ye are justified in the name of the Lord Jesus, and by the Spirit of our God.

1 Peter 1:2. Elect according to the foreknowledge of God the Father, through sanctification of the Spirit, unto obedience and sprinkling of the blood of Jesus Christ: Grace unto you, and peace, be multiplied.

Romans 8:12. Therefore, brethren, we are debtors, not to the flesh, to live after the flesh.

13. For if ye live after the flesh, ye shall die: but if ye through the Spirit do mortify the deeds of the body, ye shall live.

14. For as many as are led by the Spirit of God, they are the sons of God.

Galatians 5:16. This I say then, Walk in the Spirit, and ye shall not fulfil the lust of the flesh.

17. For the flesh lusteth against the Spirit, and the Spirit against the flesh: and these are contrary the one to the other: so that ye cannot do the things that ye would.

18. But if ye be led of the Spirit, ye are not under the law.

22. But the fruit of the Spirit is love, joy, peace, longsuffering, gentleness, goodness, faith.

23. Meekness, temperance: against such there is no law.

24. And they that are Christ's have crucified the flesh with the affections and lusts.

1 John 3:6. Whosoever abideth in him sinneth not: whosoever sinneth hath not seen him, neither known him.

7. Little children, let no man deceive you: he that doeth righteousness is righteous, even as he is righteous.

LESSON OUTLINE

LESSON EXPOSITION

INTRODUCTION

An individual is justified when he accepts Christ as Savior—he is accepted by God as being in right standing with Him. The person also experiences regeneration—a cleansing and renewal within the heart. Regeneration is just the beginning of the Christian life, however; now sanctification begins. And through sanctification, the Holy Spirit provides the believer with the power to live a separated life—a life of holiness.

The call to the sanctified life has always been a call to heroism. Both the Bible and church history document that its challenge has never been answered by weaklings or worldlings. Such dedication has always called for volunteers—conscripts would be too weak of motive to submit to God in this fashion. Those who have fought in the cause of holiness have been characterized by some as "Christian commandos"—those who volunteered for the place of greatest dan-ger in the mission that required the greatest courage. Holiness has never really been a popular cause, not because it lacks appeal but because there have always been more cowards in the world than heroes.

The New Testament records that John the Baptist, who was filled with the Holy Spirit from birth, lived a life of rugged holiness and preached with the fire of God blazing from his heart and lips. But when he refused to soften or compromise his message even for the lecherous Herod, his life was doomed; and finally his head was served on a platter by the beautiful Salome to the passion-crazed Herodias. The platter held his head, but it couldn't hold his blood! That had already flowed into the reservoir of the holiness heritage.

I. SEPARATED TO GOD
   (2 Thessalonians 2:13;
   1 Corinthians 6:11; 1 Peter 1:2)

A. A Divine Work
   (2 Thessalonians 2:13)

13. But we are bound to give thanks alway to God for you, brethren beloved of the Lord, because God hath from the beginning chosen you to salvation through sanctification of the Spirit and belief of the truth.

The Oxford Dictionary defines *sanctification* as "the action of the Holy Ghost in sanctifying or making holy the believer, by the implanting within him of the Christian graces and the destruction of the sinful affections." Here's another definition: "Sanctification is the work of God's free grace, whereby we are renewed in the whole man after the image of God, and are enabled more and more to die unto sin and live unto righteousness."

The source of sanctification is identified in the New Testament as follows:

1. *God the Father:* "And the very God of peace sanctify you wholly; and I pray God your whole spirit and soul and body be preserved blameless unto the coming of our Lord Jesus Christ" (1 Thessalonians 5:23). "Jude, the servant of Jesus Christ, and brother of James, to them that are sanctified by God the Father, and preserved in Jesus Christ, and called" (Jude 1).

2. *Jesus Christ the Son:* "For both he that sanctifieth and they who are sanctified are all of one: for which cause he is not ashamed to call them brethren" (Hebrews 2:11). "Wherefore Jesus also, that he might sanctify the people with his own blood, suffered without the gate" (Hebrews 13:12).

3. *The Holy Spirit:* "That I should be the minister of Jesus Christ to the Gentiles, ministering the gospel of God, that the offering up of the Gentiles might be acceptable, being sanctified by the Holy Ghost" (Romans 15:16).

In 2 Thessalonians 2:13, Paul attributed the whole process of salvation from beginning to end to the will and action of God, according to W.F. Adeney. He writes: "In the beginning God chose His people for Himself. Salvation is no afterthought coming in to redeem the failure of creation. It was all planned from the first. When God made man He foresaw sin and determined on redemption. The process is sanctification of the Spirit. This is the divine side. Prior to it is the great atoning work of Christ. But that

work is done for us that we might receive the Spirit of God as its fruit. Now we are looking at the work of God in us. God purifies and consecrates His people by an inspiration of His own Spirit. No safety is possible for the guilty, no glory for the unholy. The cleansing process must come before the great end can be reached. Belief of the truth is the human side of the process. It is useless for us to wait for our sanctification. It will not come without our active reception of it. It comes on certain conditions being fulfilled by us. Truth is the vehicle that conveys it into our hearts. Faith is the door that opens to receive it. The end is deliverance from all evil. We can have no glory while we are in the mire of sin and wretchedness. But when we are delivered, God will not leave us like drowning men on a barren rock, saved from present destruction indeed, but with dreary future prospects. He will not have completed His work with us till He has exalted us into the region of His own glory" *(Pulpit Commentary).*

B. A Sharp Distinction
(1 Corinthians 6:11; 1 Peter 1:2)

11. And such were some of you: but ye are washed, but ye are sanctified, but ye are justified in the name of the Lord Jesus, and by the Spirit of our God.

Paul reminded the Corinthians of all that God had done for them. Now they had an obligation to use their bodies for His service and glory—to live consecrated lives to God. Sanctification requires both separation from the world and complete consecration to God. Separation from the world and union with Christ produce consistent Christian living.

On his spiritual quest, the Christian must recognize the nature of worldliness if he is to succeed in his journey. He is helpless to protect himself against the onslaughts of the Enemy unless he has some knowledge of what to expect and what to prepare for.

The world—that is, a human society that has left God out—does not know or accept its Creator as Savior. It has constantly spurned the divine offer of redemption in Christ.

Worldliness represents the substitution of personal interests and human sufficiency for God at the very center of an individual's life. On the other hand, sanctification is separation from the world; a liberation from society's worldly pursuits; and a holiness of lifestyle and conduct, brought about by the cleansing, justifying blood of Christ, and wrought in us by the Holy Spirit.

1 Peter 1:2. Elect according to the foreknowledge of God the Father, through sanctification of the Spirit, unto obedience and sprinkling of the blood of Jesus Christ: Grace unto you, and peace, be multiplied.

The Holy Spirit sanctifies the people of God. The Bible teaches that without holiness no one will see the Lord (Hebrews 12:14). These words are full of meaning, for holiness is the sum of all Christian graces. It is that heavenly-mindedness which ever turns us to things divine and rules the life and fills the soul, leaving no room in our hearts for this present evil world. No power of man can effect this change of heart; it is the peculiar work of the Holy Spirit.

God's election of His people, the drawing of His chosen to Himself through the sanctifying influences of His Spirit, must result in obedience. "If we live in the Spirit," Paul said, "let us also walk in the Spirit" (Galatians 5:25). He whose path is daily illuminated by the indwelling grace of the Holy Spirit must walk with God like Enoch and before God like Abraham—in the consciousness of God's presence. Recognizing that God's eye is on us and God's presence is with us, more and more the purpose of our lives becomes to please Him in all things and to do His will. "Thy will be done" is the prayer of God's elect, filling our hearts and fashioning our lives after the example of our Lord.

Peter said the foundation of our election is the blood of Jesus Christ: "Unto . . . sprinkling of the blood of Jesus Christ." The Trinity—Father, Son, and Spirit—is engaged in the work of lifting us from the bondage of corruption into the life of holiness wherein we have as much desire to do right as once we had to do wrong.

Appropriately, mention of the blood follows that of obedience, as if to remind us that the best obedience could not save us apart from the precious blood of Christ.

How would you encourage a believer to live separated to God?

II. RENOUNCING SIN (Romans 8:12-14; Galatians 5:16-21)

A. Deliverance (Romans 8:12-14)

12. Therefore, brethren, we are debtors, not to the flesh, to live after the flesh.

13. For if ye live after the flesh, ye shall die: but if ye through the Spirit do mortify the deeds of the body, ye shall live.

14. For as many as are led by the Spirit of God, they are the sons of God.

It is the power of the Spirit that enables us to live as sons of God. This idea is not limited to a concept of life beyond the grave but includes life in this present world, enabling us to live a life of victory over sin. To be a child of God but with no power to live up to all that this name implies, is a mockery to God. It also suggests the absence of spiritual life. Paul said in Romans 8:13, "If ye live after the flesh, ye shall die."

The apostle Paul informed us in verse 14 that "as many as are led by the Spirit of God, these are sons of God." The leadership to which he referred was that suggested in verses 12 and 13. In these verses, we find a reiteration of what Paul had already talked about in the preceding section, but with this valuable addition: "If ye, through the Spirit, do mortify [put to death] the deeds of the body, ye shall live." Therefore, there is provision through the indwelling presence of the Holy Spirit not only for the accomplishment and assurance of sonship but also for a life of victory as children of God. Paul specified the Holy Spirit as the direct agent in mortifying the flesh. We are enabled to live as victorious sons of God because the Holy Spirit accomplishes this death to self for us when we consider it so by faith. No wonder Paul believed we have a responsibility not to live after the flesh but to live after the Spirit. It is not only our privilege but also our obligation to live a life of practical holiness. God has provided all that is needed to make such living possible through the Holy Spirit.

B. Sanctification (Galatians 5:16-21)

(Galatians 5:19-21 is not included in the printed text.)

16. This I say then, Walk in the Spirit, and ye shall not fulfil the lust of the flesh.

17. For the flesh lusteth against the Spirit, and the Spirit against the flesh: and these are contrary the one to the other: so that ye cannot do the things that ye would.

18. But if ye be led of the Spirit, ye are not under the law.

Sanctification in the New Testament is reflected in two objectives: negatively, putting off the old man, removing the principle of evil and destroying its power in the life; positively, putting on the new man which is renewed in righteousness. This makes possible the growth of righteousness until it controls all one's being—thoughts, feelings, and actions—until the individual is conformed to the image of our Lord Jesus Christ.

The apostle Paul often referred to the death of the old man and commanded the believer to get away from the sins which characterized his life before he was re-created in Christ Jesus. He spoke of the principle involved: "Likewise reckon ye also yourselves to be dead indeed unto sin, but alive unto God through Jesus Christ our Lord. Let not sin therefore reign in your mortal body, that ye should obey it in the lusts thereof" (Romans 6:11, 12). In Colossians, he said, "Mortify therefore your members which are upon earth; fortification, uncleanness, inordinate affection, evil concupiscence, and covetousness which is idolatry. . . . But now ye also put off all these; anger, wrath, malice, blasphemy, filthy communication out of your mouth" (3:5, 8).

Paul weighs the life of sin against the life of righteousness. He stresses the negative aspect of sanctification with the warning that we are to flee the sins listed in Galatians 5:19-21. Why? Because sanctification demands the elimination of those remnants of the old man that would keep the Christian from being his spiritual best for Christ.

The putting off process is essentially negative. But Christianity has never been a negative faith. Unfortunately, some people seem to think they have passed the test of sanctification if they do not drink, dance, smoke, or do a variety of other things they consider unwholesome. But this is only one part of the story. We must preserve the negative and warn Christians to refrain from certain activities and amusements that are either dangerous to their own spirituality or harmful to their testimony. But beyond the negative there is the positive. We remove some things only to replace them with others that excel them—as diamonds do pieces of glass.

Describe your experience of sanctification.

III. EMBRACING RIGHTEOUS-
    NESS (Galatians 5:22-25;
    1 John 3:6, 7)

A. Produce Fruit (vv. 22, 23)

22. But the fruit of the Spirit is love, joy, peace, longsuffering, gentleness, goodness, faith.
23. Meekness, temperance: against such there is no law.

The sanctified believer enjoys a quality of life which sets him apart from other Christians. That life is the result of the inward working of the Holy Spirit and manifests itself outwardly in the fruit of the Spirit. The Bible never tells us that we shall be free from temptation or exempt from trials, tribulations, difficulties, and hardships. In fact, the fruit of the Spirit suggests these very things. These graces do not become a part of our spiritual equipment until they have been perfected through testing. For example, long-suffering becomes long-suffering only when one has been sufficiently provoked to develop the quality. Faith increases and becomes triumphant when it has engaged in warfare against unbelief and has been strengthened in the conflict.

The fruit of the Spirit is involved in all of the believer's relationships. Love, joy, and peace relate to the inner man. They cannot be manifested externally in one's life and behavior unless they first exist internally. Long-suffering and goodness relate to the treatment of one's fellowmen. Kindness reflects one's attitude of life; goodness his will and heart; and long-suffering his conduct in contact with others. Sanctification thus sets one right with both self and others. Faith, meekness, and temperance relate to one's God. Meekness suggests the attitude, faith the will and heart, and temperance the course of action. The balanced, sanctified life produces universally right relationships—to self, to others, and to God (Lindsell and Woodbridge, *A Handbook of Christian Truth*).

B. Crucify the Flesh (v. 24)

24. And they that are Christ's have crucified the flesh with the affections and lusts.

The believer must surrender the control of himself and his life to God. Until this is done, self remains on the throne of the heart; and the Holy Spirit will not fill a self-controlled life. Christ and Christ alone must be King. Paul wrote, "I beseech you therefore, brethren, by the mercies of God, that ye present your bodies a living sacrifice, holy, acceptable unto God, which is your reasonable service" (Romans 12:1). "Neither yield ye your members as instruments of unrighteousness unto sin: but yield yourselves unto God, as those that are alive from the dead, and your members as instruments of righteousness unto God" (Romans 6:13). We must do the yielding. We must open the doors of our hearts. This act must be done willingly and definitely.

C. Walk in the Spirit (v. 25)

(Galatians 5:25 is not included in the printed text.)

It is of the utmost importance that a Christian recognize the enmity of the world. This does not mean that the Christian will always be persecuted, but it does mean that the distinctive spirit of the world is antagonistic and opposed to the Spirit of God.

If a man is wholly dedicated to God and has the purpose of pleasing Him in his daily walk, he will separate himself from that which is distinctively of the world. It has been said he will be in the world as a ship is in the sea; but the world will not be in him, as the sea is not in the ship.

D. Do Righteousness (1 John 3:6, 7)

6. Whosoever abideth in him sinneth not: whosoever sinneth hath not seen him, neither known him.

7. Little children, let no man deceive you: he that doeth righteousness is righteous, even as he is righteous.

Sinning is altogether inconsistent with abiding in Christ. It is altogether opposed to the true knowledge of Christ. It is contrary to the principles which always mark God's children. God's children are reborn—born to a life of righteousness and love. They have to fight against the world's selfishness and sin, and in so doing they fight along with the One who was manifested to destroy the works of the devil.

Participation in the divine life precludes the practice of sin. We abide in Christ by believing on Him, loving Him, communing with Him, drawing our strength from Him. And in so far as the child of God abides in Christ, he is separated from sin.

To what extent must a Christian be involved in the world?

REVIEW QUESTIONS

1. What does it mean to be separated to God?

2. What distinction does Paul make in 1 Corinthians 6:11?

3. How does one experience deliverance from sin?

4. What is the believer's responsibility in renouncing sin?

5. What sets the believer apart from unbelievers?

GOLDEN TEXT HOMILY

"THE VERY GOD OF PEACE SANCTIFY YOU WHOLLY; AND I PRAY YOUR WHOLE SPIRIT AND

SOUL AND BODY BE PRESERVED BLAMELESS UNTO THE COMING OF OUR LORD JESUS CHRIST" (1 Thessalonians 5:23).

Sanctify. Oops, here we are dealing with one of those unpopular S words. Some others are *sin, submission, sacrifice,* and *suffering.*

In reaction against legalism many individuals have rejected sanctification—the process of being holy and living holy. It's the old throwing-out-the-baby-with-the-bathwater principle. But in doing so, they have totally overlooked the very nature of God. He is holy and desires us to be holy. But He goes beyond that by working in us to accomplish that holiness.

God wants to take an active part in our lives. Through the work of the Holy Spirit, He enables us to successfully fulfill the instructions given in the preceding verses. We aren't on our own. God doesn't expect or demand without providing the means to accomplish His wishes.

This passage reminds us that sanctification isn't a matter of just one aspect of our being. Holiness isn't just a matter of our exterior appearance and lifestyle. It begins within our soul and spirit and then springs outward into our daily living.

God desires to be involved in our total being through the ministry of the Holy Spirit. He wants to keep us pure and holy so we will be ready to meet Jesus at the time of His second coming to earth.

A line from a song seems appropriate here. "He didn't bring us this far to leave us." Our God is faithful and will accomplish all He has promised. All we have to do is allow the Holy Spirit to work within us.—**Jerald Daffe, D.Min., Chairman, Bible and Christian Ministries, Lee College, Cleveland, Tennessee**

SENTENCE SERMONS

THE HOLY SPIRIT sets apart believers from sin for holy living.
—Selected

JUSTIFICATION puts us in right relationship with God, while sanctification exhibits the fruit of that relationship—a life separated from a sinful world and delivered unto God.
—William Evans

REPENTANCE is to be sorry enough for sins to renounce them.
—H. Bert Ames

EVANGELISM APPLICATION

LIVING A HOLY LIFE IS A POWERFUL TESTIMONY TO THE UNSAVED.

There is a class of coal called "blind coal," because it burns without showing any flame. But although it shows no flame, it may provide good heat. Though it cannot be seen, it may still be felt. There are blind-coal Christians, very useful ones, who are not seen so much as felt. Still it is better to have both flame and heat, both lip testimony and life testimony *(Handfuls on Purpose).*

DAILY BIBLE READINGS

M. Called to Consecration.
   Exodus 19:3-14
T. A Holy People.
   Deuteronomy 7:6-11
W. Set Apart for Service.
   2 Chronicles 29:3-11
T. Sanctified by the Truth.
   John 17:13-19
F. Kept Blameless.
   1 Thessalonians 5:16-24
S. Cleansed by the Blood.
   Hebrews 9:11-14

The Spirit Guides Believers

Study Text: John 14:25-27; 16:12-15; Acts 8:29; 10:19, 20; 13:2-4; 15:28; 1 Corinthians 2:9-16

Objective: To recognize that the Holy Spirit leads believers, and follow His direction.

Golden Text: "When he, the Spirit of truth, is come, he will guide you into all truth" (John 16:13).

Central Truth: The Holy Spirit uses a variety of means to guide believers.

Evangelism Emphasis: The Holy Spirit will guide believers as they seek to lead others to Christ.

PRINTED TEXT

1 Corinthians 2:9. But as it is written, Eye hath not seen, nor ear heard, neither have entered into the heart of man, the things which God hath prepared for them that love him.

10. But God hath revealed them unto us by his Spirit: for the Spirit searcheth all things, yea, the deep things of God.

12. Now we have received, not the spirit of the world, but the spirit which is of God; that we might know the things that are freely given to us of God.

13. Which things also we speak, not in the words which man's wisdom teacheth, but which the Holy Ghost teacheth; comparing spiritual things with spiritual.

14. But the natural man receiveth not the things of the Spirit of God: for they are foolishness unto him: neither can he know them, because they are spiritually discerned.

John 14:25. These things

have I spoken unto you, being yet present with you.

26. But the Comforter, which is the Holy Ghost, whom the Father will send in my name, he shall teach you all things, and bring all things to your remembrance, whatsoever I have said unto you.

16:12. I have yet many things to say unto you, but ye cannot bear them now.

13. Howbeit when he, the Spirit of truth, is come, he will guide you into all truth: for he shall not speak of himself; but whatsoever he shall hear, that shall he speak: and he will shew you things to come.

14. He shall glorify me: for he shall receive of mine, and shall shew it unto you.

15. All things that the Father hath are mine: therefore said I, that he shall take of mine, and shall shew it unto you.

Acts 8:29. Then the Spirit said unto Philip, Go near, and

join thyself to this chariot.

10:19. While Peter thought on the vision, the Spirit said unto him, Behold, three men seek thee.

20. Arise therefore, and get thee down, and go with them, doubting nothing: for I have sent them.

13:2. As they ministered to the Lord, and fasted, the Holy Ghost said, Separate me Barnabas and Saul for the work whereunto I have called them.

3. And when they had fasted and prayed, and laid their hands on them, they sent them away.

15:28. For it seemed good to the Holy Ghost, and to us, to lay upon you no greater burden than these necessary things.

LESSON OUTLINE

   I. PROVIDES SPIRITUAL WISDOM

      A. Spiritual Instruction

      B. Spiritual Wisdom

  II. REVEALS GOD'S WORD

      A. Divine Teacher

      B. Spiritual Guide

 III. DIRECTS IN MINISTRY

      A. Philip

      B. Peter

      C. Barnabas and Saul

      D. James and the Jerusalem Council

LESSON EXPOSITION

INTRODUCTION

A favorite topic in many circles today is the waning power of the church. The church is often unjustly represented as an emaciated body with the death rattle already in its throat. Those of us who love the church and have spent most of our lives working in it know that in spite of all its weaknesses and failings, it is still the institution that is making a deeper impression on the lives of men and nations than any other agency in the world.

Most Christians would admit that many local churches are woefully lacking in the dynamic power that characterized the church during the days immediately following the Day of Pentecost. Many do not have the spiritual power to cope with contemporary conditions. It is also true that many of those who make up the membership of the average church lack the victory-giving power that God intended that Christians should possess.

What is the remedy for spiritual impotency? What can believers and churches do to be energized again?

Realizing the absence of spiritual power, many churches have tried to hold their own by becoming entertainment centers. We do need to be cautious about drifting into extreme theatricals which can cause churches to deteriorate into third-class amusement centers.

The church can be successful only as it appropriates the power provided. The promise of this power came from the lips of Jesus just before He left the world. "Ye shall receive power," He said, and then he continued, "Ye shall be witnesses." We must allow the Holy Spirit to guide us if we want to accomplish God's will.

I. PROVIDES SPIRITUAL WISDOM (1 Corinthians 2:9-16)

A. Spiritual Instruction (vv. 9-12)

(1 Corinthians 2:11 is not included in the printed text.)

9. But as it is written, Eye hath not seen, nor ear heard, neither have entered into the heart of man, the things which God hath prepared for them that love him.

10. But God hath revealed them unto us by his Spirit: for the Spirit searcheth all things, yea, the deep things of God.

12. Now we have received, not the spirit of the world, but the spirit which is of God; that we might know the things that are freely given to us of God.

In verse 9 Paul talks about man's way of acquiring knowledge. It is a way that is completely inadequate for gaining the wisdom of God. Man has three channels for receiving knowledge: through the "eye gate," through the "ear gate," and through the reasonings of the "heart" (or mind). In dealing with purely human things, these channels work fairly satisfactorily. But in dealing with the things of God, they cannot even scratch the surface. The greatest spiritual realities are unseen to the physical eye, unheard by the physical ear, infinitely beyond the thinking ability of the natural mind. Paul quoted the essence of Isaiah 64:4 in dealing with this subject, although he did not use the precise words. He said God has prepared wonderful things for those who love Him. However, these are not gained by human standards.

The things that Paul refers to in verse 9 can be learned in only one way—by revelation from God through the Holy Spirit (v. 10). The point is not that He will reveal them some day but that He has already revealed them to Christians by the work of the Holy Spirit. Note that Paul referred to some truths as "the deep things of God." In chapter 3, the apostle distinguished between the "milk" and the "meat" of God's Word. This suggests that there are some things of God which are comparatively easy to understand and others that are very deep (G. Coleman Luck, *First Corinthians*).

People are able to understand the feelings and problems of other people because they are all human beings. They all have a similar nature and have had many of the same experiences. Conversely, however, they are unable to comprehend the reactions of a lower order of being, such as an animal, or of a higher, such as an angel, because they do not have the nature of either of these. Then how much more is it to be expected that the natural man is unable to understand anything about an infinite God. The Spirit of God alone is capable of such comprehension. So it is quite logical that if these truths are to be known by man at all, they must be revealed by the Spirit.

Paul stated that Christians have not received the "spirit of the world." He was referring to the spirit of the natural man with his human wisdom. But believers have received the gift of the Holy Spirit so that He might reveal to them the wonderful spiritual possessions

God has given them (G. Coleman Luck).

B. Spiritual Wisdom (vv. 13-16)

(1 Corinthians 2:15, 16 is not included in the printed text.)

13. Which things also we speak, not in the words which man's wisdom teacheth, but which the Holy Ghost teacheth; comparing spiritual things with spiritual.

14. But the natural man receiveth not the things of the Spirit of God: for they are foolishness unto him: neither can he know them, because they are spiritually discerned.

The apostles spoke the deep things of God, not in human words, but in words taught by the Holy Spirit. This makes it clear that inspiration extends not only to the thoughts expressed but also to the words used to express these thoughts. Weymouth translates the last phrase of verse 13, "adapting spiritual words to spiritual truths."

The unregenerate man in his fallen condition cannot understand the things of God. It is not simply that he refuses to receive these things; he really thinks they are foolishness. It is difficult to understand, but true, that no matter how intelligent he may be, he does not have the capacity to "know them, because they are spiritually discerned" (v. 14). In the natural, it is not unusual for people to consider as foolish those things they do not understand. How much more this is true in the realm of spiritual matters. Many people who are highly educated, but unregenerate, make fun of the things of God.

On the other hand, the man who has experienced the new birth and is spiritually mature discerns and understands even these deep things of God. He is in a realm so different from the natural man, that the latter cannot understand him at all: "He himself is judged of no man" (v. 15).

Paul closed this section with a quotation from Isaiah 40:13. No one is able to teach or instruct the Lord Jehovah. The fact is that the natural man is unable even to understand the things of God, nor is he able to understand the spiritual man, who has "the mind of Christ" (v. 16).

Why is it so difficult to reach many of the highly educated with the message of Christ?

II. REVEALS GOD'S WORD (John 14:25-27; 16:12-15)

A. Divine Teacher (John 14:25-27)

(John 14:27 is not included in the printed text.)

25. These things have I spoken unto you, being yet present with you.

26. But the Comforter, which is the Holy Ghost, whom the Father will send in my name, he shall teach you all things, and bring all things to your remembrance, whatsoever I have said unto you.

There seems to have been a brief interval of time at this point while Jesus considered all the things He had said to His disciples, with the feeling that much would not be understood or even remembered. He knew they would need divine enlightenment, and He reminded His disciples again of the One whom the Father would send after He left them.

Jesus told us three important

things about the Holy Spirit in these verses. First, He explained to whom the Holy Spirit is sent—the Holy Spirit is not sent to the world, but to the disciples. Jesus had said earlier that the world could not receive Him. Those who do not have the Savior cannot have the Holy Spirit.

Second, Jesus told us how the Holy Spirit is sent. He is described as the one "whom the father will send in my name" (v. 26) and as the one "whom I will send unto you from the Father" (15:26). This is called the procession of the Holy Spirit. The Holy Spirit is sent in the name of Jesus because, as Redeemer, Jesus comprises the total sphere of redemption which the Holy Spirit operates. The Holy Spirit mediates all the blessings of salvation to us because He comes in the name of Jesus.

Third, Jesus told us why the Holy Spirit is sent. "He shall teach you all things, and bring all things to your remembrance, whatsoever I have said unto you" (14:26). There is both an immediate and an ultimate meaning in these words. The immediate meaning was to the disciples, to whom Jesus had spoken many things which they did not fully understand. The Holy Spirit would instruct them in every point of divine truth. The ultimate meaning carries the thought of inspiration. The Holy Spirit would bring to the disciples' remembrance those facts which He deemed worthy of inclusion in God's written revelation (Roy L. Laurin, *John: Life Eternal*).

So it is clear that the teaching ministry of the Holy Spirit was predicted by Christ as a means of providing the necessary revelation for the ministry of the apostles, and its fulfillment is found first in them. The teaching of the Holy Spirit is extended, however, to all Christians, having the peculiar character of illuminating the written Scriptures. The work of the Spirit in teaching is characteristic. The Word of God is written by inspiration of the Holy Spirit, and its divine author, the Spirit of truth, is its best teacher.

To Christians who are filled with the Spirit, it is possible for the Spirit to reveal the deep things of God today. The unbeliever is unable to understand even the simple truths understood by those who are Spirit-taught. The appalling ignorance of many Christians concerning the things of God is directly traceable to their failure to seek the blessing of a life filled with the Spirit (John F. Walvoord, *The Holy Spirit*).

In verse 27 we have the divine benediction of Jesus upon His disciples. He is blessing them with conditions and protections that will surround them in His absence. It is His legacy. He is bestowing His own treasure upon His heirs. It is the gift of an untroubled heart, which is priceless to its possessor.

B. Spiritual Guide (John 16:12-15)

12. I have yet many things to say unto you, but ye cannot bear them now.

13. Howbeit when he, the Spirit of truth, is come, he will guide you into all truth: for he shall not speak of himself; but whatsoever he shall hear, that shall he speak: and he will shew you things to come.

14. He shall glorify me: for he shall receive of mine, and shall shew it unto you.

15. All things that the Father hath are mine: therefore said I, that he shall take of mine, and shall shew it unto you.

The fact that the disciples were in no condition to receive further revelations from Christ demonstrates their need for the Holy Spirit. Jesus would not press upon them what they were not ready to receive (v. 12). The apostles were prejudiced. They had their hearts set on an earthly messianic kingdom. They could not tolerate the thought of Christ leaving them and returning to the Father. But the Lord could not at that time ascend the throne of David. Israel had rejected Him; and bitter would be the outcome for them, though most merciful would be the outcome for the Gentiles. It would take the Holy Spirit to help the disciples see all of this.

There are three classes of people who need to be guided: those who are blind, those who are too weak to walk alone, and those journeying through an unknown country. In each of these senses the Holy Spirit guides us. By nature we are spiritually blind, and He guides us into the way of truth. As babes in Christ, He teaches us to walk. Then as travelers through this world, He points out the narrow road that leads to the heavenly city.

In order to be led by the Holy Spirit, we must be yielded to Him. There has to be obedience on our part to the will of God.

No matter how gifted, cultured, or educated an unregenerate person may be, he will have distorted views of Christ. It is interesting, though, how apt we are to listen attentively to someone who has attained success in worldly matters and presents himself as an authority on the things of God and the soul.

The man who knows the Holy Spirit will not have any trouble knowing about the glorious Savior. It was when John, on Patmos, was "in the Spirit" (Revelation 1:10) that he had the glories of the Christ revealed unto him. So glorious was the Christ manifested to John that he tells us, "When I saw him [Jesus], I fell at his feet as dead" (Revelation 1:17).

The poverty of the spiritual life of many Christians today results from human conceptions of Christ. The real Christ, whose glory transcends even the glories of the noonday sun, will never be seen or known except by revelation of the Holy Spirit.

When we hear men classify Jesus Christ with the great men of earth, we may know that they have never had a Spirit revelation of the glorious God-man. He, the Christ, stands out among all of earth's great ones, not by comparison but by contrast.

What is it that makes the works and writings of the apostles outstanding in all centuries of Christian history? Is it not because the glories of the Lord Jesus Christ were revealed to them by the Holy Spirit, so that all they wrote, spoke, or did was with the thought of turning the eyes of their fellowmen onto the glorious Son of God.

Give us Spirit-led men in our churches today, men who have looked into the blessed face of our Savior as the Holy Spirit reveals Him in the Word, and we shall again "turn the world upside down" (Acts 17:6).

Why is it so difficult for believers to yield to the Holy Spirit?

III. DIRECTS IN MINISTRY (Acts 8:29; 10:19, 20; 13:2-4; 15:28)

A. Philip (8:29)

29. Then the Spirit said unto Philip, Go near, and join thyself to this chariot.

Philip was experiencing a great revival in Samaria. People were receiving Christ, unclean spirits were being cast out, and healings were occurring. Then the Holy Spirit directed Philip to go south to the desert. Without hesitation, Philip obeyed. No doubt he wondered why God should take him away at this time from a work that was being so abundantly blessed and ask him to go down into this hot, southern country where there could not possibly be as important a center for preaching as the city of Samaria. Nevertheless, he instantly obeyed. Success had not made him independent of or indifferent to the Lord's leading.

This is the first time in the Book of Acts that we see the Holy Spirit no longer moving upon a multitude but being the personal guide of one believer. As a result of his obedience, Philip was able to lead the Ethiopian eunuch to Christ, and tradition says this man was responsible for the gospel reaching Africa.

B. Peter (10:19, 20)

19. While Peter thought on the vision, the Spirit said unto him, Behold, three men seek thee.

20. Arise therefore, and get thee down, and go with them, doubting nothing: for I have sent them.

By allowing the Holy Spirit to direct his ministry, Peter was able to be involved in ushering in a new epoch in church history. His ministry to Cornelius led the way for the admission of Gentiles into the Christian church. This was significant because so far the members of the church had been Jews only.

C. Barnabas and Saul (13:2-4)

(Acts 13:4 is not included in the printed text.)

2. As they ministered to the Lord, and fasted, the Holy Ghost said, Separate me Barnabas and Saul for the work whereunto I have called them.

3. And when they had fasted and prayed, and laid their hands on them, they sent them away.

Paul's title "Apostle to the Gentiles" (see Romans 11:13) has also been well stated as "Missionary to the Nations." Chapter 13 of Acts records a new departure, the first foreign missionary journey, from a new center—not Jerusalem but Antioch (v. 1), center of Gentile Christianity. In some respects this journey is a model for all similar service, for the emphasis is on the Holy Spirit of God in His directing the men of God in their ministry.

D. James and the Jerusalem Council (15:28)

28. For it seemed good to the Holy Ghost, and to us, to lay upon you no greater burden than these necessary things.

Acts 15 records what has been called "the Magna Carta of the Christian Church" and also its first conference or council. Another great problem of Christianity was to be settled by the laying down of a principle concerning salvation by faith and not by works, the keeping of the Mosaic Law. It was a battle for Gentile Christian liberty, the first encounter of which is recorded in 6:1-6, the second in 11:1-18, and which was now to be renewed and brought to a finish. In chapter 11, the Gentiles had been shown to be entitled to eternal life. But what were to be the conditions? The Holy Spirit led them to conclude that it was not essential for Gentiles to become Jews in order to be Christians so long as they were true to God in other respects. W.H. Griffith Thomas says this decision was a victory for freedom over bondage, breadth over narrowness, universality over nationality, and Christianity over sectarianism. This became the great theme of the entire Epistle to the Galatians.

How can one know he is being directed by the Holy Spirit?

REVIEW QUESTIONS

1. What did Paul say about spiritual instruction in 1 Corinthians 2?
2. Contrast spiritual wisdom and human wisdom.
3. Is the Holy Spirit a divine teacher? Explain.
4. What directions did the Holy Spirit give Philip? Peter?
5. How was the Holy Spirit involved in the Jerusalem Conference?

GOLDEN TEXT HOMILY

"WHEN HE, THE SPIRIT OF TRUTH, IS COME, HE WILL GUIDE YOU INTO ALL TRUTH" (John 16:13).

The Holy Spirit is a person. He is the third person of the Trinity and is now the administrator of the work of God in and through the church. Among His many duties is that of leading us into all truth so that we may know what the will of God is for our lives. Jesus said, "Ye shall know the truth, and the truth shall make you free" (John 8:32). It is only as the Holy Spirit teaches and leads us that we can really know the truth. Paul clearly indicated that there are some things that cannot be known by natural wisdom and learning but that must be taught to us by the Holy Spirit.

Jesus indicated to His disciples before He went back to heaven that there were some things that He himself could not teach them. He told them that when the Holy Spirit should come, He would lead them into all truth and teach them the things they needed to know.

One cannot really know the truth about Christ except as it is revealed to him by the Holy Spirit. The Bible was written under the inspiration of the Holy Spirit, and it is only as we are taught by the Holy Spirit that we can understand the truth as it is given to us in the Word of God. The Holy Spirit is the supreme Teacher. Let Him be your guide, and you will know the truth as it is given to us in Christ—and through the Bible.
—Selected

SENTENCE SERMONS

THE HOLY SPIRIT uses a variety of means to guide believers.
—Selected

THE HOLY SPIRIT has the habit of taking the words of Jesus out of their scriptural setting and putting them into the setting of our personal lives.
—Oswald Chambers

HE WHO IS plenteously provided

for and directed by the Holy Spirit from within needs but little from without.

—Johann Von Gothe

EVANGELISM APPLICATION

THE HOLY SPIRIT WILL GUIDE BELIEVERS AS THEY SEEK TO LEAD OTHERS TO CHRIST.

There is no such thing as soul-winning without the Holy Spirit. A church can do a reformative work without the Holy Spirit, but a church cannot do a regenerative work without the Holy Spirit. A man may be won to a preacher, a church member, or a church, without the working of the Holy Spirit, but if a person is to be brought to true repentance for sin and become a child of God, it will be by the transforming power of the Holy Spirit.

ILLUMINATING THE LESSON

Klaus Harms, a church leader of northern Germany, was attending a conference for ministers when a young member of the group said, "It is not necessary to prepare one's sermons, because the Holy Spirit will, according to His promise, give the words which ought to be spoken." Dr. Harms answered, "'I am 75 years old and I have preached for 50 years, but I must confess that on only one occasion was I conscious of the Holy Spirit speaking to me in the pulpit. But He spoke to me often as I left the pulpit, and what He said was, 'Klaus, you have been lazy'" *(Pentecostal Preaching Is Different).*

DAILY BIBLE READINGS

M. Guiding Family Members.
   1 Chronicles 28:11-21
T. Guidance in Difficulties.
   2 Chronicles 20:14-30
W. Guidance Through Troubles.
   Psalm 143:1-12
T. Guiding a Seeking Soul.
   Acts 8:29-38
F. Guiding Into Missions.
   Acts 16:6-10
S. Guidance for the Future.
   Acts 27:21-26

The Spirit Empowers for Service

Study Text: Luke 24:44-49; Acts 1:8; 2:1-4; 4:7-31; 1 Corinthians 12:4-11, 27-31; 14:26

Objective: To discover the Holy Spirit's power that is available to believers and earnestly seek His empowerment for service.

Golden Text: "Ye shall receive power, after that the Holy Ghost is come upon you: and ye shall be witnesses unto me both in Jerusalem and in all Judea, and in Samaria, and unto the uttermost part of the earth" (Acts 1:8).

Central Truth: Believers need the power of the Holy Spirit to serve God effectively.

Evangelism Emphasis: Believers are empowered by the Spirit to witness.

PRINTED TEXT

Luke 24:49. And, behold, I send the promise of my Father upon you: but tarry ye in the city of Jerusalem, until ye be endued with power from on high.

Acts 2:1 And When the day of Pentecost was fully come, they were all with one accord in one place.

4. And they were all filled with the Holy Ghost, and began to speak with other tongues, as the Spirit gave them utterance.

1 Corinthians 12:7. But the manifestation of the Spirit is given to every man to profit withal.

8. For to one is given by the Spirit the word of wisdom; to another the word of knowledge by the same Spirit;

9. To another faith by the same Spirit; to another the gifts of healing by the same Spirit;

10. To another the working of miracles; to another prophecy; to another discerning of spirits; to another divers kinds of tongues; to another the interpretation of tongues:

11. But all these worketh that one and the selfsame Spirit, dividing to every man severally as he will.

Acts 4:8. Then Peter, filled with the Holy Ghost, said unto them, Ye rulers of the people, and elders of Israel,

10. Be it known unto you all, and to all the people of Israel, that by the name of Jesus Christ of Nazareth, whom ye crucified, whom God raised from the dead, even by him doth this man stand here before you whole.

13. Now when they saw the boldness of Peter and John, and perceived that they were unlearned and ignorant men, they marvelled; and they took knowledge of them, that they had been with Jesus.

23. And being let go, they

went to their own company, and reported all that the chief priests and elders had said unto them.

24. And when they heard that, they lifted up their voice to God with one accord, and said, Lord, thou art God, which hast made heaven, and earth, and the sea, and all that in them is:

29. And now, Lord, behold

their threatenings: and grant unto thy servants, that with all boldness they may speak thy word,

31. And when they had prayed, the place was shaken where they were assembled together; and they were all filled with the Holy Ghost, and they spake the word of God with boldness.

LESSON OUTLINE

I. PROMISED POWER
   A. The Charge
   B. The Promise
   C. The Promise Kept
II. GIFTS FOR SERVICE
   A. The Gifts
   B. The Body
   C. The Edifying
III. BOLD WITNESS
   A. The Question
   B. The Answer
   C. The Surprise
   D. The Dilemma
   E. The Release

LESSON EXPOSITION

INTRODUCTION

The great need of every Christian and every church is in the New Testament word *power*, which has in it the omnipotence of God.

Jesus did not leave us to speculate about the source of this power. Between the words "Ye shall receive power" and "Ye shall be witnesses" (Acts 1:8), He told us that the power would proceed from the Holy Spirit.

It has been well said that in trying to keep abreast of the world, the church has lost the spirit of power. We have vied with the world for the spectacular. Now it is time for us to try "Upper Rooms." We have tried everything else. Now it is time for a prostrated civilization to turn to God and realize that there is omnipotent power available through the Holy Spirit.

The great need of the church is not more eloquence, money, members, methods, or organization, but a new recognition of the place of the person and work of the Holy Spirit in the life of its members and ministers. Partnership with the Holy Spirit is indispensable for the accomplishment of the work of God.

I. PROMISED POWER
(Luke 24:44-49; Acts 1:8; 2:1-4)

A. The Charge (Luke 24:44-49)

(Luke 24:44-48 is not included in the printed text.)

49. And, behold, I send the promise of my Father upon you: but tarry ye in the city of Jerusalem, until ye be endued with power from on high.

Luke records that prior to His ascension Jesus opened the

disciples' perception that they might understand the Scriptures. However, we are not to suppose that the disciples knew nothing about the sacred writings extant at that time. We are simply to understand that Jesus showed His disciples the full meaning of passages which up to that time had been hidden from their eyes. Above all, He showed them the interpretation of prophetic passages concerning the time of the Messiah.

We all need to have our understanding enlightened. "The natural man receiveth not the things of the Spirit of God: for they are foolishness unto him: neither can he know them, because they are spiritually discerned" (1 Corinthians 2:14). Pride, prejudice, and love of the world may blind our minds and throw a veil over our eyes in the reading of the Scriptures. We may see the words but not understand them. But all will change when we are taught from above.

Jesus spoke in a remarkable way about His death on the cross. He did not speak of it as a misfortune, or as something to be lamented, but as His own willing sacrifice. He declared that it "behooved" Him to suffer, that is, it was necessary. But then he reminded the disciples that He must also "rise from the dead the third day" (Luke 24:46).

Note the first truths which Jesus told His disciples to preach after He would have left them. They were to preach repentance and remission of sins in His name among all nations.

Repentance and remission of sins are the first elements of truth to be presented to every person, everywhere. Without repentance and remission resulting in conversion, we are not eligible to participate in the kingdom of God.

Jesus concluded His appearance to His disciples with His charge to be witnesses to the things they had personally observed. They were to repeat the story of God's eternal purpose as fulfilled in the person of His Son. Jesus did not give this commission to be enacted by human strength, however, but in God's strength. The disciples were to remain in the city of Jerusalem until they were endued with God's strength and power.

B. The Promise (Acts 1:8)

(Acts 1:8 is not included in the printed text.)

The last recorded promise of Jesus to His disciples was "Ye shall receive power, after that the Holy Ghost is come upon you: and ye shall be witnesses unto me both in Jerusalem, and in all Judaea, and in Samaria, and unto the uttermost part of the earth" (Acts 1:8). In this statement Jesus directed the attention of the disciples away from the restoration of a kingdom to Israel to personal power for witnessing. *Power* means effectiveness. We will be made effective. We will be so blessed of God that our witnessing will have a saving effect upon people. We will be able to witness with power.

C. The Promise Kept (Acts 2:1-4)

(Acts 2:2, 3 is not included in the printed text.)

1.   And when the day of Pentecost was fully come, they were all with one accord in one place.

4. And they were all filled with the Holy Ghost, and began to speak with other tongues, as the Spirit gave them utterance.

The word *Pentecost* is a Greek term which means "fiftieth." It refers to the fact that the long-standing Feast of Pentecost was celebrated on the fiftieth day after the offering of the barley sheaf on the day following the Passover Sabbath. The feast was the second of three annual Jewish feasts occurring between the Passover and the Feast of Tabernacles. In the Old Testament it bears the names "Feast of Weeks," "Feast of Harvests," and "Day of the Firstfruits."

The word *all* refers back to Acts 1:15, which speaks of all the disciples assembled in Jerusalem, men and women, particularly the 120, and not the apostles only. The expression of "all together in one place" (2:1, *NIV*) is most striking in that it points to a perfect unity of heart, thought, and purpose among the disciples.

Luke states that "when the day of Pentecost was fully come," suddenly from heaven came a sound "as of a rushing mighty wind" (v. 2). God's mighty works often occur suddenly and unexpectedly. There is no evidence that the disciples experienced a storm, but only that they heard a sound like a tempestuous wind. The word here translated *wind* means "blowing, blast, breath." The literal translation is that the disciples heard "a sound as of a mighty blast being borne along."

The natural interpretation of this verse is that the sound, not a wind, filled the house. Just as the phenomena of light and sound indicate the presence of invisible energy, so the sound of wind in this instance told of the coming of the divine Spirit.

Next, the disciples experienced the visible phenomenon of cloven tongues—of tongues parting asunder, like fire, which sat upon each of them. Here again, it is not said that there were actual tongues of fire, but that the tongues had the semblance of fire.

An unknown scholar has said: "We can hardly fail to see the meaning of the symbol. These witnesses were to speak to their fellowmen the things of God, and hence the emblem of the tongue. The power which was to glow in their message was the burning power of God the Holy Ghost, and hence the emblem of fire."

Luke states that all the people in the Upper Room were filled with the Holy Spirit (v. 4). What a vital difference the coming of the Spirit in His fullness made to those first disciples! The weak became strong; the timid became bold; the carnal became spiritual.

How did the disciples know they were filled with the Holy Spirit? They "began to speak with other tongues" (2:4). R. Hollis Gause states: "A careful study of the language of Acts 2:4 shows a causative relationship between being filled with the Spirit and speaking in tongues: 'And they were all filled with the Holy Spirit, and they began to speak with tongues because [*kathos*, because] the Spirit was giving them inspiration to speak.' When they were filled with the Spirit, the Spirit became the agent and origin of their speech. They were not empowered to speak before the Holy Spirit filled them. This is the force of Luke's language; they began to speak and kept on speaking because the Holy Spirit continued to give them the speech. The origin of this speech is also reflected in the sublimity of their speech; their utterances were oracular or inspired in their nature. The Holy Spirit's presence is signaled by His speech" *(Living in the Spirit: The Way of Salvation).*

What is the effect of attempting to witness for Christ if we are not endued with the power of the Holy Spirit in our lives?

II. GIFTS FOR SERVICE
    (1 Corinthians 12:4-11,
    27-31; 14:26)

A. The Gifts (1 Corinthians 12:4-11)

(1 Corinthians 12:4-6 is not included in the printed text.)

7. But the manifestation of the Spirit is given to every man to profit withal.

8. For to one is given by the Spirit the word of wisdom; to another the word of knowledge by the same Spirit;

9. To another faith by the same Spirit; to another the gifts of healing by the same Spirit;

10. To another the working of miracles; to another prophecy; to another discerning of spirits; to another divers kinds of tongues; to another the interpretation of tongues:

11. But all these worketh that one and the selfsame Spirit, dividing to every man severally as he will.

The Corinthian church members had been endowed with spiritual gifts, but some of those so endowed by the Spirit had not accepted a proportionate enrichment of grace with their endowment. Hence, their gifts had engendered strife and dis-

order in the church. The gifts had created pride in those who complimented themselves with ostentatious displays of self-importance. In others, the gifts had aroused envy.

To counteract and correct such disorders, Paul directed the attention of the people to the origin and use of spiritual gifts. He plainly declared that the gifts were imparted by the Spirit according to His own sovereign will, without any reference to the merits or attainments of the people themselves. Spiritual gifts had been bestowed not for the promotion of favored individuals, but for the benefit of the church, in worship and service—"for the profit of all" (v. 7, *NKJV*). This is the point of 1 Corinthians 12, as well as 1 Corinthians 14.

Before Paul identified any particular gifts of the Spirit, he talked about the administration of the gifts. The Holy Spirit not only baptizes believers into the body of Christ, but He also endows them with power to become functioning members.

The operation of the Holy Spirit through His gifts makes evident His presence in the church. Spiritual gifts, in fact, are necessary avenues of revelation and necessary avenues of adoration, which give special enlightenment and blessings to the services. Spiritual gifts are also necessary instruments of power for service.

The gift "word of wisdom" (v. 8) is the ability of spiritually endowed individuals in the church to judge rightly and to follow sound courses of action. Wisdom also includes the idea of the development and use of manual skills, as in the case of Hiram, who was "filled with wisdom" in the craft of metallurgy (1 Kings 7:13, 14).

Wisdom, as a spiritual gift, is the miraculous enlightenment of the spiritual mind by the Holy Spirit. One scholar indicates that it is to be expected that a Christian's mental perception will repudiate carnal suggestions and readily respond to the influence of the Spirit; but being filled with the Spirit effects a spiritual transformation of the believer's mind and gives him ever-deepening insights into the divine will. Such wisdom is supernatural and is described by Paul in 1 Corinthians 2:15: "But he that is spiritual judgeth all things, yet he himself is judged of no man."

The "gift of knowledge" includes in its function the supernatural and the miraculous. Knowledge, in the sense of a spiritual gift, is the declaration of some aspect of divine omniscience through Spirit-filled human beings in the church, implementing a sovereign purpose that is in the mind of God.

The gift of faith (v. 9) is faith that impregnates godly desires with divine power, whether they be in spoken words or in acts of obedience. Its essential functions are to afford divine protection, to provide for physical needs, and to aid in one's work.

Divine healing is a basic fundamental Christian belief and has the backing of the Holy Scriptures. That healing is divine means it proceeds from God. The word healing means "the restoring of a sick person to health." Thus, divine healing means the restoring of a sick person to health by divine means.

A miracle has been defined as a supernatural intervention in the ordinary course of nature, a temporary suspension of the accustomed order, an interruption of the system of nature as we know it (v. 10). Harold Horton is of the opinion that the gift of the working of miracles operates by the energy or dynamic force of the Spirit in reversals or suspensions of natural laws. A miracle is a sovereign act of the Spirit of God irrespective of laws or systems.

Prophecy, in its simplest form, is divinely inspired utterance. It is entirely supernatural. As speaking with tongues is supernatural utterance in an unknown tougue, so prophecy is supernatural utterance in the prophet's own tongue. But it is a manifestation of the Spirit of God, and not one of the human mind.

The word discerning means "judging through." Robinson defines it as "a distinguishing, a discerning clearly." The basic idea seems to be that discernment is "a piercing of all that is merely outward, a seeing through, then a forming of a judgment based on that insight.

Tongues may be defined as supernatural speaking in a language unfamiliar to the speaker and his hearers. Speaking in tongues has nothing to do with linguistic ability or with the human mind or intellect. It is a manifestation of the Holy Ghost's employing human speech.

As a manifestation of the Spirit, interpretation of tongues is vastly superior to human thought and volition. This gift may be defined as the inspired explanation (in a commonly understood language) of an inspired but not understandable utterance. Interpretation of tongues makes possible and meaningful the use of tongues for worship and edification in the meeting.

Spiritual gifts are numerous and varied, but they are all given by the same Spirit, that is, the Holy Spirit (v. 11), who apportions them as He wills. Gifts are given not for personal, competitive rivalry but for the church's corporate advantage. Gifts are many, but the Spirit is one. Gifts vary but the Spirit is unchangeable as the source of the gifts.

B. The Body (1 Corinthians 12:27-31)

(1 Corinthians 12:27-31 is not included in the printed text.)

The apostle did not really imagine all Christians being alike and doing the same thing. It was his belief that the church should function as a healthy body. In order for this to occur, God has placed in the church those essentials that make this possible. His list includes apostles, prophets, teachers, miracles, gifts of healings, helps, governments, and diversities of tongues. Each of these work together for the good of the whole body.

C. The Edifying (1 Corinthians 14:26)

(1 Corinthians 14:26 is not included in the printed text.)

Verse 26 gives a cameo picture of worship in the early church. Each member was invited to participate as the Lord directed. One would want to sing a psalm. Another would be led to share a doctrine. Someone might have a revelation that would be given in a tongue and then interpreted. Apart from some kind of God-given order, there could never be edification.

Does the Holy Spirit bestow upon every Christian a gift? Explain.

III. BOLD WITNESS (Acts 4:7-31)

A. The Question (v. 7)

(Acts 4:7 is not included in the printed text.)

Peter and John had been arrested for healing the crippled man at the gate of the Temple. The Jewish rulers revealed their spiritual blindness when they asked the question, "By what power or by what name have ye done this?"

It has been said, "There is none so blind as he who will not see." This is the precise category the Jewish religious leaders fell into. They knew very well, from Peter's sermon the previous day, the power they claimed as their source. The question itself confirms that they recognized a miracle had occurred; the man born blind could now see. That was indisputable. And to make a blind person well was to do a good thing. But if they could discredit the means of healing, then they would be justified in their attempts to silence the disciples' preaching and teaching in the name of the One they had sentenced to death as a blasphemer. And they refused to bring themselves to admit they had committed so grave an error of judgment. To do so would be to acknowledge He was the Son of God as He had claimed He was and that He had risen from the grave as His disciples claimed He had. How easily they could have repented of their evil deed and received divine forgiveness. But they would not!

B. The Answer (vv. 8-12)

(Acts 4:9, 11, 12 is not included in the printed text.)

8. Then Peter, filled with the

Holy Ghost, said unto them, Ye rulers of the people, and elders of Israel,

10. Be it known unto you all, and to all the people of Israel, that by the name of Jesus Christ of Nazareth, whom ye crucified, whom God raised from the dead, even by him doth this man stand here before you whole.

Peter answered the question of the rulers without hesitation, as the Holy Spirit inspired him, by saying that the healing had occurred through the authority of Jesus Christ of Nazareth—the same One they, the Sanhedrin, had crucified but God had raised from the dead.

Peter continued his speech by rising to a sublime height of inspiration. He glorified Christ as the neglected stone spoken of in Psalm 118:22, which had now become the chief cornerstone in the building. He declared that man can be saved only through the name of Jesus Christ.

C. The Surprise (v. 13)

13. Now when they saw the boldness of Peter and John, and perceived that they were unlearned and ignorant men, they marvelled; and they took knowledge of them, that they had been with Jesus.

It was indeed a mark of holy boldness that Peter should address the Sanhedrin in the manner he did. He might have spared himself further persecution, at least for a time, had he merely answered the religious leaders' question with the simple reply "By the name of Jesus of Nazareth." He wasn't compelled to mention His curcifixion or resurrection—except by the compelling of the Holy Spirit. The surprise for us

is that this is the same Peter who forsook Christ in the garden and denied Him three times during the trial. The difference, of course, was the infilling of the Spirit. The power of the Holy Spirit enabled Peter and John not only to maintain fellowship with Christ but also to give a strong testimony to His grace.

D. The Dilemma (vv. 14-22)

(Acts 4:14-22 is not included in the printed text.)

The Jewish leaders simply did not know what to do. Christ's threat to their influence and authority had not ceased with His death. Here it was, as powerful and perplexing as ever. They could not punish the apostles for healing a poor cripple. So for the present, they had to be satisfied with forbidding them to preach or teach in the name of Jesus. Even that, however, was an exercise in futility, since Peter and John answered courageously that they must obey God rather than men and that they must tell what they had seen and heard in the life of the Messiah.

E. The Release (vv. 23-31)

(Acts 4:25-28, 30 is not included in the printed text.)

23. And being let go, they went to their own company, and reported all that the chief priests and elders had said unto them.

24. And when they heard that, they lifted up their voice to God with one accord, and said, Lord, thou art God, which hast made heaven, and earth, and the sea, and all that in them is:

29. And now, Lord, behold their threatenings: and grant unto thy servants, that with all boldness they may speak thy

word,

31. And when they had prayed, the place was shaken where they were assembled together; and they were all filled with the Holy Ghost, and they spake the word of God with boldness.

As soon as Peter and John were released, they hastened to report to the other apostles and Christians anxiously awaiting them, probably in the Upper Room. The report was so inspiring that the entire group burst forth in praise and thanksgiving, together with petitions for continued boldness to speak the truth.

God answered the prayers of the Christian group at once. He manifested Himself by shaking the building where they were assembled. He also filled them with the Holy Ghost, thus reequipping them to preach the Word with boldness.

Is there a lack of boldness in preachers today concerning preaching the Word? Explain.

REVIEW QUESTIONS

1. What charge did Jesus give His followers prior to His ascension?

2. What did Christ say would happen to His disciples after He had ascended?

3. Were the words of Jesus fulfilled? Explain.

4. List the gifts recorded by Paul in 1 Corinthians 12:8-10.

5. Evaluate Peter's speech before the Jewish leaders.

GOLDEN TEXT HOMILY

"YE SHALL RECEIVE POWER AFTER THAT THE HOLY GHOST IS COME UPON YOU AND YE SHALL BE WITNESSES UNTO ME BOTH IN JERUSALEM AND IN ALL JUDEA, AND IN SAMARIA, AND UNTO THE UTTERMOST PART OF THE EARTH" (Acts 1:8).

After all that Jesus did and taught, the main thing He had on his heart before His ascension was that the disciples needed to receive the power of the Holy Spirit in order to carry out the mission of the church—evangelizing the world.

This passage shows us the importance of the Holy Spirit in the church today. David Watson wrote that if God were to take the Holy Spirit away from the church today, 95 percent of what we are doing would continue and no one would know the difference. Then he said that if God had taken the Holy Spirit from the early church, 95 percent of what they were doing would have ceased and everybody would have known the difference.

Let us examine three outstanding challenges that have direct bearing on the need for the Holy Spirit:

First, the Lord's commandment (vv. 4, 5). Jesus commanded the disciples not to leave Jerusalem but to "wait for the promise of the Father."

Second, the disciples challenge (vv. 6, 7). The disciples interrupted Jesus with a question about prophecy. They wanted to know if Jesus would restore the kingdom to Israel at that time. They seemed to be more interested in political development than spiritual enduement. Jesus informed them that prophetic developments were in the hand of the Father. Then He brought them back on track.

Third, the Lord's challenge (v. 8). Jesus said to the disciples, "Ye shall receive power after that the Holy Ghost is come upon you." Then He said, "Ye shall be witnesses unto me both in Jerusalem, and in all Judaea, and in Samaria, and unto the uttermost part of the earth." Notice the absolute certainty of the two *shalls.*

Jesus places priority on power and service! Such admonition was directed to the disciples, but also to all believers of all time.—**F.J. May, D.Min., Professor, Church of God School of Theology, Cleveland, Tennessee**

SENTENCE SERMONS

BELIEVERS need the power of the Holy Spirit to serve God effectively.

—Selected

GOD CAN DO tremendous things through people who don't care who gets the credit.

—*Draper's Quotations for the Christian World*

HE WHO serves God and has divine help for Kingdom service has a good Master.

—Selected

BELIEVERS are empowered by the Holy Spirit to witness for Christ.

—Selected

EVANGELISM APPLICATION

BELIEVERS ARE EMPOWERED BY THE SPIRIT TO WITNESS.

The story is told of a believer who was burdened for the soul of a blacksmith in his town. The believer struggled with himself before he could approach the man. When he returned from his interview, he buried his head in his hands and said to his wife, "I just made a fool of myself; I stuttered out a few words and then just blubbered." But before his wife could respond, a knock came to the door. It was the blacksmith. Approaching the believer, he said, "Sir, if you are so concerned about my soul, surely I ought to be, too." They settled the matter on their knees that day; and the blacksmith became one of America's great preachers. The Holy Spirit can use the "blubbering" of an earnest believer as well as the eloquence of a trained minister to bring men to Christ.

ILLUMINATING THE LESSON

If we study the lives of the men of God in the Old Testament, we invariably find their successes linked to the Holy Spirit. Without Him, they failed. With Him, they gloriously triumphed and accomplished that which was humanly impossible. They did not have the abiding presence of the Spirit in their day as we have had since Pentecost. He came upon them for specific service. This was the case in the lives of Gideon, Samson, David, and others.

When we open the doors of the Gospels, we are faced with the omnipotent work of the Holy Spirit in the Incarnation and throughout the life of Jesus.

The same Holy Spirit who formed the physical body of Christ at the Incarnation is the One who is today forming the spiritual body of Christ out of believers.

DAILY BIBLE READINGS

M. The Spirit Provides Skills.
Exodus 31:1-11
T. The Spirit Provides Help.
Numbers 11:16-25
W. Strength for Battle.
Judges 7:7-14
T. Christ's Power.
Luke 4:14, 15, 33-37
F. God's Power.
1 Corinthians 1:18-25
S. Power to Overcome.
Philippians 4:10-13

The lessons for the winter quarter (December, January, February) are presented under three distinct units of study: "Celebrating Advent" (lessons 1-4); "Let's Study the Bible" (lessons 5-8); and "God's Word in Psalm 119" (lessons 9-12).

Unit One is a special study of the prophetic announcement of Christ's coming as a virgin-born child, the actual Incarnation, and various responses to His birth.

Unit Two, "Let's Study the Bible," seeks to add the additional application of not only studying the Bible, but also applying it to our own lives as well as sharing it with others.

Unit Three focuses on specific passages about the Word of God from the familiar Psalm 119.

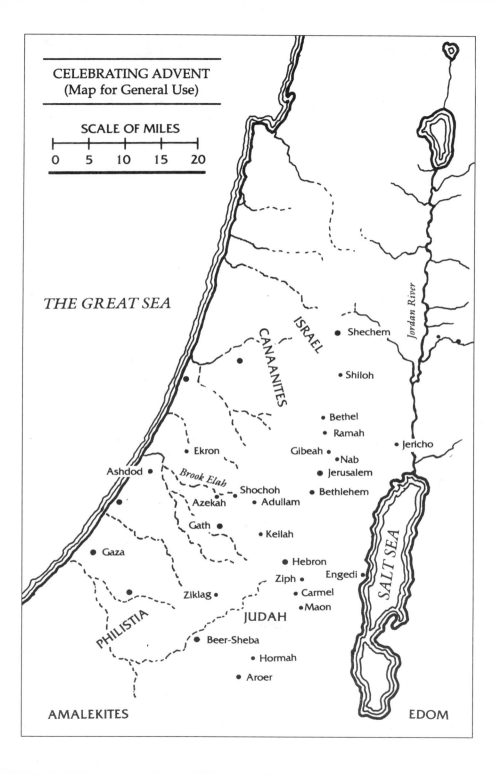

CELEBRATING ADVENT
(Map for General Use)

SCALE OF MILES

0   5   10   15   20

THE GREAT SEA

CANAANITES

ISRAEL

Jordan River

Shechem

Shiloh

Bethel

Ramah

Gibeah

Jericho

Ekron

Nab

Ashdod

Jerusalem

Brook Elah

Shochoh

Bethlehem

Azekah

Adullam

Gath

Keilah

Gaza

Hebron

Ziph

Engedi

SALT SEA

Ziklag

Carmel

Maon

PHILISTIA

JUDAH

Beer-Sheba

Hormah

Aroer

AMALEKITES

EDOM

The Savior's Coming Foretold

Study Text: Genesis 3:15; Deuteronomy 18:15, 18; Isaiah 7:14; 9:6, 7; 53:1-6; Micah 5:2; Matthew 2:5, 6; Galatians 4:4

Objective: To review prophecies concerning the Savior's birth and appreciate the eternal plan of salvation.

Golden Text: "The Lord himself shall give you a sign; Behold, a virgin shall conceive, and bear a son, and shall call his name Immanuel" (Isaiah 7:14).

Central Truth: The prophets foretold the Savior's coming to provide redemption.

Evangelism Emphasis: The prophets foretold the Savior's coming to provide redemption.

PRINTED TEXT

Genesis 3:15. And I will put enmity between thee and the woman, and between thy seed and her seed; it shall bruise thy head, and thou shalt bruise his heel.

Deuteronomy 18:15. The Lord thy God will raise up unto thee a Prophet from the midst of thee, of thy brethren, like unto me; unto him ye shall hearken.

Isaiah 53:3. He is despised and rejected of men; a man of sorrows, and acquainted with grief: and we hid as it were our faces from him; he was despised, and we esteemed him not.

4. Surely he hath borne our griefs, and carried our sorrows: yet we did esteem him stricken, smitten of God, and afflicted.

5. But he was wounded for our transgressions, he was bruised for our iniquities: the chastisement of our peace was upon him; and with his stripes we are healed.

6. All we like sheep have gone astray; we have turned every one to his own way; and the Lord hath laid on him the iniquity of us all.

Galatians 4:4. But when the fulness of the time was come, God sent forth his Son, made of a woman, made under the law.

Isaiah 7:14. Therefore the Lord himself shall give you a sign; Behold, a virgin shall conceive, and bear a son, and shall call his name Immanuel.

9:6. For unto us a child is born, unto us a son is given: and the government shall be upon his shoulder: and his name shall be called Wonderful, Counsellor, The mighty God, The everlasting Father, The Prince of Peace.

7. Of the increase of his government and peace there shall be no end, upon the throne of David, and upon his kingdom, to order it, and to establish it with judgment and with justice from henceforth even for ever. The zeal of the Lord of hosts

will perform this.

Micah 5:2. But thou, Bethlehem Ephratah, though thou be little among the thousands of Judah, yet out of thee shall he come forth unto me that is to be ruler in Israel; whose goings forth have been from of old, from everlasting.

Matthew 2:5. And they said unto him, In Bethlehem of Judaea: for thus it is written by the prophet,

6. And thou Bethlehem, in the land of Juda, art not the least among the princes of Juda: for out of thee shall come a Governor, that shall rule my people Israel.

LESSON OUTLINE

I. NEED OF THE SAVIOR
   A. A Promise of a Savior
   B. A Prophet Like Moses
   C. A Suffering Savior
   D. In the Fullness of Time
II. PROMISE OF THE SAVIOR
   A. A Virgin-born Son
   B. A Wonderful Name
III. PROMINENCE OF THE SAVIOR
   A. Jesus—God and Man
   B. Jesus—Heaven's Most Precious Gift

LESSON EXPOSITION

INTRODUCTION

The first four lessons in this quarter are collectively titled "Celebrating Advent." In some parts of Christendom, the four weeks leading up to Christmas are called the Advent season. Advent, like Lent, was originally meant to be a time of reflection and sobriety during which a believer fasted and did penance. The word *advent* comes from the Latin *adventus* and corresponds closely to the Greek word *parousia*. Both *adventus* and *parousia* can be translated "coming" or "arrival."

When theologians speak of the return of Christ, they use the New Testament term *parousia*. There is one additional term with which we should be familiar as we study about the birth of our Lord: *epiphaneia*, a Greek word meaning "appearance," which is used for both the first and second comings of Christ.

The Advent season has been extended in modern times by several weeks in order for the Christmas merchants to prepare everyone for the joyous season of yuletide. The commercialization of Christmas, crass as it is, should not deter believers from setting aside a time to reflect on and commemorate the incarnation of God's Son into the world.

While the word *incarnation* is not used by the New Testament writers, the components of the word are often used in referring to the Son of God becoming a man and living on earth. The most simple doctrinal statement of the Incarnation is found in John 1:14: "And the Word was made flesh [*kai ho Logos sarx egeneto*]." "The Word" (*logos*, a thought or concept or the expression or utterance of a thought) can refer only to Him who was the perfect reflection of His Father, our Lord and Savior Jesus Christ.

The importance of the Incarnation is that God became a man ("flesh"). Without becoming any less God, the Son of God took upon Himself humanity for the express purpose of fulfilling the divine eternal plan to save fallen man from sin. Paul, writing to the Colossians, said that Jesus reconciled us "in the body of his flesh" (1:22). Concerning Jesus' humanity, the New Testament declares that He was sent "in the . . . flesh" (Romans 8:3), appeared "in the flesh" (1 Timothy 3:16), came "in the flesh" (1 John 4:2), suffered "in the flesh" (1 Peter 4:1), died "in the flesh" (3:18) and made peace "in his flesh" (Ephesians 2:15).

This lesson begins immediately following the fall of Adam and Eve and their sentencing by the Lord as they stand with the devil for judgment.

I. NEED OF THE SAVIOR
   (Genesis 3:15; Deuteronomy
   18:15, 18; Isaiah 53:1-6;
   Galatians 4:4)

A. A Promise of a Savior
   (Genesis 3:15)

15. And I will put enmity between thee and the woman, and between thy seed and her seed; it shall bruise thy head, and thou shalt bruise his heel.

With these words, the Bible addresses for the first time a war in the heavens, waged between the forces of good and evil. It is the first promise of a Savior and a prophecy about the way the most important battle ever to be fought would end.

God was not caught by surprise at mankind's sin. Somewhere in the timeless past—before the earth was created, before man and woman walked among the flowers and

friendly animals of the Garden's confines—the Trinity devised a plan of action to deal with sin and sinners.

God hates sin but loves the sinner! Therein lies the eternal problem. He is a holy God and will not permit His holiness to be tainted even minutely by allowing sin and holiness to coexist in His kingdom. What was He to do? The law of *holiness* demanded that the wages of sin was to be death (Romans 6:23) and that mankind was to be banished from the holy presence of God. The law of *love*, however, pleaded that the judgment of death not be eternal and that a way be found to bring man back to fellowship with his Creator.

B. A Prophet Like Moses
   (Deuteronomy 18:15, 18)

   (Deuteronomy 18:18 is not included in the printed text.)

15. The Lord thy God will raise up unto thee a Prophet from the midst of thee, of thy brethren, like unto me; unto him ye shall hearken.

As with the promise of a Savior spoken of in Genesis 3:15, this text also provides a first—it establishes the office and role of the prophet. There were three institutional offices in Israel with the divine commission to lead the people of God. These were prophet, priest, and king. The words and work of the prophet were always prefaced with "Thus saith the Lord . . . " (more than 350 times).

While the king ruled as subregent in a theocracy (a nation ruled by God) and the priest represented the people in their search for holiness and godlikeness, it was the prophet who continually spoke for

God. Like the congress, the courts, and the presidency of the United States of America today, the triumvirate of prophet, priest, and king provided safeguards over the government of both church and state in Israel. The visit of the prophet Nathan to King David after the king had sinned is a good example of the way these safeguards worked. Also, when the nation went into a spiritual decline, it was the task of the prophet to call the people to revival that they might be cleansed from sin and thus allow the continuance of the covenant church in the Old Testament.

The people of Israel asked, "How shall we know the word which the *Lord hath not spoken* [through the prophets]?" (Deuteronomy 18:21). The response from Jehovah was, "When a prophet speaketh in the name of the Lord, if the thing follow not, nor come to pass, that is the thing which the Lord hath not spoken, but the prophet hath spoken it presumptuously: thou shalt not be afraid of him" (v. 22).

Paul the apostle, speaking of New Testament prophesy (or preaching) told the Galatians, "Though we, or an angel from heaven, preach any other gospel unto you than that which we have preached unto you, let him be accursed" (1:8).

Prophet, priest, and king led the children of Israel through the Word, the Temple, and the throne—but the special task of the prophet was to assure that a pure, refreshing stream flowed from the mind of God, through the mouth of the prophet, to the hearts of the people.

The term *prophet* derives from the Hebrew word *nabiy*, and it is used not only for the office of prophet but also for those who held no office in the state of Israel (and later in the church of Jesus Christ). Anyone who spoke the words of God, accurately and fully, was a prophet. That the coming Prophet would be "from among their brethren, like unto [Moses]" (Deuteronomy 18:18), was God's notification to Israel that the Messiah would be a leader of stature, born as a man, and from among the people of Israel.

A vast majority of the books of the Bible were written by Old Testament prophets, among whom were Moses, Isaiah, Jeremiah, Ezekiel, and Daniel. Because they wrote big books, they were called major prophets. Some of the early prophets wrote small books, so they were called minor prophets.

One of these minor prophets foretold a day when the Holy Spirit would be offered to all believers: "And it shall come to pass afterward, that I will pour out my spirit upon all flesh; and your sons and your daughters shall prophesy" (Joel 2:28). The prophecy was fulfilled on the Day of Pentecost just after the death and resurrection of Jesus Christ (cf. Acts 2:16-17). Some of the Old Testament prophets—some great leaders, some almost unknown—are quoted in the historical books of the Bible.

When Jesus came to earth that first Christmas, He was the "Thussaith-the-Lord" incarnate, God the Father's very own Word (John 1:1, 14). At the first advent, God's thoughts turned into a baby—then a little boy, a teen, and finally a man in His prime. And like no other person, He spoke about things just the way they were. Even His enemies said, "Never man spake like this man" (John 7:46).

There will come a day, however, when prophecy will no longer be needed, and it will pass away (see 1 Corinthians 13:8-10), but the Great Prophet is forever.

C. A Suffering Savior
   (Isaiah 53:1-6)

(Isaiah 53:1, 2 is not included in the printed text.)

3. He is despised and rejected of men; a man of sorrows, and acquainted with grief: and we hid as it were our faces from him; he was despised, and we esteemed him not.

4. Surely he hath borne our griefs, and carried our sorrows: yet we did esteem him stricken, smitten of God, and afflicted.

5. But he was wounded for our transgressions, he was bruised for our iniquities: the chastisement of our peace was upon him; and with his stripes we are healed.

6. All we like sheep have gone astray; we have turned every one to his own way; and the Lord hath laid on him the iniquity of us all.

The work performed by Jesus Christ, the Son of God, the suffering Messiah, on the cross at Calvary—and described here in Isaiah 53—is called the *Atonement*. The apostle Paul described the Atonement in these words: "But God commendeth his love toward us, in that, while we were yet sinners, Christ died for us. . . . For as by one man's disobedience [Adam] many were made sinners, so by the obedience of one [Jesus Christ] shall many be made righteous" (Romans 5:8, 19).

This is the gospel—the good news: "For God so loved the world, that he gave his only begotten Son, that whosoever believeth in him should not perish, but have everlasting life" (John 3:16).

Yet Jesus was rejected as Messiah by the nation of Israel (John 1:11) and was so despised by the religious leaders that they crucified Him. Just before He was nailed to the cross for their (and our) sins, the crowd cried, "Crucify him!" (John 19:15). "And the men that held Jesus mocked him, and smote him. And when they had blindfolded him, they struck him on the face, and asked him, saying, Prophesy, who is it that smote thee? And many other things blasphemously spake they against him" (Luke 22:63-65).

Notice four things (Isaiah 53:5) that Christ provided through His death—He paid for our *transgressions* with His wounds, our *iniquities* with His bruises, our *peace* with His chastisement, and our *healing* with His stripes. Finally (v. 6), Jesus provided the only sacrifice for sin that God would ever recognize.

D. In the Fullness of Time
   (Galatians 4:4)

4. But when the fulness of the time was come, God sent forth his Son, made of a woman, made under the law.

All of history until the first Advent was only a preparation for the coming of the Lord Jesus Christ to earth in the flesh—God building a bridge from His own suffering to span the chasm which separated lost mankind from its Creator. And like all things that God does, it was done exceptionally well—endlessly complex, yet so simple a child could understand.

The Old Testament message is the story of God's love for a small group of continually disgruntled people and His protection of them from all the efforts by time and the forces of evil to destroy them off the face of the earth. For in this people was to be found the hope of all mankind—the covenant community, the Bible, the belief in one God, and the hope that a Messiah would someday come.

Every thrust of the Enemy became another useful tool for the propagation of the glorious gospel message of God's love (read the story of Esther). Finally, the day arrived. The only bright light on the religious horizon was seen in the religion of the Jews, who were now dispersed to the far corners of the earth. Heathen religion was in total disarray and the world hungered for spiritual and intellectual sources in which to trust.

Almost the whole known world was a part of the vast Roman Empire and shared many things in common: a universal peace; good Roman roads that stretched throughout the empire; a single, excellent language which could be read or spoken by almost everyone; and the protection of Roman citizenship, Rome's soldiers, and its government.

Finally, in our text, Paul was explaining to the Galatians that when the time was full, or when the time was filled up, "God sent forth his Son, made of a woman, made under the law, to redeem them that were under the law, that we might receive the adoption of sons" (vv. 4, 5).

Raymond T. Stamm says, "Jewish apocalyptics believed that their God was the creator of the universe, and arbiter of the destinies of all men and nations. Nothing could happen that was not his doing, either directly or indirectly through angels and men. He had a time for everything and everything happened exactly on time" (*The Interpreter's Bible*). They were partially right—at least on these points: the promised Savior came exactly when the time was right, when all circumstances had been readied, and precisely when the prophets had predicted He would come.

> *There is a tide in the affairs of men,*
> *Which, taken at the flood,*
> *leads on to fortune;*
> *Omitted, all the voyage of their life*
> *Is bound in shallows and in miseries.*
>
> —Shakespeare,
> *Julius Caesar*, Act IV, sc. 3

What things made the time right for Jesus' coming?

II. PROMISE OF A SAVIOR
(Isaiah 7:14; 9:6, 7)

A. A Virgin-born Son (7:14)

14. Therefore the Lord himself shall give you a sign; Behold, a virgin shall conceive, and bear a son, and shall call his name Immanuel.

One of the signs God gave to Israel about the coming Messiah was that He would be born of a virgin. What a wonderful sign! He could have said that the Christ would be born on a rainy morning, or be as beautiful as any woman, or that He would have six digits on each extremity. However, those things happen too frequently to be considered marks of divinity. But to be born of a virgin—now, that's a sign only God could give.

This sign of God was not only notable, but it had also been adopted by false religion from the time the tower was built in Babylon. The big difference is these religions are still looking for a virgin mother and child—ours has already come. Except for the one born in a stable in Bethlehem, there has never been a virgin birth.

As to the old argument that Isaiah used the Hebrew word *almah*, which refers to all unmarried young women, there is little doubt that the people of Israel interpreted the word in this instance as *virgin*. It was accepted in Jewish society that *all maidens* were virgins. In fact, the betrothed husband at the time of marriage could insist on proof that his bride was a virgin. Then, too, Jewish scholars when translating the Book of Isaiah into Greek used the Greek word *parthenos*, which *always* signified a virgin.

The name *Emmanuel*, which means "God with us" (Matthew 1:23), was to be the child's name to mark again the truth that the promised Messiah would be totally and completely both God and man.

B. A Wonderful Name (9:6, 7)

6. For unto us a child is born, unto us a son is given: and the government shall be upon his shoulder: and his name shall be called Wonderful, Counsellor, The mighty God, The everlasting Father, The Prince of Peace.

7. Of the increase of his government and peace there shall be no end, upon the throne of David, and upon his kingdom, to **order it, and to establish it with judgment and with justice from henceforth even for ever. The zeal of the Lord of hosts will perform this.**

The names God has used to reveal His character, personality, and plans for mankind are now also seen as the names of His Son. In Bible times, names were carefully chosen because of their meaning rather than for the beauty of their sound as they rolled from the tongue.

Just as Jesus used parables and other mnemonic devices to enhance the retention of His teachings, so God throughout the Old Testament introduced Himself through various names. These names often revealed a work that God was doing, or would do, for His covenant people. A powerful example is found in the manner in which God is addressed as *Elohim*, "the eternal and almighty God," when He commanded Abraham to sacrifice his son Isaac (Genesis 22:1, 2). The lad, seeing they had brought no sacrifice, asked, "Where is the lamb for a burnt-offering?" (22:7). His father had responded, "My son, God will provide himself a lamb" (v. 8).

When at last God allowed Abraham to see the majestic parable He was teaching on Mount Moriah—that God the Father will provide a lamb in the form of His own Son to be a sacrifice for us all—Abraham called God by the name *Jehovah-jireh* ("God will see to it" or "God will provide"). Thus we see in the names of God revealed to Abraham both His stern justice and His overwhelming love.

While our text separates the names *Wonderful* and *Counselor* into two different names for the

Messiah, modern translators are probably more nearly correct when they combine them to employ the word *wonderful* as an adjective describing the kind of counselor Messiah would be. Thus, the coming Christ would be named Wonderful Counselor, Mighty God, Everlasting Father, and Prince of Peace.

These names reveal that the Messiah will be the source of all wisdom and knowledge—*Wonderful Counselor*, powerful and divine, *Mighty God*. He will be a father in every sense of the word, from having begotten us as children to caring for us in every situation forever—*Everlasting Father*. He will also, in the course of time, be the One who will bring peace (in the sense of the Hebrew word *shalom*—harmony and wholeness) as the *Prince of Peace*.

What can we learn from the various names God calls Himself?

III. PROMINENCE OF THE SAVIOR (Micah 5:2; Matthew 2:5, 6)

A. Jesus—God and Man (Micah 5:2)

2. But thou, Bethlehem Ephratah, though thou be little among the thousands of Judah, yet out of thee shall he come forth unto me that is to be ruler in Israel; whose goings forth have been from of old, from everlasting.

To discover the unimaginable value of the treasure which God gave to the world that first Advent, we should compare two places—Bethlehem and heaven—though there is in fact no comparison that could reasonably be made between them. The first is a tiny, little-known village in a nondescript, poor nation, militarily attached to a barbaric empire, on a third-rate planet (Earth) circling an insignificant star (our sun), in a mediocre galaxy somewhere in space.

The village of Bethlehem, one of many which dotted the hostile landscape of early Palestine, is important to us today mostly because it was the birthplace of our Savior Jesus Christ. Further back in time, however, this obscure town, clinging to a ridge in the hill country, had been put on the map of important locales in Israel when the prophet Samuel selected the boy David from Bethlehem to be the second king of Israel.

In a cosmic sense, Bethlehem, which means "house of bread," will forever be remembered as the portal through which the Almighty God and Creator of the universe surged into the lives of mortal men forever. It is the place where, in the most ignoble of surroundings, the Lord of Lords, the King of Kings, the Prince of Peace, heaven's greatest treasure, awoke to the noise of cattle and other barnyard animals and was wrapped in soft cloth and laid in a manger.

John the Revelator saw a vision of heaven. He described its beauty the only way he could, in the metaphors of this earth—streets of gold, gates of pearl, foundations of dazzling and precious stones, a crystal river flowing through its center bordered by bounteous fruit trees producing their fruits continually (Revelation 22).

Though the throne room of God was described as one of utter beauty and those who approached it were awed by both the magnificence of it and the immensity of the authority that flowed from it, there can be no adequate description given before we actually see the city and throne of God in person. It is here, in the heavenly Jerusalem, that the affairs of state, the conduct of the wars of the universe, the oversight of the church of every age and all the other official duties of God and His courtiers are conducted.

The Incarnation brought these two locales—heaven and Bethlehem —together for one magnificent moment after which nothing in all the universe would ever again be the same!

B. Jesus—Heaven's Most Precious Gift (Matthew 2:5, 6)

5. And they said unto him, In Bethlehem of Judaea: for thus it is written by the prophet,

6. And thou Bethlehem, in the land of Juda, art not the least among the princes of Juda: for out of thee shall come a Governor, that shall rule my people Israel.

The words of our text were being spoken in the royal palace in Jerusalem by the wisest men King Herod could muster. The questions were about a promised Messiah and where He was to be born. Herod wanted to know the answers in order to destroy any possible challenger to his uneasy throne. The wise men from the East waited for the answers because they sought to worship Him.

We need to be absolutely certain that we recognize the importance of not only the geographic locations in this cosmic drama but also—and especially—the importance of the personalities involved. Magi, wise

men who may have thought the star they saw was an angel delivering the new king to earth, represented the greatest knowledge to be found on earth. Herod, in his royal regalia, with far-flung palaces and a retinue of beautiful people to assuage his every whim—represented the outrageous limits to which earthly kings could fall.

Everywhere the crowds milled about, unaware that heaven had somehow merged with earth—that the very God himself was being born in Bethlehem. Let us be clear in our understanding that the Messiah was not an emanation *from* God—He was and is God. That One born in the stable is not a part of God (John 1:1); He is God! Jesus Christ is not part man and part God—He is *all* man and *all* God (Philippians 2:5, 6).

Someone said, facetiously we imagine, that though one will not likely lose his soul if he does not fully understand the trinity of God, he might lose his mind if he tries too hard to understand it! However limited our understanding of God is as He rules, loves, judges, and administers the affairs of this universe in the form of three personalities—Father, Son, and Holy Spirit—we can celebrate together the wonder of wonders that such a magnificent God thought us important enough to send His only Son to redeem us.

How can we best describe the trinity of God?

REVIEW QUESTIONS

1. What was the first promise that God would provide a Savior?

2. What four specific things was

the Messiah to do for us in His death?

3. How did Herod's advisers know where the Messiah was to be born?

4. What is the Incarnation?

5. Why did the nation of Israel need the office of a prophet?

GOLDEN TEXT HOMILY

"THE LORD HIMSELF SHALL GIVE YOU A SIGN; BEHOLD, A VIRGIN SHALL CONCEIVE, AND BEAR A SON, AND SHALL CALL HIS NAME IMMANUEL" (Isaiah 7:14).

A review of the Old Testament prophecies of Christ always leaves me in awe of Scripture. The degree of accuracy with which the coming Messiah was described is astounding. Nothing illustrates this idea better than this text. Commentators define *sign* as a "miracle" or "visible illustration." What greater miracle could there be than the supernatural conception of an obscure Judean girl? Of all the messianic prophecies, this particular one was so miraculous because no other person in the entire human history would ever be the product of such a birth.

The word *virgin* as it is used here also has the meaning of "young girl," and Bible historians conclude that this scripture also had an immediate, historical fulfillment in the lineage of King Ahaz. The gospels of Matthew and Luke later cite this scripture in reference to Mary, in the context of a literal virgin. Thus the Bible often has long-range as well as short-range applications.

What is the relevance of this verse to you and me? It assures me that our God knows us by experience through Christ, and that we have abundant life from One who Himself, as a human being, knew the power of life and death. God truly is "with us."—**Dennis W. Watkins, Director of the Office of Legal Services for the Church of God, Cleveland, Tennessee**

SENTENCE SERMONS

THE PROPHETS FORETOLD the Savior's coming to provide redemption.

—Selected

GOD PROVED HIS LOVE on the cross. When Christ hung, and bled, and died, it was God saying to the world—I love you.

—Billy Graham

O MY SAVIOR, make me see how dearly thou hast paid for me.

—Richard Crashaw

THE CROSS OF JESUS CHRIST is not the cross of a martyr, but the door whereby God keeps open house for the universe.

—Oswald Chambers

DAILY BIBLE READINGS

M. Type of the Savior.
   Genesis 50:16-21
T. Only One Savior.
   Isaiah 45:20-25
W. Invitation of the Savior.
   Matthew 11:28-30
T. All Have Sinned.
   Romans 3:10-23
F. The Free Gift. Romans 5:8-19
S. Sacrifice Needed.
   Hebrews 10:1-10

The Virgin Birth

Study Text: Luke 1:26-38, 46-55

Objective: To acknowledge the significance of Christ's miraculous birth and worship Him.

Time: The Gospel According to Luke was written between A.D. 58 and 70.

Place: The Gospel According to Luke was probably written at Caesarea or Rome.

Golden Text: "A virgin shall be with child, and shall bring forth a son, and they shall call his name Emmanuel, which being interpreted is, God with us" (Matthew 1:23).

Central Truth: Jesus, God's Son, was born of a virgin.

Evangelism Emphasis: Jesus, the virgin-born Son of God, came to save sinners.

PRINTED TEXT

Luke 1:26. And in the sixth month the angel Gabriel was sent from God unto a city of Galilee, named Nazareth,

27. To a virgin espoused to a man whose name was Joseph, of the house of David; and the virgin's name was Mary.

28. And the angel came in unto her, and said, Hail, thou that art highly favoured, the Lord is with thee: blessed art thou among women.

29. And when she saw him, she was troubled at his saying, and cast in her mind what manner of salutation this should be.

30. And the angel said unto her, Fear not, Mary: for thou hast found favour with God.

31. And, behold, thou shalt conceive in thy womb, and bring forth a son, and shalt call his name JESUS.

32. He shall be great, and shall be called the Son of the Highest: and the Lord God shall give unto him the throne of his father David:

33. And he shall reign over the house of Jacob for ever; and of his kingdom there shall be no end.

34. Then said Mary unto the angel, How shall this be, seeing I know not a man?

35. And the angel answered and said unto her, The Holy Ghost shall come upon thee, and the power of the Highest shall overshadow thee: therefore also that holy thing which shall be born of thee shall be called the Son of God.

36. And, behold, thy cousin Elisabeth, she hath also conceived a son in her old age: and this is the sixth month with her, who was called barren.

37. For with God nothing shall be impossible.

38. And Mary said, Behold the handmaid of the Lord; be it unto me according to thy word. And

the angel departed from her.

46. And Mary said, My soul doth magnify the Lord,

47. And my spirit hath rejoiced in God my Saviour.

48. For he hath regarded the low estate of his handmaiden:

for, behold, from henceforth all generations shall call me blessed.

49. For he that is mighty hath done to me great things; and holy is his name.

DICTIONARY

Gabriel (GAY-bree-el)—Luke 1:26—An angel of God who announced Jesus' birth.

Galilee (GAL-i-lee)—Luke 1:26—The country between the Jordan River and Mediterranian Sea.

Nazareth (NAZ-uh-reth)—Luke 1:26—The city in Galilee where Jesus grew up.

LESSON OUTLINE

I. THE ANGEL'S ANNOUNCE-MENT

    A. Two Worlds

    B. Mary, the Mother of Jesus

    C. Jesus, the Son of Mary

II. MARY'S SUBMISSION

    A. A Physical, Social, and Spiritual Quandary

    B. Mary's Surrender

III. THE MAGNIFICAT

    A. Mary's Psalm

    B. The Adoration of Mary

LESSON EXPOSITION

INTRODUCTION

Belief in the virgin birth of Christ has long been a vital part of the Evangelical credo. And though the liberal theologians of this century would like us to believe that the doctrine which declares that the Messiah was born of a virgin mother is a new thing to these last gen-erations, exactly the opposite is true.

From the words chosen by the New Testament writers to describe this glorious event, through the writings of the early-church fathers, and all through the cen-turies from the Advent to the Dark Ages, the truth of the Virgin Birth has been held dear by believers all over the world. It is these liberal scholars themselves who have introduced faulty theology, dredged from the darkest moments in church history, and heralded their teachings as superior to that of conservative scholarship and Evangelical thinking today. Born-again, Bible-believing seekers of the truth will lift their voices in concert to declare, "We believe in the Virgin Birth" (Evangelical credo).

To understand our lesson more fully, we must picture the times as they were just prior to the coming of Christ. Life among the people of the myriad small villages of Israel was relatively simple. Theirs was mostly an agrarian existence, bare-ly surviving by coaxing the simple necessities from the soil, or performing mundane tasks, such as that of Joseph of Nazareth—a carpenter.

The family of a young girl named Mary had arranged for her to be betrothed to Joseph, and the two of them were happily looking forward to their coming marriage, which would be celebrated with their families and friends. This time of courtship was special and romantic as the lovers planned their lives together—with the possibly older Joseph adding his wisdom to the youthful enthusiasm of his teenage sweetheart.

Unknown to the two of them, just beyond a curtain which separated the spirit world from the physical world so familiar to Joseph and Mary was the bustling of last-minute activity. The messengers of the great King, the God of the universe, readied themselves to pierce the heavens and enter the realm of time with a marvelous message to a shocked and shy young girl.

One would be prone to say without warning—but there had been sufficient "warning." A continual declaration through more than 2,000 years of written Hebrew history declares that God would provide a Savior, a Messiah (the Anointed One, the Christ) who would bridge the vast chasm between God, the Creator, and man, the created.

But as with so many other things, the prophesies about the Messiah had been muddled and muddied, argued and disclaimed, debated endlessly, spiritualized and carnalized until it was almost impossible to understand the true meaning of the message from God.

There were a few who would not allow their faith in a coming Messiah to be extinguished and met regularly in the Temple to await the momentous event (Luke 2:25, 26, 36-38). For the most part, however, the people went about their daily lives, unaware that a celestial curtain was already being parted. It was the "fulness of the time," and hardly anyone cared.

And then it happened!

I. THE ANGEL'S ANNOUNCE-MENT (Luke 1:26-33)

A. Two Worlds (v. 26)

26. And in the sixth month the angel Gabriel was sent from God unto a city of Galilee, named Nazareth.

J. Patterson-Smyth introduces us to the unveiling of the eternal plan of God by helping us to see beyond the curtain which separated the divine from the hustle and bustle of people going about their everyday lives. "Who could dream," he said, "that in that simple setting [Nazareth in Galilee] should be wrought the Miracle of the Ages! The Unseen World, so long watching its preparation with enthralling interest, were now shifting to earth the drama of redemption" (*People's Life of Christ*).

The words "in the sixth month" refer to a half-year span between the announcement of Jesus' birth by Gabriel to Mary and his earlier announcement to Zacharias—that the old priest and his elderly wife, Elizabeth, were to have a son (Luke 1:13). Since the couple were well past their childbearing years and Elizabeth was barren (v. 7), Zacharias doubted and asked for a sign that what the angel said would actually come to pass (vv. 18-20).

Now, six months later, Gabriel returned to tell Elizabeth's cousin (kinsman) Mary (v. 36) that she also would bear a son (v. 31); and under even more miraculous conditions than those experienced by her relative—it was to be a *virgin birth.*

Gabriel, whose name means "man of God," is a heavenly creature; he is first introduced to the Bible readers in Daniel 8:16 and 9:21, where he was called "the man Gabriel." This great angel's special function is that of *revealer* of the graciousness and wonderful purposes of the Lord God to His people.

The Jewish Targum placed Gabriel in Genesis 37:15, speaking to the lad Joseph; then in Deuteronomy 34:6, at the secret burial of Moses; and also in 2 Kings 19:35, at the massacre of the Assyrians outside Jerusalem— though the angel involved in each of these was not identified as Gabriel by name.

In a special Hebrew sense, "where the messenger of God is, there is God Himself" (*Interpreter's Bible*). Thus, with the arrival of Gabriel in Nazareth, the continuing saga of the redemption of mankind had moved to earth.

The New Testament reveals a continual spiritual incursion into the world related to the life of Jesus: at His birth (Luke 2:8-14), baptism (Matthew 3:16, 17), temptation (Matthew 4:11), transfiguration (Mark 9:2-8; 2 Peter 1:16-18), resurrection (Matthew 28:2-7), and ascension (Acts 1:10, 11). From Gabriel and the angels who "hailed His birth on the Bethlehem plains, down to the two [men] in white who appeared at His ascension," there was a continual parting of the eternal curtain, visitors "from another world, voices, appearances, indications not to be questioned of a sphere outside our own, intensely interested in the drama of our redemption.

"We believe that world is equally around us still. If we cannot see it, it is only that the light is wrong, that the glare of this world obscures it. Just as happens every day when the glare of the sunlight revealing to us every little flower and leaf and insect shuts out from us the great Universe which stands forth in the midnight sky, the light is wrong for it. If we never got darkness to correct our vision we might never believe in that starry world at all. Maybe only the closing of our eyes in the darkness of death will put us in the right light for seeing that spirit world. But we firmly believe that it is around us all the same as it so manifestly was in the life of Jesus" (J. Patterson-Smyth, *People's Life of Christ*).

B. Mary, the Mother of Jesus
   (vv. 27-30)

27. To a virgin espoused to a man whose name was Joseph, of the house of David; and the virgin's name was Mary.

28. And the angel came in unto her, and said, Hail, thou that art highly favoured, the Lord is with thee: blessed art thou among women.

29. And when she saw him, she was troubled at his saying, and cast in her mind what manner of salutation this should be.

30. And the angel said unto her, Fear not, Mary: for thou hast found favour with God.

Mary's Family History. Luke 1:32 leads us to believe that Mary herself was of the line of David, though her relative (cousin) Elizabeth was said to be "of the daughters of Aaron" (v. 5). Jesus Christ, her son, was described as being of "the seed of David according to the flesh" (Romans 1:3; see also Acts 2:29, 30; 2 Timothy 2:8). There is no problem placing Mary in the line of David, since there was no prohibition against marriage to members of Israelite clans other than their own.

That Mary and Joseph were poor is attested to by the humble offering made for her purification in the Temple 40 days after the birth of Jesus. Not being able to afford a lamb, she offered the sacrifice of the poor, "a pair of turtledoves, or two young pigeons" (Luke 2:24; see Leviticus 12:8).

Mary's Virginity. That Mary was a virgin at the time of the birth of Christ is verified by Scripture. The Virgin Birth is a fact—even though the New Testament testimony is exclusive to only two New Testament writers. Jesus said "that in the mouth of two or three witnesses every word may be established" (Matthew 18:16; see also Deuteronomy 17:6; 2 Corinthians 13:1).

One of the two who gave witness that Mary was a virgin was Matthew, the tax collector turned disciple, who wrote: "Now the birth of Jesus Christ was on this wise: When as his mother Mary was espoused to Joseph, *before they came together*, she was found with child of the Holy Ghost. . . . But while he thought on these things, behold, the angel of the Lord appeared unto him in a dream, saying, Joseph, thou son of David, fear not to take unto thee Mary thy wife: *for that which is conceived in her is*

of the Holy Ghost. And she shall bring forth a son, and thou shalt call his name JESUS: for he shall save his people from their sins. Now all this was done, that it *might be fulfilled* which was spoken of the Lord by the prophet [Isaiah], saying, *Behold, a virgin shall be with child*, and shall bring forth a son, and they shall call his name Emmanuel, which being interpreted is, God with us" (1:18, 20-23, italics are author's emphasis).

A second witness was Luke the physician, a doctor who traveled with Paul on some of his missionary trips. Luke said, "And in the sixth month [after the conception of John the Baptist] the angel Gabriel was sent from God unto a city of Galilee, named Nazareth, *to a virgin* espoused to a man whose name was Joseph, of the house of David; and *the virgin's name was Mary*" (1:26, 27, italics are author's emphasis).

These "two witnesses" were sufficient to establish the credibility of the doctrine for the early church, and they are also enough for us.

Liberal critics would make much of the fact that Isaiah—in his prophecy "A virgin shall conceive, and bear a son, and shall call his name Immanuel" (7:14)—used the Hebrew word *almah*, which implies simply an unmarried woman of marriageable age, rather than a more specific term which designated a young woman of marriageable age who had never engaged in sexual intercourse.

Two answers come to mind quickly: First, contrary to what the foes of the doctrine try to expound, there is no single word in the Hebrew language which denotes a young woman of marriageable age who has never had sexual relations with a man. It is only possible to make that statement by using more than a single word. Second, *almah* (an unmarried young woman) was understood by Jewish society to be a virgin.

It is also important to note that in the Greek version of the Old Testament, the Septuagint, published just prior to the time of the birth of Christ, the Hebrew word *almah* was translated with the Greek word *parthenos*, which specifically denotes a young woman who had never engaged in sexual intercourse. Since this translation was designed to be read by the Jews of the Dispersion, who were scattered all over the world and often could no longer speak or read Hebrew, those who studied *this* Bible were looking for a Messiah born of a *virgin*.

Also, Isaiah prefaced his prophecy with these words: "The Lord himself shall give you a sign." That an unmarried woman should bear a son would not constitute a "sign"— rather, it would be a disgrace. But if a virgin, a woman who had never engaged in sexual intercourse, would give birth to a son, that would be a sign only the Lord could provide.

Mary's Betrothal. Mary's family had, in the manner of Jewish marriage ritual, espoused her to a man named Joseph (Matthew 1:18). Betrothal (or espousal) to a man was a solemn and sacred event, which in legal terms was the equivalent of marriage. So special is the bond denoted by the word *betrothal* (Hebrew: *aras*) that the prophet Hosea used it to describe the covenant relationship between God and Israel (2:19, 20).

In all ways except for two—entering into sexual liaison and the social obligation that the woman remain in the home of her parents until the final marriage ceremony had been performed—the betrothed couple were married. In fact, often the betrothed of the woman was called, or considered to be, her husband (Matthew 1:18-20, 24, 25; see also Genesis 19:14 [*NIV*]; Judges 14:15; 15:1 [*NIV*]).

Mary was thus *married* to Joseph; but in the true spirit of Jewish marriage customs, she was still a virgin and would remain such until her marriage was completed in an elaborate wedding ritual. Betrothal did not include sexual relations. In fact, there was a vast and clear distinction between betrothing a wife and having "taken her."

The betrothal was the customary first step in a relationship meant to be fully consummated at a future date. Mary herself lent full credence to her virginity when she responded to the announcement of the angel Gabriel (that she was to have a son) with the words, "How shall this be, seeing I know not a man?" (Luke 1: 34). In Gabriel's contact with Joseph, the same theme was repeated several times (Matthew 1:18-20; 23, 25).

Mary's Husband, Joseph. Joseph was surely a good man—for he made the right decisions at the right time, every time. Like Mary, he was placed in a great quandary. What would people think? Would their own families be able to accept that this son was from God?

But the thing that surely must have bothered them both the most was the possibility that the holiness standards they upheld would be besmirched—standards they had worked so hard to maintain in such difficult times.

There was no doubt at all that the birth of this child would be misunderstood by those nearest to Mary and Joseph. For them to appear to be intimate during their courtship was at the least a breach of Jewish customs and at the worst a violation of the laws of God.

If Joseph put his betrothed away, even quietly, the birth of the child would leave her open to charges of adultery—and Jesus would be branded as illegitimate.

What was he to do?

Joseph had a dream (Matthew 1:20-25) in which the angel of the Lord told him, "Fear not to take unto thee Mary thy wife: for that which is conceived in her is of the Holy Ghost."

The great Christian writer S.D. Gordon said concerning Joseph's position: "The time had come. The nation's deliverance was at hand. And he [Joseph] was to have a share . . . only an incidental part; yet what a privilege to have even that part.

"And he accepted gratefully the sacred trust committed to him of being *the friend* of the holy woman through whom God was working out His great plan."

It must have been a wonderful morning for Mary when Joseph, smiling, came to tell her about the visit of an angel in the night.

We don't know much about Joseph. After Jesus was 12 years old, Joseph seems to have simply dropped out of the picture. Perhaps he died early—but not too early to teach "his" son to be a good carpenter and make yokes for both oxen and men that were light and easy to carry (see Matthew 11:29, 30).

Doctor Gordon continues, "That word *husband* took on a new fineness of meaning as Joseph became the friend and protector of the woman whom God had chosen to bring to birth His Only Begotten [Son]" (*Quiet Talks About the Babe of Bethlehem*).

C. Jesus, the Son of Mary
   (vv. 31-33)

31. And, behold, thou shalt conceive in thy womb, and bring forth a son, and shalt call his name JESUS.

32. He shall be great, and shall be called the Son of the Highest: and the Lord God shall give unto him the throne of his father David:

33. And he shall reign over the house of Jacob for ever; and of his kingdom there shall be no end.

How easy it is for us to get so involved in Mary and Joseph, Zacharias and Elizabeth, Gabriel, and all the other bit players in the great drama of the Christmas story and leave out the most important One—Jesus, the son of Mary, the Son of God.

That the baby was to be called *Jesus* was revealed independently to both Joseph and Mary. They did not choose the name Jesus; they would not have known how. The name Jesus was the final revelation, by which God had regularly through the ages revealed His character, purpose, and will to mankind. Now a tiny baby whose name means "God is salvation" has come into the world to tell us about the great love of the Father and His desire that everyone should be reconciled to Him.

The name of God and the names of those in the Godhead were so important in the scheme of eternal things that the Lord specifically forbade that His name be taken in vain in the third of the Ten Commandments: "Thou shalt not take the name of the Lord thy God in vain; for the Lord will not hold him guiltless that taketh his name in vain" (Exodus 20:7).

The name of Jesus is the greatest name in all the world. Hugh Jeter, in a study on divine healing, said, "There are three ways by which a person may obtain a great name. He may inherit it, earn it, or have it conferred on him. There is no name on earth or in heaven greater than the name of Jesus Christ. The writer of the Epistle to the Hebrews said that Christ is the *heir of all things*, the One who made the worlds and upholds all things by the word of His power and, comparing Him with the angels, said, 'He hath *by inheritance* obtained a more excellent name than they' (Hebrews 1:2-4). The fact that He lived a perfect life and purchased redemption for the human race certainly *earned for Him* the greatest name of all earthly heroes.

"Besides this *God has conferred upon Him* a name above all names. 'Wherefore God also hath highly exalted him, and given him a name which is above every name: that at the name of Jesus every knee should bow, of things in heaven, and things in earth, and things under the earth; and that every tongue should confess that Jesus Christ is Lord, to the glory of God the Father' (Philippians 2:9-11).

"All creatures in three worlds or domains (angels, men, and demons) must acknowledge the absolute supremacy of that name!" (*By His Stripes*, Gospel Publishing House).

What makes us believe that Joseph and Mary were poor?

II. MARY'S SUBMISSION
(Luke 1:34-38)

A. A Physical, Social, and Spiritual Quandary (vv. 34-37)

34. Then said Mary unto the angel, How shall this be, seeing I know not a man?

35. And the angel answered and said unto her, The Holy Ghost shall come upon thee, and the power of the Highest shall overshadow thee: therefore also that holy thing which shall be born of thee shall be called the Son of God.

36. And, behold, thy cousin Elisabeth, she hath also conceived a son in her old age: and this is the sixth month with her, who was called barren.

37. For with God nothing shall be impossible.

When the angel told Mary that she was to bear a child, she asked, "How shall this be, seeing I know not a man?" With these words, she expressed both her condition as a virgin and her quandary as a young, unmarried Jewish girl.

First, there had never in the history of the world been a *virgin birth*. No wonder she was "troubled at his [the angel's] saying" (v. 29). How disturbing this must have been for a teenage girl in those long-ago years.

Then she must have thought, *What will everyone think when they realize that I'm pregnant? Will my parents understand? Will my friends understand? Will my pastor understand? And what about Joseph—could he ever understand? How can I hold my head up and face them?*

The angel had called her "highly favoured" and "blessed . . . among women" (v. 28). *But I don't see a blessing,* she may have thought. *All I see is hardship and suffering.*

Little could she know that these questions that perplexed her now would pale in comparison to the problems that would face her as she would someday watch her son be nailed to a cross.

After the birth of Jesus, when she and Joseph went to the Temple to make a sacrifice, an old man named Simeon added to her quandary by prophesying that a sword would pierce through her soul in relation to this child (2:34, 35).

By her gracious conduct and holy life, Mary taught us that being blessed and highly favored does not always mean life will be tranquil and easy, filled with riches and glory, or that the future will be bright and happy every day.

In fact, the most profound sign of favor with God comes through our willingness to suffer for the Lord, to accept His will by faith, and to toil endlessly in His fields.

B. Mary's Surrender (v. 38)

38. And Mary said, Behold the handmaid of the Lord; be it unto me according to thy word. And the angel departed from her.

We're not sure that Mary knew even after the prophecy of Simeon what she must suffer. And certainly as a young teenage girl, it is not likely that she was strong enough or mature enough to understand and accept such tidings. Nevertheless, Mary showed remarkable maturity in her responses to the angel, especially in her words "Be it unto me according to thy word."

Just like that, it was decided, "Tell God to do with me as He wishes." Whatever might be, she was willing. Whatever sacrifice of reputation, relationships, or love—"be it unto me."

And that was enough for Gabriel. Like that he was gone.

If it was difficult for Mary to make these decisions and face the consequences while in the presence of an angel, imagine how difficult it must have been now that he was gone, and all that remained was the memory of his being there and the echo of his words.

She may have thought, *What have I got myself into?* But her surrender to God was real and permanent. She, like her son, would have to face whatever the future held—in faith that God does "all things well" (Mark 7:37).

How would a teenage girl today react to the angel Gabriel's visit?

III. THE MAGNIFICAT
    (Luke 1:46-55)

A. Mary's Psalm (vv. 46-55)

(Luke 1:50-55 is not included in the printed text.)

46. And Mary said, My soul doth magnify the Lord,

47. And my spirit hath rejoiced in God my Saviour.

48. For he hath regarded the low estate of his handmaiden: for, behold, from henceforth all generations shall call me blessed.

49. For he that is mighty hath done to me great things; and holy is his name.

The *Magnificat*, or Mary's psalm, is in fact the first of three psalms found in the story of Christ's infancy in the Gospel of Luke. Its name was derived from the first word of the text in Latin ("My soul doth magnify") and was modeled after the song of Hannah in 1 Samuel 2:1-10. There is no reason to believe that it was the work of anyone but Mary—a woman expecting a child, exuding joy and confidence in God and His promises to and through her.

Miriam (whose name means the same as Mary) sang her song of triumph when God destroyed the army of Pharaoh in the Red Sea (Exodus 15:20, 21). Deborah, the judge, sang a song of victory with Barak, her general of the army, when God gave them victory over Sisera (Judges 5:1-31). Mary also sang her song of praise for what God had done, was doing, and would do in the future through her son.

There would be long, lonely vigils beside the bed of her child; meals to cook; clothes to make and repair; hours of teaching, loving, and coaxing Him to be the very best. Others might have been able to do all this—but God thought Mary could do it best.

Mary, God blessed you! And so do we!

B. The Adoration of Mary

(The following paragraphs are not related to the printed text, but should be a part of the study of Mary, the mother of Jesus.)

The virgin mother of Jesus must surely have been a lovely, holy woman. The Gospels speak of her that way. And she was strong, as only a woman of great faith could be. She was willing to sacrifice her reputation among family and friends, and possibly the love of the man to whom she was betrothed, to do the will of God. If any woman could ever be called *blessed*, it was she.

There is, however, no scripture to support, nor genuine historical reason to believe, that Mary's body was "assumed" into heaven after her death so that it might not see corruption or that she was, or is, worthy of any special *adoration*.

We give her thanks; we honor her; however, adoration belongs only to God!

Name two other women in the Bible besides Mary who sang their hymns of joy after some great event.

REVIEW QUESTIONS

1. Who was the angel that brought the message of Jesus' birth to both Mary and Joseph? What was his special task as a messenger of God?

2. Why was the birth of John the Baptist considered a miracle? Compare the situation of Zacharias and Elizabeth with that of Abraham and Sarah.

3. Discuss Mary's quandary about the message of the angel.

4. Discuss the family ties between Jesus and John the Baptist? Do you think they were friends as boys?

5. Discuss the difference between the adoration of Mary and giving her honor.

GOLDEN TEXT HOMILY

"A VIRGIN SHALL BE WITH

CHILD, AND SHALL BRING FORTH A SON, AND THEY SHALL CALL HIS NAME EMMANUEL" (Matthew 1:23).

According to *Halley's Bible Handbook,* Matthew is said to be the "most widely read book in all the world." Thus, the fact of the virgin birth of Jesus becomes knowledgeable to all the world. From the miraculous union of the divine nature and human nature, Jesus, the Son of God, was conceived (Matthew 1:20; Luke 1:34, 35). Mary is the only virgin that ever became, or ever will become, a mother in this fashion. The Jews, and even some so-called Christians, try desperately to refute this miracle birth; but for the true Christian believer the Scriptures leave no room to doubt as to the authenticity of the virgin birth of Jesus— Emmanuel (Isaiah 7:14; Matthew 1:23; Luke 1:27, 34, 35).

Emmanuel—"God with us." God with us then, God with us now! In the Old Testament ages God manifested Himself as Jehovah; in the Gospels, God manifested Himself in the person of Jesus Christ, the Son—"God with us"; and after the Ascension, He manifests Himself in the indwelling, empowering Holy Spirit (John 14:16-18; 1 John 4:4).

God is *with* us, and *in* us, through the miracle of faith. God is with us—saving from sin, comforting us, defending us, enlightening us, protecting us from Satan's darts, guiding us, keeping us from yielding to Satan's temptations and sinning, sanctifying us, infilling us with the Holy Spirit, healing us, empowering us for service for God and mankind.

Jesus was born of God's nature and human nature; He is very God and perfect man. Because of His humanity He relates with humankind. He experienced all the temptations that we do. He felt pain, loneliness, hunger, thirst, weariness; He was poor; He shed tears (Hebrews 4:15).

We live in a sinful, sick, strife-ridden, suffering, cruel, revengeful world. So did Jesus! He understands our every need.

Emmanuel—God with us and in us, and we with Him now and eternally!—**Karl W. Bunkley, (Retired), Former General Sunday School President, International Pentecostal Holiness Church, Oklahoma City, Oklahoma**

SENTENCE SERMONS

JESUS, GOD'S SON, was born of a virgin.

—Selected

THE LIGHT that shines from the humble manger is strong enough to lighten our way to the end of our days.

—*Vita-Rays*

THE TURKS are of the opinion that it is no uncommon thing for a virgin to bear a child. I would by no means introduce this belief into my family.

—Martin Luther

I BELIEVE that Christ was born of a virgin because I have read it in the Gospel.

—St. Augustine

EVANGELISM APPLICATION

JESUS, THE VIRGIN-BORN SON OF GOD, CAME TO SAVE SINNERS.

Jesus, the Word, is the gospel. The gospel is founded not only on the universal Christ but upon the incarnate Jesus as well. "You cannot say 'Christ' until you have first said 'Jesus,' for Jesus puts content into Christ—the content of His own life lived out among us. The universal Christ is defined by the historic Jesus. You cannot know God or the Holy Spirit or Christ until you have first known Jesus. The gospel begins with Jesus. It begins, not with a word, but with the Word made flesh. Had it begun with a word, it would have been a philosophy. Had it been a philosophy, it would have been *good views*. It was a fact; hence it was *good news*. To present the Christian faith as primarily a philosophy of life is to place it alongside other philosophies of life—above them, but one of them. This makes the issue the question of the best ideas. But Jesus never presented good views— He announced good news. And He was good news. He came to present Himself as the good news, the forgiveness and love of God in the flesh." (E. Stanley Jones, *The Way*

to Power and Poise).

The *good news*, the gospel, is God's greatest revelation to mankind. Jesus did not come to bring the gospel—He is the gospel! And this Word from God—Jesus incarnate—is no namby-pamby sentimental view of life. Like Himself, His followers must from the first read the fine print that requires they also *take up their cross and follow Jesus to His*.

DAILY BIBLE READINGS

M. A Miraculous Birth.
   Genesis 21:1-7
T. A Deliverer Promised.
   Judges 13:1-5
W. A Desired Son.
   1 Samuel 1:10-20
T. The Angel's Visit. Luke 1:11-20
F. Preparing the Way.
   Luke 1:76-80
S. Joseph's Obedience.
   Matthew 1:18-25

The Incarnation (Christmas)

Study Text: John 1:1-14

Objective: To appreciate the true meaning of Christmas and observe it with adoration and obedience to Christ.

Time: Birth of Christ—possibly 5 B.C. John's message was probably written midsummer A.D. 26.

Place: Birth of Christ—Bethlehem; John's message was probably written near Jerusalem.

Golden Text: "The Word was made flesh, and dwelt among us, (and we beheld his glory, the glory as of the only begotten of the Father,) full of grace and truth" (John 1:14).

Central Truth: The wonder of the Christmas story is that God, in Christ, became flesh.

Evangelism Emphasis: The Christmas season offers a wonderful opportunity to share the good news.

PRINTED TEXT

John 1:1. In the beginning was the Word, and the Word was with God, and the Word was God.

2. The same was in the beginning with God.

3. All things were made by him; and without him was not any thing made that was made.

4. In him was life; and the life was the light of men.

5. And the light shineth in darkness; and the darkness comprehended it not.

6. There was a man sent from God, whose name was John.

7. The same came for a witness, to bear witness of the Light, that all men through him might believe.

8. He was not that Light, but was sent to bear witness of that Light.

9. That was the true Light, which lighteth every man that cometh into the world.

10. He was in the world, and the world was made by him, and the world knew him not.

11. He came unto his own, and his own received him not.

12. But as many as received him, to them gave he power to become the sons of God, even to them that believe on his name:

13. Which were born, not of blood, nor of the will of the flesh, nor of the will of man, but of God.

14. And the Word was made flesh, and dwelt among us, (and we beheld his glory, the glory as of the only begotten of the Father,) full of grace and truth.

LESSON OUTLINE

LESSON EXPOSITION

INTRODUCTION

The Christmas season offers an excellent time to share the good news (the gospel) of Christ's incarnation, His coming into the black void of sin in the world with the light of hope. The message of the season is "For God so loved the world, that he gave his only begotten Son . . ." (John 3:16) and "He that spared not his own Son . . . how shall he not with him also freely give us all things?" (Romans 8:32).

The message of John the Baptist was "Behold the Lamb of God!" (John 1:36). The Incarnation would not be complete without this picture of a Lamb—God's sacrificial Lamb. The Bible, from beginning to end, is the story of the Lamb—from Exodus 12:5, the story of the Passover lamb, to Revelation 22:3, where the crucified Christ is the victorious Lamb of God.

Revelation is specifically the "book of the Lamb"—telling us about the worthy Lamb (4:11), the slain Lamb (5:6), the blood of the Lamb (12:11), the Lamb's wife (21:9), the Lamb as the light (21:23), the "Lamb's book of life" (21:27), and the throne of the Lamb (22:1, 3).

Isaac and his father, Abraham, went up Mount Moriah to make a sacrifice to the Lord. The lad asked, "Behold the fire and the wood: but where is the lamb for a burnt-offering?" Abraham responded, with what would be one of the greatest prophecies in the Bible: "My son, God will provide himself a lamb" (Genesis 22:7, 8).

The Incarnation is the story of God the Son coming into the world as a tiny baby, growing into manhood, and dying on a cross to demonstrate the love of God the Father. His words and His life were a living parable about a God so advanced above mankind that He could not tell them how much He loved them, so His Son agreed to come and be a man, speak the language of men, feel the pain of men, be tempted to sin like men—and still be able to live in such a manner that men would see the love of His Father and be drawn to Him.

This is the "good news" of Christmas—that the babe in the manger is God in the flesh! He came to Bethlehem on His way to the Cross.

I. THE ETERNAL CHRIST
(John 1:1-5)

A. Jesus the Word of God (v. 1)

1. In the beginning was the Word, and the Word was with God, and the Word was God.

The *Logos*, the "Word," is a Greek term meaning "someting said; a thought or concept or the expression of that concept." John tells us from the first that Jesus was the expression of the very thoughts of God—in human form.

Notice that He is not the *words* of God but the *Word* of God. If you want to know what God thinks, you must not only listen to what Jesus says but also look at what He does.

Jesus speaks to us about God with a personal knowledge of God, because *He is God.* The Lord said, "As the heavens are higher than the earth, so are my ways higher than your ways, and my thoughts than your thoughts" (Isaiah 55:9). Because the world could not know God (no man had ever seen Him [1 John 4:12]) and because He was too far above us for us to reach Him, God must reach down to us. He sent His Son as an ambassador from heaven to show us the things He wanted us to know.

Jesus is the "express image" of the Father (Hebrews 1:3). Adam was also created in that same image. God said, "Let us make man in our image, after our likeness. . . . So God created man in his own image, in the image of God created he him; male and female created he them" (Genesis 1:26, 27).

When Adam fell into sin, the image of God in him was marred so badly that men no longer knew what God looked like. Jesus came not only to reveal the image of God but also to give mankind the opportunity to regain that perfect image lost in the Fall. The aim of every Christian should be to "come in the unity of the faith, and of the knowledge of the Son of God, unto a perfect man, unto the measure of the stature of the fulness of Christ" (Ephesians 4:13).

The work of Christ on the cross enables us to become a new creation, partaking of the divine nature of God. The new man in Christ is being formed in the believer (Galatians 2:20; 4:19). "Hereby perceive we the love of God, because he laid down his life for us" (1 John 3:16).

The grace of God, the unmerited favor of a gracious God, is at the heart of all that Christ does and says. Peter described this unmerited favor as "the manifold grace of God" (1 Peter 4:10). How descriptive this is of the work of Christ. The word *manifold* means "multifaceted" or "many-faceted" and refers to the facets of a diamond—or, more specifically, a prism. When the pure white light of the sun shines through a prism, all the colors of the rainbow are radiated through the facets, providing a wonderful display of colored lights.

Peter tells us the grace of God is like this prism—God's pure grace—like the white light of the sun, which cannot be seen by the naked eye. When His grace is directed into the prism of the life of Christ, the invisible white light takes on the colors of God's favor, healing, atonement, care, and love. In Jesus, the express image of God, all the attributes of a loving God are mirrored. Peter said, "We . . . were eyewitnesses of his majesty" (2 Peter 1:16). John declared, "The Word was made flesh, and dwelt among us, (and we beheld his glory . . .) full of grace and truth" (John 1:14).

B. Jesus the Eternal Christ (v. 2)

2. The same was in the beginning with God.

The word *beginning* probably has the same thought here as the word translated "beginning" in Genesis 1:1: "In the beginning God created the heaven and the earth."

The word translated "God" is the Hebrew word *Elohim* (*El,* "the strong One," and *alah,* "to swear, to bind oneself by an oath, or to be faithful"). It is the plural word used in Genesis 1:26, 27, when God (*Elohim*) said, "Let *us* make man in *our* image, after *our* likeness."

Jesus was God (John 1:1), and He was with God always. The concept of "having neither beginning of days, nor end of life . . . like unto the Son of God" (Hebrews 7:3) is difficult for our finite minds to comprehend. To us, everything must start somewhere and end somewhere! But with God, there is no time—no beginning and no end.

The Son of God was a part of the Godhead always. He did not come into existence in a manger in Bethlehem (nor in Mary's womb at conception). He was in the beginning with "the everlasting [eternal] God" (Romans 16:26), and He was with God before the beginning as we know it.

God is not only the God of eternity but also the Lord over time. Time as we know it does not exist in the heavenly realm but came into being when God created the earth and ordered it to spin on its axis and around the sun at a precise speed, thus creating periods which we have designated as "time." "This is the day which the Lord hath made" (Psalm 118:24). Time will exist only so long as God decrees it, and it will end when He declares that it end.

C. Jesus the Creator (v. 3)

3. All things were made by him; and without him was not any thing made that was made.

As has already been mentioned, Jesus was in the beginning with God, and He was God. The Creator God (*Elohim*)—the Trinity—is comprised of God the Father, God the Son, and God the Holy Spirit. This plurality of persons said, "Let *us* make man in *our* image" (Genesis 1:26). John said of Jesus, "All things were made by *him*"; and again he said in the Book of Revelation, "*Thou* hast created all things, and for thy pleasure they are and were created" (4:11; see also Colossians 1:15-19).

To the Jews, this revelation that Jesus was Creator of all things would come as a complete surprise. The *Shema,* Israel's most sacred writing, declared, "The Lord our God is one Lord!" That Jesus should have claimed to be "the Son of God" was too much for them to accept.

To the Gentiles, Paul declared that they could see God in His creation: "For the invisible things of him [God] from the creation of the world are clearly seen, being understood by the things that are made, even his eternal power and Godhead; so that they are without excuse" (Romans 1:20). The Jews too could have seen the Godhead in the creation and in their Bible, if they had cared to; and some, like the apostles and many in the early church, did.

If we look for it, God's power is easy to see. It is all around us in the magnificence of the structure of a plant, in the order of the universe, and in the "fearfully and wonderfully made" body of a man (Psalm 139:14). The psalmist said, "When I consider the heavens, the work of thy fingers, the moon and the stars, which thou hast ordained; what is man, that thou art mindful of him?" (Psalm 8:3, 4).

But while His power is visible in the lightning and the storm, His majesty in the starlit heavens (Psalm 19:1), His glory in this wonderful earth, His control in the tides of the sea and in the rain which falls to replenish the aquifers and provide an unlimited source of life-giving water—His love is much more difficult to perceive.

The only way God could adequately explain to man how much He loved him was by sending His Word, who was exactly like Him. Philip said, "Lord, shew us the Father." Jesus responded, "Hast thou not known me, Philip? *he that hath seen me hath seen the Father.* . . . Believest thou not that I am in the Father, and the Father in me? the words that I speak unto you I speak not of myself: but the Father that dwelleth in me, he doeth the works" (John 14:8-10).

God the Father, God the Holy Spirit, and God the Son—are all God. They are God, eternally existing in three persons—not three Gods, but *one God.* This is the trinity of God, the Godhead. John wrote, "The Word was *with God,* and the Word [Jesus] *was God*" (1:1).

D. Jesus the Life (v. 4)

4. In him was life; and the life was the light of men.

Life is one of the greatest themes of the Bible. It is symbolized by the "tree of life," first seen in Genesis 2:9, where it was one of two special trees God planted in the Garden of Eden. When John the Revelator speaks to us about another Garden, a place called heaven, he tells us that the "tree of life" will then be seen again in the midst of the city, growing on both sides of the crystal river which flows out of the throne of God (Revelation 22:1, 2).

It is significant that the waters of this river of life flow from God's throne. For God, through His Son Jesus, is the source of all life—the wellhead, or spring, from which life originates.

John said, "In him [Jesus] was life" (John 1:4); Paul called Him "Christ, who is our life" (Colossians 3:4); and Peter said of those who crucified Jesus, "[You] killed the Prince of life" (Acts 3:15).

Wherever Jesus was, there was life—whether it was in the Creation, when He breathed into Adam's nostrils the breath of life "and man became a living soul" (Genesis 2:7), or when He touched the casket of the dead son of the widow of Nain "and he that was dead sat up, and began to speak" (Luke 7:15). At the tomb of Lazarus, He called His friend, dead for four days, out of the grave. Someone has said that unless Jesus had called specifically for Lazarus to come forth, all the graves would have burst open and all those who were dead since the creation of the earth would have risen!

One day, that will happen: "The Lord himself shall descend from heaven with a shout, with the voice of the archangel, and with the trump[et] of God: and the dead in Christ shall rise first: Then we which are alive and remain shall be caught up together with them in the clouds, to meet the Lord in the air: and so shall we ever be with the Lord" (1 Thessalonians 4:16, 17).

Where Jesus was, there was life. Maybe that is why He died before the two thieves who were crucified beside Him on Calvary. They could die after Him, but not in His presence.

Isn't it ironic that He who *came to give life* also "*came . . . to give his life* a ransom for many"? (Mark 10:45). "Therefore doth my Father love me, because *I lay down my life*, that I might take it again. No man taketh it from me, but *I lay it down of myself.* I have power to lay it down, and I have power to take it again" (John 10:17, 18).

Life was very important to Jesus—not just living, but abundant living! He said, "I am come that they might have life, and . . . have it more abundantly" (10:10). He told the great Jewish leader Nicodemus, "God so loved the world, that he gave his only begotten Son, that whosoever believeth in him should not perish, but have everlasting life" (3:16).

E. Jesus the Light (vv. 4, 5)

4. In him was life; and the life was the light of men.

5. And the light shineth in darkness; and the darkness comprehended it not.

Light and life are inextricably entwined. There cannot be one without the other. Thus, it is not strange that John placed them together (v. 4). In our spiritual life, the same is true. Jesus tells us that He is both "the life" and "the light" (John 14:6; 8:12). We too can become lights—though lesser lights—as He shines through us. But while we may share with others the life of Jesus through the gospel, *He alone is life!*

Life is an attribute of God which man cannot give and has no right to arbitrarily take away.

Light and darkness are antagonists in a fight for predominance in the world. This celestial war has been waged since before the fall of man in the Garden of Eden. Satan and evil are the emissaries of darkness, while Jesus is the champion of light. Sometimes darkness seems about to win, but John said, "And the darkness comprehended it not" (v. 5). The word *comprehended* is derived from the Greek word *katalambano*, probably best translated "overcome." The darkness will not overcome the Light. Jesus promised the disciples as they began to build the fledgling Christian church that "the gates of hell shall not prevail against it" (Matthew 16:18).

The church is to be the repository of the light, that is, the truth of the gospel. Jesus is the Light; the church is the lampstand (Revelation 1:20). We as Christians ("little Christs") are to reflect His light to the world around us.

Spiritual darkness is a state of mind that rejects the things of God and is conformed to "the pattern of this world" (Romans 12:2, *NIV*). Jesus said that He was rejected for the reason that "men loved darkness rather than light, because their deeds were evil" (John 3:19).

Isaiah, prophesying about the coming of Jesus, said, "Arise, shine; for thy light is come" (60:1). And He did come—nearly 2,000 years ago—to a manger in Bethlehem. Imagine how awful a place this world would be if He had not come.

The Bible declares that when Jesus came, He was the fulfillment of the prophecy found in Isaiah 9:2: "The people which sat in darkness saw great light" (Matthew 4:16).

Jesus, like most young preachers, began His ministry at home. He went into the synagogue on the Sabbath, stood and read from the prophecy of Isaiah (61:1, 2): "The Spirit of the Lord is upon me, because he hath anointed me to preach the gospel to the poor; he hath sent me to heal the broken-hearted, to preach deliverance to the captives, and recovering of sight to the blind, to set at liberty them that are bruised, to preach the acceptable year of the Lord" (Luke 4:18, 19). If He had stopped there, He may have been lauded as a fine preacher; but He had the unmitigated gall to say, "This day is this scripture fulfilled in your ears" (v. 21).

"Who does He think He is?" may have been whispered across the room. "Is not this Joseph's son?" (v. 22). They became so angry about this hometown boy claiming to be the fulfillment of messianic prophecy that they tried to kill Him. "But he passing through the midst of them went his way" (v. 30). How sad. The Giver of life was standing in their synagogue, offering to make this great city the headquarters of the greatest spiritual movement that would ever sweep the earth, but instead He "went his way."

It may have been at the Jewish Festival of Lights that Jesus announced, "I am come a light into the world, that whosoever believeth on me should not abide in darkness" (John 12:46).

In the end, light will be provided for those of the light. In fact, Jesus himself will be the eternal light that turns out the sun and moon and shines like the day for those who have accepted Him (Revelation 21:23). But those who reject the Light shall, like Judas, go to their own place (Acts 1:25). They "shall be cast out into outer darkness" (Matthew 8:12).

What does the "manifold grace of God" mean?

II. WITNESS TO CHRIST
   (John 1:6-9)

A. A Man Named John (v. 6)

6. There was a man sent from God, whose name was John.

John the Baptist was Jesus' cousin (kin) and they were linked together even before either of them were born. Mary, the mother of Jesus, spent three months with Elizabeth, the mother of John, just after she conceived and when Elizabeth was already six-months expectant with her son John.

Unlike Jesus' own brothers, John believed in Jesus from the first and recognized that Jesus was the prophesied Messiah. Probably his mother told him so, since she and Mary had divine signs of Jesus' special birth.

And the respect between them was mutual. Jesus declared, "Among them that are born of women there hath not risen a greater than John the Baptist" (Matthew 11:11). Now that is some high praise!

Several things about John are noteworthy. Among them is his commission—he was sent by God (John 1:6). He came in fulfillment of messianic prophecy, was the last of the Old Testament prophets, and was Jesus' first convert in the New Testament.

John was prophesied to be the forerunner of Christ, a messenger commissioned on official business to go ahead of the King of kings and announce His arrival (see Luke 3:4, 5; Isaiah 40:3-5). John's mission was to set the stage for Jesus' ministry and then graciously retire from the spotlight. He said himself, "He must increase, but I must decrease" (John 3:30).

John's message was clear: "[Jesus is] the Lamb of God who taketh away the sin of the world" (1:29); He was the Son of God (v. 34); and He was the One who would baptize with the Holy Spirit (v. 33).

John made no claims for himself: "Are you the Christ?" "I am not the Christ." "Are you Elijah?" "No! I'm not!" "Well, then," they asked, "who are you?" He responded, "I am the voice of one crying in the wilderness, Make straight the way of the Lord" (see vv. 19-23).

Two of Jesus' disciples—one of whom was John the Beloved, the writer of five books of the Bible— were originally disciples of John the Baptist. When they heard Jesus speak, they followed Him (John 1:35-37).

John the Baptist was the ideal witness; he was obsessed with his mission—so important was it that he lived in the wilderness and ate the coarsest of foods, fasted and prayed often, and talked endlessly about the Messiah. He told those who came to him that Jesus alone spoke for God—"He that cometh from above is above all. . . . And what he hath seen and heard, that he testifieth . . . He that believeth on the Son [of God] hath everlasting life" (3:31, 32, 36).

John, like us, had doubts sometimes. After wicked Herod had thrown him into prison, John, thinking that Jesus was moving more slowly toward establishing His kingdom than he had thought He would, sent messengers to ask, "Art thou he that should come, or do we look for another?" (Matthew 11:3).

He must have been satisfied with Jesus' answer—for John especially would understand that in Jesus' answer He was telling John the works He did were the exact fulfillment of the prophecies concerning the Messiah's mission. And perhaps John could be classified as the first Christian martyr, losing his head at the request of Herod's wife (Matthew 14:1-12) before he could see his own prophecies and proclamations concerning the identity of Jesus as the Christ come to pass.

B. John the Baptist—A Little Light (vv. 7-9)

7. The same came for a witness, to bear witness of the Light, that all men through him might believe.

8. He was not that Light, but was sent to bear witness of that Light.

9. That was the true Light, which lighteth every man that cometh into the world.

John did not say that he was not a light, only that he was not *that Light,* because *that Light* was "the true Light, which lighteth every man that cometh into the world" (v. 9).

John saw himself as something like the morning star that heralds the coming of the sun (Isaiah 58:10). John's light was necessary but not nearly as important as Jesus, "the light of the world" (John 8:12), through whom God's children will shine, reflecting their Lord.

John the Baptist introduced the Christian church to water baptism—a public profession of an inward confession—a symbol of the believer's death with Christ (down into the water) and resurrection (up out of the water).

Water baptism is a symbol of the cleansing work of the Holy Spirit, since we are washed in the blood of Christ (Revelation 1:5) and made clean daily by the washings of the Holy Spirit (1 Corinthians 6:11; Hebrews 10:22).

What was the primary work of John the Baptist?

III.   THE WORD BECAME FLESH
       (John 1:10-14)

A.   Rejected by His Own
     (vv. 10-13)

10. He was in the world, and the world was made by him, and the world knew him not.

11. He came unto his own, and his own received him not.

12. But as many as received him, to them gave he power to become the sons of God, even to them that believe on his name:

13. Which were born, not of blood, nor of the will of the flesh, nor of the will of man, but of God.

"He came unto his own," but they rejected Him. John the Baptist said, "No man receiveth his testimony" (John 3:32). He was the light that shone into a dark world, but "*men loved darkness rather than light,* because their deeds were evil" (3:19).

Isn't it strange that He who made the world (Revelation 4:11) was rejected by His own creation! In their own minds, there were several reasons that justified their actions.

First, they expected an earthly king. The Messiah, as they saw Him, was to break the yoke of impe-rial Rome and to restore the grandeur of the Israel of old. They could not accept a Christ who preached that freedom was internal and that when men see and accept the true light of freedom, they will free themselves from oppression.

Second, they wanted changes—but not spiritual changes. When Jesus demanded that their lives be changed so that they could love their "neighbor"—even if the neighbor was a loathed Samaritan (Luke 10:25-37)—that proved too much for them to accept. When He said, "Sell whatsoever thou hast, and give to the poor . . . and come, take up the cross, and follow me," they went away grieved (Mark 10:21, 22).

Third, they could never accept Jesus because He allowed His followers to say He was the Son of God. "We have a law," the highest court of the land said, "and by our law he ought to die, because he made himself the Son of God" (John 19:7). But He was the Son of God—God said so. When Jesus came out of the water of baptism, "the heavens were opened unto him, and he saw the Spirit of God descending like a dove, and lighting upon him: and lo a voice from heaven, saying, This is my beloved Son, in whom I am well pleased" (Matthew 3:16, 17).

Fourth, they could never accept a Messiah who was "cursed" by hanging on a tree (Deuteronomy 21:23). They did not know that Jesus came to take our curse, for "the Lord thy God turned the curse into a blessing unto thee, because the Lord thy God loved thee" (Deuteronomy 23:5).

Oh, if only they could have heard with their hearts His cry for them: "O Jerusalem, Jerusalem . . . how often would I have gathered thy children together, even as a hen gathereth her chickens under her wings, and ye would not!" (Matthew 23:37). God loved them so much "that he gave his only begotten Son" (John 3:16).

B. The Incarnation (v. 14)

14. And the Word was made flesh, and dwelt among us, (and we beheld his glory, the glory as of the only begotten of the Father,) full of grace and truth.

"The Word [Christ] was made flesh" are perhaps the most incongruous words in this or any language. For the "Word"—the *Logos*, the expression of God's love for His creation—is very God. He dwelt in the heavens, in beautiful palaces, in a city with golden streets, and sat on a throne, while the angels sang "Holy, holy, holy, Lord God Almighty!" That the Word (Christ) could become a man, lay aside the glory He had with His Father (Philippians 2:6, 7), and be born in a feed trough in a barn—in a nondescript town, in a backward country, in barbaric times—defies all logic.

But this is the message of the gospel, the good news: "God sent not his Son into the world to condemn the world; but that *the world through him might be saved*" (John 3:17).

The Christmas message says:
O little town of Bethlehem,
  How still we see thee lie!
Above thy deep and dream less sleep
  The silent stars go by;
Yet in thy dark streets shineth
  The everlasting Light;
The hopes and fears of all the years
  Are met in thee tonight.

—Phillips Brooks and
Lewis H. Redner

Why do you think God's plan of salvation included Jesus' becoming a man?

REVIEW QUESTIONS

1. Why is Jesus called the Lamb of God?
2. What does *logos* mean?
3. What can we learn about God from a study of His creation?
4. Who was the first Christian martyr? (Debate: Stephen or John the Baptist?)
5. What is the good news that the believer is to share with the lost?

GOLDEN TEXT HOMILY

"THE WORD WAS MADE FLESH, AND DWELT AMONG US, (AND WE BEHELD HIS GLORY, THE GLORY AS OF THE ONLY BEGOTTEN OF THE FATHER,) FULL OF GRACE AND TRUTH" (John 1:14).

The bedrock of our Christian hope is this: "The Word was made flesh." The only Son of God is eternal, yet He took on flesh, walked and lived among men. Through Christ we can have a proper relationship with God.

The greatest fact of all time is that Jesus Christ, the Son of God, lived on this earth and was crucified. He died for the sins of men and was resurrected from the dead. We often hear people use the words "Jesus is the reason for the season," but do they understand that Jesus is the Son of God? There are many who know not Christ and celebrate Christmas through tradition and purposes other than a love and appreciation for Him. We who have partaken of Christ are involved in the greatest adventure of all time.

We who understand that Christmas represents the eternal, living Son of God should spread the good news to others. The only way to understand, appreciate, and be recipients of God's love and gifts is through regeneration. As a man, He lived on earth and revealed the living Word of God. Our celebration of Christmas should be motivated by our love and appreciation for all He has done for us.**—Harvey L. Davis, Retired Consultant, Jackson, Mississippi**

SENTENCE SERMONS

THE WONDER of the Christmas story is that God, in Christ, became flesh.

—Selected

CHRISTMAS BEGAN in the heart of God. It is complete only when it reaches the heart of man.

—*Religious Telescope*

THE SON OF GOD became a man to enable men to become the sons of God.

—C.S. Lewis

THE HINGE OF HISTORY is on the door of Bethlehem's stable.

—Ralph W. Sockman

DAILY BIBLE READINGS

M. Promised Savior.
      Isaiah 7:10-16
T.   An Eternal Kingdom.
      Isaiah 9:1-7
W. The Message Foretold.
      Isaiah 40:1-5
T.   Birthplace Announced.
      Micah 5:2-4
F.   Christ Is Born. Luke 2:1-7
S.   Shepherds Worship.
      Luke 2:8-20

Responding to Christ's Coming

Study Text: Luke 2:21-38

Objective: To examine responses to Christ's birth and offer praise for His coming.

Time: The Gospel According to Luke was probably written between 58 and 70 A.D.

Place: The Gospel According to Luke was probably written at Caesarea or Rome.

Golden Text: "The shepherds returned, glorifying and praising God for all the things that they had heard and seen, as it was told unto them" (Luke 2:20).

Central Truth: Christ's coming gives us reason to rejoice and share the good news.

Evangelism Emphasis: Christ's coming gives us reason to rejoice and share the good news.

PRINTED TEXT

Luke 2:21. And when eight days were accomplished for the circumcising of the child, his name was called JESUS, which was so named of the angel before he was conceived in the womb.

22. And when the days of her purification according to the law of Moses were accomplished, they brought him to Jerusalem, to present him to the Lord;

25. And, behold, there was a man in Jerusalem, whose name was Simeon; and the same man was just and devout, waiting for the consolation of Israel: and the Holy Ghost was upon him.

26. And it was revealed unto him by the Holy Ghost, that he should not see death, before he had seen the Lord's Christ.

27. And he came by the Spirit into the temple: and when the parents brought in the child Jesus, to do for him after the custom of the law,

28. Then took he him up in his arms, and blessed God, and said,

29. Lord, now lettest thou thy servant depart in peace, according to thy word:

30. For mine eyes have seen thy salvation,

31. Which thou hast prepared before the face of all people;

32. A light to lighten the Gentiles, and the glory of thy people Israel.

33. And Joseph and his mother marvelled at those things which were spoken of him.

34. And Simeon blessed them, and said unto Mary his mother, Behold, this child is set for the fall and rising again of many in Israel; and for a sign

which shall be spoken against;

35. (Yea, a sword shall pierce through thy own soul also,) that the thoughts of many hearts may be revealed.

36. And there was one Anna, a prophetess, the daughter of Phanuel, of the tribe of Aser: she was of a great age, and had lived with an husband seven years from her virginity;

37. And she was a widow of about fourscore and four years, which departed not from the temple, but served God with fastings and prayers night and day.

38. And she coming in that instant gave thanks likewise unto the Lord, and spake of him to all them that looked for redemption in Jerusalem.

DICTIONARY

Simeon (SIM-ee-un)—Luke 2:25—A godly man of Jerusalem who lived to see baby Jesus at the Temple.

Anna . . . the daughter of Phanuel (fa-NU-el), of the tribe of Aser (AA-ser)—Luke 2:36—A prophetess of Jerusalem who was present at the Temple when baby Jesus was brought for dedication.

LESSON OUTLINE

I. OFFERING OBEDIENCE
  A. An Obedient Household
  B. Obedience to the Law
  C. An Obedient Name
  D. Sacrificial Obedience

II. OFFERING BLESSING
  A. Simeon, a Man God Could Use
  B. Simeon's Song of Blessing
  C. Simeon's Sorrowful Blessing

III. OFFERING THANKSGIVING
  A. Anna, a Widow
  B. The Secret of a Happy, Godly Life

LESSON EXPOSITION

INTRODUCTION

The period just following

Christmas week is sometimes the saddest one of the year. It is in that time that so many lonely people take the most extreme measures to solve their problems . . . they sometimes take their own lives. For those who had no family or friends to be with on Christmas, this can be a time of sad reflection. Some also, just returning from a great week of gaiety with family, now find their lives too difficult or too boring to go on.

For the believer, however, this should be a week of contemplation about the gift of God—His Son, who came to bring life, "and that . . . more abundantly" (John 10:10). Life is supposed to be good, wholesome, healthy, and enjoyable, for that is what Jesus wants for us.

Whatever it is that may be needed by the believer, remember that the Word of God declares: "He that spared not his own Son, but delivered him up for us all, how shall he not with him also freely give us all things?" (Romans 8:32). You have no problem that is too hard for God.

Our lesson this week takes a look at three very serious situations in which tragedy and disaster could have easily been the outcome. But there were also three things that combined to make life special—obedience, blessing, and thanksgiving.

The obedience of a young couple with a tiny baby, just starting their married life together; the blessing of a child and His mother by a man who waited in solitude for the baby to be born; and the thanksgiving of an elderly, godly lady named Anna—all these were enough to make these three households very special to God.

In *obedience, blessing,* and *thanksgiving,* all three found happy solutions and lives worth living.

I. OFFERING OBEDIENCE
(Luke 2:21-24)

A. An Obedient Household (v. 21)

21. And when eight days were accomplished for the circumcising of the child, his name was called JESUS, which was so named of the angel before he was conceived in the womb.

The Bible portrays Jesus as our example in all things, beginning with the things He learned at home, things which were later incorporated into His lifestyle, such as obedience to the law, the keeping of the Sabbath, and attendance at the synagogue—"as his custom was" (Luke 4:16).

There was nothing unusual about the circumcision of the eight-day-old infant Christ—every other Jewish male child was also circumcised on the eighth day—except that

everything that was done to Jesus and everything He did in conformity with the law demonstrated the validity of the scripture in Galatians 4:4, 5: "But when the fulness of the time was come, God sent forth His son, made of a woman, made under the law, to redeem them that were under the law."

God chose a law-abiding family to be the earthly family of His Son. Even the time and place of His birth were ordered by law. Mary and Joseph went to Bethlehem to pay their taxes. The circumcision on exactly the eighth day shows the same subjection to law. Many today seem to think that rejection of the laws and institutions that have been approved by centuries of use is a sign of strength, and thus institutional Christianity is discarded. We need to learn from Jesus and His family how to live by law and then learn from Jesus to outgrow the need of law—because when we love as God commands us to love, we do *naturally* the things that law demands.

The family unit as ordained by God—father, mother, and children—is the basic building block of society. When that unit is broken down and the family is destroyed, society has no chance at all of being orderly, law-abiding, and God-fearing. But when, like Joshua, the head of the household declares his allegiance to God and claims his wife and children for God, society has a foundation upon which to build a democratic, free, God-fearing nation. "As for me and my house, we will serve the Lord" (Joshua 24:15).

B. Obedience to the Law (v. 22)

22. And when the days of her

purification according to the law of Moses were accomplished, they brought him to Jerusalem, to present him to the Lord.

Obedience to the law of God was important to Jesus. We can be sure He learned that at home. Not once—even while He changed the ritual, outward law to a law written on the heart—did Jesus ever disparage His followers for, or discourage them from, keeping the Old Testament law. His own little family kept the law in every detail— "after the custom of the law" (v. 27)—and He followed that pattern throughout His life. Jesus learned obedience to the law and to God through His parents, who presented him to the Lord, "as it is written in the law of the Lord" (vv. 22, 23), when he was eight days old.

Even as a man, Jesus went to the synagogue every Sabbath day and listened to cold, dry rationale. He who was the fount of all wisdom sat at the feet of the teachers of the Law, because it had been "the custom" of His family to do so.

No doubt, Jesus studied the Law, at least in part, at His mother's feet. At 12 years of age He mystified the teachers of the Law with His "understanding and answers" (vv. 46, 47) as He listened to them and asked them questions. Later, He chided the "Sadducees, who say that there is no resurrection," by saying, "Ye do err, not knowing the scriptures, nor the power of God" (Matthew 22:23, 29). Jesus, of course, knew both the Scriptures and the power of God intimately from His boyhood.

Because of His righteous nature and the holiness home that nourished Him, "Jesus increased in wisdom and stature, and in favour

with God and man" (Luke 2:52).

C. An Obedient Name (v. 21)

21. And when eight days were accomplished for the circumcising of the child, his name was called JESUS, which was so named of the angel before he was conceived in the womb.

For this point, it is necessary to return to verse 21 and discuss the name of Jesus. Names have little meaning to us today, except as a means for distinguishing one person from another. It would be disastrous to have all the children in a family named "John" or "Mary." In the Bible, though, a name usually denoted some hope of the parents for the child's future; or it honored God, the father, mother, or nation; or it conveyed some other worthy idea.

J. Theodore Mueller says, "A person [today], for instance, may be called 'Mr. Free King,' and be neither free nor a king, while our Lord's name is truly and fully what it denotes" (*Baker's Dictionary of Theology*).

The name *Jesus* means "God is the Savior" or "God is my Savior." It is the name above all names; and "at *the name of Jesus* every knee should bow . . . in heaven . . . in earth, and . . . under the earth; and . . . every tongue should confess that Jesus Christ is Lord" (Philippians 2:10, 11).

The writer of the Book of Hebrews presented a strange idea when he said, "Though he were a Son, yet learned he obedience by the things which he suffered" (5:8). That Jesus should *learn obedience* should not shock us. That's how we all became obedient, if we did. We learned it. And usually we learned it at home. But there is also an obedience that is learned through suffering.

The Bible says, "For consider him [Jesus] that endured such contradiction [*antilogia*—opposition, rebellion, hostility, *disobedience*] of sinners against himself. . . . My son, despise not thou the chastening [*paideia*—instruction in obedience] of the Lord . . . for whom the Lord loveth he chasteneth. . . . For what son is he whom the father chasteneth not?" (Hebrews 12:3, 5-7).

Even the name of Jesus was given in obedience to the direction of the angel to both Joseph and Mary—"Thou shalt call his name JESUS" (Matthew 1:21; Luke 1:31). The parents of Jesus were themselves obedient to God, to the law, and to the angel. No wonder Jesus "learned obedience"!

D. Sacrificial Obedience
(vv. 23, 24)

(Luke 2:23, 24 is not included in the printed text.)

For the custom of presenting every firstborn to the Lord, we have to go back to the night when God "smote all the firstborn in the land of Egypt" (Exodus 12:29) but spared the lives of all the firstborn of Israel who had in obedience to God slain the Passover lamb and sprinkled its blood on the doorposts and lintels. The pascal lamb took the place of the firstborn in the households of Israel. Its life was given for theirs. In exchange for this redemption, the Lord claimed the firstborn of man and beast (see Exodus 13:2).

As was their consistent pattern of obedience, Joseph and Mary brought the sacrifice required by

law for Mary's purification ceremony—"a pair of turtledoves, or two young pigeons" (Luke 2:24).

The spiritual principles of the rite remain although the observance of this particular Levitical law has been abrogated in the church that Christ established. As a matter of fact, the idea has been broadened to include not only the firstborn son, but every child who is born into the church family is to be dedicated to the Lord and accepted by the church as part of the community of faith. The church as well as the parents are to accept the responsibility of providing a spiritually nurturing atmosphere for all the children in the fellowship of Christians.

Why does the Word of God say, "To obey is better than sacrifice" (1 Samuel 15:22)?

II. OFFERING BLESSING
(Luke 2:25-35)

A. Simeon, a Man God Could Use
(vv. 25-27)

25. And, behold, there was a man in Jerusalem, whose name was Simeon; and the same man was just and devout, waiting for the consolation of Israel: and the Holy Ghost was upon him.

26. And it was revealed unto him by the Holy Ghost, that he should not see death, before he had seen the Lord's Christ.

27. And he came by the Spirit into the temple: and when the parents brought in the child Jesus, to do for him after the custom of the law.

The second of the three households represented in our lesson this week is that of Simeon. Though we don't know much about him other than what the Scriptures tell us here, we can surmise a few things. First, like most men and women of the Bible, his name was significant; it meant "hearken, hear, or listen." No name ever fit a man more, for he was constantly in tune with the Holy Spirit, and he *listened* when the Spirit told him the baby Jesus was in the Temple.

We can infer from verses 26 and 29 that he was probably an older man. Like Anna (vv. 36, 37), he frequented the Temple. It had been revealed to him by the Spirit that he would see the Messiah in his life-time. When he said, "Now lettest thou thy servant depart in peace" (v. 29), he was using language that alluded to a master freeing his slave. Verse 25 seems to imply that he was well known in Jerusalem for "waiting for the consolation of Israel"—that is, the coming of Messiah.

Simeon was a devout man. It goes without saying that the man God uses is devout. The word *devout* is derived from a Greek word meaning "good" or "well." He was a *good* man. Over the years, the word has also come to mean "religious," or "pious," depicting a man who is devoted to God.

When Paul was at Athens, he was honored by the learned men of that city with the opportunity to witness from Mars Hill, a place sacred to them. He began his mes-sage by saying, "For as I passed by, and beheld your devotions" (Acts 17:23). The easiest way to tell what a man is, is to determine what he is devoted to. Simeon was thoroughly devoted to the Lord.

Simeon waited for the coming of the Lord. There were only a few men (or women) in the Bible of whom it was said, "The Holy Ghost was upon him" (v. 25). Whenever it did, it was because the Spirit of God wished to reveal something about God to mankind. It is meaningful that Luke used the words "it was revealed unto him by the Holy Ghost" (v. 26).

As it is with so many Christians today, fewer and fewer Hebrew believers were expecting the coming of the Lord's Messiah in their own lifetime. They said, "[The] lord delayeth his coming" (Matthew 24:48) and "Where is the promise of his coming?" (2 Peter 3:4). But Simeon looked for the Messiah . . . and he was not disappointed.

Simeon allowed the Spirit to guide him. Simeon's name in Hebrew was pronounced *Shim-on*; it came from the word *shama* meaning "hear" or "hearing." The "Shema" is a word very dear to the Jewish people and the title of the words of the Law which begin "Hear, O Israel: The Lord our God is one Lord" (Deuteronomy 6:4). These words are repeated by orthodox Jews every day of their lives. Simeon had long ago heard the Holy Spirit tell him he would live to see the Messiah, and he kept on listening. Then the call came, "and he came by the Spirit into the temple."

B. Simeon's Song of Blessing
   (vv. 28-32)

28. Then took he him up in his arms, and blessed God, and said,

29. Lord, now lettest thou thy servant depart in peace, accord-ing to thy word:

30. For mine eyes have seen thy salvation,

31. Which thou hast prepared before the face of all people;

32. A light to lighten the Gentiles, and the glory of thy people Israel.

When Mary and Joseph brought the baby Jesus to Jerusalem to perform Mary's purification rites (v. 22; see Leviticus 12:6-8), the Spirit alerted Simeon that the end of his long wait had come, and he came to the Temple.

The old man knew as soon as he saw Him that this was the Christ that the prophets had spoken about for centuries, and he broke into a song of joy: "Lord . . . mine eyes have seen thy salvation" (vv. 29, 30). As he blessed God for His faithfulness, he spoke of the child who was to be "a light to lighten the Gentiles" (v. 32; see also Isaiah 42:6, 7; 52:10) and of "the glory of thy people Israel" (v. 32; see also Revelation 12). Jesus was to bring salvation for both the Gentiles and the Jews.

The song of Simeon is called the *Nunc Dimittis* (derived from the Latin words which begin the hymn of joy, "Now lettest thou . . . depart" (Luke 2:29). This and two other songs from the Gospel of Luke became the earliest hymns sung by the Christian church. The others were the *Benedictus*, the song of Zacharias, the father of John the Baptist (Luke 1:68-79), and the *Magnificat*, the song of Mary (Luke 1:46-55).

C. Simeon's Sorrowful Blessing
   (vv. 33-35)

33. And Joseph and his mother marvelled at those things which were spoken of him.

34. And Simeon blessed them, and said unto Mary his mother, Behold, this child is set for the fall and rising again of many in Israel; and for a sign which shall be spoken against;

35. (Yea, a sword shall pierce through thy own soul also,) that the thoughts of many hearts may be revealed.

After all that Joseph and the mother of Jesus had seen and heard about this child, it was remarkable that they could still *marvel.* He was the Son of God, conceived of a virgin mother and the Holy Spirit; His coming was announced by an archangel; a heavenly choir sang at His birth; it was foretold that He would be a light for the Gentiles and for His nation Israel and that He was the fulfillment of more than 2,000 years of written prophecy. What more could be said?

Until then, the prophecies on the child Jesus had been pleasant ones. But the prophet Simeon (for that is what he became that day) changed all that and began to paint a dreary, dark picture of sadness for Mary—and ultimately for her son as well.

As difficult as it was for them to understand—and even for us who have witnessed it through the Bible account and the saving work of Christ in us—salvation can come only by the surrogate (substitutional) suffering and death of another (a sinless One) for sinners.

In the Book of Romans, Paul explained the theology of sin and redemption: "Wherefore, as by one man sin entered into the world, and death by sin; and so death passed upon all men, for that all have sinned. . . . But not as the offence . . . is the free gift. For if through the offence of one many be dead, much more the grace of God, and the gift by grace, which is by one man, Jesus Christ, hath abounded unto many. . . . For as by one man's [Adam] disobedience many were made sinners, so by the obedience of one [Jesus Christ] shall many be made righteous. . . . That as sin hath reigned unto death, even so might grace reign through righteousness unto eternal life by Jesus Christ our Lord" (5:12, 15, 19, 21).

Isaiah told about Jesus' awful death: "His visage was so marred more than any man. . . . He hath no form nor comeliness; and when we shall see him, there is no beauty that we should desire him" (52:14; 53:2). From our view of Him on the cross, we see Him bloody, bruised, and whipped; a crown of thorns had been pushed into the tender skin of His brow; spit ran down His face and mingled with His precious blood. Gangrene, starting at the open wounds where the nails had pierced His hands and feet, had turned His lovely smile into a grimace of pain. There was "no beauty that we should desire him."

"But he was wounded for our transgressions, he was bruised for our iniquities: the chastisement of our peace was upon him; and with his stripes we are healed" (53:5). This was the kind of message that was slowly sinking into Mary and Joseph's heart and mind.

Simeon told Mary that her heart would be pierced through, or broken, reminding her that she must be strong if her son was to be strong. Mary, like Jesus, was prophetically named; for "Mary" is derived from the Hebrew word *mar*, which means "bitter" or "sorrowful." It is the word from which we get "myrrh." Myrrh is an expensive spice which was used in Israel for the embalming of the dead, and

was one of the gifts of the wise men who came to see the baby Jesus at His birth. Even then, their gift spoke prophetically of the Messiah's death.

An artist once painted a most poignant picture. It showed the boy Jesus working with Joseph beside their carpenter shop. It had been a long day, and Jesus was tired. The lad had lifted His arms to stretch. His shadow fell on the building behind Him, where the artist had painted a cross on which the boy's small hands were nailed. Even then, the shadow of the Cross loomed over Him.

I don't know when Jesus first began to see the Cross before Him, but it was always there. And because Jesus was willing to give His life on it, we are saved.

What is the relationship between Simeon's name and the Shema?

III. OFFERING THANKSGIVING (Luke 2:36-38)

A. Anna, a Widow (v. 36)

36. And there was one Anna, a prophetess, the daughter of Phanuel, of the tribe of Aser [Asher]: she was of a great age, and had lived with an husband seven years from her virginity.

Anna was an elderly woman, who was widowed after seven years of marriage. From the way the text is worded, we don't know if she had been a widow for 84 years or was 84 years old when she met the holy family in the Temple. In either case, she had been a widow for a long time and was quite old.

To be a widow in a poor land like Israel was very hard, even though the

Lord had made provisions for such needy people to glean after the harvesters in the fields (Deuteronomy 24:19- 21) and Jewish families were commanded to take care of their own. Paul told Timothy to "honour widows that are widows indeed. But if any widow have children or nephews, let them learn first to shew piety at home, and to requite their parents: for that is good and acceptable before God. . . . But if any provide not for his own, and specially for those of his own house, he hath denied the faith, and is worse than an infidel" (1 Timothy 5:3, 4, 8).

Still, if anyone had reason to be bitter and unhappy, it would be a widow who lost the love of her life while still in her twenties, and was forced to live alone for all those years. But Anna would not be bitter—she could not be—she was too busy serving the Lord she loved so much. She turned her sorrow into joy by devoting her life to God and the service of others. Each day she went to the Temple to pray and, like Simeon, was one of those "that looked for redemption in Jerusalem" (Luke 2:38).

There are several ways this lady of "grace"—for that is what her name means (Old Testament, *Hannah* or *Channah*)—buoyed up her spirit when she could have blamed God and been angry for her predicament. Anna's godly lifestyle is a good example for today's single adults, widows or widowers, and others who are forced, or choose, to live alone to develop a happy and productive Christian life.

B. The Secret of a Happy, Godly Life (vv. 37, 38)

37. And she was a widow of about fourscore and four years, which departed not from the temple, but served God with fastings and prayers night and day.

Anna stayed in church. Luke said she "departed not from the temple." Usually, the first words from our mouths in times of sorrow and discouragement are "Why *me*? Why did this happen to me when everybody else is so happy? If God loves me, why is He allowing me to suffer this terrible calamity?"

Then, having blamed God for all the bad things in our lives, we leave the church. Ironic, isn't it, that the only safe haven we have is abandoned first? We exchange the love of fellow believers for the fickle love of the world.

But Anna did not do that; she stayed in church.

Anna worshiped God. Anna's priorities were right. She stayed in church, worshiped God, fasted and prayed, witnessed to others, gave thanks in all things, and looked for the coming of the Lord. Some would say, "Well, how do you know that Anna wasn't a gossip with a long tongue, or a person of low morals?" There is no mention of these things. Of course there was no reason to mention them, since one who stays in church, worships God, fasts and prays, witnesses faithfully of her salvation, and looks for the return of her Lord is one who can be trusted with your life. She has reached a high level of maturity in her godly life.

Anna fasted and prayed. Fasting, together with prayer, is an excellent means of cleansing the soul of negative thinking and opening ourselves spiritually for God to do some wonderful things in our lives. And not only does prayer and fasting benefit us in our own personal spiritual lives, but it also enables us to assist our pastor and the church in powerful ways that no one else can. There are always those problems in the church which can be solved only by prayer and fasting (Mark 9:29).

Since widows and other singles who have only themselves to take care of sometimes have an extra amount of time, they can either use it to feel sorry for themselves as they mope around the house or they can use it as an opportunity to pray and fast and make their presence in God's church powerfully felt.

38. And she coming in that instant gave thanks likewise unto the Lord, and spake of him to all them that looked for redemption in Jerusalem.

Anna gave thanks. A thankful heart has no room for bitterness, hostility, hatred, or spite. You can trust God "that all things work together for good to them that love God, to them who are the called according to his purpose" (Romans 8:28). Then if you know that, you can trust God to "supply all your need according to his riches in glory by Christ Jesus" (Philippians 4:19). Finally, because "all things work together for good" and God supplies "all your need," you can give "thanks always for all things" (Ephesians 5:20) and in every situation of your life "give thanks: for this is the will of God in Christ Jesus concerning you" (1 Thessalonians 5:18).

Those who are alone sometimes need a shoulder to cry on or perhaps provisions or sustenance. Therefore, if you are alone, stay in the church. While others around you may have husbands or wives, families, and children—*you have*

the comfort of the Holy Spirit! (John 14:16, 17). The word *Comforter* in Greek is *Parakletos*, "One called alongside to help." No other friend could ever do more.

Anna witnessed about her faith. "She *spake of him* to all them that looked for redemption in Jerusalem" (v. 38). When the tempter tries to lead us into temptation, we can overcome him "by the blood of the Lamb, and by the word of [our] testimony" (Revelation 12:11). The best way to maintain a holy walk is to walk with and talk about Jesus.

There are many ways to witness for Christ, but Anna seems to have gotten to the heart of what Christian witness is all about—she witnessed *about Him,* and she witnessed *to all* who would listen.

Anna looked for the coming of the Lord. In times of revival or persecution, we begin afresh to look for the return of Christ in the air to rapture the church. Our ardor for His coming seems to run hot and cold, but Simeon and Anna looked for the Lord all their lives; and then He came. Peter said, "The day of the Lord will come as a thief in the night [unexpectedly]" (2 Peter 3:10).

Paul, writing to Titus, called the coming of the Lord "that blessed hope" (2:13). He also comforted the Thessalonians who had lost loved ones in death with these words: "For the Lord himself shall descend from heaven with a shout, with the voice of the archangel, and with the trump[et] of God: and the dead in Christ shall rise first: Then we which are alive and remain shall be caught up together with them in the clouds, to meet the Lord in the air: and so shall we ever be with the Lord" (1 Thessalonians 4:16, 17).

Why are lonely people often bitter against God?

REVIEW QUESTIONS

1. Why were dietary and sanitary laws so important to the early Israelites?
2. Where do men and women usually first learn obedience?
3. What were Simeon's heartbreaking words to Mary?
4. What does the name *Anna* or *Channah* mean in the Hebrew language?
5. How did Anna prevent bitterness, loneliness, and spiritual despair?

GOLDEN TEXT HOMILY

"THE SHEPHERDS RETURNED, GLORIFYING AND PRAISING GOD FOR ALL THE THINGS THAT THEY HAD HEARD AND SEEN, AS IT WAS TOLD UNTO THEM" (Luke 2:20).

The central theme of our lesson is "Responding to Christ's Coming," and has several groups of people in mind. The shepherds were one of these groups. Though our Golden Text focuses on their "glorifying and praising God for all the things that they had heard and seen," this is only one part of their response. Luke also says, "When they had seen Him they made widely known the saying which was told them concerning this Child" (v. 17, NKV).

Here are two sides of the coin of responsibility regarding the Christian revelation. We have heard the good news, and we have experienced the wonder of Christ in our lives. What should our response be? It must be twofold: both vertical and horizontal. We must *glorify* and *praise* God. Both of these verbs in Greek are in the present tense, indicating continuous action. Having heard of Christ and met with Him in saving power, we should spend the rest of our lives in glorifying and praising God, a holy exercise which will spill over into and continue throughout eternity.

And we too should make "known . . . the saying which was told [us] . . ." (v. 17)—the Word of God, the gospel, which has been disclosed in Christ for all mankind—and we must make it known far and wide. This saving Word is for all nations, and for every creature, and for the whole wide world.—**Noel Brooks, D.D. (Retired), Avon, England, Writer,** *Adult Sunday School Teacher Quarterly,* **International Pentecostal Holiness Church, Oklahoma City, Oklahoma**

DAILY BIBLE READINGS

M. Desire.
    Acts 16:25-31
T. Confess.
    Psalm 51:1-13
W. Repent.
    Jonah 3:1-10
T. Believe.
    John 9:35-39
F. Submit.
    Acts 22:1-10
S. Follow.
    Matthew 4:17-22

The Bible—God's Word

Study Text: Psalm 19:7-14; Jeremiah 36:1-28; 2 Timothy 3:14-17; Hebrews 4:12; 2 Peter 1:19- 21

Objective: To investigate the background of the Bible and stand on its reliability in today's world.

Golden Text: "All scripture is given by inspiration of God, and is profitable for doctrine, for reproof, for correction, for instruction in righteousness" (2 Timothy 3:16).

Central Truth: The Bible is God's Word and the authority for our faith.

Evangelism Emphasis: The integrity of the Bible must be upheld as a witness to God's marvelous grace.

PRINTED TEXT

2 Peter 1:19. We have also a more sure word of prophecy; whereunto ye do well that ye take heed, as unto a light that shineth in a dark place, until the day dawn, and the day star arise in your hearts:

20. Knowing this first, that no prophecy of the scripture is of any private interpretation.

21. For the prophecy came not in old time by the will of man: but holy men of God spake as they were moved by the Holy Ghost.

2 Timothy 3:14. But continue thou in the things which thou hast learned and hast been assured of, knowing of whom thou hast learned them;

15. And that from a child thou hast known the holy scriptures, which are able to make thee wise unto salvation through faith which is in Christ Jesus.

16. All scripture is given by inspiration of God, and is profitable for doctrine, for reproof, for correction, for instruction in righteousness:

17. That the man of God may be perfect, throughly furnished unto all good works.

Hebrews 4:12. For the word of God is quick, and powerful, and sharper than any twoedged sword, piercing even to the dividing asunder of soul and spirit, and of the joints and marrow, and is a discerner of the thoughts and intents of the heart.

Psalm 19:7. The law of the Lord is perfect, converting the soul: the testimony of the Lord is sure, making wise the simple.

8. The statutes of the Lord are right, rejoicing the heart: the commandment of the Lord is pure, enlightening the eyes.

9. The fear of the Lord is clean, enduring for ever: the judgments of the Lord are true and righteous altogether.

10. More to be desired are they than gold, yea, than much fine gold: sweeter also than

honey and the honeycomb.

11. Moreover by them is thy servant warned: and in keeping of them there is great reward.

12. Who can understand his errors? cleanse thou me from secret faults.

13. Keep back thy servant also from presumptuous sins; let them not have dominion over me: then shall I be upright, and I shall be innocent from the great transgression.

14. Let the words of my mouth, and the meditation of my heart, be acceptable in thy sight, O Lord, my strength, and my redeemer.

LESSON OUTLINE

LESSON EXPOSITION

INTRODUCTION

The word *Bible* is from the Greek word *biblia* (books), and is akin to *biblos* (book) and *byblos* (papyrus). Originally, the collection of writings we call the inspired Word of God were known as "the Books," but later the plural Greek word was made singular and the Bible became "*the* Book."

The Bible is the book of all time . . . read by billions of people, translated into more than 1,100 languages, revered and honored, cursed and burned—it is certainly *the* Book.

The Bible has changed more lives, overthrown more dictators, shaped the destiny of more nations, developed more humane institutions, and set more people free from slavery than all the books ever published—taken together.

As we start this series of lessons on the study of the Bible, we will take a detailed look at its origin, its purpose, its place in history and in our lives, and its divine destiny (see Psalm 119:89; Isaiah 40:8; Hebrews 2:1-3; 1 Peter 1:25).

These should be exciting and inspiring lessons for all who wish to know more about God's will as it is revealed in His Word, how God came to speak to us in this manner, and how this revelation can change our lives.

I. HOW WE GOT OUR BIBLE (Jeremiah 36:4-6, 17, 18, 23, 27, 28; 2 Peter 1:19-21)

A. Anointed Men Wrote It (Jeremiah 36:4-6, 17, 18, 23, 27, 28)

(Jeremiah 36:4-6, 17, 18, 23, 27, 28 is not included in the printed text.)

Our lesson text in Jeremiah,

provides an illustration of how God inspired men to write what has become known as the Holy Bible, God's Word, the Scriptures, or simply the Book! We are told in verse 1, and again in verse 27, that "the word of the Lord came to Jeremiah." Later, as Baruch the scribe presented the manuscript to the princes of King Jehoiakim, they asked him, "Tell us now, How didst thou write all these words at his mouth?" Baruch replied, "He [Jeremiah] pronounced all these words unto me with his mouth, and I wrote them with ink in the book" (vv. 17, 18).

The Bible is in the words of men, but it is the work of the Holy Spirit, revealing God's Word (Christ) to His people. The writers were people much like you and me—some movers and shakers, some ordinary men, and some not so ordinary. Moses, who wrote the Books of the Law, was the son of slave parents. He became the adopted son of an Egyptian princess, then was the revolutionary leader of the new nation of Israel.

David was a shepherd boy who fought a giant and became Israel's greatest king and the "sweet psalmist" of God.

Jonah was a man running from God, who, after being swallowed by a whale (a big fish) was at last ready to take God's Word to an evil city-state called Nineveh.

Daniel was a slave in Babylon who refused to lower his spiritual standards and became the third highest ruler in the most powerful empire on earth to that day.

Perhaps these men were not ordinary in the way we view the ordinariness of ourselves, but still we are able to identify with many of their characteristics—both good and bad. They too had their weaknesses and strengths, failures and successes. Some were good writers; others were not as skilled.

The *New Testament* writers ran the gamut from a doctor of medicine (Luke) and a doctor of theology (Paul) to a civil servant (Matthew) and fishermen (Peter and John). The only criteria for writers of Holy Scripture was that they be "holy men" and open to the moving of "the Holy Ghost" (2 Peter 1:21).

The *Old Testament* writers—who were often more formal than their New Testament counterparts who wrote mostly letters to friends and churches—wrote for kings and nations. Thus they were almost unanimous in their declarations that the words they spoke came directly from God: "Then came the word of the Lord to Isaiah" (38:4). "The word of the Lord came unto me" (Jeremiah 1:4; Ezekiel 3:16).

Almost every one of the minor prophets prefixed their writings with similar words (Jonah 1:1; Micah 1:1; Zephaniah 1:1; Haggai 1:1; Zechariah 1:1; Malachi 1:1).

When these men finished writing, there were 66 separate books—39 in the Old Testament (old covenant) and 27 in the New Testament (new covenant). They were written over a period of 1,500 years, in several regions of the world and in several languages. The Old Testament was written mostly in Hebrew and the New Testament mostly in Greek. Some of the Old Testament and a very small portion of the New Testament scriptures were written in Aramaic. Aramaic was the language of the streets in Israel during the ministry of Jesus on earth, just as koine Greek was the popular language of the remainder of the world at that time.

There is no holy language of the Bible. It was meant to be read and understood by the common people; and to facilitate that, it has been translated into more than a thousand languages today, from German to Tutsi, so that God can speak plainly to all the inhabitants of His earth. The completed Book is a seamless whole, without error; and it is the greatest book ever written.

Rightly dividing the Word. Paul told Timothy, "Study to shew thyself approved unto God, a workman that needeth not to be ashamed, rightly dividing the word of truth" (2 Timothy 2:15). To tell the true from the false has always been a problem for believers, but that was especially true in the early church when there was not yet a set standard by which one knew what was considered the inspired Word of God and what was simply good teachings by good men (or false teachings by charlatans and heretics).

In the very next verse after our text in 2 Peter 1:19-21, the apostle said of his former words about prophecy in "old time" (v. 21) that "there were false prophets also among the people [in the Old Testament], even as there shall be false teachers among you" (2:1).

A great number of books, letters, and sermons were already being spoken of (by their writers mostly) as anointed. But the only writings Peter acknowledged as "Scripture" at this point in his life, and that of the young church, were the writings of Paul (2 Peter 3:15, 16) and the complete Old Testament.

What constitutes the Word of God? We live in a time when the Holy Bible is recognized as a *finished* work. All that God wants to say to us as believers and the church has been said. All that is needed to be saved, cleansed, live a holy life, and grow into the image of Jesus has been provided for us in the Word of God.

John the Revelator, in the last book of the Bible, said, "For I testify unto every man that heareth the words of the prophecy of this book, If any man shall add unto these things, God shall add unto him the plagues that are written in this book: and if any man shall take away from the words of the book of this prophecy, God shall take away his part out of the book of life, and out of the holy city, and from the things which are written in this book" (Revelation 22:18, 19).

When He gave the Commandments, God warned Israel, "Ye shall not add unto the word which I command you, neither shall ye diminish ought from it" (Deuteronomy 4:2).

Paul wrote to the Galatians, "There be some that trouble you, and would pervert the gospel of Christ. But though we, or an angel from heaven, preach any other gospel unto you than that which we have preached unto you, let him be accursed" (1:7, 8).

There was but one gospel then, and there is but one gospel today. The "good news" is the same for all men, from all nations, in all times.

The Canon. The Word of God— composed of the Old and New Testaments, written by men and inspired by the Holy Spirit—is a finished work and it can never be amended, changed, added to, or terminated.

God not only entrusted the writing of these Scriptures to men, but

He also gave them the task of separating the wheat from the chaff and determining with the guidance of the Holy Spirit which of the books being written by men and women of the early church were to be included in the canon of Scripture. "Canon" (Greek, *kanon*) referred to anything straight that could be used for a ruler or straight edge. It was also a model, paradigm, boundary, or standard. The books of the Old Testament and the New Testament, which are accepted as the inspired Word of God, are called the canon of Scripture.

But for Timothy to "rightly divide" the Word of God was not so easy when there was no real consensus in his day of what constituted the Bible. He could be certain, of course, that when Paul spoke of Scripture, or the Word of God, he was first of all referring to the Old Testament, which is almost exactly the same today as it was then.

For many years—aside from the writings of Paul and Peter, the Gospels, and the Acts of the Apostles—there was little unanimity as to what constituted the New Testament.

In the early days, several books circulated through the church which claimed to be inspired, among them being the *Epistle of Barnabas*, the *Didache*, the *Shepherd of Hermas*, and *1 and 2 Clement*. At least five books (inspired and uninspired) were attributed to Peter, among them being the *Gospel of Peter*, the *Preaching of Peter*, and the *Apocalypse of Peter*.

The books of Hebrews, James, 2 and 3 John, 2 Peter, Jude, and Revelation were disputed by scholars for many years. Around the year 200, the books of the New Testament as we know them today became accepted as God's Word for the people of the new covenant.

In the early church, in addition to the problem of what constituted the Word of God, was another difficulty to "rightly dividing the word of truth"—there were no chapter-and-verse divisions. Both the Old Testament and the New Testament were written much as any other book or letter is written today, as a single unit, and it was very difficult to find a particular word from the Lord. By the time of the birth of Christ, the Jewish scribes had given the Old Testament the chapters and verses with which we are familiar, and divided the books of the old covenant into three divisions: the Law, the Prophets, and the Writings.

The chapter-and-verse divisions of the New Testament were not finalized until 1551, a millennium and a half after the books were written.

Our English translations. At the very first, the leaders of the church were so protective of the Word of God that they refused to allow it to be translated from the original languages. They believed that the word structure and the very words themselves, as spoken by the writers, were sacrosanct and would be destroyed if translated from the Hebrew and Greek.

As the Catholic Church became stronger, the Bible was translated into Latin, which was the language of the Mass and the prayers of the church—and was thus considered a holy language.

With the translation of the Bible into Latin began an idea that only the priest could really understand what the Bible meant to say, thus the average layperson would only be confused if he studied it for himself.

At last, the Bible was chained to the pulpit in the church so common people would not even be allowed to touch it, for fear they would pollute even its covers.

We owe the fact that we can read the Bible for ourselves to such bold, godly men as John Wycliffe (1320-1384), who braved the wrath of both the king and the church to translate the Latin Bible into the language of the people. Not only did the government burn his Bibles (handwritten in English), but when Wycliffe died the church had his body exhumed and burned for his crime against humanity. State authorities ruled that anyone caught reading the Scriptures in the "common tongue" would forfeit land, cattle, and their life and the goods of their heirs forever.

William Tyndale was born exactly a hundred years after the death of Wycliffe. During that hundred years the printing press had been invented, and a renaissance of learning had begun on the continent. Tyndale studied first at Oxford under the tutelage of several enlightened scholars, then at Cambridge, where he was the student of Erasmus, the great New Testament Greek scholar. Tyndale, with a heart burning to give the man on the street the Word of God, once said to a learned man, "If God spare my life ere many years, I will cause a boy that drives the plough to know more of the scripture than you do."

Tyndale translated the Vulgate into English, and though only a few fragments of his original work remains, 80 percent of the King James Version is taken from that Bible. On October 6, 1536, he was strangled and burned. His last words were "Lord, open the King of England's eyes" (*Interpreter's Dictionary of the Bible*).

The King James Version of 1611, though called the *Authorized Version*, was never authorized by king or parliament—and the Protestant church took 50 years to finally accept it. The excellence of that translation, however, is shown in the fact that 400 years later it is the most widely read English Bible in the world.

B. Holy Men Spoke It
   (2 Peter 1:19-21)

19. We have also a more sure word of prophecy; whereunto ye do well that ye take heed, as unto a light that shineth in a dark place, until the day dawn, and the day star arise in your hearts:

20. Knowing this first, that no prophecy of the scripture is of any private interpretation.

21. For the prophecy came not in old time by the will of man: but holy men of God spake as they were moved by the Holy Ghost.

Peter said, "Holy men of God spake . . ." (v. 21). When the Lord wants a job done, He always looks for holy men. In the year that King Uzziah died, the prophet Isaiah had a vision of God in the Temple. The seraphim (special angels that surround the throne of God) cried, "Holy, holy, holy, is the Lord of hosts" (Isaiah 6:3). The holiness of God was so strong in that place that Isaiah cried out, "Woe is me! for I am undone; because I am a man of unclean lips, and I dwell in the midst of a people of unclean lips: for mine eyes have seen the King, the Lord of hosts" (v. 5).

As Isaiah trembled before the Lord, one of the seraphim took a live coal in his hand and touched it to Isaiah's lips and said, "Thine iniquity is taken away, and thy sin purged" (v. 7). Then he heard the voice of the Lord saying, "Whom shall I send, and who will go for us?" (v. 8).

The mission God sent this prophet on was to prepare the nation of Israel and the world for the coming of a Savior who, Isaiah prophesied, would be "wounded for our transgressions . . . bruised for our iniquities," chastised for our peace, and striped (beaten with a whip) for our healing (53:5). When his sin was purged, he was quick to answer, "Here am I; send me" (6:8).

In order to be used of God, a man must be sanctified of God and made holy. This work is done by the infilling of the Holy Spirit—which was symbolized by the "live coal . . . from off the altar" (Isaiah 6:6); "fire" (Matthew 3:11); and "cloven tongues like as of fire, [which] sat upon each of them" at Pentecost (Acts 2:3).

Peter tells us that we have a "more sure word of prophecy" (2 Peter 1:19) than that provided under the old covenant. The importance of the Old Testament was that it pointed the way to the New, to the coming of the Son of God in the flesh to reconcile all men to God. God himself has put His stamp of approval on the work of His Son, and Peter and the other disciples were witnesses to it.

Peter believed he was about to go on to his reward (vv. 14, 15), and he wanted to leave a record of the truth, "that ye may be able after my decease to have these things always in remembrance" (v. 15).

The apostle said, "No prophecy of the scripture is of any private interpretation" (v. 20)—that is, no true prophecy is from a man himself!

God's highest honor must surely be reserved for those holy men He chose to be special instruments of the Holy Spirit—the writers of the Word of God.

C. The Holy Spirit Breathed It
   (2 Peter 1:21)

21. For the prophecy came not in old time by the will of man: but holy men of God spake as they were moved by the Holy Ghost.

Peter said, "Holy men of God spake as they were *moved* [Greek, *pheromenoi*, as wind in a sail moves a ship along] by the Holy Ghost." The word *spirit* (Hebrew, *neshamah*; Greek, *pneuma*—both mean "breath" or "wind") is first seen in the Creation story: "And the Lord God formed man of the dust of the ground, and *breathed* into his nostrils the *breath* of life" (Genesis 2:7). Jesus made an interesting play on the words *breath* and *wind* in His conversation with Nicodemus: "I tell you the truth, no one can enter the kingdom of God unless he is born of water and the *Spirit*. Flesh gives birth to flesh, but the *Spirit* gives birth to *spirit*. You should not be surprised at my saying, 'You must be born again.' The *wind* blows wherever it pleases. You hear its sound, but you cannot tell where it comes from or where it is going. So it is with everyone born of the *Spirit*" (John 3:5-8, *NIV*).

While it was men who wrote the Bible, in their flawed handwriting and with marks of their humanity showing everywhere, the Holy Spirit "breathed" upon the work of these very human individuals and inspired them to write collectively, cohesively, and without error the most memorable book in the world—the Holy Bible!

The work of the Bible is to reveal the mystery of God's plan in eternity through His Son, who became "flesh, and dwelt among us" (John 1:14). This mystery has been "revealed unto his holy apostles and prophets [the writers] by the Spirit [the Author]" (Ephesians 3:5; see also vv. 3, 4).

What is meant by "No prophecy of the scripture is of any private interpretation"?

II. AUTHORITY OF THE BIBLE
(2 Timothy 3:14-17)

A. The Word of God Corrects Our Lives (vv. 14, 15)

14. But continue thou in the things which thou hast learned and hast been assured of, knowing of whom thou hast learned them;

15. And that from a child thou hast known the holy scriptures, which are able to make thee wise unto salvation through faith which is in Christ Jesus.

Timothy had learned the Scriptures first at the knees of two lovely Christian ladies—his mother and his grandmother (2 Timothy 1:5). His lessons in theology had continued under the tutelage of the apostle Paul and, finally, in his own studies of the Word.

Paul told his "son in the Lord" that "the holy scriptures" (*hiera grammata,* "are able to make thee wise unto salvation" (3:15). The

Word of God is absolutely necessary to the work of salvation, for "faith [to be saved] cometh by hearing, and hearing by the word of God" (Romans 10:17).

We are cleansed "with the washing of water by the word" (Ephesians 5:26), and those that are saved become "doers of the word" (James 1:22; Romans 2:13).

John told us that Jesus is the "Word [which] was with God, and . . . was God" (John 1:1). He is the exact image of God, giving expression to God's love for all mankind in His salvation plan. Without the Word (Jesus Christ and the Holy Scriptures) there is no salvation. "And this is the record, that God hath given to us eternal life, and this life is in his Son. He that hath the Son hath life; and he that hath not the Son of God hath not life. . . . And we know that the Son of God is come, and hath given us an understanding [the Scriptures], that we may know him that is true, and we are in him that is true, even in his Son Jesus Christ. This is the true God, and eternal life" (1 John 5:11, 12, 20).

B. The Word of God Directs Our Lives (v. 16)

16. All scripture is given by inspiration of God, and is profitable for doctrine, for reproof, for correction, for instruction in righteousness.

The Word provides sound doctrine. The word *doctrine* is derived from the Greek words *didache* and *didaskalia,* meaning "to teach." It is the mission of both the Word of God and the Spirit of God to teach the believer, safeguard the church, and judge the world. Sound doctrine is the first line of defense against heresy.

Paul told Timothy, "Preach the word. . . . For the time will come when they will not endure sound doctrine, but according to their own desires, because they have itching ears, they will heap up for themselves teachers; and they will turn away from the truth, and be turned aside to fables" (2 Timothy 4:2-4, *NKJV*).

When the Word of God abides in us, Satan and his messengers cannot "wrest" (twist, distort) the Scriptures to their own interpretation. In every circumstance we are given the proper response to error (Psalm 56:1-5; 2 Peter 3:16). The Lord's response to Satan's use of Scripture in the temptation in the wilderness was to "rightly divide" the Word and turn it back against His tempter.

The Word provides discipline. The writer of Hebrews said: "For the word of God is quick [alive], and powerful, and sharper than any twoedged sword, piercing even to the dividing asunder of soul and spirit, and of the joints and marrow, and is a discerner of the thoughts and intents of the heart. . . . All things are naked and opened unto the eyes of him with whom we have to do" (4:12, 13).

God knows us; and He provides reproof, correction, and instruction in righteousness (2 Timothy 3:16). He also chastens and disciplines: "God dealeth with you as with sons; for what son is he whom the father chasteneth not?" (Hebrews 12:7).

Discipline (Greek, *paideia*) is not so much punishment as it is constant, ongoing instruction and training in how to live the Christian life. If we stay in the Word, we will stay in the center of God's will.

C. The Word of God Perfects Our Lives (v. 17)

17. That the man of God may be perfect, throughly [thoroughly] furnished unto all good works.

Perfect is a New Testament word with a host of meanings. In our text, the Greek word *artios* speaks of being "completely equipped for service." *Teleios* (James 1:4) means "complete or perfect in mental and moral character." *Katartizo* means "to mend, or to restore to perfection" (2 Corinthians 13:9).

Jesus Christ, as the Word of God, provides us with imputed righteousness (perfection) (Hebrews 10:14), which we have simply by believing on Jesus as our Savior. That is, so far as God is concerned, when we become "sons of God" we are "perfectly righteous" before Him.

There is another perfection, a perfection we will not attain until "he shall appear, [and] we shall be like him" (1 John 3:2). This is a perfection toward which every believer should, however, be striving—to become restored to the "measure of the stature of the fulness [the full stature] of Christ" (Ephesians 4:13)—to be like Christ in every way.

The church also is being perfected by the Word of God. In Ephesians 5:25-27, Paul continued, "Christ also loved the church, and gave himself for it; that *he might sanctify and cleanse it with the washing of water by the word*, that he might present it to himself a glorious church, not having spot, or wrinkle, or any such thing; but that it should be holy and without blemish" (Ephesians 5:25-27).

What are some ways the Bible talks about "perfection"?

III. IMPACT OF THE BIBLE
(Hebrews 4:12; Psalm 19:7-14)

A. The Word of God Works in Us
(Hebrews 4:12)

12. For the word of God is quick, and powerful, and sharper than any twoedged sword, piercing even to the dividing asunder of soul and spirit, and of the joints and marrow, and is a discerner of the thoughts and intents of the heart.

It is through the Word of God that Christians are born again (1 Peter 1:23; see also James 1:18). Jesus' disciples are clean through the Word (John 15:3), and the true child of God is one in whom the Word of God abides (John 5:38). The Word is said to be "quick," that is, it is alive (from the Greek word *zao*, "to live").

"The entrance of thy words giveth light" (Psalm 119:130) could just as easily read "giveth *life*," for light and life are inextricably entwined. Where the Word of God is, there is *light* and there is *life*.

The Word not only brings life, but it also discerns the inner man, discovering the secret places of the heart and even reading the very thoughts we think. God knows us through and through. There is nothing hidden from Him. Because of that, He will judge us rightly and "will bring to light the hidden things of darkness, and will make manifest the counsels of the hearts" (1 Corinthians 4:4, 5).

The Word and the Spirit are able to judge the believer in the hidden things of the heart, because our body is the house of God: "Know ye not that ye are the temple of God, and that the Spirit of God dwelleth in you? . . . The temple of God is holy, which temple ye are" (1 Corinthians 3:16, 17). God has always demanded that His people be holy: "Ye shall be holy; for I am holy" (Leviticus 11:44, 45).

The Old Testament Tabernacle and later the Temple were *holy places*, sanctified and cleansed so that God, *a holy* God, could dwell there. There was the *Holy Place*, where only the priests could go, and the *Holy of Holies*, where the high priest went once a year to offer a sacrifice for the people. The priest wore *holy garments* (Exodus 39:1) and were anointed with a *holy oil* (37:29).

The image of God, lost in the Fall, is restored as we become more and more like Jesus. It is the Word and the Spirit that accomplish that work in us.

B. The Word of God Works in the World Outside Us (Psalm 19:7-14)

7. The law of the Lord is perfect, converting the soul: the testimony of the Lord is sure, making wise the simple.
8. The statutes of the Lord are right, rejoicing the heart: the commandment of the Lord is pure, enlightening the eyes.
9. The fear of the Lord is clean, enduring for ever: the judgments of the Lord are true and righteous altogether.
10. More to be desired are they than gold, yea, than much fine gold: sweeter also than honey and the honeycomb.
11. Moreover by them is thy servant warned: and in keeping of

them there is great reward.

12. Who can understand his errors? cleanse thou me from secret faults.

13. Keep back thy servant also from presumptuous sins; let them not have dominion over me: then shall I be upright, and I shall be innocent from the great transgression.

14. Let the words of my mouth, and the meditation of my heart, be acceptable in thy sight, O Lord, my strength, and my redeemer.

The Word of God not only changes men, but it also changes the world in which men live. Man and his habitation were brought into existence by the Word of God (the Logos), Jesus Christ the Creator of all things (John 1:1-3; Revelation 4:11). The ordered universe and man made "in the image of God" were to work together in perfect fellowship with their Creator. And just as redeemed mankind longs for the return of the Lord to set all things right, so does all creation groan and travail toward that day (Romans 8:22).

This is still the plan of God for His creation, man and the universe, in fellowship and harmony—and God the Lord and Master of all!

What are some ways the Word of God has impacted the world socially?

REVIEW QUESTIONS

1. Who were the writers of the Bible?

2. Who was the author of the Bible?

3. What does *spirit* mean in Hebrew and Greek?

4. How does the Word of God discipline believers?

5. What do we mean by the Spirit's working in the world as well as in us?

GOLDEN TEXT HOMILY

"ALL SCRIPTURE IS GIVEN BY INSPIRATION OF GOD, AND IS PROFITABLE FOR DOCTRINE, FOR REPROOF, FOR CORRECTION, FOR INSTRUCTION IN RIGHTEOUSNESS" (2 Timothy 3:16).

As the apostle Paul wrote to Timothy with specific instructions and charges concerning the faith and practice of the church, he emphasized the importance of preaching and teaching the inspired (God-breathed) Word of God. Paul knew that the best defense against false teachers and false doctrines is to stand firmly on what the Scriptures say.

In 2 Timothy 3:16 Paul emphasized four outstanding uses of Scripture that are profitable to the spiritual well-being of members of the body of Christ.

First, the Word of God is profitable for *doctrine*. It is the textbook which clearly spells out the teachings and doctrines concerning God and His marvelous relationships with His creation—past, present, and future.

Second, the Word of God is the authority used in *reproving*, or rebuking, false teachers who teach anything contrary to the Scripture.

Third, the Word of God is the means by which *corrections* are made in the teachings and the practice of the Christian faith.

Fourth, the Word of God is profitable for *instructing*, or training, people so they may be fully equipped to perform the ministries

God has called them to do.

With this fourfold function of the Word of God, we would do well to be certain that we stand squarely on the Scripture as the foundation of our faith and practice. This is the only way we can be absolutely sure that we are in harmony with the divine will of God.—**F.J. May, D.Min., Professor, Church of God School of Theology, Cleveland, Tennessee**

SENTENCE SERMONS

THE BIBLE IS God's Word and the authority for our faith.

—Selected

THE BIBLE grows more beautiful, as we grow in our understanding of it.

—Johann Von Goethe

WHY IS IT that our children can't read the Bible in school, but they can in prison?

—Marshalltown Times Republic

NO ONE ever graduates from Bible study until he meets the Author face-to-face.

—Everett Harris

EVANGELISM APPLICATION

THE INTEGRITY OF THE BIBLE MUST BE UPHELD AS A WITNESS TO GOD'S MARVELOUS GRACE.

David was a shepherd boy who became king. Maybe if he had known how many difficult things he would encounter as the greatest of all the kings of Israel, he might have refused the offer of Samuel the prophet and remained with his sheep.

This great monarch was a good man who sometimes did bad things. But since he loved the Lord with all his heart, he always repented of his sins and returned to God for forgiveness.

Before David became king, his life was continually threatened by Saul, his predecessor. He knew what it was to live in "the valley of the shadow of death." He also knew what it was to be a shepherd, and he set to music the shepherd's song as a symbol of the comfort and protection the believer has from God and His Word. "Thy rod and thy staff they comfort me" (Psalm 23:4) may be likened to the Spirit and the Word which live in us—both of which are said to "comfort" (John 14:16; 1 Thessalonians 4:18).

DAILY BIBLE READINGS

M. The Ten Commandments.
Exodus 20:1-4, 7, 8, 12-17
T. The Strength of the Word.
2 Samuel 22:29-37
W. Reverence for the Word.
Nehemiah 8:1-10
T. Source of Faith.
Romans 10:13-17
F. God Has Spoken.
Hebrews 1:1-4
S. The Everlasting Word.
1 Peter 1:22-25

Study the Word

Study Text: Joshua 1:8; Job 23:12; Psalm 1:1-6; Proverbs 1:2-7; Jeremiah 15:16; John 5:39; Acts 17:10-12; 2 Timothy 2:15-19

Objective: To discover the benefits of studying the Bible and commit to daily study of God's Word.

Golden Text: "Study to shew thyself approved unto God, a workman that needeth not to be ashamed, rightly dividing the word of truth" (2 Timothy 2:15).

Central Truth: The Bible is God's divine revelation of Himself.

Evangelism Emphasis: An understanding of God's Word contributes to effective witnessing.

PRINTED TEXT

Joshua 1:8. This book of the law shall not depart out of thy mouth; but thou shalt meditate therein day and night, that thou mayest observe to do according to all that is written therein: for then thou shalt make thy way prosperous, and then thou shalt have good success.

John 5:39. Search the scriptures; for in them ye think ye have eternal life: and they are they which testify of me.

2 Timothy 2:15. Study to shew thyself approved unto God, a workman that needeth not to be ashamed, rightly dividing the word of truth.

16. But shun profane and vain babblings: for they will increase unto more ungodliness.

17. And their word will eat as doth a canker: of whom is Hymenaeus and Philetus;

18. Who concerning the truth have erred, saying that the resurrection is past already; **and overthrow the faith of some.**

19. Nevertheless the foundation of God standeth sure, having this seal, The Lord knoweth them that are his. And, Let every one that nameth the name of Christ depart from iniquity.

Job 23:12. Neither have I gone back from the commandment of his lips; I have esteemed the words of his mouth more than my necessary food.

Jeremiah 15:16. Thy words were found, and I did eat them; and thy word was unto me the joy and rejoicing of mine heart: for I am called by thy name, O Lord God of hosts.

Acts 17:10. And the brethren immediately sent away Paul and Silas by night unto Berea: who coming thither went into the synagogue of the Jews.

11. These were more noble than those in Thessalonica, in that they received the word with

all readiness of mind, and searched the scriptures daily, whether those things were so.

12. Therefore many of them believed; also of honourable women which were Greeks, and of men, not a few.

Psalm 1:1. Blessed is the man that walketh not in the counsel of the ungodly, nor standeth in the way of sinners, nor sitteth in the seat of the scornful.

2. But his delight is in the law of the Lord; and in his law doth he meditate day and night.

DICTIONARY

Hymenaeus (Hi-me-NEE-us) and Philetus (fi-LEE-tus)—2 Timothy 2:17—Men who are remembered only for the evil they did.

Berea (ber-EE-ah)—Acts 17:10—A city of southwest Macedonia.

Thessalonica (THES-ah-lah-NY-kah)—Acts 17:11—A city of Macedonia.

LESSON OUTLINE

I. COMMAND TO STUDY
- A. Meditate Upon the Word
- B. Search the Word
- C. A Workman Without Shame
- D. Know the Word
- E. Stand on the Word

II. NECESSITY FOR STUDY
- A. Disciplined Study
- B. The Joy of Study
- C. The Importance of Corporate Study

III. BENEFITS OF STUDY
- A. The Word Brings Stability
- B. The Word Produces a Fruitful Life
- C. The Wise Seek Instruction

LESSON EXPOSITION

INTRODUCTION

This generation is extremely fortunate to have the Word of God so available to us. Never before have there been so many fine translations, excellent commentaries, and extensive word studies that were so obtainable and so inexpensive. Scholars have defined even the most remote passages, and studies in Greek and Hebrew are taught in almost every university in the land.

That has not always been the case. There have been times in the past when the Bible was forbidden to the common people and only the priests were allowed to read it. In England, for many years the Bible was chained to the pulpit in the church, and Bible language experts were forbidden to translate it into the language of the people, with threats of flogging and even death.

Once in Israel the Bible was lost for many years, only to be found, of all places, in the Temple, probably covered by debris from the constant building programs. The Bible tells us, "Hilkiah the priest found a book of the law of the Lord given by Moses. And Hilkiah . . . said . . . I have found the book of the law in the house of the Lord" (2 Chronicles 34:14, 15).

For so many Christians today, the Word of God is lost in the house of the Lord. They hear the Word at church, but never take it home and practice it. Sure, we have Bibles in almost every room, but they are seldom opened—though dusted regularly and placed in prominent view.

David said that the man who is blessed of God delights "in the law [Word] of the Lord; and in his law doth he meditate day and night" (Psalm 1:2). To meditate means to spend an exceedingly great time mulling over the Word, thinking about it, letting the Word become a vital part of our mental makeup.

The psalmist prayed, "Let the . . . meditation [thoughts] of my heart, be acceptable in thy sight, O Lord, my strength, and my redeemer" (Psalm 19:14). Meditation for the Eastern Jew and Christian was often accompanied by the low moanings, or the soft sounds, of one reading or memorizing verses from the Scriptures. Paul told the believers at Ephesus to "[speak] to yourselves in psalms and hymns and spiritual songs, singing and making melody in your heart to the Lord; giving thanks always for all things unto God and the Father in the name of our Lord Jesus Christ" (5:19, 20).

Israel was admonished, "Lay up these my words in your heart and in your soul, and bind them for a sign upon your hand, that they may be as frontlets between your eyes. And ye shall teach them [to] your children, speaking of them when thou sittest in thine house, and when thou walkest by the way, when thou liest down, and when thou risest up" (Deuteronomy 11:18-19).

We will get the most spiritual benefit from this series on the study of the Word if we commence from the beginning to put into practice what we are learning. There is nothing that pleases God so much as finding a man or woman who reads and studies—and is a doer of the Word.

I. COMMAND TO STUDY (Joshua 1:8; John 5:39; 2 Timothy 2:15-19)

A. Meditate Upon the Word (Joshua 1:8)

8. This book of the law shall not depart out of thy mouth; but thou shalt meditate therein day and night, that thou mayest observe to do according to all that is written therein: for then thou shalt make thy way prosperous, and then thou shalt have good success.

The instruction of Joshua to *meditate* on the Word of God day and night is the first use of the Hebrew word *hagah* ("to murmur, ponder, imagine, meditate, mourn, or mutter") in the Bible. The Greek equivalent in the New Testament is *meletao* ("to imagine, to resolve in the mind") and is akin in both English and Greek to *muse*—"thinking deeply about a thing."

The negative form of the word *muse* is probably more common in English today—*amuse*, "without thinking." The letter *a* before a word in Greek makes the word negative—"without" or "not." Amusement is the biggest industry in the world, and the greatest enemy of meditation. Theaters, carnivals, clubs, beaches, skiing, bowling, card playing, and especially radio and television all take time from our meditation on God's Word. While such recreational activities are not wrong, they are amusements—things designed to keep a person from thinking.

Amusements in themselves are not wrong until or unless they shut out the Spirit that comes in "a still small voice" (1 Kings 19:12).

If we are to know the Word of the Lord, we must read it, contemplate it, memorize it, make it a part of us. To escape the things that keep us from "musing" on the Bible, perhaps we should rise early (or stay up late) and, in a quiet place, daily store up the Words of life in our soul. The *Word*, the *life*, and the *soul* are the only eternal things we possess—everything else is amusement.

B. Search the Word (John 5:39)

39. Search the scriptures; for in them ye think ye have eternal life: and they are they which testify of me.

A study of the Word of God must be comprehensive if we are to know the mind of God for our lives. God's will can be clearly discerned from our study of the Bible, but not from single-verse, once-a-week devotions.

This scripture above does not say, "Search the scriptures; for in them ye have eternal life." It says "in them *ye think* ye have eternal life." There was no one who searched the scriptures more than the Pharisees to whom Jesus was speaking. But they were only interested in finding "proof texts" for the things they wanted to believe.

"Search the scriptures," Jesus said. Rightly divide the Word and see what it really says. When you do, you will find that "they . . . testify of me." If your studies fail to lead you to a personal relationship with Jesus Christ, you haven't really searched the scriptures, for He is the Word of God incarnate.

Jesus said to these Pharisees, "Ye think ye have eternal life," but the Scriptures "testify of me." It seems as if He was saying, "you missed that point completely. And if you miss that point, you have missed it all." And they had, for Jesus said to them, "I know you, that ye have not the love of God in you" (v. 42).

The Bible is not a magical book of incantations from which we can draw our select "proof texts" and think we have studied it. I knew a man once who studied the Bible day in and day out—but for the express purpose of arguing about the "latter days." He frightened himself with the knowledge he gained, but he did not know Christ as Savior through all that study.

Paul's words to Timothy sum up the real reason we should study the Word—"to shew thyself approved."

C. A Workman Without Shame (2 Timothy 2:15)

15. Study to shew thyself approved unto God, a workman that needeth not to be ashamed, rightly dividing the word of truth.

Studying the Word of God is work! But it is work concerning which we should never be ashamed. Some are ashamed to be seen with a Bible because they think it brands them as fanatic or holier-than-thou. Some Christians are ashamed because they are totally deficient in their knowledge of the Word. Still others *should be* ashamed for *knowing the Word* and failing to be *doers of the Word.*

I am reminded of one workman who "needeth not to be ashamed." His name was Jacob. He dug a deep well and took stones from the region and lined it. When the well was more than 2,000 years old, Jesus the Lord of life came by and drank from its cool water. The well is now more than 4,000 years old, and pilgrims still drink from the same spring that fed it so long ago. Jacob was a well-digger who did not need to be ashamed. Jacob did not know that one day God himself would drink from his well—but I don't think he could have made it better if he had known.

Timothy was told he was to "rightly divid[e] [Greek, *orthotomeo*, cut straight] the word of truth." He was never to twist the Word for his own benefit or to cut it in such a way that it would become "Timothy's word" instead of God's Word: "Knowing this first, that no prophecy of the scripture is of any private interpretation" (2 Peter 1:20).

The study of the Word of God requires that we allow the Holy Spirit to guide us in the selection of our reading and the times that we set aside for study—and that we listen to Him as He teaches us all things and brings all things to our remembrance (John 14:26). When the Spirit is invited to be the honored teacher in our study sessions, we will always know "what is the mind of the Spirit," and "the will of God" (Romans 8:27).

D. Know the Word
   (2 Timothy 2:16-18)

16. But shun profane and vain babblings: for they will increase unto more ungodliness.

17. And their word will eat as doth a canker: of whom is Hymenaeus and Philetus;

18. Who concerning the truth have erred, saying that the resurrection is past already; and overthrow the faith of some.

Hymenaeus and Philetus had "erred" in their teachings, and their false doctrine was eating into the church at Ephesus like "a canker." The Greek word for *canker* is *gaggraina*, translated "gangrene" or "an ulcer." When Christians fail to study the Word of God with the Holy Spirit to help them "rightly divide" it (to cut it straight), they run the risk of misinterpreting what God is saying.

When believers depend on a few self-made leaders to determine what they believe, they often drift off into false doctrine. The greatest value of the "elder system" is that older Christians who have studied the Bible for many years and know the truth can challenge false teaching, nipping it in the bud before it has a chance to spread like gangrene and disease the entire body.

There are some things in the Bible that are "hard to be understood, which they that are unlearned and unstable wrest . . . unto their own destruction" (2 Peter 3:16). But if the student of the Word will persevere in a spiritual search for answers, the Spirit will illuminate even the most difficult passages.

Those who search the Word looking for "new truth" that has never before been preached waste their time and God's. If the Spirit wishes to reveal something "new" for your own personal life, He will do so. But the Word of God is a finished work. It has stated its truths, and men over the centuries have studied them, gleaned them, sifted them, and sought the Spirit's guidance for an understanding of them. *There is no new truth!*

Study your Bible for personal guidance and to find the perfect will of God for your life, and you will be that rock that keeps false doctrine from creeping into your local church—and maybe the larger church as well. The true child of God is not "unlearned and unstable" (v. 16). He will not be "tossed to and fro, and carried about with every wind of doctrine" (Ephesians 4:14).

The Sadducees tried to confuse Jesus with what looked like a contradiction in the Old Testament law. They did not know that the One with whom they debated was the Word of God made flesh. Jesus *knew* the Word! As strange as that is to say, He not only was the Word, but He also knew the written Word intimately. To those who would challenge the truth, He said, "Ye do err, not knowing the scriptures, nor the power of God" (Matthew 22:29).

E. Stand on the Word
(2 Timothy 2:19)

19. Nevertheless the foundation of God standeth sure, having this seal, The Lord knoweth them that are his. And, Let every one that nameth the name of Christ depart from iniquity.

It is good to have faith, but it is better to have faith in something that is worthy of our faith. While I may have faith that a rickety old chair will support my weight, my faith may be jolted when the chair collapses beneath me. But the "foundation of God [the Word] standeth sure." It is worthy of our faith.

We can take the Scriptures at face value. For though "heaven and earth shall pass away . . . my words shall not pass away" (Matthew 24:35).

It is assuring to the child of God to know that he is known in heaven. Jesus said, "I am the good shepherd, and *know my sheep*, and am known of mine" (John 10:14). The Lord knows those who are His.

We cannot stand on the Word of God when we don't know *where* the Word stands nor *what* it says. So "study to shew thyself approved unto God" (v. 15).

What do we mean by "meditating on the Word of God"?

II. NECESSITY FOR STUDY
(Job 23:12; Jeremiah 15:16; Acts 17:10-12)

A. Disciplined Study (Job 23:12)

12. Neither have I gone back from the commandment of his lips; I have esteemed the words of his mouth more than my necessary food.

If we are to be workmen who are not ashamed of their work for God, we must discipline ourselves to study the Bible. A thorough knowledge of the Scriptures is never a result of casual reading.

Job said that an understanding of God's commandments was more important to him than eating. His words reveal at least two things: (1) Job placed the disciplined study of the Scriptures before even the most important things in his life (such as, eating); and (2) regular fasting (not eating) is a necessary corollary to the understanding of the deeper things of God.

Disciplined study requires that we schedule specific times each day to read the Bible and that those study times be important enough to us that we set aside everything else to keep our daily appointments with God.

In-depth study necessitates that we read the *whole* Bible, not only those portions that we find spiritually uplifting. There is a place for devotional reading; perhaps we read a scripture on prayer before we begin our daily prayer times or select a precious promise from the little box at our workstation before we start the day at the factory or office.

Disciplined study, however, requires that we know something about the *entire* Bible, and that means plodding through those seemingly long, dull chapters in Jeremiah and Ezekiel. If we are saying that the Word is "verbally inspired," we are saying that God gave us every word of it. In that case, we need to read every word of it.

Esteem the words of God, and He will multiply your blessings and make you "like a tree planted by the rivers of water . . . and whatsoever [you do] shall prosper" (Psalm 1:3).

B. The Joy of Study
(Jeremiah 15:16)

16. Thy words were found, and I did eat them; and thy word was unto me the joy and rejoicing of mine heart: for I am called by thy name, O Lord God of hosts.

In literary circles there is a term that is often used for the time when a reader comes across something new, inspiring, or pleasant in what he is reading. It is called the "aha" moment. How many times do you recall that while reading the Bible you came across a scripture that made your heart miss a beat and your mind thrill with joy as the Holy Spirit showed you something?

When you are a serious student of the Word, those moments come often. There is a special joy—unlike any other in all the world—in finding the "*treasure* hid in a field" or the "*pearl* of great price" (Matthew 13:44, 46) right in the middle of some of the dullest portions of Scripture.

Eliphaz had one of those "aha" moments. He described it this way: "Then a spirit passed before my face; the hair of my flesh stood up" (Job 4:15). What a thrill when the Spirit of God passes before our faces and the hair on our arms and heads bristle with the awe of the Holy Presence.

Then there are those lines from the song of Deborah when the mother of the dead Sisera, not yet knowing her son has been killed, tries to find other excuses for her son being so late returning from the battle with the Israelites (Judges 5:28-30). Even though he was an enemy, our hearts went out to his brokenhearted mother.

There is no joy greater than that found in the precious hours spent with the Lord in His Word. It is at these times that the Spirit teaches us about eternal things, mysteries hidden in the heavenlies, and gives us divine wisdom to live for Jesus.

C. The Importance of Corporate Study (Acts 17:10-12)

10. And the brethren immediately sent away Paul and Silas by night unto Berea: who coming thither went into the synagogue of the Jews.

11. These were more noble than those in Thessalonica, in that they received the word with all readiness of mind, and searched the scriptures daily, whether those things were so.

12. Therefore many of them believed; also of honourable women which were Greeks, and

of men, not a few.

After Paul and Silas had ministered to the Jews and Gentiles at Thessalonica, certain of the Jews stirred up the city against them and forced them to flee in the night to Berea. Time after time, it was their own people, the Jews, who had troubled these missionaries the most. One wonders why they didn't just "shake the dust off their feet" (see Matthew 10:14) toward the entire Jewish nation and take their good news of salvation to only the Gentiles.

But in Berea they went immediately to the synagogue and told the local Jews about Jesus before reaching out to their Gentile neighbors.

How nice it must have seemed to Paul and Silas to find that these Jews "were more noble than those in Thessalonica" (v. 11). The difference was that the Jews at Berea "received the word with all readiness" and "searched the scriptures daily" to see "whether those things [preached by the missionaries] were so."

They listened attentively to Paul and Silas and then went to the Word of God to determine for themselves if what was preached was from God. Their example was a fine one for us today. While we should trust our leaders in the Lord, we personally, and the local church corporately, are responsible to go to the Bible and compare *what we hear* from the pulpit with *what we read* in the Word.

False doctrine cannot creep into the congregation that studies the Word together. When the study of the Scriptures is central to a local church and is built into its regular system of worship, that church will teach about Jesus—and that church will win souls! (v. 12). In the end it is not fellowship suppers or basketball that draw men and women to Christ but the preaching, teaching, and study of the unadulterated Word of God.

What particular "aha" experience have you had in your study of the Bible?

III. BENEFITS OF STUDY
(Psalm 1:1-6; Proverbs 1:2-7)

A. The Word Brings Stability
(Psalm 1:1, 2)

1. Blessed is the man that walketh not in the counsel of the ungodly, nor standeth in the way of sinners, nor sitteth in the seat of the scornful.

2. But his delight is in the law of the Lord; and in his law doth he meditate day and night.

Someone has said that in the first verse of Psalm 1 the psalmist has, in reverse order, described the descent of a righteous man into sin. First he *sits* with those who are scornful of spiritual things, who have no room for guidance from God. Second, he *stands* (he sides) with sinners rather than his brethren. Finally, he *walks* in the guidance of the false teachers and heretics. Paul described that kind of man this way: "Christ is become of no effect unto you . . . ye are fallen from grace" (Galatians 5:4).

But the psalmist did not stop there; he said that the man who refrains from these things (sitting, standing, and walking with sinners) will be blessed of God. This man, because he "delight[s] . . . in the law of the Lord" and "meditate[s]" upon it "day and night," will never take even the first step away from the Lord.

The counsel of the Lord (in the study of the Word) is the single most important factor in stabilizing the man of God in the Christian life. When we know the Word and meditate on it, then act upon it through the Spirit's guidance, we will never be led astray.

The psalmist tells us that the man whose "delight is in the law of the Lord" (v. 2), will be like a tree—solid and steadfast. He says that this tree was planted by a gardener (or transplanted) beside a river. Here in the fertile alluvial soil of the riverbank, with its taproot drinking directly from the deep and abundant supply of water, the tree will be fruitful and a blessing to its owner.

B. The Word Produces a Fruitful Life (Psalm 1:3-6)

(Psalm 1:3-6 is not included in the printed text.)

This firmly planted tree will bring "forth his fruit in his season; his leaf also shall not wither; and whatsoever he doeth shall prosper" (v. 3). The man or woman who delights in the study of God's Word will be strong, healthy, and fruitful.

There are those today who are preoccupied with the words "whatsoever he doeth shall prosper." It has become one of the proof texts used to validate the teaching that the Christian can ask anything from the Lord and He is thereby obligated to supply it. But at no time in the history of the church have believers expected to receive monetary or material recompense for serving the Lord.

The prosperity of God has never meant—nor does it mean now—that

Christians can expect to become wealthy, receive the plaudits of men, and have anything their (lustful) hearts desire. James said, "Ye ask, and receive not, because ye ask amiss, that ye may consume it upon your lusts" (4:3).

The Greek term hedone ("lust") is from the root handano, which means "to please." James was saying, "you don't receive anything from God because you ask amiss, that you may consume it on your own pleasure."

The law of love is giving, not getting! The man the Lord prospers is one who is willing to give it all away (see Luke 18:21-24) and follow his Master to the Cross.

God's idea of prosperity is found in the meanings of the word shalom (peace)—a state of wholeness, health, security, spiritual completeness, and sufficient prosperity for a good life.

"The wicked are not so" (v. 4) reminds us that there are trees that bear fruit and trees that do not. Jesus spoke this parable: "A certain man had a fig tree planted in his vineyard; and he came and sought fruit thereon, and found none" (Luke 13:6). Jesus' parable was about the people of Israel (and those who would follow Him) who were planted in a special vineyard, given special attention from God, and expected to bring forth fruit for Him.

When the owner of the vineyard (the Creator) found no fruit on the fig tree, He said, "Behold, these three years I come seeking fruit on this fig tree, and find none: cut it down; why cumbereth it the ground?" (vv. 6-9). And Matthew 7:19 says, "Every tree that bringeth not forth good fruit is hewn down, and cast into the fire."

If a tree or a man fails to fulfill the purpose for which it was planted in the garden of God—for shade, beauty, berries, apples, flowers, or figs—it shall not be allowed to "use up the ground" (Luke 13:7, *NKJV*).

C. The Wise Seek Instruction
   (Proverbs 1:2-7)

(Proverbs 1:2-7 is not included in the printed text.)

Solomon said, "A wise man will hear . . . but fools despise wisdom and instruction" (Proverbs 1:5, 7). Those who will not listen to the *voice* of God will feel the *wrath* of God. Those who love and fear God and have been born again by the precious blood of Jesus Christ shall "have eternal life" (John 3:15), but "the ungodly shall perish" (Psalm 1:6).

That "a wise man will hear, and will increase learning" (Proverbs 1:5) speaks volumes about the study of God's Word. It does not say the "intellectual man" or the "simple man"—for both can be wise in the Word if they are willing to listen to the Holy Spirit. Seek wisdom from the Word as you would silver and hidden treasures, "then shalt thou understand righteousness, and judgment" (2:4, 9).

The study of God's Word is a privilege we have today that has been denied to most of the Christians who lived during the past 2,000 years. Where there are such great blessings, there are also great responsibilities.

Discuss what it means to be "fruitful" and what real prosperity is.

REVIEW QUESTIONS

1. Discuss the need to set aside a specific time daily for the study of the Word.

2. What do we mean by "a workman that needeth not to be ashamed" (2 Timothy 2:15)?

3. What does "sit, stand, and walk" (see Psalm 1:1) mean to you?

4. How does a knowledge of the Word of God retard the spread of false teaching?

5. What is meant by "whatsoever he doeth shall prosper" (Psalm 1:3)?

SENTENCE SERMONS

THE BIBLE IS God's divine revelation of Himself.
—Selected

AN UNDERSTANDING of God's Word contributes to effective witnessing.
—T.Z. Koo

IT IS NOT POSSIBLE ever to exhaust the mind of Scriptures. It is a well that has no bottom.
—St. John Chrysostom

ONE WHO uses the Bible as his guide never loses his sense of direction.
—Draper's Quotations for the Christian World

DAILY BIBLE READING:

M. Parental Obligation.
   Deuteronomy 6:20-25
T. Desire for His Word.
   Psalm 19:7-14
W. Rejecting God's Word.
   Jeremiah 36:2, 3, 21-24, 29-31
T. Power of the Word.
   Matthew 4:1-11
F. The Word Is Our Weapon.
   Ephesians 6:11-20
S. Witness of the Word.
   1 John 5:1-13

Apply the Word

Study Text: Deuteronomy 6:4-9; Matthew 13:1-9, 18-23; Hebrews 5:12-14; James 1:21-25

Objective: To know that God expects us to obey His Word, and apply it to our lives.

Golden Text: "Be ye doers of the word, and not hearers only, deceiving your own selves" (James 1:22).

Central Truth: Believers benefit when they apply the Word of God to their lives.

Evangelism Emphasis: Doing the Word of God is a powerful witness to the unbeliever.

PRINTED TEXT

Matthew 13:18. Hear ye therefore the parable of the sower.

19. When any one heareth the word of the kingdom, and understandeth it not, then cometh the wicked one, and catcheth away that which was sown in his heart. This is he which received seed by the way side.

20. But he that received the seed into stony places, the same is he that heareth the word, and anon with joy receiveth it;

21. Yet hath he not root in himself, but dureth for a while: for when tribulation or persecution ariseth because of the word, by and by he is offended.

22. He also that received seed among the thorns is he that heareth the word; and the care of this world, and the deceitfulness of riches, choke the word, and he becometh unfruitful.

23. But he that received seed into the good ground is he that heareth the word, and understandeth it; which also

beareth fruit, and bringeth forth, some an hundredfold, some sixty, some thirty.

Hebrews 5:12. For when for the time ye ought to be teachers, ye have need that one teach you again which be the first principles of the oracles of God; and are become such as have need of milk, and not of strong meat.

13. For every one that useth milk is unskilful in the word of righteousness: for he is a babe.

14. But strong meat belongeth to them that are of full age, even those who by reason of use have their senses exercised to discern both good and evil.

Deuteronomy 6:4. Hear, O Israel: The Lord our God is one Lord:

5. And thou shalt love the Lord thy God with all thine heart, and with all thy soul, and with all thy might.

6. And these words, which I command thee this day, shall be in thine heart:

7. And thou shalt teach them

diligently unto thy children, and shalt talk of them when thou sittest in thine house, and when thou walkest by the way, and when thou liest down, and when thou risest up.

8. And thou shalt bind them for a sign upon thine hand, and they shall be as frontlets between thine eyes.

9. And thou shalt write them upon the posts of thy house, and on thy gates.

James 1:22. But be ye doers of the word, and not hearers only, deceiving your own selves.

LESSON OUTLINE

I.   RESPONSE TO THE WORD
- A. Three Immortal Losers
- B. One Eternal Winner
- C. Infants in the Word
- D. Fathers—on Earth and in Heaven

II. TEACH THE WORD
- A. Teaching Love—With All Thine Heart
- B. Teaching Love—With All Thy Mind
- C. Teaching Love—With All Thy Soul
- D. Teaching Love—With All Thy Strength

III. DO THE WORD
- A. The Engrafted Word
- B. Doers and Hearers

LESSON EXPOSITION

INTRODUCTION

To be a *doer* of the Word, one must first be a *hearer* of the Word (or a reader of the Word). You cannot do what the Bible says if you don't know what the Bible says. A "doer" has read, studied, meditated upon, and allowed the Word to be implanted in his heart. Jesus himself, who was the Word incarnate, was a doer of the Word. He said to those who questioned His sonship, "If I do not the works of my Father, believe me not. But if I do [if I am a doer of the Word], though ye believe not me, believe the works [that I do]" (John 10:37, 38).

Scholars of the Bible and those who have read it for a great number of years are not the only ones who can witness for Christ. The newest believer is expected to be "holding forth the word of life" (Philippians 2:16). We do not have to have all the answers to be a witness of what Christ has done for us. Paul gave good advice to those who are new in the Lord: "Whereto we have already attained, let us walk . . ." (3:16)—that is, you are responsible to walk and witness at the spiritual level you have reached in your life with Christ.

We should be doers of the Word from the first day we open the Bible as newborn believers. Whatever the Scriptures instruct us to do, we should make at least some effort to comply. If you failed in your compliance, try again and again. The young Christian must realize that believers grow into the likeness of Christ. A good gauge of how much of Christ is in my life is best gauged by how much of the Word is in my life.

I. RESPONSE TO THE WORD
(Matthew 13:18-23; Hebrews
5:12-14)

A. Three Immortal Losers
(Matthew 13:18-22)

18. Hear ye therefore the parable of the sower.

19. When any one heareth the word of the kingdom, and understandeth it not, then cometh the wicked one, and catcheth away that which was sown in his heart. This is he which received seed by the way side.

20. But he that received the seed into stony places, the same is he that heareth the word, and anon with joy receiveth it;

21. Yet hath he not root in himself, but dureth for a while: for when tribulation or persecution ariseth because of the word, by and by he is offended.

22. He also that received seed among the thorns is he that heareth the word; and the care of this world, and the deceitfulness of riches, choke the word, and he becometh unfruitful.

These verses refer to a situation in which three individuals hear the Word of God and believe—then for some reason they allow their salvation to be lost. This parable of Jesus relates only some of the many things that can draw the believer away from Christ and back into his old way of life. Peter graphically described this turning back as a "dog [that] turned to his own vomit again; and the sow [hog] that was washed to her wallowing in the mire" (2 Peter 2:22). The writer of the Book of Hebrews speaks plainly about the consequences of turning spitefully and blasphemously away from the Lord once a person has made a start to serve Him.

It is a sad thing to see those who have served the Lord for many years turn their backs on their families, their churches, their friends, and the Lord for one adulterous affair. It is almost as sad to see those who are only beginning their Christian lives choose to turn back to lives of sin; for imagine what they could have been—perhaps another Moses, or Paul, or John the Beloved. Perhaps those individuals could have someday reformed the church, like Martin Luther or John Calvin, or given their lives for the publication of the Word or been great missionaries. But we will never know!

The parable of the sower speaks of four converts; three began, but only one endured (see Matthew 7:13, 14). The first of those heard the Word, but didn't understand it. The "wicked one" soon came and caught away (stole) the Word by which he had been saved. A second convert was likened to a seed that fell on a stone. It sprang up but soon "withered away, because it lacked moisture" (Luke 8:6). The third was the seed that tried to grow among the thorns.

The devil stole the Word. The first man was "he which received seed by the way side" (Matthew 13:19). He heard the Word but failed to understand it. Because the Word of salvation had no opportunity to be engrafted into his life, Satan and all his workers could easily pull him back into the society and lifestyle from which he was saved.

Someone has said the *wayside* has a connotation of "a rougher side of life; a place where immorality is rampant and sin controls lives." In such a place one tends to become calloused and cynical, making it very difficult for the Word to take hold and grow.

Adversity and persecution stole the Word. The second of the individuals who heard and responded to the Word received it with joy and thankfulness. But the message fell on "stony places [rocky ground]," and when tribulation or persecution arose "because of the word [for the gospel's sake]," he fell away (vv. 20, 21). Times of difficulty may either make the man of God stronger or drive him away from the Lord altogether.

But our God is the God of the second chance (and third, and fourth . . .). He told Israel, "When thou art in tribulation, and all these things are come upon thee . . . he will not forsake thee, neither destroy thee" (Deuteronomy 4:30, 31).

This man fell away because he had no "taproot," that large root that bores straight down into the ground until it finds streams of water from which to drink. The psalmist tells us the man who "meditate[s] day and night" on the Word is like the tree that is "planted by the rivers of water," where the taproot can carry nutrients and refreshment to the rest of the tree's body (Psalm 1:2, 3). Without such roots in the Word of God, we, like the tree, are subject to being blown over and destroyed. Without such an anchor, we will be "tossed to and fro, and carried about with every wind of doctrine" (Ephesians 4:14).

Cares and riches choke the Word. When Israel was in the wilderness for 40 years and so poor that they were dependent upon God for their every need, they served and trusted Him. But the Lord, "which knoweth the hearts" of men (Acts 15:8), knew that when they became prosperous and burdened down with the cares of the world, they would desert Him for the god of riches. God told Moses, "For when I shall have brought them into the land which I sware unto their fathers, that floweth with milk and honey; and they shall have eaten and filled themselves, and waxen fat; then will they turn unto other gods, and serve them" (Deuteronomy 31:20).

One day a young ruler came to Jesus and asked how he could be saved. When Jesus responded that he must sell what he had and give it to the poor, the young man "went away sorrowful: for he had great possessions" (Matthew 19:21, 22). No one could have been more sorrowful at his departure than the Lord of Glory, who came to give His life for this man's sins and ours.

The thorns and thistles of this life's indulgences began to grow around the man in Jesus' third example (13:22), choking out time for the Word or for spiritual things, and—like the young ruler—he went away sad.

A great man of God once told a story about a wild goose which was flying south with his companions when he spied a barn and pigpen below. In the pigpen was a goose's favorite meal—corn. So he decided that he could catch up with the remainder of the flock at the rear of the formation if he went down for just one ear.

But one ear of corn turned to two, then to three—and the goose said with confidence, "There's plenty to eat here. I'll catch my flight as they go north in the spring. But each spring and fall he found himself more and more bogged down in the mire of the pigpen. Finally, after several years, as the wild geese flew overhead, he made a final determination that he would now, at last, join them.

But to his sorrow and amazement, he could not fly! He had lost his ability to soar into the skies; his place with the flock was lost forever; and as his former companions flew away into the bright blue heavens, he found himself stuck in the mud and filth of the earth—he was an earthbound barnyard fowl.

With our heads bowed in sorrow, we call these first three men "losers"—they came to Jesus and began in the Word of God but then dropped away.

B. One Eternal Winner
   (Matthew 13:23)

23. But he that received seed into the good ground is he that heareth the word, and understandeth it; which also beareth fruit, and bringeth forth, some an hundredfold, some sixty, some thirty.

Usually where there are losers, there are also winners. Out of that group of young men and women praying in the altar—tears streaming down their faces—there are some who will someday say with the apostle Paul: "The time of my departure is at hand. I have fought a good fight, I have finished my course, I have kept the faith: Henceforth there is laid up for me a crown of righteousness, which the Lord, the righteous judge, shall give me at that day: and not to me only, but unto all them also that love his appearing" (2 Timothy 4:6-8).

Only God knows which of those who begin will win the race of life and which will fall along the wayside. And we need not know; for every man or woman who seeks Christ in our church should be given the same opportunities to succeed in their pursuit of the spiritual life.

The parable gives us three reasons why the "winner" was triumphant, while the others failed. First, he heard the Word of God with a heart prepared to receive it. Second, he understood the Word of God and knew what was expected of him as a believer. Third, he began to produce fruit. He was a hearer as well as a doer of the Word, and the result was a fruitful Christian life.

The vital difference between a winner and a loser in the kingdom of God is the role the Word of God is allowed to play. Jesus said, "Whosoever cometh to me, and heareth my sayings [My Word], and doeth them, I will shew you to whom he is like: He is like a man which built an house, and digged deep, and laid the foundation on a rock: and when the flood arose, the stream beat vehemently upon that house, and could not shake it: for it was founded upon a rock" (Luke 6:47, 48).

C. Infants in the Word
   (Hebrews 5:12, 13)

12. For when for the time ye ought to be teachers, ye have need that one teach you again which be the first principles of the oracles of God; and are become such as have need of milk, and not of strong meat.
13. For every one that useth milk is unskilful in the word of righteousness: for he is a babe.

In psychology, certain life passages are called "the feeding cycle." In the simplest of language, the feeding cycle consists of a time when (1) we must be fed (babies), (2) when we feed ourselves (children and teens), and (3) when we are able to feed others (adults).

Growth is expected in the Christian. The writer of Hebrews told those to whom he wrote: "When . . . ye ought to be teachers [able to feed others], ye have need that one teach you [you can't even feed yourself]. . . . For every one that useth milk is unskilful in the word of righteousness: for he is a babe [who must be fed]" (5:12, 13).

Peter tells us there is nothing wrong with drinking milk, and advises the newborn in Christ who are not yet able to eat spiritual meat to "desire the sincere milk of the word, that ye may grow thereby" (1 Peter 2:2). *Growth* is a significant word in the Christian's life. The writer of our text was saying, in effect: "Considering the time you've been Christians, you should be grown men and women in the Lord by now. But you have not grown at all! You are still babies who must be fed, perhaps even have your food deposited in your mouth by a loving mother."

Anything that has life must grow or die. The beautiful baby who lisps his pretty little words as a 2-year-old would greatly alarm his parents if he still needed help to walk, talk, and eat at age 10 or 20.

Paul admonished the Corinthian church: "And I, brethren, could not speak unto you as unto spiritual, but as unto carnal, even as unto babes in Christ. I have fed you with milk, and not with meat: for hitherto ye were not able to bear it, neither yet now are ye able. For ye are yet carnal [fleshly or of this world]" (1 Corinthians 3:1-3).

The apostle told the Jewish-Christian teachers in Rome, "[You] are confident that you yourself are a guide to the blind, a light to those who are in darkness, an instructor of the foolish, a teacher of babes, [but you have only a] form of knowledge and of the truth in the law" (Romans 2:19, 20, *NKJV*).

The master teacher was Jesus himself. In fact, the words *teacher* and *master* were held in such high regard by both the Jews and the Greeks that the same Greek word, *didaskalos*, was used for both.

From the first moment after being saved, the new convert should be a witness—for there is no time when his witness is better received by his family and friends than just after his life begins to change into the likeness of Christ. But a witness does not need to be an expert in theology, nor is it absolutely necessary that the thing he witnesses about happened directly to him. He could be simply an eyewitness (see John 1:14, 15; 2 Peter 1:16-18).

Everyone should be a witness to what he has seen and heard about the Savior who did such wonderful things for him—but not everyone is qualified to teach. To be a teacher of the Word of God, one must study and understand the Word and live the Word he teaches. Paul told the church at Colosse, "Let the word of Christ dwell in you richly in all wisdom; teaching and admonishing one another in psalms and hymns and spiritual songs, singing with grace in your hearts to the Lord" (Colossians 3:16; see also 2 Timothy 2:15; 3:16, 17).

Then, too, the position of teacher is so important that God appoints those He wants to teach His Word. Paul said to Timothy, "The appearing of our Saviour Jesus Christ . . . hath abolished death, and hath brought life and immortality to light through the gospel: whereunto I am appointed a preacher, and an apostle, and a teacher" (2 Timothy 1:10, 11). To the Ephesians he said, "But unto every one of us is given grace according to the measure of the gift of Christ. . . . And he gave some, apostles; and some, prophets; and some, evangelists; and some, pastors, and teachers; for the perfecting [equipping] of the saints, for the work of the ministry, for the edifying of the body of Christ" (Ephesians 4:7, 11, 12).

D. Fathers—on Earth and in Heaven (Hebrews 5:14)

14. But strong meat belongeth to them that are of full age, even those who by reason of use have their senses exercised to discern both good and evil.

Our Father in heaven. Long before we begin to understand about "our Father which art in heaven" (Matthew 6:9), most of us had earthly fathers who demonstrated the love and care of our Father God. My father was, and is, the spiritual and moral patriarch of his family. For more than 50 years he and my mother have modeled a life of prayer and Bible study (a chapter while breakfast got cold). They were a godly example of regular church attendance, working in their church (my mom taught the same Primary Girls class for more than 40 years), and supporting their pastor and church in whatever way the leadership asked.

But for some, the father model has been so marred by divorce, abuse, molestation, and mental and emotional degradation that it is difficult for those children to see God as a "caring Father." Where these circumstances exist, mature men and women of God must step into the shoes of those degenerate parents.

Fathers as mentors. As God the Father is the head of all things spiritual and heavenly, so He has ordained the father to be the head of his household in all matters reflecting on the family. Where the family is left without a father through death, divorce, or other reasons; statistically, that home has a greatly reduced hope of surviving and thriving as a coherent and working unit. From the Creation, the family has been solid and secure—but then Daddy went away.

American society is awash with broken homes, delinquent children, illegitimate births, rising drug use in all levels of society, easy and stigma-free divorce, and a growing number of homes in which the children are being reared by single parents. Christian fathers are needed to reverse this tide.

However, fathers, don't assume that your own children are drug-free and that they have steered clear of experimental sex. Neither should you assume that your own marriage cannot fail. While there are so many places a Christian father can act as mentor to boys and girls in desperate and hopeless states—working with slum kids, feeding the poor, providing clothing to those without, and visiting the sick and those in prison—your first responsibility is to your own family! Your children must be nurtured, loved, taught, encouraged, and prepared for the time when they will have families of their own and will need to pass on the love you are teaching them today.

Once we have heard the Word, what should be our response—as new-born believers, as maturing Christians, as elders?

II. TEACH THE WORD
(Deuteronomy 6:4-9)

A. Teaching Love—With All Thine Heart (vv. 4-6)

4. Hear, O Israel: The Lord our God is one Lord:
5. And thou shalt love the Lord thy God with all thine heart, and with all thy soul, and with all thy might [mind and strength].
6. And these words, which I command thee this day, shall be in thine heart.

The *Shema* is the greatest creed of Israel; it is named for the first word (the Hebrew for *hear*) in verse 4. There are two commandments in our text—"Thou shalt love the Lord . . . with all thine heart" (v. 5) and "These words, which I command thee . . . shall be in thine heart" (v. 6)

At first there may seem to be a contradiction. We may question, "How can love be commanded?" The ordinary concept of relationships and feelings of affection that come and go with a whim cannot be commanded. But there is nothing ordinary about God's love, or the love He demands from us.

There are loves which can, or at least should be able to, be commanded.

First, love for God is commanded in the home. God told Israel, "These words, which I command thee this day . . . thou shalt teach them diligently unto thy children" (vv. 6, 7). The home was meant to be the cornerstone of society, the base upon which our love for God our Father and His Son Jesus Christ could

withstand every attack of the Enemy. If the home is built upon a rock (Matthew 7:24, 25), and the church is an exemplary pattern of the godly home; then governments and legislatures, judges, and the entire scope of freedom's laws will continue and endure until Jesus comes.

Second, love for God is commanded for our nation. "And thou shalt do that which is right and good in the sight of the Lord: that it may be well with thee [as a nation]" (Deuteronomy 6:18).

While the home provides the perpetuation of the godly life of a nation, the nation itself also has a responsibility for the continuity of the laws and customs by which God is glorified. The people, in turn, are responsible that the nation preserve its sense of the "holy."

Since a stable nation preserves the peace and tranquillity needed by the Christian family to practice its faith openly and under the protection of those in authority, the Christian is commanded to support those in positions of power and authority with our prayers and taxes (and with military service when necessary). The writer of Hebrews declared, "Obey them that have the rule over you, and submit yourselves: for they watch for your souls" (13:17). Paul wrote to Timothy, "I exhort therefore, that, first of all, supplications, prayers, intercessions, and giving of thanks, be made for all men; for kings, and for all that are in authority; that we may lead a quiet and peaceable life in all godliness and honesty" (1 Timothy 2:1, 2). Solomon gave a very good reason to pray for those in authority: "When the righteous are in authority, the people rejoice: but when the wicked beareth rule, the people mourn" (Proverbs 29:2).

"Blessed is the nation whose God is the Lord; and the people whom he hath chosen for his own inheritance" (Psalm 33:12).

B. Teaching Love—With All Thy Mind (v. 7)

7. And thou shalt teach them diligently unto thy children, and shalt talk of them when thou sittest in thine house, and when thou walkest by the way, and when thou liest down, and when thou risest up.

The words "teach them diligently" characterize the heart of religious instruction—diligently, without fail, always. For we know that the final result of diligent religious teaching is not religious knowledge, but changed lives and hearts. Sporadic and heartless training results in a soft, spineless religious experience for the teacher and confusion and indecision for the trainee.

Moses was instructed to tell the new nation that they were to "love the Lord thy God with all thine heart, and with all thy soul, and with all thy might." Then, Jesus included a fourth dimension of man's duties to those in Deuteronomy—man is to love God with all his mind as well (Matthew 22:37).

When one thinks of loving God with the mind, we aren't sure how to separate that from soul and heart. At times in Bible usage, each of these is used to denote the center of a man's being. The Greek root word *nous*, translated "mind" in the New Testament and Septuagint, refers to that part of man that makes decisions, contemplates, thinks, recalls the past, plans the future. The mind is reflective and purposes man's conscious movements.

The Lord told Moses that the minds of the children are to be filled with the law of the Lord. They are to talk about God, His love, and His law all day long and into the night as they go to bed.

Paul told Christians also to fill their minds with worthy and pure things: Whatever is true, honest, just, pure, lovely, of good report, of any virtue, of any praise—"think on these things" (Philippians 4:8). The writer of Proverbs added a sobering thought to the importance of the mind: "For as he thinketh in his heart, so is he" (Proverbs 23:7).

C. Teaching Love—With All Thy Soul (v. 8)

8. And thou shalt bind them for a sign upon thine hand, and they shall be as frontlets between thine eyes.

The children of Israel were commanded to bind the law of God on their hands as well as on the frontlets they wore between their eyes. We may, if we take a very liberal view, think these outward signs of the people's confession of faith were no more than the ritualistic garments and charms worn by religions all around them. But the reference to hands and the wearing of frontlets were, and are, rife with meaning.

Because God was teaching His people things that were new to them, He bid them to make His law the most important thing in their lives outside of Jehovah himself. All Israel was commanded to wear the most significant laws before their eyes as frontlets (see also Exodus 13:1-16 [note especially vv. 8, 9, 16]; Deuteronomy 11:13-21). By the time of the New Testament, the frontlets (from the Hebrew *tuph*, "to bind") had become known as phylacteries.

Someone once said, "I don't want to be tied down in the work of the church." The pastor responded, "Is tied down all you are—Jesus was nailed down." Since Jesus was nailed to the Father's eternal purpose, may we at least bind ourselves to it!

The hands have always performed a vital function in the Kingdom. The Lord Jehovah told a prophet of old, "Behold, I have graven thee [all my people] upon the palms of my hands" (Isaiah 49:16). How marvelous! The eternal God has marked the names, or likeness, of each of us in His hand that we may forever be before His face.

Centuries before His Son trod the Via Dolorosa and death-hardened soldiers nailed His hands and feet to a cross, God the Father had spoken of His love for us, by saying, in effect, "I have the scars of Calvary already in My hand."

D. Teaching Love—With All Thy Strength (v. 9)

9. And thou shalt write them upon the posts of thy house, and on thy gates.

It took strength to join with such a massive rebellion as that begun by the slave children of Israel, to put one's very life on the line, and then plaster the symbol of rebellion on the front door of the house. There were no halfway revolutionaries in this group. Either one trusted God and His spokesman or he took his chances right along with the Egyptians.

But once his mind was made up, once he had decided to make the break with Egypt, he mustered all the strength he could find, walked to the front of the house and—there in front of everyone—he made known his determination to serve God. Because he applied the blood, he and his entire household was passed over by the death angel. The success of our church and our nation lies in having fearless Christian men and women who will "love the Lord [their] God . . . with all [their] strength" (Mark 12:30).

Timothy was told, "For God hath not given us the spirit of *fear* [Greek, *dilia*, better translated "a timid spirit"]; but of *power*, and of *love*, and of a sound *mind*" (2 Timothy 1:7). A timid witness is a contradiction in terms. *Enthusiasm* (from the Greek words *en theos*, "inspired by God") is the best way to describe the life the Christian should live before the world. To be *enthusiastic* about God and to witness about Him daily takes a mind determined to "love the Lord thy God . . . with all thy strength."

Immediately following the outpouring of the Holy Spirit on the New Testament church, the Bible says: "Now when they [the elders of the Jews] saw the boldness of Peter and John, and perceived that they were unlearned and ignorant men, they marvelled; and took knowledge of them, that they had been with Jesus" (Acts 4:13). Because God's love for us through Jesus Christ's death on the cross was the *boldest* act in all of time and eternity, we who are recipients of that love should also show our love for Him in boldness. When we love God with all our hearts, minds, souls and strengths, now as then, we will demonstrate to the lost that we have "been with Jesus."

Describe how we are to teach love and to whom?

III. DO THE WORD
(James 1:21-25)

A. The Engrafted Word (v. 21)

(James 1:21 is not included in the printed text.)

The central idea of verse 21 is the engrafting (or implanting) of the Word of God in the life of the believer. Fritz Rienecker says, metaphorically something is placed deep into a man, and it is expected to grow to be a part of his nature (*A Linguistic Key to the Greek New Testament*, Vol. 2). One of the best illustrations of implanting is seen in today's heart-transplant operations, where an outside organ is grafted into the body of a dying person. If the transplant is successful, the body has absorbed the new heart so completely that it is now a growing, living part of the body into which it was placed.

James tells us to strip off the dirty clothes of immoral, sinful living ("lay apart all filthiness"), and meekly allow the saving Word of God to be implanted in us. The Word then, residing in us, is our guide in all things. The standards of the world are not our measuring sticks. When the Word has become a part of our very being, God through that Word will provide all the instruction we need to live a separated, holy, Spirit-filled, witnessing life for Christ. At every turn of the road, "whether you turn to the right or to the left, your ears will hear a voice behind you, saying,

'This is the way; walk in it' "(Isaiah 30:21, *NIV*).

Jesus Christ himself—the Word of God incarnate—also, like His words, dwells in us to cleanse us from sin, to purify us in holiness, to change us into His likeness, and to guide us in all ways.

B. Doers and Hearers (vv. 22-25)

(James 1:23-25 is not included in the printed text.)

22. But be ye doers of the word, and not hearers only, deceiving your own selves.

Early church fathers, and even the great reformist Martin Luther, had a problem accepting the Book of James as a part of the holy canon of Scripture. From the surface it appears that the writer of this little book took a stance just opposite that of the acclaimed apostle Paul.

Faith and works are both gifts from God, however; and both are necessary to salvation. Paul advised the Philippians to "work out your own salvation with fear and trembling" (2:12). And to the Ephesians, Paul said, "For by grace are ye saved through faith; and that not of yourselves: it is the gift of God: not of works, lest any man should boast. For we are his workmanship, created in Christ Jesus unto good works, which God hath before ordained that we should walk in them" (2:8-10).

James said, in effect, "Now that you've believed, it's time to put your beliefs to work." He also said, "Faith, if it hath not works, is dead" (2:17). "The faith that is not followed by works is dead . . . and the works that are not preceeded by faith is dead" (*The Speaker's Bible*).

Explain the apparent inconsistencies between the emphasis on doing in the Book of James and Paul's strong emphasis on faith.

REVIEW QUESTIONS

1. Discuss the difference between "witnessing" and "teaching the Word."

2. Why did the rich young ruler go away sad? Does the Lord ask the same of us that He asked that young man when we get saved?

3. What caused the seed (new converts) of the sower to go back into the world? Why was the one convert able to hold on, while the others failed?

4. What are some things God has commanded us to love?

5. What did the Lord mean when He said, "I have graven thee upon the palms of my hands" (Isaiah 49:16)?

SENTENCE SERMONS

BELIEVERS BENEFIT when they apply the Word of God to their lives.
—Selected

NO TEACHER should strive to make others think as he thinks, but to lead them to the living Truth—to the Master himself—of whom alone they can learn anything.
—George MacDonald

THE TEACHER is like the candle which lights others in consuming itself.
—Italian Proverb

EVANGELISM APPLICATION

DOING THE WORD OF GOD IS A POWERFUL WITNESS TO THE UNBELIEVER.

Charles L. Allen preached a sermon about the man with the withered hand (Mark 3:1-5). He said of him, "He could think of a lot of things he wanted to do, but his hand was withered. He could not translate his thoughts into deeds. The hand represents action and his hand was withered. . . . In fact, to some extent we are all afflicted with this handicap of the withered hand. We have so many good things in mind that we never put into deeds" (Charles L. Allen, *The Touch of the Master's Hand*).

Those who see a need and hold back their largesse, or those who plan without any intention of fulfilling their unspoken commitments to God and man, or those who dream of days of greatness and make no attempt to bring their dreams to pass—their hands are withered.

But listen to the Master as He says, "Stretch forth thine hand." And when we do, we will be healed—and the "withered hand" can become a helping hand.

DAILY BIBLE READINGS

M. Keep God's Commandments.
Deuteronomy 8:1-6
T. Proclaim His Word.
Jeremiah 11:1-6
W. The Greatest Commandments.
Matthew 22:34-40
T. Living in the Word.
Colossians 3:12-17
F. Pattern for Living. Titus 2:1-8
S. Communicate the Word.
Titus 2:9-15

Declare the Word

Study Text: Deuteronomy 4:2; 12:32; Psalms 12:6; 18:30; Proverbs 30:5, 6; Acts 8:26-40; 18:24-28; 2 Timothy 4:1-5

Objective: To recognize the need for declaring the Word of God and to uphold its standards.

Golden Text: "Preach the word; be instant in season, out of season; reprove, rebuke, exhort with all longsuffering and doctrine" (2 Timothy 4:2).

Central Truth: Declaring the Word is the privilege and responsibility of every believer.

Evangelism Emphasis: Declaring the Word is the privilege and responsibility of every believer.

PRINTED TEXT

Acts 8:34. And the eunuch answered Philip, and said, I pray thee, of whom speaketh the prophet this? of himself, or of some other man?

35. Then Philip opened his mouth, and began at the same scripture, and preached unto him Jesus.

18:24. And a certain Jew named Apollos, born at Alexandria, an eloquent man, and mighty in the scriptures, came to Ephesus.

25. This man was instructed in the way of the Lord; and being fervent in the spirit, he spake and taught diligently the things of the Lord, knowing only the baptism of John.

26. And he began to speak boldly in the synagogue: whom when Aquila and Priscilla had heard, they took him unto them, and expounded unto him the way of God more perfectly.

27. And when he was disposed to pass into Achaia, the brethren wrote, exhorting the disciples to receive him: who when he was come, helped them much which had believed through grace.

28. For he mightily convinced the Jews, and that publickly, shewing by the scriptures that Jesus was Christ.

Deuteronomy 4:2. Ye shall not add unto the word which I command you, neither shall ye diminish ought from it, that ye may keep the commandments of the Lord your God which I command you.

Psalm 18:30. As for God, his way is perfect: the word of the Lord is tried: he is a buckler to all those that trust in him.

Proverbs 30:5. Every word of God is pure: he is a shield unto them that put their trust in him.

6. Add thou not unto his words, lest he reprove thee, and thou be found a liar.

2 Timothy 4:1. I charge thee

therefore before God, and the Lord Jesus Christ, who shall judge the quick and the dead at his appearing and his kingdom;

2. Preach the word; be instant in season, out of season; reprove, rebuke, exhort with all longsuffering and doctrine.

3. For the time will come when they will not endure sound doctrine; but after their own lusts shall they heap to themselves teachers, having itching ears;

4. And they shall turn away their ears from the truth, and shall be turned unto fables.

5. But watch thou in all things, endure afflictions, do the work of an evangelist, make full proof of thy ministry.

DICTIONARY

Apollos (uh-POL-us), born at Alexandria (AL-eg-ZAN-dre-ah)—Acts 18:24—An educated Jew from Egypt.

Ephesus (EF-eh-sus)—Acts 18:24—The capital city in the Roman state of Asia in New Testament days.

Aquila (AK-wi-lah) and Priscilla (pri-SIL-uh)—Acts 18:26—A husband-and-wife team who had fled from Rome because of the emperor's edict.

Achaia (a-KA-yuh)—Acts 18:27—A Roman province in New Testament times.

LESSON OUTLINE

I. TESTIFY OF CHRIST

    A. Lay Leaders—Philip the Deacon

    B. Preachers—Apollos the Evangelist

    C. Teachers—Aquila and Priscilla

II. UPHOLD THE WORD

    A. The Finished Word

    B. The Perfect Word

    C. The Pure Word

III. TEACH RIGHT DOCTRINE

    A. Teaching the Church

    B. Reaching the Backslider

    C. Preaching to Sinners

LESSON EXPOSITION

INTRODUCTION

The task of the church universal is to bring in the "day of the Lord" . . . to restore all things to Christ and to His Father in a glorious age to come. It is the will of God that all men come to a saving knowledge of Christ. And while God has called some men and women to specific offices and given them extraordinary gifts to preach and evangelize the lost throughout the whole world, it is the specific task of every believer to win the lost and teach the convert. It's true that Christ gave the church "some, apostles; and some, prophets; and some, evangelists; and some, pastors and teachers [or, pastor-teachers]; for the perfecting of the saints, for the work of the ministry, for the edifying of the body of Christ" (Ephesians 4:11, 12), but every believer is to testify of Christ (Mark 16:15, 16; Acts 1:8).

And like those called to the

special preaching offices, every believer has been given two powerful tools with which to accomplish the work. They are baptized with the Holy Spirit and given the Word of God. Our greatest fear, though, is that the men and women in the pews will "quench the Spirit" and ignore the Word. The Bible on the table is good; the Bible in our hearts is better; the Bible, empowered by the Holy Spirit, overflowing from our lips, is best of all.

It is not necessary to be a master of the Word to be qualified to declare the Word. Even if you became proficient in the Greek and Hebrew languages, and if you spent years in institutions of higher learning and most of every day in a personal study of the Bible, you still could not master it. God never meant for you to master it, but that it should master you.

This is not to say that you should not give the study of the Word of God a priority place in your life—it should be studied until it saturates your very mind, soul, body, and spirit. Then the Holy Spirit will take what you have read and meditated on and turn it into food for those God has given you to testify to or teach.

In each local church there are three groups with the task of "testifying" of Christ. In this study we will call them "preachers," "teachers," and "reachers." They are (1) the professional leader— the pastor (Greek, *poimen*); (2) the elected or selected laymen who teach and instruct in and out of the church— the deacons (Greek, *diakonos*); and (3) the body of laity (Greek, *laos*). Our study will take a look at representatives from each of these groups.

I. TESTIFY OF CHRIST
(Acts 8:26-40; 18:24-28)

A. Lay Leaders—Philip the Deacon
(8:26-40)

(Acts 8:26-33, 36-40 is not included in the printed text.)

34. And the eunuch answered Philip, and said, I pray thee, of whom speaketh the prophet this? of himself, or of some other man?

35. Then Philip opened his mouth, and began at the same scripture, and preached unto him Jesus.

This Philip—who preached to the crowds in Samaria, did great miracles of healing, and was chosen to witness to the Ethiopian eunuch in the desert near Gaza—was the same Philip chosen by the apostles to be a deacon (Acts 6:5). He is not Philip the disciple, but simply a layman filled with the Holy Spirit (6:3) and obedient to God's call.

After the death of Stephen (Acts 7:59, 60), the first Christian martyr, the church at Jerusalem scattered throughout Judea and Samaria, leaving only the apostles in the Jews' capital city. One of those who made the most of his forced evacuation was Philip the deacon. Philip began to preach in the city of Samaria, and "the people with one accord gave heed unto those things which Philip spake, hearing and seeing the miracles which he did. . . . And there was great joy in that city" (8:6, 8).

When the apostles in Jerusalem heard of the great revival in Samaria, they sent Peter and John to lay hands on Philip's converts that they might be filled with the Holy Spirit (vv. 14-17). Verse 26 says, "The angel of the Lord spake unto Philip. . . ." This could have been in a vision or in a dream by night. The angel may have spoken to him silently in his heart—we do not know. But we do know that the Lord gave this deacon a mission and pointed him in the right direction (south). "And he arose and went" (v. 27).

What a change this must have seemed to Philip. From the crowds in the city he was directed into the desert. Luke's expressive "behold" (Greek, *idou*) expresses the English idea of "look!" and probably reveals that what Philip saw when he arrived at the Gaza road was a sight to behold. There he found a man of a different race and culture, traveling along in what was described as a chariot surrounded by a great retinue of brightly colored attendants, and who was reading from Isaiah 53 in the Old Testament.

The man in the "chariot" was a eunuch, treasurer of the nation of Ethiopia, under Candace the queen. He was a nobleman, "of great authority [Greek, *dunastes*]" (v. 27). He had traveled over a thousand miles to Jerusalem to worship, thus indicating he was a convert to Judaism, though as a eunuch he could not have full membership in that faith (Deuteronomy 23:1).

While at Jerusalem he may have heard about the man "Jesus" who was put to death by the Jews because they said He claimed to be the Son of God. He may have heard also that some were saying He had risen from the grave. As he rode he was reading about One who was led as "a lamb to the slaughter" (Isaiah 53:7; Acts 8:32).

Philip used the nobleman's interest in what he read in the prophecy of Isaiah to open a conversation with him and "began at the same scripture, and preached unto him

Jesus" (v. 35). If the Christian witness is to lead men and women to Christ, they must be able to "declare the Word," to begin with any part of the Scriptures and show through them and the whole Bible that "Jesus Christ is the Son of God" (v. 37).

We do not know how long Philip and the eunuch rode together toward Gaza; but somewhere down that dusty desert road, they came upon a place with water—a stream or a pool—and the Eunuch asked to be baptized. "They went down both into the water" (v. 38).

The writer tells us that after the eunuch was baptized, "the Spirit of the Lord caught away Philip, that the eunuch saw him no more" (v. 39). Whether this was a supernatural occurrence or something totally different, we are not sure, but we do know that right away Philip was somewhere else *declaring the Word!*

Whereas a city had been won with great flair at Samaria, there in the desert the seed was quietly sown for the conversion of an entire nation. The change came through an obedient layman and a converted eunuch—after a meeting on a dirt road in the desert.

B. Preachers—Apollos the
   Evangelist (18:24-28)

24. And a certain Jew named Apollos, born at Alexandria, an eloquent man, and mighty in the scriptures, came to Ephesus.

25. This man was instructed in the way of the Lord; and being fervent in the spirit, he spake and taught diligently the things of the Lord, knowing only the baptism of John.

26. And he began to speak boldly in the synagogue: whom

when Aquila and Priscilla had heard, they took him unto them, and expounded unto him the way of God more perfectly.

27. And when he was disposed to pass into Achaia, the brethren wrote, exhorting the disciples to receive him: who, when he was come, helped them much which had believed through grace:

28. For he mightily convinced the Jews, and that publickly, shewing by the scriptures that Jesus was Christ.

In our study about declaring the Word, Apollos represents for us the clergy. Like Paul, he was highly educated (v. 24). Unlike Paul—who was "brought up in this city [Jerusalem] at the feet of Gamaliel, and taught according to the perfect manner of the law of the fathers" (22:3)—Apollos' education had been steeped in the Hellenist, or Greek, studies of his home city of Alexandria in Egypt. His ideal teacher would have been the great Jewish philosopher of Alexandria, Philo Judaeus, who would greatly influence the Coptic church in the years to come.

There are only a few verses that mention Apollos and his ministry. When he arrived on the scene in Ephesus (18:24), the Word tells us that he "spake and taught diligently the things of the Lord" (v. 25). But his message was flawed—he knew nothing of the baptism of the Holy Spirit or water baptism in the name of the Father, Son, and Holy Ghost. What he knew about Jesus had been learned as a disciple (or a student) of John the Baptist.

Like Paul, Apollos would be considered a "doctor of the law" and an authority on both the Jewish Scriptures and the teachings of Christ. Aquila and Priscilla had learned about the Lord from the lips of the great apostle Paul himself while he stayed at their house in Corinth and they made tents together (18:3). When they heard the eloquent man speak, they realized that he had not heard the whole story, and so they took him aside and instructed him. To Apollos' credit, he did not allow his intellect and education to hinder his learning more about Jesus from common lay folks like Aquila and Priscilla.

In the first four chapters of Paul's first letter to the Corinthian church, the apostle addressed a problem that had arisen in the young church. After his departure, there had arisen a conflict between several religious parties at Corinth. The apostle said, "Every one of you saith, I am of Paul; and I of Apollos; and I of Cephas [Peter]; and I of Christ. Is Christ divided? was Paul crucified for you? or were ye baptized in the name of Paul?" (1 Corinthians 1:12, 13).

Apollos too would have none of this hero worship, and when the Corinthian church asked that he come back for an evangelistic trip, he refused. Paul said diplomatically, "As touching our brother Apollos, I greatly desired him to come unto you with the brethren: but his will was not at all to come at this time; but he will come when he shall have convenient time" (1 Corinthians 16:12).

Through the years we find Apollos always loyal to his friend and (through Aquila and Priscilla) his mentor. Little is known of Apollos except that he was a scholar, a gentleman, an eloquent minister of the gospel, a fellow laborer, and loyal companion and friend. But, then, what more could you ask of any man than that?

C. Teachers—Aquila and Priscilla (18:26)

26. And he began to speak boldly in the synagogue: whom when Aquila and Priscilla had heard, they took him unto them, and expounded unto him the way of God more perfectly.

How often, as a young preacher, it has been necessary for an older saint in the church to take me home with them for Sunday dinner and "expound unto [me] the way of God more perfectly." I found that all the lessons I learned in college and seminary were insufficient to prepare me for "the real world," and those who "had been there" could keep me from making a lot of mistakes.

Aquila and Priscilla are outstanding role models for lay men and women who would serve God to the fullest. As they made their living by making tents, they sat at the feet of the great apostle Paul and learned about Jesus. Their home was opened to him while he was in Corinth (Acts 18:3), and seemed to have been used as a house church whenever they moved from city to city (Romans 16:3-5). It even seems from the words of Paul that they had gone so far as to risk their very lives in the protection of the man of God.

I am especially impressed that they were people who didn't need to have the limelight. Paul took them to Ephesus and then left them there while he went on to Jerusalem (Acts 18:18, 19), when surely they had expected to go with him. When Apollos needed further teaching,

they did not criticize him, nor embarrass him, but "they took him unto them[selves] [Greek, *proslambano*] and expounded [Greek, *ektithemi*, "set forth" or "explained"] to him the way of God more perfectly" (v. 26).

They took the evangelist aside quietly, or took him home with them, and gently, as befitted his standing and office, told him about the baptism of the Holy Spirit and baptism in water in the name of the Father, Son, and Holy Spirit.

It is interesting to note that in an age when women "belonged" to their fathers or husbands and were literally their property, Aquila and Priscilla are never mentioned alone. They are always seen as a team—and in three of the six references to them by name in Scripture, Priscilla (or Prisca as she is sometimes known) is named ahead of her husband, reversing the normal order for listing a man and wife (Acts 18:18; Romans 16:3; 2 Timothy 4:19).

What Christian virtue did Apollos most demonstrate when he allowed a lay couple in the church to teach him?

II. UPHOLD THE WORD
    (Deuteronomy 4:2; 12:32; Psalms 12:6; 18:30; Proverbs 30:5, 6)

A. The Finished Word
    (Deuteronomy 4:2; 12:32)

(Deuteronomy 12:32 is not included in the printed text.)

2. Ye shall not add unto the word which I command you, neither shall ye diminish ought from it, that ye may keep the commandments of the Lord your God

which I command you.

There are a number of ways that God reveals Himself—through nature and creation itself (Romans 1:20), through the heavens (Psalm 33:6), through the Holy Spirit internally (John 14:26) and by way of prophecy (Hebrews 1:1), through the life of His Son (John 1:18), and finally through the entirety of the Holy Scriptures (John 5:39). There is nothing, however, that can replace the written Word, nor surplant it. The Bible is the final statement of the eternal God as to His all-encompassing plans for mankind.

The words "Ye shall not add unto the word . . . neither shall ye diminish ought from it" are in complete agreement with John the Revelator, who completed the writing of the Scriptures with these words: "For I testify unto every man that heareth the words of the prophecy of this book, If any man shall add unto these things, God shall add unto him the plagues that are written in this book: and if any man shall take away from the words of the book of this prophecy, God shall take away his part out of the book of life, and out of the holy city, and from the things which are written in this book" (Revelation 22:18, 19).

Though the Word of God was written by men, its author is the Holy Spirit. "For the prophecy came not in old time by the will of man: but holy men of God spake as they were moved by the Holy Ghost" (2 Peter 1:21). The ideas contained in the Word are the ideas of God, for "no prophecy of the scripture is of any private [or one's own] interpretation [or idea]" (1:20). God will not allow any man to contaminate the purity of the Word, or the perfection of the Word by taking away from it or adding to it.

B. The Perfect Word
(Psalms 12:6; 18:30)

(Psalm 12:6 is not included in the printed text.)

30. As for God, his way is perfect: the word of the Lord is tried: he is a buckler to all those that trust in him.

Someone has said that if we can believe the first words of the Bible, "In the beginning God created the heaven and the earth" (Genesis 1:1), we can believe all the rest of it. How true, for if God created all things from nothing, is anything too hard for Him? Satan and his forces have begun with those first words about the Creation and sought to destroy mankind's confidence in the truth and trustworthiness of Scripture.

If the evolutionist can take away Creation, then there is no Garden of Eden, no Adam and Eve, no fall from grace, and no sin to be dealt with. However, the perfect Word is adamant that God did create man "in his own image" (1:27) and sinless and that our first parents fell from favor with their Creator and committed sin. It is plain that "by one man [Adam] sin entered into the world, and death by sin" (Romans 5:12), and through Adam "all have sinned, and come short of the glory of God" (3:23).

If there is no sure Word—if all things are relative and every man is left to his own devices, and each does "that which [is] right in his own eyes" (Judges 21:25)—there can be only confusion and chaos.

But God has not left us alone. He declares through His Son Christ Jesus, "Lo, I am with you alway"

(Matthew 28:20). We know that "his work is perfect" (Deuteronomy 32:4), and we can know the "perfect will of God" (Romans 12:2, *NKJV*).

C. The Pure Word
(Proverbs 30:5, 6)

5. Every word of God is pure: he is a shield unto them that put their trust in him.

6. Add thou not unto his words, lest he reprove thee, and thou be found a liar.

The Word of God is not only finished and perfect, but it is also pure (see Ephesians 5:26). One of the words for *pure* in the Greek (*eilikrines*) is also defined as "genuine" or "sincere." The Latin for "sincere" is *sine cera*, meaning "without wax." It is said that in the ancient marketplaces cracked pottery was often stuffed with wax to make them appear usable. However, when the buyer took the vessel home and placed it over the fire, the wax melted and the broken pot was revealed for what it really was—worthless.

The Word of God is pure and undefiled. Though it has passed through many translations and hands on its journey down nearly 2,000 years of time, the Holy Spirit has not allowed it to be defiled or destroyed. Satan attacks the purity of the Scriptures, for he knows that if he can prove any portion of the Word less than the whole truth, the enemies of God can drive a stake through the heart of the gospel and destroy it in the eyes of the world.

Why is it important for us to believe in the Creation story in the first chapter of the Book of Genesis?

III. TEACH RIGHT DOCTRINE
(2 Timothy 4:1-5)

Just as there are three (sometimes distinct and sometimes not) groups within the church that proclaim the gospel—the professionals (evangelists and pastors), the selected or elected local church officials (deacons), and the membership of the church (lay men and women)—so there are also three groups to whom the church ministers its teaching: the converted who make up the church body, the backslider, and the lost who have not yet been reached with the gospel.

Each of these groups must be ministered to in a manner unique to their particular needs from the Word. We will call these proclamations: teaching the church, reaching the backslider, and preaching to sinners.

A. Teaching the Church (vv. 1, 2)

1. I charge thee therefore before God, and the Lord Jesus Christ, who shall judge the quick and the dead at his appearing and his kingdom;

2. Preach the word; be instant in season, out of season; reprove, rebuke, exhort with all longsuffering and doctrine.

The task of teaching in the church is first of all the responsibility of the pastor. Paul told the Ephesian church, "[God]" gave . . . pastors and teachers [or pastor-teachers]; for the perfecting of the saints, for the work of the ministry [of the saints], for the edifying [building; Greek, *oikodome*, from *oikos*, house] of the body of Christ" (Ephesians 4:11, 12). The pastor is to train and build up (as a carpenter builds a house) the lay men and women that they may be the ministers.

The pastor must employ the Word of God to comfort the bereaved and to assure those who grieve that the Lord is coming again (1 Thessalonians 4:18). He or she must lead the new converts into a systematic study of the Word for themselves (2 Timothy 2:15), encouraging them to leave the basic things and press on toward spiritual perfection (Ephesians 4:13-15; Hebrews 6:1). He is to *exhort* (Greek, *parakaleo*, "to beseech, comfort, guide with tenderness") with all kindness and love (Acts 27:22; 2 Corinthians 9:5; Hebrews 3:13). And he is to reprove and rebuke where necessary for the health and life of the local church and the individual member.

Since the pastor cannot do all things by himself, he is to train others to teach and minister the gospel (2 Timothy 2:2). He is to encourage the laity in their task of winning souls, as well as direct the ministry of deacons and teachers within the church (1 Peter 5:1-3).

B. Reaching the Backslider
   (vv. 3, 4)

3. For the time will come when they will not endure sound doctrine; but after their own lusts shall they heap to themselves teachers, having itching ears;

4. And they shall turn away their ears from the truth, and shall be turned unto fables.

Timothy was instructed by Paul to expect that some would fall away from the Lord and drift back into the world. It is not the teachers who are spoken of as having itching ears but those who have fallen away.

The "itching ears" refers to the very human desire to hear "something new"—the sensational. Luke said the people in Athens gathered regularly on Mars Hill just to hear "some new thing" (Acts 17:21). When the church was young, many teachers "tickled the ears" with their false doctrine and led away entire households from the true faith (see Titus 1:10, 11). Things have changed very little in that regard—for the cults, the Eastern religions, as well as the modern gods of pleasure, ease, and amusement still teach their false doctrines and draw men and women away from their faith in Christ.

In the Old Testament there were "soothsayers," people who spoke soothing, pleasant-sounding words, and "wise men," who deemed their wisdom greater than anyone else's. But in whatever clothing they come—they bring something new for "itching ears," and the weak fall away.

C. Preaching to Sinners (v. 5)

5. But watch thou in all things, endure afflictions, do the work of an evangelist, make full proof of thy ministry.

Is it possible that we have the preaching and teaching ministries backward? The church is to be taught and sinners are to be preached to; thus, it appears that the preachers should be teaching and the teachers preaching. That is, the laity are the "chosen generation, a royal priesthood, an holy nation, a peculiar people; that ye should shew forth the praises of him who hath called you out of darkness into his marvellous light" (1 Peter 2:9).

Jesus said that all Spirit-filled

believers would be "witnesses" (Acts 1:8), and all the followers of Jesus were told to "go ye therefore, and teach all nations, baptizing them in the name of the Father, and of the Son, and of the Holy Ghost" (Matthew 28:19). In response to this command, the lay men and women of the early church went "from house to house" and the Lord gave them converts every day (Acts 2:46, 47).

Why does the church have several different kinds of teachers?

REVIEW QUESTIONS

1. Why did Aquila and Priscilla think they were qualified to teach Apollos?

2. What do we mean when we say the Word of God is a finished work?

3. Are "prophecies" received from the Spirit on a level of authority with the Bible?

4. What is the pastor's first responsibility to the local church?

5. What kind of teaching draws people away from God?

GOLDEN TEXT HOMILY

"PREACH THE WORD; BE INSTANT IN SEASON, OUT OF SEASON; REPROVE, REBUKE, EXHORT WITH ALL LONGSUFFERING AND DOCTRINE" (2 Timothy 4:2).

Upon approaching one's departure from this life, it is natural to become more intensely concerned about our eternal destiny—and that of others. Hence, Paul was not only interested about Timothy's own ministry, but he was also concerned about those whom Timothy's ministry would touch. So, for the fatherly advice Paul gave to his son in the ministry, these were his instructions:

Preach the Word. This is our accountability—to preach the Word. It is the preached Word of God that He promises will not return to Him without results (Isaiah 55:11). Jesus said, "They [the words that He has spoken] are spirit, and they are life" (John 6:63).

Be instant in season and out of season. The minister is to perform his calling when he feels like it and when he doesn't; when people listen and when they don't. The King's business demands diligence and faithfulness. Souls are committed to our charge. In fact, a woe is pronounced upon those who refuse His call (1 Corinthians 9:16). He accepts no excuses for our negligence.

Reprove and rebuke. Those who indulge in lifestyles not according to His Word need to be reminded there is present and future judgment if not forgiven. Problems arise in homes, churches, and communities if discipline is compromised or absent altogether.

Exhort, encourage, lift up, and strengthen. Only when sound doctrine is proclaimed can these be accomplished. And it must be done with love and patience.

The reason for this advice becomes evident in the verses that follow. Times of deception are ahead. Our only protection is that we hide the Word of God in our hearts so that we might not sin against Him (Psalm 119:11). Let us take heed.—**Fred H. Whisman, (Lt. Col.), Group II Chaplain, Civil Air Patrol, Chattanooga, Tennessee**

SENTENCE SERMONS

DECLARING THE WORD is the privilege and responsibility of every believer.

—Selected

TO TEACH is to learn.

—Joseph Joubert

A TEACHER affects eternity; he can never tell where his influence stops.

—Henry Gardner Adams

ILLUMINATING THE LESSON

Tribute to a Great Teacher

Teachers are the great unsung heroes and heroines of the world. Whatever we have achieved in our lives has been the result of the teaching we received at home, at school, at work, in our environs, and at church. Through the years I have been blessed to have had some of the greatest teachers enter my life, sometimes for only a short time, to nurture me along. The names of many of those teachers have long been forgotten, and I cannot quote verbatim a single bit of wisdom from any of them. But the sum total of the wisdom which they imparted to me has molded and shaped my life—they gave me a well-rounded education.

One teacher in my life stands out above all the rest. He taught me college Spanish, and a whole lot more. The passing years have reduced the Spanish to a few scattered and simple phrases, but the "more" which I learned from Dr. Charles Beach will never be forgotten.

Charles Beach and his wife, Lois, both taught a full schedule of English and foreign languages, but always had time to visit the city hospitals and comfort the sick. He had a goal of witnessing to at least one lost person for Christ each day. He turned that personal vision into the "Pioneers for Christ," a college witness team that has carried the gospel around the world. He helped found and greatly influenced the Lay Ministries Department and served on its national board for many years.

If I could live my life again, and know what I know now, I think I would be a college professor and model my life after that of my mentor and friend, Dr. Charles R. Beach, teacher exemplary.

DAILY BIBLE READINGS

M. Commanded to Teach.
   Deuteronomy 4:5-14
T. Teaching the Scriptures.
   2 Chronicles 17:3-10
W. The Word Reveals Christ.
   Luke 24:25-32
T. The Word Edifies.
   Ephesians 4:11-16
F. Exemplify the Word.
   1 Peter 3:8-16
S. Warning About the Word.
   Revelation 22:16-21

The Word Purifies

Study Text: Psalm 119:1-16

Objective: To learn that God cleanses believers with His Word and seek to live a pure life.

Time: Scholars differ on the date of Psalm 119, but a consensus of opinions favor the Davidic kingdom period 1000—961 B.C.

Place: The place of the writing of Psalm 119 is uncertain, but probably Jerusalem.

Golden Text: "Wherewithal shall a young man cleanse his way? by taking heed thereto according to thy word" (Psalm 119:9).

Central Truth: Living according to God's Word brings purity of life.

Evangelism Emphasis: Christians must proclaim biblical morality to an immoral society.

PRINTED TEXT

Psalm 119:1. Blessed are the undefiled in the way, who walk in the law of the Lord.

2. Blessed are they that keep his testimonies, and that seek him with the whole heart.

3. They also do no iniquity: they walk in his ways.

4. Thou hast commanded us to keep thy precepts diligently.

5. O that my ways were directed to keep thy statutes!

6. Then shall I not be ashamed, when I have respect unto all thy commandments.

7. I will praise thee with uprightness of heart, when I shall have learned thy righteous judgments.

8. I will keep thy statutes: O forsake me not utterly.

9. Wherewithal shall a young man cleanse his way? by taking heed thereto according to thy word.

10. With my whole heart have I sought thee: O let me not wander from thy commandments.

11. Thy word have I hid in mine heart, that I might not sin against thee.

12. Blessed art thou, O Lord: teach me thy statutes.

13. With my lips have I declared all the judgments of thy mouth.

14. I have rejoiced in the way of thy testimonies, as much as in all riches.

15. I will meditate in thy precepts, and have respect unto thy ways.

16. I will delight myself in thy statutes: I will not forget thy word.

LESSON OUTLINE

I. BLESSINGS OF PURITY

   A. Blessed Are Those Who Seek the Lord

   B. Blessed Are Those Who Walk in the Word

   C. Blessed Are Those Who Keep the Word

II. DESIRE FOR PURITY

   A. Love the Lord and Honor His Word

   B. Praise the Lord and Keep His Word

III. DIRECTIONS FOR PURITY

   A. Thinking and Being

   B. Hiding and Sharing the Word

   C. Joy, Meditation, and Delight

LESSON EXPOSITION

INTRODUCTION

With this lesson, we begin a four-week study of Psalm 119. David, the shepherd-king, wrote many of the psalms, and some scholars attribute this one to David also. Although there are specific verses that could easily apply to periods and circumstances of David's life, there is no conclusive proof that he is the author of this psalm. However, comparisons of points in this psalm with David's life and writings can be illuminating. The poems and songs composed by David and others and played on the harp were called "psalms" (originally and literally, "twangings," for the twanging or plucking of the harp strings). The word has come to mean "songs."

Psalm 119 is the longest chapter in the longest book in the Bible. It is an acrostic poem, with every eighth verse beginning with a different letter of the Hebrew alphabet. Psalm 119 is dedicated to the praise of the Word of God and uses a synonym for the word *law* in all but two of its 176 verses. The sacred name of God is used 22 times, once for each letter of the Hebrew alphabet.

Some psalms make us want to clap our hands and dance: "Bless the Lord, O my soul: and all that is within me, bless his holy name. Bless the Lord, O my soul, and forget not all his benefits" (Psalm 103:1, 2).

When we read others, we feel the crushing weight of sin or despair and become sad and morose: "Behold, I was shapen in iniquity; and in sin did my mother conceive me. . . . Purge me with hyssop, and I shall be clean: wash me, and I shall be whiter than snow. . . . Hide thy face from my sins, and blot out all mine iniquities. Create in me a clean heart, O God; and renew a right spirit within me. Cast me not away from thy presence; and take not thy holy spirit from me. Restore unto me the joy of thy salvation" (Psalm 51:5, 7, 9-12).

Mostly, however, as with our own lives, the Psalms neither aspire to reach the peaks nor plumb the depths, but are concerned with Israel and the psalmist's everyday walk with God, the study of the Word of God, and worship in the Temple.

Many of the lyrics of songs and choruses we sing today are taken directly from the Psalms. Because Hebrew poetry does not always resemble what we think of as poetry, we may tend to forget that they were as stylized as the work of any poet or songwriter today.

I. BLESSINGS OF PURITY
(Psalm 119:1-4)

The converted person is "purified" by "obeying the truth through the Spirit" (1 Peter 1:22) and is cleansed by the Word of God (Psalm 119:9; John 15:3; 17:17; Ephesians 5:26). There are many Hebrew words that connote "pure" or "clean" (e.g., *tahor*, "clean or pure ceremonially, ethically, or morally"; *barar*, "clean as polished, purged, or washed"; *zak*, "clean, pure, righteous"; *paz* or *tsaraph*, "cleaned or made pure by refining, or smelting"). In the Greek, three different words are used for *pure*, (*katharos*, "made pure by refining, pruning, or cleaning"; *hagnos*, "holy, chaste, or sacred"; and *eilikrines*, from the root word for "sun," meaning "found pure or sincere when examined in sunlight").

In one way or another, all these words relate to sanctification (the separation or setting apart of something or someone for God's service—the sacred, as opposed to the profane). It is in the difference between the requirements of outward purity (rituals) and heart purity (the work of Christ, the Word, and the Holy Spirit in the converted man or woman) that Christianity differs most from Judaism. The availability of the spiritual cleansing promised in Zechariah 13:1 has never been appropriated by Israel as a nation, though the offer still stands: "In that day there shall be a fountain opened to the house of David and to the inhabitants of Jerusalem [and to all men] for sin and for uncleanness." The promise

was fulfilled in Jesus Christ—"But if we walk in the light, as he is in the light, we have fellowship one with another, and the blood of Jesus Christ his Son cleanseth us from all sin" (1 John 1:7).

It was because of sin (impurity) that mankind was separated from a holy God in the Garden of Eden: "By one man sin entered into the world, and death by sin" (Romans 5:12). "But God commendeth his love toward us, in that, while we were yet sinners, Christ died for us . . . For as by one man's disobedience many were made sinners, so by the obedience of one shall many be made righteous" (vv. 8, 19). The writer of the Epistle to the Hebrews explains our purification in this way: "We are sanctified through the offering of the body of Jesus Christ once for all" (10:10).

The internal holiness applied to our lives as Christians is purchased by Christ on the cross, made effective by the Word, and maintained by the Holy Spirit. This cleansing action (purity, sanctification) provides the only means by which we can be restored to fellowship with our righteous God. Jesus commanded us in His Sermon on the Mount, "Be ye therefore perfect, even as your Father which is in heaven is perfect" (Matthew 5:48). It is purity through the Word that is the main thrust of our study.

A. Blessed Are Those Who Seek the Lord (vv. 1, 2)

1. Blessed are the undefiled in the way, who walk in the law of the Lord.

2. Blessed are they that keep his testimonies, and that seek him with the whole heart.

In Psalm 63:1, David said, "Early

will I seek thee: my soul thirsteth for thee, my flesh longeth for thee in a dry and thirsty land, where no water is." He knew the benefits of seeking the Lord through His Word. He knew that real blessing, or happiness, comes only from God our Father, the fountain of all blessings. A pure man immersed in the pure Word of a pure God is the only lasting blessing to be obtained anywhere in this world. "Blessed" and "happy" are tied firmly together. The best blessings—and those that bring true happiness—are those which are spiritual and rooted in faith in Christ Jesus.

The Hebrew word *esher* and the Greek word *makarios*, both translated "blessed," could just as easily have been translated "happy." While in the English language *happiness* is derived from the word *hap* and relates to "happenstance" or luck, there is none of that connotation in these Bible words. This happiness is more aligned with *joy*, which comes only through the Word. Jesus said, "These things have I spoken unto you, that my joy might remain in you, and that your joy might be full" (John 15:11). Concerning our joy He also said, "And now come I to thee; and these things I speak in the world, that they might have my joy fulfilled in themselves" (17:13).

There is no peace, no joy, no happiness, and no blessing aside from God and His Word. Those who abide in the Word are blessed: "Blessed is the man that walketh not in the counsel of the ungodly, nor standeth in the way of sinners, nor sitteth in the seat of the scornful. But his delight is in the law of the Lord; and in his law doth he meditate day and night. And he shall be like a tree planted by the rivers of water, that bringeth forth his fruit in his season; his leaf also shall not wither; and whatsoever he doeth shall prosper" (Psalm 1:1-3).

B. Blessed Are Those Who Walk in the Word (v. 3)

3. They also do no iniquity: they walk in his ways.

The special promise of this verse is that those who walk in the ways of the Lord shall be kept from sin. Verse 11 of this psalm says, "Thy word have I hid in mine heart, that I might not sin against thee." When Jesus was tempted by Satan during His wilderness temptation, He turned to the Scriptures to rebut the devil (Luke 4:1-13). He knew that "the word of God is quick, and powerful, and sharper than any twoedged sword, piercing even to the dividing asunder of soul and spirit, and of the joints and marrow, and is a discerner of the thoughts and intents of the heart" (Hebrews 4:12). We too are directed to "take the helmet of salvation, and the sword of the Spirit, which is the word of God" (Ephesians 6:17).

We are directed to walk in the Word, as Jesus walked: "He that saith he abideth in him ought himself also to walk, even as he walked" (1 John 2:6). We are assured that if we walk like Jesus, we shall also walk with Jesus (Revelation 3:4).

If we walk in the Word, we walk under special protection: "He that dwelleth in the secret place of the most High shall abide under the shadow of the Almighty. . . . A thousand shall fall at thy side, and ten thousand at thy right hand; but it shall not come nigh thee. . . . There shall no evil befall thee. . . . For he shall give his angels charge over thee, to keep thee in all thy ways" (Psalm 91:1, 7, 10, 11; see also Isaiah 35:9).

Knowing that "the steps of a good man are ordered by the Lord" (Psalm 37:23), the psalmist requested of God, "Order my steps in thy word: and let not any iniquity have dominion over me" (119:133). We should all heed the words of the wise man, Solomon, the son of David, who admonished us: "My son, keep thy father's commandment, and forsake not the law of thy mother: Bind them continually upon thine heart, and tie them about thy neck. When thou goest, it shall lead thee; when thou sleepest, it shall keep thee; and when thou awakest, it shall talk with thee. For the commandment is a lamp; and the law is light; and reproofs of instruction are the way of life" (Proverbs 6:20-23).

C. Blessed Are Those Who Keep the Word (v. 4)

4. Thou hast commanded us to keep thy precepts diligently.

The Word of God is precious beyond imagination. There is no revelation of God and no way to know God without the Bible—no gospel (good news), no knowledge of the baby Jesus born in a manger, no record of the most holy life ever lived, no Cross, no resurrection, and no eternal life—for "the gospel of Christ . . . is the power of God unto salvation to every one that believeth" (Romans 1:16). Therefore we are not only to walk in the light of the Word, but we are also to "keep" (Hebrew, *shamar*, "guard, keep watch over as a sentinel") the "precepts diligently."

We are to place a guard over the Word entrusted to our keeping, for Satan would like to snatch it from us. Jesus said of some who had received the Word, "These are they by the way side, where the word is sown; but when they have heard, Satan cometh immediately, and taketh away the word that was sown in their hearts" (Mark 4:15).

Paul spoke of the same kind of "keeping" as is in our text above: "And the peace of God, which passeth all understanding, shall keep your hearts and minds through Christ Jesus" (Philippians 4:7). He then told how we are kept by the peace of God: "Finally, brethren, whatsoever things are true, whatsoever things are honest, whatsoever things are just, whatsoever things are pure, whatsoever things are lovely, whatsoever things are of good report; if there be any virtue, and if there be any praise, think on these things. Those things, which ye have both learned, and received, and heard, and seen in me, do: and the God of peace shall be with you" (vv. 8, 9).

Perhaps the most effective way to guard the Word is to make it so much a part of us that we cannot be separated from the Scripture in us. The prophet said, "Thy words were found, and I did eat them; and thy word was unto me the joy and rejoicing of mine heart" (Jeremiah 15:16). "And these words, which I command thee this day, shall be in thine heart" (Deuteronomy 6:6). "Let the word of Christ dwell in you richly in all wisdom" (Colossians 3:16).

Discuss some ways the Word of God keeps us from sinning.

II. DESIRE FOR PURITY
(Psalm 119:5-8)

The most straightforward demand made upon us to live a pure life was made by the apostle Peter: "Wherefore gird up the loins of your mind . . . not fashioning yourselves according to the former lusts in your ignorance: but as he which hath called you is holy, so be ye holy in all manner of conversation; because it is written, Be ye holy; for I am holy" (1 Peter 1:13-16). Two things stand out in these verses. First, we are to practice holy living (*conversation,* "lifestyle") because the God we serve is holy. Second, the way to holiness is found in the restructuring of the mind ("gird up the loins of your mind"). The illustration Peter used of girding up the loins was familiar to his readers. This meant lifting the hem of a robe so it wouldn't drag in the mud and mire. Then a belt was tied around the waist to hold the robe up.

Likewise, the child of God is to lift the pure mind from the mire and sin of the world and "gird it" tightly so it doesn't slip back and become soiled (see Ecclesiastes 9:8; Revelation 3:4). Paul told the Ephesians that the church (including, of course, the individuals who constitute it) is bought by the blood of Christ, "that he might sanctify and cleanse it with the washing of water by the word" (5:26).

A. Love the Lord and Honor His Word (vv. 5, 6)

5. O that my ways were directed to keep thy statutes!
6. Then shall I not be ashamed, when I have respect unto all thy commandments.
So precious is the law of God that the psalmist desired to "keep" ("to guard, watch over, as guarding treasure)" the statutes of the Lord. Though one must return to the original language to get the full effect of his words, the psalmist was saying in essence, "Oh that my ways (the path I take, my manner of life, my habits) would all work together to guard as a great treasure the precious Word of God."

To desire purity is to desire the Lord *and* His Word. Jesus said, "If a man love me, he will keep my words: and my Father will love him, and we will come unto him, and make our abode with him" (John 14:23). The apostle John would later say that we could not with truth say we loved the Lord if we failed to do what He told us to do (1 John 2:4, 5). In Psalm 138:2, David said, "Thou hast magnified thy word above all thy name"—or better translated "You have made Your name and Your Word great."

It is impossible to separate God and His Word. We cannot love one and despise the other or fail to honor one or the other. The written Word of God (the Bible—both the Old Testament and the New Testament together) and the incarnate Word (the Son of God—the Logos) both were given to reveal the love of God for a fallen world.

In a time when there is little respect for God and religion, for parents, teachers, law-enforcement officers, and others in general, the Word of God demands nothing less than our wholehearted respect and honor. Like Paul, we must declare, "I am not ashamed of the gospel of Christ: for it is the power of God unto salvation to every one that believeth" (Romans 1:16).

Love and the law of God are inseparable; three times in this 119th psalm, the psalmist said he loved God's Word (vv. 97, 113, 163). In fact, the Word is called the "law," and love is a fulfillment of the law. To love God is the first commandment (Matthew 22:37-40), and to love one's neighbor is to fulfill the "royal law" (James 2:8).

Verse 6 of Psalm 119 may also be translated, "I will not be put to shame, when my eyes are transfixed on Your Word." How wonderful it is to know that the heart of our purity and right relationship with God is His Word—the written Word and the incarnate Word.

Here, and in several other places in the Psalms, the Hebrew word *buwsh* is rendered "ashamed." One of its meanings is "to turn pale," as opposed to being "ruddy" and healthy. One could be said to have "lost his glow" when he is ashamed.

B. Praise the Lord and Keep His Word (vv. 7, 8)

7. I will praise thee with uprightness of heart, when I shall have learned thy righteous judgments.

8. I will keep thy statutes: O forsake me not utterly.

The greatest praise we could ever extend to God is to love Him and live for Him. The psalmist said that when he had learned God's Word, he would praise Him "with uprightness of heart." This conveys that holy living is praise to the Lord. Paul expressed this same concept in his letter to the Philippians: "Being filled with the fruits of righteousness, which are by Jesus Christ, unto the glory and praise of God" (1:11).

Jesus was from the Jewish tribe of Judah; *Judah* means "praise." Deuteronomy 10:21 says, "He [God] is thy praise." When Israel was threatened by the Ammonites and Moabites, longtime enemies, Jehoshaphat and the people sought help from God. God promised them He would deliver them without their having to fight. They believed God and went into battle praising the Lord. "When they began to sing and to praise," God gave them the victory (2 Chronicles 20:22).

Praise is the expressed happiness of a born-again people. It is quite impossible to be found, forgiven, freed, and favored by the God of the universe and not give vent somehow to our feelings of joy. The psalmist did not try to hide his emotions when he said, "Thy statutes have been my songs" (Psalm 119:54). He meant that he had put the law to music . . . to use as praise!

Someone said, "Let me make the songs of a country, and let who will make the laws." People can be moved with music who could not be driven by law. When we accept our relationship to the commandments of God and determine that they are God's best for us, we too will begin to sing and praise.

Why is it important for the Christian to "guard" the Word?

III. DIRECTIONS FOR PURITY (Psalm 119:9-16)

A. Thinking and Being (vv. 9, 10)

9. Wherewithal shall a young man cleanse his way? by taking heed thereto according to thy word.

10. With my whole heart have I sought thee: O let me not wander from thy commandments.

The early years of a man's life are

those filled with the most temptation to go wrong. The psalmist, knowing what it was to be a youth with the normal temptations of youth, determined that while those around him might fail the Lord, he would live an exemplary godly life. David was an excellent example of the sentiment of these verses. Because he began to trust God so early in life, he was able to face the giant Goliath on the battlefield, to slay him, and to win a mighty victory for the army of Israel—while he was still a teenager.

When Israel desired a king in the time of the judges, the people clamored for a big, tall man named Saul. They wanted Saul to be their king—but God wanted David. Saul was a big man who acted like a little boy. David was a boy who lived like a big man. The Word says, "The Lord hath sought him a man after his own heart" (1 Samuel 13:14). Then the Lord said at the end of His search, "I have found David my servant" (Psalm 89:20).

David's son, the wise Solomon, said, "Remember now thy Creator in the days of thy youth, while the evil days come not, nor the years draw nigh, when thou shalt say, I have no pleasure in them" (Ecclesiastes 12:1). When a young man or woman makes a decision to serve God, the question arises as to how they shall cleanse their ways—that is, how can a youth live holy in a soiled world? The answer: "By taking heed thereto according to thy [God's] word."

The mind is the control center for one's actions. What an individual thinks determines what he does. "For as he thinketh in his heart, so is he" (Proverbs 23:7). I am what I think, but not necessarily what I think I am. If I think I am Napoleon Bonaparte, it does not mean I am Napoleon Bonaparte; but it does mean I am suffering from mental delusions. I am not necessarily what I think I am, but I am what I think.

Repeated thoughts, good or bad, mold the character for good or bad; and the longer one holds an erroneous idea, the harder it is to break that pattern of thinking. The older an unconverted person gets, the less the chances are that he or she will ever accept the Lord as Savior. Some years ago, before the highways were paved, a sign was seen at the forks of a road which read, "Choose your rut carefully. You will be in it for a long time!" It is important what youth think, for often they continue to think it for a lifetime.

The deadliest sins—as well as the greatest actions for good—begin in the mind! The primary concern of many of the Jews was with the outward appearance. But Jesus explained, "Ye have heard that it was said by them of old time, Thou shalt not commit adultery: But I say unto you, That whosoever looketh on a woman to lust after her hath committed adultery with her already in his heart" (Matthew 5:27, 28).

If one covets, he is a thief. If he is angry enough to kill, he is a murderer. And the truth of the Word of God is this: If one covets long enough, he will steal. If the anger is intense enough and remains long enough, he will kill. Therefore we plead with our youth, "Keep thy heart [mind] with all diligence; for out of it are the issues of life" (Proverbs 4:23).

Jesus set the perfect example for youth. He "increased in wisdom [mentally] and stature [physically], and in favour with God [spiritually] and man [socially]" (Luke 2:52).

B. Hiding and Sharing the Word (vv. 11-13)

11. Thy word have I hid in mine heart, that I might not sin against thee.
12. Blessed art thou, O Lord: teach me thy statutes.
13. With my lips have I declared all the judgments of thy mouth.

Jesus said, "The kingdom of heaven is like unto treasure hid in a field; the which when a man hath found, he hideth, and for joy thereof goeth and selleth all that he hath, and buyeth that field" (Matthew 13:44). The psalmist used an expression much like that in the parable Jesus was telling. He said, "Thy word have I hid in mine heart." He had found the Word of God to be such a treasure that he had hid it away as one would hide pearls and diamonds. He tucked it safely away where it could never be stolen. But though it couldn't be taken away by any means, he was willing to give it away free to any who would take it: "With my lips have I declared all the judgments of thy mouth."

There is a "secret place of the most High" (Psalm 91:1) where anything we commit to God is safely guarded by Him. Like an exceptionally fortified strongbox at the bank, we can stash there our most prized possessions—our marriage covenant, the love and respect of family members for each other, our assurances of salvation, and so many other precious things. But the paradoxes of Christianity are never more visible than here in this celestial bank. For the things we

have stored there for protection are the things we want most to share with others.

Some things can be kept only if they are given away! The best way to keep the Word of God is to share it! The Word of God, like the love of God, grows most when given away!

The psalmist pleaded, "Teach me thy statutes" (119:12). We don't know how old the songwriter was when he penned these lines. Maybe he was still a youth. Or maybe he was aged and physically ailing. But this we do know: One is never too young or too old to learn more about the Word of God.

C. Joy, Meditation, and Delight (vv. 14-16)

14. I have rejoiced in the way of thy testimonies, as much as in all riches.
15. I will meditate in thy precepts, and have respect unto thy ways.
16. I will delight myself in thy statutes: I will not forget thy word.

Has there ever been a time in your life when you failed the Lord so miserably you lost your Christian joy? There was a time in David's life when he had committed a great sin and lost the sweetness of his fellowship with Jehovah. When Nathan the prophet confronted him with the words, "Thou art the man" (2 Samuel 12:7) and the sure knowledge that his newborn son would not live, David was a man without joy.

He then confessed his sin and cried, "Create in me a clean heart, O God; and renew a right spirit within me. Cast me not away from thy presence; and take not thy holy spirit from me. Restore unto me the joy of thy salvation" (Psalm 51:10-12).

Sin takes away the presence of the Holy Spirit and steals our joy. Since joy is a fruit of the Spirit (Galatians 5:22), when the Spirit departs, so does our joy (see Romans 14:17). It is interesting to find that the "disciples were filled with joy, and with the Holy Ghost" (Acts 13:52; see also 1 Thessalonians 1:6). Sin is the only thing that can rob us of our joy in the Lord, for He said, "These things have I spoken unto you, that my joy might remain in you, and that your joy might be full" (John 15:11). He also said, "I will see you again, and your heart shall rejoice, and your joy no man taketh from you" (16:22).

Joy belongs to us by the bucketful. The prophet told us, "Therefore with joy shall ye draw water out of the wells of salvation" (Isaiah 12:3). The psalmist said he would meditate on God's precepts, and whoever does finds delight in it.

How may we as God's children lose our joy?

REVIEW QUESTIONS

1. Who wrote the Psalms, and on what musical instrument were they first played?
2. Why is it important that Christians live pure lives?
3. Why does Satan want to take the Word of God away from you?
4. What Jewish tribe was Jesus from, and what does its name mean?
5. What is the only thing that can take your joy from you?

GOLDEN TEXT HOMILY

"WHEREWITHAL SHALL A

YOUNG MAN CLEANSE HIS WAY? BY TAKING HEED THERETO ACCORDING TO THY WORD" (Psalm 119:9).

Purity seems to be a word that is openly mocked and publicly scorned. In our world, purity is not only considered old-fashioned but also useless and cruel. Yet thousands reap daily the grim harvest of immorality, impurity, and unrestrained living. One young person said of his sickness, "It's not my fault—the government should do something."

God has our best interest at heart. He knows how life can be lived so as to maximize joy, fulfillment, and true happiness. His Word is our guide to freedom, not a rule book of mournful living. It is sad that many have the mistaken notion that God is only interested in restricting our activities and spoiling our fun—when in fact, He joyfully wants our lives to be brimming over with life at its fullest.

To accomplish this, God requires that we say no to certain activities and behaviors. We must understand that His *no* to us has in it protection and provision—protection from harmful, destructive, and sometimes subtle invasions from the enemy of our souls. He calls for purity to protect us. There is also provision in each no—a provision of His grace for a better choice, a provision for a higher level, a provision for deeper joy. We must trust His protection and receive His provision.

Thank God for His Word. It is not an obsolete ranting of a disconnected being; it is rather a living love letter from a faithful and compassionate Father who pleads for us to follow purity and find fullness of joy—**Michael S. Stewart, Senior Pastor, First Assembly of God, Raleigh, North Carolina**

EVANGELISM APPLICATION

CHRISTIANS MUST PROCLAIM BIBLICAL MORALITY TO AN IMMORAL SOCIETY.

The laws of God, which some have found severely binding and chafing, were themselves turned into songs by the psalmist. The yoke that some found so heavy was lightened by praise. The children of God are able to not only live by the commandments of God but also to live happily and rejoice that they have been given the law.

I heard a story once about two young ladies who worked together at a department store during their last year of high school. When they graduated, they went their separate ways. Several years had gone by when they just happened to meet on the street one day.

After exchanging greetings, one asked the other, "Are you still working?"

"No, I don't work anymore," came the response. "I got married!"

Some would laugh . . . but what a paean to love! Though she probably worked as hard or harder than her friend who labored every day in the department store—whatever work this young wife did was a "labor of love." Because she loved her husband so much, she was willing to give all her time to her home and family with joy.

Because we love God, we want to please Him. Whatever He asks of us we will do—and sing while we do it. There is no labor there—just love!

ILLUMINATING THE LESSON

The ermine is a special kind of weasel. Though it looks much like any other weasel, the fur of the ermine turns yellow-white in winter—all but the tip of the tail which remains black. The fur is beautiful and the animals are rare, thus during medieval times the wearing of ermine was restricted to royalty. Later it would become a part of the robes of high judge, symbolizing the majesty of the law.

The ermine is proud of his beautiful fur and works hard to keep it spotless. Hunters, knowing the pride of the ermine, spread filth around the entrance to its den while the animal is away. When the little creature returns to his home and finds the doorway smeared with slime, he refuses to enter and stands with his back to the place of safety and fights the hunter's dogs to his death—he would rather have a bloody coat than a dirty one! He would rather die than soil himself.

Paul advised Timothy, his son in the Lord, "Let no man despise thy youth; but be thou an example of the believers, in word, in conversation, in charity, in spirit, in faith, in purity" (1 Timothy 4:12). The psalmist asked, "How can a young man cleanse his way? By taking heed according to Your word" (119:9, *NKJV*).

DAILY BIBLE READINGS

M. Passion for Purity.
Psalm 119:137-144
T. Guard Against Immorality.
Proverbs 6:20-29
W. God's Word Is Pure.
Proverbs 30:3-9
T. The Word Sanctifies.
John 17:6-19
F. Right Thinking.
Philippians 4:4-9
S. Pure Wisdom. James 3:13-18

The Word Guides

Study Text: Psalm 119:25-40, 105-112

Objective: To know that God has a purpose for our lives and follow His plan.

Golden Text: "Thy word is a lamp unto my feet, and a light unto my path" (Psalm 119:105).

Time: Scholars differ on the date of Psalm 119, but a consensus of opinions favor the Davidic kingdom period 1000-961 B.C.

Place: The place of the writing of Psalm 119 is uncertain, but probably Jerusalem.

Central Truth: God's Word gives direction to our lives.

Evangelism Emphasis: The Word directs the Christian to lead others to Christ.

PRINTED TEXT

Psalm 119:25. My soul cleaveth unto the dust: quicken thou me according to thy word.

26. I have declared my ways, and thou heardest me: teach me thy statutes.

27. Make me to understand the way of thy precepts: so shall I talk of thy wondrous works.

28. My soul melteth for heaviness: strengthen thou me according unto thy word.

29. Remove from me the way of lying: and grant me thy law graciously.

30. I have chosen the way of truth: thy judgments have I laid before me.

31. I have stuck unto thy testimonies: O Lord, put me not to shame.

32. I will run the way of thy commandments, when thou shalt enlarge my heart.

33. Teach me, O Lord, the way of thy statutes; and I shall keep it unto the end.

34. Give me understanding, and I shall keep thy law; yea, I shall observe it with my whole heart.

35. Make me go in the path of thy commandments; for therein do I delight.

36. Incline my heart unto thy testimonies, and not to covetousness.

37. Turn away mine eyes from beholding vanity; and quicken thou me in thy way.

38. Stablish thy word unto thy servant, who is devoted to thy fear.

39. Turn away my reproach which I fear: for thy judgments are good.

40. Behold, I have longed after thy precepts: quicken me in thy righteousness.

105. Thy word is a lamp unto my feet, and a light unto my path.

106. I have sworn, and I will

perform it, that I will keep thy righteous judgments.

107. I am afflicted very much: quicken me, O Lord, according unto thy word.

108. Accept, I beseech thee, the freewill-offerings of my mouth, O Lord, and teach me thy judgments.

109. My soul is continually in my hand: yet do I not forget thy law.

110. The wicked have laid a snare for me: yet I erred not from thy precepts.

111. Thy testimonies have I taken as an heritage for ever: for they are the rejoicing of my heart.

112. I have inclined mine heart to perform thy statutes alway, even unto the end.

LESSON OUTLINE

I. NEED FOR GUIDANCE

    A. In Times of Despair

    B. When We Need Strength and Understanding

    C. In Times of Drudgery

II. PRAYER FOR GUIDANCE

III. DETERMINE TO FOLLOW

    A. Follow After Light

    B. Follow After Life

    C. Follow After Law

    D. Follow After Longevity

    E. Follow After the Lord

LESSON EXPOSITION

INTRODUCTION

David prayed to the Lord: "For thy name's sake lead me, and guide me" (Psalm 31:3). Everything we do as Christians—whether good or bad—reflects on the character of God (His character is revealed in His name). When we sin and miss the mark of our calling, we soil the good name of God. For that reason, the psalmist was careful to ask for God to lead and guide him.

There are three special types of guidance provided by the Word of God: the guidance that leads us to salvation, the guidance that takes us through this life with its many pitfalls, and the guidance that leads us home to be with Jesus eternally. The Word is active in all of these (1 Samuel 2:9; Psalm 73:24; Colossians 3:2; John 14:3; Jude 24). Then, there are also special times of guidance in which the Word of God works, such as times of despair when we are in need of help far beyond our own strength. It is then that God's Spirit seems the most precious.

We also need personalized and specific guidance when we witness to our family and friends in order to win them to Christ.

There are other extremely critical times when guidance is especially necessary: in the selection of a life mate, in choosing and training for a vocation, in the rearing and discipline of our children to assure that they choose to serve God, and in numerous other choices which we must make. In the following passages, it seems that the psalmist's special cry for guidance comes from times of despair, troubled times, hurting times. It is this guidance which we will study today.

I. NEED FOR GUIDANCE
(Psalm 119:25-32)

A. In Times of Despair (vv. 25, 26)

25. My soul cleaveth unto the dust: quicken thou me according to thy word.

26. I have declared my ways, and thou heardest me: teach me thy statutes.

The Lord said, "Call upon me in the day of trouble" (Psalm 50:15). Some people thought once they were saved, there wouldn't be any more trouble or sadness. They expected that the Christian life was the Garden of Eden revisited. In fact, many came to Christ in a time of despair, thinking that the Savior would immediately abolish all suffering and bring about a paradise here on earth for them and their families. And He will—but not yet. In the meantime, the race of man is cursed, along with the rest of creation, through the Fall.

Paul said about the problem of pain: "For we know that the whole creation groaneth and travaileth in pain together until now. And not only they, but ourselves also, which have the firstfruits of the Spirit, even we ourselves groan within ourselves, waiting for the adoption, to wit, the redemption of our body. For we are saved by hope: but hope that is seen is not hope: for what a man seeth, why doth he yet hope for?" (Romans 8:22-24).

The greatest despair in all the world comes when all hope of immortality is gone—to stand at the casket of a loved one and wonder if we will ever meet again. When we are young we think we will live forever. But one day we look in the mirror and wrinkled skin and gray hair confirm our worst fear—we are growing old. Many have thrown off the shackles of traditional religion, and for them there is now only the fear that the ground which accepts the cold lifeless body will be the final resting place. Again, Paul must have felt this, for he said, "If Christ be not risen . . . they also which are fallen asleep in Christ are perished. If in this life only we have hope in Christ, we are of all men most miserable" (1 Corinthians 15:14, 18, 19).

Perhaps the psalmist stared death in the face; in whatever situation he found himself, he cried out, "My soul cleaveth unto the dust: quicken thou me [give me life]" (119:25). Men fear that they are no more than "the beasts that perish" (Psalm 49:20). Peter said of the brevity of life, "For all flesh is as grass, and all the glory of man as the flower of grass. The grass withereth, and the flower thereof falleth away" (1 Peter 1:24).

But there is more! Paul continued his discourse on suffering and death, "For I am persuaded, that neither death, nor life, nor angels, nor principalities, nor powers, nor things present, nor things to come, nor height, nor depth, nor any other creature, shall be able to separate us from the love of God, which is in Christ Jesus our Lord" (Romans 8:38, 39).

When the son born to David and Bathsheba was critically ill, the great poet-king fasted and prayed that the Lord would spare the child. He fell into a dark depression and refused to eat or make any social amenities. At last, when the child was dead, he accepted the situation and said, "But now he is dead, wherefore [why] should I fast? can I bring him back again? I shall go to him, but he shall not return to me"

(2 Samuel 12:23).

One day the suffering will be over forever. John the Revelator saw that great day and said: "And I heard a great voice out of heaven saying, Behold, the tabernacle of God is with men, and he will dwell with them, and they shall be his people, and God himself shall be with them, and be their God. And God shall wipe away all tears from their eyes; and there shall be no more death, neither sorrow, nor crying, neither shall there be any more pain: for the former things are passed away" (Revelation 21:3, 4).

B. When We Need Strength and Understanding (vv. 27-29)

27. Make me to understand the way of thy precepts: so shall I talk of thy wondrous works.

28. My soul melteth for heaviness: strengthen thou me according unto thy word.

29. Remove from me the way of lying: and grant me thy law graciously.

Sometimes, with the tears still staining their cheeks, young and old will turn their eyes to the sky and ask questions like these: "Why, Lord?. . . Why must I suffer in this way?. . . If the devil causes all our problems, why didn't You just kill him long ago?. . . I've tried everything I know to do, Lord; why must I suffer so much?"

Job, the great sufferer, was visited by his friends. They had all the questions he did. *Why?* they thought. But "they sat down with him upon the ground seven days and seven nights, and none spake a word unto him: for they saw that his grief was very great" (Job 2:13). When three of these "comforters" finally spoke—they said all the wrong things. I'm not sure that aside from the Word of God there is a right answer—and even then—in the midst of our grief and sorrow, we may not want to hear even the Lord's voice.

The psalmist said, "Make me to understand. . . . My soul melteth for heaviness" (vv. 27, 28). In other words, "Lord, I'm in the middle of a great sadness—help me to understand it! Please!"

At the very southernmost tip of England is a place called Land's End. There is a house there with a sign which reads, "The last house and the first house in England." Whether it is the first or last house depends on which way you're going. The cross of Calvary was the very last place in suffering, defeat, and discouragement—but the first place in healing, victory, and joy!

The Cross is a perfect picture of right at whatever cost! It is perfect love—a suffering, helpless Savior, dying as a bloody spectacle for the amusement of the crowd. It is God in total submission, total surrender, and total humility.

And though it may look like the end of the world—the Word of God has comfort and guidance through every hard situation. God cares—He and His Son have suffered everything you could ever suffer so He can guide you safely through the perils of this life and onward and upward to victory.

C. In Times of Drudgery (vv. 30-32)

30. I have chosen the way of truth: thy judgments have I laid before me.

31. I have stuck unto thy testimonies: O Lord, put me not to shame.

32. I will run the way of thy

commandments, when thou shalt enlarge my heart.

Here are three strong affirmations: "I have chosen. . . . I have stuck. . . . I will run. . . ." All of us will have to make those same defining statements about our relationship with Christ: "As for me and my house, we will serve the Lord" (Joshua 24:15). "This one thing I do . . . I press toward the mark for the prize of the high calling of God in Christ Jesus" (Philippians 3:13, 14). "Let us run with patience the race that is set before us, looking unto Jesus the author and finisher of our faith" (Hebrews 12:1, 2).

It seems that running with patience, or even plodding along at a slow walk, is what serving Christ is like more often than not. True, there are times when we fly with the eagles—but those over-the-housetop experiences in which we soar above all the everyday, mundane labors and simple hard work do not come every day. I think Isaiah had it right when he said, "But they that wait upon the Lord shall renew their strength; they shall mount up with wings as eagles; they shall run, and not be weary; and they shall walk, and not faint" (40:31).

Notice his order of events: "Mount up with wings"—sometimes. "Run, and not be weary"—more often. "Walk, and not faint"—most of the time. Jeremiah got tired of plodding, and said, "Oh that I had in the wilderness a lodging place of wayfaring men; that I might leave my people, and go from them!" (9:2).

He was so tired of the rat race. Like us sometimes, he just wanted out. And that's not bad—for though we must make our peace with the certainty of drudgery, even Jesus and His disciples needed rest from the toils of their journey. He said, "Come ye yourselves apart into a desert[ed] place, and rest a while: for there were many coming and going, and they had no leisure so much as to eat" (Mark 6:31).

Resting is not quitting, however. Jesus also said, "I must walk to day, and to morrow, and the day following" (Luke 13:33). In the language of His times, He was saying, "I must keep on laboring until the task is done." If only we can realize that "he that endureth to the end shall be saved" (Matthew 10:22) and will work until Jesus comes or calls—for He has promised: "Be thou faithful unto death, and I will give thee a crown of life" (Revelation 2:10).

Why is the Cross so comforting in difficult times?

II. PRAYER FOR GUIDANCE
    (Psalm 119:33-40)

33. Teach me, O Lord, the way of thy statutes; and I shall keep it unto the end.

34. Give me understanding, and I shall keep thy law; yea, I shall observe it with my whole heart.

35. Make me go in the path of thy commandments; for therein do I delight.

36. Incline my heart unto thy testimonies, and not to covetousness.

37. Turn away mine eyes from beholding vanity; and quicken thou me in thy way.

38. Stablish thy word unto thy servant, who is devoted to thy fear.

39. Turn away my reproach which I fear: for thy judgments are good.

40. Behold, I have longed after thy precepts: quicken me in thy righteousness.

It seems that the psalmist meant for these verses collectively to form a prayer; thus we would do them an injustice to separate them into various studies. For that reason we will pursue a view which would embrace the whole rather than to dissect them. The psalmist has leaped from the words "when thou shalt enlarge my heart" (v. 32) into a seven-step spiritual growth program (there are eight steps, but the last repeats the fifth).

In essence, he was asking God, "teach me . . . give me understanding . . . make me to walk in Your commandments . . . incline my heart to Your law . . . establish Your Word . . . turn away my reproach . . . enliven me [or give me life]" (vv. 33-40). When we begin our prayer with the words "teach me," the logical end result is *life.*

When the psalmist said, "Turn away mine eyes from beholding vanity [Hebrew, *shav*, emptiness or nothingness]" (v. 37), he used a word close in meaning to Solomon's "vanity of vanities" (Ecclesiastes 1:2). The latter is a translation of the Hebrew word *hebel*, meaning "vapor" or "air." When the Preacher said, "All is vanity" (12:8), he concluded that every nonspiritual pursuit in the world is just "eating air."

The Word and prayer—brought together in these eight verses—form a marvelous "one-two punch," which will always result in a victorious Christian life.

Discuss how the Word of God and prayer together form a weapon for the Christian.

III. DETERMINE TO FOLLOW
(Psalm 119:105-112)

A. Follow After Light
(vv. 105, 106)

105. Thy word is a lamp unto my feet, and a light unto my path.

106. I have sworn, and I will perform it, that I will keep thy righteous judgments.

When we walk as the Lord directs us, we have a lighted pathway (John 12:35; Ephesians 5:8) and will not stumble into sin. Proverbs 6:23 says, "For the commandment is a lamp; and the law is light; and reproofs of instruction are the way of life."

Light and the Word are inextricably woven together. Where there is the Word, there is light. "The entrance of thy words giveth light; it giveth understanding unto the simple" (Psalm 119:130). Where there is an absence of the Word, there is darkness. It is interesting to note that before God began His life-giving work during the Creation, "the earth was without form, and void; and darkness was upon the face of the deep. . . . And God said, Let there be light: and there was light" (Genesis 1:1-3).

Light is a prerequisite for life. Jesus revealed to us that He is the "light of the world" and the "light of life" (John 8:12). Those who saw Him saw a "great light" (Isaiah 9:2; Matthew 4:16). Since God "spoke" the light into existence (Genesis 1:3), and Jesus is called the "Word [Logos] of God," we can be sure that Jesus' coming as Savior and the allusion to Him as a "great light" in

Matthew is a direct reference to the light that lit the world in the Creation. Those to whom Christ preached were seeing the same personage who was the Great Light that came into a formless and void world and prepared it for the coming of life.

B. Follow After Life (vv. 107, 108)

107. I am afflicted very much: quicken me, O Lord, according unto thy word.

108. Accept, I beseech thee, the freewill-offerings of my mouth, O Lord, and teach me thy judgments.

Jesus said, "The words that I speak unto you, they are spirit, and they are life" (John 6:63). The word *quicken* in our text (Hebrew, *chayah*) has a great number of meanings, but basically refers to "living" or having "life . . . more abundantly" (John 10:10). It is important to note that Jesus is the Word, or Logos (1:1), and through the Word comes life (5:24). In 14:6, Jesus said, "I am the way, the truth, and the life: no man cometh unto the Father, but by me." The Word (Jesus) and life are always bound together. He is the Creator. John said, "In the beginning was the Word, and the Word was with God, and the Word was God. The same was in the beginning with God. All things were made by him; and without him was not any thing made that was made. In him was life; and the life was the light of men" (1:1-4).

But as wonderful as Creation life is, as wonderful as salvation life is, there is much more. In the text above, the psalmist said, "Quicken me [give me life], O Lord, according unto thy word." He was saying,

"Give me all of life that's according to Thy Word." So, with that in mind, let's explore some of the ways "plain living" is expanded through obeying the Word of God:

1. *The Word is our healer* (Hebrew chayah, "to restore to health/life"). The mission of Jesus in the world was to culminate in His death on the cross. Through His death, the Atonement, He purchased several things for us— among them were salvation, restoration, and healing. Isaiah 53:5 says, "He was wounded for our transgressions, he was bruised for our iniquities: the chastisement of our peace was upon him; and with his stripes we are healed."

The word *life*, as used in the Bible includes the healing of body, soul, and spirit—all of which were purchased in the Atonement. Jesus healed great numbers of people who came to Him (Matthew 12:15; 15:30; Luke 4:40; 5:15; 9:11). It was an express purpose of His coming (Psalm 107:20; Matthew 8:16). According to the Word of God, we can be healed from sickness and disease.

2. *The Word is our peace* (Hebrew chayah, "to lift out of discouragement and despair"). Along with physical healing, Jesus provided for mental healing. One of His greatest gifts was a peace which could not be taken away from the child of God under any circumstances (John 14:27). Paul tells us in Colossians 1:20 that we have "peace through the blood of his [Jesus'] cross." The promise of the angels at Jesus' birth was "peace" (Luke 2:14); the gospel was called the "gospel of peace" (Romans 10:15; Ephesians 6:15); peace is listed as one aspect of the fruit of

the Spirit (Galatians 5:22); it guards our heart (Philippians 4:7) and rules our heart (Colossians 3:15). The Lord is "God of peace" (1 Thessalonians 5:23; Hebrews 13:20), "Lord of peace" (2 Thessalonians 3:16), "King of peace" (Hebrews 7:2), and "He is our peace" (Ephesians 2:14).

3. *The Word is our prosperity* (Hebrew *chayah*, "life in the fullest; to live prosperously"). Someone said, "Non-Christians don't have to become Christians to be blessed by God—all they have to do is live around Christians and blessings rub off on them." When a believer lives by the law of God, the laws of prosperity begin to work.

C. Follow After Law (v. 109)

109. My soul is continually in my hand: yet do I not forget thy law.

The psalmist was saying, "I live daily with life and death in my hand." So do we. Every decision we make affects us in our relationship with God. Either we are learning to live by His wonderful law and becoming more like His Son (1 Peter 2:21) or we are being broken on the rocks of folly.

When God committed to Moses and to Israel the Ten Commandments (Exodus 20) and the ceremonial and social laws that accompanied them, He was letting His people in on a secret which He had long kept to Himself. God is the original promoter of law and order. Everything in His realm works on specific principles. When those principles are obeyed, the one who obeys is rewarded. When those principles are disobeyed, the one who disobeys is punished (Romans 2:12-16).

If you don't believe this, plant a seed in the ground, fertilize it, and watch it grow. "For whatsoever a man soweth, that shall he also reap" (Galatians 6:7). Near it, plant a rock! Whether the laws of the harvest or the laws of the Temple—their results are equally sure. Whether the laws of thermodynamics or the "royal law" (James 2:8,which demands that one love his brother)—neither can be injudiciously broken without penalty.

But God's special intent in the giving of both the natural and spiritual laws is the blessing of mankind. He created this world for Adam and Eve and their offspring, and daily He cares for and maintains it, along with the wild lilies and the sparrows (Matthew 6:28-30; Luke 12:6). Without God and His laws, the world would be back where it began (Genesis 1:2)—in chaos.

While the natural laws can be and are treated objectively, God's spiritual laws in my life are subjective in nature. Once, a "law of sin and death" reigned in me; but through faith in the accomplished work of Jesus Christ on the cross, a new law now controls my life—"For the law of the Spirit of life in Christ Jesus hath made me free from the law of sin and death" (Romans 8:2).

D. Follow After Longevity (vv. 110, 111)

110. The wicked have laid a snare for me: yet I erred not from thy precepts.

111. Thy testimonies have I taken as an heritage for ever: for they are the rejoicing of my heart.

The heritage of the righteous is not only life but also long life—as well as eternal life (Titus 3:7). The latter part of the fifth commandment provides for a long life for those who honor their parents. Jehovah specifically admonished Israel, "Honour thy father and thy mother: that thy days may be long upon the land which the Lord thy God giveth thee" (Exodus 20:12). Jesus, on several occasions, spoke of the hypocricy of the Pharisees in relation to caring for their parents, and Paul reiterated the Exodus text and added "which is the first commandment with promise" (Ephesians 6:2, 3).

As with all of God's promises, long life is based on keeping both spiritual and natural laws. The righteous will live longer (on an average) because of the manner in which they treat their souls, bodies, and minds in relation to the spiritual and natural laws to which all of us are subject. For instance, the person who refuses to use harmful drugs, alcohol, and tobacco, and keeps his body in good physical condition with meaningful exercise and manual labor, will have a distinct advantage over those who do not.

Whatever we do to build up or tear down our spirits, minds, or bodies will be returned to us abundantly. The Word of God says specifically, "Be not deceived; God is not mocked: for whatsoever a man soweth, that shall he also reap. For he that soweth to his flesh shall of the flesh reap corruption; but he that soweth to the Spirit shall of the Spirit reap life everlasting" (Galatians 6:7, 8). Note these spiritual and natural laws of sowing and reaping: (1) If we sow, we will reap; (2) we reap what we sow; (3) we reap more than we sow.

Peace and satisfaction are benefi-cial to the mental conditioning necessary to live long and productive lives. Those who can find no peace and fall into despair often take their own lives. Sin works to destroy the body, while righteousness builds it up. And the benefits of lives lived in the will of God are cumulative and are passed on through the genes to the children of the righteous (Deuteronomy 7:9-11; Psalm 105:8).

And while the Old Testament law promised long life on the earth, the atoning work of Christ on the cross promises that the righteous "should not perish, but have everlasting life" (John 3:16, 36; 5:24; 6:40; see also Matthew 25:46).

The apostle Paul told the Romans that "the wages of sin is death; but the gift of God is eternal life through Jesus Christ our Lord" (6:23). The "wages" (result) of sin is death, while the "gift" (grace) of God is life. In the broadest sense, death and life refer to much more than breathing and ceasing to breathe. Death (Greek, *thanatos*) encompasses all the problems and miseries arising from, or as a result of, sin. Life (Greek, *zoe*) refers to all that derives from association with the Creator of life and the fullness of fellowship with Him—here on earth (the good life) and in heaven (life eternal).

E. Follow After the Lord (v. 112)

112. I have inclined mine heart to perform thy statutes alway, even unto the end.

Ultimately it is the Lord who guides. The great fisherman said, "Because Christ also suffered for us, leaving us an example . . . follow his steps" (1 Peter 2:21). The steps we are commanded to follow are stained with the blood of countless miles walked over stony ground to carry a message of hope to a hopeless people . . . stained with the blood of the sins of every man from Adam until today . . . stained with His own precious blood from the wounds in His feet. Yes, the path we have chosen is one of sacrifice and suffering. One day the suffering will all be over; but today "follow his steps," for "if we suffer [with him], we shall also reign with him" (2 Timothy 2:12).

My Guide
There is no path in this desert waste,
For the winds have swept the shifting sands,
The trail is blind where the storms have raced,
And a stranger, I, in these fearsome lands.
But I journey on with a lightsome tread;
I do not falter nor turn aside,
For I see His figure just ahead—
He knows the way—my Guide.

—Robert J. Burdette, 1948

What is one sure result of following the footsteps of the Lord?

REVIEW QUESTIONS

1. What is the most despairing time in our lives? In your life?

2. What are several problems for which we need God's guidance?

3. What does the Hebrew word for vanity mean?

4. What are some spiritual meanings for *light* in the Bible?

5. How does the Word of God say our hearts are to be guarded?

GOLDEN TEXT HOMILY

"THY WORD IS A LAMP UNTO MY FEET, AND A LIGHT UNTO MY PATH" (Psalm 119:105).

God's Word has been a lamp and instrument of light from the very beginning of Creation. Adam and Eve failed to obey the Word of God, the source of spiritual light, when they ate of the forbidden tree in the Garden. Because of their failure in the beginning, man is in spiritual darkness until God in His mercy allows His Spirit to shine the light of God's Word on his path. The psalmist knew how important the Word of God was as a light to shine upon the path he traveled.

When David had sinned with Bathsheba, the prophet Nathan had to come to make him aware of his sin. He told David the story of the poor man who had only one ewe sheep and the rich man who had many sheep but took the poor man's only sheep. The prophet was God's mouthpiece, as if God were speaking directly to David about his sin. Conviction penetrated David's heart. He confessed his sin to God, and God forgave him (2 Samuel 12).

We need the light of God's Word to shine on the path that we are traveling in this world. Not every path has the light of God's Word shining on it. Indeed, Satan and the secular minds have suggested many paths of life, but only God knows the pitfalls and erroneous views of life's paths. We need to know the Word of God so that we will not stumble in the Christian walk. If the light of God's Word illumines the path, those who follow will not stumble in darkness and lose their way. May God's Word light our path like the noonday sun.**—Charles G. Wiley, Pastor, Church of God, Graham, Texas**

SENTENCE SERMONS

GOD'S WORD gives direction to our lives.

—Selected

OTHER BOOKS were given for our information; the Bible was given for our transportation.

—The Defender

MANY THINGS in the Bible I cannot understand, many things in the Bible I only think I understand, but there are many things in the Bible I cannot misunderstand.

—The Encyclopedia of Religious Quotations

EVANGELISM APPLICATION

THE WORD DIRECTS THE CHRISTIAN TO LEAD OTHERS TO CHRIST.

The story is told of a little lost boy who was found by a policeman and taken to the station house downtown. He didn't know his last name or his address, and at first it looked as if it would be a major task to find his parents. Then the lad remembered something important—there was a large church across from his house with a big lighted cross on top of it.

"If you'll take me to the cross," the boy said, "I can find my way home from there."

In Luke 15, Jesus spoke of three lost things—a lost sheep (v. 4), a lost coin (v. 8), and a lost son (v. 13). Sin has blinded us to our need of a loving Father, and we have become lost. But like the little lost boy, there is help for us at the Cross. Jesus said, "The Son of man is come to seek and to save that which was lost" (Luke 19:10).

ILLUMINATING THE LESSON

God has never left His people without guidance. When the children of Israel set out from Egypt toward the Promised Land, the psalmist tells us, "In the daytime also he led [guided] them with a cloud, and all the night with a light of fire" (Psalm 78:14).

But when they were ensconced in the new land, the Lord led through the high priest, who sought the Lord's direction through two stones in the breastplate. "And thou shalt put in the breastplate of judgment the Urim and the Thummim; and they shall be upon Aaron's heart, when he goeth in before the Lord: and Aaron shall bear the judgment [guidance] of the children of Israel upon his heart before the Lord continually" (Exodus 28:30).

We don't know how the Urim (Hebrew, "lights") and Thummim (Hebrew, "perfection") worked. They could have been cast as lots, and the way they fell showed the will of the Lord. Some have suggested that they sparkled and shone and the twinkling lights guided the high priest. Nevertheless, the priests soon fell out of favor and the office of prophets came into being.

Today, we have a direct line to God through the Holy Spirit (Romans 8:26, 27) and the Holy Scripture (2 Timothy 3:16, 17; 1 John 2:5, 6). They will never lead us astray—and they will never disagree.

DAILY BIBLE READINGS

M. Submit to God's Guidance. Psalm 32:8-11
T. Trust in the Lord. Proverbs 3:1-10
W. A Superior Way. Isaiah 55:8-13
T. Follow the Shepherd. John 10:1-11
F. Jesus Is the Way. John 14:6-14
S. Guided by the Spirit. John 16:7-14

The Word Comforts

Study Text: Psalm 119:49, 50, 57-64, 73-80, 89-94

Objective: To discover the comfort found in God's Word and receive His strength.

Time: Scholars differ on the date of Psalm 119, but a consensus of opinions favor the Davidic kingdom period 1000-961 B.C.

Place: The place of the writing of Psalm 119 is uncertain but probably Jerusalem.

Golden Text: "This is my comfort in my affliction: for thy word hath quickened me" (Psalm 119:50).

Central Truth: Believers can find strength and comfort in God's Word.

Evangelism Emphasis: God's Word is the answer for hurting and desperate people.

PRINTED TEXT

Psalm 119:57. Thou art my portion, O Lord: I have said that I would keep thy words.

58. I intreated thy favour with my whole heart: be merciful unto me according to thy word.

59. I thought on my ways, and turned my feet unto thy testimonies.

60. I made haste, and delayed not to keep thy commandments.

61. The bands of the wicked have robbed me: but I have not forgotten thy law.

62. At midnight I will rise to give thanks unto thee because of thy righteous judgments.

63. I am a companion of all them that fear thee, and of them that keep thy precepts.

64. The earth, O Lord, is full of thy mercy: teach me thy statutes.

Psalm 119:49. Remember the word unto thy servant, upon which thou hast caused me to hope.

50. This is my comfort in my affliction: for thy word hath quickened me.

73. Thy hands have made me and fashioned me: give me understanding, that I may learn thy commandments.

74. They that fear thee will be glad when they see me; because I have hoped in thy word.

75. I know, O Lord, that thy judgments are right, and that thou in faithfulness hast afflicted me.

76. Let, I pray thee, thy merciful kindness be for my comfort, according to thy word unto thy servant.

77. Let thy tender mercies come unto me, that I may live: for

thy law is my delight.

78.   Let the proud be ashamed; for they dealt perversely with me without a cause: but I will meditate in thy precepts.

79. Let those that fear thee turn unto me, and those that have known thy testimonies.

80. Let my heart be sound in thy statutes; that I be not ashamed.

89. For ever, O Lord, thy word is settled in heaven.

90. Thy faithfulness is unto all generations: thou hast established the earth, and it abideth.

91. They continue this day according to thine ordinances: for all are thy servants.

92. Unless thy law had been my delights, I should then have perished in mine affliction.

93. I will never forget thy precepts: for with them thou hast quickened me.

94. I am thine, save me; for I have sought thy precepts.

LESSON OUTLINE

I. STEADFAST IN THE WORD

   A. Steadfastness Is a Requirement

   B. Steadfastness Results in Praise and Victory

   C. Steadfastness Is Determined by Our Choice of Friends

II. COMFORT DURING ADVERSITY

   A. Adversity Provides Opportunity for God's Best

   B. Adversity Allows for Contemplation

   C. Adversity Provides Opportunity for Witness

III. THE WORD IS RELIABLE

   A. The Word Is Unchanging and Unchangeable

   B. The Word Is All-Sufficient

LESSON EXPOSITION

INTRODUCTION

At some point in life, we all need to be comforted. How sad are the words of Jeremiah in Lamentations 1:2: "She weepeth sore in the night, and her tears are on her cheeks: among all her lovers she hath none to comfort her: all her friends have dealt treacherously with her, they are become her enemies."

These words of Jeremiah could be the opening statement for a great sweeping novel. They speak, instead, of the sorrow of a nation which had just been destroyed by a fierce foreign army and whose people were without homes, lands, or personal possessions; they had even been stripped of their dignity. But perhaps the saddest of all the thoughts expressed here are in the words "She hath none to comfort her." The Hebrew word for *comfort* (nacham) expresses deep feelings of sorrow or pity—but there was none to express sympathy for and give comfort to Israel.

Perhaps the deep longing for someone to feel our hurts and griefs with us is the reason why God said, "I will never leave thee, nor forsake thee" (Hebrews 13:5) and why Jesus sent the Holy Spirit to be our Comforter when He went back to the Father after His earthly ministry. The lesson today deals with several avenues of God's comfort through His Word—but especially in times of adversity.

I. STEADFAST IN THE WORD
(Psalm 119:57-64)

A. Steadfastness Is a Requirement (vv. 57-60)

57. Thou art my portion, O Lord: I have said that I would keep thy words.
58. I intreated thy favour with my whole heart: be merciful unto me according to thy word.
59. I thought on my ways, and turned my feet unto thy testimonies.
60. I made haste, and delayed not to keep thy commandments.

Steadfastness is one of the characteristics most valued in the spiritual kingdom. The Lord himself said "No man having put his hand to the plow, and looking back, is fit for the kingdom of God" (Luke 9:62). James, in a study of faith, said the man who wavers is not dependable, he is of two minds, and he will receive nothing from God when he prays (1:6-8).

Conversely, those who neither look back nor waver in their loyalty to their Lord are praised. The psalmist used some key phrases to describe how one remains steadfast. First, he told the Lord, "I have said that I would keep thy words" (119:57). Second, "I intreated [sought] thy favour with my whole heart" (v. 58). Third, "I thought on my ways, and turned my feet" (v. 59). And fourth, "I made haste, and delayed not to keep thy command-

ments" (v. 60).

When a man seriously thinks on his ways, he will change them. Such thinking is seldom the philosophical kind, nor from a scientific standpoint—rather, it is the deep, brooding of a soul dissatisfied with its condition and longing for something that is lasting and satisfying.

The Prodigal Son was far from home, alone, and without any personal resources; but "when he came to himself, he said, How many hired servants of my father's have bread enough and to spare, and I perish with hunger! I will arise and go to my father, and will say unto him, Father, I have sinned against heaven, and before thee, and am no more worthy to be called thy son: make me as one of thy hired servants. And he arose, and came to his father" (Luke 15:17-20).

It is the active work of the Holy Spirit which draws men and women to Christ. Without this attraction (conviction) there is no salvation. There is, however, a work (decision) that must be made by each person who would come to Christ (Revelation 22:17). These words of the psalmist, "I thought . . . and turned;" the words of the Prodigal, "I will arise"; and the words concerning the Prodigal, "and he arose," all speak of eternal decisions of the soul.

Good intentions must be followed by steadfast action if one is to be grounded in Christ. How a convert starts his spiritual journey usually determines whether he becomes more and more like Christ or falls beside the way.

B. Steadfastness Results in Praise and Victory (vv. 61, 62)

61. The bands of the wicked have robbed me: but I have not forgotten thy law.
62. At midnight I will rise to

give thanks unto thee because of thy righteous judgments.

A better translation of verse 61 might be, "The cords of the wicked bind me . . . "— that is, "I am kept from doing what I want to do," or "I am robbed of my freedom." Nevertheless, the psalmist said in the next verse, "At midnight I will rise to give thanks." It is interesting that praise and victory are often linked so closely.

Paul and Silas, in the course of their missionary journey, were beaten and falsely imprisoned in the city jail in Philippi, a Roman colony (Acts 16:23). Since Paul was a Roman citizen, he could have yelled loudly about his mistreatment and he would have been quickly released (v. 37). He chose rather to join Silas in prayer and praise.

David and the two Christian missionaries—separated by centuries in time, but each robbed of their freedom—chose the midnight hour to praise the Lord (Psalm 119:62; Acts 16:25). The midnight hour represents the darkest time or the most painful part of affliction. Anybody can praise God when the sun is shining, when God is in His heaven and everything is right with the world. But these men knew a "God . . . who giveth songs in the night" (Job 35:10) and that "he that keepeth thee will not slumber" (Psalm 121:3). They knew where they had placed their trust and that God was the same in the night as He was in the day.

Though God is light—pure light—He and His Word can often be found in the darkest of places. We are told that when Moses approached God about the Law and the Commandments, he "drew near unto the thick darkness where God

was" (Exodus 20:21). There is no place so distant or so dark that God is not there. The psalmist said, "If I make my bed in hell, behold, thou art there" (Psalm 139:8).

To get up from one's bed in the midnight hour to pray often provides answers to the difficult questions encountered in a hectic day. It's a good time—there are fewer distractions and our minds have had time to settle down since arriving back home from the day in the marketplace. But whether or not the hour we select is midnight, the perfect day begins with prayer, continues with obedience, and ends with praise.

C. Steadfastness Is Determined by
   Our Choice of Friends
   (vv. 63, 64)

63. I am a companion of all them that fear thee, and of them that keep thy precepts.
64. The earth, O Lord, is full of thy mercy: teach me thy statutes.

"Amnon had a friend" (2 Samuel 13:3). What sweet words those are at first glance. But when we later learn that this friend devised a scheme for David's son to desecrate and dishonor his own sister to satisfy his lustful cravings, we have to think again about how "sweet" they are.

The psalmist said, "I am a companion of all them that fear thee." It is right and good that Christians seek out those of like faith as companions, mates, and friends. These *good* friends help make us better Christians.

The psalmist also said the Lord "is full of . . . mercy." We need to know that comfort and mercy can never be selfish things. In the Christian life, we are comforted not only for our immediate adversity but that we may also in turn comfort others in the same way. Paul told the Corinthian church, "Blessed be God, even the Father of our Lord Jesus Christ, the Father of mercies, and the God of all comfort; who comforteth us in all our tribulation, that we may be able to comfort them which are in any trouble, by the comfort wherewith we ourselves are comforted of God. . . . And our hope of you is stedfast, knowing, that as ye are partakers of the sufferings, so shall ye be also of the consolation" (2 Corinthians 1:3, 4, 7).

The Christian life is not a solo experience. In fact, the words *solo* and *Christian* are oxymoronic. Even when we are not with others, we are not alone. The Holy Spirit lives in us: "Your body is the temple of the Holy Ghost" (1 Corinthians 6:19). God the Father lives in us: "Ye are the temple of the living God; as God hath said, I will dwell in them, and walk in them; and I will be their God, and they shall be my people" (2 Corinthians 6:16). God has promised us, "I will never leave thee, nor forsake thee" (Hebrews 13:5). Jesus declared, "For where two or three are gathered together in my name, there am I in the midst of them" (Matthew 18:20). And so it seems there is never a time that we can't have the consolation of divine companionship, even if all our earthly friends forsake us.

From the day when God addressed the plight of the newly created Adam and said, "It is not good that the man should be alone" (Genesis 2:18), His pattern has been that "God setteth the solitary in families" (Psalm 68:6). In a day when the ideal family is difficult to find, the church fellowship (Greek,

koinonia) can often step in and fill that void.

The Christian life is for sharing, and the sweetest part of it is the loving fellowship of believers with each other. We are inseparably a part of the body of Christ, the *ecclesia*, the "called-out ones." The body cannot survive without all its parts—we need each other in times of adversity, and in the good times too.

Here is a little story by an unknown author, in poem form, about three friends who really needed each other's help:

Faith, Fact and *Feeling*
Three men were walking on a wall, / Feeling, Faith and Fact; / Feeling got an awful fall / And Faith was taken back. /
Faith was so close to Feeling, / He fell too; / But Fact remained and pulled Faith up, / And that brought Feeling too!

What are some ways to restimulate joy in our Christian experience?

II. COMFORT DURING ADVERSITY (Psalm 119:49, 50, 73-80)

A. Adversity Provides Opportunity for God's Best (vv. 49, 50)

49. Remember the word unto thy servant, upon which thou hast caused me to hope.

50. This is my comfort in my affliction: for thy word hath quickened me.

The psalmist was saying, "God, remember Your Word to Your servant! It's my only hope. It's my comfort in this affliction. Only the Word keeps me alive." I don't know what great trouble this songwriter was in, but he saw only one source of help—the promises of the Lord.

God's Word has always been a comfort to God's children. In time of trouble, we can turn to its "exceeding great and precious promises" (2 Peter 1:4) and find that God has provided for whatever experience we are suffering, and He will see us through it.

God's Word has often spoken just the right word during the midnight hour of a great trial, a temptation, or time of suffering. As we read, our hearts are softened, a glow spreads through us, and peace fills our troubled minds. The solution comes. For each of us and for every situation that solution is different. Sometimes God resolves the problem; sometimes the problem does not go away, but God gives us strength to go through it.

Paul comforted those in the Thessalonian church whose loved ones had died since accepting the Lord. They feared their loved ones would not be a part of the rapture of the church. Paul told them, "For the Lord himself shall descend from heaven with a shout, with the voice of the archangel, and with the trump of God: and the dead in Christ shall rise first: Then we which are alive and remain shall be caught up together with them in the clouds, to meet the Lord in the air: and so shall we ever be with the Lord" (1 Thessalonians 4:16, 17). Then he admonished them, "Wherefore comfort one another with these words" (v. 18).

Paul, at the close of his earthly ministry, was imprisoned in Rome. His response to his troubles is an excellent illustration of how a child of God should react to adverse situations. In his second letter to Timothy, he expressed sadness at being forsaken by Demas, "having loved this present world," but appreciation for Luke's being there (4:10, 11).

In verse 9, the apostle had encouraged Timothy to visit him "shortly." Before the end of the chapter he amended his invitation to read, "Do thy diligence to come before winter" (v. 21). In his time of trouble an old friend would be such a blessing. Then as he thought about it, maybe two old friends would be better—so he said, "Take Mark, and bring him with thee: for he is profitable to me for the ministry" (v. 11).

Paul's only other request concerned some items he wished Timothy to bring with him: "The cloke [cloak] that I left at Troas with Carpus, when thou comest, bring with thee, and the books, but especially the parchments" (v. 13). The *parchments* almost surely were copies of the Old Testament Scriptures.

Were we in Paul's predicament, most of us would be upset with God, upset with the church, and crying about our need for a television or at least a radio in our cell. But to Paul, good friends, a good coat, good books, and the Word of God were all the comfort the great man needed. He said, "I have learned to be content whatever the circumstances" (Philippians 4:11, *NIV*).

Likewise, let us too look to the Word of God and godly friends for comfort for ourselves and others who suffer adversity.

B. Adversity Allows for
   Contemplation (vv. 73-77)

73. Thy hands have made me and fashioned me: give me understanding, that I may learn thy commandments.

74. They that fear thee will be glad when they see me; because I have hoped in thy word.

75. I know, O Lord, that thy judgments are right, and that thou in faithfulness hast afflicted me.

76. Let, I pray thee, thy merciful kindness be for my comfort, according to thy word unto thy servant.

77. Let thy tender mercies come unto me, that I may live: for thy law is my delight.

Our relationship to Christ and to the members of His spiritual body is very much like the workings of the human body. While we do not enjoy pain and suffering, these are not the real problems we are facing. Pain is usually a symptom of something worse that is unseen—such as when the excruciating pain of a tooth reveals decay in its roots.

In the previous verses the psalmist said, "It is good for me that I have been afflicted; that I might learn thy statutes" (v. 71) and "Before I was afflicted I went astray: but now have I kept thy word" (v. 67). Sometimes God allows us to be in trouble so that we can see ourselves, our surroundings, the situation, our friends, our strengths, and our weaknesses.

Just as the little saplings that are never tested by the wind grow into weak and spindly trees, we do not have the opportunity to grow our strongest until we have weathered the storms of adversity. Christians who weather troubled times only grow stronger and more

reliant on God and His Word.

Troubles help us to remember who the real "Boss" is (v. 73), that "it is he that hath made us, and not we ourselves" (100:3). We learn in trials to lean on the fellowship of believers, for we know "they . . . will be glad when they see me" (119:74). When we have come safely through the storm, we will realize that the wind and rain were the purging work of the Holy Spirit, that God "in faithfulness hast afflicted" us (v. 75), and that it was His "tender mercies" working through the trials (vv. 76, 77).

C. Adversity Provides Opportunity for Witness (vv. 78-80)

78. Let the proud be ashamed; for they dealt perversely with me without a cause: but I will meditate in thy precepts.

79. Let those that fear thee turn unto me, and those that have known thy testimonies.

80. Let my heart be sound in thy statutes; that I be not ashamed.

David was often disappointed that evil appeared to triumph over good. "Shew me a token for good," he said to the Lord, "that they which hate me may see it, and be ashamed: because thou, Lord, hast holpen me, and comforted me" (Psalm 86:17). He petitioned the Lord to give him something that he could show to the world and say, "See! God is a good God!" When we are afflicted, we may worry that our unsaved friends and neighbors will only see the pain we suffer and overlook the joy inside us.

But we need not worry. It is how we conduct ourselves during hardships that most often impresses the world with the beauty of Christ. I remember a story about a farmer who, on the very night he was converted, made a pledge to give everything he owned to God. The next day, his pastor heard that all the farmer's crops had been eaten by a massive swarm of locusts. The preacher rushed to the farm to comfort the new Christian.

"I'm so sorry about your awful calamity," the minister said somberly.

"Well, it wasn't so awful really," the farmer responded.

"How can you say that when you've lost this year's entire crop?" the preacher asked.

"Last night," said the farmer, "I gave those crops to the Lord. If He wants to feed them to His locusts, that's His business."

I am still blessed today, many years later, by that farmer's response to what could have been a devastating situation. He demonstrated for us the overwhelming comfort of the Lord, no matter what calamity may befall us.

During adversity is a perfect time for us to witness of the good things God is doing. We can declare with the psalmist, "Come and see the works of God" (Psalm 66:5).

What was the thing Paul most wanted Timothy to bring to him in Rome?

III. THE WORD IS RELIABLE
(Psalm 119:89-94)

A. The Word Is Unchanging and Unchangeable (vv. 89-91)

89. For ever, O Lord, thy word is settled in heaven.

90. Thy faithfulness is unto all generations: thou hast established the earth, and it abideth.

91. They continue this day according to thine ordinances: for all are thy servants.

Here we see terms like *settled, established, abideth,* and *continue* to describe the unchanging and unchangeable Word of God. Each of these words are formed from the idea "to take a stand or station" as a guard would take a firm position and be willing to give his life to defend his position. "For ever, O Lord, thy word is settled in heaven" (v. 89). The prophet Isaiah joined the psalmist in declaring the Scriptures to be eternal: "The grass withereth, the flower fadeth: but the word of our God shall stand for ever" (40:8).

Jesus said, "Heaven and earth shall pass away: but my words shall not pass away" (Luke 21:33). And not only will the Scriptures remain forever, but they will also remain without error. "For verily I say unto you," He said, "Till heaven and earth pass, one jot or one tittle shall in no wise pass from the law, till all be fulfilled" (Matthew 5:18).

David declared of the Word of God: "The law of the Lord is perfect, converting the soul. . . . The commandment of the Lord is pure" (Psalm 19:7, 8). The purity of the law is maintained by God himself. The Lord said to Jeremiah, "I am watching to see that my word is fulfilled" (Jeremiah 1:12, *NIV*). And to keep it pure and unchanged, the Lord says to us: "Ye shall not add unto the word which I command you, neither shall ye diminish ought from it, that ye may keep the commandments of the Lord your God which I command you" (Deuteronomy 4:2). "And if any man shall take away from the words of the book of this prophecy, God shall take away his part out of the book of life, and out of the holy city, and from the things which are written in this book" (Revelation 22:19).

B. The Word Is All-Sufficient (vv. 92-94)

92. Unless thy law had been my delights, I should then have perished in mine affliction.

93. I will never forget thy precepts: for with them thou hast quickened me.

94. I am thine, save me; for I have sought thy precepts.

Nothing in the animal or vegetable kingdom is static—all living things are either growing or decaying. The psalmist spoke of this process as "perished" (v. 92), "quickened" (v. 93), and "saved" (v. 94). In the New Testament this pattern of growth and decay is seen in Paul's words to the Galatians: "Be not deceived; God is not mocked: for whatsoever a man soweth, that shall he also reap. For he that soweth to his flesh shall of the flesh reap corruption; but he that soweth to the Spirit shall of the Spirit reap life everlasting" (6:7, 8).

Corruption [Greek, *phthora,* "perishing, decaying, or destruction"] is the result of being cut off from one's life-giving resources. To speak of "perishing on the vine" means the veins that stretch between the life-giving vine and a branch or the fruit of that vine has been somehow clogged and vital nourishment withheld. The affected branch or fruit shrivels and falls off the vine.

Perishing is a process. One does not shrivel and fall from Christ the Vine (John 15:5-7) in the course of a few minutes. Corruption is a gradual falling away, sinking into sin, and the loss of a desire for holy things. But like a malignant can-

cer, the end result is sure without radical surgery by the Master Physician.

However, as Paul said, we have been freed from the law of sin and death (Romans 8:2). And "now being made free from sin, and become servants to God, ye have your fruit unto holiness, and the end everlasting life" (6:22).

What will happen to anyone who adds to or takes away from the Scriptures?

REVIEW QUESTIONS

1. What do you do in the darkest part of a trial or affliction?

2. Why is it so important to choose the right friends?

3. Why did the psalmist say, "It is good for me that I have been afflicted" (Psalm 119:71)?

4. How can affliction be one of the best witnesses for the Lord?

5. Defend the following statement: "God's Word is unchanging and eternal."

GOLDEN TEXT HOMILY

"THIS IS MY COMFORT IN MY AFFLICTION: FOR THY WORD HATH QUICKENED ME" (Psalm 119:50).

Words properly arranged and fitly spoken have a therapeutic value. Many people pay large sums of money to engage in an exchange of words with a therapist because it makes them feel better. Scripture says, "A soft answer turneth away wrath" (Proverbs 15:1) and "A word fitly spoken is like apples of gold in pictures of silver" (25:11). The therapeutic quality of words is brought to the forefront by Jesus: "These things have I spoken unto you, that my joy might remain in you, and that your joy might be full" (John 15:11).

The text goes beyond the ordinary therapy of words in our exchange with one another. The issue here is the fact that God is the speaker. The result of this spoken Word also goes far beyond the ordinary. In a sense God himself is present in His words. The truth of the matter is that God and His Word are the same. "In the beginning was the Word, and the Word was with God, and the Word was God" (John 1:1). When God speaks, there is power. He spoke, and meaningless mass became an orderly world. In the darkness He called for light, and the darkness disappeared. At a grave he called, "Lazarus," and the dead came to life.

Why wouldn't we be comforted and quickened by His Word? To Mary in the garden He said, "Weep not," and her tears were dried. To the disciples barricaded in an upper room for fear, He said, "It is I," and their fear was dispelled!

The word *quickened* used in the text has a wealth of meanings in the Hebrew language. It means "to give life, revive, renew, restore; to nourish; to make whole." Knowing what His Word does, we can be comforted in our afflictions. In the face of death, His Word gives life. In the face of sorrow, His Word restores. In our times of weakness, His Word revives us. Regardless of how fractured we may be, His Word makes us whole!—**R.B. Thomas, D.Litt., Vice President, Church of God School of Theology, Cleveland, Tennessee**

SENTENCE SERMONS

BELIEVERS can find strength and comfort in God's Word.

—Selected

GOD'S WORD IS the answer for hurting and desperate people.

—Selected

PRAYER LIFTS the heart above the battles of life and gives it a glimpse into the resources of God's Word, which spells victory and hope.

—C. Neil Strait

FAITH IN GOD and His Holy Word is the antidote for anxiety.

—*The Encyclopedia of Religious Quotations*

DAILY BIBLE READINGS

M. Assurance. Genesis 28:10-15
T. Comfort. Psalm 23:1-6
W. Healing. Luke 8:43-48
T. Companionship.
    John 14:21-27
F. Encouragement.
    Romans 15:1-7
S. Hope.
    1 Thessalonians 4:13-18

The Word Sustains

Study Text: Psalm 119:113-120, 161-176

Objective: To find hope in the Word and praise God for His help.

Time: Scholars differ on the date of Psalm 119, but a consensus of opinions favor the Davidic kingdom period 1000-961 B.C.

Place: The place of the writing of Psalm 119 is uncertain, but probably Jerusalem.

Golden Text: "Hold thou me up, and I shall be safe: and I will have respect unto thy statutes continually" (Psalm 119:117).

Central Truth: The Word of God sustains those who trust in Christ.

Evangelism Emphasis: The Word of God presents the hope of salvation to the unsaved.

PRINTED TEXT

Psalm 119:113. I hate vain thoughts: but thy law do I love.

114. Thou art my hiding place and my shield: I hope in thy word.

115. Depart from me, ye evildoers: for I will keep the commandments of my God.

116. Uphold me according unto thy word, that I may live: and let me not be ashamed of my hope.

117. Hold thou me up, and I shall be safe: and I will have respect unto thy statutes continually.

118. Thou hast trodden down all them that err from thy statutes: for their deceit is falsehood.

119. Thou puttest away all the wicked of the earth like dross: therefore I love thy testimonies.

120. My flesh trembleth for fear of thee; and I am afraid of thy judgments.

161. Princes have persecuted me without a cause: but my heart standeth in awe of thy word.

162. I rejoice at thy word, as one that findeth great spoil.

163. I hate and abhor lying: but thy law do I love.

164. Seven times a day do I praise thee because of thy righteous judgments.

165. Great peace have they which love thy law: and nothing shall offend them.

166. Lord, I have hoped for thy salvation, and done thy commandments.

167. My soul hath kept thy testimonies; and I love them exceedingly.

168. I have kept thy precepts and thy testimonies: for all my ways are before thee.

169. Let my cry come near before thee, O Lord: give me

understanding according to thy word.

170. Let my supplication come before thee: deliver me according to thy word.

171. My lips shall utter praise, when thou hast taught me thy statutes.

172. My tongue shall speak of thy word: for all thy commandments are righteousness.

173. Let thine hand help me; for I have chosen thy precepts.

174. I have longed for thy salvation, O Lord; and thy law is my delight.

175. Let my soul live, and it shall praise thee; and let thy judgments help me.

176. I have gone astray like a lost sheep; seek thy servant; for I do not forget thy commandments.

LESSON OUTLINE

LESSON EXPOSITION

INTRODUCTION

In this last lesson on our study of the Word from Psalm 119, we are especially concerned with God's care for His children through His Word. Though the word *providence* (Greek, *pronoia*) is neither an Old Testament nor a New Testament term in the sense the Christian church has come to use it (in Acts 24:2, it should be translated "foresight"), the idea of God's provident care is found throughout the Bible and was a prominent teaching of Jesus (Matthew 5:45; 6:25-34; 10:29-31).

Our Father's largesse extends from His creation of this great universe for our pleasure to the care of the sparrows and the dressing of the lilies of the fields (Matthew 6:28-30). We are instructed to request our daily provisions when we pray (6:9-13) and, by faith, to have absolute confidence in God's love and care.

I. THE WORD IS A REFUGE
(Psalm 119:113-120)

The idea of a refuge, or safe place, was very important to the

Jewish people at the time the Psalms were written. And even though we are not imperiled by the beast of the desert or the violent whims of nature to quite the extent they were, even today we need a safe place—a refuge to which we can flee and feel secure.

Something as simple as a rock projecting up from the ground in a wilderness could be extremely vital if one should be caught in a windstorm or a cold rain, or if one needed shade from the sun or was fleeing from a lion. "And a man [the Christ] shall be as an hiding place from the wind, and a covert from the tempest; as rivers of water in a dry place, as the shadow of a great rock in a weary land" (Isaiah 32:2).

A. God's Word Is a Refuge for the Mind (v. 113)

113. I hate vain thoughts: but thy law do I love.

The King James Version's translation of "vain thoughts" from the Hebrew word *céeph,* should be translated instead as "the halfhearted" or "the double-minded." The psalmist was declaring emphatically that he hated those with a divided mind, especially concerning their trustworthiness. There is no place in the kingdom of God for a person with a "half mind." The halfhearted patriot will sit back in times of trouble and allow his country to go into slavery. The halfhearted worker will produce a shoddy product. And for those who make a profession of serving God, Jesus told us, "No man can serve two masters: for either he will hate the one, and love the other; or else he will hold to the one, and despise the other. Ye cannot serve God and mammon [possessions]" (Matthew 6:24).

The psalmist wrote in 119:10, "With my whole heart have I sought thee." Such a claim could never be truthfully uttered by a man with "half a mind." Israel's shepherd boy who became king, was certainly no halfhearted man. Although the authorship of this psalm is uncertain, the sentiments of this verse definitely apply to David. In fact, the wholeheated faith and works of David may have inspired his son Solomon to write, "Whatsoever thy hand findeth to do, do it with thy might" (Ecclesiastes 9:10).

When Israel came back from exile in Babylon, they found Jerusalem in shambles. The Temple, the homes, the walls, and the businesses that had been within the walls were destroyed and burned. It was a heartrending sight and could have been a time of total discouragement had it not been for Nehemiah, the great prophet who pulled the people together into a team of workers. Nehemiah 4:6 says, "So built we the wall; and all the wall was joined together unto the half thereof: for the people had a mind to work." In the face of their enemies and with the taunts of those who said the job could never be done, they built the wall and restored the city, because they put their whole heart into the task.

The apostle Paul was a man driven with a passion for the gospel of Jesus Christ. Possibly no one has served God with such fervor through so many afflictions (Acts 16:23, 24; 2 Corinthians 11:23-27), nor could declare more truthfully than he, "I bear in my body the marks of the Lord Jesus" (Galatians 6:17). Paul gave us the secret of his great success when he said, "This one thing I do, forgetting those things which are behind, and reaching forth unto those things which are before, I press toward the mark for the prize of the high calling of God in Christ Jesus" (Philippians 3:13, 14).

Jesus said, "Thou shalt love the Lord thy God with all thy heart, and with all thy soul, and with all thy mind" (Matthew 22:37). James may have even coined a Greek word to describe the kind of man who gets nothing from the Lord when he prays: "A double minded [*dipsuchos*, "two-spirited"] man is unstable in all his ways" (James 1:8).

B. God's Word Is a Hiding Place (vv. 114, 115)

114. Thou art my hiding place and my shield: I hope in thy word.

115. Depart from me, ye evildoers: for I will keep the commandments of my God.

David was the greatest king the nation of Israel ever knew. So great was he that the Messiah to come would be known as "the son of David" (Matthew 22:42-45), and the prophets would foretell that He would sit on the throne of David (Isaiah 9:7; 16:5; Luke 1:32). But the man David, like most men, did not have an easy life. After he was anointed by Samuel to be the next king, Saul, the reigning king, began to persecute him, and David was forced to flee for his life and hide in caves and among the rocks in the hills. David came to appreciate these hiding places. Even in his later years when his son Absalom sought to overthrow his throne (2 Samuel 15:6), David was forced to flee and hide, sometimes even hiding among Israel's enemies.

The Christian life, however, was never meant to be lived out in hiding. Our orders are to take the battle to the Enemy (Mark 16:15-18). We need not think that Satan will defeat us—we know how the story ends (Revelation 21:1-4). We also have "exceeding great and precious promises" (2 Peter 1:4) and assurance that the church (and thereby we also) will stand through whatever comes against it (Matthew 16:18).

In this spiritual war between "principalities and powers" and the forces of righteousness, there are those times when the child of God needs to hide—to get away for a while and rest, to let wounds heal and build strength for the next conflict. And while we are there, the hiding place of prayer can become a "communication center," a quiet place where the child of God can send and receive messages from our heavenly headquarters.

The psalmist wisely told us that the best hiding place is in the Word of God. We never have far to go to find strength and rest in times of weariness—only as far as the Book.

C. God's Word Is a Sure Place (vv. 116, 117)

116. Uphold me according unto thy word, that I may live: and let me not be ashamed of my hope.

117. Hold thou me up, and I shall be safe: and I will have respect unto thy statutes continually.

The words "uphold me" (Hebrew, *camak*) and "hold . . . me up" (Hebrew, *caád*) mean almost identically the same thing and are words all of us have cried out to God at one time or another. They ring with the urgency of the shrill little voice that reached up to us during some scary time and said, "Hold me, Daddy!" And every time, our heavenly Father—just like earthly fathers, reached down and lifted us up.

But as much as gladness fills those words, so does sadness. For while the heavenly Father was picking us up, He was allowing sinful men to "lift up" His Son on a cross. Jesus explained, "And I, if I be lifted up from the earth, will draw all men unto me" (John 12:32). Jesus was lifted up that we might be picked up.

D. God's Word Is a Holy Place
   (vv. 118, 119)

118. Thou hast trodden down all them that err from thy statutes: for their deceit is falsehood.

119. Thou puttest away all the wicked of the earth like dross: therefore I love thy testimonies.

Trodden (Hebrew, *calah*, "tossed aside, flouted, made light of, despised"), along with *dross* (Hebrew, *ciyg*, "refuse, garbage, that which is thrown away"), demonstrates God's attitude toward sin.

The Bible is called "the Holy Bible." It was written by "holy men" (2 Peter 1:21; see also Ephesians 3:5). It is a revelation of a holy God. The psalmist saw the holiness of God and declared that God has walked on sinners and cast aside the wicked like garbage. In an age when our schools stress the self-worth of everyone—and a favorite slogan is "God don't make no junk!"—the psalmist's brash words still allege that a holy God will cast away sinners like refuse or junk.

How wonderful it is that God has given us a holy place to which we can flee and escape the confusion, the uproar, the turbulence, the chaos, the bitterness. For a while we can hide in His holy place, the Word, where there is peace, tranquillity, hope, love, and assurance that God has everything under control. The Bible is a holy hiding place.

E. God's Word Is an Awesome
   Place (v. 120)

120. My flesh trembleth for fear of thee; and I am afraid of thy judgments.

This generation—having almost exhausted its supply of superlatives lauding "medical marvels," "electronic wizardry," "space exploration," and "transportation ingenuity"—is extremely difficult to impress. We are scared a tiny bit by the horror shows, wince a little at the violence on television, and are impressed somewhat by the rich and famous; but most of the things that would have awed other ages elicit only a yawn. But to study the Word of God is to be awed by it!

"My flesh trembleth for fear of thee; and I am afraid of thy judgments" (v. 120). While we can understand a little of the psalmist's emotions from the word *tremble*, the word from which it was translated is much stronger (*camar*, "to bristle up, to shiver, to stand up"). Eliphaz said, "Then a spirit passed before my face; the hair of my flesh stood up" (Job 4:15). When the aura of God came before Eliphaz, he said, on essence, "I was scared to death!"

God and His Word are awesome! While there are no superlatives grand enough to express God's greatness and power, as nothing in this world is exactly like God and thus nothing is adequate to describe Him—and while the terms "omnipotent," "omniscient," "omnipresent," and "eternal" say very little to a word- and idea-sated people—no one has ever come into the presence of God without shivering and trembling with awe (see Isaiah 6:1-5; Ezekiel 1:1, 28).

Why was a refuge so important in David's times?

II. THE WORD BRINGS PEACE
(Psalm 119:161-168)

The word *peace* (Greek, *eirene*), refers first of all to harmony and a lack of discord between people and things. Nations are said to be at peace when there is a state of national tranquillity and its citizens are free of the ravages of war. But just as nations can be at war and require peace, so can the individual—both internally and externally. God and His Word are the great bringers of peace (Acts 10:36). Peace is a place (in Christ), a process (growing in grace), and a person (God).

A. Peace Through Sufficiency
(vv. 161, 162)

161. Princes have persecuted me without a cause: but my heart standeth in awe of thy word.
162. I rejoice at thy word, as one that findeth great spoil.

The conclusion of a war and the ensuing peace are brought about by the stronger defeating the weaker. Through most of history this statement has been true: "To the victor belong the spoils." The defeated country was often looted by the conqueror, and the wealth of the people and nation was taken away. The spoils of war in our text (Hebrew, *shalal*) refers to the booty taken from the enemy after a war. Jesus referred to this practice (Luke 11:22); and it was prophesied of Jesus, "Therefore will I divide him a portion with the great, and he shall divide the spoil with the strong; because he hath poured out his soul unto death" (Isaiah 53:12).

Built into the word *peace* is the idea of "security, safety, and prosperity," which are the natural results of harmony between nations and individuals. Not only does the winner of a battle enjoy the wealth of the loser, but the peace that follows allows the economy of the nation to soar—factories work to manufacture items of peace; workers are hired, and their salaries allow them to buy the things made in the plants and shops of the country. In peacetime, everybody prospers.

The Word of God brings peace, and with that peace come the "spoils," or results of peace. When peace comes into our lives, a great number of other good things come with it. Paul said: "The peace of God, which passeth all understanding, shall keep [guard] your hearts and minds through Christ Jesus. Finally, brethren, whatsoever things are true, whatsoever things are honest, whatsoever things are just, whatsoever things are pure, whatsoever things are lovely, whatsoever things are of good report; if there be any virtue, and if there be any praise, think on these things. Those things, which ye have both learned, and received, and heard, and seen in me, do: and the God of peace shall be with you" (Philippians 4:7-9).

B. Peace Through Praise
(vv. 163-165)

163. I hate and abhor lying: but thy law do I love.

164. Seven times a day do I praise thee because of thy righteous judgments.

165. Great peace have they which love thy law: and nothing shall offend them.

The words *lying* and *law* are diametrically opposed in the psalmist's mind. One cannot lie and depend on the Word of God for his honor and character. The *law* is the *truth.* John 17:17 declares, "Thy word is truth." But while God is truth, Satan is a liar. "There is no truth in him [the devil]. When he speaketh a lie, he speaketh of his own: for he is a liar, and the father of it" (8:44).

The psalmist said he praised the Lord seven times a day for His "righteous judgments." The word *seven* refers to infinity and is called the number of God. The psalmist was not saying we are to praise God one, two, three . . . up to seven times—but to praise God continually. This same idea is contained in the New Testament admonition "Pray without ceasing" (1 Thessalonians 5:17). While one cannot praise or pray to God in actual conscious activity 60 minutes an hour, 24 hours a day, one can live in such a manner that his entire life is made up of perpetual prayer and praise.

Verse 165 says that nothing shall offend those who are in the Word. To *offend* (Hebrew, *mikshowl*) could also speak of being a stumbling block to those who trust in the Word. The believer who trusts in the Bible to guide in every circumstance will find nothing to stumble over; the path will always be lighted, and there will be divine protection at all times.

C. Peace Through Assurance of Salvation (vv. 166-168)

166. Lord, I have hoped for thy salvation, and done thy commandments.

167. My soul hath kept thy testimonies; and I love them exceedingly.

168. I have kept thy precepts and thy testimonies: for all my ways are before thee.

The tranquil state of the soul that has trusted Christ for salvation is, indeed, the greatest peace. In God alone is eternal assurance and everlasting peace. The psalmist said, "I have hoped for thy salvation" (v. 166); and in a manner of speaking, that is all he could do at that time—since the work of Christ the Savior on the cross was not yet accomplished, except in the mind of God. Israel was yet subservient to the law and looked forward with hope to the coming of the great Messiah (the Anointed One)—though they could neither understand nor accept the idea of a "suffering Savior" or that Messiah would be both the son of David and the Son of God.

The apostle Paul tells us, "Now in Christ Jesus ye who sometimes were far off are made nigh by the blood of Christ. For he is our peace" (Ephesians 2:13, 14). On the night before He was crucified (in the most tumultuous, uneasy and disquieting times of His earthly life), Jesus bequeathed to His disciples their most precious heritage. He said, "Peace I leave with you, my peace I give unto you: not as the world giveth, give I unto you. Let not your heart be troubled, neither let it be afraid" (John 14:27).

This peace is based on a relationship with the "God of peace" (Philippians 4:9) and on a sure knowledge that we have been born again and are coheirs with Christ (Romans 8:17) to the riches of God. Regardless of what may befall us as pilgrims in this world (see Hebrews 11:10, 13-16), Jesus has gone to prepare us a better place and will return to take us there (John 14:1-3).

What kind of things just naturally come with peace?

III. THE WORD GIVES HOPE
      (Psalm 119:169-176)

A. We Have Hope Because
    Christ Is the Word
    (vv. 169-173)

169. Let my cry come near before thee, O Lord: give me understanding according to thy word.
170. Let my supplication come before thee: deliver me according to thy word.
171. My lips shall utter praise, when thou hast taught me thy statutes.
172. My tongue shall speak of thy word: for all thy commandments are righteousness.
173. Let thine hand help me; for I have chosen thy precepts.

Three times in the verses above (vv. 169, 170, 172), the psalmist spoke of the "word." It is precisely this term in the Greek language that was adopted by the New Testament writers to describe who Jesus was. John said, "In the beginning was the Word [Logos], and the Word was with God, and the Word was God" (1:1). John

used the term *Logos* to show that Jesus is exactly like His Father. Paul wrote that He "is the [express] image of the invisible God, the first-born of every creature" (Colossians 1:15).

What God the Father is, Jesus is; what Jesus is, God the Father is! They are exactly alike. Since "no man hath seen God" (John 1:18), the Son of God came to reveal Him and show the world what He was like. "God . . . hath in these last days spoken unto us by his Son . . . who [is] the brightness of his glory, and the express image of his person" (Hebrews 1:1-3).

Our hope is in the Word. Having seen Jesus, we have learned about forgiveness, love, and salvation.

B. We Have Hope Because Christ
    Is Our Salvation (vv. 174, 175)

174. I have longed for thy salvation, O Lord; and thy law is my delight.
175. Let my soul live, and it shall praise thee; and let thy judgments help me.

Salvation (Hebrew, *yeshuwah*) also means "deliverance, prosperity, victory" and is the word from which the name Jesus is derived. When the psalmist said, "I have longed for thy salvation, O Lord," he could not have realized how important this word would be to the entire rebuilding of the relationship of mankind with his God.

Jesus' very name means "salvation," as indicated by Matthew: "Thou shalt call his name JESUS: for he shall save his people from their sins" (1:21). The order of salvation (Latin, *ordo salutis*) is a process somewhat outlined by Paul in Romans 8:29, 30 and includes all the things God does to redeem restore us, and return us to our place as sons of God.

The mission of Jesus which sent Him to the cross was "to seek and to save that which was lost" (Luke 19:10). In fact, Peter declared: "Be it known unto you all, and to all the people of Israel, that by the name of Jesus [which means "salvation, healing, wholeness"] Christ of Nazareth, whom ye crucified, whom God raised from the dead, even by him doth this man stand here before you whole. This is the stone which was set at nought of you builders, which is become the head of the corner. Neither is there salvation in any other: for there is none other name under heaven given among men, whereby we must be saved" (Acts 4:10-12).

All Israel longed for the Lord's salvation (Jesus). We have Him as our blessed Savior and eternal hope.

C. We Have Hope Because Christ Is Our Shepherd/King (v. 176)

176. I have gone astray like a lost sheep; seek thy servant; for I do not forget thy commandments.

The words of the psalmist in this verse are reminiscent of Israel's shepherd-king, David. David knew sheep. He was called from tending his sheep so the prophet Samuel could anoint him to be the future king of Israel (see 2 Samuel 7:8). He knew that when a sheep was lost, it did not find its own way home. Contrary to folk wisdom contained in the nursery rhyme about Little BoPeep's sheep, if sheep are left alone, they do not come home, wagging their tails behind them.

In this last verse of Psalm 119,

the psalmist beseeched the Great Shepherd to "seek thy servant." And in the parable of the lost sheep, Jesus said, "What man of you, having an hundred sheep, if he lose one of them, doth not leave the ninety and nine in the wilderness, and go after that which is lost, until he find it? And when he hath found it, he layeth it on his shoulders, rejoicing" (Luke 15:4, 5).

In the beautiful lyrics of the shepherd psalm, David declared, "The Lord is my shepherd" (Psalm 23:1). First Peter 2:25 declares, "Ye were as sheep going astray; but are now returned unto the Shepherd." Jesus said, "I am the good shepherd: the good shepherd giveth his life for the sheep" (John 10:11).

Jesus is not only the Good Shepherd, but He is also "the Lamb of God" (John 1:29)—the Passover Lamb, the sacrificial lamb of which Abraham prophetically spoke when he said, "My son, God will provide himself a lamb for a burnt-offering" (Genesis 22:8). In the Book of Revelation, John saw Jesus standing as "a Lamb as it had been slain" (5:6). Immediately, however, the slain Lamb became the center of all adoration. As John continued, those about the throne were "saying with a loud voice, Worthy is the Lamb that was slain. . . . And every creature which is in heaven, and on the earth, and under the earth, and such as are in the sea, and all that are in them, heard I saying, Blessing, and honour, and glory, and power, be unto him that sitteth upon the throne, and unto the Lamb for ever and ever" (vv. 12, 13).

In what ways is Jesus both our shepherd and our king?

REVIEW QUESTIONS

1. In modern times, why do we need a refuge for the mind?

2. On what construction did Nehemiah and his workers have "a mind to work"?

3. What, according to the apostle Paul, is to "[guard] your hearts and minds"?

4. How did those around Jesus discover what His Father was like?

5. What is the meaning of the name *Jesus*?

GOLDEN TEXT HOMILY

"HOLD THOU ME UP, AND I SHALL BE SAFE: AND I WILL HAVE RESPECT UNTO THY STATUTES CONTINUALLY" (Psalm 119:117).

The three distinct facets of this verse—supplication, security, and salvation—are the theme cry of the whole psalm, which builds praise in the writer's heart for the Word of God.

With this, the psalmist had peace; he had no fear. In the Christian life, peace and fear are incompatible. Where there is fear there can be no peace; conversely, where the peace of God abides, fear is excluded. Just as light dispels darkness, peace erases fear.

Did the psalmist draw upon some secret supply of security and safety? No, Jehovah, through His Word, provided strength. Did he have a secret formula for inducing Jehovah's favor? Not at all. The key that unlocks the doors of peace and fearlessness is faith—taking God at His Word. The exercise of faith and trust dispels fear and instills a sense of security. This psalmist's state of heart has been alluded to by many others, including Isaiah, who said, "I will trust, and not be afraid" (12:2).

When we are surrounded by foes and dangers, faith brings the peace that dispels fear. To trust only when things are favorable is to sail only with the wind, to believe only when we can see. Let us seek the kind of faith that will enable us to trust God and produce praise, come what will.

If we want to have continuous love and respect for God's Word, we must take God at His word.

Stated negatively, God may not always will to save us "out of trouble." Herein is the acid test of faith with praise. It's easy to trust the Lord in the sunlight. It's something else to trust in the dark. God's will is always right; and if He does not remove the trouble, He will give us grace in it. His peace and joy may be ours in trouble. It is up to us to cultivate the roots of faith. Oh, for the faith of perfect trust! "God is our refuge and strength, a very present help in trouble" (Psalm 46:1).—**Willie F. Lawrence, D. D., Pastor, Church of God, Moline, Illinois**

DAILY BIBLE READINGS

M. God Is Our Refuge.
   2 Samuel 22:1-7

T. Miraculous Provision.
   1 Kings 17:8-16

W. Continuous Care.
   Nehemiah 9:20-25

T. Free From Worry.
   Matthew 6:25-34

F. Secure in God's Love.
   Romans 8:31-39

S. Renewed Day by Day.
   2 Corinthians 4:8-18

INTRODUCTION
TO SPRING
QUARTER

The month of March begins the spring quarter series of lessons, which is divided into two distinct units. Unit One (lessons 1-6) is presented under the theme "Book of Hebrews." The Book of Hebrews is rich in its teaching on the present ministry and priesthood of Christ. Those who witnessed the passing of the Jewish priesthood, and who felt that with it a divinely ordained system of salvation had vanished, must have been greatly reassured by the teaching that this man, Christ Jesus, "[for] ever hath an unchangeable priesthood" (Hebrews 7:24).

Unit Two (lessons 8-13) is titled "Lessons From the Patriarchs." The lessons in this series cover incidents in the lives of Abraham, Lot, Isaac, Jacob, Esau, and Joseph.

Lessons 7 and 14 focus on our special day studies of Easter and Pentecost. The quarter of lessons taken as a whole is certain to bring new insights and inspiration for service to our Lord.

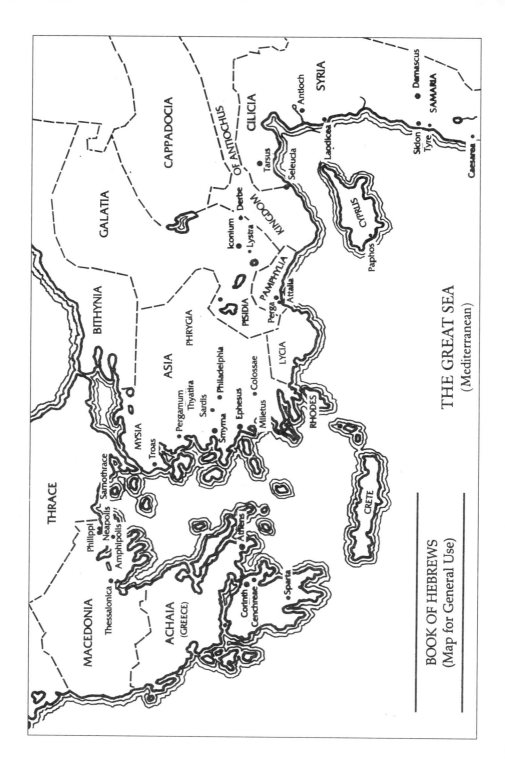

THE GREAT SEA
(Mediterranean)

BOOK OF HEBREWS
(Map for General Use)

The Superiority of Jesus Christ

Study Text: Hebrews 1:1 through 3:6

Objective: To acknowledge the superiority of Christ as Lord over all and worship Him.

Time: The Book of Hebrews was probably written between A.D. 64 and 70.

Place: The place of the writing of the Book of Hebrews is uncertain. Many Bible scholars suggest Rome.

Golden Text: "Holy Brethren . . . consider the Apostle and High Priest of our profession, Christ Jesus" (Hebrews 3:1).

Central Truth: Jesus Christ is infinitely superior to everyone and everything in creation.

Evangelism Emphasis: Jesus Christ is the only way to eternal life.

PRINTED TEXT

Hebrews 1:1. God, who at sundry times and in divers manners spake in time past unto the fathers by the prophets,

2. Hath in these last days spoken unto us by his Son, whom he hath appointed heir of all things, by whom also he made the worlds;

3. Who being the brightness of his glory, and the express image of his person, and upholding all things by the word of his power, when he had by himself purged our sins, sat down on the right hand of the Majesty on high;

4. Being made so much better than the angels, as he hath by inheritance obtained a more excellent name than they.

2:9. But we see Jesus, who was made a little lower than the angels for the suffering of death, crowned with glory and honour; that he by the grace of God should taste death for every man.

10. For it became him, for whom are all things, and by whom are all things, in bringing many sons unto glory, to make the captain of their salvation perfect through sufferings.

11. For both he that sanctifieth and they who are sanctified are all of one: for which cause he is not ashamed to call them brethren,

12. Saying, I will declare thy name unto my brethren, in the midst of the church will I sing praise unto thee.

13. And again, I will put my trust in him. And again, Behold I and the children which God hath given me.

14. Forasmuch then as the children are partakers of flesh and blood, he also himself likewise took part of the same; that through death he might destroy

him that had the power of death, that is, the devil;

15. And deliver them who through fear of death were all their lifetime subject to bondage.

3:3. For this man was counted worthy of more glory than Moses, inasmuch as he who hath builded the house hath more honour than the house.

4. For every house is builded by some man; but he that built all things is God.

5. And Moses verily was faithful in all his house, as a servant, for a testimony of those things which were to be spoken after;

6. But Christ as a son over his own house; whose house are we, if we hold fast the confidence and the rejoicing of the hope firm unto the end.

LESSON OUTLINE

LESSON EXPOSITION

INTRODUCTION

We live in a spiritual world. People are seeking after spirits. Perhaps humanity is more spiritually-minded now than at any other time in history. The new spirituality is not about the Holy Spirit, nor does it acknowledge the only name by which there is salvation—the name of Jesus. The new age of spirituality talks about the spirit within each person, the spirits all around us, and the transcendent realities that promise to bring peace and unity to the earth.

Hebrews 1 is as contemporary as the morning newspaper, as relevant as any new book on the market, and as penetrating and mesmerizing as any paid programming on late-night television. The message of Hebrews 1 is that Christ is without equal. All spirits bow down to Christ; He formed the worlds. The Lord is the only Son of the heavenly Father. Christ is the very Word that controls the world.

The first chapter of Hebrews cuts through all of the false spirituality postured in our world today. The New Age religion is a system that worships the wrong god. Transcendent thought is a religion that has created altars sacrificing the Scripture. The spirituality of today attracts multitudes toward a light that burns with a flame separate from Christ's. To ignore the message of Hebrews 1 is to lose a valuable resource for addressing one of the greatest challenges facing the church today.

I. GREATER THAN ANGELS
(Hebrews 1:1-6)

A. Proclamation Through the Son (vv. 1, 2)

1. God, who at sundry times and in divers manners spake in time past unto the fathers by the prophets,

2. Hath in these last days spoken unto us by his Son, whom he hath appointed heir of all things, by whom also he made the worlds.

The Word of God is the communication of humanity's redemption. Communication is important for commerce, education, government and many other vital functions of society. However, no other communication can match the quality of God's Word.

God communicated directly through the prophets in Old Testament times. When the prophet spoke, he or she became the mouthpiece of God. The proclamation was "Thus saith the Lord." Nations were changed, sins uncovered, and multitudes brought to repentance by God's utterances through the prophets.

When Jesus came, God superseded all former means of communication by speaking through His Son. Former proclamations were incomplete. But now, perfectly, the divine Word came, by incarnation, to fallen humanity. Prophecy continues today through the Holy Spirit and in accordance with God's Holy Scripture. The perfect, redemptive Word, however, is Christ Jesus.

"Appointed heir of all things, by whom also he made the worlds" (v. 2) indicates the very power of God's Word through Christ. Bursting through the Son were royalty and creation—creation not only of the earth but of all things. The writer spoke of the means by which God "wrote" the universe into existence before he ever penned human words.

Describe Christ's role as the Word of the Father. How can we acknowledge Christ as the Creator of all things?

B. Position of Authority (vv. 3, 4)

3. Who being the brightness of his glory, and the express image of his person, and upholding all things by the word of his power, when he had by himself purged our sins, sat down on the right hand of the Majesty on high;

4. Being made so much better than the angels, as he hath by inheritance obtained a more excellent name than they.

Christ was the divine instrument who executed the sovereignty of the Father on earth. To achieve this role, Christ sacrificed himself for the sins of the world. He now sits at the right hand of Authority, next to the Father. Superior to creation, Christ the Creator now exercises authority over all creation.

Inheritance (v. 4) is an important term, because it verifies the deity of Christ. He is of the same essence as the heavenly Father. Christ is not of the same essence as the angels or any other spirit being. Christ, the Mediator of divine authority on earth, is very God in essence as well as in power.

What unique relationship does Christ have with the heavenly Father? How is Christ above all beings, especially those that are spiritual?

C. Praise by the Angels for the Son (vv. 5, 6)

(Hebrews 1:5, 6 is not included in the printed text.)

No other creature—whether physical, angelic, or spiritual—is like Christ. Who else, asks verse 5, does the heavenly Father address as "My Son"? This is not just an expression Jesus was actually "begotten."

Begotten (v. 5) implies "of the same being." The heavenly Father's relationship with Christ is unlike any other in all of the universe. The Father and Son are distinct; yet they are in divine relationship with each other.

The worldview of many at the time the Book of Hebrews was written was that angelic and spirit beings performed acts of power and authority that rivaled those of Christ. By quoting from Psalms 2:7; 89:26; 97:7, the writer demonstrates that Christ has no rival. In fact, the angels worship Him (Revelation 5:11, 12).

II. CONQUEROR OF DEATH
(Hebrews 2:9-18)

A. Salvation Through Suffering (vv. 9, 10)

9. But we see Jesus, who was made a little lower than the angels for the suffering of death, crowned with glory and honour; that he by the grace of God should taste death for every man.

10. For it became him, for whom are all things, and by whom are all things, in bringing many sons unto glory, to make the captain of their salvation perfect through sufferings.

Position is meaningless unless it is used to accomplish something

worthy and beneficial. Christ, in His unique and divine position, carried out the word and will of the Father. He did so in order to bring salvation and blessing to those who believe on Him.

The heart of Christ's work for humanity was His death on the cross. The irony of the Cross is that without strength, Christ overcame the sentence of death. His suffering was the means for conquering the pain and sentence of sin. Suffering was not a terminal condition for the Savior; it was the vehicle Grace used to terminate the grip Satan had on humankind.

The root of the Greek term for *suffering (pathema)* is *pathos*, which emphasized "intense feeling and experience." The suffering Christ experienced on our behalf was especially painful to Him personally and internally. The pain is graphically depicted in what we know from Scripture about the physical scars, bruises, and brokenness He experienced which eventually led to His death. The physical pain was enormous; however, the internal agony was even greater.

The personal endurance of Christ and suffering purchased our salvation. Christ's pain on the cross was not in vain. Most New Age philosophies avoid suffering; instead they advertise peace. But Christ suffered so that we might not only have peace in this world but eternal peace as well.

B. Solidarity In Christ (vv. 11-13)

11. For both he that sanctifieth and they who are sanctified are all of one: for which cause he is not ashamed to call them brethren,

12. Saying, I will declare thy name unto my brethren, in the midst of the church will I sing praise unto thee.

13. And again, I will put my trust in him. And again, Behold I and the children which God hath given me.

The message of Christ in Hebrews is not only about Christ, but it is also about Christ's work for all those who will come to Him as Lord and Savior. Christ brings all who believe on Him into fellowship with Him. His supremacy is used to forge an eternal union with His body of believers.

The solidarity of Christ with the Christian speaks of the intimacy of Christ's work. Not only is Christ exalted, but He is also extended to the believer. *Brethren* is the personal term used to convey the relationship of close union between the believer and Christ. This Savior is not lifted up to be lifted beyond any of us. He is Lord in order that He might love us.

Both Psalms and Isaiah are quoted in verses 12 and 13 to document the desire of Christ for relationship with believers. Psalms 18:2 and 22:22 along with Isaiah 8:18 and 12:2 convey the threefold message that He is in the midst of believers. We believers are his brethren, and as such we have been given unto Him by the heavenly Father.

C. Supremacy Over Death
(vv. 14-16)

(Hebrews 2:16 is not included in the printed text.)

14. Forasmuch then as the children are partakers of flesh and blood, he also himself likewise took part of the same; that through death he might destroy him that had the power of death, that is, the devil;

15. And deliver them who through fear of death were all their lifetime subject to bondage.

Christ's victory over death not only exalts our Savior, but it also benefits the believer. Verse 14 rings with the message of the Savior's victory through death, and verse 15 sings of the believer's deliverance from death. Verse 16 declares that precisely because Christ is not merely another spirit or an angel, He is able to bring victory and deliverance from death.

Today, the Christian must combat the New Age philosophy that Christ is just another spirit or emanation. If Christ is not the Lord, the Creator, and the only begotten of the Father, then His death is just another death and He is just another who made a contribution to the peace we all seek, rather than the door of our salvation.

How important is it to combat the false doctrine of the New Age? How is Christ unique as the one and only Son of God the Father? How does the New Age try to preach that there are other ways to peace and salvation besides Jesus Christ?

D. Sacrifice of a High Priest
(vv. 17, 18)

(Hebrews 2:17, 18 is not included in the printed text.)

Drawing on this knowledge of the Old Testament high priest—a lesson Hebrew readers would understand—the writer declares Christ as the only High Priest for their salvation. The high priest was unrivaled in the religious ritual of Israel. No other person was designated and purified to offer the sacrifice for sins before Almighty God. In the same way, the only person in eternity who could offer the redeeming sacrifice for forgiveness from sin was Christ.

III. FAITHFUL SON OF GOD
(Hebrews 3:1-6)

A. Appointment of Christ (vv. 1, 2)

(Hebrews 3:1, 2 is not included in the printed text.)

Christ was appointed by God the Father to do the work He did. He performed it faithfully—so faithfully that at His death He could proclaim, "It is finished" (John 19:30). Just as Moses was faithful in God's house, the writer says, so Jesus was faithful to the One who appointed him.

B. Acclaim Above Moses (vv. 3-5)

3. For this man was counted worthy of more glory than Moses, inasmuch as he who hath builded the house hath more honour than the house.

4. For every house is builded by some man; but he that built all things is God.

5. And Moses verily was faithful in all his house, as a servant, for a testimony of those things which were to be spoken after.

Jesus' work is above price and reward. The image of the builder and the building emphasize the supremacy of His work. Just as the architect is more important than the house he builds, so also is Christ more worthy of honor and glory than His creation. He preceded Moses and He made Moses. He assigned to Moses his task. This work was necessary but it was secondary to the supreme work of Christ. God is the builder of all things.

Moses, a servant in God's house, testified by his faithfulness to things that would come later.

Compare Moses' work with Christ's? How does Christ make it possible for us to do the works we do today? In what ways can you honor Christ as the supreme Savior?

C. Acquisition of Christ's Faithfulness (v. 6)

6. But Christ as a son over his own house; whose house are we, if we hold fast the confidence and the rejoicing of the hope firm unto the end.

Look at the faithfulness of Christ alongside the faithfulness of believers. In Christ's work, He created us. He died to redeem us. He is building us into His own house (Ephesians 2:19-22). He is faithful in this task.

The believer's work, on the other hand, is to believe by "hold[ing] fast the confidence" and "rejoicing [in] the hope" found in Christ. Christ is constructing a house of total and complete redemption; however, we must be faithful in order to remain in His house and receive the full benefits of redemption.

"Hold fast" (Greek, *katecho*) means, in today's vernacular, "to keep a strong grip." The concept is similar to a life-giving, life-sustaining grip, a matter of life and death. It means holding on as though our lives depend on it. The content of our salvation is sure, but it is our job to hold on to it.

Confidence is translated from a

term which speaks of something so real and viable that it does not have to be hidden. *Rejoicing* comes from a combination of Greek terms emphasizing something that could be justifiably proclaimed and boasted of. There is no second-guessing the work of Christ. Christ is supreme and His work indestructible, open, and unashamed. The writer's message is to hold on to Christ's work until the very end.

REVIEW QUESTIONS

1. Describe in your words the false spirituality of our world today?

2. How important is it to combat the false doctrine of the New Age?

3. Do believers recognize Christ's power above the power of all beings, seen and unseen?

4. How is Moses' work an illustration of Christ's work as the High Priest for our salvation?

5. What did the writer mean when he encouraged the readers to "hold fast"?

GOLDEN TEXT HOMILY

"HOLY BRETHREN . . . CONSIDER THE APOSTLE AND HIGH PRIEST OF OUR PROFESSION, CHRIST JESUS" (Hebrews 3:1).

The Book of Hebrews emphasizes the fact that Jesus Christ is greater than all the patriarchs. Therefore, this particular text strongly appeals to those who are redeemed. "Holy brethren" is the title given to the intended hearers. It is the writer's purpose to make known the effectiveness of the gospel so that all who hear will consider and become "holy brethren."

From this point on there flows an extensive characterization of Jesus. He is not just another apostle who has come to *tell* of salvation; He is also the Apostle, or Sent One, who has come to *be* our salvation. He is the "High Priest of our confession" (*NASB*). Under the law the high priest went every year to make atonement with the blood of sacrificed animals. Jesus is superior to the high priests of the Law, and superior to the sacrifices also. Scripture reads, "Without shedding of blood is no remission [of sin]" (9:22). As High Priest of our confession, He has placed us in relationship with Him as His holy brethren.

When we consider His office of superiority, we suddenly and solemnly are brought face to face with our own character. Do we consider Christ greater than the prophets, angels, Moses, and Joshua? Do we consider that He is the Mediator of our relationship with the Father? Do we consider ourselves "holy brethren"? Have we considered His calling? Do we confess Christ with our lips only or with our life also? Do we consider Christ as just a spectator in our lives, or has He become Lord of our life?

Consider the Holy Brother who is our Apostle, High Priest, and Lord. He has been sent to complete and perfect our faith in God. How wonderful it is that we are partakers of His blessed holy calling and not just hearers of it. Truly He is superior!—**Aaron D. Mize, Chaplain I, Parchman, Mississippi**

SENTENCE SERMONS

JESUS CHRIST IS infinitely superior to everyone and everything in creation.

—Selected

JESUS CHRIST IS the only way to eternal life.

—Selected

CHRIST IS not valued at all unless He is valued above all.
—**Saint Augustine**

JESUS CHRIST, the condescension of divinity, and the exaltation of humanity.
—**Phillips Brooks**

EVANGELISM APPLICATION

JESUS CHRIST IS THE ONLY WAY TO ETERNAL LIFE.

There are many claims today about the work of spirits. Many more claims are made about the way to achieve eternal peace. We are told that we can tap into the "inner source" of peace—that it is *within* each of us. We are told that there are many spirits and many paths to peace and divinity. We are told that Jesus was just a spiritual success story who can be a path for some today.

Christ is the only way to eternal peace. There is a spirit within each person, but it is not bent toward peace. Rather, each person has a sinful nature that is contrary to God. Without the saving work of Christ, every person is destined for eternal destruction.

Christ died on the cross, making salvation possible for everyone who will believe in Him. He provided deliverance from the bondage of sin and the sentence of an eternity in hell. Spirits cannot save lost humanity. Christ's work is the only way to salvation.

Today the task of evangelism is not only to proclaim Christ but also to denounce the preaching of other paths to peace. To accept the New Age doctrine of diversity of spirits and alternative works of righteousness negates the message of salvation through Christ. Nevertheless, Jesus Christ is not just the way to peace and eternal life; He is the only way.

ILLUMINATING THE LESSON

The *Canadian Magazine* commented on Hitler's use of the swastika. It said:

If [Hitler's] National Reich Church had been established, the swastika would have replaced the Cross. Point 30 of the proposed National Reich Church's 30-point program, drawn up during the war, read: "On the day of its foundation, the Christian cross must be removed from all churches, cathedrals, and chapels. . . . It must be superseded by the only unconquerable symbol, the swastika." History is the commentary on the folly of Hitler's dreams and on the futility of all who would seek to destroy the Church of Christ (from the *Parsons Bible Illustrator*).

There have been, and will continue to be, many challenges and counterfeits of Christ's work. All challenges to the deity, work, and lordship of Christ will ultimately fail.

DAILY BIBLE READINGS

M. Lord Over Angels.
   Psalms 103:19 through 104:4
T. Superior Sacrifice.
   Isaiah 53:7-12
W. Anointed Messiah.
   Isaiah 61:1-3
T. Superior Son. Matthew 17:1-5
F. Exalted Son. Philippians 2:5-11
S. Glory of the Son.
   Colossians 1:15-20

Christ, Our High Priest

Study Text: Hebrews 4:13-16; 5:1-10

Objective: To examine Christ's ministry as the Great High Priest and come boldly to Him in faith.

Time: The Book of Hebrews was probably written between A.D. 64 and 70.

Place: The place of the writing of the Book of Hebrews is uncertain. Many Bible scholars suggest Rome.

Golden Text: "Let us therefore come boldly unto the throne of grace, that we may obtain mercy, and find grace to help in time of need" (Hebrews 4:16).

Central Truth: Because Jesus is the eternal High Priest, believers can approach God with confidence.

Evangelism Emphasis: Sinners can find forgiveness in the atoning work of Christ.

PRINTED TEXT

Hebrews 4:13. Neither is there any creature that is not manifest in his sight: but all things are naked and opened unto the eyes of him with whom we have to do.

14. Seeing then that we have a great high priest, that is passed into the heavens, Jesus the Son of God, let us hold fast our profession.

15. For we have not an high priest which cannot be touched with the feeling of our infirmities; but was in all points tempted like as we are, yet without sin.

16. Let us therefore come boldly unto the throne of grace, that we may obtain mercy, and find grace to help in time of need.

5:1. For every high priest taken from among men is ordained for men in things pertaining to God, that he may offer both gifts and sacrifices for sins:

2. Who can have compassion on the ignorant, and on them that are out of the way; for that he himself also is compassed with infirmity.

3. And by reason hereof he ought, as for the people, so also for himself, to offer for sins.

4. And no man taketh this honour unto himself, but he that is called of God, as was Aaron.

5. So also Christ glorified not himself to be made an high priest; but he that said unto him, Thou art my Son, to day have I begotten thee.

6. As he saith also in another place, Thou art a priest for ever after the order of Melchisedec.

7. Who in the days of his flesh, when he had offered up prayers and supplications with

strong crying and tears unto him that was able to save him from death, and was heard in that he feared;

8. Though he were a Son, yet learned he obedience by the things which he suffered;

9. And being made perfect, he became the author of eternal salvation unto all them that obey him;

10. Called of God an high priest after the order of Melchisedec.

DICTIONARY

Aaron (AIR-ohn)—Hebrews 5:4—The oldest brother of Moses.

Melchisedec (mel-KIZ-ih-dek)—Hebrews 5:6—Priest and king who worshiped God in the time of Abraham.

LESSON OUTLINE

I. CHRIST UNDERSTANDS US

   A. The Perception of Christ

   B. The Position of Christ

   C. The Provision of Christ

II. OUR PRIEST FOREVER

   A. The Foundational Calling

   B. The Fulfilled Origin

   C. The Forever Priest

III. CHRIST PROVIDES SALVATION

   A. The Suffering Savior

   B. The Special Author of Salvation

   C. The Supreme Priest of Salvation

LESSON EXPOSITION

INTRODUCTION

Christ ministers as our High Priest before the heavenly Father. His unique position makes the sacrifice He provided on our behalf unequaled. His position comes as a result of the Father's will and is responsive to the Father's purposes. The sacrifice itself is Christ's own body, making the sacrifice per-

fect. The work of this High Priest is perfect in position, process, and performance.

The believer needs to recognize the unique work of Christ as our High Priest. There is no way in which His work can be replaced. The believer is required to depend on this work.

Hebrews 4 and 5 communicate the great principles behind Christ's work as the believer's High Priest. The knowledge conveyed in these chapters encourages the believer to continually value and commit to that work. The chapters summarize the origin of God's plan of redemption, explain Christ's work, survey the position of Christ as our High Priest, and probe the responsibility of every individual to respond to His work.

I. CHRIST UNDERSTANDS US (Hebrews 4:13-16)

A. The Perception of Christ (v. 13)

13. Neither is there any creature that is not manifest in his sight: but all things are naked and opened unto the eyes of him with whom we have to do.

All the deeds of the nation were to be accounted for to God under the Old Testament law. Even the intents of the heart were to be judged by God. It was the work of the high priest to make atonement for all the sinful works of the nation. Nothing could be left unaddressed by the system of sacrifices and intercession offered by the high priest.

Similarly, the work of Christ as High Priest had to be thorough, perfect. All the deeds, thoughts, and intents of every person who would come to Christ had to be covered by His blood. Verse 13 assures the reader that Christ the High Priest is perfect in His ability to uncover all sin, corruption, and evil.

B. The Position of Christ
   (vv. 14, 15)

14. Seeing then that we have a great high priest, that is passed into the heavens, Jesus the Son of God, let us hold fast our profession.

15. For we have not an high priest which cannot be touched with the feeling of our infirmities; but was in all points tempted like as we are, yet without sin.

Christ is the High Priest who intercedes on behalf of sinners. The position He holds is twofold. He has a position of authority before the Father from which to offer his death as a sacrifice for our salvation. Also, His experiences as a human allow Him to personally identify with the deepest needs we have. This enables us to trust in His supreme sacrifice for our sins.

What hinders people from applying Christ's sacrifice to their own experience?

Jesus' lofty position, indicated by the phrase "passed into the heavens," far exceeds the position earthly High Priests had. They could approach only the Holy of Holies on earth. However, Christ is in the heavens with before the heavenly Father himself, directly offering His sacrifice before the Father.

The personal position of Christ includes His incarnate experience of humankind's infirmities or weaknesses. Christ did not sin, but He became sin and felt the burden of our pain, weaknesses, and temptations. Christ's sacrifice is not an irrelevant matter, but is custom-tailored to bring our deepest sin and infirmity before the Father for redemption.

The word *tempted* (v. 15), from the Greek *peira*, means "ascertain, assay, test." Christ's temptations were a matter of His being tested. A matter may be ascertained yet not known by experience. Christ's temptations provided Him with sufficient understanding of the human condition. He knew full well about sin without having sinned. His victory over temptation enabled Him to offer a perfect sacrifice without ever having committed sin.

C. The Provision of Christ (v. 16)

16. Let us therefore come boldly unto the throne of grace, that we may obtain mercy, and find grace to help in time of need.

Our own confidence about Christ's work is important. There is no question that the nature of Christ's sacrifice is perfect. What we do with His sacrifice is the great question, however.

The writer has been emphasizing the specific and personal

applications of Christ's work. In verse 13, He knows everything about every one of our lives. In verses 14 and 15, Christ understands the specific sin that each of us has committed. Therefore, Christ's sacrifice was not a general act but a profoundly personal act designed for the specific sins of every individual.

The word *boldly* emphasizes that every sinner has a personal invitation to come and receive forgiveness. Rather than a general issuance of redemption, there is an individual invitation with our own name on it. It is an invitation to come personally and be reconciled unto the Father.

What hinders people from believing in the personal nature and application of Christ's sacrifice? What can we do to convince people that Christ died for them individually?

II. OUR PRIEST FOREVER
(Hebrews 5:1-6)

A. The Foundational Calling
(vv. 1-4)

1. For every high priest taken from among men is ordained for men in things pertaining to God, that he may offer both gifts and sacrifices for sins:
2. Who can have compassion on the ignorant, and on them that are out of the way; for that he himself also is compassed with infirmity.
3. And by reason hereof he ought, as for the people, so also for himself, to offer for sins.
4. And no man taketh this honour unto himself, but he that is called of God, as was Aaron.

The foundation of Christ's ministry is that He has been "ordained" by the heavenly Father to be our High Priest. *Ordained* comes from the Greek term, *kathistemi*. The term emphasizes "placing or setting into place." Christ was not simply given an office, but He was put into a position by the heavenly Father from which He could offer the supreme sacrifice for our sins.

No earthly High Priest could be a priest without having a direct lineage to Aaron, the original high priest. The writer assures us that Christ's lineage is greater than that of Aaron's, for His lineage goes all the way back to the Father himself, who directly appointed or set Him in place as High Priest.

B. The Fulfilled Origin (v. 5)

5. So also Christ glorified not himself to be made an high priest; but he that said unto him, Thou art my Son, to day have I begotten thee.

The role of Christ as High Priest comes from the fact that He is the Son of the Father. Not only does He have a direct appointment from the heavenly Father to be High Priest (vv. 1-4), but He is also in direct relationship with the Father as His Son.

Glorified and begotten are concepts more powerful than *ordained*. *Glorified* conveys the divine nature of Christ as High Priest. God the Son offered His life to God the Father. Christ, the sacrifice, and Christ, the High Priest who administered the sacrifice, were one, and that One was divine. The sacrifice to the Holy God was the most perfect of sacrifices because of the High Priest's glorified nature.

Explain the significance of the

Son's being offered as a sacrifice to the heavenly Father.

Begotten conveys the personal relationship between the Son and the Father. There was a familial unity between the One who offered the sacrifice and the One who received the sacrifice. This relationship assured the consummation and reception of the sacrifice. Rather than a cold, aloof ritual, the sacrifice of the Son was given in sincerity and obedience. The reception of the sacrifice was sealed with the stamp of the love between the heavenly Father and the Divine Son.

C. The Forever Priest (v. 6)

6. As he saith also in another place, Thou art a priest for ever after the order of Melchisedec.

This is a quotation from Psalm 110:4. The order of Melchisedec refers to the Old Testament priest who combined the offices of priest and king. Abram paid a tithe to Melchisedec in gratitude for the blessings of God. When the King of Sodom tried to ingratiate Abram to him, Abram refused. He would be indebted to God, not to the King of Sodom.

Instead of rituals of purification, Christ offers, in similar fashion, the sacrifice of Himself and establishes for the believer a direct relationship with the heavenly Father. Melchisedec represented a direct relationship with God but foreshadowed the coming of something better. Christ is the fulfillment and perfection of this type and shadow through His sacrifice of himself and His perfect relationship with the Father.

III. CHRIST PROVIDES SALVATION (Hebrews 5:7-10)

A. The Suffering Savior (vv. 7, 8)

7. Who in the days of his flesh, when he had offered up prayers and supplications with strong crying and tears unto him that was able to save him from death, and was heard in that he feared;

8. Though he were a Son, yet learned he obedience by the things which he suffered.

After discussing the nature of Christ's position and work as our High Priest, His suffering becomes the topic in verses 7-10. Suffering is at the heart of the sacrifice of Christ. The power in suffering involves the denial of self. The interest of the Savior was not Himself, but the pleasure of the heavenly Father. Obedience pleased the Father, and suffering was involved in that obedience.

The term *suffered* comes from the Greek *pascho*. The word emphasizes not only the agony but also the "purposeful vexation" laid upon the Savior. Christ's sacrifice was for a purpose. Verse 7 conveys a sense of the agony of the suffering that Christ endured in being sacrificed. The cries and tears of the Savior are described. Verse 8 says He learned from His sufferings. Christ's suffering was obedience, not mere self-flagellation or meaningless slaughter. He knew His call to be the sacrificial lamb, and He obediently carried it out.

What is the heart of the sacrifice of Christ? How is Christ qualified to offer the supreme sacrifice for our sins? How is the sacrifice of Christ applied to our lives?

B. The Special Author of Salvation (v. 9)

9. And being made perfect, he became the author of eternal salvation unto all them that obey him.

Christ is the perfect High Priest and therefore is the author of eternal salvation for all who obey Him. There are three critical aspects of the work of Christ for salvation: "perfect," "author," and "obey."

Perfect describes the work of the heavenly Father in Christ our High Priest. The term comes from the Greek word, *teleioo*. The word refers to a "goal" and "purpose." Verse 1 refers to the ordaining of Christ for the position of High Priest. The work of perfecting was the work of His position as High Priest. Christ was perfectly fitted by the heavenly Father for the purpose and work of being our High Priest.

Author refers to an aspect of the work of Christ our High Priest. The word comes from the Greek term *aitios*, which involves causing something. Christ, exalted and glorified as our High Priest, has become the personal mediating cause of eternal salvation on the grounds of His finished work. No one else, no other cause, and certainly no earthly source was responsible for salvation. Christ is the first and only cause that brought about forgiveness.

Obey refers to our response to the sacrifice offered by Christ, our High Priest. The term comes from a compound Greek word which means "to hear and respond." The sacrifice of Christ is applied to our lives as we respond in obedience to Him. His sacrifice does not overwhelm any individual. The perfection of the sacrifice does not guarantee that all people will receive it.

C. The Supreme Priest of Salvation (v. 10)

10. Called of God an high priest after the order of Melchisedec.

The *obedience, authorship,* and *perfection* of the sacrifice of Christ the High Priest are all three summarized in verse 10. *Obedience* was the response of Abram when he rejected the offer of the King of Sodom, affirming the blessing of Melchisedec. The King of Sodom tempted Abram by asking him to give credit to himself and the other kings for the victory won. Abram refused, obedient to the blessing that he had received from God through Melchisedec. In similar fashion, the believer today must remain obedient and dependent on God, rejecting the temptation to turn to the offers and temptations of the world for false relief from sin.

"The order of Melchisedec," the high priest who delivered the blessing to Abram, refers to the *authorship*. Melchisedec was faithful in his priestly function, thus assuring that the blessing would be carried out.

Perfection was present in that the calling from God guaranteed the divine nature of the blessing. The blessing that Abram received was not earthly in origin but direct from the perfect hand of God.

The perfect sacrifice of the High Priest, Christ Jesus, is without question the only sacrifice sufficient for our deliverance from the bondage of sin. The work of the Father, the work of Christ, and their relationship together as heavenly Father and Divine Son make the sacrifice for our sins without equal. The tragedy is that so many today still rebel and neglect such a great sacrifice, neglecting the deliverance available to them.

REVIEW QUESTIONS

1. What are some of the reasons individuals don't apply the work of Christ to their lives as they should?

2. Do you believe that as you approach the heavenly Father through Christ, He knows your name as well as the nature of your needs?

3. In what way can we claim that Christ has made a perfect sacrifice for the believer today?

4. What is the heart of the sacrifice of Christ?

5. What are the three elements that make the sacrifice of Christ our High Priest without equal? Explain.

GOLDEN TEXT HOMILY

"LET US THEREFORE COME BOLDLY UNTO THE THRONE OF GRACE, THAT WE MAY OBTAIN MERCY, AND FIND GRACE TO HELP IN TIME OF NEED" (Hebrews 4:16).

The idea of standing before the throne of an all-powerful God who is capable of destroying both body and soul can be horrifying. In the wilderness, the Israelites trembled in the presence of God and begged Moses to stand before God for them. Most of us are keenly aware of our sins and, like Adam, we would rather look for a place to hide than stand before the holy throne of God as we are.

But God requires us to present ourselves before His throne in order to receive forgiveness. In the Old Testament this was accomplished by the high priest going into the veiled Most Holy Place to make atonement for the sins of the people, so that the judgments of God would not come upon them. All others were prohibited from entering the Most Holy Place.

The work of Jesus Christ changed the way of approaching God. As a result of His sinless life and sacrificial death, the throne of judgment has become a throne of grace. The closed veil has become an open door. The prohibition has become an open invitation.

Our attitude of approaching God no longer has to be one of fear, but one of boldness. Through our faith in Christ, we can be confident that God will forgive our sins. We can be confident as well that we will be able to find the sustaining grace of God when we need it most. Because of Christ, we can receive both forgiveness of past sins and the power to live an overcoming life at God's throne of mercy and grace.—**Richard L. Pace, Chaplain (MAJ), U.S. Army, Fort Bragg, North Carolina**

SENTENCE SERMONS

BECAUSE JESUS CHRIST IS the eternal High Priest, believers can approach God with confidence.
—Selected

SINNERS CAN FIND forgiveness in the atoning work of Christ.
—Selected

CHRIST IS full and sufficient for all His people. . . . He is priest to make atonement for them.
—John Spencer

EVANGELISM APPLICATION

SINNERS CAN FIND FORGIVENESS IN THE ATONING WORK OF CHRIST.

Sinners can never find salvation on their own. The corrupted state of a sinner nullifies even the access of the sinner to the Father to petition for his or her own deliverance. Even the most devout humans could not achieve their own salvation, much less that of others.

Only the work of Christ is sufficient to bring release from the bondage of sin and to offer forgiveness from God. Christ is divine, appointed the High Priest, and is Himself the pure sacrifice offered in our behalf. Christ's work has already been accomplished. The forgiveness of sins is not a work to be done, but a reality to be applied.

The application of forgiveness is the obligation of the sinner today. The sinner must come to God in repentance and obedience. The person must confess his sins and testify that Christ is Lord. Once a believer, the new Christian must continue to hold fast to the salvation that Christ has provided.

The atoning work of Christ makes the believer's access to the heavenly Father possible. A relationship with God, beginning with forgiveness, is the reward of Christ's atoning work. Atonement makes access possible.

ILLUMINATING THE LESSON

Christ did not offer His sacrifice grudgingly, but willingly. He was not overwhelmed and forced to offer Himself as a sacrifice. On the contrary, Christ gave Himself in obedience and commitment to the will and love of the heavenly Father.

In World War I, a young French soldier was seriously wounded. His arm was so badly smashed that it had to be amputated. He was a magnificent specimen of young manhood, and the surgeon was grieved that he must go through life maimed. So he waited beside his bedside to tell him the bad news when he recovered consciousness. When the lad's eyes opened, the surgeon said to him: "I am sorry to tell you that you have lost your arm." "Sir," said the lad, "I did not lose it; I gave it—for France."

Jesus was not helplessly caught up in a mesh of circumstances from which He could not break free. Apart from any divine power He might have called in, it is quite clear that to the end He could have turned back and saved His life. He did not lose His life; He gave it. The Cross was not thrust upon Him; he willingly accepted it—for us (William Barclay, *Gospel of John*).

DAILY BIBLE READINGS

M. Priestly Ministry.
   Exodus 28:1-3, 36-43
T. A Call to Priesthood.
   1 Samuel 3:1-10
W. Responsibility of Priesthood.
   Malachi 2:1-8
T. Interceding Priest.
   John 17:20-26
F. Holy Priesthood. 1 Peter 2:4-10
S. Kingdom of Priests.
   Revelation 1:4-8

Christ's Unique Priesthood

Study Text: Hebrews 7:1-28

Objective: To understand the basis of Christ's priesthood and receive the benefits of His perfect sacrifice.

Time: The Book of Hebrews was probably written between A.D. 64 and 70.

Place: The place of the writing of the Book of Hebrews is uncertain. Many Bible scholars suggest Rome.

Golden Text: "Wherefore [Christ] is able also to save them to the uttermost that come unto God by him, seeing he ever liveth to make intercession for them" (Hebrews 7:25).

Central Truth: Jesus Christ, the eternal High Priest, has made the perfect sacrifice for sins.

Evangelism Emphasis: Jesus Christ, the eternal High Priest, has made the perfect sacrifice for sins.

PRINTED TEXT

Hebrews 7:1. For this Melchisedec, king of Salem, priest of the most high God, who met Abraham returning from the slaughter of the kings, and blessed him;

2. To whom also Abraham gave a tenth part of all; first being by interpretation King of righteousness, and after that also King of Salem, which is, King of peace;

3. Without father, without mother, without descent, having neither beginning of days, nor end of life; but made like unto the Son of God; abideth a priest continually.

15. And it is yet far more evident: for that after the similitude of Melchisedec there ariseth another priest,

16. Who is made, not after the law of a carnal commandment, but after the power of an endless life.

17. For he testifieth, Thou art a priest for ever after the order of Melchisedec.

18. For there is verily a disannulling of the commandment going before for the weakness and unprofitableness thereof.

19. For the law made nothing perfect, but the bringing in of a better hope did; by the which we draw nigh unto God.

20. And inasmuch as not without an oath he was made priest:

21. (For those priests were made without an oath; but this with an oath by him that said unto him, The Lord sware and will not repent, Thou art a priest for ever after the order of Melchisedec:)

22. By so much was Jesus made a surety of a better testament.

23. And they truly were many priests, because they were not suffered to continue by reason of death:

24. But this man, because he continueth ever, hath an unchangeable priesthood.

25. Wherefore he is able also to save them to the uttermost that come unto God by him, seeing he ever liveth to make intercession for them.

26. For such an high priest became us, who is holy, harmless, undefiled, separate from sinners, and made higher than the heavens;

27. Who needeth not daily, as those high priests, to offer up sacrifice, first for his own sins, and then for the people's: for this he did once, when he offered up himself.

DICTIONARY

Melchisedec (mel-KIZ-ih-dek)—Hebrews 7:1—Priest and king who worshiped God in the time of Abraham.

LESSON OUTLINE

I. KING-PRIEST PORTRAYED

   A. Blessing and Meeting

   B. Being Without Beginning or Ending

   C. Bringing Tithe

II. A GREATER PRIEST

   A. Changing the Priesthood

   B. Changing the Priest

   C. Changing the Provision

III. PERFECT SACRIFICE

   A. The Unchangeable Priest

   B. The Undefiled Priest

   C. The Unmovable Priest

LESSON EXPOSITION

INTRODUCTION

Hebrews 7 analyzes the principles of Melchisedec as a priest and illustrates how those principles are resident in the position and work of Christ as our priest. The order of Melchisedec's priestly work stands unique from the order of the priesthood of the law. The principles of Melchisedec's service as priest are superior in many ways, and the nature of that superiority is presented in this lesson.

God chose to accomplish His plan of redemption through the nation of Israel. Since God is a God who moves through history, He chose the historical people of Israel as the vehicle through which He would bring salvation. Preliminary to the perfect work of redemption, a system of sacrifices was instituted in the Old Testament, or old covenant, which proved to be imperfect.

Christ was the fulfillment of the old covenant and the establishment of a new covenant. The new covenant was foretold through the priestly order of Melchisedec. Melchisedec was a royal priest of God who brought a blessing to Abraham in Genesis 14. In Psalm 110, David foretold the fulfillment of the priestly order of Melchisedec in Christ.

Hebrews 7 presents the full story of Christ's work as our divine priest. The sacrifice He made in behalf of all who would repent and be obedient to Him is a lasting sacrifice. Unlike the Old Testament means of appeasing the Father, the means provided by Christ's sacrifice is sufficient and it is eternal.

I. KING-PRIEST PORTRAYED (Hebrews 7:1-10)

A. Blessing and Meeting (v. 1)

1. For this Melchisedec, king of Salem, priest of the most high God, who met Abraham returning from the slaughter of the kings, and blessed him.

Royalty is the first principle conveyed about Melchisedec's priesthood. He came as a king to the office of priest. His authority superseded that of other priests. Governmental and religious law was changed by this priest. His work would alter the legal life as well as the moral life of an individual. In similar fashion, Christ came as the royal Son of the Father to fill the position of priest. Christ's priestly work would also remove the legal bondage pertaining to sin.

Melchisedec was a priest who came to Abraham and met him where he was. Rather than having to journey to a tabernacle or special place of sacrifice, the priest came to the person in need. In the same way, Christ as our priest came to us—first through the Incarnation, next through the Holy Spirit, and eventually in His Second Coming of judgment at the end time.

Blessing was another principle of the priestly order of Melchisedec. Intercession for sin and sacrifice for transgression were regular duties of a priest. However, Melchisedec brought a blessing from God to Abraham. In the same way, Christ functions as priest by bringing

blessings to whoever accepts Him as Lord and priest in their lives.

How do you perceive the priestly function of Christ today? Why is it necessary to know the distinctive connection between Melchisedec's work and Christ? What are the benefits?

B. Being Without Beginning or Ending (vv. 2, 3)

2. To whom also Abraham gave a tenth part of all; first being by interpretation King of righteousness, and after that also King of Salem, which is, King of peace;

3. Without father, without mother, without descent, having neither beginning of days, nor end of life; but made like unto the Son of God; abideth a priest continually.

The order of Melchisedec as a priest is an eternal order. There was no known origin to Melchisedec's priesthood and there was no known ending. He is interpreted in these two verses as being of an eternal priesthood. The priestly order of Melchisedec is given in Scripture without beginning or ending.

"King of righteousness" refers to the holiness of God himself. The word *righteousness* emphasizes the standard by which something is judged. The word *Melchisedec* is literally made up of the Hebrew word for "king" and the word for "righteousness." Since Melchisedec is the "king of righteousness," He is of the divine standard of God himself. The work of this priestly order is in perfect alignment with the holiness of God. Christ's work as priest is in the same perfection of divine righteousness.

"King of Salem," meaning "king of peace," refers to the result of the righteous work of Melchisedec. He is called the king of Salem in Genesis 14:18. *Salem* comes from the Hebrew term *shalom*, a word usually translated "peace." Hence, he is referred to as the king of peace.

"Abideth" (v. 3) indicates the major significance of the eternality of this priesthood. Christ's work of redemption goes on continually. It is sufficient and will never fail.

What does "King of Salem" mean? What is the significance of the term abideth?

C. Bringing Tithe (vv. 4-10)

(Hebrews 7:4-10 is not included in the printed text.)

Honor is given to God through the order of the priesthood of Melchisedec. Tithing was the act performed by Abraham to honor God as the only source of his blessing. Melchisedec was the priest who mediated this tithe to God the Father.

Similarly, the work of Christ is to take our offerings and tithe to the Father. Thereby, the Father is honored by our gifts to Him. We were not worthy to bring our tithe directly to Him. However, the perfect priest is Christ, who brings our gifts to the Father in our behalf.

II. A GREATER PRIEST
    (Hebrews 7:11-22)

A. Changing the Priesthood
    (vv. 11-14)

(Hebrews 7:11-14 is not included in the printed text.)

Christ as priest transcended the Levitical priesthood of the Old

Testament. The law ordered the priesthood to come from the tribe of Levi and descend from Aaron. Christ, however, was from the tribe of Judah.

The author states that there was another priesthood, that of Melchisedec, which predated the priesthood of Aaron. The priesthood of Melchisedec took precedence over that of Aaron. The precedent had already been demonstrated in the divine call of Melchisedec, in his representation of Abraham, and in the royal nature of his priesthood.

The superiority of Melchisedec's priesthood was necessary (v. 12) because Aaron's priesthood would be corrupted. Aaron's priesthood had not maintained the purity and anointing that God had originally intended. Further, there was a beginning and, therefore, an ultimate ending of that priesthood. But the priesthood of Melchisedec was without beginning and ending.

B. Changing the Priest (vv. 15-17)

15. And it is yet far more evident: for that after the similitude of Melchisedec there ariseth another priest.

16. Who is made, not after the law of a carnal commandment, but after the power of an endless life.

17. For he testifieth, Thou art a priest for ever after the order of Melchisedec.

The priesthood of the Old Testament law was destined to be insufficient because the law itself was carnal. Though the priests were purified according to the law, the law itself was impure. Rooted in carnality, sin would never be ultimately purged by a Levitical priest.

By comparison, the order of the priesthood of Melchisedec was rooted in eternity. The "endless life" (v. 16) refers to the manner in which Melchisedec is described in Scripture as one without beginning or ending. The origin of Melchisedec is rooted in God. God himself gave birth to the priest Melchisedec. This is why many interpret the priest Melchisedec to be a forerunner of Christ himself.

Psalm 110:4 is quoted by the writer in verse 17 in order to connect Christ prophetically with the priestly order of Melchisedec. The Old Testament predates the Levitical priesthood with the priesthood of Melchisedec. Likewise, Hebrews points out the precedence of the order of Melchisedec over the Levitical priesthood. The prophecy of the psalmist would establish the connection of Christ with this supreme priestly order.

In what way was the priesthood in the Old Testament insufficient? What made the changing of the Old Testament system of the priesthood inevitable?

C. Changing the Provision
   (vv. 18-22)

18. For there is verily a disannulling of the commandment going before for the weakness and unprofitableness thereof.

19. For the law made nothing perfect, but the bringing in of a better hope did; by the which we draw nigh unto God.

20. And inasmuch as not without an oath he was made priest:

21. (For those priests were made without an oath; but this with an oath by him that said unto him, The Lord sware and will not repent, Thou art a priest for ever after the order of Melchisedec:)

22. By so much was Jesus made a surety of a better testament.

The provision of the priesthood had to be changed for two reasons. First, the old priesthood created by the law was imperfect. "Weakness" and "unprofitableness" (v. 18) were the marks of the old priesthood. *Weakness* came from a Greek term which means "without strength." The work of the old priesthood always fell short. *Unprofitableness* came from a Greek term which emphasized "having no advantage." The work of the old priesthood could not produce anything of any lasting benefit.

The second reason the old priesthood had to be changed was the prophetic word from God that had already established a higher order of priesthood. In this case God did not use the law, but spoke this order of the priesthood directly into existence. *Oath* was a term which meant that something was declared to be into existence by an affirming word. The strength of the oath was only as strong as the person speaking it into existence. In this case, the Almighty God established a priesthood that was divine in origin and sustenance.

Psalm 110:4, quoted by the writer again in verse 21, cites the prophetic covenant spoken by God that established the priesthood of Christ according to the order of Melchisedec. Verse 22 identifies the prophetic covenant of this priesthood with Jesus.

What is the significance of an oath? Of a covenant? Why is Christ's work as priest unchangeable?

III. PERFECT SACRIFICE
(Hebrews 7:23-28)

A. The Unchangeable Priest
(vv. 23, 24)

23. And they truly were many priests, because they were not suffered to continue by reason of death:

24. But this man, because he continueth ever, hath an unchangeable priesthood.

The principle of Melchisedec's order is extended by Christ, because He is eternal. The order of Melchisedec itself was enough to transcend the priesthood of the law. Added was the eternal nature of Christ. Priests under the law were multiplied because their priesthood ended with the death of each priest. However, since Christ lives forever, there is no other priest who ministers in our behalf except Him.

"Unchangeable" is the mark of Christ's work as our priest. The sin removed from us is a perfect and enduring work because the Priest who administers the sacrifice in our behalf is perfect, enduring, and eternal.

B. The Undefiled Priest (vv. 25, 26)

25. Wherefore he is able also to save them to the uttermost that come unto God by him, seeing he ever liveth to make intercession for them.

26. For such an high priest became us, who is holy, harmless, undefiled, separate from sinners, and made higher than the heavens.

The position of Christ's priesthood is after the order of Melchisedec, established by the oath of the Father himself and is eternal because He is eternal. The work of Christ as our priest is just as perfect, just as established, and just as eternal.

Christ's work is able to "save." The Old Testament sacrifice and work of the priests went only so far as to satisfy God's demand for justice. The individual for whom the sacrifice was made remained in the same fallen condition. Christ's work transforms the individual and satisfies God's justice. The bondage of sin is broken as the person is saved from sin. Salvation emphasizes deliverance.

The heart of Christ's work as our priest is to make *intercession*. The term emphasizes "something affirmed in the behalf of another." Christ's position as our intercessor is continuous. Salvation is continuous for the believer because the life of the Intercessor is continuous. The believer should be reminded of the constant work of Christ. If there would ever be a time that Christ was not before the Father in behalf of the Christian, the provision for salvation would be withdrawn.

C. The Unmovable Priest
(vv. 27, 28)

(Hebrews 7:28 is not included in the printed text.)

27. Who needeth not daily, as those high priests, to offer up sacrifice, first for his own sins, and then for the people's: for this he did once, when he offered up himself.

Christ offered up the sacrifice of Himself one time only. In the Old Testament it was necessary to offer sacrifices daily because the priests offering the sacrifices were not perfect. Not only that, but the sacrifices themselves were inadequate. No matter how unblemished the sacrifice, it was still not perfect.

Christ fulfilled a dual role both as Sacrifice and High Priest. In His role as Sacrifice, He was the perfect offering. He offered Himself once and for all. This means that the payment required by the heavenly Father was fully satisfied. In His role as High Priest, He was perfect and pure. His perfection means that the demands of the heavenly Father for redemption from sin were fulfilled.

The believer today can have confidence in salvation because of the perfection of the sacrifice made in behalf of all who would believe upon Christ. God chose to require a system of sacrifices in the Old Testament to appease His wrath. The Old Testament system was imperfect, having to be constantly maintained and renewed. However, Christ, having a divinely instituted position as our High Priest, uniquely of the priestly order of Melchisedec, was able to perfectly offer a perfect sacrifice. Christ continues today as our intercessor on the foundation of the perfect sacrifice He made in our behalf.

REVIEW QUESTIONS

1. How do people today fail to recognize the fuller ramifications of Christ's work in their behalf?

2. What does "King of righteousness" mean as a description of Melchisedec?

3. How does the priesthood of Melchisedec and Christ transcend the Old Testament priesthood?

4. Why did the writer of Hebrews quote Psalm 110:4 when referring to the priesthood of Christ?

5. Why is Christ's sacrifice in our behalf an eternal sacrifice?

GOLDEN TEXT HOMILY

"WHEREFORE [CHRIST] IS ABLE ALSO TO SAVE THEM TO THE UTTERMOST THAT COME UNTO GOD BY HIM, SEEING HE EVER LIVETH TO MAKE INTERCESSION FOR THEM" (Hebrews 7:25).

The theme of the Book of Hebrews shows the superiority of Christ to that which has gone before and to that which is to come.

When the writer said, "He is able to save," he was indicating that the priesthood of Christ combines intercession with the power to save. It should be noted this is the third time His ability has been stressed in this epistle. In 2:18, we are told that because of His temptations in the flesh, "He is able to succour [help] them that are tempted." In 4:15, the writer said that because of the days of Christ's humanity, we have a High Priest who is able to sympathize with us when we are tempted.

The Golden Text gives us the great assurance that He is able to save (deliver) even in the utmost circumstances. This truth about the ability of Christ is of great importance to the Christian faith. It is basic to everything in the believer's life and experience.

He is able to save "to the uttermost." This phrase in the Greek means "completely," and it is found in only one other place in the Scripture—Luke 13:11. The Satan-afflicted woman "was bowed together, and could in no wise lift up herself." A more accurate description of her condition is given in the *New English Bible,* indicating she was "quite unable to stand up straight." What a picture of too many believers today—they face ever downward, looking at earthly things. With no power to lift themselves unto God, definitely hampered, they are Satan-bound. Christ instantly made straight the bent back. So now, as our High Priest, He can save completely those who draw near to God by Him, because "he is always living to plead on their behalf" (NEB).—
Luther E. Painter, D.Min. (Retired), Assistant Professor of Religion, Lee College, Cleveland, Tennessee

SENTENCE SERMONS

JESUS CHRIST, the eternal High Priest, has made the perfect sacrifice for sins.

—Selected

AS PRIEST, CHRIST'S work is that of mediation, reconciling man, an enemy with God, back to God. Peace is made through a sacrifice of which He is both the priest and the sacrifice.

—William W. Stevens

AS PRIEST, Christ not only offers sacrifice, He also mediates. He can intercede for us because He knows our weakness.

—William W. Stevens

EVANGELISM APPLICATION

JESUS CHRIST, THE ETERNAL HIGH PRIEST, HAS MADE THE PERFECT SACRIFICE FOR SINS.

There are many opinions today about salvation. World religions declare different paths to deliverance from sin. Modern mystics conjure up all kinds of spirits in search of an escape from this world. New Age philosophies present the enrichment of the inner potential of individuals in an effort to achieve lasting peace. But none of these paths and provisions are sufficient to remove the guilt brought on by sin.

Sin has eternal consequences. A relationship with the one eternal God has been violated and broken.

Though we live temporal lives, our sin created lasting effects throughout time. Only an eternal solution that transcends time is adequate to remove sin and reconcile individuals back into relationship with the eternal God.

Christ's sacrifice as the High Priest in behalf of all who would believe on Him is the only way a person can be saved. No other means except this sacrifice has eternal rewards. Christ is Himself eternal. He was the sacrifice, and He offered the sacrifice. Thus, the sacrifice and its provision are eternal because of who Christ is.

Salvation is perfect in its work because the sacrifice given was perfect. There is no lacking in this sacrifice. No sin is left without forgiveness. No sin is too great or too vile. The perfect Sacrifice perfectly removes the guilty stain of sin.

DAILY BIBLE READINGS

M. King of Righteousness.
   Genesis 14:18-24
T. Triumphant Priest.
   Psalm 110:1-7
W. Cleansing Ministry.
   Zechariah 3:1-10
T. Obedient Priest.
   Romans 5:12-21
F. Righteous in Christ.
   2 Corinthians 5:17-21
S. Blessings in Christ.
   Ephesians 1:3-12

The Superior Covenant

Study Text: Hebrews 8:1-13; 9:15-28; 10:9-18

Objective: To examine the limitations of the old covenant and embrace and celebrate the new covenant in Christ.

Time: The Book of Hebrews was probably written between A.D. 64 and 70.

Place: The place of the writing of the Book of Hebrews is uncertain. Many Bible scholars suggest Rome.

Golden Text: "This is the covenant that I will make with them after those days, saith the Lord, I will put my laws into their hearts, and in their minds will I write them" (Hebrews 10:16).

Central Truth: God established the new covenant in Christ to fulfill the demands of the law.

Evangelism Emphasis: Salvation does not come through our works, but through the work

PRINTED TEXT

Hebrews 8:6. But now hath he obtained a more excellent ministry, by how much also he is the mediator of a better covenant, which was established upon better promises.

7. For if that first covenant had been faultless, then should no place have been sought for the second.

10. For this is the covenant that I will make with the house of Israel after those days, saith the Lord; I will put my laws into their mind, and write them in their hearts: and I will be to them a God, and they shall be to me a people.

9:15. And for this cause he is the mediator of the new testament, that by means of death, for the redemption of the transgressions that were under the first testament, they which are called might receive the promise of eternal inheritance.

24. For Christ is not entered into the holy places made with hands, which are the figures of the true; but into heaven itself, now to appear in the presence of God for us:

25. Nor yet that he should offer himself often, as the high priest entereth into the holy place every year with blood of others;

26. For then must he often have suffered since the foundation of the world: but now once in the end of the world hath he appeared to put away sin by the sacrifice of himself.

27. And as it is appointed unto men once to die, but after this the judgment:

28. So Christ was once

offered to bear the sins of many; and unto them that look for him shall he appear the second time without sin unto salvation.

10:9. Then said he, Lo, I come to do thy will, O God. He taketh away the first, that he may establish the second.

10. By the which will we are sanctified through the offering of the body of Jesus Christ once for all.

14. For by one offering he hath perfected for ever them that are sanctified.

15. Whereof the Holy Ghost also is a witness to us: for after that he had said before,

16. This is the covenant that I will make with them after those days, saith the Lord, I will put my laws into their hearts, and in their minds will I write them;

17. And their sins and iniquities will I remember no more.

18. Now where remission of these is, there is no more offering for sin.

LESSON OUTLINE

LESSON EXPOSITION

INTRODUCTION

Hebrews 8—10 reviews the supremacy of the covenant established by Christ. The covenant of Christ is compared to the Old Testament covenant, but it can also be compared to any attempt to find salvation outside of Jesus Christ.

Three aspects of salvation are especially borne out in Hebrews 8—10 that have never been and will never be copied by any person, religion, or New Age system: (1) The covenant of Christ came from God himself. (2) God places the covenant of Christ within the heart of the believer. (3) God has made the covenant of Christ eternal.

By contrast, modern-day covenants, as well as the covenant of the Old Testament, are made of earthly materials by imperfect humans. These covenants are falsely manufactured by individuals within their own hearts. Finally, the effects of these covenants are not sound, much less eternal.

The believer can marvel at the covenant of Christ because of the comparative failure of all other attempts to reconcile lost humanity to God. The analysis of Hebrews

8—10 marvels at the work of the new covenant and reveals the failure of all other covenants, especially the covenant of the Old Testament law.

I. NEW COVENANT NEEDED
(Hebrews 8:1-13)

A. A Firmer Covenant Needed
(vv. 1-6)

(Hebrews 8:1-5 is not included in the printed text.)

6. But now hath he obtained a more excellent ministry, by how much also he is the mediator of a better covenant, which was established upon better promises.

The authority and eternity of Christ as our High Priest has been the emphasis of Hebrews 1—7. Hebrews 8:1, 2 summarizes those two emphases; verse 1 says that Christ is at the position of authority at the right hand of the Father, and verse 2 reviews the fact that the sanctuary and the sacrifices offered by Christ are divine and not earthly in origin.

Attention in chapter 8 turns to the effects of Christ's work as our High Priest. The main effect is the establishing of a covenant between God and man. The covenant is a relationship which reconciles man back to God, bringing fellowship and peace between them.

Former covenants established by the Old Testament Law were not adequate. They were weak in that they only covered relationships on earth. The requirement that remained was for a covenant that would reach into heaven. God's original intent when He gave the instructions for the Tabernacle to Moses was to establish a reconciling covenant addressing the requirement of heavenly things (v. 5; Exodus 25:40). The pattern for the Tabernacle shown to Moses was from heaven and bore a heavenly standard. Earthly material could never perfectly meet the standards of a heavenly design. The foundation of the Old Testament Law was an insufficient platform from which to reach those heavenly things spoken of by the Father to Moses.

Hebrews 8:6 reveals that Christ has a firmer foundation from which to establish a new covenant that is perfect and wholly adequate. Christ's work as High Priest is a "better covenant, which was established upon better promises." *Promises* referred to the fundamental strength of the covenant. The future prospects of the success of the covenant were not based on the ability of earthly priests, but on Christ, the Son of God.

Why was a covenant with a firmer foundation needed?

B. A Faultless Covenant Needed
(vv. 7-9)

(Hebrews 8:8, 9 is not included in the printed text.)

7. For if that first covenant had been faultless, then should no place have been sought for the second.

Verses 7-9 continue to emphasize the need for another covenant by stressing two important points. First, the covenant of the Old Testament was not faultless. Second, the people of the old covenant had not been faultless in maintaining the covenant.

The Old Testament covenant contained imperfect sacrifices, included an imperfect tabernacle, and failed to cover sin eternally.

Verses 8-12 quote Jeremiah 31:31-34. Verses 8 and 9 indicate that God would eventually establish another covenant with His people because the old covenant was faulty.

The people of the Old Testament who were to be faithful to the covenant and pass it on to their posterity had not been without fault. The old covenant had become corrupted by their disobedience. The transmission of the covenant had passed through disobedient hands and lives. As a result, the foremost person seeking another covenant was God himself (see v. 7).

C. A Forgiving Covenant Needed (vv. 10-13)

(Hebrews 8:11-13 is not included in the printed text.)

10. For this is the covenant that I will make with the house of Israel after those days, saith the Lord; I will put my laws into their mind, and write them in their hearts: and I will be to them a God, and they shall be to me a people.

Forgiveness would be at the core of the new covenant. The old covenant emphasized appeasement of God's wrath. The new covenant would emphasize mercy and the removal of the memory of their sins from the mind of God (v. 12).

Three aspects of the new covenant would make it superior to the old covenant: First, whereas the old covenant had a weak foundation, the new covenant would come from God himself. The writer continued to quote from Jeremiah 31:31-34, where God said that He would personally create the new covenant.

Second, whereas the old covenant was faulty, the new covenant would be written by God himself upon the hearts of individuals. The substance of the covenant would be that God would continue to reconcile His people (v. 10). The new covenant would not be sustained by imperfect and disobedient priests but by the reconciling hand of God. The heart of God's reconciling work would be mercy and forgiveness. The forgiveness of God in the new covenant would replace the failure of people in the old covenant.

Third, the new covenant would be eternal. Unlike the old, it would never "vanish away" (v. 13). The new covenant would not only outlast the old covenant but would also establish an eternal relationship of righteousness between God and His people.

Thus the new covenant of God contrasts with the old covenant of the Old Testament Law and with humanity's attempts to establish a relationship with God without Jesus Christ. Christ is the only covenant that God himself has perfectly and eternally established to bring people to Himself. All other beliefs, systems and attempts to know God are not firm in their foundation; they are faulty in substance and therefore not eternal.

What is the role of Christ in the new covenant? What is the role of the heavenly Father?

II. NEW COVENANT ESTABLISHED (Hebrews 9:15-28)

A. The New Mediator (vv. 15-23)

(Hebrews 9:16-23 is not included in the printed text.)

15. And for this cause he is the mediator of the new testa-

ment, that by means of death, for the redemption of the transgressions that were under the first testament, they which are called might receive the promise of eternal inheritance.

Life was required by God to redeem life. A sacrifice was the means established by God to satisfy the guilt of sin. Death was brought about with the Fall in Genesis 3. Ultimately, the giving of life was the only sacrifice sufficient to overcome the death of sin. The Old Testament Law and covenant had a system of life-giving sacrifices to temporarily satisfy God's demand for sin. The life-giver, the one who was the sacrifice, was called "mediator."

Mediator came from a Greek term, *mesites*, which means "someone who stands in the middle." This term signified someone who stood between two people and made a relationship possible between them that could not be possible without this intervention. Because of the sin and imperfection of people, the relationship between God and individuals was not possible. Sin had brought about death to the relationship. Christ as Mediator made the relationship possible.

The primary requirement to make the relationship between God and individuals possible was the "redemption of transgressions" (v. 15). Christ satisfied that requirement by taking upon Himself the transgressions of the people. He then was slain, thereby slaying the transgressions and the punishment they bore. The life-giving sacrifice of the Mediator, who was bearing the transgressions of the unrighteous, satisfied the requirements so that the relationship between God

and man would become possible.

Even more than the reestablishment of the relationship broken by the Fall, an "eternal inheritance" (v. 15) was founded by Christ the Mediator. This inheritance indicates the depth of the relationship. Christ's mediation was so perfect that we were able to become sons and daughters of the heavenly Father. Our reunion is so complete that we are brought into family relationship; the result is not just righteousness but also paternal love.

B. The New Manner (v. 24)

24. For Christ is not entered into the holy places made with hands, which are the figures of the true; but into heaven itself, now to appear in the presence of God for us.

The new covenant, with Christ as the new Mediator, accomplishes our redemption in a completely different manner than the old attempted to do. The old covenant represented distant approaches to the heavenly Father. Those mediators, priests and sacrifices could only go to "holy places" that were made by human hands and were thus imperfect. They were mere "figures" or "copies" of true reality. They did not stand in heaven, in the physical presence of God. The perfect Mediator appears in heaven, in the very presence of God himself.

Do you know of any religious leaders and movements today that might be compared to the old covenant's attempt to find salvation?

C. The New Measure (vv. 25, 26)

25. Nor yet that he should

offer himself often, as the high priest entereth into the holy place every year with blood of others;

26. For then must he often have suffered since the foundation of the world: but now once in the end of the world hath he appeared to put away sin by the sacrifice of himself.

Not only was the new covenant established by a new mediator (Christ) and in a new manner (in the very presence of God) but also the new covenant was represented by a new standard. The old covenant was inferior. The mediator was not involved in the sacrifice itself except to offer it. In this sense the mediator was removed from the sacrifice.

Christ gave 100 percent to the sacrifice by making Himself the sacrifice. The purity of His sacrifice was in its content and in the commitment of the One giving it. Christ was completely committed to the redemption of the lost. He gave the covenant mediation in full measure by investing Himself. He did not negotiate and mediate our salvation with reservations. He gave the full measure of Himself to the process. Oh, what a Savior!

D. The New Magnitude (vv. 27, 28)

27. And as it is appointed unto men once to die, but after this the judgment:

28. So Christ was once offered to bear the sins of many; and unto them that look for him shall he appear the second time without sin unto salvation.

The new magnitude of the covenant established by Christ is that the burden of sin's punishment is now removed for those who repent and serve the Lord. The severity of sin's penalty was certain death. Death came with the Fall and was part of the certainty of sin's guilt. However, just as certain was the all-sufficient sacrifice of Christ.

Christ's perfect sacrifice "was once offered to bear the sins of many" (v. 28). *Once* stresses the magnitude of Christ's sacrifice. So perfect, His sacrifice needed to be offered only once. *Bear* conveys the extent to which the sacrifice was efficient. All of the guilt of sin is borne by that one sacrifice.

The word *many* declares that the effect of the sacrifice reaches to everyone who believes. The sacrifice of Christ was not only perfect within itself, but it was perfect in the distance it covered—it reached thoroughly into every individual's heart who would believe.

The reconciling work of Christ's sacrifice is not only a spiritual reality within the hearts of believers, but it is also a work that will transform the very body of the Christian at the second coming of Christ. Thus transformed, the believer will be ushered into the heavenly presence of the Father. Those who "look for Him" also "love his appearing" (2 Timothy 4:8). Loving the appearing of the Lord implies repenting of sins and renewing one's desires. There must be a heavenly desire for an eternal reunion in the heavenly presence of the Father.

Compare modern-day attempts at establishing covenants to the new covenant of Christ.

III. NEW COVENANT RESULTS
  (Hebrews 10:9-18)

A. Fulfilling God's Will for
  Sanctification (vv. 9-14)

(Hebrews 10:11-13 is not included in the printed text.)

9. Then said he, Lo, I come to do thy will, O God. He taketh away the first, that he may establish the second.

10. By the which will we are sanctified through the offering of the body of Jesus Christ once for all.

14. For by one offering he hath perfected for ever them that are sanctified.

The perfect sacrifice of Christ in the new covenant also means the end product of a perfected life. The perfection is in the sanctifying work of the sacrifice of Christ. Not only did Christ's sacrifice remove the guilt and sentence of sin, but it also did the work of sanctification.

Perfected (v. 14) is translated from the Greek term *teleioo*, which means "to make perfect." The term had no inherent value in and of itself. The definition of the word depended on the particular goal. In this case, the sacrifice of Christ enabled the believer to be "perfected" according to the goal and standard of God's requirements.

Sanctified came from the Greek term *hagiazo*. Sanctification is meaningful because of the God to whom we are sanctified. We are sanctified to be devoted to God, and our sanctification is only as strong as our devotion to God. Christ's sacrifice is sufficient and satisfies those devoted to God. Through the work of Christ we have been consecrated to the Father.

B. Fulfilling God's Witness of the Holy Ghost (vv. 15, 16)

15. Whereof the Holy Ghost also is a witness to us: for after that he had said before,

16. This is the covenant that I will make with them after those days, saith the Lord, I will put my laws into their hearts, and in their minds will I write them.

The work of the Holy Spirit is very important in the new covenant of Christ. The Holy Spirit working within the life of the believer is the means by which God writes the new law of the covenant upon the heart of the Christian. This is the fulfillment of Jeremiah 31:31-34.

The work of the Holy Spirit is a witness to the believer of the presence of God's new covenant in Christ. The present reality is the presence of the new covenant within the believer's heart. This reality is not affirmed mentally, socially, or confessionally. It is a work of God himself. The Holy Spirit reassures the believer of the reality of the covenant. Whatever genuine confidence a Christian has about personal salvation comes from God's Holy Spirit.

Heart refers to the inner feelings and spirituality of the believer. In the reflective depths of the heart the Christian is reassured of salvation. The Holy Spirit quickens the spirit of the believer, giving yearnings and longings which reassure one of deliverance from the bondage of sin.

Mind refers to the activation of the mental and inner life of a person. What one does with the work of the Spirit within the heart begins largely in the mind. God intervenes in the working of mind, writing His laws in our innermost king. His new covenant in Christ guides our mental process, affecting what we do and where we are headed.

C. Fulfilling God's Requirement for Remission (vv. 17, 18)

17. And their sins and iniquities

will I remember no more.

18. Now where remission of these is, there is no more offering for sin.

Complete and whole, not partial and imperfect, is the work of God's new covenant. God brings new realities in the heart and mind of the believer by writing His new covenant in their hearts (v. 16). Jeremiah 31:33, 34 prophesied that the sins and iniquities of the believer would be remembered no more. Before God's people had to continually work with an imperfect covenant in order to have any chance at being reconciled to Him; now one supreme sacrifice in Christ is eternally sufficient.

The parallel application of the message of the new covenant is that any attempt at our own salvation, whether under the Old Testament law or by some other means, will only result in continued sin and iniquity. Attempts today are made in the form of New Age philosophy, modern-day spiritism, world religions, inner peace, a new world order, and so forth. Not only do these fail to bring reconciliation with God, but they perpetuate sin and iniquity. In God's eyes, their evil continues. The bondage of sin does not end without the new covenant in Christ. No other religion, philosophy, or spirit can make the claim of being originated by God himself.

REVIEW QUESTIONS

1. What were some of the weaknesses of the Old Testament law?

2. How would you describe the new covenant established in Christ?

3. What are some of the modern-day attempts to develop covenants in order to remove the guilt of sin

and be reconciled with God?

4. What is the heavenly nature and connection of the new covenant established in Christ?

5. How is the covenant of Christ reflected in the work of the Holy Spirit?

GOLDEN TEXT HOMILY

"THIS IS THE COVENANT THAT I WILL MAKE WITH THEM AFTER THOSE DAYS, SAITH THE LORD, I WILL PUT MY LAWS INTO THEIR HEARTS, AND IN THEIR MINDS WILL I WRITE THEM" (Hebrews 10:16).

There is always a battle or confrontation within us regarding right and wrong. If this were not true, we would never be tempted of Satan to do wrong in our speech, deeds, thoughts, and so forth. God was well aware that the old covenant and the law were not accomplishing righteousness in the lives of His people. The new covenant, which is wrought through Christ and His sacrifice, gives us a new incentive in that Christ is our model and we are to be like (imitate) Him. God promised to put these laws into our hearts (the very source of life flow) and into our minds (the storehouse of knowledge and wisdom) that we may know Him and live for Him. We are true disciples when we learn of Him personally and walk as He walked. God's covenant is in Jesus' sacrifice and the pouring out of His blood for us to experience new life in our actions, speech, and attitudes.

God's commandments, not our own whims and ideas, bond us to Him and fit us into His building. I urge you to allow God's words to lodge in your heart and mind so you may pattern all your life after

Jesus Christ, our Lord and Savior.—**Marion H. Starr, Pastor, Marion, South Carolina**

SENTENCE SERMONS

GOD ESTABLISHED the new covenant in Christ to fulfill the demands of the law.

—Selected

SALVATION does not come through our works, but through the work of Christ on the cross.

—Selected

THE COVENANT between God and His created ones is a covenant with God setting both the conditions of acceptance and the consequences of violation.

—William W. Stevens

EVANGELISM APPLICATION

SALVATION DOES NOT COME THROUGH OUR WORKS, BUT THROUGH THE WORK OF CHRIST ON THE CROSS.

Humanity's works are feeble attempts to find peace with God. The distance between the sinner and God is obvious through the continuing strife and evil that is in the world. Universally, individuals today seek reconciliation with God (whom they may call a "higher power" or "mystic reality") and freedom from the bondage of sin and evil. Regrettably, the search continues because no one has found a lasting way to be reconciled to God and find personal peace apart from Jesus Christ.

Many have attempted secularism and materialism. Some individuals still think that accomplishments, knowledge, and material things can bring peace and reconciliation. However, more and more people are in despair about the futility of the material, and are turning to spiritual realities. The danger is that they are not seeking the Holy Spirit but pagan and human spirits.

Only the cross of Christ and the work of the Holy Spirit can bring salvation. The cross of Christ was the one and only perfect sacrifice that satisfied the requirement of the heavenly Father for redemption from sin. The Holy Spirit applies and sustains the work of the Cross within the heart of the believer. Individuals must respond to the Cross by believing in Christ, repenting of all their sins, and following the Lord in obedience.

DAILY BIBLE READINGS

M. Believe God's Covenants.
   Genesis 15:1-6
T. Covenant Commandments.
   Deuteronomy 5:7-21
W. Covenant Renewal.
   Joshua 24:14-21
T. New Covenant
   Foretold. Jeremiah 31:31-34
F. New Covenant Celebrated.
   Matthew 26:26-29
S. New Covenant Freedom.
   Galatians 4:21-31

Dynamics of Faith

Study Text: Hebrews 11:1-40; 12:1, 2

Objective: To discover how God views faith and exercise faith in Him.

Time: The Book of Hebrews was probably written between A.D. 64 and 70.

Place: The place of the writing of the Book of Hebrews is uncertain. Many Bible scholars suggest Rome.

Golden Text: "Without faith it is impossible to please [God]: for he that cometh to God must believe that he is, and that he is a rewarder of them that diligently seek him" (Hebrews 11:6).

Central Truth: God is pleased when we have faith in Him and obey His Word.

Evangelism Emphasis: Faith in Christ is essential to salvation.

PRINTED TEXT

Hebrews 11:1. Now faith is the substance of things hoped for, the evidence of things not seen.

5. By faith Enoch was translated that he should not see death; and was not found, because God had translated him: for before his translation he had this testimony, that he pleased God.

6. But without faith it is impossible to please him: for he that cometh to God must believe that he is, and that he is a rewarder of them that diligently seek him.

7. By faith Noah, being warned of God of things not seen as yet, moved with fear, prepared an ark to the saving of his house; by the which he condemned the world, and became heir of the righeousness which is by faith.

8. By faith Abraham, when he was called to go out into a place which he should after receive for an inheritance, obeyed; and he went out, not knowing whither he went.

9. By faith he sojourned in the land of promise, as in a strange country, dwelling in tabernacles with Isaac and Jacob, the heirs with him of the same promise.

10. For he looked for a city which hath foundations, whose builder and maker is God.

13. These all died in faith, not having received the promises, but having seen them afar off, and were persuaded of them, and embraced them, and confessed that they were strangers and pilgrims on earth.

14. For they that say such things declare plainly that they seek a country.

15. And truly, if they had

been mindful of that country from whence they came out, they might have had opportunity to have returned.

16. But now they desire a better country, that is, an heavenly: wherefore God is not ashamed to be called their God: for he hath prepared for them a city.

39. And these all, having obtained a good report through faith, received not the promise:

40. God having provided some better thing for us, that they without us should not be made perfect.

12:1. Wherefore seeing we also are compassed about with so great a cloud of witnesses, let us lay aside every weight, and the sin which doth so easily beset us, and let us run with patience the race that is set before us,

2. Looking unto Jesus the author and finisher of our faith; who for the joy that was set before him endured the cross, despising the shame, and is set down at the right hand of the throne of God.

DICTIONARY

Enoch (E-nuk)—Hebrews 11:5—A man who walked with God.
Noah (NO-uh)—Hebrews 11:7—A God-fearing man who obeyed God, built an ark, and saved his family.

LESSON OUTLINE

I. FAITH PLEASES GOD

   A. The Evidence Obtained

   B. The Testimony Owned

   C. The Diligence Offered

II. FAITH SEES THE PROMISE

   A. The Insight of Godly Fear

   B. The Inheritance of a Faithful Sojourner

   C. The Intent of the Faithful

   D. The Issue of Not Receiving Promises

   E. The Inspiration of Heavenly Faith

III. FAITH FINISHES THE RACE

   A. Conquering to Finish

   B. Conquered, Yet Finishing

   C. Conquest Finished through Christ

LESSON EXPOSITION

INTRODUCTION

Hebrews 11 and 12 present one of the most thorough descriptions of godly faith. These verses present a model for our faith today. It is so easy to seek after a faith that is not pleasing to God, that is empty and void, that does not accomplish what God intends to accomplish through us. Definitions, illustrations, and principles for genuine faith are presented. Dynamics of faith to be exercised are given in these chapters. The work of Christ as our High Priest reaches practical application in these chapters, describing what it is like to live in the reality of the sacrifice Christ made for those who believe in Him.

I. FAITH PLEASES GOD
(Hebrews 11:1-6)

A. The Evidence Obtained (vv. 1-4)

(Hebrews 11:2-5 is not included in the printed text.)

1. Now faith is the substance of things hoped for, the evidence of things not seen.

Faith occurs within the heart of a believer and is the element that places an individual in right relationship with God.

The language of Hebrews 11:1, 2 comes from the world of the ancient legal courts. Illustrating a trial, the two verses present the dynamics of the Christian life as subject to the verdict of God, the Judge. In the trial, the term *substance*, from the Greek term, *hupostasis*, indicates the evidence presented to the court and used to establish the case. *Evidence* (v. 1) (the Greek term *elegchos*) indicates the "convicting piece of evidence" that is sure to win the case. Finally, a *good report* (v. 2) is the verdict that they had a positive witness borne to them.

Most important of all three concepts is the goal of receiving a favorable verdict, or a "good report." No matter what the proof—not even if a decisive piece of evidence sufficient to win the case is presented—the case is not over until the verdict is decided. Faith is the evidence, the conclusive piece of evidence sufficient to win the case before Almighty God. Faith in Christ brings a "good report" from the heavenly Father.

Define faith in your words. What principles in Hebrews 11 guide us in exercising our faith today?

B. The Testimony Owned (v. 5)

5. By faith Enoch was translated that he should not see death;

and was not found, because God had translated him: for before his translation he had this testimony, that he pleased God.

Throughout Hebrews 11, the goal of our faith is to receive a "good report" from the Father. Several terms in verses 3-8 convey the concept of receiving a good report from God. In verse 3, the creation was God's good report. Verse 4 tells of God's good report about Abel's life and sacrifice. In verse 7, Noah became "heir of righteousness," signifying a commendable report by God.

Enoch's good report in verse 5 was God's witness about him. The report was so good that God translated him from earth to heaven. The Greek term for *translated (metatithema)* means "to transfer to another place." The word illustrates going from one reality to another. Enoch left this earthly reality and moved to the heavenly presence of the Lord. The translation was not mystical or merely spiritual; it was a physical reality.

Testimony (v. 5) is the same Greek term used for "good report" (v. 2). The substance of the testimony was that "he pleased God." *Pleased* is a term in the text which emphasizes that Enoch desired to satisfy the heart of God. Enoch not only wanted to satisfy the requirements of God, he desired to please the heart of God. Faith is not just getting what we pray for; neither is it just satisfying the laws of God. Genuine faith draws us close to the heart of God, fulfilling His desires for our life.

How do we know when we have obtained a good report? How do we know that Enoch received the good report from God?

C. The Diligence Offered (v. 6)

6. But without faith it is impossible to please him: for he that cometh to God must believe that he is, and that he is a rewarder of them that diligently seek him.

Pleasing God is the theme of verse 6. Faith at it's core is a desire to please God. That desire must be carried out in diligence. *Ekzeteo,* the Greek term, means "to search carefully." It implies intensity. The same word describes both the kind of intensity with which the prophets looked for the salvation of God (1 Peter 1:10) and the kind of intensity with which all men must look for salvation. Romans 3:11 says that men are away from God because they don't seek Him diligently.

Many today think that faith and pleasing God can be a casual acceptance of what God offers. On the contrary, one must possess a heart that intensely desires to please the heavenly Father. The diligence with which a person seeks God reveals how much that person believes that God exists. It shows how much faith one has in God.

If God exists at all, then he is truly God and can command the absolute faith of the individual. When one really believes in God, he or she has a strong desire to affirm Him as God. That person will seek God with intensity. Believing in God completely motivates one to seek God diligently. This intense faith is the dynamic that pleases God.

II. FAITH SEES THE PROMISE (Hebrews 11:7-16)

A. The Insight of Godly Fear (v. 7)

7. By faith Noah, being warned of God of things not seen as yet, moved with fear, prepared an ark to the saving of his house; by the which he condemned the world, and became heir of the righeous-ness which is by faith.

Another aspect of faith is godly fear. "Moved with fear" indicates that godly fear was the primary motivation of Noah. He was not merely afraid. Rather, he had received a word from the Lord and was responding to that word. He respected the impending consequences of God's judgment upon the earth. His godly fear was an appropriate response to the foretold destruction that would come as the result of judgment. In godly fear Noah received the salvation offered by the Lord.

Faith is not merely praying for something and receiving it. Godly faith is rooted in godly fear. Godly fear is based in the reality of who God is and what He has said. A contemporary translation of the term *fear* is "to be overwhelmed." Godly fear is to be overwhelmed by who God is and what He has promised to do. Godly fear cannot merely be compared to fright or terror. Much more than earthly examples can illustrate godly fear comes from the awesome presence of God that encompasses all a person is and all the circumstances that surround him or her.

Fear of God is one of the primary ingredients of faith in God. "Warned of God," Noah then possessed faith that was "moved with fear." The result was obedience to God and the saving of his family.

B. The Inheritance of a Faithful Sojourner (vv. 8, 9)

8. By faith Abraham, when he was called to go out into a place which he should after receive for an inheritance, obeyed; and he went out, not knowing whither he went.

9. By faith he sojourned in the land of promise, as in a strange country, dwelling in tabernacles with Isaac and Jacob, the heirs with him of the same promise.

Another element of godly faith is obedience. Abraham did not believe and then receive the inheritance. Rather, in faith he obeyed God and thereby received the inheritance that God had promised him. Faith was incomplete without obedience.

Obedience answered the call of God. God had called Abraham to a certain place in order to receive the inheritance. The place was a land beyond his native Ur. The calling of God is important precisely because it is God himself who is doing the calling. The call was to the land and inheritance that Abraham would receive. It was important because it was God who had called him. Because the call comes from God, one must respond in faith and obedience.

What do we learn about the nature of faith from Enoch? from Noah? from Abraham? How can we apply these principles to our faith today?

There was resistance to the obedient steps of Abraham. He stepped into a "strange" or foreign land. The territory was unfamiliar to him and the inhabitants of the land regarded him as hostile (Genesis 12). Nevertheless, Abraham's obedience was sure. His obedience demonstrated the reality of his faith. Sometimes today the reception of the promise is said to be the demonstration of faith. However, the story of Abraham provides evidence that obedience to the call of God is actu-ally the demonstration of faith, even before the reception of the promise or the answer to prayer.

C. The Intent of the Faithful
   (vv. 10-12)

(Hebrews 11:11, 12 is not included in the printed text.)

10. For he looked for a city which hath foundations, whose builder and maker is God.

The attraction that stirred Abraham to great faith and obedience was the work of God. Abraham was not believing for earthly recompense for his faith; he was motivated by what God was doing. God had called him. God had sustained him. God had prepared a place and a city for him to inhabit at the end of his journey. The work of God, not the answer to his prayer, was the fulfillment of his faith.

Today, the answer to prayer is made the focus of our faith. Abraham, however, did not pray for anything. He was merely responsive to what God was doing and what God had called him to do. There is no record of either a great petition on the part of Abraham, or of the great fulfillment of that prayer. Abraham was seeking what he had not even prayed for. He was seeking something, a city, built by God himself. Yet Abraham had neither asked for it nor did he deserve it. He was not looking to have any of his "God-given" rights fulfilled. Abraham was seeking God's call and work.

D. The Issue of Not Receiving Promises (v. 13)

13. These all died in faith, not having received the promises, but having seen them afar off, and were persuaded of them, and embraced them, and confessed

that they were strangers and pilgrims on the earth.

Receiving the promises of God in this life is not the litmus test, much less the apex of faith. You may have faith and not have all your prayers answered. The promises of God are not magic formulas merely waiting for the right kind of faith. The test of faith does not depend on the fulfillment of all the promises of God on this earth. Some of His promises await their fulfillment in another world.

What is the primary goal of faith, as it is defined by some today? What is the relationship between faith and receiving what we pray for? what God has promised us?

The apex of faith is to please God, to receive a good report from Him (v. 2). The focus of faith is not what happens in this life on earth, but what will happen after this life. People of godly faith are strangers and pilgrims on the earth. The fulfillment of the promises of God will never be fully accomplished on this earth or in this life.

The word *promises* does not refer to Christ. The term is in the plural, referring to the multitude of promises that God made to the saints of old, listed in 11:4-12, and to many other men and women of faith.

The phrase *not having received* is the theme, the very heart of the writer's instruction about faith in this section. Faith is not based on receiving. Tragically, faith has today become centered in receiving. If you do not receive, you must not be a person of faith. The faith that created the worlds (v. 3), the faith of Abel (v. 4), the faith of Enoch (vv. 5, 6), the faith of Noah (v. 7), and the

faith of Abraham and Sara (vv. 8-12) was not strong because they received what they asked for, or what they were promised by God. On the contrary, their faith looked heavenward and was strong and pleasing before God in spite of not receiving all of the promises.

E. The Inspiration of Heavenly Faith (vv. 14-16)

14. For they that say such things declare plainly that they seek a country.

15. And truly, if they had been mindful of that country from whence they came out, they might have had opportunity to have returned.

16. But now they desire a better country, that is, an heavenly: wherefore God is not ashamed to be called their God: for he hath prepared for them a city.

Confession about receiving earthly things is not the key to faith. To declare that your faith will yield an earthly reward to be enjoyed merely upon earth and to have value only upon earth is not to confess in faith. A declaration of faith states your desire for greater things—things beyond this earth.

The confession of the saints in Hebrews 11 was for a heavenly country and city. Verse 15 states that earthly cities and blessings can be inhabited, one can return to them at anytime. However, a "better" faith is to seek after the heavenly city prepared by God.

God is ashamed of faith that does not desire heavenly things first and foremost. God is preparing better things beyond this earthly life. This kind of faith minimizes heaven, counting it a secondary goal. It reduces the heavenly preparation of God to a subsidiary role and elevates the accumulation of riches, success, and many other such confessions made in the name of faith.

III. FAITH FINISHES THE RACE (11:32-40; 12:1, 2)

A. Conquering to Finish (vv. 32-34)

(Hebrews 11:32-34 is not included in the printed text).

The list of the faithful includes descriptions of the conquering of many foes. Faith is a victorious experience. In faith many enemies are conquered. The sick are healed. Miracles take place. The course of history is changed by God's divine providence. All of these things are accomplished "through faith" (v. 33) in the Lord.

B. Conquered, Yet Finishing (vv. 35-39)

(Hebrews 11:35-38 is not included in the printed text.)

39. And these all, having obtained a good report through faith, received not the promise.

Faith is not a formula for conquering every foe. Faith endures as well as conquers. Sometimes the foe is not removed. Verse 36 begins a list of other faithful saints who were tortured and not delivered, tried and not rescued, imprisoned and not released, slain and not spared, and left with no place to dwell. Rather than a secondary list, the accomplishments of these "others" are called "worthy" (v. 38). They are worthy far beyond any measure of this world. Nothing on earth is as valuable as the enduring faith that these others possessed.

The ultimate reward of faith is the "good report" from God. The "good report" has been the theme and goal throughout the chapter (rf.

v. 2). What God thinks of us, whether we appear to have conquered or to have been conquered, is more important than what any other thinks of us or our faith. The best evaluation of faith is not what I accomplish with my faith, but what God is able to say about my faith.

C. Conquest Finished through Christ (Hebrews 11:40; 12:1, 2)

11:40. God having provided some better thing for us, that they without us should not be made perfect.

12:1. Wherefore seeing we also are compassed about with so great a cloud of witnesses, let us lay aside every weight, and the sin which doth so easily beset us, and let us run with patience the race that is set before us,

2. Looking unto Jesus the author and finisher of our faith; who for the joy that was set before him endured the cross, despising the shame, and is set down at the right hand of the throne of God.

Rather than glossing over experiences of pain and suffering when talking about faith, it is important to build on the idea that greater faith comes when one endures through an intense struggle rather than being delivered from it. The suffering of the "others" listed (beginning in the middle of 11:35) is climaxed when the suffering of Jesus is described (12:2). In fact, the "witnesses" (12:1) are not so much the success stories listed earlier in chapter 11, but the "others" listed in the latter part of the chapter. The suffering of Jesus, with His resurrection, is the climactic model for the faith of the believer. The essence of our faith is that we suffer with Him now, and await resurrection.

The faith of the Cross, not just in the Cross, is the beginning and ending of our faith. *Author* means the "one who takes a lead in." *Finisher* means the "one who perfects" something. The example of the suffering Savior on the Cross is where genuine faith comes from and is directed. This kind of faith is a far cry from the idea that we can say a few words and phrases, or follow the teaching of an individual, and have our faith multiplied. Godly faith comes from God through the suffering of the Cross.

Does this mean that we have to literally die on a cross. No, but it does mean that Christ's death on the Cross is not just the means of our faith but the example of our faith. Verses 3 and 4 exhort believers to not be weary but ready to endure, and to thereby possess the faith that God is building within us.

Laying aside sin, having patience, running with endurance, and following the example of the suffering Christ, who regarded the shame of the Cross lightly, are the kinds of things that make for genuine godly faith. In chapter 11, pleasing God, having godly fear, and being obedient are presented as elements of faith. Not receiving, looking beyond this earth, and seeking the heavenly home prepared by God are also mentioned later in chapter 11 as the elements of the essence of the believer's faith. May we grow up unto the full measure of the stature of the Cross in receiving the kind of faith that only comes from God. May we lay aside the temptation to exercise and confess an earthly faith which desires temporal things above heavenly.

REVIEW QUESTIONS

1. What is the ultimate goal of faith?

2. What is the definition of "good report" as it relates to faith?

3. What elements make up godly faith?

4. What is the primary goal of our faith?

5. Does suffering have anything to do with faith? Explain.

GOLDEN TEXT HOMILY

"WITHOUT FAITH IT IS IMPOSSIBLE TO PLEASE [GOD]: FOR HE THAT COMETH TO GOD MUST BELIEVE THAT HE IS, AND THAT HE IS A REWARDER OF THEM THAT DILIGENTLY SEEK HIM" (Hebrews 11:6).

In Hebrews 11, the great chapter on faith, there are many mountain peaks of inspiration that reach high into the purified atmosphere of God's divine power. Our Golden Text is certainly one of them. This verse teaches us that we can actually bring pleasure to our heavenly Father by simply believing Him.

Verse 5 tells us of Enoch, one man who had the testimony that he pleased God. How? Enoch walked with God in faith (Genesis 5:24). Pleasing God is just that simple—developing a relationship of trust and fellowship with God, just as a son would have with his earthly father. This text shows us the way to do this.

First, we must believe that God really exists. There are three special ways to express this belief. We come to God through His Word, through worship, and through prayer.

Next, we must believe He keeps His promises; that "he is a rewarder of them that diligently seek him." Our diligence in seeking God is like Enoch's walking with God continually. As Corrie ten Boon said, it is not a matter of having "great faith in God, but of having faith in a great God."

Believing God pleases Him. The

passage in Hebrews 10:38 tells us that God has no pleasure in the person who shrinks back from Him in fear and unbelief. But He does have pleasure in the person who simply believes Him. In fact, He welcomes us to approach His throne with boldness, "that we may obtain mercy, and find grace to help in time of need" (Hebrews 4:16).— **F.J. May, D.Min., Professor of Pastoral Studies, Church of God School of Theology, Cleveland, Tennessee**

SENTENCE SERMONS

GOD IS PLEASED when we have faith in Him and obey His Word.

—Selected

FAITH IN CHRIST is essential to salvation.

—Selected

IF WE DESIRE an increase of faith, we must consent to its testings.

—A.W. Tozer

FAITH SEES the invisible, believes the incredible, and receives the impossible.

—The Free Methodist

ILLUMINATING THE LESSON

The value of heavenward faith far exceeds faith that rests on earthly achievements and comforts. Many times heavenward faith must endure great hardship.

An evangelist said, "I have a friend who, during the depression, lost a job, a fortune, a wife, and a home. But he tenaciously held to his faith—the only thing he had left.

"One day he stopped to watch some men building a stone church. One of them was chiseling a triangular piece of rock. 'What are you going to do with that?' asked my friend.

"The workman said, 'Do you see that little opening way up there near the spire? Well, I'm shaping this down here so that it will fit up there.' Tears filled the eyes of the heartbroken man as he walked away. It seemed that God had spoken through the workman to explain the ordeal through which he was passing."

Perhaps you have recently suffered a great loss. Or maybe you are experiencing physical or emotional pain. The outward man seems to be "perishing." Yet, if you know the Lord as your Savior, you need not despair. All these things are under the loving hand of your heavenly Father, who is using them to prepare you for heaven.

DAILY BIBLE READINGS

M. Faith to Obey. Genesis 6:13-22
T. Walk by Faith. Genesis 12:1-9
W. Faith Rewarded. Genesis 22:1-13
T. Touch of Faith. Mark 5:25-34
F. Test of Faith. John 6:5-13
S. Faith in Jesus' Name.
   Acts 3:1-10

Marks of a Godly Life

Study Text: Hebrews 12:4-29; 13:1-25

Objective: To consider practical aspects of godly living and submit to God's authority.

Time: The Book of Hebrews was probably written between A.D. 64 and 70.

Place: The place of the writing of the Book of Hebrews is uncertain. Many Bible scholars suggest Rome.

Golden Text: "Follow peace with all men, and holiness, without which no man shall see the Lord" (Hebrews 12:14).

Central Truth: The Bible clearly reveals how Christians should live for God's glory.

Evangelism Emphasis: The godly conduct of believers testifies to the transforming power of Christ.

PRINTED TEXT

Hebrews 12:4. Ye have not yet resisted unto blood, striving against sin.

5. And ye have forgotten the exhortation which speaketh unto you as unto children, My son, despise not thou the chastening of the Lord, nor faint when thou art rebuked of him:

6. For whom the Lord loveth he chasteneth, and scourgeth every son whom he receiveth.

7. If ye endure chastening, God dealeth with you as with sons; for what son is he whom the father chasteneth not?

8. But if ye be without chastisement, whereof all are partakers, then are ye bastards, and not sons.

9. Furthermore we have had fathers of our flesh which corrected us, and we gave them reverence: shall we not much rather be in subjection unto the

Father of spirits, and live?

10. For they verily for a few days chastened us after their own pleasure; but he for our profit, that we might be partakers of his holiness.

11. Now no chastening for the present seemeth to be joyous, but grievous: nevertheless afterward it yieldeth the peaceable fruit of righteousness unto them which are exercised thereby.

14. Follow peace with all men, and holiness, without which no man shall see the Lord:

15. Looking diligently lest any man fail of the grace of God; lest any root of bitterness springing up trouble you, and thereby many be defiled;

13:1. Let brotherly love continue.

2. Be not forgetful to entertain strangers: for thereby

some have entertained angels unawares.

3. Remember them that are in bonds, as bound with them; and them which suffer adversity, as being yourselves also in the body.

4. Marriage is honourable in all, and the bed undefiled: but whoremongers and adulterers God will judge.

7. Remember them which have the rule over you, who have spoken unto you the word of God:

whose faith follow, considering the end of their conversation.

8. Jesus Christ the same yesterday, and to day, and for ever.

17. Obey them that have the rule over you, and submit yourselves: for they watch for your souls, as they that must give account, that they may do it with joy, and not with grief: for that is unprofitable for you.

LESSON OUTLINE

LESSON EXPOSITION

INTRODUCTION

Hebrews presents the ministry of Christ as priest and sacrifice for the believer. The majority of the book teaches the reader about the nature and eternal ramifications of Christ's work. This work is especially applied to the life of the believer in two areas, in faith and in practice. The discussion of faith begins at 10:31 and continues to the end of chapter 12. The practical applications of the book is the theme of the majority of chapter 13.

Christian conduct is a necessary part of our response to Christ's work in us. Salvation is not by works; however, legitimate salvation will manifest authentic works. At least three categories of works are emphasized in chapter 13: submission, righteousness, and conduct. All of these are relational. The essential paradigm is that the work of Christ, the foundation of the relationship between God and the individual, will manifest itself in the working relationship the believer has with others.

I. SUBMISSION TO DISCIPLINE (Hebrews 12:4-11)

A. The Standard of Discipline (v. 4)

4. Ye have not yet resisted unto blood, striving against sin.

Living the Christian life of faith is the theme of Hebrews 12. After presenting the examples of faith in Hebrews 11, the writer describes the nature of the believer's life of faith. Verses 1-3 introduces the life of faith by referring to examples of faith in chapter 11 and the example of Christ on the cross.

The standard for Christian living is to develop a life of submission to the example of the cross of Christ. Resisting and putting aside sin as a matter of faith and discipline are central concerns. Putting away sin is urged in verse 1; Christ's example is given. Next, the author talks about resisting sin.

Christ died on the cross so that the believer may live without the bondage of sin. Sinning is not necessary but must be resisted by the believer. Every effort, even resisting "unto blood," must be made in order to live without sin. "Blood" does not refer to giving one's own blood or sacrifice in order to obtain salvation. Rather, the word refers to the intense degree to which the Christian must strive for the standard of a sinless life.

How important is Christian conduct to the believer? What are expressions of the work of Christ within a Christian? What are evidences of submission within a life?

B. The Scourging of Discipline (vv. 5, 6)

5. And ye have forgotten the exhortation which speaketh unto you as unto children, My son, despise not thou the chastening of the Lord, nor faint when thou art rebuked of him:

6. For whom the Lord loveth he chasteneth, and scourgeth

every son whom he receiveth.

Personal discipline includes and goes beyond the minimal standard of "striving against sin" (v. 4). It involves a relationship with the heavenly Father that sometimes includes chastening. *Chastening* comes from the Greek term, *paideia.* The term emphasizes the overall training of an individual, particularly a child.

Submission to the discipline of chastening is based on the parent-child relationship between the believer and the heavenly Father. That relationship is rooted in love. Because the Lord loves His children, He takes care to train and chasten them. The chastening is not necessarily pleasant.

If a child of God does not recognize the roots of love and parental relationship, the temptation may be to despise the discipline of the Lord. "Despise" (v. 5) is included in a quotation from Proverbs 3:11, 12. The theme of the Father's love is affirmed elsewhere in the Old Testament (see also Psalm 94:12). The Greek term used in Hebrews 12 is *oligoreo.* The word means "to care little for." The implication is to belittle or minimize the value of something. Despising the discipline of the Lord's chastening is to fail to realize the love behind the training, and the benefit it will bring.

How does God choose to chasten his beloved? What does it mean for a believer to choose to reject the discipline of the Lord? When are difficulties not necessarily the chastening of the Lord?

C. The Sonship of Discipline (vv. 7-11)

7. If ye endure chastening,

God dealeth with you as with sons; for what son is he whom the father chasteneth not?

8. But if ye be without chastisement, whereof all are partakers, then are ye bastards, and not sons.

9. Furthermore we have had fathers of our flesh which corrected us, and we gave them reverence: shall we not much rather be in subjection unto the Father of spirits, and live?

10. For they verily for a few days chastened us after their own pleasure; but he for our profit, that we might be partakers of his holiness.

11. Now no chastening for the present seemeth to be joyous, but grievous: nevertheless afterward it yieldeth the peaceable fruit of righteousness unto them which are exercised thereby.

Not only is the discipline of chastening part of the Father-child relationship, it is also a necessary part of that relationship. If there is no discipline or rigorous training, then there is little or no evidence of a parental relationship.

Tragically, believers today feel that knowing Christ should mean that all pain and discomfort are removed. God uses discomfort, trial, and enduring circumstances in our lives to train us. Discipline is not a blissful experience. Working hard, changing attitudes, removing harmful habits, developing new abilities, and learning how to endure hardship are all part of the chastening process of the Lord.

Some mistake chastening for punishment. Punishment is part of God's process of judgment. Judgment may complement and lead to chastening. However, the emphasis of chastening is on training in order to improve and develop. The heavenly Father does not arbitrarily inflict pain upon His children. Quite the contrary, the Father introduces rigor in the lives of His children so that they may be able to reap greater blessings. The supreme example is the endurance of Christ on the cross which yielded salvation for you and me (vv. 2, 3).

II. LIVING RIGHTEOUSLY
(Hebrews 12:14-17)

A. Living Among People (v. 14a)

14a. Follow peace with all men.

The result of the chastening of the Lord is the ability to live among others in this world. Just as discipline is a necessary part of the Christian life, so is the ability to live a godly life among others. The reward of a right relationship with God is the development that comes through godly discipline. The reward of godly discipline and chastening is the ability to live rightly with others in this world.

"Follow peace with all men" is not a philosophy but a command of the Father. The chastening of the Lord is, in part, to prepare the believer for living according to God's commands. The Christian does not merely live according to philosophies or nice precepts. Rather, the commands of the Lord guide the believer's life. The goal of the commandment is not to give us peace or tranquility; it is to fulfill the commandment of the Lord.

What are some benefits of God's chastening? What does the term righteous mean? What are some characteristics of living righteously with others?

B. Living Before God (vv. 14b, 15a)

14b. And holiness, without which no man shall see the Lord:

15a. Looking diligently lest any man fail of the grace of God.

Holiness emphasizes devotion to the Lord. Just as the relationship of peace with others results from faithful obedience to the Lord, so holiness reflects faithful devotion to the Father. Holiness is not an abstract philosophy or code, as peace is not a mere philosophy. Holiness is a commitment to the God of holiness.

The heart of the devotion to holiness is the ability to see the Lord, both now and at His future coming. Holiness bears the fruit of purity in character and living. However, the root of holiness from which the fruit develops is devotion.

C. Living With Ourselves (v. 15b-17)

(Hebrews 12:16, 17 is not included in the printed text.)

15b. Lest any root of bitterness springing up trouble you, and thereby many be defiled.

A failure to live holy and devoted to God allows another root to develop—the root of bitterness. Bitterness stems from the failure to properly respond to the chastening and discipline of the Lord. Bitterness comes from the refusal to look to the Lord for the ability to live peacefully with others. Bitterness springs up when the cares of this world overcome the Christian's ability to remain focused on the Lord.

Bitterness comes from the Greek term, *pikria.* The word is strong, with connotations of poison. Bitterness produces a bitter, if not lethal, fruit. The fruit may look good on the outside, but the inside is deadly. Failing to respond to the discipline of the Lord by living peaceably with others and holy unto God results in corruption in a life that may otherwise look good on the outside. True Christian living avoids internal corruption and bitterness.

In verses 16 and 17, the writer reminds his readers of the foolish, profane action of Esau who was willing to sell his birthright for present gratification. He showed little or no regard for the future blessing of the birthright, but was willing to sacrifice it to satisfy the hunger pains he felt.

Here, as in some other cases in the Old Testament, the word *repentance* may mean "change of mind." It may refer to Issac or to God, against whose will Isaac would not go. Esau desired that he be given the blessing—indirectly a request for the birthright that Jacob had usurped from him. But he was rejected; he found no repentance (change of mind on the part of the bestower).

How does bitterness develop in the believer's life? What are some characteristics of bitterness? How is Esau's action repeated in today's world?

III. CHRISTIAN CONDUCT (Hebrews 13:1-8, 17)

A. Love as the Rule of Conduct (vv. 1-6)

(Hebrews 13:5, 6 is not included in the printed text.)

1. Let brotherly love continue.

2. Be not forgetful to entertain strangers: for thereby some have

entertained angels unawares.

3. Remember them that are in bonds, as bound with them; and them which suffer adversity, as being yourselves also in the body.

4. Marriage is honourable in all, and the bed undefiled: but whoremongers and adulterers God will judge.

The final chapter of Hebrews is no accident. The book portrays a picture of the ministry of Christ as sacrifice and priest for the believer. The end of the book begins to relate the role of faith to applying the ministry of Christ. The final conclusion of the book is about the roles of love and relationships. Christ taught that by love one for another, especially in the body of believers, others would know that Christians are true followers of Christ (John 13:34, 35). Hebrews ends with the same affirmation.

Four primary relationships are mentioned in the first six verses. The relationships include: those between members of the body of Christ, those with strangers, those with the imprisoned, and those between husband and wife. No apparent reason is given for the order or for listing these first in this summary chapter about relationships. They are clustered at the beginning with verses 5 and 6 forming a transition to the rest of the chapter. The four areas may have precedent over the rest of the chapter because of the transition of verses 5 and 6.

The four relationships are especially challenging to the faith of the believer. Relationships in the body of Christ are especially important for witness (John 13:34-35). Being open to strangers is important because they may be special oppor-

tunities from the Lord, as indicated by the comment regarding angels. The reference is to literal angels and is documentation that angels are real. The believer should be aware of the possibility of meeting them.

Relationships with those in bonds is important because of the need for sensitivity to those who suffer pain, injustice, and estrangement. Christ himself led the way in providing an example of this kind of sensitivity (Isaiah 61:1; Matthew 25:36). God especially takes the relationship between husband and wife seriously and will personally judge those who violate it.

Verses 5 and 6 affirm that right relationships with others, especially in the categories mentioned in verses 1-4, are important because they reflect the dependency we have on the Lord. Certainly, one of the biggest lessons we learn in relating to others is that it takes the Lord to make relationships work. We depend on Him.

B. Lordship as the Guide of Conduct (vv. 7, 8)

7. Remember them which have the rule over you, who have spoken unto you the word of God: whose faith follow, considering the end of their conversation.

8. Jesus Christ the same yesterday, and to day, and for ever.

Together, these two verses confirm dependency on the lordship of Jesus Christ. The rule of others first is affirmed. And then a simple worshipful statement, almost like an utterance repeated in worship services, affirms the overriding presence of Jesus and His lordship over all authorities.

The particular authorities mentioned in verse 7 may be those outside of the church. However, the phrase, "who have spoken unto you the word of God," may refer to religious or church authorities. Some interpreters take the phrase to mean that authorities, by virtue of their position, whether sacred or secular, speak with direct or indirect instruction from the Lord. Others interpret the phrase to mean religious authorities, assuming that the word of God is spoken more directly by believers.

Not only do the authorities speak the word of God but also the message of verse 8: "Jesus Christ, the same yesterday, and to day, and for ever." This message affirming the authority of Jesus seems to represent the message of church authorities more than that of civil authorities. Therefore, the admonition is to submit to leaders in the church.

A definite character trait of the Christian is the affirmation of the authority of the Lord and the authorities, especially those in the church. Recognition of both sources of authority go hand in hand. Allegiance to Christ comes first, but the secondary accountability is not negated.

C. Loyalty as the Profit of Conduct (v. 17)

17. Obey them that have the rule over you, and submit yourselves: for they watch for your souls, as they that must give account, that they may do it with joy, and not with grief: for that is unprofitable for you.

The admonition in verses 7 and 8 to "remember" authorities is extended now to "obey them." The essential meaning of the Greek word for *remember* is "to remain." The form of the word "to remember"

is "to cause something to remain," or "to remain over and over" within someone's mind. The admonition is to bring to mind, over and over, those who are in authority. The expression is not only a reference to memory, but also an affirmation to care. To care about the authorities by keeping them in mind, to not forget them or think little of them, is the emphasis of the expression.

Obey comes from the root Greek concept, *peitho*, meaning, "to be persuaded." Mere consent or going through the motions of assent was not the meaning of *obey*. The term emphasizes acting with the persuasion that the ruler is correct. The idea of persuasion does not mean putting authorities to a test and following them if we are persuaded that they are worth following. Rather, the task of being persuaded is the responsibility of the reader. The individual is to work through whatever personal difficulties exist in order to be persuaded of and obedient to authorities.

Verse 17 conveys the important responsibility placed upon authorities in the church. Because the task was so important, the authorities did not need the extra burden of trying to convince others of the importance of their responsibilities. Authorities in the church were to be valued because they had an important task—one that should be recognized, not criticized or questioned. This does not mean that authorities are above examination or accountability. Rather, the minimum was to at least recognize the weight of the responsibility laid upon them.

The work of the cross of Christ means that there is also a responsibility on the believer. The believer is to recognize the transformation of character and relationships that are to take place as a consequence of the cross. Submission, righteousness, and good conduct are minimal core values that come with being a Christian.

REVIEW QUESTIONS

1. How important is Christian conduct to the believer?
2. How does God choose to chasten his beloved?
3. What are some characteristics of righteous living with others?
4. How does bitterness develop in the believer's life?
5. What does the term *remember* mean in 13:7?

GOLDEN TEXT HOMILY

"FOLLOW PEACE WITH ALL MEN, AND HOLINESS, WITHOUT WHICH NO MAN SHALL SEE THE LORD" (Hebrews 12:14).

Exemplary lessons from the lives of the heroes of faith and a strong admonition to endure the spiritual race precede the Golden Text. Obstacles and hindrances in the Christian life can be discouraging and sap our spiritual energy.

We can also become despondent in failing to see purpose in the difficulties that result from the chastening love of the Father (Hebrews 12:5-11). It's been said that the struggle of life can make us either bitter or better. The message is clear and urgent—don't be incapacitated by the blows of life, but pick yourself up and get moving down the road to restoration. "Lift up the hands which hang down . . . the feeble knees; and make straight paths for your feet . . . [so] that which is lame . . . [may] be healed" (Hebrews 12:12, 13).

Often, failures and difficulties turn us against God and against people. Unless we are restored, we can ultimately be infected by a cancerous "root of bitterness" (Hebrews 12:15). Disliking ourselves, rationalizing our sin, and standing up for our rights cause us to be continually at variance with others. Cutting ourselves off from God's spiritual blessing and favor, we begin to lose those characteristics (holiness) that set us apart as believers.

Regarding this spiritually perilous condition, the Biblical writer gives a strong exhortation of both encouragement and warning. Instead of striking out and reacting to people, we should strive to live in peace with everyone, including those who are the source of our hurts. Supernatural love for others and determined trust in spite of circumstances are distinguishing traits of those who see dimly—as through a dark glass—now, but will one day see Him face to face.—**John J. Secret, Chaplain (Capt.), United States Air Force, APO, New York, New York**

SENTENCE SERMONS

THE BIBLE clearly reveals how Christians should live for God's glory.

—Selected

THE GODLY CONDUCT of believers testifies to the transforming power of Christ.

—Selected

RIGHTEOUSNESS as exemplified by Christ is not merely the absence of vice or the presence of virtue. It is a consuming passion for God which sends you forth in His name to establish His kingdom.

—Irving Peake Johnson

EVANGELISM APPLICATION

THE GODLY CONDUCT OF BELIEVERS TESTIFIES TO THE TRANSFORMING POWER OF CHRIST.

The godly conduct of the believer is based in the work of Christ. Godly conduct is not just good works. Godly conduct is, by nature, Christ-transformed conduct. Good works reflect a good nature. However, godly conduct reflects the work of Christ within the believer.

The believer reflects Christ in his godly conduct. Christ should be seen though the behavior of the believer. Witness for the believer is not just verbal but is also behavioral. Witnessing verbally is important because it clarifies and identifies the source and nature of our conduct. Acting out the transformation brought on by the indwelling Christ is a necessary part of the believer's witness to the world.

Two perils face the believer regarding his godly conduct. The first is merely act out good works, motivated by philosophy or human mentors. The believer's mentor is, first of all, Christ. The second peril is to rely on works exclusively to be his witness. The behavior of the believer, in order to present a full witness of the Savior, must both reflect love for other believers and be affirmed by verbal testimony.

ILLUMINATING THE LESSON

Submission is an important aspect of Christian conduct. The nature of submission calls for the believer to do things that may not immediately appear to yield results. Although results are delayed, they are sure. Sometimes it is necessary to slow down in order to make progress.

An interesting thing about flight in outer space is that you must "slow down in order to catch up." If two satellites, or spacecraft, desire to rendezvous, the one making the approach cannot accelerate, it must decelerate. If it increases its speed, the craft will go into a higher orbit, but if it decreases its speed, it will drop into a lower orbit and actually gain on the craft ahead of it. Most rendezvous are designed so that the approaching craft comes in from a higher orbit and "slows down in order to catch up." As a result, the craft drops into place by decelerating.

In a sense, this is how we best discover God's will for our own lives. If we struggle spiritually and emotionally to please God, we only make it hard on ourselves and will probably move further away from God's perfect will. The best way to serve God is to submit our lives to his control. The more we yield ourselves to his power, the more power we find available to use for service.

DAILY BIBLE READINGS

M. Live in God's Presence.
   Psalm 15:1-5
T. Love God's Word.
   Psalm 19:7-14
W. A Pure People.
   Zephaniah 3:9-13
T. Speak God's Word.
   Acts 13:42-47
F. Walk in Love. Romans 13:8-10
S. Live in Holiness.
   1 Corinthians 6:9-11, 18-20

Death Destroyed (Easter Lesson)

Study Text: 1 Corinthians 15:1-58

Objective: To affirm that Christ has conquered death and live in the hope of eternal life.

Time: The Book of 1 Corinthians was written between A.D. 55 and 57.

Place: The Book of 1 Corinthians was written at Ephesus.

Golden Text: "Now is Christ risen from the dead, and become the firstfruits of them that slept" (1 Corinthians 15:20).

Central Truth: Christ defeated sin and death by His death and resurrection.

Evangelism Emphasis: Faith in Christ is the only way to receive eternal life.

PRINTED TEXT

1 Corinthians 15:20. But now is Christ risen from the dead, and become the firstfruits of them that slept.

21. For since by man came death, by man came also the resurrection of the dead.

22. For as in Adam all die, even so in Christ shall all be made alive.

23. But every man in his own order: Christ the first-fruits; afterward they that are Christ's at his coming.

24. Then cometh the end, when he shall have delivered up the kingdom to God, even the Father; when he shall have put down all rule and all authority and power.

25. For he must reign, till he hath put all enemies under his feet.

26. The last enemy that shall be destroyed is death.

48. As is the earthy, such

are they also that are earthy: and as is the heavenly, such are they also that are heavenly.

49. And as we have borne the image of the earthy, we shall also bear the image of the heavenly.

50. Now this I say, brethren, that flesh and blood cannot inherit the kingdom of God; neither doth corruption inherit incorruption.

51. Behold, I shew you a mystery; We shall not all sleep, but we shall all be changed,

52. In a moment, in the twinkling of an eye, at the last trump: for the trumpet shall sound, and the dead shall be raised incorruptible, and we shall be changed.

53. For this corruptible must put on incorruption, and this mortal must put on immortality.

54. So when this corruptible shall have put on incorruption, and this mortal shall have put

on immortality, then shall be brought to pass the saying that is written, Death is swallowed up in victory.

55. O death, where is thy sting? O grave, where is thy victory?

56. **The sting of death is sin; and the strength of sin is the law.**

57. But thanks be to God, which giveth us the victory through our Lord Jesus Christ.

58. **Therefore, my beloved brethren, be ye stedfast, unmoveable, always abounding in the work of the Lord, forasmuch as ye know that your labour is not in vain in the Lord.**

LESSON OUTLINE

I. CHRIST IS RISEN

    A. Christ as the Firstfruits of the Resurrection

    B. The Victory of the Resurrection

II. BELIEVERS SHALL RISE

    A. The Resurrected Body

    B. The Heavenly Image of the Resurrection

III. VICTORY OVER DEATH

    A. The Resurrection Trumpet of God

    B. The Steadfast Victory of the Resurrection

LESSON EXPOSITION

INTRODUCTION

The resurrection of Jesus brings eternal victory to the believer. Much of the attack of the enemy of the Christian has been through the earthly body. At the resurrection, final victory over death and the onslaught of Satan will be the inheritance of each believer. A new, resurrected body, independent of earthly substance, will be received. Paul proclaimed that despite what is not known about the final resurrection, it is still a fact. He further explained much of what can be confessed about the resurrected body of the Christian.

Death is a cruel consequence of sin. This fact is reflected by the comparative beauty of life. The reality of death is as cruel as life is precious. Death is the cessation of life. Life may hold many good qualities and relationships, but the power of death is such that all of the beauty of life is taken away by its evil grasp.

Individuals were created to live eternally with God. Despite its finality, God has prepared a way beyond death. There is a reality beyond death. The termination of life is not the last event in the existence of an individual. Each person has an eternal destiny. Death is a door to the existence beyond life. For the believer this existence is in a resurrected body.

The witness of the Bible speaks of the resurrected body of the saints. Saints will not remain as spirits. They will be known and will have a body. This body will not bear the imperfections of the past; nor will it depend on the flesh and the fallen things of earth. Rather, it will be a perfect creation of God, dependent on the Spirit of God. This lesson text looks at the nature of the resurrected body of the saints.

I. CHRIST IS RISEN
(1 Corinthians 15:20-26)

A. Christ as the Firstfruits of the Resurrection (vv. 20-23)

20. But now is Christ risen from the dead, and become the firstfruits of them that slept.

21. For since by man came death, by man came also the resurrection of the dead.

22. For as in Adam all die, even so in Christ shall all be made alive.

23. But every man in his own order: Christ the firstfruits; afterward they that are Christ's at his coming.

In 1 Corinthians, Paul responded to various issues raised by the Corinthian church. In chapter 15, Paul taught about resurrection. He responded to "some among you that [were saying] there is no resurrection of the dead" (v. 12). This was a very critical heresy. Paul was careful to point out that the doctrine of the Resurrection was very important for the eternal life and faith of the saints. He not only emphasized the reality of the resurrection of the saints, but He also clarified the nature of the resurrected body of the believer.

In verses 1-11, Paul discussed the historical evidence for the bodily resurrection of Christ. In verses 12-19, he stressed the importance of belief in the Resurrection. In verses 20-28, he explained that Christ would lead Christians in the final resurrection.

"Firstfruits" (v. 20) refers to the fact that Christ is the first One to be resurrected and that the saints will follow in like manner. *Firstfruits* was not used merely to indicate the fruit that first came in a crop; it was also used to indicate that more fruit would follow. The term pledged that there would be other fruit in

like manner, and it was a sign to the farmer of what would follow. Likewise, the certainty of Christ's resurrection was a pledge of the certainty of our resurrection.

Paul elaborated the forerunning of Christ's resurrection in verse 21. The explanatory word used is *for*, illustrating verses 19 and 20. Paul explained that we have a hope because of the work of Christ.

The point is made that death existed because of the action of Adam. There was no effort to prove the truthfulness of this claim—it was an established fact. Paul proceeded to tell of the effect of Adam's life, sin, and death.

The Resurrection is a powerful part of the victory of the believer. In order to erode the faith of the believer, Satan is especially determined to tempt the Christian to doubt the reality of the resurrection of the body. Will the believer actually have a body as part of the resurrection, or will we just be spirits that ascend to heaven? Paul clearly stated that we will have an actual body, not only at the resurrection of the righteous, but in heaven also. In fact, having an actual body is a significant part of the victory and power of the resurrection work of Christ.

How certain is the resurrection of the believer? What truth did Paul present to make this point?

In verses 22 and 23, Paul identified the One who makes the resurrection of the believers a certainty. That One is Jesus. Adam had made death certain; now Christ makes the resurrection of the believer certain.

The actions of Adam and Christ

were applied to the Christian. The word *but* (v. 23) indicated that man was not excluded at death. Rather, he was included in the resurrection through the work of Christ. Paul told the Corinthians that the resurrection of the Christian would move him from death to life, just as Christ lived beyond death.

The "order" (*tagma*) of the resurrection is given in verse 23. This Greek word was used only here in the New Testament. It was a military word designating the soldier who waited for the decision of the commander. The emphasis here is on the Christian waiting for the direction or signal of Christ at the resurrection. Christ rose as the "firstfruits." The Christian will be "in his own order" to rise thereafter. The order and response of the believer will be at the coming of Christ in the clouds. "They that are Christ's" will rise to meet Him in the air in the resurrection of the saints.

B. The Victory of the Resurrection (vv. 24-26)

24. Then cometh the end, when he shall have delivered up the kingdom to God, even the Father; when he shall have put down all rule and all authority and power.

25. For he must reign, till he hath put all enemies under his feet.

26. The last enemy that shall be destroyed is death.

The time of the resurrection would be the time of the "end." The first description of the end is that it would be the time when Christ would deliver the Kingdom to the Father. The work of Christ in the church will be presented to the heavenly Father. He will present it as a completed vessel. Paul was pointing out that Christ is now working in the life of the Christian for a definite purpose, to present him to the Father at the resurrection of the saints.

The second description of the end is that it would mean the time when Christ would establish His reign over all principalities and powers. There will be powers and forces, seen and unseen, which will continue for a time to come against the work of Christ. However, when the resurrection of the believers takes place, just before the Great Tribulation begins, the beginning of the end of Satan's work will start. The work of victory will continue through the Tribulation and the Millennium until Satan will be cast into eternal punishment. This will complete the work of establishing Christ's reign, which began at the resurrection of Christ and will continue through the eventual resurrection of the believer.

In verses 25 and 26, Paul emphasized Christ's power for two major reasons. First, he wanted to communicate Christ's ability to conquer death. In verse 12, Paul had identified the skeptics who said there was no resurrection of the dead. Paul combated this argument by declaring that death has no power over the resurrection of the saints. Christ's power had established the reality and certainty of the resurrection. Whereas the doubter said that there will be no resurrection, Paul said that Christ's power is greater than death.

The second reason Paul wanted to emphasize Christ's power was to establish confidence and understanding for the Corinthians about death itself. Death was to be understood not as a mighty, unconquerable foe. This feeling was understandable in light of the finality of death over this earthly life. However, Paul assured the Christian that resurrection is just as definite as death. This is because of the power of Christ at His Resurrection. The believers' resurrection is as certain as Christ's.

II. BELIEVERS SHALL RISE
(1 Corinthians 15:35-49)

A. The Resurrected Body
(vv. 35-47)

(1 Corinthians 15:35-47 is not included in the printed text.)

These verses emphasize what will occur to the body of the believer—it will be resurrected. The Christian will not be a ghost, or some mystic force. The body of the believer will be changed, but it will be an actual body. These verses emphasize that the body of the believer will be resurrected (v. 38). The structural makeup of the body and the manner in which it will be created at the resurrection is known only to God. Paul did not emphasize the manner of creation of the resurrected body but only the fact that God would do it.

In verses 39-41, Paul emphasized that the glory of the resurrected body would be different from the body that believers had on earth. The term *glory* referred to the most outstanding and identifying characteristics of the body. He pointed out that there are distinctions between men and beasts. There are also distinctions of earthly bodies and of heavenly bodies at the resurrection. The specific nature of that glory, or distinction, is the emphasis of the latter portion of this section.

Verses 42-47 list a number of comparisons between the body before and after the resurrection. These categories include: corruptible versus incorruptible, dishonor versus glory, weakness versus power, natural versus spiritual, and earthly versus heavenly. All of these point out the superiority and new reality of the resurrected body. In each item which describes the nature of the resurrected body, the Creator is God himself. It will be a real body, entirely dependent on the Lord.

What is the reality which makes the resurrected body of the saints a definite occurrence in the future?

B. The Heavenly Image of the Resurrection (vv. 48, 49)

48. As is the earthy, such are they also that are earthy: and as is the heavenly, such are they also that are heavenly.

49. And as we have borne the image of the earthy, we shall also bear the image of the heavenly.

The emphasis of these two verses is upon the reality of the heavenly realm applied to the resurrected bodies of the saints. The saints of God are going to receive bodies composed of heavenly elements. Those heavenly elements will not make them any less real. The bodies will be as real as heaven itself.

The word *image* is translated from the Greek term *eikon*. The emphasis of the word is on likeness. The resurrected body will have a likeness to the things of heaven. That likeness will first be dependent on God as its source of sustenance and strength. The likeness of the body will not be reliant on the natural things of earth. It will be a heavenly body, contingent on the same things of God that the things of heaven depend on for their existence.

III. VICTORY OVER DEATH
(1 Corinthians 15:50-58)

A. The Resurrection Trumpet of God (vv. 50-54)

50. Now this I say, brethren, that flesh and blood cannot inherit the kingdom of God; neither doth corruption inherit incorruption.

51. Behold, I shew you a mystery; We shall not all sleep, but we shall all be changed,

52. In a moment, in the twinkling of an eye, at the last trump: for the trumpet shall sound, and the dead shall be raised incorruptible, and we shall be changed.

53. For this corruptible must put on incorruption, and this mortal must put on immortality.

54. So when this corruptible shall have put on incorruption, and this mortal shall have put on immortality, then shall be brought to pass the saying that is written, Death is swallowed up in victory.

In verse 50 Paul explains the relationship between the resurrected body and the inheritance of God's kingdom. Believers will have to take on the resurrected body in order to inherit the completion of the kingdom of God as it is presented to the Father by Christ (v. 24). Verses 51-58 are a summary of the doctrine and teaching of the Resurrection. They proclaim the circumstances in which the body of the believer will actually be changed from an earthly body to a heavenly one.

The resurrection will be a "mystery." Although Paul taught about the resurrection and its circumstances, much was still left unsaid. The time when the resurrection will take place was not revealed. The specific biological construction of the resurrected body was not revealed. The way the corruptible body would become incorruptible was not revealed. Nevertheless, Paul confirmed the fact and hope of the resurrected body. Though the resurrection is certain, there is still some "mystery" about it.

Paul revealed some information about the nature of the mystery in the second half of verse 51: "We shall not all sleep, but we shall all be changed." *Sleep* represents death. Not all will die before Christ's coming. The words *we* and *all* are general in application; they did not refer specifically to the initial readers at Corinth. Some Christians would be alive at the resurrection of the saints. They would be changed. *Changed* means to alter the condition of something or someone. Those alive at the resurrection would be transformed from a natural to a spiritual body.

Verse 52 elaborates on the change mentioned in verse 51. The timing is discussed first. The length of time in which the change would take place is called "*a* moment, in the twinkling of an eye." *Moment* is translated from a Greek word made up of two words—*a*, meaning "not," and *temno*, meaning "to cut." Together they form the word *atomos*. The English word *atom* comes from this word. It means "an indivisible unit." The word *atom,* when originally created in ancient Greece, represented the smallest unit of the universe. After units of nature were divided, there would be a final indivisible unit.

Moment refers to the smallest unit of time. The smallest unit of time expressed in typical English conversation is "in a split second." This might be a more accurate interpretation of the term.

"Twinkling of an eye" expresses another extremely short unit of time. In human experience the twinkling of an eye is so effortless and brief it goes unnoticed. Humans rarely perceive the event of an eye blinking unless it is slow, deliberate, and intentional. The speed of the change from the natural body to the spiritual body will be so quick it will be practically beyond human perception.

After the timing of the resurrection, verse 52 elaborates on the moment at which the resurrection will take place. It will occur with the signal of the "last trump." This "trump" is part of the prophetic description of the end time. This is the "trump of God" which will proclaim the time for the resurrection to take place (1 Thessalonians 4:16).

Besides the length of time and the signal of the change, Paul also indicated the nature of the "raised" body—it will be "incorruptible." This is the same description given in verse 42. The body will be changed to one that is not subject to decay or the corruption of sin.

Verses 53 and 54 give the mandate or necessity for change. The first word in verse 53, *for*, indicates the necessity of the change. This is reemphasized by the word *must*. In verse 54 Paul gave the purpose of the resurrection. The body must be changed in order for death to be conquered. The victory over death which Paul taught was prophesied in Isaiah 25:8. Paul quoted it in verse 54: "Death is swallowed up in victory." It celebrated the victory of the believer over death.

What does the term immortality mean in the lesson text?

B. The Steadfast Victory of the Resurrection (vv. 55-58)

55. O death, where is thy sting? O grave, where is thy victory?

56. The sting of death is sin; and the strength of sin is the law.

57. But thanks be to God, which giveth us the victory through our Lord Jesus Christ.

58. Therefore, my beloved brethren, be ye stedfast, unmoveable, always abounding in the work of the Lord, forasmuch as ye know that your labour is not in vain in the Lord.

The victory of the believer at the resurrection is deliverance from the sting of sin. Verses 55-58 declare this victory. Death for the believer is a step toward acquisition of the heavenly, resurrected body. The unbeliever goes through death as the passage to eternal judgment and damnation.

Christ's work and sacrifice has removed the stigma and sting of death. Death is a time for celebration rather than tragedy. The believer rather has the hope of eternal life. This passage has clarified and amplified the hope and reality of the resurrected body after death. The glory of that body is also a cause for encouragement and celebration.

That resurrection hope is the basis of Paul's final exhortation for believers to be encouraged. The benefits and reality of the resurrected body are to be a source of edification for believers. Paul's exhortation is to be "stedfast, unmoveable, always abounding in the work of the Lord" (v. 58). These benefits are possible because the reality of the resurrected body gives ultimate purpose and direction for the believers. This is the reason Paul exhorts them that their labor is "not in vain." The hope of the resurrection of the believers shines on all the pathways of the Christian to give direction and purpose.

REVIEW QUESTIONS

1. How important is the doctrine of the Resurrection of the saints to the believer?

2. What does the term *firstfruits* indicate?

3. What will the resurrected body be like?

4. What is the significance of the resurrected body depending on the creation of God?

5. What does the term *moment* signify in the lesson text?

GOLDEN TEXT HOMILY

"NOW IS CHRIST RISEN FROM THE DEAD, AND BECOME THE FIRSTFRUITS OF THEM THAT SLEPT" (1 Corinthians 15:20).

A terrible plague is sweeping our world. I am not speaking of cancer, AIDS, or heart disease. Even though each of these is terrible, the worst plague today is death! Death, a plague? Yes, it kills more people spiritually than all other deadly methods.

To die physically is a sad thing. "It is appointed unto men once to die" (Hebrews 9:27). To die physically and not to live spiritually is even worse. To neglect salvation means eternal death and separation from God! Death transports the lost into spiritual damnation apart from God. Many believe the lie of physical death that this life is all there is.

Some men and women actually come to Christ because of the threat of death. In the face of dealing with a terminal illness, some hard hearts are humbled to repentance. At the funeral of a lost loved one, some family members may finally yield to the prayers of a parent or beloved relative to hear the gospel message and come with them by faith into the Promised Land. Death is the final enemy that will one day be put under the feet of Christ!

The resurrection of Christ offers the cure for death, both physically and spiritually. Christ is the answer to the "whys" of this life. Jesus came that whoever believes in Him shall not perish! (John 3:16). Death is already defeated, eternally! Will you accept His righteousness? Believe on the Lord Jesus Christ, and you will be saved (Acts 16:31).— **Eugene Wigelsworth, M.S.W., M.Div., Senior Chaplain, Pasquotank Correctional Institution, Elizabeth City, North Carolina**

SENTENCE SERMONS

CHRIST DEFEATED sin and death by His death and resurrection.

—Selected

SOME DIE without having really lived, while others continue to live in spite of the fact they have died.

—*The Encyclopedia of Religious Quotations*

DEATH IS NOT a period but a comma in the story of life.

—Amos Traver

THOSE WHO HOPE for no other life are dead even in this life.

—Johann Von Goethe

EVANGELISM APPLICATION

FAITH IN CHRIST IS THE ONLY WAY TO RECEIVE ETERNAL LIFE.

People today would like to receive eternal life. There is a fear about death and a quest for life. Life can be so pleasant; who wants to give up the good things of life? The very thought of death can be painful, and who wants to experience that pain? Life is preferred, sought after, and preserved at all costs. The deception is that people today actually think they can conquer death. They live as though they will never die.

The reality that weighs on all of life is the certainty of death. No matter who you are, no matter how long you may have lived, you will face death one day. No one can add one day of life past that eternal appointment we have with finitude. There is only one way to conquer death, and that is to live eternally.

The only way to receive eternal life is by faith in Christ. He has already done the work. Only faith in His work brings eternal life. Faith is not a partnership, but a complete confidence in what Jesus has done. Faith is not a contract, but a covenant accepted by believing totally in Christ. Faith is not exchange, but a gift of grace given to all who repent and call on the name of the Lord.

The reality of the resurrected body has been explained in 1 Corinthians 15. This is the body the believer will inhabit for eternity. Understanding the certainty of the resurrected body is the key to many of the doubts some have about the reality of heaven. Heaven will be an eternal home for the new body and existence of the believer. However, none of the joys of the resurrected body are possible unless a person comes to know Christ as Lord and Savior.

ILLUMINATING THE LESSON

A beggar stopped a lawyer on the street in a large Southern city and asked him for a quarter. Taking a long, hard look into the man's unshaven face, the attorney asked, "Don't I know you from somewhere?"

"You should," came the reply. "I'm your former classmate. Remember, second floor, old Main Hall?"

"Why Sam, of course I know you!" Without further question the lawyer wrote a check for $100.

"Here, take this and get a new start. I don't care what's happened in the past, it's the future that counts." And with that he hurried on.

Tears welled up in the man's eyes as he walked to a bank nearby. Stopping at the door, he saw through the glass well-dressed tellers and the spotlessly clean interior. Then he looked at his filthy rags. "They won't take this from me. They'll swear that I forged it," he muttered as he turned away.

The next day the two men met again. "Why Sam, what did you do with my check? Gamble it away? Drink it up?"

"No," said the beggar, as he pulled it out of his dirty shirt pocket and told why he hadn't cashed it.

"Listen, friend," said the lawyer. "What makes that check good is not your clothes or appearance, but my signature. Go on, cash it!"

The Bible says, "Whosoever shall call upon the name of the Lord shall be saved" (Romans 10:13). That promise is a "negotiable note" of infinite value. And as sinners, all we need to do is "exchange" it by faith for eternal life. Don't let the "tattered clothes" of your past keep you from cashing God's "check" of salvation.—*Parsons Illustrations*

DAILY BIBLE READINGS

M. Hope of Resurrection.
   Job 19:23-27
T. Resurrection Foretold.
   Psalm 16:8-11
W. Order of Resurrection.
   John 5:24-29
T. Promise of Resurrection.
   John 11:23-26
F. Resurrection of Believers.
   Revelation 20:4-6
S. Resurrection of Unbelievers.
   Revelation 20:12-15

Making Difficult Decisions

Study Text: Genesis 12:1-9; 13:1-18

Objective: To realize that life offers many opportunities and determine to make godly choices.

Time: The Book of Genesis was written between 1450 and 1400 B.C.

Place: The general belief is that Moses received this revelation while on Mount Sinai in the wilderness.

Golden Text: "By faith Abraham, when he was called to go out into a place which he should after receive for an inheritance, obeyed; and he went out, not knowing whither he went" (Hebrews 11:8).

Central Truth: Believers can make wise choices by trusting in God's Word.

Evangelism Emphasis: Accepting Christ as Savior is life's most important decision.

PRINTED TEXT

Genesis 12:4. So Abraham departed, as the Lord had spoken unto him; and Lot went with him: and Abraham was seventy and five years old when he departed out of Haran.

5. And Abraham took Sarai his wife, and Lot his brother's son, and all their substance that they had gathered, and the souls that they had gotten in Haran; and they went forth to go into the land of Canaan; and into the land of Canaan they came.

6. And Abraham passed through the land unto the place of Sichem, unto the plain of Moreh. And the Canaan-ite was then in the land.

7. And the Lord appeared unto Abraham, and said, Unto thy seed will I give this land: and there builded he an altar unto the Lord, who appeared unto him.

13:8. And Abraham said unto Lot, Let there be no strife, I pray thee, between me and thee, and between my herdmen and thy herdmen; for we be brethren.

9. Is not the whole land before thee? separate thyself, I pray thee, from me: if thou wilt take the left hand, then I will go to the right; or if thou depart to the right hand, then I will go to the left.

10. And Lot lifted up his eyes, and beheld all the plain of Jordan, that it was well watered every where, before the Lord destroyed Sodom and Gomorrah, even as the garden of the Lord, like the land of Egypt, as thou comest unto Zoar.

11. Then Lot chose him all the plain of Jordan; and Lot journeyed east: and they separated themselves the one from the other.

12. Abraham dwelled in the land of Canaan, and Lot dwelled in the cities of the plain, and pitched his tent toward Sodom.

13. But the men of Sodom were wicked and sinners before the Lord exceedingly.

14. And the Lord said unto Abraham, after that Lot was separated from him, Lift up now thine eyes, and look from the place where thou art northward, and southward, and eastward, and westward:

15. For all the land which thou seest, to thee will I give it, and to thy seed for ever.

16. And I will make thy seed as the dust of the earth: so that if a man can number the dust of the earth, then shall thy seed also be numbered.

17. Arise, walk through the land in the length of it and in the breadth of it; for I will give it unto thee.

DICTIONARY

Sichem (SIGH-kem)—Genesis 12:6—The same as Shechem (SHE-kem). A personal name and the name of a city in Ephraim.

Moreh (MO-reh)—Genesis 12:6—The plain of Moreh is near Schechem where Abraham erected an altar to the Lord.

Canaanites (KAY-nun-ites)—Genesis 12:6—Descendants of Canaan (KAY-nun), who was the son of Ham.

Sodom (SOD-um) and Gomorrah (goh-MOR-ruh)—Genesis 13:10—Cities remembered primarily for their wickedness.

Zoar (ZO-er)—Genesis 13:10—An ancient Cannanite city.

LESSON OUTLINE

I. DEALING WITH CHANGE

  A. Responding to the Voice of God

  B. Reacting to the Threats of People

  C. Renewing Commitments to Original Promises

II. DEALING WITH CONFLICT

  A. Evolution of Conflicts

  B. Earnest of Relationships

  C. Exchange of Commitments

III. CHOICES REFLECT VALUES

  A. Assessing Before Choosing

  B. Acclimating to Your Choices

  C. Acquiring the Curse or Blessing of Your Values

LESSON EXPOSITION

INTRODUCTION

Change, decision, and consequences—these are inevitable in the believer's life. God uses each of these to guide us to continued renewal. The individual is tempted to resist change, to make compromising decisions, and to deny consequences. Nevertheless, God uses each of these elements to mold the Christian into the image of Christ.

The encounter between Abraham and Lot was an example of God's using change, decision, and consequences to mold the lives of these two men. They did not want conflict, but change and circumstance brought conflict to them. When confronted with a critical decision, they had to make value-based choices. The character of their choices brought definite consequences from the Lord.

Genesis 13 is alive with the challenge of the choices the people of God must make. The conflict between the herdsmen of Abraham and Lot is so similar to the contentions that members of a local church enter into—fighting over "water rights" when there is a lost and dying world to be won to Christ. The compromise that settled into Lot's heart, choosing the riches of Sodom rather than working out a solution with Abraham, is so much like the easy, quick fixes that Christians settle into when they avoid working together with other believers. The sober tragedy of Lot finding himself in the middle of Sodom's wickedness is so much like someone finding out almost too late that he or she has drifted too far from the heavenly shore and too close to the waterfall of the world.

I. DEALING WITH CHANGE
(Genesis 12:1-9)

A. Responding to the Voice of God (vv. 1-5)

(Genesis 12:1-3 is not included in the printed text.)

4. So Abraham departed, as the Lord had spoken unto him; and Lot went with him: and Abraham was seventy and five years old when he departed out of Haran.

5. And Abraham took Sarai his wife, and Lot his brother's son, and all their substance that they had gathered, and the souls that they had gotten in Haran; and they went forth to go into the land of Canaan; and into the land of Canaan they came.

Change is inevitable. Life, by its very nature, presents change—even to believers. God does not change, but He has created life in such a way that things change all around us. The nature of the world that God created means that the believer must depend on God to know how to react to the changes and decisions taking place.

Genesis 12:1-3 presents one of the most powerful promises in all of Scripture. The promises changed Abraham's life, gave birth to a nation, and affected the peoples of the earth for the rest of history. The promises regarded Abraham, his children, and all of his posterity. Whether those who encountered Abraham and his descendants would be a blessing and be blessed was wrapped up in the content of these promises.

The responsibility laid on Abraham to obey the command of God was as heavy as the promises were powerful. God commanded him to leave his native land and go to a far country. No doubt the difficulties in leaving were great. Some of his relatives went with him, including Lot, his nephew. Initially, Abraham had left his native land of Ur (11:31; see also Acts 7:2-4) and settled in Haran, where he was living when God called him. He then continued to the land of Canaan. Nevertheless, Abraham took a necessary step in the process of change; he responded to the voice of God.

What changes are inevitable in the believer's life today? How can the believer be equipped to face these changes?

B. Reacting to the Threats of
   People (v. 6)

6. And Abraham passed through the land unto the place of Sichem, unto the plain of Moreh. And the Canaanite was then in the land.

When Abraham first arrived in the land that he was instructed by God to enter, it was a land of rich promise. The place he entered (Shechem) was where the conquering army of Joshua would later gather (Joshua 24:1) when they had won victory and possessed the land. However, at this time, Abraham was severely threatened.

The reference to the presence of the Canaanites in verse 6 is short, but significant. The Canaanites were pagan. They presented an omnious threat to Abraham. The reference captures Abraham's initial fear. His family and the promises God had given to him were threatened, from Abraham's perspective.

C. Renewing Commitments to
   Original Promises (vv. 7-9)

(Genesis 12:8, 9 is not included in the printed text.)

7. And the Lord appeared unto Abraham, and said, Unto thy seed will I give this land: and there builded he an altar unto the Lord, who appeared unto him.

Into the midst of Abraham's fear of the Canaanites, God spoke to him. God assured Abraham that He would give the land to him and his descendants. Abraham believed the promises and reassurance of God. He built an altar, affirming his faith in God's work.

The believer must also affirm faith in God's promises, despite the presence of danger and opposition. Just because a Christian initially responds to the promises of God does not mean that there will not be resistance. Reassurance from God and reaffirmation of faith by the believer is an ongoing part of the process of change. As new challenges are met, simply looking back to initial commitments is not enough. New assurances come from God and new affirmations must be offered to God.

II. DEALING WITH CONFLICT
    (Genesis 13:1-9)

A. Evolution of Conflicts (vv. 1-7)

(Genesis 13:1-7 is not included in the printed text.)

Many times decisions are forced upon us as believers. We do not ask for them; they come to us. Circumstances, situations, relationships, even relatives bring decisions and problems to us. The problems do not come because of what we have done, but because of what others have done to us or to each other.

Why do conflicts arise? Is a person always responsible for conflicts that may be present? What are some ways in which conflicts arise?

Neither Abraham nor Lot were looking for trouble. In fact, they had traveled together and shared the same commitments. Thus far, their relationship had been very fruitful. In fact, not only had they been successful together, but the relationship had been mutually beneficial for them. Together and individually, they had amassed considerable success.

They now found themselves in a circumstance in which the land could not support their cattle. Added to this pressure was the conflict that arose between the herdsmen that worked for them. Both Abraham and Lot loved the Lord. Abraham was experiencing the revival of his prior commitments to the Lord by renewing his sacrifice at the very place he had earlier been strengthened by the Lord. Nevertheless, trouble arose and came to him.

B. Earnest of Relationships (v. 8)

8. And Abraham said unto Lot, Let ther be not strife, I pray thee, between me and thee, and between my herdmen and thy herdmen; for we be brethren.

In the midst of conflict, Abraham and Lot provided leadership by affirming relationships. Neither denied the conflict. They just reaffirmed their relationship. A specific solution was not yet fully developed, but they knew the foundation for a resolution was their prior relationship as family and committed partners.

Conflict is not resolved by patent solutions as much as on solid relationships. Without a foundation of relationships, any conflict may persist without resolution. With a foundation of relationships, regardless of the nature of the conflict, resolution is always possible. The affirmation of relationships is the earnest (down payment pledge) for resolution.

C. Exchange of Commitments (v. 9)

9. Is not the whole land before thee? separate thyself, I pray thee, from me: if thou wilt take the left hand, then I will go to the right; or if thou depart to the right hand, then I will go to the left.

The resolution between Abraham and Lot was rooted in their relationship together. Abraham was flexible enough to abide by either side of Lot's decision. He was willing to go to either the right or the left. Most of all, he wanted to work with whatever Lot decided. Being willing to exchange commitments for the sake of relationship was more important than the particular decision. The content of choice was secondary to the partnership of choice.

What are some guiding principles for resolving conflicts? What is the role and responsibility of each person involved in a conflict for finding an answer? What is the role of the Lord in the resolution of a conflict?

In the church today, relationship is vital to the decision-making process. Many times, individuals are more willing to sacrifice relationships in order to preserve an ideology or abstraction than they are to root themselves in relationships and press for a solution that is mutually together within the body of believers. The body of is just as important as the substance of a choice. Truth must be spoken in love (Ephesians 4:15).

III. CHOICES REFLECT VALUES (Genesis 13:10-18)

A. Assessing Before Choosing (vv. 10, 11)

10. And Lot lifted up his eyes, and beheld all the plain of Jordan, that it was well watered every where, before the Lord destroyed Sodom and Gomorrah, even as the garden of the Lord, like the land of Egypt, as thou comest unto Zoar.

11. Then Lot chose him all the plain of Jordan; and Lot journeyed east: and they separated themselves the one from the other.

After Abraham's commitment to abide by whatever choice his nephew, Lot, made, Lot assessed his choices. The description implies the prize of the land. Lot chose the better land. The land was prized because it was fertile and well watered. The comparisons are striking. The land was like the "garden of the Lord," which some interpreters take to imply the Garden of Eden. The land was also compared to the fertile lands of mighty Egypt.

"As thou comest unto Zoar" (v. 10) was a reference to the expansiveness of the fertility of the land. Zoar was a small town located in the southwestern part of the region. The name of the town meant "small" or "insignificant." The richness of the region extended to even the most remote and insignificant location, represented by the reference to Zoar. Tiny Zoar would later be the refuge of Lot (19:22, 23).

What was in Lot's heart when he chose the land of Sodom?

The phrase "chose him all the plain" (v. 11) implies that Lot was perhaps selfish in his choice. He wanted all of the plain. He was not inclined to share or bargain with Abraham. This would force Abraham to remain where he was, and eventually to retreat to poorer, much less fertile, territory.

Both Lot and Abraham made their own assessment of the choices they faced. Abraham had assessed the value of relationships and chosen to be faithful to God and Lot. Lot had assessed the bounty of the land and made a choice to hoard it. This would eventually cost him his family and the nearness of his relationship with God.

B. Acclimating to Your Choices (v. 12)

12. Abraham dwelled in the land of Canaan, and Lot dwelled in the cities of the plain, and pitched his tent toward Sodom.

Both men adjusted to the consequences of their choices. Abraham was able to rest in the integrity of his choice to honor relationships with Lot and the Lord, although he had to continue to live under the threat of the Canaanites in a less fertile land. Lot lived in the fertile plain, intentionally without Abraham. The text is careful to note that not only did he live in the same plain as the city of Sodom, but the expression "toward Sodom" indicates he lived very near Sodom. The emphasis is that Lot was especially drawn to Sodom, not just to the fertility of the land. "Pitched his tent" is a stronger reference than "dwelled." It emphasized that Lot became a part of the ethos and culture of Sodom.

C. Acquiring the Curse or Blessing of Your Values (vv. 13-18)

(Genesis 13:18 is not included in the printed text.)

13. But the men of Sodom were wicked and sinners before the Lord exceedingly.

14. And the Lord said unto Abraham, after that Lot was separated from him, Lift up now thine eyes, and look from the place where thou art northward, and southward, and eastward, and westward:

15. For all the land which thou seest, to thee will I give it, and to thy seed for ever.

16. And I will make thy seed as the dust of the earth: so that if a man can number the dust of the earth, then shall thy seed also be numbered.

17. Arise, walk through the land in the length of it and in the breadth of it; for I will give it unto thee.

The choices a believer makes reflect his values and relationship to God. In summarizing verses 13-18, one significant fact is that the choice Lot and Abraham made bore distinctive consequences. The most critical factor about Sodom was not the richness of the region but the relationship of the inhabitants to the Lord. In particular, the men of Sodom were extremely wicked in the eyes of the Lord. Later, in Genesis 19, they are described as homosexual. The term *sodomy* has become synonymous with homosexuality. Though the text is not explicit in indicating as to whether Lot had prior knowledge about the homo-

sexuality of the city, many interpreters feel that he did know, but was drawn by the richness of the land. Though Lot no doubt never intended to be influenced by the sin of Sodom, he was affected to the near point of destruction.

Abraham received the blessing of the Lord. Though the land he possessed was not as fertile, God was still able to bring blessing to Abraham. The condition of Abraham's heart was a more important variable than the richness of the soil.

Riches do not guarantee success; nor does poverty predict failure. Critical decisions are made throughout the life of the believer. These decisions affect the destiny of the individual's life. Being perceptive of God's leading, maintaining good relationships with others despite conflicts, and making value-based, godly choices despite the temptation to compromise—these are very important in Christian living.

REVIEW QUESTIONS

1. Why is it important to listen for God's direction for our lives?

2. What should Abraham and Lot have done to settle the conflict between them?

3. How important is maintaining relationships in the midst of a decision to be made?

4. What consideration did Abraham give to Lot when he made his choice? Did Abraham have a choice?

5. What was the consequence of Abraham's decision?

GOLDEN TEXT HOMILY

"BY FAITH ABRAHAM, WHEN HE WAS CALLED TO GO OUT

INTO A PLACE WHICH HE SHOULD AFTER RECEIVE FOR AN INHERITANCE, OBEYED; AND HE WENT OUT, NOT KNOWING WHITHER HE WENT" (Hebrews 11:8).

I had been living in my present home for a year. The people next door and the community were unknown to us. We only knew that God had opened a door of opportunity, so we stepped through, seizing the moment of decision for His glory.

Another year later we look back. We now know the people we live next door to. We have found favor in the community, as well as a church with loving friends who even share the goodness of their summer garden. We have met many new friends—some just good neighbors, some with status in the community, but each finding a welcome at our home. Our children not only adjusted to the new environment, but they met the challenge to excel in school and in meeting new friends.

Like Abraham, our journey to a new place had to start with faith in God. It could have begun with selfish ambition, but that would have worn out quickly. It could have started with fear, but that would have kept us locked behind doors of insecurity. As a family we chose to start with faith, and faith has sustained us in this journey. Abraham knew in his heart that God would take the journey with him. He knew in his heart that God's way was the best. When I face new situations in this journey of life, my faith is renewed and challenged. By faith, I obey the Word of God and declare that God is faithful to me.—**Florie Brown Wigelsworth, M.Div., Elizabeth City, North Carolina**

SENTENCE SERMONS

BELIEVERS can make wise choices by trusting in God's Word.
—Selected

ACCEPTING CHRIST as Savior is life's most important decision.
—Selected

DECISION IS a sharp knife that cuts clean and straight.
—Gordon Graham

THE PERSON who insists on seeing with perfect clearness before he decides, never decides.
—Henri-Frederic Amiel

EVANGELISM APPLICATION

ACCEPTING CHRIST AS SAVIOR IS LIFE'S MOST IMPORTANT DECISION.

Life is filled with choices. Some believe that the most critical part of life is made up of the choices that we make. The importance of choices is demonstrated by the value of good choices and the consequences of bad choices. Individuals are certainly affected by the quality and consequences of the choices they make.

There is a decision that is more critical than any other decision a person can make. The most critical choice is the decision to accept or reject Christ. The decision is important for at least three reasons: First, Christ has made an eternal offer that was purchased with His own life's blood. Second, the very nature of a person's heart is forever altered by the choice he makes. Finally, where a person spends eternity, whether heaven or hell, depends on the choice made.

The possibility of a decision for Christ is granted through the grace, mercy, and work of Jesus. The opportunity and the occasion is granted to each individual. The consequences of the choice are out of one's control; the Lord has determined the result of the choice. Still, the choice is in the hands of the individual. The most valuable choice a person can make is to take up the offer given by Christ, choose to repent and follow Him, and thereby receive the eternal consequences of His love and power.

ILLUMINATING THE LESSON

God forgives us when we confess our iniquity and plead the cleansing blood of Christ. There are certain sins and decisions, however, which irreversibly damage the human body; and as a result, their effects may be transmitted to others. What a person sows "in the flesh," his poor children eventually may have to reap. The following account is dated, but nevertheless, timelessly true. *The Dallas Morning News* of March 21, 1971, featured a column by Sue Connally which carried this heartrending account:

"The shrill, piercing cry, almost inhuman in its intensity and timbre, tears its way into your conscience. Once you've heard it, you can never forget it. The sound is made by a baby only one day old. But this is not a normal child; it was introduced to life 'hooked' on heroin! The typical, disturbing scream means that the pain and rigor of withdrawal are already taking place. This little one became addicted when the woman carrying it used drugs. Muscles in the tiny body are taut, the rigid arms and legs flail incessantly, and the high-pitched cry continues for hours.

"Such children, although showing intense hunger, can't retain their feedings. The tremors that rack them are so severe their bassinets shake. Occasionally there are even convulsions. 'They could never rest, but would run themselves to death,' says Dr. Dolores Carruth, 'unless we sedate them.'"

Can you imagine babies being born screaming for a "fix"? That's what sin does! (from *Parsons Illustrator*).

DAILY BIBLE READINGS

M. Choose to Believe God. Numbers 13:26-30
T. Follow the Lord. 1 Kings 18:17-21
W. Hear Wise Council. Proverbs 4:20-27
T. Choose to Follow Christ. Matthew 4:18-22
F. Remain With Christ. John 6:60-69
S. Choose to Live Right. 1 Peter 5:5-10

Trusting in God's Promises

Study Text: Genesis 15:1-6; 17:1-9; 21:1-5

Objective: To know that God's promises are certain and believe His Word.

Time: The Book of Genesis was written between 1450 and 1400 B.C.

Place: The general belief is that Moses received this revelation while on Mount Sinai in the wilderness.

Golden Text: "[Abraham] staggered not at the promise of God through unbelief; but was strong in faith, giving glory to God" (Romans 4:20).

Central Truth: Because God's promises are reliable, we can trust our lives to Him.

Evangelism Emphasis: God has promised to receive all who come to Him in faith.

PRINTED TEXT

Genesis 15:1. After these things the word of the Lord came unto Abraham in a vision, saying, Fear not, Abraham: I am thy shield, and thy exceeding great reward.

2. And Abraham said, Lord God, what wilt thou give me, seeing I go childless, and the steward of my house is this Eliezer of Damascus?

3. And Abraham said, Behold, to me thou hast given no seed: and, lo, one born in my house is mine heir.

4. And, behold, the word of the Lord came unto him, saying, This shall not be thine heir; but he that shall come forth out of thine own bowels shall be thine heir.

5. And he brought him forth abroad, and said, Look now toward heaven, and tell the stars, if thou be able to number them: and he said unto him, So shall thy seed be.

6. And he believed in the Lord; and he counted it to him for righteousness.

17:1. And when Abraham was ninety years old and nine, the Lord appeared to Abraham, and said unto him, I am the Almighty God; walk before me, and be thou perfect.

7. And I will establish my covenant between me and thee and thy seed after thee in their generations for an everlasting covenant, to be a God unto thee, and to thy seed after thee.

8. And I will give unto thee, and to thy seed after thee, the land wherein thou art a stranger, all the land of Canaan, for an

everlasting possession; and I will be their God.

9. And God said unto Abraham, Thou shalt keep my covenant therefore, thou, and thy seed after thee in their generations.

10. This is my covenant, which ye shall keep, between me and you and thy seed after thee; Every man child among you shall be circumcised.

21:1. And the Lord visited Sarah as he had said, and the Lord did unto Sarah as he had spoken.

2. For Sarah conceived, and bare Abraham a son in his old age, at the set time of which God had spoken to him.

3. And Abraham called the name of his son that was born unto him, whom Sarah bare to him, Isaac.

4. And Abraham circumcised his son Isaac being eight days old, as God had commanded him.

5. And Abraham was an hundred years old, when his son Isaac was born unto him.

DICTIONARY

Eliezer (EL-ih-EE-zer) of Damascus (duh-MAS-kus)—Genesis 15:2—Abraham's chief servant who was from Damascus, a city northeast of Lake Galilee.

LESSON OUTLINE

I. BELIEVE GOD'S PROMISES
  A. Assurance from the Promises
  B. Adjustments from the Promises
  C. Accounting for the Promises

II. COVENANT BLESSINGS
  A. Issuing Covenant Blessings
  B. Establishing Covenant Blessings
  C. Ascribing Covenant Blessings

III. GOD KEEPS HIS WORD
  A. God Speaks His Word
  B. Individuals Subscribe to the Word
  C. Circumstances Submit to the Power of the Word

LESSON EXPOSITION

INTRODUCTION

A promise is only as strong as the one making the promise. The promises of God are as reliable as God himself. A believer can walk away from the promises and thereby be removed from their blessings. On the other hand, the believer can trust in God's promises—it is God who makes the promise in the first place—and thereby receive their benefits. The key is to trust in God himself, the Promise-giver.

Genesis 15-21 focuses on God's promises to Abraham and Sarah. They were fearful, even rebellious, concerning the promises. They could have removed themselves completely from them. However, God was faithful to His promises, and Abraham and Sarah looked in faith to God for their fulfillment.

The concept of covenant is

important for understanding the nature of God's promises. A covenant is not created and sustained by two parties. The party originating the covenant establishes and sustains it. In the case of God's covenants, they are not cocreated by the recipients. On the contrary, the covenants are simply declared by God.

When a person does not keep God's covenants, the covenant is not destroyed. An individual cannot destroy a contract that he did not create. A person can fail to keep the covenant and thereby be removed from it but God's covenant is rooted in God himself. Abraham and Sarah discovered the profound strength of God's own covenant with them, though they wavered at times from fully receiving the benefits.

I. BELIEVE GOD'S PROMISES (Genesis 15:1-6)

A. Assurance from the Promises (v. 1)

1. After these things the word of the Lord came unto Abraham in a vision, saying, Fear not, Abraham: I am thy shield, and thy exceeding great reward.

Assurance is built on commitment. "After these things" indicates that the foundation for this assurance had just taken place. Abraham, in the verses prior to Genesis 15:1, committed himself wholeheartedly to God. He told the King of Sodom that he would not receive anything from him. He did not want anyone to say, "I have made Abraham rich" (14:23). Abraham wanted all the credit and glory to go to God. Abraham's commitment was the basis for his confident assurance in God's promises.

Verse 1 has three parts: an admonition to not fear, the commitment by God to protect Abraham, and the promise that the Lord himself was Abraham's reward. These parts are interrelated, with the last point being foundational to the others. Not fearing helps the believer stay under God's protection. Delighting oneself in the Lord is the inner motivation that keeps a person under that protection.

How is a covenant created? How is it sustained?

B. Adjustments from the Promises (vv. 2, 3)

2. And Abraham said, Lord God, what wilt thou give me, seeing I go childless, and the steward of my house is this Eliezer of Damascus?

3. And Abraham said, Behold, to me thou has given no seed: and, lo, one born in my house is mine heir.

Abraham's response to God's assurance was, "But what will you do for me?" The person of God was not enough; he wanted what God could give him. For the believer, the blessing of God's presence must be more important than anything God may do for us. The Creator himself is sufficient reward. God never stops acting in our behalf, and His works are sure. However, our concern with what God gives us so easily overshadows our focus on who He is.

Abraham expressed disappointment in his circumstances in verses 2 and 3, thus questioning God's wisdom and ability. He asked, in essence, "God, is this the way You are going to fulfill Your promise?" Abraham was sincere in that He wanted to see the accomplishment of God's promises. He believed that

God would bless his posterity. Both Abraham and Sarah "judged Him faithful who had promised" (Hebrews 11:11). So he wondered aloud to God if the way God would fulfill the promise was through a servant in his household.

The tragedy of Abraham's suggestion at this point is obvious. It shows a lack of confidence in God's methods. Many people today do not question God's promises, but they question the method God chooses to fulfill those promises. Faith relates not only to the promise of God, but to the method God chooses to use to fulfill the promise.

Why do you think Abraham suggested using his servant rather than trusting in God for the fulfillment of His promise?

C. Accounting for the Promises (vv. 4-6)

4. And behold, the word of the Lord came unto him, saying, This shall not be thine heir; but he that shall come forth out of thine own bowels shall be thine heir.

5. And he brought him forth abroad, and said, Look now toward heaven, and tell the stars, if thou be able to number them: and he said unto him, So shall thy seed be.

6. And he believed in the Lord; and he counted it to him for righteousness.

In verses 4-6, God announces the method by which He will fulfill His promises. He informed Abraham that his attempt to adjust God's methods of fulfillment was unacceptable. God's method was as sure as His promise, demonstrating Abraham's inability in contrast to God's ability. Abraham

could not fulfill the promise that God had given him.

Abraham came to agree with God. Abraham realized that his own fears were not right or acceptable before God, and he realized his inability, his woeful inadequacy in contrast to God's ability.

The text describes Abraham's response to God as being faith. Faith is not only an affirmation of God but also an admission about our own condition. The more we realize our own inability, the more we are drawn to God's ability. Faith is distrusting our own attempts and trusting God's accomplishments.

II. COVENANT BLESSINGS (17:1-10)

A. Issuing Covenant Blessings (vv. 1-6)

(Genesis 17:2-6 is not included in the printed text.)

1. And when Abraham was ninety years old and nine, the Lord appeared to Abraham, and said unto him, I am the Almighty God; walk before me, and be thou perfect.

In chapter 17 the covenant concept presented to Abraham is a foundational aspect of trusting God. Covenanting is an important method by which God gives assurance to the believer. God's covenanting is the foundation for His relationship with His people. Understanding the nature of God's covenanting process and gaining insight into the nature of His covenants with His people greatly increases the trust of the believer.

A covenant is not a contract but a pact issued by God. A contract is a bilateral agreement held together by the strength of the contracting parties. By comparison, a covenant is a one-way, unilateral arrangement established by one party. The covenant's strength is based on the strength of the party that issues it. The person to whom the covenant is extended can walk away, rejecting it and its benefits. The key difference is that the covenant of God, unlike a contract, is a unique gift from God, not the product of humanity.

God issued to Abraham a covenant calling him to be faithful and, thereby, blessed. God's covenant was that Abraham would be the father of many nations.

In verse 1, the Lord introduced Himself to Abraham by a new name, El Shaddai, "Almighty God." The use of the name El Shaddai, which speaks of God as a bountiful giver, reveals that the Lord has reappeared to renew His promises and covenant, to amplify the nature of the promises, and to clarify the conditions expected of Abraham and his descendants. In renewing the promises, He repeats certain factors which He had announced earlier, especially the everlasting nature of the promise and the possession of the land of Canaan. But He adds that Abraham will become "a father of many nations" (v. 5) and that "kings shall come out of [him]" (v. 6).

Lee Haines comments on the matter of the kings in this manner: "It is clear from the Biblical record that not only Israel, but also the Ishmaelites and Edomites, as well as perhaps other desert tribes, were descendants from Abraham. Israel and Edom both had kings, and the former included some of the most illustrious in human history: David, Solomon, Hezekiah, Josiah, and the greatest of all, Jesus Christ. These promises were abundantly fulfilled by the God of bountiful giving" (*The Wesleyan Bible Commentary*, Vol. 1).

Abram's name would now be, "Abraham" (v. 5). Becoming the father of many nations would not be the result of Abraham's action, but of God's.

What was Abraham's response to the covenant established by God? What should the believer's response be today to God's covenants and promises?

B. Establishing Covenant
Blessings (vv. 7, 8)

7. And I will establish my covenant between me and thee and thy seed after thee in their generations for an everlasting covenant, to be a God unto thee, and to thy seed after thee.

8. And I will give unto thee, and to thy seed after thee, the land wherein thou art a stranger, all the land of Canaan, for an everlasting possession; and I will be their God.

God issued the covenant to Abraham (vv. 1-6); consequently, the covenant would be established in Abraham and his seed (vv. 7, 8). God's covenant concerns those who are faithful to Him. God was investing in Abraham and his descendants. The investment was to be "everlasting" (v. 7). Only God could establish something for eternity. The powerful reality was that God was doing an infinite work within a finite person.

God's covenant was to "give" (v. 8) the land of Canaan to Abraham and his descendants. The land would be the blessing of God to them. Abraham would not earn it or deserve it. Earning the land would be the profit of labor. Deserving the land would be a compensation. The land would be a blessing. Blessings are gifts; they are granted from the heart of God to the believer.

God had a purpose in the blessing that He would give Abraham and his descendants; He wanted them to know God for who He is. Twice—at the end of verses 7 and 8—God declares that as a result of the blessing, they would know God as God. The power of the blessing is not in its content but in the way it reflects God. A blessing, more than anything else, makes a statement. It can only be attributed to God's matchless person and to His being the one and only God.

What were the blessings Abraham would receive through God's covenant?

C. Ascribing Covenant Blessings (vv. 9, 10)

9. And God said unto Abraham, Thou shalt keep my covenant therefore, thou, and thy seed after thee in their generations.

10. This is my covenant, which ye shall keep, between me and you and thy seed after thee; Every man child among you shall be circumcised.

My, keep, and *circumcised* are key terms in verses 9 and 10. They describe the implications of God being known as God in the life of Abraham and his descendants (vv. 7, 8). Abraham was to "keep" the covenant because it was God's ("my") covenant. The indication that Abraham was keeping the covenant was the act of "circumcision."

Keep refers to the fact that God issued the covenant and Abraham was to respond. The covenant was not created by God and Abraham; God alone created the covenant. Abraham's response to God was to

"keep" the covenant.

Keep is also the term used to describe Adam's care of the Garden of Eden that God had created (2:15). The word is similarly used to describe Noah's care of the animals God brought into the ark (6:19, 20). Further, Noah was "to keep seed alive upon the face of all the earth" (7:3).

My emphasizes that God created the covenant. Rather than a contract kept alive only by the strength of each partner, this covenant was created and is sustained by God.

However, Abraham had a responsibility toward the covenant. If he neglected the covenant, Abraham would be driven from the blessings of the covenant as Adam and Eve had been driven from the Tree of Life. Just as the keeping of Noah related to the animals and maintaining them and their seed alive, so Abraham was to apply the life of the covenant to his seed or descendants. Circumcision was an act which represented the keeping of God's own covenant and applying it to the children of Abraham.

III. GOD KEEPS HIS WORD (Genesis 21:1-5)

A. God Speaks His Word (vv. 1, 2)

1. And the Lord visited Sarah as he had said, and the Lord did unto Sarah as he had spoken.

2. For Sarah conceived, and bare Abraham a son in his old age, at the set time of which God had spoken to him.

As the animals in the ark benefited from being kept by Noah in response to what God had commanded, so Abraham and Sarah benefited from Abraham's keeping the covenant that God had created. Their seed was blessed just as the seed of the animals was continued in the Ark.

As God initiated the covenant, so God initiated the child that was born to Abraham and Sarah. Verse 1 reads, "And the Lord visited Sarah." While Abraham was the husband of Sarah and the child was from their union, the emphasis of the text is on the work of God. Neither Isaac nor any other child is born merely because a man and a woman come together. Perceiving a child as merely the result of sexual union is a man-centered interpretation of the miracle of birth. Conception resulting from this union is actually a gift from the Lord. The phrase "set time" further affirms that the conception came in God's own timing and was not merely that of Abraham and Sarah.

Since the idea of covenanting depends so heavily on God's own action, the believer's response calls for trust in God and His actions. The Lord is trustworthy; therefore, His covenant is trustworthy. The significance of Genesis 21 is that God carries out His covenant. God's Word is reliable because what He speaks He will carry out.

B. Individuals Subscribe to the Word (vv. 3, 4)

3. And Abraham called the name of his son that was born unto him, whom Sarah bare to him, Isaac.

4. And Abraham circumcised his son Isaac being eight days old, as God had commanded him.

Isaac means, "he laughs." The name reflects the circumstances under which he was born. His mother had laughed at the prospect of having a child (18:11-15). In spite of the unbelief of Sarah, God still fulfilled the covenant. God requires us to believe in Him. At times, God moves in spite of our

belief. Ultimately, every person will be dealt with by the Lord in regard to his faith and keeping of the covenant (17:9, 10). God, because of His grace and mercy, often works in our behalf in spite of what we do. Isaac's birth was a testimony to God's faithfulness.

As an act of faithfulness, in keeping the covenant that God had given to him, Abraham circumcised Isaac. While Isaac's name reflected the disbelieving spirit of Sarah, the text highlights the new obedience of Abraham and Sarah by noting that he was circumcised.

Full obedience is indicated by the text as well. Not only was Isaac circumcised, but he was also circumcised according to the way that God had commanded. That is, when he was eight days old, Abraham obeyed the command to circumcise his son.

While God is faithful to His Word, there is an obligation of the believer to be faithful in obedience to God's Word. While God is completely trustworthy, the believer must trustfully respond to God. God provided the son, Isaac; and Abraham responded by circumcising him.

C. Circumstances Submit to the Power of the Word (v. 5)

5. And Abraham was an hundred years old, when his son Isaac was born unto him.

Circumstances had to yield to God's Word. Sarah's laughter did too. God moved to bring forth Isaac in spite of Sarah's laughter and her age. He also moved in spite of the physical limitations of Abraham's age. Isaac was a product of the Word of God and God's faithfulness, not the abilities of Sarah or Abraham.

Many times we mistake the requirement of obedience to the

Word for the power of the Word itself. The Word stands on the power of God. God does not need our response in the same way that we need His Word. God desires the responsiveness of His people, but it is a matter of our survival for us to have God's Word.

The testimony of the birth of Isaac is that God is faithful in His covenant and promises. He is trustworthy. Even though there were doubts and mitigating circumstances that to the finite mind would have threatened the fulfillment of His promises, God still acted on the covenant that He had established with Abraham. Abraham had a devout obligation to keep the requirements of the covenant. He could have removed himself from the promises of the covenant, but he did not. As a result, He received the faithful promises that God had established.

REVIEW QUESTIONS

1. How can a person fully trust in the promises of God?

2. How did Abraham indicate a lack of trust in God's promise to him about Sarah's bearing children?

3. How would you define a "covenant?"

4. How does God establish His covenant today in the lives of His people?

5. What does the term keep indicate about Abraham's relationship with God and His covenant?

GOLDEN TEXT HOMILY

"[ABRAHAM] STAGGERED NOT AT THE PROMISE OF GOD THROUGH UNBELIEF; BUT WAS STRONG IN FAITH, GIVING GLORY TO GOD" (Romans 4:20).

Having concluded a masterful argument, Paul makes a powerful statement of fact. "Now is Christ risen from the dead, and become the firstfruits of them that slept" (1 Corinthians 15:21). He is referring to Leviticus 23:10, 11, "Ye shall bring a sheaf of the firstfruits of your harvest unto the priest: And he shall wave the sheaf before the Lord, to be accepted for you: on the morrow after the sabbath the priest shall wave it." A clear explanation of this passage is offered by William Barclay in his *Letters to the Corinthians:*

"The law laid it down that some sheaves of barley must be reaped from a common field. They must not be taken from a garden or an orchard or from specially prepared soil. They must come from a typical field. When the barley was cut, it was brought to the temple. There it was threshed with soft canes so as not to bruise it. It was then parched over the fire in a perforated pan so that every grain was touched by the fires. It was then exposed to the wind so that the chaff was blown away. It was then ground in a barley mill, and the flour of it was offered to God. That was the firstfruits. And it is very significant to note that not until after that was done could the new barley be bought and sold in the shops and bread be made from the new flour. The firstfruits were a sign of the harvest to come; and the resurrection of Jesus was a sign of the resurrection of all believers which was to come."

So even as the new barley could not be used until the firstfruits had been offered, so our resurrection could not occur until Jesus was first raised from the dead and offered as the firstfruits.—**Thomas Griffith Jr., D.Min., Pastor, Porterville, California**

SENTENCE SERMONS

BECAUSE GOD'S PROMISES are reliable, we can trust our lives to Him.

—Selected

GOD HAS PROMISED to receive all who come to Him in faith.

—Selected

YOU MAY TRUST the Lord too little, but you can never trust Him too much.

—Anonymous

TRUST GOD for great things; with your five loaves and two fishes, He will show you a way to feed thousands.

—Horace Bushnell

ILLUMINATING THE LESSON

God's promises are reliable. As a result, the believer can trust in His promises. It would be foolish to rely on unreliable promises. Such foolish trust is illustrated by the following story:

The scene is a four-engine airliner. The pilot's voice comes across the intercom: "Those of you on the left side of the plane have probably noticed that one of our engines has failed. Do not be alarmed. We can still fly on three engines, but we will probably arrive about 15 minutes late." A few minutes later the pilot's calm voice was heard again: "Those of you on the right side of the plane are probably aware that a second engine has failed. Do not be alarmed. We can make it on two engines, though we will probably be at least 30 minutes late now." A few minutes later the pilot spoke to the passengers: "It has just come to my attention that a third engine has failed. Please do not be alarmed. We can make it to the airport on one engine. However, we will arrive approximately 45 minutes late." One passenger turned to another and said, "Boy, I hope that fourth engine doesn't fail, or we could be up here all night!" (from *Parsons Illustrator*).

The passenger's trust was clouded by faulty assumptions. God's promises are reliable, they will not fail us. Keeping our perspective on Jesus through the work of the Holy Spirit, the believer can fully trust in God's promises and not be afraid.

DAILY BIBLE READINGS

M. Unconditional Promise.
   Genesis 9:8-17
T. Eternal Covenant.
   Psalm 111:1-10
W. Promise to Restore.
   Jeremiah 33:10-15
T. A Sure Promise.
   Romans 4:13-22
F. Promise of Salvation.
   1 Peter 1:3-9
S. Promise of Inheritance.
   Revelation 21:1-7

Intervene and Intercede

Study Text: Genesis 14:8-16; 18:17-33

Objective: To grasp the seriousness of Satan's attack on families and be ready to intervene and intercede on their behalf.

Time: The Book of Genesis was written between 1450 and 1400 B.C.

Place: The general belief is that Moses received this revelation while on Mount Sinai in the wilderness.

Golden Text: "I know him, that he will command his children and his household after him, and they shall keep the way of the Lord, to do justice and judgment" (Genesis 18:19).

Central Truth: God calls and equips His people to rescue those ensnared by Satan.

Evangelism Emphasis: God calls and equips His people to rescue those held captive by Satan.

PRINTED TEXT

Genesis 14:14. And when Abram heard that his brother was taken captive, he armed his trained servants, born in his own house, three hundred and eighteen, and pursued them unto Dan.

15. And he divided himself against them, he and his servants, by night, and smote them, and pursued them unto Hobah, which is on the left hand of Damascus.

16. And he brought back all the goods, and also brought again his brother Lot, and his goods, and the women also, and the people.

18:17. And the Lord said, Shall I hide from Abraham that thing which I do;

18. Seeing that Abraham shall surely become a great and mighty nation, and all the nations of the earth shall be blessed in him?

19. For I know him, that he will command his children and his household after him, and they shall keep the way of the Lord, to do justice and judgment; that the Lord may bring upon Abraham that which he hath spoken of him.

20. And the Lord said, Because the cry of Sodom and Gomorrah is great, and because their sin is very grievous;

21. I will go down now, and see whether they have done altogether according to the cry of it, which is come unto me; and if not, I will know.

22. And the men turned their faces from thence, and went toward Sodom: but Abraham stood yet before the Lord.

23. And Abraham drew near,

and said, Wilt thou also destroy the righteous with the wicked?

24. Peradventure there be fifty righteous within the city: wilt thou also destroy and not spare the place for the fifty righteous that are therein?

25. That be far from thee to do after this manner, to slay the righteous with the wicked: and that the righteous should be as the wicked, that be far from thee: Shall not the Judge of all the earth do right?

32. And he said, Oh let not the Lord be angry, and I will speak yet but this once: Peradventure ten shall be found there. And he said, I will not destroy it for ten's sake.

33. And the Lord went his way, as soon as he had left communing with Abraham: and Abraham returned unto his place.

DICTIONARY

Hobah (HO-ba) . . . Damascus (duh-MAS-kus)—Genesis 14:15—Hobah is an area north of Damascus.

Sodom (SOD-um) and Gomorah (goh-MOR-ruh)—Genesis 18:20—Cities remembered primarily for their wickedness.

LESSON OUTLINE

I. PREPARE FOR BATTLE

   A. Arming to Pursue

   B. Activating to Win

   C. Acquiring to Save

II. STAND FOR MORAL PRINCIPLES

   A. Presence of the One Moral God

   B. Potential of a Moral Person

   C. Practice of Moral Relationships

III. PLEAD FOR THE LOST

   A. The Cry for Justice

   B. The Cry for Intervention

   C. The Cry for God's Mercy

LESSON EXPOSITION

INTRODUCTION

God's justice and judgment have often been misunderstood. People feel that God is cruel in His judgment. Others feel that God judges regardless of the damage done to the innocent. Still others perceive God as dispensing destruction regardless of the pleas of intercessors to hold back His judgment.

The story of Abraham and Lot is a story of God's true judgment. It is true that God's judgment is based on His mercy. God protects the innocent and dispenses His judgment with divine sensitivity for the hurting. He sought out the righteous who had suffered because of sin in Sodom and Gomorrah. Deliverance was theirs, turning the time of destruction for the cities to a time of redemption for the righteous.

God heard the intercession of Abraham, not for the cities, but for the suffering righteous. Abraham's intervention sought the heart of God, not the rescuing of the cities. The Lord did not respond to Abraham because He valued the population of the cities; rather, because He is a God who blesses the righteous. The righteousness and mercy of God made possible Abraham's intercession.

Genesis 14 and 18 unfolds the tragedy that awaits the sinner and the blessing that awaits the intercessor. The focus of these chapters is on God and His action. The intercession of Abraham was powerful because it joined with the mercy that was already in God's heart. God was already seeking the cry of the righteous in Sodom and Gomorrah before Abraham ever interceded. When Abraham prayed, the Lord responded with even greater mercy, delighting in communion with Abraham the intercessor. The believer should be stirred by these passages to seek God in an even greater fashion in the days that remain before the mighty judgment of God comes in these last days.

I. PREPARE FOR BATTLE
(Genesis 14:8-16)

A. Arming to Pursue (vv. 8-14)

(Genesis 14:8-13 is not included in the printed text.)

14. And when Abram heard that his brother was taken captive, he armed his trained servants, born in his own house, three hundred and eighteen, and pursued them unto Dan.

A period of time after Lot had moved to Sodom, a group of four kings from Mesopotamia led an invasion of the area east of the Jordan which extended into southern Canaan. The invaders fought on until they had captured and gathered the spoil of the five cities of the plain. These five cities of the plain were probably located at the southern end of the Dead Sea.

According to the record, the five cities had been subjugated under Chedorlaomer, king of Elam. They apparently served Chedorlaomer without serious opposition for 12 years, but in the 13th year they rebelled. Consequently, Chedor--laomer and his allies marched on the area in a move to punish the rebels. They fought violently and plundered the cities along the entire route. When the battle was waged on the shores of the Dead Sea, the invaders were victorious and the kings of Sodom and Gomorrah fell into the slime or asphalt pits, which were plentiful in that area. With the kings of Sodom and Gomorrah gone, the remnant of the army fled into the mountains. The cities were pillaged, and Lot and all he had were taken away.

Verse 13 indicates that a person who had escaped from the invaders when they plundered Sodom and Gomorrah came and told Abraham of the fate that had befallen Lot. It is evident from Abraham's quick action that the news touched him deeply.

The description of Abraham's armed response emphasizes the closeness of Abraham and his household. Lot is referred to as a very close kinsman, a "brother." The servants Abraham used to respond to the threat were described as being "born in [Abram's] own house" (v. 14). Out of this sense of familial unity, Abraham responded to the plight of Lot.

Abraham's response was not an act of war but an act of impassioned intervention. By it's very nature, intervention springs from some essential motivation. Abraham's motivation was love for a kinsman. The implication of the text is that the servants who responded had a very similar motivation as well.

The fervent motivation of

Abraham and his servants explains the immediacy of their response. The beginning and ending portions of verse 14 imply a very quick response: "And when Abram heard . . . [he] pursued them unto Dan." Further, the response was intense because Dan was in the far north of the region, requiring a persistent pursuit for several days.

How can the believer intervene in behalf of the needy today?

B. Activating to Win (v. 15)

15. And he divided himself against them, he and his servants, by night, and smote them, and pursued them unto Hobah, which is on the left hand of Damascus.

Not only did Abraham arm himself in quick response, but he followed through, effectively activating his troops, until they won. They had to commit several critical steps in completing their mission. The first was to quickly arm themselves. The second was to pursue their foe just as quickly. The third step was to strategically place themselves in position, dividing, in order to win. The fourth step was to make a critical adjustment and attack when the enemy was most vulnerable—at night.

It is reasonable to assume that the force Abraham attacked was not the main force of the confederation of the kings, but only a group armed and carrying some of the captives. Abraham's force was not an army by any means—it only numbered 318 (v. 14). Though the enemy was no doubt not the main army, it evidently outnumbered Abraham's men. Nevertheless, Abraham was determined enough and made the required adjustments in order to defeat the enemy.

Two facts stood out in Abraham's victory. First, Abraham won soundly, pursuing the enemy for some distance. Hobah lay between Dan and Damascus, some distance from the point where Abraham no doubt first encountered the enemy. Second, Abraham was able to take back the captured people and possessions. This second aspect of his victory is the emphasis of verse 16.

What kind of adjustments did Abram make in order to be victorious?

C. Acquiring to Save (v. 16)

16. And he brought back all the goods, and also brought again his brother Lot, and his goods, and the women also, and the people.

"Brought back" reflects the ultimate nature of Abraham's victory. The victory was not merely for Abraham's gain, but it benefited those he was intervening for. Personally, Abraham did not need to fight. No damage had been done to him, his property, or the personnel that worked for him. His victory was purely for the sake of intervention.

The power of intervening for another is that it moves a person beyond oneself. God, moved by love, gave His only begotten Son to save the world (John 3:16). Intervention for others is being moved by love. Self-centeredness is being moved only by what affects one personally. The selfish person will not intervene for others because from that person's perspective, there is no reason to do so.

II. STAND FOR MORAL PRINCIPLES (Genesis 18:17-19)

A. Presence of the One Moral God (v. 17)

17. And the Lord said, Shall I hide from Abraham that thing which I do?

Intervention and intercession reflect not only the love and compassion of a person, as illustrated in Genesis 14, but also the moral condition of the intervener. In the case of Genesis 18, the moral nature of God is reflected in His intervention for Abraham.

Abraham had no descendants. God's intervention would provide a miraculous means for him to have a child; likewise, miraculous intervention would bring judgment on Sodom and Gomorrah. The time of blessing for righteous Abraham would be a time of destruction for wicked Sodom and Gomorrah. God knows when to bring blessing and when to bring destruction, because He is a moral God. Whereas Abraham presently had no descendants, and Sodom and Gomorrah fared lavishly, God in His judgment would reverse the circumstances by giving Abraham descendants through the ages and cutting off Sodom and Gomorrah forever.

Is there evidence of godly morality based on Scripture in today's society? How can the believer exhibit moral principles that God would have us follow?

B. Potential of a Moral Person (v. 18)

18. Seeing that Abraham shall surely become a great and mighty nation, and all the nations of the earth shall be blessed in him?

God perpetuates His morality through righteous children. God continually ordains our sons and daughters to be a significant part of the extension of His righteousness on earth. Moral potential is maximized through our children. Being upright is not just an individual venture. To be complete, an ethical person must be concerned for the morality of the next generation and other generations to come.

Moral potential is not fulfilled in national programs or moral statements. Ethics are not complete when they are established only in a current generation—future generations are the ultimate goal. Children fulfill morality and they reflect the true morality of previous generations. Is there much of God in us? How much of God is in our children? Both parents and children are responsible for their own walk before God. However, the morality of a succeeding generation is at least a partial commentary on the moral potential of the previous generation.

C. Practice of Moral Relationships (v. 19)

19. For I know him, that he will command his children and his household after him, and they shall keep the way of the Lord, to do justice and judgment; that the Lord may bring upon Abraham that which he hath spoken of him.

There are four parts to the upright relationship between God and Abraham: (1) Abraham would be concerned for the righteousness of his family; (2) he would personally "keep the way of the Lord"; (3) he would maintain justice and carry out judgment; (4) he would be blessed of God.

The concern of Abraham for his children and future generations was discussed in verse 18. Abraham's personal moral obligation before God would be met. The phrase "the way of the Lord" was a reference to one's manner of personal living.

Justice referred to the ability to make godly decisions, the godly principles on which those decisions were made, and the personal qualities of making decisions as a just person. *Judgment* referred to the carrying out of decisions of justice. Righteousness became active, behavioral reality through godly judgment.

Blessings from God bestowed on the moral person was a strong teaching in the Old Testament. There would be times of testing, but that was part of the moral formation of the individual. Ultimately, there would be a reward for godliness.

How did Abraham demonstrate an upright and moral life? What did God recognize in Abraham that made him a moral person?

III. PLEAD FOR THE LOST
(Genesis 18:20-33)

A. The Cry for Justice (vv. 20, 21)

20. And the Lord said, Because the cry of Sodom and Gomorrah is great, and because their sin is very grievous;

21. I will go down now, and see whether they have done altogether according to the cry of it, which is come unto me; and if not, I will know.

The cry of Sodom and Gomorrah was a cry for justice. Their noted penchant for sexual sins is legendary, yet Biblical. Centuries later Ezekiel would say: "This was the iniquity of . . . Sodom: she and her daughter had pride, fullness of food, and abundance of idleness; neither did she strengthen the hand of the poor and needy. And they were haughty and committed abomina-

tion before Me; therefore I took them away as I saw fit" (Ezekiel 16:49, 50). Apparently, the magnitude of their gross and vile sins, coupled with the cries of countless victims of their immorality and lawlessness, rose to God in a mighty complaint.

Sin always brings hurt and destruction. God's judgment addresses the pain caused by sin, as well as the sin itself. The Hebrew word for *grievous* means "burdensome and heavy." The weight of the sin of these cities added to the severity of the resulting pain and suffering. God's judgment was in response to sin's affront—not only to Him, but also to humanity. The only justice for the enormity of their evil and disobedience was certain retribution.

B. The Cry for Intervention (vv. 22-31)

(Genesis 18:26-31 is not included in the printed text.)

22. And the men turned their faces from thence, and went toward Sodom: but Abraham stood yet before the Lord.

23. And Abraham drew near, and said, Wilt thou also destroy the righteous with the wicked?

24. Peradventure there be fifty righteous within the city: wilt thou also destroy and not spare the place for the fifty righteous that are therein?

25. That be far from thee to do after this manner, to slay the righteous with the wicked: and that the righteous should be as the wicked, that be far from thee: Shall not the Judge of all the earth do right?

The requirement to intervene and intercede is rooted in the fact that when we intercede we are following the heart of God in listening for the cry of those who suffer because of evil. The intercessor is heard by God because God recognizes that the intervener has first heard what He hears—the cries which result from sin. God was listening for the cries of the suffering in Sodom and Gomorrah, and Abraham was able to say that he had heard those cries as well.

The cry of those who suffered because of sin was the basis of God's destruction and the foundation of His deferral of destruction. God's justice is never so severe that greater damage is done to the victim while trying to punish the offender. God's first priority in judgment is the condition of the innocent. Worldly systems of justice too often focus on the offender and almost forget the condition and safety of the victim.

Knowing God's first priority for the innocent, Abraham appealed to God. Abraham was not seeking to spare the two cities. He wanted to make sure that the righteous were not slain while the evildoers were being slain. God ultimately did this very thing. God visited the city, separated the victims from the offenders, and provided a safe haven for them. God deferred His judgment long enough to provide a way of escape for the righteous. This same principle will continue to be used by God all the way to the rapture of the church, just before the Tribulation.

C. The Cry for God's Mercy
(vv. 32, 33)

32. And he said, Oh let not the Lord be angry, and I will speak yet by this once: Peradventure ten shall be found there. And he said, I will not destroy it for ten's sake.

33. And the Lord went his way, as soon as he had left communing with Abraham: and Abraham returned unto his place.

Intercession is possible because of who God is. Abraham was a man of faith. However, it was the person of God and not the person of Abraham that made intercession possible. Regardless of Abraham's good intentions, he would have never been able to approach God, much less plead for the mercy of God for the righteous that may have been in Sodom, except for the nature of God which is open to the cry of the intercessor. In fact, God is seeking intercessors who will appeal for His mercy. Further, God requires that believers be intercessors.

Intercession does not bring something new to the attention of God; rather, the intercessor affirms what God already knows. The affirmation of the cry of the intercessor relates to one of the deepest purposes of intercession—"communing" (v. 33) with God. The intercessor is not only praying that someone will be spared from the judgment of God; but also intercession is entering into communion with God. It is seeking to know the heart of God and, ultimately, to walk with Him. The intercessor affirms the mercy that is present in God's judgment. God responds to the intercessor in communion, hearing the appeal of the intercessor and responding with mercy.

Godly intercessors today must not see a God who barely hears them. Instead, godly intercessors should approach God in full confidence, knowing that He desires to hear their cry. God is already aware of the need brought to Him by the intercessor. He desires communion with the intercessor and is ready to respond with mercy.

REVIEW QUESTIONS

1. What should motivate the believer to be an intervener and intercessor today?

2. How is the victory obtained in these last days of intercession as the final judgment of the Lord approaches?

3. What seems to be the basis of morality today?

4. What difference did the morality of Abraham make in his relationship before God and the world?

5. How can the believer be an intercessor and intervener today?

GOLDEN TEXT HOMILY

"I KNOW HIM, THAT HE WILL COMMAND HIS CHILDREN AND HIS HOUSEHOLD AFTER HIM, AND THEY SHALL KEEP THE WAY OF THE LORD, TO DO JUSTICE AND JUDGMENT" (Genesis 18:19).

Why did the Lord have such great confidence in Abraham? The Lord's answer: "I know him." Abraham understood "the way of the Lord" and was committed to walking in it. He did not stop with understanding the Lord's will; he also practiced it. Knowing Abraham's faith and his devotion to personal integrity and holiness, the Lord was confident that the patriarch would be a good father and would provide the kind of leadership that his children and family needed.

Good fathers are neither hatchet men nor tyrants. But they are people of authority. For example, Abraham would "command his children and his household after him." As every father should, he had a positive influence on his family and taught them to acknowledge him as the priest of his home.

The father's exercise of leadership in the family is very important. In fact, it is a qualification for a church leader. The apostle Paul said, "If anyone does not know how to manage his own family, how can he take care of God's church?" (1 Timothy 3:5, *NIV*). Family management is a matter of caring, loving and shepherding—not a matter of ruling, dominating, and controlling. It is a matter of commitment to wife and children and of exercising proper discipline. The family is our children's first school. It is there that the foundation should be laid for a personal knowledge of Christ and for holy and productive living. Fathers have a great responsibility and a great opportunity.

As fathers we cannot afford to wait for the church to grow our children spiritually!—**French L. Arrington, Ph.D., Professor of New Testament Greek and Exegesis, Church of God School of Theology, Cleveland, Tennessee**

SENTENCE SERMONS

GOD CALLS AND EQUIPS His people to rescue those ensnared by Satan.

—Selected

SOUL-WINNING is not the art of bringing people from down where they are up to where you are. It is bringing them to Christ.

—George L. Smith

HE WHO PRAYS for his neighbor will be heard for himself.

—Hebrew Proverb

DAILY BIBLE READINGS

M. A Boy Intervenes.
1 Samuel 17:32-37, 49

T. A Woman Intervenes.
Esther 4:10-17

W. A Layman Intercedes.
Nehemiah 1:3-11

T. A Father Intercedes.
Matthew 17:14-18

F. Friends Intervene. Mark 2:1-5

S. The Church Intercedes.
Acts 12:1-11

Facing Family Conflict

Study Text: Genesis 25:21-34; 27:1-46; 33:1-11

Objective: To see that godly families can be wounded, and minister healing and reconciliation to them.

Time: The Book of Genesis was written between 1450 and 1400 B.C.

Place: The general belief is that Moses received this revelation while on Mount Sinai in the wilderness.

Golden Text: "Then they cry unto the Lord in their trouble, and he saveth them out of their distresses. He sent his word, and healed them, and delivered them from their destructions" (Psalm 107:19, 20).

Central Truth: Although godly families suffer the effects of sin, God is able to heal their wounds.

Evangelism Emphasis: God desires to redeem every sinner.

PRINTED TEXT

Genesis 25:27. And the boys grew: and Esau was a cunning hunter, a man of the field; and Jacob was a plain man, dwelling in tents.

28. And Isaac loved Esau, because he did eat of his venison: but Rebekah loved Jacob.

29. And Jacob sod pottage: and Esau came from the field, and he was faint:

30. And Esau said to Jacob, Feed me, I pray thee, with that same red pottage; for I am faint: therefore was his name called Edom.

31. And Jacob said, Sell me this day thy birthright.

32. And Esau said, Behold, I am at the point to die: and what profit shall this birthright do to me?

33. And Jacob said, Swear to me this day; and he sware unto him: and he sold his birthright unto Jacob.

34. Then Jacob gave Esau bread and pottage of lentiles; and he did eat and drink, and rose up, and went his way: thus Esau despised his birthright.

27:34. And when Esau heard the words of his father, he cried with a great and exceeding bitter cry, and said unto his father, Bless me, even me also, O my father.

35. And he said, Thy brother came with subtilty, and hath taken away thy blessing.

41. And Esau hated Jacob because of the blessing wherewith his father blessed him: and Esau said in his heart, The days of mourning for my father are at hand; then will I slay my brother

Jacob.

33:4. And Esau ran to meet him, and embraced him, and fell on his neck, and kissed him: and they wept.

8. And he said, What meanest thou by all this drove which I met? And he said, These are to find grace in the sight of my lord.

9. And Esau said, I have enough, my brother; keep that thou hast unto thyself.

10. And Jacob said, Nay, I pray thee, if now I have found grace in thy sight, then receive my present at my hand: for therefore I have seen thy face, as though I had seen the face of God, and thou wast pleased with me.

11. Take, I pray thee, my blessing that is brought to thee; because God hath dealt graciously with me, and because I have enough. And he urged him, and he took it.

DICTIONARY

Esau (EE-saw)—Genesis 25:27—The firstborn twin of Isaac and Rebecca. His twin brother was Jacob.

Edom (EE-dum)—Genesis 25:30—The land where Esau's descendants lived.

LESSON OUTLINE

I. DYSFUNCTION IN THE FAMILY
    A. Division Brings Dysfunction
    B. Despair Brings Dysfunction
    C. Deception Brings Dysfunction

II. THE PAIN OF CONFLICT
    A. The Pain of Subversion
    B. The Pain of Secrecy
    C. The Pain of Severity

III. HEALING THE BROKENNESS
    A. Brokenness Healed by Grace
    B. Brokenness Healed by Giving
    C. Brokenness Healed by Godliness

LESSON EXPOSITION

INTRODUCTION

The desperation of today's society is reflected in the deprivation of contemporary families. Families are being deprived of godliness and purity, the strength that gave birth to the family in the beginning. God intended for the family to reflect His love and holiness. To the contrary, little in modern culture remains of the divine love and sanctity with which God marked the family at the dawn of time.

Without the power of God's love and purity, a cycle of dysfunction and conflict develops. Genesis 25—33 tells the tragic story of this cycle in Abraham's first descendants. Though Abraham received powerful faith from the Lord, the following generations were not guaranteed the same faith. Graft and deception marked the family of Isaac until the love and holiness of

God flowed within the family, creating faith.

Isaac, Rebekah, Esau, and Jacob were not very different from contemporary families. They had a great heritage of faith, but they crumbled personally. Although Isaac's faith was apparently strong, he was deceived. Rebekah was drawn astray by her love for one child and her disappointment with another child. Esau was self-centered, sacrificing the fruits of tomorrow on the altar of today. Jacob was self-serving, ambitious enough to violate sacred commitments to family members. All of these characteristics are repeated over and over in modern families.

I. DYSFUNCTION IN THE FAMILY (Genesis 25:21-34)

A. Division Brings Dysfunction (vv. 21-28)

(Genesis 25:21-26 is not included in the printed text.)

27. And the boys grew: and Esau was a cunning hunter, a man of the field; and Jacob was a plain man, dwelling in tents.

28. And Isaac loved Esau, because he did eat of his venison: but Rebekah loved Jacob.

Immediately after the birth of the twins (vv. 21-34), the Scripture tells of a division between the two boys. There was a foretelling of division when Jacob grabbed Esau's heel in birth (v. 26). The boys were different in their preferences and mannerisms. Esau was an outdoorsman and Jacob preferred to stay indoors. There was nothing wrong in being different. However, the Scripture possibly notes division beginning in the family when verse 28 states that Isaac loved Esau and

Rebekah loved Jacob.

What are the consequences of self-centeredness in the family? When did competition between Esau and Jacob begin?

Love and unity foster functionality in a family; division and preference breed dysfunction. Not every family member is exactly alike; nor can each family member expect to be treated in precisely the same way. However, there must be a commitment to harmony and unity in the midst of differences. Though a family member may disagree with another, each person must be able to work through those disagreements and still love one another.

B. Despair Brings Dysfunction (vv. 29-32)

29. And Jacob sod pottage: and Esau came from the field, and he was faint:

30. And Esau said to Jacob, Feed me, I pray thee, with that same red pottage; for I am faint: therefore was his name called Edom.

31. And Jacob said, Sell me this day thy birthright.

32. And Esau said, Behold, I am at the point to die: and what profit shall this birthright do to me?

Stress in the modern home would be an equivalent of the fatigue of Esau in that ancient home. Esau was vulnerable and unwise because he had come to a point of exhaustion. Nothing is said to condemn the fainted condition of Esau. He may have justifiably been hunting for food for the family. However, the stress that his body was under became the occasion for preexisting divisions within the family to rise and bring dysfunction. The division was wrong, and the stress was perhaps understandable; but the two in combination brought dysfunction to the home.

How was the self-centeredness of Esau and Jacob displayed? What are the effects of stress in the family?

Today, both division and stress are enemies to the home. Division should never begin in the first place, and stress must be monitored and managed as much as possible. It is hard to deal with relational stresses when one's body is exhausted. Working long hours, bearing burdens for weeks on end, and living as though the world is going to cave in at any moment— these facts set the modern family up for a downfall of lethal proportions. Esau negotiated foolishly out of exhaustion; and Jacob, observing Esau's fatigue, deceptively took advantage of him.

Tragically, both Esau and Jacob looked at family relatinoships as something as something that could be bartered. Esau felt the birthright was of no "profit" in his condition. Jacob "sold" the pottage in return for a family possession. To the contrary, Jacob should have nurtured his brother out of love; Esau should have realized that the birthright was a family possession and that he had little right, because of his position as firstborn, to barter a family possession. Self-centeredness, "what I can get out of something," is the alter on which family commitments are sacrificed over and over. Though society may function with profits and losses, the family con only function out of sacrificial nurture and commitment.

C. Deception Brings Dysfunction (vv. 33, 34)

33. And Jacob said, Swear to me this day; and he sware unto him: and he sold his birthright unto Jacob.
34. Then Jacob gave Esau bread and pottage of lentiles; and he did eat and drink, and rose up, and went his way: thus Esau despised his birthright.

Dysfunction reached fruition when the Scripture notes that "Esau despised his birthright." *Despised* is translated from the Hebrew term *bazah*, which means "to have a severe contempt for something." The term was used of Michal (Saul's daughter) when she observed David dancing before the Lord (2 Samuel 6:16; 1 Chronicles 15:29). It was also used by Nathan the prophet when he described the way David felt toward the commandments of God and murdered Uriah the Hittite (2 Samuel 12:9). If Esau merely rejected his birthright and considered it worthless, other terms would have been used in the Hebrew text (e.g., *qalal* in Genesis 16:4, 5; *ma'ac* in Leviticus 26:43 and Numbers 11:20). On the contrary, a deep-seated bitterness and vile feeling toward his family birthright arose within Esau.

How was Jacob affected by the sale of Esau's birthright? How was the family to be affected by the sale of the birthright?

Notice that Esau's feeling was not to his brother alone but to the birthright—that is, his family's possession. Esau did not care—he even loathed his family. Self-centeredness and bartering his family commitments eventually come full circle and turn to bitterness toward the family. Jacob felt he could use his family's possession for his own gain, but discovered that his family's value was a cause of his bitterness.

II. THE PAIN OF CONFLICT (Genesis 27:30-41)

A. The Pain of Subversion (vv. 30-34)

(Genesis 27:30-33 is not included in the printed text.)

34. And when Esau heard the words of his father, he cried with a great exceeding bitter cry, and said unto his father, Bless me, even me also, O my father.

Dysfunction in the home leads to open conflict. The seeds of bitterness, deception, and self-centered bartering in the home of Isaac, Rebekah, Esau, and Jacob erupted in open conflict. Jacob continued on a path of deception and Esau continued on a path of bitterness. Esau sought the love of his father, continually feeding him and pleasing him. Jacob continued to use the love of his mother to gain personally at the expense of his family.

The conflict occurred when both Rebekah and Jacob deceived Isaac. Deception grows within a family, bringing polarization. Members choose sides. Factions in families grow whenever there is a diminished capacity to love each member of the family, seeking overall unity. Commitment to one another is destroyed by self-centeredness.

Eventually, pain to the family comes as a result of deception and self-centeredness. Esau's cry erupted not only because he had lost the birthright, but also because he had a volcano of bitterness from despising his family and birthright (25:34). The pain came from the subversion of two brothers who wanted to sell and profit from their family heritage. Family commitments may have a cost, but the cost of subverting the family for personal gain is even greater.

B. The Pain of Secrecy (vv. 35-37)

(Genesis 27:36, 37 is not included in the printed text.)

35. And he said, Thy brother came with subtilty, and hath taken away thy blessing.

The pain of subversion is made possible by the sin of secrecy. Not only did Jacob take the inheritance from Esau, but he maneuvered around his brother to complete his wickedness. Family sins are secret sins. Not only are they held secret from those outside of the family but also from those inside the family. Secrecy is another form of lying when it is used to perpetuate sin. Lying to his father in order to perpetuate a lie to his brother, and joining in a lie with his mother, Jacob secured the birthright for himself.

How was the pain of Esau reflected? What would it take to bring peace and reconciliation between Esau and Jacob?

The pain of Jacob's secrecy was that he took something away from his father and his brother that was not his. His subtilty led to theft of his own family members. Although Esau had participated and was to blame for the pain inflicted by selling his birthright, now the blame for the pain inflicted by seditious subtilty shifted to Jacob and his mother.

C. The Pain of Severity (vv. 38-41)

(Genesis 27:38-40 is not included in the printed text.)

41. And Esau hated Jacob because of the blessing wherewith his father blessed him: and Esau said in his heart, The days of mourning for my father are at hand; then will I slay my brother Jacob.

The spiral of pain inflicted in the family of Isaac, Rebekah, Esau, and Jacob increased until it reached the severe point of open hatred. What was once sold between two brothers, then secretly taken from a father, was now openly exposed to vehement hatred. Family dysfunction is on an inevitable spiral; which, if left unchecked, will continue to grow in severity until it erupts in open, strong, violent emotion.

The severity of pain for Esau moved him to do the unthinkable. It was the exact opposite of what a family member should do. Esau should have had an innate, God-given urge to protect, defend, and love his own brother. However, the spiral of self-centeredness and deception resulted in a desire to kill his brother. Dysfunction, without the intervention of the Lord, can lead to death in a family.

III. HEALING THE BROKEN-
    NESS (Genesis 33:1-11)

A. Brokenness Healed by Grace
    (vv. 1-5)

(Genesis 33:1-3, 5 is not included in the printed text.)

4. And Esau ran to meet him, and embraced him, and fell on his neck, and kissed him: and they wept.

By Genesis 33, the two brothers had completely changed. The story of Jacob's transformation is carefully told in chapters 28-32. He had had an encounter with God and with a deceptive father-in-law. He returned in humility seeking reconciliation with his brother. Esau appeared on the scene (33:4) as suddenly as his anger once erupted toward Jacob. This time, however, he ran in humility to his brother, embracing and kissing him.

Only a miraculous intervention of God could have turned the tide between these two brothers. Events happened in both of their lives; however, without God's intervention all efforts to be transformed and reconciled would have failed.

In contemporary families, aids and resources for family enrichment and intervention are absolutely vital. Yet, in the deepest valleys, especially those that have run too long and too deep, where the course of conflict will not subside or even turn, God still moves the waters and brings calm to a family. The story is one of grace. Only by God's own intervention—out of His grace and His grace alone—do we find the keys to turn the tragedies that confront families today.

B. Brokenness Healed by Giving
   (vv. 6-8)

(Genesis 33:6, 7 is not included in the printed text.)

8. And he said, What meanest thou by all this drove which I met? And he said, These are to find grace in the sight of my lord.

Giving is the result of God's grace. Once God had demonstrated

Himself in Jacob's life, Jacob had to turn to his brother with a giving heart. Jacob had once been self-centered, willing to barter and manipulate his entire family in order to gain something for himself. Now, he was more than willing to freely give to His brother.

Jacob's attitude toward his brother had completely changed. Whereas Jacob previously used his brother, he now honored his brother. Jacob once took from his brother; now he gave to his brother. Jacob once deceived his brother; now he called him respectfully, "my lord." Honor had replaced hatred. Healing had replaced hypocrisy. Humility had replaced haughtiness. A home is known and nurtured by the manner in which its members treat one another.

C. Brokenness Healed by
   Godliness (vv. 9-11)

9. And Esau said, I have enough, my brother; keep that thou hast unto thyself.

10. And Jacob said, Nay, I pray thee, if now I have found grace in thy sight, then receive my present at my hand: for therefore I have seen thy face, as though I had seen the face of God, and thou wast pleased with me.

11. Take, I pray thee, my blessing that is brought to thee; because God hath dealt graciously with me, and because I have enough. And he urged him, and he took it.

Jacob's motivation for a renewed relationship with his brother came from God. Jacob did not give to his brother to meet a need his brother had. He gave to his brother to be a blessing to him. He gave to his brother because he felt as though he was giving to God. He gave to his brother because God had given to him. He gave because God had already met his needs. Thus four principles form the basis for giving in the home: (1) being a blessing, (2) giving to God, (3) realizing that God has given to us, and (4) recognizing that God has satisfied our own needs.

Family functionality is an act of faith. When we love a family member, we love God. When we give honor to a family member, we are being faithful to God. Family members may not deserve a blessing, but we give to them in order to be a blessing . . . and because God has blessed us. Family members may not want to receive from us, but we urge them to receive because God has put that desire in our hearts. Family members may continue to be self-centered, but we give to them because God has satisfied our needs. Faith as the foundation of a family turns conflict into communion.

REVIEW QUESTIONS

1. Where does dysfunction begin in the family?

2. What was the family result of self-centeredness on the part of Esau and Jacob?

3. How deeply was Esau affected by the sale of his birthright?

4. What is the effect of secrecy in a family?

5. How can reconciliation be brought about in a family that is dysfunctional?

GOLDEN TEXT HOMILY

"THEN THEY CRY UNTO THE LORD IN THEIR TROUBLE, AND HE SAVETH THEM OUT OF THEIR DISTRESSES. HE SENT HIS WORD, AND HEALED THEM, AND DELIVERED THEM FROM THEIR

DESTRUCTIONS" (Psalm 107:19, 20).

As a prison chaplain, I have worked with and ministered to many families facing extreme social conflict. Whenever healing took place, Psalm 107:19, 20 would begin to work in their lives.

A young black man facing a death sentence for the rape/murder of a young white woman, approached me in tears, needing healing for his wounded soul. He was seeking a sense of relief from his pain and sorrow. We talked about the forgiveness God offers to all who accept. He assured me he had prayed and felt God had forgiven him for his act of violence, but the pain was still there. He talked of his deep sorrow. He felt if he could talk to the family of his victim, and let them know how sorry he was, it would in some way help relieve their pain. He felt he would be able to deal with his pain too.

The Scripture says God will go before us and make the crooked paths straight (Isaiah 45:2). Not many days after my conversation with this man, I received a call from a grieving mother and father. They were Christians, and had prayed for the salvation of the man who killed their daughter, but still struggled with forgiveness. They asked about the possibility of meeting with this man and letting him know that because of God's love, they could forgive him. I was able to arrange a meeting between them.

The meeting took place at our Maximum Security facility. We met in a small room with no windows, no air-conditioning. A small fan in the corner of the room moved the hot humid air through the room, not an ideal setting for such a meeting.

When we are not able to deal with the guilt and anger, however, or when we are not able to extend forgiveness to those whom we have wronged or those who have wronged us, we will be totally consumed by inner turmoil. Placing ourselves in partnership with God enables us to work through our problems. We cannot do it without God. God won't do it without our being submitted to His will.

Here in this small room, three people cried "unto the Lord in their trouble. . . . He sent his word, and healed them, and delivered them from their destructions."

God "is able to do exceedingly abundantly above all that we ask or think" (Ephesians 3:20).—**Ronald M. Padgett, Chaplain, Director of Religious Programs, Mississippi Department of Corrections, Parchman, Mississippi**

SENTENCE SERMONS

ALTHOUGH GODLY FAMILIES suffer the effects of sin, God is able to heal their wounds.

—Selected

THE CHRISTIAN HOME is the Master's workshop where the process of character molding is silently, lovingly, faithfully, and successfully carried on.

—Richard Milner

DAILY BIBLE READINGS

M. Brothers Reconciled.
Genesis 33:1-4
T. A Father Grieves.
2 Samuel 18:31 through 19:4
W. Promise of Healing. M a l a c h i 4:1-6
T. Anointing for Healing.
Luke 4:18-21
F. A Father Forgives.
Luke 15:17-24
S. Healing Through Confession.
James 5:13-16

Patience in Adversity

Study Text: Genesis 37:1-20; 39:1-23; 41:38-46

Objective: To realize that every person is challenged by adversity and rely upon God for deliverance.

Time: The Book of Genesis was written between 1450 and 1400 B.C.

Place: The general belief is that Moses received this revelation while on Mount Sinai in the wilderness.

Golden Text: "We know that all things work together for good to them that love God, to them who are the called according to his purpose" (Romans 8:28).

Central Truth: In His perfect time, God delivers those who wait on Him.

Evangelism Emphasis: The Holy Spirit can use adversity to draw sinners to Christ.

PRINTED TEXT

Genesis 39:7. And it came to pass after these things, that his master's wife cast her eyes upon Joseph; and she said, Lie with me.

8. But he refused, and said unto his master's wife, Behold, my master wotteth not what is with me in the house, and he hath committed all that he hath to my hand;

9. There is none greater in this house than I; neither hath he kept back any thing from me but thee, because thou art his wife: how then can I do this great wickedness, and sin against God?

10. And it came to pass, as she spake to Joseph day by day, that he hearkened not unto her, to lie by her, or to be with her.

11. And it came to pass about this time, that Joseph went into the house to do his business; and there was none of the men of the house there within.

12. And she caught him by his garment, saying, Lie with me: and he left his garment in her hand, and fled, and got him out.

20. And Joseph's master took him, and put him into the prison, a place where the king's prisoners were bound: and he was there in the prison.

21. But the Lord was with Joseph, and shewed him mercy, and gave him favour in the sight of the keeper of the prison.

22. And the keeper of the prison committed to Joseph's hand all the prisoners that were in the prison; and whatsoever they did there, he was the doer of it.

23. The keeper of the prison

looked not to any thing that was under his hand; because the Lord was with him, and that which he did, the Lord made it to prosper.

41:38. And Pharaoh said unto his servants, Can we find such a one as this is, a man in whom the Spirit of God is?

41. And Pharaoh said unto Joseph, See, I have set thee over all the land of Egypt.

42. And Pharaoh took off his ring from his hand, and put it upon Joseph's hand, and arrayed him in vestures of fine linen, and put a gold chain about his neck;

43. And he made him to ride in the second chariot which he had; and they cried before him, Bow the knee: and he made him ruler over all the land of Egypt.

DICTIONARY

Pharaoh (FAY-row)—Genesis 41:38—The title given to the kings of Egypt.

LESSON OUTLINE

I.   CHALLENGED BY ADVERSITY
   A. Peace Before Adversity
   B. Pressure of Adversity
   C. Problems From Adversity

II. SUSTAINED BY ADVERSITY
   A. The Lord's Mercy
   B. The Lord's Mastery
   C. The Lord's Ministry

III. DELIVERED FROM ADVERSITY
   A. Spirit Indwelling
   B. Set Over Others
   C. Secure From Harm

LESSON EXPOSITION

INTRODUCTION

The ultimate test of the reality of any religion is what it does with the suffering of the innocent. Pagan religions send sufferers into an abstract world of metaphysical mysticism. Carnal religions send sufferers into carnage and self-flagellation. Christianity retrieves righteous sufferers under the wings of a caring and sovereign God.

In the life of Joseph, the God of the ages was the God of all-sufficiency. Whatever adversity he encountered, he had the assurance of God's sovereign Word and the all-sufficiency of God's present safe haven. God spoke to him early in life, assuring him there was a divine destiny laid up for his future. As his life unfolded, God intervened and directed the destiny of Joseph's life.

Adversity for the child of God is not marked by present tragedy; it is marked by the presence of a sovereign God. Present realities reveal only a fraction of the fuller reality for the child of God. Serving an eternal God means our lives are constantly held in the perspective of the Eternal. Adversity does not write the meaning of our lives. God, who was with us before the adversity, is with us during the adversity and will be with us after the adversity.

The trick of the Enemy is to convince the believer that adversity is eternal. No adversity lasts forever, except the eternal judgment of hell awaiting those who do not accept Christ as Lord and Savior. God's work in the life of Joseph demonstrates that adversity not only has an ending, but can also be used by God to provide a doorway to fulfilling God's ultimate will. Adversity does not originate with God, but God eventually ends the adversity and uses it for His glory.

I. CHALLENGED BY ADVERSITY (Genesis 39:1-20)

A. Peace Before Adversity (vv. 1-6)

(Genesis 39:1-6 is not included in the printed text.)

Typically, the trauma of adversity comes after a time of tranquillity. It may seem as though there has been only adversity but there usually is some memory of peace before the storm. In the case of Joseph, the peace was from the Lord. Joseph became "prosperous" (v. 2) even though he was a servant under an Egyptian master, Potiphar. In fact, Joseph's life was a testimony to his master (v. 3). The master made Joseph overseer of his house and many of his possessions. Further, the master's house prospered as a result of Joseph's presence. Finally, the master placed complete confidence and trust in Joseph, making him manager of all his possessions.

B. Pressure of Adversity (vv. 7-12)

7. And it came to pass after these things, that his master's wife cast her eyes upon Joseph; and she said, Lie with me.

8. But he refused, and said unto his master's wife, Behold, my master wotteth not what is with me in the house, and he hath committed all that he hath to my hand;

9. There is none greater in this house than I; neither hath he kept back any thing from me but thee, because thou art his wife: how then can I do this great wickedness, and sin against God?

10. And it came to pass, as she spake to Joseph day by day, that he hearkened not unto her, to lie by her, or to be with her.

11. And it came to pass about this time, that Joseph went into the house to do his business; and there was none of the men of the house there within.

12. And she caught him by his garment, saying, Lie with me: and he left his garment in her hand, and fled, and got him out.

Pressure follows peace in the cycle of adversity. Joseph did not ask for pressure; nor did he do anything that deserved pressure. Adversity for the believer is frequently brought on by outside temptation and attack. If it seems like you have done everything right and adversity still comes, you are much like Joseph. You are innocent, but still you come under pressure that could very well lead to adversity.

The wife of Potiphar, the very man that God had used to be such a blessing to Joseph, now became the instrument of great turmoil. She insisted that Joseph have illicit relationships with her. Joseph refused her advances, responding with gratefulness about his master and faithfulness about his God. He tried to reason with her and respond righteously to her. The heart of his resistance was based on faith. He knew that it would be a sin against God to compromise (v. 9).

The pressure of Potiphar's wife was persistent; she continued daily in her advances. Joseph, just as persistently, refused her. Despite the pressure of adversity, consistent faithfulness is extremely important. Even though there would inevitably be a time when the woman would turn her advances into adversity, Joseph remained faithful, not fatalistic.

While continuing to be faithful in the business of his master, Joseph found himself in the grip of the woman. Note that adversity was initiated by the evildoer. God ultimately would work these events for Joseph's good; but at this point, he was in the clutches of his attacker. Thankfully, Joseph escaped and fled from the woman.

Even though we may be faced with the inevitability of adversity, and even though it may appear that the evildoer has gained the advantage, the believer must continue to remain faithful in resisting those advances and not despairing.

Why do bad things happen to believers? What good would be accomplished in Joseph's life through adversity?

C. Problems From Adversity
   (vv. 13-20)

(Genesis 39:13-19 is not included in the printed text.)

20. And Joseph's master took him, and put him into the prison, a place where the king's prisoners were bound: and he was there in the prison.

Lying is the ultimate weapon of evil. As God is truth and reigns in justice, so evildoers dwell in lying and revel in corruption. Essentially, the attack of Satan on the innocent is an effort to speak evil of their good, to misrepresent their accomplishments and destroy their deeds. The master's wife did all of these things by completely falsifying her misfortune and portraying Joseph as the evildoer rather than herself.

When adversity comes, the things that were once the occasion for great blessing become the very instruments of destruction the devil uses. The household of Potiphar had once been Joseph's success; now it was used to destroy him. The power he once possessed was used to claim abuse of privilege. The affinity he had with Potiphar was used to insinuate illicit intimacy with his wife. Adversity may not always destroy our world, but our world may be used in adversity to destroy us. Joseph's world of blessing became the very instrument that would put him in bondage.

Did success shield Joseph from adversity? What was the primary tool used to bring adversity to Joseph?

II. SUSTAINED BY ADVERSITY
    (Genesis 39:21-23)

A. The Lord's Mercy (v. 21)

21. But the Lord was with Joseph, and shewed him mercy, and gave him favour in the sight of the keeper of the prison.

As great as the adversity was for Joseph, the words "But the Lord . . ." made all the difference. Those words convey his source of strength. While in prison, Joseph had none of the things he previously had, except the thing that made the difference—the presence of the Lord.

Whereas God had previously given Joseph blessing and prosperity, now, in the midst of adversity, He was giving him mercy. The Hebrew term for *mercy* is *checed*. It is also translated as "lovingkindness" in other passages in the Bible. The emphasis of the word was on love and kindness; and in the context of this verse, the further emphasis was on faithfulness of presence.

God was assuring Joseph He was with him as he had always been. Many times our focus is on God's actions and not on His presence. God's actions change. They are always consistent with His nature, but He will not always do for us individually what He has done in the past. Like Joseph, we may be surrounded by family; we may be surrounded by a deep pit; we may be surrounded by captors; we may be surrounded by blessing; or we may be surrounded by deception and imprisonment. These were all circumstances of Joseph's life. In the midst of these places in his life, the key was to abide in the assurance that God was still faithfully with him, working all things for Joseph's good.

Evidence of God's abiding with Joseph is in the second part of verse 21. Joseph found favor in the eyes of the keeper of the prison. God was still moving in Joseph's life. *Mercy* is not a passive or diluted term. God's merciful presence is an active reality. God is always working, despite adversity. Just as

the Lord had used every other phase of Joseph's life for overcoming, God would use the prison as a platform for Joseph's advancement once again.

What is the greatest tool God gives the believer to overcome adversity? How is the believer to overcome adversity today?

B. The Lord's Mastery (v. 22)

22. And the keeper of the prison committed to Joseph's hand all the prisoners that were in the prison; and whatsoever they did there, he was the doer of it.

Joseph was given the same position in prison that he had been given in Potiphar's house (v. 6). The function was the same, but the format was different. God had given abilities of leadership to Joseph. He was a gifted administrator. God had told him through dreams that he would be a great administrator. God made him the chief manager of Potiphar's household and possessions. Now, God made him the steward of all the prison. In the future, God would make Joseph the supervisor of all the affairs of the Pharaoh of Egypt. God's gifts operated through him, regardless of circumstances.

What would you rather have— the gifts of God working in your life, or the circumstances of life creating a life for you? The answer is obvious—the gifts of God. But we so often rely on circumstances. We think we can only function if conditions are just right. Who would suspect that a prison would be a place for gifts of administration to operate? Nevertheless, God used

Joseph mightily in prison. The gifts of God are not dictated by circumstances. Circumstances, no matter what they are, are always used by God as the tools for His will to be fulfilled in our lives. The circumstances may not be God's will, but they are always tools that He can use through us (see Romans 8:28).

C. The Lord's Ministry (v. 23)

23. The keeper of the prison looked not to any thing that was under his hand; because the Lord was with him, and that which he did, the Lord made it to prosper.

The Lord's ministry not only applied to Joseph but also to the keeper of the prison. Potiphar prospered because of God's blessings on Joseph. The prison keeper was prospering, and Pharaoh would eventually prosper. The ministry of the Lord through Joseph meant blessings for those around him.

The power of those who are faithful despite adversity is that blessing eventually comes, not only to them, but to those around them. This secondary blessing is a reason to remain faithful. Not only is our life at stake but the lives of others as well. They are responsible for their own lives; however, there are blessings God intends for them that will only come if we remain faithful. Adversity is not only a threat to us but also to those who may be around us.

Credit for good things happening to the prison keeper was not Joseph's but the Lord's. Critically, the text makes the point that the story is not about a great man named Joseph but about the God of Joseph.

Is adversity certain to come

upon believers today?

III. DELIVERED FROM ADVERSITY (Genesis 41:38-46)

A. Spirit Indwelling (vv. 38-40)

(Genesis 41:39, 40 is not included in the printed text.)

38. And Pharaoh said unto his servants, Can we find such a one as this is, a man in whom the Spirit of God is?

Finally, the witness of God through Joseph reached Pharaoh. Through all the adversity that Joseph endured, his testimony of the Lord was held in the balance. At stake was whether or not He would be glorified through Joseph. A great witness and testimony of God's greatness was at stake. God gained tremendous glory because of the faithfulness of Joseph in the midst of adversity.

The Spirit of the Lord was the source of Joseph's faithfulness. The Spirit's work was ultimately revealed to Pharaoh through Joseph's interpretation of Pharaoh's dreams (vv. 1-37). The work of the Holy Spirit is the key for the believer in the midst of adversity. Pharaoh bore witness to the work of God's Spirit, as indicated in verse 38. The Holy Spirit gave Joseph what he needed all through his experiences. God's presence was manifested through the presence of the Spirit. The Lord was with Joseph and was working through him by the Holy Spirit. The declaration of the Pharaoh was a forerunner of the unfolding witness of the work of the Holy Spirit in the Old Testament.

B. Set Over Others (vv. 41, 42)

41. And Pharaoh said unto

Joseph, See, I have set thee over all the land of Egypt.

42. And Pharaoh took off his ring from his hand, and put it upon Joseph's hand, and arrayed him in vestures of fine linen, and put a gold chain about his neck.

God restored aspects of Joseph's life that had previously been promised, fulfilled, and then taken away. When Joseph was a youth, God had revealed to him in a dream that he would rule over others. Joseph saw the dream partially fulfilled when he was in Potiphar's house. Then the fulfillment of God's promise was seemingly taken away by adversity. Ultimately, God restored and even brought greater fulfillment of what He had revealed to Joseph. Joseph now was placed over all the subjects and possessions of the Pharaoh in Egypt. Giving Joseph authority had been at the heart of God's plan from the beginning. Adversity appeared to take that away, but amazingly the Almighty God actually used adversity to accomplish what He had intended for Joseph all along.

C. Secure From Harm (vv. 43-46)

(Genesis 41:44-46 is not included in the printed text.)

43. And he made him to ride in the second chariot which he had; and they cried before him, Bow the knee: and he made him ruler over all the land of Egypt.

Joseph rode in Pharaoh's chariot, secure from all harm. He ruled over the subjects of the realm who once threatened to harm him. This image of a secure and strong Joseph is the picture of the believer today. The believer is not threatened by adversity. Rather, like Joseph, adversity is merely the tool

God uses to ensure greater security for eternal victory over evildoers and Satan himself.

The greatest danger facing the believer is that in the midst of adversity, one might leave the presence of a merciful God. God was always the center of Joseph's life. God brought Joseph through each diversity and made him prosper. It was not Joseph's ability or a stroke of good fortune. He was not just a good man making the best out of a bad situation. Joseph prospered over adversity because he never gave up on what God was doing in His life. Likewise, in the midst of our adversity, no matter what may be taken away, we do not have to let go of the presence of a faithful, Almighty God. God is awesome—more awesome than any adversity.

REVIEW QUESTIONS

1. Are believers immune from adversity? Explain.

2. How did adversity enter into Joseph's life?

3. What did the Lord use to aid Joseph in the midst of his adversity?

4. Was the prosperity brought to Potiphar and Pharaoh because of their kind treatment to Joseph? Why, or why not?

5. What different kinds of adversity did Joseph endure during his lifetime?

GOLDEN TEXT HOMILY

"WE KNOW THAT ALL THINGS WORK TOGETHER FOR GOOD TO THEM THAT LOVE GOD, TO THEM WHO ARE THE CALLED ACCORDING TO HIS PURPOSE" (Romans 8:28).

This is a remarkable statement

for the apostle Paul to make, especially when we consider how much he suffered because of his love for God and His truth. He had been imprisoned, stoned, beaten with stripes, and yet after all of this he could say, "All things work together for good to them that love God." It is imperative for Christians to have faith in the character of God, not in the circumstances.

God is a loving heavenly Father who only does what is best for His children. We, His children, must believe this fact.

There is a purpose in all things. God allows things to happen in our life to lift us from indifference. We must strive to learn to avoid murmuring by remembering that even unfavorable circumstances are intended by God to work out His highest goal in our lives. We must believe and accept the fact that as Christians, we will profit sooner or later from God's providential dealings. We can look forward to the day when we can look back to the path where God has led us and realize in a beautiful way that God did all things well.

Many Christians, with feelings of deep humility and gratitude, acknowledge that they never had serious thoughts of eternity and never really knew the greatness of the love of Christ until the day adversity came into their lives.

Let us thank God for the discipline of trial, because our trials have often proved to be our greatest blessings.—**O.W. Polen, D.D., Coordinator of Special Projects, Pathway Press, Cleveland, Tennessee**

SENTENCE SERMONS

IN HIS PERFECT TIME, God delivers those who wait on Him.
                              —Selected

THE HOLY SPIRIT can use adversity to draw sinners to Christ.
                              —Selected

ILLUMINATING THE LESSON

Horatio G. Spafford, a successful Chicago lawyer, lost most of his wealth in the financial crisis of 1873. He sent his wife and four daughters on a trip to France, but on their way, their ship was struck by another, and sank. Of 225 passengers, only 87 survived.

Mrs. Spafford was among the survivors, but the four daughters perished. As soon as she reached land, she telegraphed to her husband: "Saved alone."

Spafford left for France to join his wife and return her to Chicago. In the depth of this bereavement, he wrote his only hymn, "It Is Well With My Soul." Perhaps the words of the first stanza will take on new meaning for you, as you ponder them:

When peace, like a river, attendeth my way,
When sorrows like sea billows roll;
Whatever my lot,
Thou hast taught me to say,
It is well, it is well with my soul.
From *Plus Magazine*, Vol. 45:6, July/August 1994

DAILY BIBLE READINGS

M. Commitment in Adversity.
    Ruth 1:3-5, 10-17
T. Strength in Adversity.
    1 Samuel 26:5-11
W. Hope in Adversity.
    Job 13:15-18
T. Victory in Adversity.
    Romans 8:35-39
F. Grace in Adversity.
    2 Corinthians 12:7-10
S. Wisdom in Adversity.
    James 1:2-5

A Lesson in Forgiveness

Study Text: Genesis 45:1-15; 50:15-21

Objective: To learn that forgiveness is consistent with God's will and forgive those who have wronged us.

Time: The Book of Genesis was written between 1450 and 1400 B.C.

Place: The general belief is that Moses received this revelation while on Mount Sinai in the wilderness.

Golden Text: "But as for you, ye thought evil against me; but God meant it unto good, to bring to pass, as it is this day, to save much people alive" (Genesis 50:20).

Central Truth: Forgiveness removes barriers to reconciliation and restoration.

Evangelism Emphasis: God forgives all who confess their sins to Him.

PRINTED TEXT

Genesis 45:1. Then Joseph could not refrain himself before all them that stood by him; and he cried, Cause every man to go out from me. And there stood no man with him, while Joseph made himself known unto his brethren.

8. So now it was not you that sent me hither, but God: and he hath made me a father to Pharaoh, and lord of all his house, and a ruler throughout all the land of Egypt.

9. Haste ye, and go up to my father, and say unto him, Thus saith thy son Joseph, God hath made me lord of all Egypt: come down unto me, tarry not:

10. And thou shalt dwell in the land of Goshen, and thou shalt be near unto me, thou, and thy children, and thy children's children, and thy flocks, and thy herds, and all that thou hast:

11. And there will I nourish thee; for yet there are five years of famine; lest thou, and thy household, and all that thou hast, come to poverty.

12. And, behold, your eyes see, and the eyes of my brother Benjamin, that it is my mouth that speaketh unto you.

13. And ye shall tell my father of all my glory in Egypt, and of all that ye have seen; and ye shall haste and bring down my father hither.

14. And he fell upon his brother Benjamin's neck, and wept; and Benjamin wept upon his neck.

50:15. And when Joseph's brethren saw that their father was dead, they said, Joseph will peradventure hate us, and will certainly requite us all the evil which we did unto him.

16. And they sent a messenger unto Joseph, saying, Thy father did command before he died, saying,

17. So shall ye say unto Joseph, Forgive, I pray thee now, the trespass of thy brethren, and their sin; for they did unto thee evil: and now, we pray thee, forgive the trespass of the servants of the God of thy father. And Joseph wept when they spake unto him.

18. And his brethren also went and fell down before his face; and they said, Behold, we be thy servants.

19. And Joseph said unto them, Fear not: for am I in the place of God?

20. But as for you, ye thought evil against me; but God meant it unto good, to bring to pass, as it is this day, to save much people alive.

21. Now therefore fear ye not: I will nourish you, and your little ones. And he comforted them, and spake kindly unto them.

DICTIONARY

Pharaoh (FAY-row)—Genesis 45:8—The title given to the king of Egypt.

Goshen (GO-shen)—Genesis 45:10—A very fertile area in the Nile delta of Egypt, where Joseph's family settled.

LESSON OUTLINE

I. WILLING TO FORGIVE
    A. The Privacy of Forgiveness
    B. The Pain of Forgiveness
    C. The Presence of Forgiveness

II. RESTORING RELATIONSHIPS
    A. God's Restorative Action
    B. God's Responding Blessing
    C. God's Reconciling Bond

III. SEEING GOD'S PROVIDENCE
    A. Humanity's Pitiful Attempts
    B. God's Powerful Response
    C. Seeing Peace at the End

LESSON EXPOSITION

INTRODUCTION

The power of forgiveness is at the heart of the gospel. A forgiving God forgave a sinning world so that forgiven men might live lives of repentance before others. The saving relationship between God and man begins with forgiveness and is maintained by the forgiving spirit of the believer. Without forgiveness, the flow of God's mercy stops and an individual loses favor with God.

Joseph is one of the best examples of the power of forgiveness. Being the second highest ruler of all Egypt, he was a powerful man and could have had anything he wanted. When he was mistreated by his brothers, Joseph's life was threatened; so he could have demanded the lives of his brothers because of their cruelty to him. However, Joseph exercised the power of forgiveness and became a mighty witness of God's mercy.

When the believer is confronted with the option of forgiving or retaliating, more than a choice is at stake. The forgiveness that God has extended to the believer is ready to flow through that believer. The recipient of forgiveness is a candidate for grace and mercy. The believer is sustained by the exercise of forgiveness. Forgiveness is not an option, or an opportunity; it is an obligation, if we are to remain obedient to a loving God.

I. WILLING TO FORGIVE
(Genesis 45:1-5)

A. The Privacy of Forgiveness (v. 1)

1. Then Joseph could not refrain himself before all them that stood by him; and he cried, Cause every man to go out from me. And there stood no man with him, while Joseph made himself known unto his brethren.

Joseph finally met his brethren who had been cruel to him and had tried to kill him. Joseph had endured great testing because of them. He could have become bitter toward them. Joseph, however, resisted bitterness and turned toward forgiveness.

Joseph requested a private audience because the issues concerned him and his brethren alone. Joseph was ready to forgive his brothers, but he knew that forgiveness was a private matter; it concerned only the individuals involved in the offense. His brothers had violated him, and no one else could bring to pass what had to take place between them. No one else could do what Joseph had to do, and no one else needed to receive what he knew he had to give.

The temptation for the believer is to avoid the direct nature of forgiveness. Essentially, an offense involves people, not circumstances, issues, or philosophies. Forgiveness is a people task. Therefore, just as Joseph asked for a private time with those who had been cruel to him, so must the believer deal with relationships in order to reach the reality of true forgiveness.

What reasons might Joseph have had for not forgiving his brothers? What is the Christian's response in the face of cruelty?

B. The Pain of Forgiveness (v. 2)

(Genesis 45:2 is not included in the printed text.)

Joseph was not without pain and agony as he faced the demands of forgiving his brethren. He was crying. His tears represented all the years of testing, separation, and trial he had endured because of the cruelty of his brothers. More than anything, however, Joseph was feeling the pain of love for his brothers. He loved them greatly. To forgive, the believer must yearn for the restoration of relationships to dominate one's spirit. It is the longing for relationship that allows the flow of forgiveness to be applied to others.

C. The Presence of Forgiveness (vv. 3-5)

(Genesis 45:3-5 is not included in the printed text.)

Verse 3 brings many of the dynamics of forgiveness into full view. "They were troubled at his presence." The word *presence* reveals that forgiveness is a matter of people. The fact is that Joseph's brothers had to deal with Joseph himself, not a memory, a law, or an explanation. The reality that they were facing Joseph himself made the occasion troubling for them.

Forgiveness requires us to deal with the very people that we need forgiveness from, or that we must forgive. The greatest reality about the dynamics of forgiveness is that God brings those individuals together who need to experience forgiveness between each other. Though the presence of Joseph was troubling, he assured his brothers that God had brought them together (v. 5), and that there was an ultimate purpose for their being with each other.

Can forgiveness be painful at times? How painful was it for Joseph to forgive his brothers? What was the response of his brothers to the grief that Joseph was experiencing?

II. RESTORING RELATIONSHIPS (Genesis 45:6-15)

A. God's Restorative Action (vv. 6-8)

(Genesis 45:6, 7 is not included in the printed text.)

8. So now it was not you that sent me hither, but God: and he hath made me a father to Pharaoh, and lord of all his house, and a ruler throughout all the land of Egypt.

Forgiveness restores relationships, beginning with one's relationship with God. God initiated the action that made possible Joseph's

forgiveness of his brothers. God spared Joseph's life and made him to prosper. God's action in Joseph's life made forgiveness of his brothers possible. If Joseph had relied on his own action to forgive his brothers, he may have found an excuse. But, in light of God's abundant work in his life, there was no excuse for not forgiving his brothers.

B. God's Responding Blessing (vv. 9-11)

9. Haste ye, and go up to my father, and say unto him, Thus saith thy son Joseph, God hath made me lord of all Egypt: come down unto me, tarry not:

10. And thou shalt dwell in the land of Goshen, and thou shalt be near unto me, thou, and thy children, and thy children's children, and thy flocks, and thy herds, and all that thou hast:

11. And there will I nourish thee; for yet there are five years of famine; lest thou, and thy household, and all that thou hast, come to poverty.

Forgiveness also led to restoration between Joseph and his father. Again, the basis of restoration was what God had done in Joseph's life, which made it possible for him to now appeal to his father.

Joseph's restoration appeal to his father and the rest of his family was a blessed one. First, God had blessed Joseph so that he might bless others. Second, the blessing that Joseph was offering was abundant. Joseph would place his father and his brothers' families in one of the most fertile regions of Egypt and the entire world—the land of Goshen. There they would be able to feed their flocks and be well-fed themselves. Third, the restoration was a protection from harm. There were still five years of famine left. The restoration of Joseph would remove those families from the perils of the famine.

How did Joseph demonstrate forgiveness and reconciliation? How do we know as believers when our forgiveness has reached further to the level of reconciliation?

C. God's Reconciling Bond
(vv. 12-15)

(Genesis 45:15 is not included in the printed text.)

12. And, behold, your eyes see, and the eyes of my brother Benjamin, that it is my mouth that speaketh unto you.

13. And ye shall tell my father of all my glory in Egypt, and of all that ye have seen; and ye shall haste and bring down my father hither.

14. And he fell upon his brother Benjamin's neck, and wept; and Benjamin wept upon his neck.

Restoration led to a deep renewal of love between Joseph and his family. The bond was special between Joseph and Benjamin, for they were both sons of Rachel. They were close brothers before all of the calamity befell Joseph. Once again, they were united as brothers who deeply loved each other.

The bond was made possible by the forgiving and reconciling spirit of Joseph. If Joseph had been bitter or angry, there may have never been the chance for renewal of fellowship and love. It was impossible for Joseph to predict his reactions

and especially the reactions of some of the brothers. Nevertheless, forgiveness assuredly paved the way for a response of reconciling love.

III. SEEING GOD'S PROVIDENCE (Genesis 50:15-21)
A. Humanity's Pitiful Attempts (vv. 15-18)

15. And when Joseph's brethren saw that their father was dead, they said, Joseph will peradventure hate us, and will certainly requite us all the evil which we did unto him.

16. And they sent a messenger unto Joseph, saying, Thy father did command before he died, saying,

17. So shall ye say unto Joseph, Forgive, I pray thee now, the trespass of thy brethren, and their sin; for they did unto thee evil: and now, we pray thee, forgive the trespass of the servants of the God of thy father. And Joseph wept when they spake unto him.

18. And his brethren also went and fell down before his face; and they said, Behold, we be thy servants.

The strongest forgiveness places the matter in God's hand. Joseph's brothers thought that Joseph was the key to the forgiveness that they had enjoyed. On the contrary, Joseph tried to tell them that God was the One responsible for his ability to forgive them. The brothers thought that Joseph only forgave them because of their father. They would still find out that true forgiveness comes from God.

When their father died, Joseph's brothers thought Joseph would kill them. They thought Joseph's forgiveness was based on Joseph's love for his father. In fact, Joseph's forgiveness was based on God's love and work in his own life.

Joseph's initial response was one of grief. He was grieved not only about his father's death but the fact that his brothers would respond in such a way. He could sense their fearfulness and he wept.

What was the source of power for Joseph's forgiveness? What was Joseph's initial reaction to his brothers' questioning of his forgiveness?

B. God's Powerful Response
   (vv. 19, 20)
   19. And Joseph said unto them, Fear not: for am I in the place of God?
   20. But as for you, ye thought evil against me; but God meant it unto good, to bring to pass, as it is this day, to save much people alive.

Joseph's immediate confession was of his dependence on God. He said that he was not God, thereby implying that judgment and vengeance belong to God who is the author of true forgiveness. The forgiveness he gave them was in God's hands. They were accountable to God, and God had forgiven them. Joseph's response was that he could do no less; he had already forgiven them. The strength of his forgiveness was the strength that God had given him.

Sensing that they were worried about their own condition, Joseph reminded them of a powerful principle. The forgiveness that they had received could not even be deterred by their wickedness. God's love and

action had superseded even their wickedness. God's work reversed the evil of their work.

Forgiveness for the believer turns the evil that someone may do to us and brings God's will to pass. God had already worked in Joseph's behalf. What Joseph's brothers had intended for evil, the Lord had turned into the good of His own will. When Joseph forgave his brothers, he was working in line with what God was doing. God's reversal of evil worked through Joseph to give a blessing instead of a cursing for his entire family.

C. Seeing Peace at the End (v. 21)
   21. Now therefore fear ye not: I will nourish you, and your little ones. And he comforted them, and spake kindly unto them.

The power of forgiveness comes from the care of God. God cares for every one of us. Therefore, we should not be threatened by those who need our forgiveness or those who have forgiven us. Forgiving is a spiritual act, rooted in faith.

Joseph reassured his brothers to believe and know that they did not have to fear. Joseph allowed the work that God had done in his own life to be transferred to his brothers through continued forgiveness. Joseph had not only been made successful by God, but he had also been comforted many times by the Lord. In the deep pit in the wilderness and in Pharaoh's prison, the comfort of the Lord had taught him how to minister comfort to his brothers.

Faith to forgive is the lesson of Joseph to us today. He exercised faith for many things throughout his eventful life. Later in life, that faith moved him to forgiveness.

Perhaps the real fiber of our faith is not known until we are required to forgive.

REVIEW QUESTIONS

1. Are there times when the believer is not required to forgive?

2. How easy is it to forgive someone?

3. What is the relationship between forgiveness and reconciliation?

4. How did Joseph's brothers misinterpret his forgiveness?

5. What is the relationship between forgiveness and faith?

GOLDEN TEXT HOMILY

"BUT AS FOR YOU, YE THOUGHT EVIL AGAINST ME; BUT GOD MEANT IT UNTO GOOD, TO BRING TO PASS, AS IT IS THIS DAY, TO SAVE MUCH PEOPLE ALIVE" (Genesis 50:20).

If ever a person had the right to hold a grudge against anyone, Joseph was that person. After the way his brothers had treated him, he would have been justified in not helping them when they were in need—at least that is the way most people would think. Children of God do not think in terms of getting even with their enemies, however—only of forgiving them. Joseph is a perfect example of one who showed the love of God toward his enemies.

We cannot be Christian and not forgive our fellowman, regardless of the offense. Human forgiveness and divine forgiveness are inextricably combined. Our forgiveness of our fellowman and God's forgiveness of us cannot be separated. In the prayer the Lord taught His disciples, He said, "Forgive us our debts, as we forgive our debtors" (Matthew 6:12). The literal meaning is, "Forgive us our sins in proportion as we forgive those who have sinned against us."

We must learn to forgive and to forget. When God forgave us of our sins, He put them away forever, never to be brought against us again. This is what is meant in Christian forgiveness. When we forgive, we are never to bring up the offense again.

Christian love, *agape*, is that unconquerable benevolence, that undefeatable goodwill, which will never seek anything but the highest good of others—no matter what they do to us, and no matter how they treat us. That love can come to us only when Christ, who is love, comes to dwell within our hearts. To be forgiven, we must forgive. That is a condition of forgiveness that only the power of Christ can enable us to fulfill.—**Excerpts from the *Evangelical Commentary*, Vol. 28**

SENTENCE SERMONS

FORGIVENESS removes barriers to reconciliation and restoration.

—Selected

GOD FORGIVES all who confess their sins to Him.

—Selected

IF YOU ARE SUFFERING from a bad man's injustice, forgive him lest there be two bad men.

—Augustine

NEVER DOES a person stand so tall as when he forgives revenge, and dares to forgive an injury.

—J. Harold Smith

EVANGELISM APPLICATION

GOD FORGIVES ALL WHO CONFESS THEIR SINS TO HIM.

The power of God's forgiveness is without comparison. God's ability to forgive is greater than the sin of any sinner. God's love to forgive is able to overcome the greatest of evils. God's mercy to forgive endures beyond all the power of the Enemy.

If a person genuinely repents and asks for forgiveness, God's mercy is so far-reaching that He will indeed forgive that person, regardless of who it is or the circumstances. All who confess their sins to Him will receive forgiveness (1 John 1:9).

God's forgiveness is rooted in His own deity and power. The repentance of the sinner does not produce forgiveness. God's forgiveness stems from the action of His own heart and will. The divine nature of God's forgiveness means that no one can counterfeit or manipulate His forgiveness. He forgives, as He wills, unaffected by the imperfections of individuals. God's choosing and His divine person assures every repentant sinner of forgiveness.

ILLUMINATING THE LESSON

A powerful illustration of forgiveness is how Louis XII of France treated his enemies after he ascended to the throne. Before coming to power, he had been cast into prison and kept in chains. Later when he did become king, he was urged to seek revenge, but he refused. Instead, he prepared a scroll on which he listed all who had perpetrated crimes against him. Behind every man's name he placed a cross in red ink. When the guilty heard about this, they feared for their lives and fled. Then the king explained, "The cross which I drew beside each name was not a sign of punishment, but a pledge of forgiveness extended for the sake of the crucified Savior, who upon His Cross forgave His enemies and prayed for them."—**From _Parsons Illustrator_**

DAILY BIBLE READINGS

M. Fruit of Forgiveness.
  2 Samuel 9:1-7
T. Blessings of Forgiveness.
  Psalm 32:1-5
W. Offer of Forgiveness.
  Psalm 86:1-7
T. Unlimited Forgiveness.
  Luke 7:44-50
F. None Righteous.
  Romans 3:21-25
S. Forgiveness Provided.
  1 John 1:5 through 2:2

The Day of Pentecost

Study Text: Deuteronomy 16:9-12; Acts 2:1-39

Objective: To understand the Holy Spirit was at work in Bible times and appreciate that He is working in the world today.

Time: The Book of Acts was probably written in A.D. 63. The events recorded in today's lesson occurred in A.D. 30.

Place: The Book of Acts was written at Jerusalem.

Golden Text: "The promise is unto you, and to your children, and to all that are afar off, even as many as the Lord our God shall call" (Acts 2:39).

Central Truth: God's plan is that all believers be filled with the Holy Spirit.

Evangelism Emphasis: The Holy Spirit makes us effective witnesses for Christ.

PRINTED TEXT

Acts 2:1. And when the day of Pentecost was fully come, they were all with one accord in one place.

2. And suddenly there came a sound from heaven as of a rushing mighty wind, and it filled all the house where they were sitting.

3. And there appeared unto them cloven tongues like as of fire, and it sat upon each of them.

4. And they were all filled with the Holy Ghost, and began to speak with other tongues, as the Spirit gave them utterance.

5. And there were dwelling at Jerusalem Jews, devout men, out of every nation under heaven.

6. Now when this was noised abroad, the multitude came together, and were confounded, because that every man heard them speak in his own language.

7. And they were all amazed and marvelled, saying one to another, Behold, are not all these which speak Galilaeans?

8. And how hear we every man in our own tongue, wherein we were born?

12. And they were all amazed, and were in doubt, saying one to another, What meaneth this?

13. Others mocking said, These men are full of new wine.

14. But Peter, standing up with the eleven, lifted up his voice, and said unto them, Ye men of Judaea, and all ye that dwell at Jerusalem, be this known unto you, and hearken to my words:

15. For these are not drunken, as ye suppose, seeing it is but the third hour of the day.

16. But this is that which was spoken by the prophet Joel;

17. And it shall come to pass in the last days, saith God, I

will pour out of my Spirit upon all flesh: and your sons and your daughters shall prophesy, and your young men shall see visions, and your old men shall dream dreams:

18. And on my servants and on my handmaidens I will pour out in those days of my Spirit; and they shall prophesy:

37. Now when they heard this, they were pricked in their heart, and said unto Peter and to the rest of the apostles, Men and brethren, what shall we do?

38. Then Peter said unto them, Repent, and be baptized every one of you in the name of Jesus Christ for the remission of sins, and ye shall receive the gift of the Holy Ghost.

39. For the promise is unto you, and to your children, and to all that are afar off, even as many as the Lord our God shall call.

LESSON OUTLINE

I. MEANING OF PENTECOST
   A. A Time of God's Harvest Blessings
   B. A Time of Unity Before God
   C. A Time of Remembering God's Deliverance

II. OUTPOURING OF THE SPIRIT
   A. The Fullness of Pentecost
   B. The Source and Overwhelming Nature of the Spirit's Work
   C. Initial Evidence of Speaking in Other Tongues
   D. Spectators at Pentecost

III. INVITATION TO RECEIVE
   A. Making a Decision About Pentecost
   B. Peter's Decision and Defense
   C. Three Prophetic Elements of Pentecost Found in Joel
   D. Reaction to the Message of Pentecost

LESSON EXPOSITION

INTRODUCTION

There are many interpretations today of what it means to be Pentecostal. The need is for Bible-based information among full-gospel believers about the meaning of the Spirit-filled life. Deuteronomy 16 and Acts 2 are two of the most definitive texts regarding Pentecost's meaning. Every Holy Ghost-baptized believer should carefully study and strive to retain the contents of these two critical passages.

The power the church received at Pentecost would launch the early believers into the world as witnesses of Christ. Luke records this powerful event in the Book of Acts. It was a time of tragedy and triumph. The church was wondering about the work of the Lord, now that He had ascended. The coming of the Spirit would answer their questions.

Christ had promised the coming of the Spirit (John 13-16; Acts 1), but they were waiting for the manifestation of that promise. The early church had heard the words of Jesus about the coming of the

Spirit. However, they still did not know the impact that event would have. It would revolutionize their witness. The flame of Pentecost would fan the hearts of multitudes.

Baptism in the Spirit would be an experience distinct from their initial believing in Christ. This lesson will look at the important elements of the baptism in the Holy Spirit. Portions of today's lesson text point out the distinctiveness of the experience, and we will compare it to conversion. The disciples who were baptized in the Holy Spirit were already believers (1:15). They had already been baptized in water, for how could Peter tell them to be baptized in water (v. 38) if he himself had not been? (See also 8:14-17). Thus, the baptism in the Holy Spirit is distinct from both conversion and water baptism.

When the baptism in the Holy Spirit first occurred, it was misunderstood and doubted. Many people surrounded the place where the disciples were. The crowd was aware that something unusual was happening to the disciples, but what did it all mean? There were some who doubted.

In the midst of the profound experience the disciples were having, despite the confusion and skepticism of the crowd, there was a powerful witness of Christ that day. The testimony and preached word were so powerful that there was a great harvest of souls.

How important is the message of Pentecost today? Were those who received the Baptism in Acts 2 and later passages already believers? Explain.

I. MEANING OF PENTECOST
(Deuteronomy 16:9-12)

A. A Time of God's Harvest Blessings (vv. 9, 10)

(Deuteronomy 16:9, 10 is not included in the printed text.)

Deuteronomy 16:9-15 is a review of the observance of Pentecost in the Old Testament. Instructions for this festival or feast were also given in Exodus 34:22, Leviticus 23:15-21, and Numbers 28:26-31. The observance was to be held on the day following seven full weeks from Passover. *Pentecost* means "fiftieth day," signifying 50 days after Passover.

Certain marks of significance were established by God regarding Pentecost. The first series of these related to the harvest of God. On the calendar, the celebration fell midway between the time of planting and the final harvest. There may already have been some early or firstfruits, but the end of the harvest had not yet come. Three things about the harvest were connected with Pentecost. First, the certainty of the harvest is signified in the reference to the sickle. Second, the personal nature of coming before God for oneself is reflected in the reference to a "freewill-offering of thine own hand." Third, the reason for praising God at Pentecost is explained in the reference to offerings of praise "according as the Lord thy God hath blessed thee."

B. A Time of Unity Before God (v. 11)

(Deuteronomy 16:11 is not included in the printed text.)

Unity among the people of God was a major factor in the celebration of Pentecost. Everyone was to come with family members and others, including "the stranger, and the fatherless, and the widow." They were to be in unity before God. This would have its complete fulfillment in Pentecost in the New Testament.

C. A Time of Remembering God's
   Deliverance (v. 12)

(Deuteronomy 16:12 is not included in the printed text.)

Underlying the celebration of Pentecost was the remembrance of deliverance. Gratefully and mindfully, the people preserved the memory of bondage-breaking. Pentecost was linked to Passover. Passover was the event which broke the bondage of Egypt. Pentecost was possible only because of the Passover. Without the provision of Passover there would have been no Pentecost. If the remembrance of where God had brought them from ever left their celebration, the legitimacy of their praises would be gone. They would still be slaves, singing in fetters—the chains of negligent ungratefulness.

II. OUTPOURING OF THE SPIRIT
    (Acts 2:1-8)

A. The Fullness of Pentecost (v. 1)

1. And when the day of Pentecost was fully come, they were all with one accord in one place.

The principles for Pentecost given by God in Deuteronomy 16 are fully realized on the Day of Pentecost in Acts 2. The fullness of Pentecost was established in the action of God himself that day. Since that day, God has continued to work through the Holy Spirit. Peter would declare in Acts 2 that the power of

Pentecost was in God's pouring out His Spirit on all flesh. The harvest, unity, and deliverance of Pentecost fully came in the Upper Room on the Day of Pentecost. It continues today.

The unity of the people was an important aspect of Pentecost. It is marked by the phrases, "one accord" and "one place." They had been with the Lord as He exhorted them about unity and love. Now they were fulfilling this command by banding together. They were a unit seeking the Lord. They were not scattered individuals seeking mere personal reward or success. Rather, they were concerned about others as well as themselves. Their desire was that God fully bless the whole group.

How does God prepare circumstances so the hearts of individuals may receive the Spirit?

B. The Source and Overwhelming
   Nature of the Spirit's Work
   (vv. 2, 3)

2. And suddenly there came a sound from heaven as of a rushing mighty wind, and it filled all the house where they were sitting.

3. And there appeared unto them cloven tongues like as of fire, and it sat upon each of them.

Luke's emphasis is on the source of the happenings on the Day of Pentecost. The power manifested in the lives of the disciples and believers gathered there came from God. Verse 2 says that the physical manifestations which occurred came from heaven. The personal manifestations in verse 4 came from the

Holy Spirit. These were from God, not man. The events and experiences could not be explained by nature. The baptism in the Holy Spirit and the manifestations which accompanied it were from God.

Verses 2 and 3 emphasize physical manifestations which occurred. These were in two categories: those that were heard and those that were seen. A sound like a mighty wind occurred. A sight of cloven tongues like fire appeared. These were visible and audible manifestations of God's power. They signified that God was doing something powerful in their midst. It was a sign to them that God was indeed present and moving in their midst.

God is still performing signs and wonders today. Miracles occur which affect the surroundings and personal lives of individuals. These have not ceased. When they occur, they draw the attention and focus of people to the power and glory of the Lord.

The first emphasis in verses 2 and 3 is on the source of the sound—it came from heaven. This continues to be emphasized throughout the description. That which occurred came from heaven. This is first and foremost: These manifestations were divine in origin.

Second, verse 2 describes the sound. The description involves a comparison. Luke does not say directly what the sound was. He merely says what it was like. The sound was similar to what one would hear from a "rushing, mighty, wind." Wind is a symbol for the Spirit. The term *wind* is the idea for *spirit* in the Old Testament. The Old Testament term for *spirit* was *ruwach*, literally "wind."

The extent of the sound of the wind is also given in verse 2. It filled the entire place where they were. As they were sitting, the power and presence of the Lord filled the place. There was room for nothing else. The focus of attention was this manifestation that came from heaven. The Spirit of the Lord began to consume their thoughts and attention.

Verse 3 describes the physical manifestations they saw. There were "cloven tongues like as of fire" (v. 3). *Cloven* comes from a term which means "divided" or "separated." Just as flames divide and flicker when they burn, these tongues divided and flickered. What they saw was comparable to fire, according to Luke. The extent of the manifestation was that it came to all of them.

What is the most important aspect of the physical manifestations in Acts 2:1-3? What does the idea regarding the source signify about the manifestations? What was the extent of these manifestations?

C. Initial Evidence of Speaking in Other Tongues (v. 4)

4. And they were all filled with the Holy Ghost, and began to speak with other tongues, as the Spirit gave them utterance.

The description moves from outward, observable manifestations inward, to personal manifestations. The outward manifestations could be heard and seen. Now the emphasis changes to what happened personally to the disciples. "And they" (v. 4) signifies that the attention is now on the infilling of those gathered in the upper room. The room had been filled with a mighty sound and wondrous sight; now they themselves would be filled. They had been amazed by what they had heard and seen. Now they themselves would personally encounter the Spirit of God.

The emphasis in verse 4 is on what they actually experienced as a result of the work of the Spirit. What occurred in this experience could be seen and heard. They spoke "with other tongues, as the Spirit gave them utterance." This speaking could be seen and heard. The speaking was the initial sign that what they were experiencing was the baptism in the Spirit.

The source of the personal manifestation is mentioned last, while the description of the physical manifestations comes first. This is opposite the order given in verse 2. However, this does not minimize the source. Rather, it draws attention to it in a different way. The source of their personal experience is significant.

This personal experience—the infilling with the Holy Spirit—came to all present. They had all participated in the unity and worship. They were all humbly and obediently waiting upon the Lord. As a result, the experience came to all of them.

The term *filled* is important. It identifies the particular experience they received. The experience—as a baptism—involved them completely. They were not divided or fragmented. They were fully involved and enraptured by the experience. Their emotions, minds, and behavior were completely focused on and filled by the experience.

The description of the experience

places significance on the phrase, "and began to speak with other tongues." This, the only description of their intense, personal experience, distinctly focuses on what happened to them. There are many other benefits such as inner peace, spiritual insight, and power to witness for Christ; however, none of these are mentioned. The aspect of speaking in other tongues is mentioned exclusively because it becomes the distinctive sign of receiving the baptism in the Holy Spirit.

The term *and*, which appears after the declaration that they were "filled," demonstrates the significance of speaking in other tongues as the initial evidence of receiving the baptism in the Holy Spirit. *And* is a "causative conjunction" in the Greek text. This indicates that the reason they knew they were filled was the fact that they spoke with "other tongues."

The same means of knowing that people had been filled with the baptism in the Holy Spirit is also given later by Peter in Acts 10:46. In that passage the believers knew that members of Cornelius' house received the baptism in the Holy Spirit "for they heard them speak with tongues."

The phrase, "other tongues," means "unknown tongues" or "unknown languages" and implies a language (or languages) unknown to the speaker, not necessarily a foreign language or language of another country or region. It could indicate a foreign language in different contexts, but in this context the focus is on the speaker. The language was simply unknown to the speaker. Whether or not the phrase implies the language of another country or region is not the point.

The fact that individuals from other countries and regions heard their own languages among the "other tongues" (v. 6) does not mean that all of the "other tongues" were languages of other countries or regions. The concern in verse 6 is with the effect on those individuals, not the languages. They were "confounded" (v. 6). The text does not limit the tongues to known languages. The purpose of the text is to demonstrate that those who were filled spoke in other tongues and those hearing the tongues were confounded.

According to verse 4, those filled with the Spirit "began to speak with other tongues, as the Spirit gave them utterance." Those filled did the speaking, but the source of the speaking was the Spirit. They spoke, but the utterance came from the Spirit. The fact that the Spirit of the Lord is the source of the experience is the emphasis in this description. The exact nature of the speaking or the manner in which it took place is not amplified. The fact that they spake with other tongues was the initial result of the baptism with the Spirit.

There is no indication that the baptism in the Holy Spirit is a unique experience which was to occur only here. This baptism also occurred in Acts 10 and then a number of years later in Acts 19. Speaking in unknown tongues was the criterion used to determine the authenticity of the infilling. The major emphasis of Acts 2:1-4 is that the experience is divine in origin.

What does the phrase "other tongues" mean?

D. Spectators at Pentecost (vv. 5-8)

5. And there were dwelling at Jerusalem Jews, devout men, out of every nation under heaven.

6. Now when this was noised abroad, the multitude came together, and were confounded, because that every man heard them speak in his own language.

7. And they were all amazed and marvelled, saying one to another. Behold, are not all these which speak Galilaeans?

8. And how hear we every man in our own tongue, wherein we were born?

The initial reaction of the crowd was marked by confusion. Luke said in verse 6 that they were "confounded." *Confounded* comes from the Greek term, *sugcheo*. It literally means "to be poured together or mixed." The crowd was confused as to the event that took place.

Their confusion was centered on the fact that they heard these disciples speaking in different languages. Each of them heard his own native language. Yet all knew that the disciples were Galilaeans. They were amazed that the disciples were speaking in so many different languages that could be understood by those present.

The message was about the "wonderful works of God" (v. 11). The text does not say that they heard the message of salvation in their own language. The gospel would be proclaimed later, primarily by Peter. He would proclaim it in his native language. The difference Spirit baptism made in his life was not to enable him to speak in a foreign language. The difference was empowerment; he was now empowered by the infilling of the Spirit.

III. INVITATION TO RECEIVE
   (Acts 2:12-18; 37-39)

A. Making a Decision About
   Pentecost (vv. 12, 13)

12. And they were all amazed, and were in doubt, saying one to another, What meaneth this?

13. Others mocking said, These men are full of new wine.

On the Day of Pentecost everyone who came into contact with those in the Upper Room had to decide what they were personally going to do in response to the blessing God was pouring out. Verses 12 and 13 describe different decisions: some questioned and others mocked what God was doing. People today must decide one way or another about how they are going to respond to God's Pentecostal outpouring.

Between verses 5-11, Luke merely describes the people as being amazed at the startling manifestation of tongues and languages. The assessment by the crowd was that they heard—from persons who would not normally know their languages and dialects—the "wonderful works of God" (v. 11).

How do people react to Pentecost today? What should the reaction of the Christian be to criticism? How important is Scripture in responding to critics of Pentecost?

In verses 12 and 13 Luke mentions others in the crowd who held a different sentiment toward those experiencing the baptism in the Holy Spirit. These were the skeptical. They were not merely confounded, they "were in doubt, . . .

mocking." *Doubt* comes from a Greek term which means "to be perplexed." It represents a deeper level of anxiety than mere confusion.

Mocking is a more serious term, indicating ridicule toward another. Whereas some were confused and others were perplexed about the outpouring of the Spirit, these mockers were seriously ridiculing the experience.

These different responses mirror those of many people today toward the Pentecostal experience. Some, confused about the meaning of the experience, may be open to receiving a message which declares the wonders of the Lord. Others may have personal struggles and perhaps anxiety about accepting the message of the baptism of the Holy Spirit. Finally, some openly ridicule the experience. Peter addressed all three responses in his sermon as he stood and declared the Pentecostal message in the rest of this chapter.

B. Peter's Decision and Defense
   (14, 15)

14. But Peter, standing up with the eleven, lifted up his voice, and said unto them, Ye men of Judaea, and all ye that dwell at Jerusalem, be this known unto you, and hearken to my words:

15. For these are not drunken, as ye suppose, seeing it is but the third hour of the day.

In face of criticism of the Pentecostal outpouring, Peter stood and defended the experience. He addressed the false interpretations of the crowd. He stated that these Spirit-filled believers were not drunk. As evidence he referred to the hour of the day. The "third hour of the day" was not the time when people usually became inebriated. It was usually known as a time of religious devotion and sacrifice.

C. Three Prophetic Elements of Pentecost Found in Joel (vv. 16-18)

16. But this is that which was spoken by the prophet Joel;

17. And it shall come to pass in the last days, saith God, I will pour out of my Spirit upon all flesh: and your sons and your daughters shall prophesy, and your young men shall see visions, and your old men shall dream dreams:

18. And on my servants and on my handmaidens I will pour out in those days of my Spirit; and they shall prophesy.

The prophecy of Joel refers to three things. First, the Spirit will be abundantly poured out on the earth. It will be poured out without respect of persons. It will fall on all ages, on men and on women, and on all areas of society. The purpose of the outpouring is to proclaim and to prophesy the Word of the Lord. Prophesy here refers both to foretelling the future plan of God and to forth-telling the Word of the Lord.

Second, the prophecy foretells in verses 19 and 20 the coming end-time judgment of the Lord. The signs and wonders mentioned indicate coming judgment. This judgment will be the end-time harvest of the Lord during the tribulation, leading to the millennium and the new heaven and new earth.

The third thing in the prophecy is the message of deliverance: "Whosoever shall call on the name of the Lord shall be saved" (Acts 2:21). The Pentecostal message is meant to be a primary vehicle for the propagation of the message of deliverance and salvation.

All three elements are vital to the message of Pentecost. Any one existing by itself creates excesses of various kinds. If there is only abundant blessing, the result is mere emotional ecstasy. If there is only judgment, the tendency is toward condemnation. If deliverance only, then a sense of escapism may develop.

D. Reaction to the Message of Pentecost (vv. 37-39)

37. Now when they heard this, they were pricked in their heart, and said unto Peter and to the rest of the apostles, Men and brethren, what shall we do?

38. Then Peter said unto them, Repent, and be baptized every one of you in the name of Jesus Christ for the remission of sins, and ye shall receive the gift of the Holy Ghost.

39. For the promise is unto you, and to your children, and to all that are afar off, even as many as the Lord our God shall call.

After listening to Peter's message, the crowd responded three ways that day. First, they "heard" the message. Second, they became "pricked" in their hearts. Finally, they asked what they must do in response to the message.

The message of Pentecost must be heard. It cannot and must not be minimized or excluded. Multitudes are moved to believe upon the Lord with the same kinds of dramatic responses when the Pentecostal message is heard today.

The term *pricked* came from a Greek term which means, "to pierce or sting sharply." The word was used in ancient literature to signify painful emotion. The conviction that came as the result of the Pentecostal message moved the hearts of the crowd deeply. It was a feeling they could not ignore.

The depth of their pain moved them to ask what they must do to be saved. Peter's primary reply was that they must repent. This was an appropriate response to the crowd, and it was critically important that Peter give it. A repentant heart is necessary for salvation. At this point a new, dynamic relationship with God begins.

As a symbol of the change brought about by repentance, Peter calls for the crowd to be baptized in water "in the name of Jesus Christ." This phrase indicates that the baptism signified a confession of faith in Jesus Christ, as distinguished from other baptisms they may have taken part in before. Such a baptism was an affirmation of their repentance and commitment to Christ, not a substitute for their faith.

Peter further admonished them to "receive the gift of the Holy Ghost." He was not pronouncing that they were filled. They still had to trust the Lord for the infilling of the baptism in the Spirit. This was not a declaration that the Spirit had been conferred at water baptism. Peter issued this as a separate command because it was a separate experience. Just as the listeners had to respond in repentance and be baptized in water to receive salvation, so they had to respond in order to receive the infilling of the baptism in the Spirit.

The Pentecostal experience is real. The record of Acts 2 makes it clear that the baptism in the Holy Spirit is a distinct experience. It is marked by the initial evidence of speaking in other tongues. The power of the Holy Spirit is given for effective witnessing to the lost. Although skepticism may be strong, the Word of Pentecost must be proclaimed today.

REVIEW QUESTIONS

1. Is the Baptism in the Holy Ghost distinct from initial believing?

2. What kind of preparation must the people of God make today in preparation for the coming of the Spirit?

3. What is the significance of the physical manifestations described in Acts 2:1-3?

4. What is the initial evidence that someone is baptized in the Holy Ghost?

5. What is the connection between the Baptism in the Holy Spirit and the preaching of the gospel?

GOLDEN TEXT HOMILY

"THE PROMISE IS UNTO YOU, AND TO YOUR CHILDREN, AND TO ALL THAT ARE AFAR OFF, EVEN AS MANY AS THE LORD OUR GOD SHALL CALL" (Acts 2:39).

It is unlikely that the writer of this scripture had a full conception of just how far the scope of his statements would extend. He may have visualized "to all that are afar off" in the terms of the area of the Middle East or even of the then-known world. But there is no way that he could have fully grasped the vast sweep of the promise of this scripture.

Many times we are too small in our thinking when it comes to the promises of God. Even while we are thinking of the infinite possibilities of what God can accomplish, we are probably underestimating Him.

There is an old saying that "what the human mind can conceive, it can achieve." But God can achieve those things that the human mind can never conceive or comprehend. It is impossible to cast the promises of God in such cosmic terms that they fully explore the range of His power.

Dedication to the cause of Christ and surrender to Him will result in signs following the believer. We have that assurance from God. We only need to take hold of that promise and live for Him whether or not the signs are always visible to us.—**Excerpts from the *Evangelical Commentary*, Vol. 18**

SENTENCE SERMONS

GOD'S PLAN IS that all believers be filled with the Holy Spirit.
—Selected

THE HOLY SPIRIT makes us effective witnesses for Christ.
—Selected

HE WHO HAS the Holy Spirit in his heart and the Scriptures in his hands has all he needs.
—Alexander Maclaren

WE MUST NOT be content to be cleansed from sin; we must be filled with the Holy Spirit.
—John Fletcher

EVANGELISM APPLICATION

THE HOLY SPIRIT MAKES US EFFECTIVE WITNESSES FOR CHRIST.

The task of winning the lost is very difficult at times. People may resist the message. Frequently, it is difficult to know what to say. The circumstances may not be exactly right for sharing the gospel. It may be discouraging to think about all the obstacles we face in witnessing.

God has provided the power of the Holy Spirit to overcome all obstacles to witnessing. God gives the believer the words to say. The Spirit prepares the heart of the unbeliever. The Holy Spirit works through circumstances. The Holy Spirit provides encouragement for the child of God who witnesses.

The believer must depend upon the power of the Spirit first and foremost. The alternative is to rely on oneself. Human ability will not win souls. That is a divine task. The difficulties to overcome are greater than any human. The sharing of the gospel can only be done effectively through the empowerment of the Holy Spirit. As a result, the believer must depend upon the Spirit's help to be an effective witness.

DAILY BIBLE READINGS

M. Spirit-Filled Craftsmen.
  Exodus 31:1-6
T. Spirit-Filled Elders.
  Numbers 11:24-29
W. A Spirit-Filled King.
  2 Samuel 23:1-5
T. Spirit-Filled Believers.
  Acts 4:23-33
F. Spirit-Filled Gentiles.
  Acts 10:44-48
S. Spirit-Filled Living.
  Galatians 5:16-25

INTRODUCTION
TO SUMMER
QUARTER

The lessons for the summer quarter (June, July, August) are presented under two distinct themes: Unit One, "Messages of Minor Prophets" (lessons 1-7), and Unit Two, "Bible Answers to Current Issues" (lessons 8-13).

Unit One draws from the books of Hosea, Joel, Amos, Zechariah, Obadiah, Jonah, Nahum, Micah, Habakkuk, Haggai, and Malachi. Their messages deal with issues that are dear to the heart of God and that are ever present in our day-to-day world.

Unit Two draws from both Old and New Testament books to bring answers to current issues that press upon the human family.

The studies of this quarter are certain to challenge the most avid Bible scholar as well as the new convert as they seek to enrich their Bible knowledge and share the gospel message.

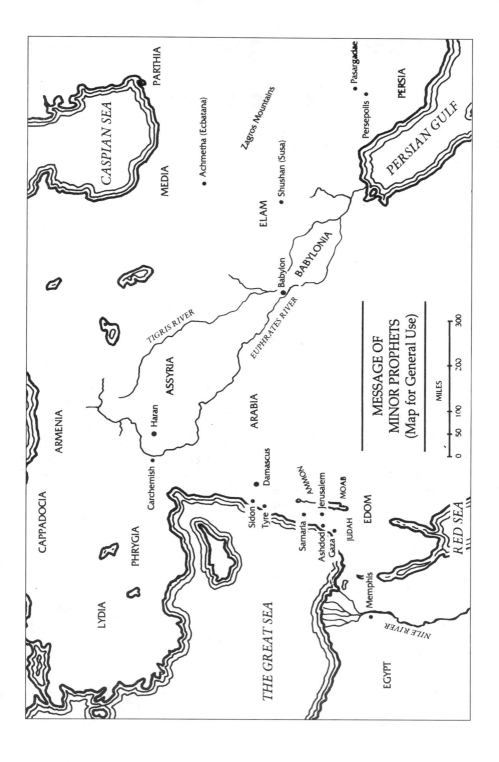

MESSAGE OF
MINOR PROPHETS
(Map for General Use)

MILES

0   50   100   200   300

Be Reconciled to God

Study Text: Hosea 4:1 through 6:11

Objective: To understand that God hates sin and strive to please Him.

Time: The Book of Hosea was written between 790 and 710 B.C.

Place: Israel (northern kingdom)

Golden Text: "Come, and let us return unto the Lord: for he hath torn, and he will heal us; he hath smitten, and he will bind us up" (Hosea 6:1).

Central Truth: God has made provision for all people to be reconciled to Him through faith in Christ.

Evangelism Emphasis: God has made provision for all people to be reconciled to Him through faith in Christ.

PRINTED TEXT

Hosea 4:1. Hear the word of the Lord, ye children of Israel: for the Lord hath a controversy with the inhabitants of the land, because there is no truth, nor mercy, nor knowledge of God in the land.

2. By swearing, and lying, and killing, and stealing, and committing adultery, they break out, and blood toucheth blood.

3. Therefore shall the land mourn, and every one that dwelleth therein shall languish, with the beasts of the field, and with the fowls of heaven; yea, the fishes of the sea also shall be taken away.

4. Yet let no man strive, nor reprove another: for thy people are as they that strive with the priest.

5. Therefore shalt thou fall in the day, and the prophet also shall fall with thee in the night, and I will destroy thy mother.

6. My people are destroyed for lack of knowledge: because thou hast rejected knowledge, I will also reject thee, that thou shalt be no priest to me: seeing thou hast forgotten the law of thy God, I will also forget thy children.

15. Though thou, Israel, play the harlot, yet let not Judah offend; and come not ye unto Gilgal, neither go ye up to Bethaven, nor swear, The Lord liveth.

16. For Israel slideth back as a backsliding heifer: now the Lord will feed them as a lamb in a large place.

17. Ephraim is joined to idols: let him alone.

18. Their drink is sour: they have committed whoredom continually: her rulers with

shame do love, Give ye.

19. The wind hath bound her up in her wings, and they shall be ashamed because of their sacrifices.

6:1. Come, and let us return unto the Lord: for he hath torn, and he will heal us; he hath smitten, and he will bind us up.

2. After two days will he revive us: in the third day he will raise us up, and we shall live in his sight.

3. Then shall we know, if we follow on to know the Lord: his going forth is prepared as the morning; and he shall come unto us as the rain, as the latter and former rain unto the earth.

DICTIONARY

Gilgal (GIL-gal)—Hosea 4:15—The first place the Israelites camped after entering the Promised Land.

Bethaven (BETH-AA-ven)—Hosea 4:15—A town in the northern mountains of the territory of Benjamin.

Ephraim (EE-fray-im)—Hosea 4:17—The dominant tribe of the northern kingdom.

LESSON OUTLINE

   I. TRUTH REJECTED

      A. God Charges Israel With Lawlessness

      B. God Points the Blame

      C. Destruction for Lack of Knowledge

  II. SHUN WICKEDNESS

      A. A Warning to Judah

      B. The Tribe of Ephraim

 III. RETURN TO THE LORD

LESSON EXPOSITION

INTRODUCTION

Hosea prophecied to the northern kingdom of Israel during the last 30 years of its existence before Samaria fell. Assyria ransacked the country in 722 B.C. and carried into captivity most of the population. During this 30 years a temporary prosperity in the land anesthetized the people to the actual danger they were in. Even though four of the six kings of the period were assassinated, the people continued to reject God and turned to idolatry more than ever.

Hosea was an unusual prophet in that his own personal life mirrored the prophecies God called him to proclaim. The first three chapters of the book bearing his name are the story of his obeying God's command to marry Gomer, a woman of less-than-reputable standing in the community. Even before marrying her, however, God warned the prophet that this wife would be unfaithful to him—that she would continue to be a prostitute. Their union would serve as a picture of God's marriage covenant with Israel and how the people had been unfaithful to God—prostituting themselves to Baal and other heathen gods.

What were Hosea's personal

feelings in the matter? Did he marry a fallen woman purely out of obedience to God's command? Or did he also genuinely love her? Did she love him? Why would God ask him to do something so painful?

We can only speculate how Hosea actually felt. He may have felt a personal reluctance to having to do something so socially unacceptable. We must remember, however, that marriages in Old Testament times were generally prearranged and were not based solely on love. With this in mind, obedience to God's unusual command would not seem so unusual. At the same time, Hosea was also putting his own reputation on the line. Marrying a harlot would certainly affect negatively how the people he was preaching to viewed him.

Another thought to ponder is the possibility that Hosea was actually attracted to Gomer's "seductive" nature. Could God have been teaching him on a personal level that the lure of illicit pleasures, like that of foreign gods, brings nothing but disappointment and pain? Man is always searching for something that will satisfy; that satisfaction comes only in a relationship with God. Anything else brings misery and disappointment. Hosea's experience mirrors what people through the ages have had to learn the hard way—the world's seductive allure ends in heartache.

Saint Augustine saw the pains he faced in life as God's being "mercifully hard upon me and besprinkling all my illicit pleasures with certain elements of bitterness, to draw me on to seek for pleasures in which no bitterness should be." (Augustine, *Confessions*, 11. 2). Hosea himself said something quite

similar: "Therefore, behold I will hedge up thy way with thorns, and make a wall, that she shall not find her paths. And she shall follow after her lovers, but she shall not overtake them; and she shall seek them, but shall not find them: then shall she say, I will go and return to my first husband; for then was it better with me than now" (Hosea 2:6, 7). In essence Hosea, like Augustine, called pain and suffering a hedge that blocks our paths to idolatry and causes us to turn back to our only source of true love.

Hosea's personal life was a reflection of Israel's prostituting themselves with foreign gods. The people did not count the cost of their actions. Instead they were captivated by the gratification of the moment. What resulted was a broken nation, a dispersed people, and ruined lives.

Whatever he felt personally about the perplexing life he was called to live, Hosea still obeyed. God often demanded extraordinary obedience from His prophets. They were assigned unusual tasks in difficult times. Hosea's noble and persistent love for his prostitute wife illustrates that his love was based on a conscious choice: he was committed to her for her sake, regardless of how she treated him. This was the same commitment God had for the people He called His own.

Gomer finally returned to Hosea—he purchased her on a slave block for a meager sum. The northern kingdom of Israel, however, seems to have been lost forever, dispersed, and intermingled with the Assyrians. Was God less faithful than Hosea? No. He restored a remnant of people through the southern kingdom from the Babylonian captivity. Also, His promises are fulfilled through Jesus Christ, and thus are extended to all mankind.

I. TRUTH REJECTED
(Hosea 4:1-6)

A. God Charges Israel With Lawlessness (vv. 1-3)

1. Hear the word of the Lord, ye children of Israel: for the Lord hath a controversy with the inhabitants of the land, because there is no truth, nor mercy, nor knowledge of God in the land.

2. By swearing, and lying, and killing, and stealing, and committing adultery, they break out, and blood toucheth blood.

3. Therefore shall the land mourn, and every one that dwelleth therein shall languish, with the beasts of the field, and with the fowls of heaven; yea, the fishes of the sea also shall be taken away.

The first three chapters of Hosea leading up to this passage are the tragic tale of the prophet's marriage to a prostitute named Gomer. It is the sad story of how he continued to love her, despite her leaving him repeatedly for illicit affairs with many men. She also forsook her three children, two of whom were likely not fathered by Hosea. He finally found her on the slave block and bought her back for half the normal price—only 15 shekels. "Fifteen shekels was the value of a slave at half-price—the price reflected that this slave was 'damaged goods'" (Stuart Briscoe, *Hearing God's Voice Above the Noise*). He still loved her despite her condition, and bought her back.

Starting with chapter 4 through the remainder of the book, Hosea turned his attention to the nation of Israel. God's people were behaving just as Gomer had done with Hosea. In these first three verses God used the image of a courtroom to lay out His prosecution case for Israel's suffering. "For the Lord brings a charge against the inhabitants of the land" (4:1, *NKJV*). Their illegal (lawless) behavior had brought violence and crisis.

B. God Points the Blame (v. 4)

4. Yet let no man strive, nor reprove another: for thy people are as they that strive with the priest.

God made it clear that no one could blame another for his own individual guilt. The people were each held accountable for their own actions. Charges were also leveled against the priests and religious leaders for their irresponsible actions. Instead of leading the people toward godliness and worship of Jehovah, they had directed them toward idolatry. This had begun many years earlier when Jeroboam I rebelled against Solomon's son, Rehoboam. He established a rival northern kingdom made up of the 10 tribes living there. Jeroboam reasoned, "It is too much for you to go up to Jerusalem. Here are your gods, O Israel, who brought you up out of Egypt" (1 Kings 12:28, *NIV*). He created two golden calves like those used in Baal worship. He also appointed his own priests, who were not descendants of Aaron. He told the people that they were to worship these "gods" in the two convenient cities of Bethel and Dan.

At first some of the residents in the northern kingdom continued to worship God, although they were already going about it in the wrong way. Gradually, however, they adopted the local pagan gods, substituting Baal for Jehovah. "Worship became a matter of convenience, a matter of identifying with the culture, a matter of simply doing things their own way rather than God's way" (Briscoe). This accommodating religion led the people to a point that they stood for nothing, understood and knew nothing, and therefore were totally ignorant of God's ways.

C. Destruction for Lack of
  Knowledge (vv. 5, 6)

5. Therefore shalt thou fall in the day, and the prophet also shall fall with thee in the night, and I will destroy thy mother.

6. My people are destroyed for lack of knowledge: because thou hast rejected knowledge, I will also reject thee, that thou shalt be no priest to me: seeing thou hast forgotten the law of thy God, I will also forget thy children.

The word *knowledge* in verse 1 is translated as *acknowledgment* in the *New International Version*. It is one of two key words for the entire Book of Hosea. The other is *knowledge* (v. 6). Because there was no knowledge of the true character of God, there was as a result no acknowledgment of Him. This deficiency opened the door for the people to slide into idolatry. From the very beginning, when the Israelites were led into Canaan, God commanded that they were to have absolutely nothing to do with the cultic religions of the local Canaanite people. The worship of pagan gods could not exist alongside the worship of Jehovah.

The Israelites had never fully obeyed God, even from the time they first reached Canaan. They quickly began to intermarry with the local pagans and take on heathen ways. Because they assimilated the gods and sins of the surrounding cultures, they no longer had a true knowledge of what was right and wrong. Therefore, this paucity of knowledge led to a lack of acknowledgment of God.

The same thing is happening today. Society is abandoning the moral authority of right and wrong. We hear phrases such as "That may be right for you, but it's not right for me." We are supposed to respect everyone's beliefs, principles, and lifestyles, no matter how disgusting they are in God's eyes— all under the guise of a "plural society." The Ten Commandments are no longer considered to be a model for man's actions. They are just "Ten Suggestions." Because men are not recognizing the Bible as their ultimate source of truth, there is a resulting lack of both *knowledge* and *acknowledgment* of God.

How much of life's troubles are the direct result of disobedience to God's commandments?

II. SHUN WICKEDNESS
  (Hosea 4:15-19)

A. A Warning to Judah (vv. 15, 16)

15. Though thou, Israel, play the harlot, yet let not Judah offend; and come not ye unto Gilgal, neither go ye up to Bethaven, nor swear, The Lord liveth.

16. For Israel slideth back as a backsliding heifer: now the Lord will feed them as a lamb in a large place.

Hosea used the situation in

Israel to give a warning also to the southern kingdom of Judah. The hope was that Judah would take what had happened in Israel as a lesson to be learned through someone else's mistakes. Likely, Hosea wrote down this admonition after Israel was attacked by Assyria in 722 B.C. Though her path was somewhat slower, Judah nevertheless followed the same pattern of sinfulness that Israel had and was also destroyed 136 years later by the Babylonians.

B. The Tribe of Ephraim (vv. 17-19)

17. Ephraim is joined to idols: let him alone.

18. Their drink is sour: they have committed whoredom continually: her rulers with shame do love, Give ye.

19. The wind hath bound her up in her wings, and they shall be ashamed because of their sacrifices.

Beginning at verse 17, Hosea refers to the northern kingdom as *Ephraim.* The name had both historical and symbolic importance. Ephraim, meaning "fruitful," was Joseph's second son. When Jacob blessed his two grandsons, he gave Ephraim the larger blessing. Later, the tribe of Ephraim became one of the leading tribes in Israel. Upon arrival in Canaan, its people were given the important region just north of Dan, Judah, and Benjamin. When the north rebelled after Solomon's death, the 10 tribes named an Ephraimite, Jeroboam, as their own king (see 1 Kings 12:16-20). Jeroboam made Shechem his capital and Bethel a religious center.

In verse 17, Hosea admonished Judah to "let him alone." God was warning the southern kingdom and her priests to avoid becoming like Israel in her idolatry and rebellion.

Being God's people means acknowledging Him in two ways. If He is to be provider, friend, and counselor, then He is also the lawgiver. Hosea 7:8 gives a clear picture of Israel's one-sidedness: "Ephraim mixes with the nations; Ephraim is a flat cake not turned over" (*NIV*). Ephraim (Israel) was like flat cakes cooked in pans over hot coals. The dough may sizzle and cook quickly on one side, but unless it is turned over, it will burn on the one side and still be soggy on the other. The Israelites claimed to be God's people; but because they had no real knowledge of Him, they were not applying His laws to their lives. In other words, they were half-baked. The warning to the southern kingdom of Judah was strong: do not follow the ways of your northern neighbors.

How can we live among pagan peoples today and not be influenced by their idolatrous ways?

III. RETURN TO THE LORD
(Hosea 6:1-3)

1. Come, and let us return unto the Lord: for he hath torn, and he will heal us; he hath smitten, and he will bind us up.

2. After two days will he revive us: in the third day he will raise us up, and we shall live in his sight.

3. Then shall we know, if we follow on to know the Lord: his going forth is prepared as the morning; and he shall come unto us as the rain, as the latter and former rain unto the earth.

Hosea was called to prophesy

during Israel's last crumbling hours as a nation, just as Jeremiah would be called to do for Judah a century later. His writings represent God's last effort to offer a chance for repentance and forgiveness. Hosea's personal tragedy illustrated the national one. It was a one-sided relationship. God's faithful love was rejected by the very people He loved and called His own.

Perhaps because of his own painful experience, Hosea could identify with the sorrow God felt over the sinfulness of His people. His own loyal love for Gomer reflected the Lord's concern for the nation. These first verses in chapter 6 are a "wishful thought" that Israel would repent. Hosea was trying to put a desire for God in the people's hearts and words in their mouths, but he was unsuccessful. The people simply did not understand the depth of their sins. Their short-sightedness kept them from seeing that very quickly they would be taken into exile, never to return.

After being exiled to Assyria, the people of Israel were hopelessly interbred with their conquerors. They lost their identity as part of God's chosen people. Only those who returned from captivity in Babylon (those from the southern kingdom) have survived to today.

God is eager to forgive His people, if only they will listen to His messenger. The problem for Israel was that the people were so engrossed in their sin—and by now so ignorant of Him—that they had no desire to turn to Him.

How do we reconcile God's promise of hope with the fact that the northern tribes were totally lost and never came back from captivity?

REVIEW QUESTIONS

1. In what has been termed a "pluralistic" society, how much should we respect the views and ideas of people around us who serve heathen gods?

2. What responsibilities do those in the ministry have for making sure people have an adequate knowledge of who God is?

3. What is required for real repentance to take place?

4. At what point does God give up on a people or an individual?

GOLDEN TEXT HOMILY

"COME, AND LET US RETURN UNTO THE LORD: FOR HE HATH TORN, AND HE WILL HEAL US; HE HATH SMITTEN, AND HE WILL BIND US UP" (Hosea 6:1).

In this verse we have one of the great examples of God's love. The preceding verses tell of the disobedience of man and how he rejected the love of God. Even though man is the object of God's love, the majority have turned aside and are going their own way. What a tragedy, for in so doing they are turning away from God's salvation, protection, and everlasting love. Man is charting his own course and is, therefore, being torn and wounded and headed for destruction.

But the Word states, "Come . . . let us return unto the Lord . . . he will bind us up." God then becomes the object of our praise. We can find the strength, hope, love, and purpose that will uphold us throughout our lives. Our thoughts, purposes, and innermost spiritual insights are sustained by the abiding knowledge that our lives are ordered by God. We are further assured by the Word of God that He cares for us and desires to heal our wounds and restore our soul.

What a beautiful picture of a God who loves depraved man and welcomes him with open arms! Although our heavenly Father sees how bad our sins are and the many transgressions we are guilty of, He asks only that we "return unto the Lord." Then God will receive us, revive us, and raise us up; and we will live in His presence (6:2).—
Jerry Puckett, Customer Service Representative, Pathway Press, Cleveland, Tennessee

SENTENCE SERMONS

GOD HAS A PROVISION for all people to be reconciled to Him through faith in Christ.

—Selected

TO TRULY KNOW GOD is to live in obedience to His Word.

—Selected

KEEP YOUR HEART OPEN to the correction of the Lord and be ready to receive His chastisement regardless of who holds the whip.

—A.W. Tozer

TO HEAR TRUTH and not accept it does not nullify truth.

—Brotherhood Journal

ILLUMINATING THE LESSON

An American military couple returned some years ago from an assignment in Japan with a humorous, yet sad, story. A local merchant in the city where they were stationed was anxious to impress the Western visitors who shopped in his establishment. At Christmas he set about to decorate for the season just like Americans do. After going to great lengths to make his store as Westernized as possible, he invited his friends to see what he had done. The visitors didn't know whether to be amused, bewildered, or appalled at what they saw. In his ignorance, the proprietor had created a large display with a Santa Claus hanging on a cross.

As ridiculous as this seems, it points out the danger of ignorance of God's Word. Can we not see signs of this same thing in the American church? Is Jesus the all-American champion of free enterprise? Is He the epitome of the American dream? Have we syncretized the culture around us into our doctrines? We must be careful to teach the pure Word, not a version that is tainted with local ideas and culture.

DAILY BIBLE READINGS

M. Guard Against Error.
   Deuteronomy 4:15-20
T. God's Way Rewarded.
   Psalm 37:1-6
W. God Is Faithful. Hosea 2:14-23
T. God's Way Rejected.
   Mark 10:17-22
F. God's Wrath Revealed.
   Romans 2:1-11
S. Live God's Way.
   Galatians 5:16-24

God's Call to Repentance

Study Text: Joel 1:1-15; 2:12-32

Objective: To recognize the consequences of turning from God and determine to live in fellowship with Him.

Time: The Book of Joel was probably written between 835 and 800 B.C.

Place: The Book of Joel was probably written at Jerusalem.

Golden Text: "Rend your heart . . . and turn unto the Lord your God: for he is gracious and merciful, slow to anger, and of great kindness" (Joel 2:13).

Central Truth: Repentance prepares a person's heart to receive God's forgiveness and restoration.

Evangelism Emphasis: God will accept all who come to Him in faith and repentance.

PRINTED TEXT

Joel 1:11. Be ye ashamed, O ye husbandmen; howl, O ye vinedressers, for the wheat and for the barley; because the harvest of the field is perished.

12. The vine is dried up, and the fig tree languisheth; the pomegranate tree, the palm tree also, and the apple tree, even all the trees of the field, are withered: because joy is withered away from the sons of men.

14. Sanctify ye a fast, call a solemn assembly, gather the elders and all the inhabitants of the land into the house of the Lord your God, and cry unto the Lord.

2:12. Therefore also now, saith the Lord, Turn ye even to me with all your heart, and with fasting, and with weeping, and with mourning.

13. And rend your heart, and not your garments, and turn unto the Lord your God: for he is gracious and merciful, slow to anger, and of great kindness, and repenteth him of the evil.

18. Then will the Lord be jealous for his land, and pity his people.

19. Yea, the Lord will answer and say unto his people, Behold, I will send you corn, and wine, and oil, and ye shall be satisfied therewith: and I will no more make you a reproach among the heathen:

20. But I will remove far off from you the northern army, and will drive him into a land barren and desolate, with his face toward the east sea, and his hinder part toward the utmost sea, and his stink shall come up, and his ill savour shall come up, because he hath done great things.

21. Fear not, O land; be glad and rejoice: for the Lord will do great things.

23. Be glad then, ye children of Zion, and rejoice in the Lord your God: for he hath given you the former rain moderately, and he will cause to come down for you the rain, the former rain, and the latter rain in the first month.

27. And ye shall know that I am in the midst of Israel, and that I am the Lord your God, and none else: and my people shall never be ashamed.

28. And it shall come to pass afterward, that I will pour out my spirit upon all flesh; and your sons and your daughters shall prophesy, your old men shall dream dreams, your young men shall see visions:

29. And also upon the servants and upon the handmaids in those days will I pour out my spirit.

LESSON OUTLINE

I.   CONSIDER YOUR WAYS

    A.   Warning of Impending Crisis

    B.   A Spiritual Plague

    C.   The Farmers' Despair

    D.   A Plea to the Priests

    E.   A Solemn Assembly

    F.   Repentance and God's Mercy

II. FREEDOM AND RESTORATION PROMISED

    A.   God's Jealousy for His Land

    B.   A Message of Comfort

III. LIFE IN THE SPIRIT

LESSON EXPOSITION

INTRODUCTION

Since there are no dates or time references in the Book of Joel, there has been much speculation concerning when it was written. Some think it was penned near the end of Judah's nationhood, somewhere around 609 B.C., and that Joel was a contemporary of Jeremiah. Others say it could have been written after the exile to Babylon in 538 B.C. or even later. Still others believe it was most likely written between 835 and 796 B.C., during the reign of King Joash, because the major empires of Assyria, Syria, and Babylon are not mentioned but the countries of Phoenicia, Philista, Egypt, and Edom are. It is certain, however, that Joel was writing specifically to the southern kingdom of Judah, warning of an impending day of judgment, which he referred to as the "day of the Lord."

Assuming the date it was written was during King Joash's reign, we remember that the young monarch was crowned king of Judah and ended a terrible period controlled by his wicked father, Ahaziah, and his equally wicked grandmother, Athaliah (see 2 Kings 8:25—11:21). There was excellent opportunity for renewal in the land—if the people would forsake their idolatry and turn to God. Otherwise, there would be a terrible judgment—in the form of a locust invasion.

All that is known about Joel himself is that he was the "son of Pethuel" (1:1). From evidence within the book, he likely lived in or near Jerusalem and was associated with the Temple worship rituals. Some have conjectured that he was a priest; but others feel this is unlikely, since he called upon the priests to go into mourning because of the nation's sins (1:13). There are many agricultural references; thus it is possible he was a farmer or shepherd.

The locust invasion he spoke of is also confusing. Whether this was an occurrence from the past or an impending catastrophe is not clear. He described the disaster with vivid language, indicating that he had either actually witnessed it or God had given him a vision of it. In either case, Joel preached with fervor that God could use a terrible natural cataclysm to stir His people to a renewed sense of awareness of His will. "Any traumatic event of nature—flood, fire, storm, or earthquake—should motivate the sensitive ear to listen again to the words of the Lord" (*Nelson's Illustrated Bible Dictionary*).

Joel was so moved by the invasion of this army of locusts that he urged the elders of Judah to tell their descendants (1:3)—their children, grandchildren, and generations not yet born—about the horror of the event. This indicates that a shameful failure existed in the land. Faith and knowledge of God were not being shared with each new generation. Centuries before, Moses had told the Israelites entering the Promised Land to remember their responsibility to teach children and grandchildren what they had experienced on the way there (see Deuteronomy 4:9, 10). Every generation of God's people must pass on the story of what God has done in their lives. Doing so will help equip the young not only to walk with the Lord but also to be ready for whatever circumstances they may encounter. In the New Testament, Paul urged Timothy: "And the things you have heard me say in the presence of many witnesses entrust to reliable men who will also be qualified to teach others" (2 Timothy 2:2, *NIV*). The people of Judah had failed to share a godly heritage with the next generation. This was a prelude to their downfall.

For most believers, this prophet's predictions of the future outpouring of the Holy Spirit (2:28-32) are his pivotal contribution to Biblical literature. Peter's quoting of Joel on the Day of Pentecost (Acts 2:16-21) gave explanation for the unusual behavior of the 120 believers who had just been filled with the Holy Spirit. Exactly as the prophet had predicted, the Holy Spirit was poured out on these followers of Jesus who were seeking God's will and guidance.

I. CONSIDER YOUR WAYS
(Joel 1:5-14; 2:12, 13)

A. Warning of Impending Crisis (1:5-7)

(Joel 1:5-7 is not included in the printed text.)

Was the invasion of the army of locusts an impending disaster or one that had already occurred? It is hard to tell. The reference to drunkards and revelers seem to indicate that the people's moral senses had been dulled. They were complacent and content. This does not sound like a nation that had recently experienced a calamity. Possibly the insect plague had not yet occurred. Strangely, times of peace, prosperity, and abundance tend to lull men to sleep. Spiritual readiness is more easily maintained during spartan times than during times of prosperity.

This writer's family was devastated by one of the recent major hurricanes that whipped the southeastern United States. If that disaster did anything, it turned attention to the fragility of life and its circumstances. Overnight, fortunes and heritages were lost. The only solace in times of such devastation is found in one's faith in God.

Joel condemned the excessive use of wine, which had led to drunkenness, revelry, and total spiritual dullness. Because of the nation's spiritual decadence, the invading locust had (or would) strip bare the grape vines and fig trees that symbolized God's blessing.

Joel told all the drinkers of wine to weep and wail, because of the destruction of the source of their wine, the grapevine. God himself lamented the devastation; He so identified Himself with this people and the land He had given them that the loss was to *His* vine and *His* fig tree (v. 7). God "doth not afflict willingly" (Lamentations 3:33); yet unless His people returned to Him, the devastation was to be complete.

B. A Spiritual Plague (1:8-10)

(Joel 1:8-10 is not included in the printed text.)

The physical aspect of the locust plague was nothing to be compared to the plague in the spiritual lives of the people. Its horror could be likened to a virgin pledged to be married but her husband was killed before the marriage could take

place (v. 8). How great would be the young woman's sorrow! Joel used this picture to tell the people of Judah and Jerusalem that they should weep over the loss of their worship of Jehovah, for the loss of the agricultural crops meant there would be nothing to give as an offering. These observances had already become nothing more than ritual; but worse than that, the people had used God's bountiful provision for them as an opportunity for drunkenness. "Therefore, as he had warned, God had taken away the privilege of offering that which symbolized purity of devotion" (*Zondervan New International Version Bible Commentary*, Vol. 1, Old Testament).

Grain, wine, and oil were all seen in Old Testament times as symbols of God's blessing. For these to be taken away was a severe chastening by the Lord. It becomes obvious that the physical devastation absolutely had a spiritual root cause.

This brings up the question: Is there always a direct cause-and-effect relationship between our actions and the tragedies that come our way? No, this is not always the case, although some actions are almost certain to guarantee calamity. Nevertheless, Matthew 5:45 assures that God makes "his sun to rise on the evil and on the good, and sendeth rain on the just and on the unjust." Much that happens in life is simply life. However, when we are surrounded by problems and difficulties, we should always ask ourselves if any sinful, irresponsible, or thoughtless action of ours might have brought on our present situation. Constant introspection to make sure we are carefully following God's will is a must in every

C. The Farmers' Despair (1:11, 12)

11. Be ye ashamed, O ye husbandmen; howl, O ye vinedressers, for the wheat and for the barley; because the harvest of the field is perished.

12. The vine is dried up, and the fig tree languisheth; the pomegranate tree, the palm tree also, and the apple tree, even all the trees of the field, are withered: because joy is withered away from the sons of men.

Joel called on the farmers and workers in the vineyards to grieve over the loss of the products of their labors. The trees he mentioned were not only important aspects of Judah's agricultural economy, but they were spiritual symbols of nourishment, refreshment, fruitfulness, joy, and abundant life as well.

D. A Plea to the Priests (1:13)

(Joel 1:13 is not included in the printed text.)

Joel then made a specific plea to the priesthood. They were to gird themselves in sackcloth and mourn. So terrible would be the plagues that there would not even be enough meat and drink to make offerings to the Lord. Putting on sackcloth and ashes had been a symbol of contrition before the Lord for many centuries. Jeremiah would later call for a similar act (Jeremiah 4:8) as he warned of the advancing Babylonian invaders.

The priesthood was called to humble themselves and mourn because the priests had failed in their duties. They had been given the responsibility for keeping the Word of God before the people. Their failure to do so had resulted in the prevailing spiritual ignorance

and moral laxity. This should serve as a stern warning to everyone in the ministry today. Spiritual leaders have been entrusted with a tremendous responsibility. They must make sure they rightly discern the Word of God and carefully teach it to the people. Because of their position in the Kingdom, they are even more accountable for their labors than those to whom less responsibility has been entrusted.

E. A Solemn Assembly (1:14)

14. Sanctify ye a fast, call a solemn assembly, gather the elders and all the inhabitants of the land into the house of the Lord your God, and cry unto the Lord.

A fast and a solemn assembly were called at times of great emergency throughout Israel's history. To call such a time of repentance would indicate that the people truly meant to change their ways. No food was to be eaten, and the people were to approach God with humility, urgent prayer, and honest sorrow for their sins. This would serve to focus their attention on the only One who could bring them through their calamity. Other times when such assemblies or fasts were called can be found in Judges 20:26; Ezra 8:21; Esther 4:16; and Jonah 3:4, 5.

F. Repentance and God's Mercy (2:12, 13)

12. Therefore also now, saith the Lord, Turn ye even to me with all your heart, and with fasting, and with weeping, and with mourning.

13. And rend your heart, and not your garments, and turn unto the Lord your God: for he is gra-

cious and merciful, slow to anger, and of great kindness, and repenteth him of the evil.

In Hebrew psychology, the heart symbolized even more than the seat of one's affections; it included the aspect of one's will as well. When God beseeched the people to turn to Him wholeheartedly, He asked that it include fasting and weeping and mourning. Their sins were so great that a simple promise to forsake them would not be sufficient to make it so. Instead, it would require a deep remorse, a solemn contemplation of their evil ways, and an earnest desire to change.

If then they would "rend their hearts" in this fashion, God would, true to His character, be gracious to His repentant children. His anger would be turned away, and he would show them the great mercy and kindness He always longs to bestow on His people.

Why does it so often take a calamity to cause people to finally turn to the Lord?

II. FREEDOM AND RESTORATION PROMISED (Joel 2:18-27)

A. God's Jealousy for His Land (vv. 18, 19)

18. Then will the Lord be jealous for his land, and pity his people.

19. Yea, the Lord will answer and say unto his people, Behold, I will send you corn, and wine, and oil, and ye shall be satisfied therewith: and I will no more make you a reproach among the heathen.

Verse 18 is the turning point in the Book of Joel. Up to now Joel had been talking about an outpouring of God's judgment on Judah. Now he switched to a future outpouring of forgiveness and restoration. God's jealousy is an expression of His deep commitment to both His people and His land. The adjective *jealous* occurs six times in the Old Testament. "The word refers directly to the attributes of God's justice and holiness, as He is the sole object of human worship and does not tolerate man's sin" (*Vine's Expository Dictionary of Biblical Words*).

Joel told the people if they would repent, God would "restore health to the environment, bring about new life, and cause the revived vegetation to yield abundant produce (2:19-27). Thus there is a close connection between the redemptive work of God and the creative work of God" (*The Word in Life Study Bible*).

God's concern for the land and environment has implications that are meaningful for us today. Since He is concerned for all life, we have an obligation to wisely manage earth's natural resources. In the latter part of the 20th century, the extremists in the environmental movement in the United States have gone so far as to put animal and vegetative life ahead of human life. This has caused some believers to write off the entire preservation issue because of such fanatic extremism. However, we should not let others' excesses cause us to forget our responsibilities to the land, natural resources, and animal life God has created and entrusted to our care.

B. A Message of Comfort (vv. 20-27)

(Joel 2:22 is not included in the printed text.)

20. But I will remove far off from you the northern army, and will drive him into a land barren and desolate, with his face toward the east sea, and his hinder part toward the utmost sea, and his stink shall come up, and his ill savour shall come up, because he hath done great things.

21. Fear not, O land; be glad and rejoice: for the Lord will do great things.

23. Be glad then, ye children of Zion, and rejoice in the Lord your God: for he hath given you the former rain moderately, and he will cause to come down for you the rain, the former rain, and the latter rain in the first month.

24. And the floors shall be full of wheat, and the fats shall overflow with wine and oil.

25. And I will restore to you the years that the locust hath eaten, the cankerworm, and the caterpiller, and the palmerworm, my great army which I sent among you.

26. And ye shall eat in plenty, and be satisfied, and praise the name of the Lord your God, that hath dealt wondrously with you: and my people shall never be ashamed.

27. And ye shall know that I am in the midst of Israel, and that I am the Lord your God, and none else: and my people shall never be ashamed.

If the people would truly repent, God would sent them restoration, rest, abundance, and other benefits as well. Before this, He would send the devastating armies back to the north. Then the land would return to full bloom, the rains would fall again, the threshing floors would be full of grain, the vats would overflow with oil and wine, families would be satisfied and full of praise—there would be a total renewal of both land and people.

Did this happen? The blessings Joel promised would come only if there was complete contrition. It is obvious that the people never fully repented. The history of the Jews reveals that they did not. Nevertheless, in spite of the captivity in Babylon, the devastation and dispersion by the Romans, and the persecution and destruction of many at the hands of Hitler, preserved a remnant of the people whom He had so lovingly called by His name. And God promises that after the final Day of Judgment, His people will never again have to go through such calamities: "The Lord will be king over the whole earth. On that day there will be one Lord, and his name the only name. The whole land . . . will be inhabited; never again will it be destroyed. Jerusalem will be secure" (Zechariah 14:9-11, *NIV*). Revelation 22:1-5 reiterates this same promise.

Can we claim God's blessings if we don't follow His commands?

III. LIFE IN THE SPIRIT
(Joel 2:28-32)

(Joel 2:30-32 is not included in the printed text.)

28. And it shall come to pass afterward, that I will pour out my spirit upon all flesh; and your sons and your daughters shall prophesy, your old men shall dream dreams, your young men shall see visions:

29. And also upon the servants

and upon the handmaids in those days will I pour out my spirit.

Joel described here a time to come when God would pour out His spirit on all people. On the Day of Pentecost, Peter quoted Joel's prophetic words to indicate that the outpouring of the Holy Spirit was the long-awaited fulfillment of Joel's prophecy (Acts 2:16-21). Prior to this time, access to God had been restricted to priests and certain special individuals. Joel's words changed everything by predicting a time when God's Spirit would be available to everyone, regardless of status, position, sex, or age. Everyone would have equal access.

In a way, then, Joel became "a spiritual grandfather of the church. Christians are now experiencing the fulfillment of Joel's promise" (*Word in Life Study Bible*). But there is still a future dimension to Joel's prediction. The gifts of the Spirit that began to flow through the people of God on the Day of Pentecost were not exhausted on that day. They are still available to all who believe in the Lord Jesus Christ and who anxiously await His return and the final establishment of His kingdom.

Discuss the correlation between Joel's prophecy and Peter's quoting of his words on the Day of Pentecost.

REVIEW QUESTIONS

1. How should we as Christians view calamities that come our way? Are they an indication of God's discipline for our sins?

2. Do you think the locust plague had already occurred or was a vision that Joel saw coming on Judah? Discuss your reasons.

3. How should Christians' view of the environment balance the irrational extremes of the environmental movement of the late 20th century?

4. To what extent was Joel's prophecy fulfilled on the Day of Pentecost?

GOLDEN TEXT HOMILY

"REND YOUR HEART . . . AND TURN UNTO THE LORD YOUR GOD: FOR HE IS GRACIOUS AND MERCIFUL, SLOW TO ANGER, AND OF GREAT KINDNESS" (Joel 2:13).

The prophet calls on the people to truly repent. Their contribution must come from the heart. Mere external displays of worship will not be sufficient to please God. However, He will respond to heartfelt repentance because of His attributes. He is gracious; He is good and benevolent in His nature. He is slow to anger; He is not quick-tempered. He is not easily provoked to punish because He is gracious and merciful. He has great kindness; He extends abundant goodness to all who turn to Him.

This description of God's attributes are timeworn. In fact, these concepts were already timeworn in Joel's day. But time and retelling cannot diminish their meaning or importance because sinners need to know and be reassured that God is gracious, compassionate, slow to anger, and abounding in love. There is no better way to describe God's nature than this. We have all done enough to merit His judgment. A compassionate God who is long-suffering deals with us in mercy. As the Prodigal Son's father welcomed back his lost child, so God reaches out to us. We need to turn out to us. We need to turn to God because of what He is like. He is a God who loved the world so much that He gave His only Son for the sake of the world, that the world through Him might be saved.— **Richard Y. Bershon, Ph.D., Chaplain, State Veterans Home, Hot Springs, South Dakota**

SENTENCE SERMONS

REPENTANCE prepares a person's heart to receive God's forgiveness and restoration.
                                    —Selected

REPENTANCE, to be of any avail, must work a change of heart and conduct.
                        —Theodore L. Cuyler

REPENTANCE may begin instantly, but reformation often requires a sphere of years.
                    —Henry Ward Beecher

SELF-KNOWLEDGE is the first condition of repentance.
                        —Oswald Chambers

ILLUMINATING THE LESSON

As we approach the end of the 20th century we can look back over a hundred years of not only bloodshed but also extreme violation of the land and environment God has blessed us with. Numerous wars, earthquakes, fires, and other natural disasters have taken a terrible toll. The dropping of the first atomic bomb on Hiroshima in 1945 gave us a glimpse of what the prophet Joel had in mind when he spoke of the Garden of Eden being turned into a wilderness (2:3).

Yet nothing is ever fully lost. One of the principles of physics is that matter cannot be destroyed. It may be changed in form, but never destroyed. It takes God, however, for complete restoration to occur.

One of the most fascinating examples of this restoration process is the fires caused by lightning in the western United States. Thousands of acres of forest land are destroyed annually by infernos begun by lightning. However, it has been discovered that this is ultimately good for the land. Old insect-infested forests give way to new growth. Very quickly the land is covered with fresh vegetation.

God knows what He is doing. He is capable of restoring the land He created. This does not, however, give us the right to abuse His blessings to us. Those who truly follow the Lord will have a respect and care for the abundance He provides.

DAILY BIBLE READINGS

M. Acknowledge Sin. Psalm 51:1-5
T. Pray for Forgiveness.
    Psalm 51:6-12
W. Repent of Sin. Acts 2:36-39
T. Set Free From Sin.
    Romans 6:15-23
F. Saved by Grace.
    Ephesians 2:1-9
S. Redeemed by Christ.
    Revelation 5:1-10

God Honors Justice

Study Text: Amos 8:1-14; Zechariah 7:8-10; 8:9-17

Objective: To acknowledge and obey God's demand for social justice.

Time: The Book of Amos was written between 760 and 753 B.C. The Book of Zechariah was written around 520 B.C. Some scholars believe chapters 9-14 were written around 480 B.C.

Place: The Book of Amos was probably written near Jerusalem. The Book of Zechariah was written in Jerusalem.

Golden Text: "Execute true judgment, and shew mercy and compassions every man to his brother" (Zechariah 7:9).

Central Truth: God rewards His people when they practice justice.

Evangelism Emphasis: Christians influence the world for Christ by practicing justice toward all people.

PRINTED TEXT

Amos 8:4. Hear this, O ye that swallow up the needy, even to make the poor of the land to fail,

5. Saying, When will the new moon be gone, that we may sell corn? and the sabbath, that we may set forth wheat, making the ephah small, and the shekel great, and falsifying the balances by deceit?

6. That we may buy the poor for silver, and the needy for a pair of shoes; yea, and sell the refuse of the wheat?

7. The Lord hath sworn by the excellency of Jacob, Surely I will never forget any of their works.

9. And it shall come to pass in that day, saith the Lord God, that I will cause the sun to go down at noon, and I will darken the earth in the clear day:

10. And I will turn your feasts into mourning, and all your songs into lamentation; and I will bring up sackcloth upon all loins, and baldness upon every head; and I will make it as the mourning of an only son, and the end thereof as a bitter day.

11. Behold, the days come, saith the Lord God, that I will send a famine in the land, not a famine of bread, nor a thirst for water, but of hearing the words of the Lord.

Zechariah 7:8. And the word of the Lord came unto Zechariah, saying,

9. Thus speaketh the Lord of hosts, saying, Execute true judgment, and shew mercy and compassions every man to his brother:

10. And oppress not the widow, nor the fatherless, the stranger, nor the poor; and let none of you imagine evil

against his brother in your heart.

8:13. And it shall come to pass, that as ye were a curse among the heathen, O house of Judah, and house of Israel; so will I save you, and ye shall be a blessing: fear not, but let your hands be strong.

14. For thus saith the Lord of hosts; As I thought to punish you, when your fathers provoked me to wrath, saith the Lord of hosts, and I repented not:

15. So again have I thought in these days to do well unto Jerusalem and to the house of Judah: fear ye not.

16. These are the things that ye shall do; Speak ye every man the truth to his neighbour; execute the judgment of truth and peace in your gates:

17. And let none of you imagine evil in your hearts against his neighbour; and love no false oath: for all these are things that I hate, saith the Lord.

DICTIONARY

Zechariah (ZEK-uh-RY-uh)—Zechariah 7:8—A prophet to the remnant which returned after the 70 years of captivity.

LESSON OUTLINE

I. INJUSTICE CONDEMNED
   A. Israel's Greedy Merchants
   B. The Pride of Jacob
   C. Days of Darkness and Mourning
   D. A Famine of Hearing the Word of God
II. SOCIAL JUSTICE COMMANDED
III. JUSTICE REWARDED
   A. A New Day of Encouragement
   B. God's Reassurance

LESSON EXPOSITION

INTRODUCTION

Amos was a prophet to the northern kingdom of Israel during a period of national optimism. Jeroboam II was king and the nation was booming. The borders of Israel were restored to almost what they had been during the days of Solomon (2 Kings 14:25). However, beneath the surface of prosperity was a terrible festering sore of greed and injustice. True worship had been replaced by ritual and hypocrisy. An air of false security was growing, combined with a callousness toward the things of God. Nothing seemed to shake the people from their spiritual stupor—neither famine, drought, plague, death, nor destruction. They would not be brought to their knees. Like a basket of overripe fruit that still looked good on the outside, they were ready for judgment.

Amos was a contemporary of both Hosea and Isaiah. He prophesied in Israel during the same time Isaiah prophesied in Judah. Although from a small town in Judah, Amos was sent by God to the north. Here he was regarded as a foreigner. A simple shepherd from the town of Tekoa, Amos' name is derived from the Hebrew root *amas,* meaning "to lift a burden, to carry." Thus his name means "burdenbearer."

Amos was not a professional prophet (or a seminary-trained theologian, as we would say today); rather, he was a simple man with a great call on his life. Since Israel had split from Judah 170 years earlier, the "sophisticated" northerners did not take kindly to criticism leveled at them by a sheep herder from the south. However, Amos followed the same pattern as the other prophets of the Old Testament—he came roaring with the authority of God.

The very first words of the book point this out: "The words of Amos, who was among the herdsmen of Tekoa, which he saw concerning Israel in the days of Uzziah king of Judah, and in the days of Jeroboam the son of Joash king of Israel, two years before the earthquake. And he said, The Lord will roar from Zion, and utter his voice from Jerusalem; and the habitations of the shepherds shall mourn, and the top of Carmel shall wither" (Amos 1:1, 2). Similarities between Amos and his prophecies and other pre-exile prophets and their messages include the following:

1. *God was angry because of the sin of the people.* The fact that Jehovah would "roar from Zion" indicates that He will tolerate sin and injustice for only so long.

2. *God was threatening cataclysmic punishment.* Two years later an earthquake struck the land.

3. *Amos had a clear call and a clear vision of the words God wanted him to speak.* Like Isaiah, he experienced the majesty of God and the authority of His Word. He left

his lowly job as a shepherd to proclaim the authority of the Word of God.

4. *Amos would not spare the message God had given him for anyone.* He was so captivated by what the Lord said that he was not afraid of what men could do to him.

In chapter 7 we see the details of how this lowly shepherd-prophet came from the south and attracted the attention of the powers of the north. He created such a stir that he finally offended even Amaziah, the high priest. This is the man who should have been proclaiming God's Word to the people but was instead protecting his own political position. In a rage he screamed at the simple shepherd-prophet: "Get out, you seer! Go back to the land of Judah. Earn your bread there and do your prophesying there. Don't prophesy anymore at Bethel, because this is the king's sanctuary and the temple of the kingdom" (Amos 7:12, 13, *NIV*).

Amos was not intimidated. He knew he was God's mouthpiece, so he delivered the message with a passion. It is always interesting to see who God uses as His voice. In Amos, He chose a lowly shepherd to confront the high priest of Bethel. No servant of the Lord should ever belittle himself, thinking that God cannot use him. What God wants is a willing instrument. God qualifies those whom He calls.

Over 200 years after Amos, another prophet was used to speak to the residents of Judah who had returned from captivity in Babylon (520-516 B.C.). Zechariah was commissioned by God to encourage the returned exiles in their unfinished task of rebuilding the Temple in Jerusalem. For a dozen years or more the project had stood half-completed. Disobedience again (as in the time of Amos) was the root cause of their problems and woes. The book begins by expressing God's frustration over their callousness. He reminded them of how their ancestors' sins caught up with them. He warned them not to be like their fathers, who refused to listen and reaped the consequences of what they had sown—judgment.

Zechariah's task was to lead the people to positive action by reminding them of the vision for the future. The Temple must be rebuilt, for it would one day be visited by the Messiah. However, the future blessing was totally contingent upon present obedience. This generation need not repeat the cycle of the history. They could avoid the problems their ancestors faced by choosing to stay faithful to God.

Although earlier prophets had a positive side to their work, most of their time was spent in giving stern warnings of coming judgment. Zechariah's task, however, was primarily one of confident encouragement. The people had already seen the terrible consequences of rebellion. They didn't need such stern warnings as their forefathers had heard.

Adding to the positive aspects of Zechariah's message is the fact that he gave more prophecies concerning the coming of the Messiah than any other Old Testament prophet besides Isaiah. The rebuilding of the Temple was just the first step in a grand drama of things to come. Zechariah stirred the hopes of the people by showing the ex-captives that a great King was coming. The detailed prophecies this prophet proclaimed were clearly fulfilled 500 years later in the life of Jesus.

I. INJUSTICE CONDEMNED (Amos 8:4-14)

A. Israel's Greedy Merchants (vv. 4-6)

4. Hear this, O ye that swallow up the needy, even to make the poor of the land to fail,

5. Saying, When will the new moon be gone, that we may sell corn? and the sabbath, that we may set forth wheat, making the ephah small, and the shekel great, and falsifying the balances by deceit?

6. That we may buy the poor for silver, and the needy for a pair of shoes; yea, and sell the refuse of the wheat?

The Book of Amos gives us a glimpse into God's perspective on social issues. Its message is especially needed in the American church as we come to the close of the 20th century. Over the past 50 years the church has surrendered its role as the primary source of help to the poor and allowed the government to take over this responsibility. However, 50 years of failed government social programs have left the nation with a bitter taste for caring for those in need. Amos' denunciation gives us fresh insight into just what our role is as a church. He tells us how God feels when the powerful exploit the poor and defenseless. He shows us that how we treat social problems is extremely important to God. We must reach out to the poor, helpless, and defenseless with generosity and concern if we are to truly be God's people.

Amos challenged the crass materialism and absence of morals among the wealthy people of Israel. They had learned this from their pagan neighbors, and many were exploiting the poor without any twinge of conscience. This was God's last appeal to Israel, warning them to repent before it was too late.

In the verses above, Amos accused the merchants and businessmen of Israel of keeping the Sabbath and the religious holidays in name only. They were anxious for these to be over so that they could get back to making money, and they were not above giving short measure and raising prices. "They even sold the sweepings to increase the weight! Yet these exploiters were careful to observe the Sabbath. Though the marketplace was deserted on the holy days, in the bustle of commerce their god—Mammon—was quite in evidence, and their true religious credo was Gain at Any Cost" (*Zondervan New International Version Bible Commentary*, Vol. 1, Old Testament).

B. The Pride of Jacob (vv. 7, 8)

(Amos 8:8 is not included in the printed text.)

7. The Lord hath sworn by the excellency of Jacob, Surely I will never forget any of their works.

God never allows His name to be clouded. The "excellency of Jacob," or the "Pride of Jacob" (*NIV*), was God's solemn vow to judge His people according to the covenant He had made with Abraham. Amos 4:2 and 6:8 give similar words the Lord spoke in declaring His promise of judgment.

C. Days of Darkness and Mourning (vv. 9, 10)

9. And it shall come to pass in that day, saith the Lord God, that I will cause the sun to go down at noon, and I will darken the earth in the clear day:

10. And I will turn your feasts into mourning, and all your songs into lamentation; and I will bring up sackcloth upon all loins, and baldness upon every head; and I will make it as the mourning of an only son, and the end thereof as a bitter day.

Did "in that day" have some eschatological implications for a judgment that is still to come? Probably not. Some of Amos' words may have been purely figurative, but the disasters that did befall Israel were real enough. Israel as a nation was destroyed by Assyria; all her people were dispersed into captivity, never to return. This was no doubt the calamity predicted here. The people's ultimate punishment was that they were absorbed into a pagan world, so much so that they never regained their identity. "The Israelites had wanted to adopt the lifestyle and customs of their neighbors, so God punished them by granting them their wish. Their idolatry, immorality and exploitation of the poor had polluted their faith in God. So God judged them by allowing them to become totally immersed in their paganism" (*The Quest Study Bible*).

D. A Famine of Hearing the Word of God (vv. 11-14)

(Amos 8:12-14 is not included in the printed text.)

11. Behold, the days come, saith the Lord God, that I will send a famine in the land, not a famine of bread, nor a thirst for water, but of hearing the words of the Lord.

Anytime men refuse to obey the Word of the Lord, they will be brought down to nothing eventually.

"Know this: The Sovereign Lord Jehovah will respond in kind to our reaction to His Word. Some who go on relentlessly hardening their hearts to what God is saying need to be alerted to the fact that they cannot do so with impunity. God could send to them a famine of hearing the Word of the Lord" (Briscoe, *Hearing God's Voice Above the Noise*).

Even though the Word may be available, if God does not anoint the ears of those who hear it, it has no value to them. If God removes His anointing from the preaching of the Word, famine results. We must always be careful to keep our lives in touch with God and His Word, so that we can continue to hear His voice calling out to us.

Is there such a thing as "sinning away one's day of grace"? Can we equate this to a "famine of hearing the Word"?

II. SOCIAL JUSTICE COMMANDED (Zechariah 7:8-10)

8. And the word of the Lord came unto Zechariah, saying,

9. Thus speaketh the Lord of hosts, saying, Execute true judgment, and shew mercy and compassions every man to his brother:

10. And oppress not the widow, nor the fatherless, the stranger, nor the poor; and let none of you imagine evil against his brother in your heart.

Zechariah was likely a child when the exiles began their return to Judah from Babylon in 538 B.C. His ministry began around 520 B.C., when God called him to give messages to those who had

returned to Jerusalem. It's hard to imagine that God's people might once again become callous after having gone through the ordeal of the Captivity, but this is exactly the message Zechariah was warning them against. God reminded the people what had happened to the people and the nation when they lost their desire for God. As history has shown repeatedly, succeeding generations have not always remembered or learned from the mistakes of their predecessors. They were carrying out religious rites, holy days, and feasts without any semblance of worship or repentance. They were even carrying out fasts, and had continued to keep the fasts throughout the Captivity, (v. 5), but this meant nothing to God if their lives lacked justice and compassion.

Zechariah challenged the people to avoid empty religion (vv. 5-7) and to show their true love for God by reflecting His justice to all. God expected the people to (1) be fair and honest with everyone, (2) never take bribes, and (3) show mercy and kindness.

Are we totally honest in all our dealings? Do we treat everyone the same, or do we show favoritism? How do we treat the poor? Are we generous, or are we selfish?

III. JUSTICE REWARDED (Zechariah 8:11-17)

A. A New Day of Encouragement (vv. 11-13)

(Zechariah 8:11, 12 is not included in the printed text.)

13. And it shall come to pass,

that as ye were a curse among the heathen, O house of Judah, and house of Israel; so will I save you, and ye shall be a blessing: fear not, but let your hands be strong.

Israel had once been a great kingdom. In the days of David and Solomon her borders extended to include great territories. When the kingdom split after Solomon's death, both Israel and Judah progressively lost cities and territories until finally both were overrun and carried away. For the small band of exiles returning to Jerusalem, the task of rebuilding the city and the Temple were overwhelming. They faced hostile neighbors who made frequent raids on their settlements. It was hard for them to believe that God would one day reign again from this city and that they would be prosperous.

Zechariah encouraged the people to finish the job of rebuilding the Temple. He stirred up hope in their hearts by showing them a glowing future. "But now" (v. 11) shows the reason for new hope. God was ready to pour out His blessings on the people as in earlier times. The days of discipline and punishment were past. He promised rich rewards. The people need not fear that He would change His mind and punish them. Nevertheless, they had to do their part, and that was to live righteously.

B. God's Reassurance (vv. 14-17)

14. For thus saith the Lord of hosts; As I thought to punish you, when your fathers provoked me to wrath, saith the Lord of hosts, and I repented not:

15. So again have I thought in these days to do well unto Jerusalem and to the house of Judah: fear ye not.

16. These are the things that ye shall do; Speak ye every man the truth to his neighbour; execute the judgment of truth and peace in your gates:

17. And let none of you imagine evil in your hearts against his neighbour; and love no false oath: for all these are things that I hate, saith the Lord.

A new day had dawned in Jerusalem. God was on the people's side. His anger against their forefathers had subsided. Punishment was past. However, there were still stipulations to His blessing. They had to be truthful in their dealings with one another. They could not plot evil against their brother. They could not allow social injustice to exist among them. They must avoid hypocrisy, superficiality, and sin.

This formula for God's blessing is still valid today. If we expect Him to answer our prayers, we must carry ourselves with honesty and integrity. Our relationship with our fellowman should mirror our relationship with God himself.

How important is it for us as children of God to reach out to the poor and to those treated unjustly by society?

REVIEW QUESTIONS

1. What responsibilities does the church today have toward the poor and underprivileged?

2. What happens when a people become so calloused to God's Word that it no longer has any effect on them? Can this be considered a famine of hearing the Word of God?

3. Discuss the importance of maintaining the proper balance between positive encouragement and threats of God's discipline in motivating people to do good.

4. What conditions are attached to God's blessings?

GOLDEN TEXT HOMILY

"EXECUTE TRUE JUDGMENT, AND SHEW MERCY AND COMPAS-SIONS EVERY MAN TO HIS BROTHER" (Zechariah 7:9).

The first requirement of obedience to God's will is dependence on Him to help us fulfill it. In this passage, God calls His people to exhibit two characteristics of true judgment—mercy and compassion, knowing they must trust Him to supply the enablement.

This is where *agape*, or divine love, outshines man's nature in exhibiting mercy and compassion for wrongdoing. God can accomplish His will through us only if we submit.

Mercifulness, required in both Old and New Testament scriptures, calls the believer to overstep the finite bounds of human nature and return an act of kindness when wronged instead of feeling justified in seeking revenge. Compassion is identified with tenderness and love, as opposed to human nature's get-even attitude.

Paul said we heap coals of fire on our enemies when we love them through acts of compassion (Romans 12:20). Individuals in rebellion against God have been won to faith in Jesus Christ when Christians showed them the love of God through acts of compassion and mercy.

A young man who faced the death penalty in a Mississippi jail because he had beaten a man senseless with his bare hands felt that kind of mercy and compassion when the victim's brother visited him in jail. Instead of revenge, the brother brought him a Bible and told him he loved him. Today, that young man is working as a Christian minister, serving God in a local church. God is able to use any circumstance to turn sinners to repentance if His children will depend on Him to enable them to show love with mercy and compassion.—**Eugene Wigelsworth, M.S.W., M.Div., Senior Chaplain, Pasquotank Correctional Institution, Elizabeth City, North Carolina**

SENTENCE SERMONS

GOD REWARDS HIS PEOPLE when they practice justice.
—Selected

DELAY IN JUSTICE is injustice.
—Walter S. Landor

AN INJURY TO ONE is the concern of all.
—Draper's Book of Quotations for the Christian World

DAILY BIBLE READINGS

M. Obey God's Law.
  Exodus 20:12-17
T. Reviewing Acts of Kindness.
  Job 31:13-22
W. Injustice of Self-Righteousness.
  Luke 6:39-42
T. Show Compassion to Others.
  Luke 10:30-37
F. Avoid Partiality. James 2:1-9
S. Love Is Just. 1 John 3:14-18

God's Judgment and Mercy

Study Text: Obadiah 1:1-21; Jonah 3:1-10; Nahum 1:1-14

Objective: To know that God's judgment on sin is certain and place our hope in His mercy.

Golden Text: "The Lord is slow to anger, and great in power, and will not at all acquit the wicked" (Nahum 1:3).

Central Truth: God judges evil but offers mercy to all people.

Evangelism Emphasis: The certainty of God's judgment should motivate believers to warn the lost.

PRINTED TEXT

Nahum 1:2. God is jealous, and the Lord revengeth; the Lord revengeth, and is furious; the Lord will take vengeance on his adversaries, and he reserveth wrath for his enemies.

3. The Lord is slow to anger, and great in power, and will not at all acquit the wicked: the Lord hath his way in the whirlwind and in the storm, and the clouds are the dust of his feet.

7. The Lord is good, a strong hold in the day of trouble; and he knoweth them that trust in him.

8. But with an overrunning flood he will make an utter end of the place thereof, and darkness shall pursue his enemies.

9. What do ye imagine against the Lord? he will make an utter end: affliction shall not rise up the second time.

Obadiah 1:17. But upon mount Zion shall be deliverance, and there shall be holiness; and the house of Jacob shall possess their possessions.

18. And the house of Jacob shall be a fire, and the house of Joseph a flame, and the house of Esau for stubble, and they shall kindle in them, and devour them;

and there shall not be any remaining of the house of Esau; for the Lord hath spoken it.

21. And saviours shall come up on mount Zion to judge the mount of Esau; and the kingdom shall be the Lord's.

Jonah 3:1. And the word of the Lord came unto Jonah the second time, saying,

2. Arise, go unto Nineveh, that great city, and preach unto it the preaching that I bid thee.

3. So Jonah arose, and went unto Nineveh, according to the word of the Lord. Now Nineveh was an exceeding great city of three days' journey.

4. And Jonah began to enter into the city a day's journey, and he cried, and said, Yet forty days, and Nineveh shall be overthrown.

5. So the people of Nineveh believed God, and proclaimed a fast, and put on sackcloth, from the greatest of them even to the least of them.

10. And God saw their works, that they turned from their evil way; and God repented of the evil, that he had said that he would do unto them; and he did it not.

DICTIONARY

Nineveh (NIN-eh-vuh)—Jonah 3:2—One of the oldest and most important cities of the world. For many years it was the capital of Assyria.

LESSON OUTLINE

I. JUDGMENT DECLARED

  A. God's Power and Jealousy

  B. God's Anger

  C. God Remembers His People

  D. Nineveh's Sentence of Death

II. DELIVERANCE PROMISED

III. MERCY EXTENDED

LESSON EXPOSITION

INTRODUCTION

Nahum was the second of the minor prophets God sent to deal with the wicked capital of Assyria. The city that was built to last forever, fortified with 200 towers and surrounded by high, thick walls, had been given the privilege of knowing Jehovah a century and a half earlier. Jonah had gone there with a doomsday message that resulted in the only incident recorded in the Bible in which an entire city repented (around 780 B.C.). During the next 150 years, however, the people returned to their immoral ways. By 732 B.C. they were again marching into the northern kingdom of Israel, destroying cities and taking people captive. Samaria, Israel's capital, fell in 722 B.C.

The Assyrian armies under King Sennacherib had even marched into Judah around 701 B.C., but God miraculously delivered Hezekiah and his people, causing the death of 185,000 Assyrians (2 Kings 19:35). Sennacherib was called back to Nineveh and was soon assassinated. This marked the beginning of the downfall of the Assyrian empire and the emergence of Babylon as the controlling power of the ancient world.

Nahum's message to the heathen kingdom was much different from Jonah's. "For everyone to whom much is given, from him much will be required" (Luke 12:48, *NKJV*) is the principle that was now applied to the rebellious people. Nineveh had been given a great opportunity through Jonah's preaching, but the people had forgotten their repentance and had returned to violence, idolatry, and the arrogant ambition to dominate the world. Nahum's preaching was not a call to repentance; it was rather a warning of destruction coming from the hand of a God whose patience had come to an end.

Although Obadiah is the shortest book in the Old Testament, it is certainly not the least important. Its 21 verses span the big picture of the Bible, from the days of the patriarchs all the way to the New Testament. Its prophecy addresses the Edomites, descendants of Esau, brother of Jacob. The long-standing feud between the offspring of these two is one of the central themes of ancient Biblical history. Although very little is known about Obadiah or exactly when he lived and wrote his prophecies, it was likely that he was from Judah. His book describes a time when the Edomites were gloating mockingly over Jerusalem's misfortunes at the hands of invaders. The Edomites themselves participated in at least four plunderings of Jerusalem. This possibly was the situation that brought on God's judgment. Jeremiah alluded to this time also; he predicted Edom's turn for judgment in Jeremiah 49:17, 18 and again in Lamentations 4:21. Obadiah reiterated the principle that God takes care of His own and brings judgment on those who harm His people.

I. JUDGMENT DECLARED
(Nahum 1:1-14)

A. God's Power and Jealousy
(vv. 1, 2)

(Nahum 1:1 is not included in the printed text.)

2. God is jealous, and the Lord revengeth; the Lord revengeth, and is furious; the Lord will take vengeance on his adversaries, and he reserveth wrath for his enemies.

Nahum was a contemporary of Zephaniah, Habakkuk, and Jeremiah, prophesying during the second half of the seventh century B.C., sometime prior to Nineveh's final destruction in 612 B.C. From 701 B.C. Nineveh had remained a constant threat and source of danger to the tiny kingdom of Judah. The idea that Nineveh could be destroyed would have seemed impossible to anyone visiting there in its heyday. The city walls have been excavated in recent years and were found to be nearly eight miles in circumference. There was also a tremendous canal and river system. The city was famous for its commerce and military strength. The very word *Nineveh* could strike terror to any foreigner who might hear it.

Judah was no match for this military giant, but there was one thing in Judah's favor—the power of a mighty God who was moved by the distress of His people. Nahum's message was one of solace for those who had been threatened constantly by the overwhelming military strength of Nineveh. The name *Nahum* means "comfort," "compassionate," or "consolation." Nahum's words of consolation could not be rightly claimed by all the people of Judah, however, because as a whole the nation had forsaken God. Even though there had been legitimate revival under Hezekiah, the tiny kingdom had slowly degenerated in its worship of Jehovah to such an extent that by Nahum's day most of the people were worshiping idols. There was a remnant, however, who could take comfort in Nahum's words. In every generation there is a remnant who do not let themselves get caught up in the vanities of the times. They remain faithful, no matter what course their nation takes.

The opening verses of Nahum's writing present a picture of the eternal power and righteousness of God. He alone has the right to carry out vengeance against those who have harmed His people. Even though God is "jealous" (v. 2), His jealousy is not the same as that of humans. When men are jealous and vengeful, they act out of selfishness. "But it is appropriate for God to insist on our complete allegiance, and it is just for Him to punish unrepentant evildoers. His jealousy and vengeance are unmixed with selfishness. Their purpose is to remove sin and restore peace to the world (Deuteronomy 4:24; 5:9)" (*Life Application Bible*).

B. God's Anger (vv. 3-6)

(Nahum 1:4-6 is not included in the printed text.)

3. The Lord is slow to anger, and great in power, and will not at all acquit the wicked: the Lord hath his way in the whirlwind and in the storm, and the clouds are the dust of his feet.

These verses portray the patience, power, holiness, and justice of the living God. "The Lord is merciful and gracious, slow to anger, and plenteous in mercy" (Psalm 103:8), but He does not allow sin to go unpunished forever. Nineveh finally fell in 612 B.C. when the Babylonians, Scythians, and Medes broke through the city's defenses after floods had eroded her walls. This was almost 150 years after Jonah came to preach repentance. Initially the Ninevites had heeded the reluctant preacher's words and turned with great remorse from their sins. They put on sackcloth and fasted, crying out for God to spare them.

Every generation needs its own revival, however; and soon the people and their descendants were back to their old ways. "One of the worst things we can ever do is repent of our repentance" (Briscoe, *Hearing God's Voice Above The Noise*). After having experienced God's forgiveness and grace, a people or nation is then much more responsible for its sins. "For unto whomsoever much is given, of him shall be much required" (Luke 12:48). Unless repentance is followed by long-term changes in action and attitude, God's justice will not allow Him to overlook sin.

To do such would be to disregard the prayers of those who have been victimized by those sins (see Nahum 1:12, 15).

C. God Remembers His People (vv. 7-11)

(Nahum 1:10, 11 is not included in the printed text.)

7. The Lord is good, a strong hold in the day of trouble; and he knoweth them that trust in him.

8. But with an overrunning flood he will make an utter end of the place thereof, and darkness shall pursue his enemies.

9. What do ye imagine against the Lord? he will make an utter end: affliction shall not rise up the second time.

These words were a comfort to those who loved the Lord but were a forewarning to those who continued in their wickedness and came against God's people. Interestingly, God always gives warning before He sends judgment. His character consistently allows for the opportunity to repent. "He is patient with you, not wanting anyone to perish, but everyone to come to repentance" (2 Peter 3:9, *NIV*). The "one " referred to in Nahum 1:11 was Sennacherib, the Assyrian king who came up against Jerusalem. This monarch experienced God's anger: "'I am against you,' declares the Lord Almighty. 'I will burn up your chariots in smoke, and the sword will devour your young lions. I will leave you no prey on the earth. The voices of your messengers will no longer be heard'" (Nahum 2:13, *NIV*).

D. Nineveh's Sentence of Death (vv. 12-14)

(Nahum 1:12-14 is not included in the printed text.)

The Assyrians were known for their cruelty. When they attacked their enemies they annihilated them and destroyed their cities. "They would carefully construct pyramids of the skulls of the vanquished" (Briscoe). Such gross wickedness was eventually repaid. This decree—"Thus saith the Lord"—reversed the fortunes of the oppressor. Though they were great and had many allies, they were cut down.

Another reversal of fortune was also decreed for Judah. The word *afflict* (v. 12) means to be "humbled and oppressed" (*Zondervan New International Version Bible Commentary*). God used a foreign power as a means of disciplining His own people, as He so often had done before and would do again. Nevertheless, a remnant of the Jews would be restored after the Captivity. The Assyrians, however, would be destroyed.

Was the repentance of the Ninevites to Jonah's preaching sincere? Does repentance ever last beyond one generation?

II. DELIVERANCE PROMISED
(Obadiah 1:17-21)

(Obadiah 1:19, 20 is not included in the printed text.)

17. But upon mount Zion shall be deliverance, and there shall be holiness; and the house of Jacob shall possess their possessions.

18. And the house of Jacob shall be a fire, and the house of Joseph a flame, and the house of Esau for stubble, and they shall kindle in them, and devour them; and there shall not be any remaining of the house of Esau;

for the Lord hath spoken it.

21. And saviours shall come up on mount Zion to judge the mount of Esau; and the kingdom shall be the Lord's.

Southeast of the Dead Sea, Edom was a barren, mountainous land inhabited by the descendants of Esau. The rivalry between Judah and Edom had lasted for centuries, making reconciliation nearly impossible. At the likely time of Obadiah's writing, Edom had joined a coalition of states united in opposition against Judah. Obadiah notes two important principles of God's working: First, God's hand extends to work in the lives of foreign nations. He builds His kingdom, often using heathen lands and peoples to do His bidding. He is working toward the ultimate establishment of His eternal kingdom. Bearing this in mind, every believer must remember the big picture of world affairs. God is very much in control of everything that takes place on the international scene.

The second principle is that the proud will be brought down. Although the Edomites lived in a desolate area, they were firmly established, fierce, and arrogant. This boastful self-sufficiency always comes under the judgment of God. "There have been kings and there have been dictators. There have been emperors and Caesars. Their kingdoms have come and gone. These rulers have one thing in common. Their bones now mold in obscure graves, but the Sovereign Lord rules. God is still on the throne" (Briscoe).

The arrogance of the Edomites ran especially deep, as indicated by the fact that scholars and archeologists can find no evidence that they worshiped any god or idol at all. "This unusual people were so self-sufficient, arrogant, and self-satisfied that they wouldn't even call upon the name of any kind of god" (Briscoe). Here was a nation who thought it had all its own answers. This attitude can be compared to the humanistic New Age movement of our own day. When man feels he is master of his own fate and makes himself into a god, he is in deep trouble with the true Sovereign of the universe. This was the hard lesson Belshazzar had to learn when Daniel interpreted the handwriting on the wall in Babylon (Daniel 5:20-28). God hates pride and ultimately brings it to judgment.

As in all the prophets, there is a positive side to Obadiah's words. In contrast to the fate of Edom, there would come deliverance on Mount Zion (v. 17). Likely, Obadiah's prophecy dealt with the return of the exiles from Babylon after the captivity. Even today the remains of the stark land of Edom bears out the fact that Edom did indeed come tumbling down. But God promised that Jerusalem would be restored. Edom's principal fortress city, Petra, sits in stark wilderness and isolation. It is one of the most formidable places on earth. God had spoken judgment on the descendants of Esau. Nothing could change that. He also spoke blessing and restoration to Jerusalem. And nothing will ever stop that either.

In summary, God is active in the affairs of all men and nations, even though they may not see Him as such. He utilizes every event on earth to His ultimate purposes. Also, pride always leads to a fall. We must continually humble our-

selves and rid ourselves of arrogance, or else we will bring about our own destruction. Peter put it this way: "Humble yourselves, therefore, under God's mighty hand, that he may lift you up in due time" (1 Peter 5:6, *NIV*). Revelation 3:19 puts God's position in perspective: "As many as I love, I rebuke and chasten: be zealous therefore, and repent."

There is never a place for arrogance or pride in God's kingdom. What is the fate of those who exalt themselves, especially at the expense of others?

III. MERCY EXTENDED
     (Jonah 3:1-10)

     (Jonah 3:6-9 is not included in the printed text.)

     1. And the word of the Lord came unto Jonah the second time, saying,

     2. Arise, go unto Nineveh, that great city, and preach unto it the preaching that I bid thee.

     3. So Jonah arose, and went unto Nineveh, according to the word of the Lord. Now Nineveh was an exceeding great city of three days' journey.

     4. And Jonah began to enter into the city a day's journey, and he cried, and said, Yet forty days, and Nineveh shall be overthrown.

     5. So the people of Nineveh believed God, and proclaimed a fast, and put on sackcloth, from the greatest of them even to the least of them.

The story of the reluctant evangelist going to Nineveh is one of the most controversial in the Bible. Is it possible that a great fish actually swallowed Jonah and kept him there for three days before spitting him out on a beach? Many feel that this should be viewed as an allegorical tale. G. Campbell Morgan puts the argument into its proper context: "Men have been looking so hard at the great fish that they have failed to see the great God."

A greater miracle than Jonah's surviving the ordeal in the fish is the fact that the city of Nineveh actually responded when Jonah finally brought them the message of impending destruction. That God went to great lengths to provide a means of repentance points out His unending mercy. Punishment is never what God wants to impose on man. What He longs for is fellowship. Notice, too, that these were noncovenant people. This should have been an obvious lesson for the people of Israel. God had not made them His chosen people so only they could be His people. Rather, they were to be the means by which all mankind could be reached for God.

As shown through the comments on Obadiah, the Ninevites were hardly a people deserving of God's mercy. They were totally corrupt and wicked. This accounts for Jonah's running away from God's command in the first place. He wanted this terrible, oppressive empire to fall. It had long been a menace to Israel. At this time in history, however, internal strife had shrunk Assyria's dominance over other kingdoms, thus giving Israel and other smaller countries breathing room. Jonah probably reasoned that if God extended mercy to these enemies, then their renewed dominance would again be detrimental to Israel.

There is another possibility to ponder. Jonah's thinking may have been influenced by the preaching of Hosea and Amos, two contemporary prophets of his day. Both of these men denounced Israel for her idolatry and arrogant rebellion against God, yet there was never any responding repentance. Jonah may have felt the shame of sensing that the Assyrians would repent when God's own chosen people had refused to do so.

Who are generally the most responsive to the gospel—those who have been preached to for years or those who hear for the first time? Explain why you believe your answer to be true.

REVIEW QUESTIONS

1. Is there a greater punishment for those who have once known God's mercy through repentance and later returned to their sins?

2. At what point does a people trample so harshly on God's mercy that He must bring judgment?

3. The Edomites were blood relatives of the Israelites. Esau and Jacob renewed their brotherly relationship. Why did their descendants become such mortal enemies?

4. The people of Nineveh seemed to have genuinely repented? Why did this not last through succeeding generations?

GOLDEN TEXT HOMILY

"THE LORD IS SLOW TO ANGER, AND GREAT IN POWER, AND WILL NOT AT ALL ACQUIT THE WICKED" (Nahum 1:3).

"The Lord is slow to anger." Why? Because He is "great in power." He has power over His own feelings. That's the picture the prophet gives here, an infinitely patient God. He does not move rapidly. He gave this city chance after chance to repent. He had sent prophet after prophet.

We must understand that God does have the capacity for anger. The Bible speaks of fleeing from the wrath to come (Matthew 3:7). Unfortunately, we believe that if we just preach a God of love, then we will fill our churches. Sinners will turn from their wickedness and be drawn to Him. However, the facts prove otherwise. For years we have forgotten the message that He is also a God of wrath. As a result, people have come to view Him as a God of permissiveness, who will let you do anything and get away with it. Because of that, we have empty churches. Instead of turning toward God, men defy Him.

We know that no one who turns to God will ever experience His vengeance. It is only when we reject His love that we force Him into employing His wrath.

If He were any less divine, we would all be in trouble. He would have long ago destroyed the earth with fire and man would have been utterly destroyed. He is our Rock; in Him we place our trust. Be not afraid of His power. He is our place of refuge.—**James L. Durel, Captain, The Salvation Army, Vacaville, California**

SENTENCE SERMONS

GOD JUDGES EVIL but offers mercy to all people.

—Selected

YOU MAY JUGGLE human laws, you may fool with human courts, but there is a judgment to come and from it there is no appeal.

—Orin Philip Giford

GOD JUDGES a man not by the point he has reached but by the way he is facing, not by distance but by direction.

—James S. Stewart

MERCY IS NOT for them that sin and fear not, but for them that fear and sin not.

—Thomas Watson

EVANGELISM APPLICATION

THE CERTAINTY OF GOD'S JUDGMENT SHOULD MOTIVATE BELIEVERS TO WARN THE LOST.

The Lord will certainly vindicate His name and punish evildoers. We live in a modern world where evil seems to be triumphing over good more every day. God's law has been pushed aside in too many people's lives and replaced by their own will. As a result, good people suffer. But remember this: God is still on the throne. Nothing escapes His attention, and justice will ultimately prevail. We don't ever need to think that the wicked get away with anything. No one can tread on God's principles with impunity. Realizing this, believers must do everything in their power to warn the lost and rescue them from the destruction they will otherwise experience as a result of their sins.

DAILY BIBLE READINGS

M. God Abhors Wickedness.
   Psalm 5:4-12
T. Trust in the Lord.
   Psalm 118:1-9
W. Salvation Promised.
   Isaiah 25:1-9
T. Salvation Provided.
   John 3:14-17
F. Living Victoriously.
   Romans 6:3-14
S. Mercy Shown. Romans 9:21-28

God's Compassionate Character

Study Text: Micah 2:1-3; 3:9-11; 6:9-16; 7:18-20

Objective: To consider God's compassionate nature and respond with gratitude.

Time: The Book of Micah was written between 735 and 698 B.C.

Place: The Book of Micah was written in Judah (southern kingdom).

Golden Text: "It is of the Lord's mercies that we are not consumed, because his compassions fail not" (Lamentations 3:22).

Central Truth: God is compassionate despite human sinfulness.

Evangelism Emphasis: God's compassion gives sinners the hope of redemption.

PRINTED TEXT

Micah 2:1. Woe to them that devise iniquity, and work evil upon their beds! when the morning is light, they practise it, because it is in the power of their hand.

2. And they covet fields, and take them by violence; and houses, and take them away: so they oppress a man and his house, even a man and his heritage.

3. Therefore thus saith the Lord; Behold, against this family do I devise an evil, from which ye shall not remove your necks; neither shall ye go haughtily: for this time is evil.

3:9. Hear this, I pray you, ye heads of the house of Jacob, and princes of the house of Israel, that abhor judgment, and pervert all equity.

10. They build up Zion with blood, and Jerusalem with iniquity.

11. The heads thereof judge for reward, and the priests thereof teach for hire, and the prophets thereof divine for money: yet will they lean upon the Lord, and say, Is not the Lord among us? none evil can come upon us.

6:9. The Lord's voice crieth unto the city, and the man of wisdom shall see thy name: hear ye the rod, and who hath appointed it.

10. Are there yet the treasures of wickedness in the house of the wicked, and the scant measure that is abominable?

11. Shall I count them pure with the wicked balances, and with the bag of deceitful weights?

12. For the rich men thereof are full of violence, and the inhabitants thereof have spoken lies, and their tongue is deceitful in their mouth.

13. Therefore also will I make thee sick in smiting thee, in making

thee desolate because of thy sins.

14. Thou shalt eat, but not be satisfied; and thy casting down shall be in the midst of thee; and thou shalt take hold, but shalt not deliver; and that which thou deliverest will I give up to the sword.

15. Thou shalt sow, but thou shalt not reap; thou shalt tread the olives, but thou shalt not anoint thee with oil; and sweet wine, but shalt not drink wine.

7:18. Who is a God like unto thee, that pardoneth iniquity, and passeth by the transgression of the remnant of his heritage? he retaineth not his anger for ever, because he delighteth in mercy.

19. He will turn again, he will have compassion upon us; he will subdue our iniquities; and thou wilt cast all their sins into the depths of the sea.

LESSON OUTLINE

I. EVIL ACTIONS
   A. Indictment Against Israel's Rulers
   B. The Results of Corruption

II. DIVINE INDICTMENT
   A. A Sentence of Judgment
   B. Results of Sins Against the Poor

III. GOD'S COMPASSION
   A. Victory Assured
   B. God's Faithfulness to the Covenant With Abraham

LESSON EXPOSITION

INTRODUCTION

The very first verses of this book indicate that Micah prophesied in the days of three kings of Judah—Jotham (739-731 B.C.), Ahaz (731-715 B.C.), and Hezekiah (715-686 B.C.). His message was primarily directed at his own country, but he also addressed the northern kingdom of Israel, predicting the fall of Samaria. Thus, much of his work took place before the fall of Israel in 722 B.C. Because so much of his preaching was a denunciation of the immorality and idolatry in his home nation, it must have taken place mainly before the sweeping religious reforms of Hezekiah. Thus, some of the credit for that revival may be attributed to his exposure of the nation's sins.

The sixth of the minor prophets, Micah was a contemporary of Isaiah and Hosea. His message was similar to that of Isaiah, but the two never traveled in the same circles and were from quite different social and economic classes. Micah was from the small village of Moresheth, 30 miles southwest of Jerusalem. While Isaiah moved in and out of the king's palace, Micah never spoke to royal audiences. Still, his calling was as strong as that of Isaiah.

Much of Micah's message was directed at two cities, Samaria and Jerusalem, the two capitals of the divided kingdom. Terrible destruction was predicted for Samaria: "Therefore I will make Samaria a heap of rubble, a place for planting vineyards. I will pour her stones into the valley and lay bare her foundations. All her idols will be broken to pieces; all her temple gifts will be burned with fire; I will destroy all her images. Since she gathered her gifts from the wages of prostitutes, as the wages of prostitutes they will again be used" (Micah 1:6, 7, *NIV*). This was also fair warning to Jerusalem, for the southern kingdom was headed in the same sinful direction and would also face judgment from the Lord. Micah's dire prediction about Samaria was a reference to the Assyrian armies' invading with an irresistible force. And though it was a foreign nation who would be sweeping down on the northern kingdom, Micah made it clear that this would be a direct intervention by God into the affairs of men.

Like other prophets, Micah had difficulty getting anyone to listen to him. The great empire of Assyria was going through a time of internal difficulty, and at least temporarily posed no major threat to the security of Israel or Judah. Consequently, the people were enjoying a time of economic affluence, but they had also blinded their eyes to their own decadence. They did not want to hear a message of judgment. Interestingly, while there was tremendous idolatry in both kingdoms, Micah's message primarily condemned the social injustice that pervaded the ruling classes of the time. The rich were taking advantage of the poor and at the same time were fooling themselves by claiming the Lord's provision and blessing.

The Book of Micah can be divided into three sections with three distinct themes: (1) judgment on both Israel and Judah (chs. 1, 2); (2) restoration and reign of the Messiah (chs. 3-5); (3) divine punishment followed by divine mercy (chs. 6, 7). Micah's writings indicted Israel and Judah for sins of oppression; bribery among judges, prophets, and priests; exploitation of the poor; cheating; violence; pride; and covetousness. God would not let these sins continue unaddressed, and certain punishment was coming. But there was also a message of future hope and restoration in Micah's ministry. Real peace and justice would prevail when the Messiah would come. The most notable of Micah's prophecies is his naming of Bethlehem as the future birthplace of the Messiah (5:2). This prophecy was given some 700 years before Jesus was born there.

Micah 4:1-3 describes a wonderful future in store for the earth at some distant time. Compare this passage with Isaiah 2:2-4 and you will find that they are almost exactly the same. Both prophets spoke of a wonderful time to come when there will be no more war. They envisioned an era of security and peace when everyone will have plenty, and to worship the Lord and walk in His ways will be the predominant thought and desire of the inhabitants of the land.

This is a message for the church today. God still speaks clearly and confirms His Word through more than one voice. Just as Micah and Isaiah expressed the same words, God confirms His Word through many witnesses. Be careful to note that a message from God will never emphasize that we act contrary to exhibiting justice toward our fellowman, loving mercy, and walking humbly with our God (Micah 6:8).

God still leads His people, by His Spirit, just as He has always done.

I. EVIL ACTIONS
(Micah 2:1-3; 3:9-11)

A. Indictment Against Israel's Rulers (2:1-3)

1. Woe to them that devise iniquity, and work evil upon their beds! when the morning is light, they practise it, because it is in the power of their hand.

2. And they covet fields, and take them by violence; and houses, and take them away: so they oppress a man and his house, even a man and his heritage.

3. Therefore thus saith the Lord; Behold, against this family do I devise an evil, from which ye shall not remove your necks; neither shall ye go haughtily: for this time is evil.

God had made strict rules about property allotments when the Israelites first came to the Promised Land. In Exodus 20:15, 17, two of the Ten Commandments—theft and covetousness—dealt with how citizens should respect the possessions of others. Because everything actually belonged to God in the first place, the people were never really to be regarded as owners but rather as stewards of parcels of land. The various tribes were given major sections of territory, and these in turn were divided into tracts among clans and families so that all would have a small area of land. The law also protected the people from having their landmarks removed (Deuteronomy 19:14). The law of redemption (Leviticus 25:23-28) showed how God ordained the way property should be managed. The Year of Jubilee (every 50th) was set as a time when all property reverted to its original owner. If a family or individual had fallen into misfortune and lost their land, it must in that year be returned to them or their heirs. "And because it was God's, it was very wrong for people to abuse or covet the property of others. If you tried to buy other people's property, you took away their divine inheritance" (Briscoe, *Hearing God's Voice Above the Noise*). This was God's plan. It was His land. The people were never to become proud, selfish landowners.

Over the centuries, however, greed had overtaken the people. The classic example was the instance of when King Ahab (873-853 B.C.) and Jezebel plotted to kill Naboth so that they could seize his property (1 Kings 21:1-16). A plague of such illegal, unethical behavior had invaded the land and was now destroying the nation from inside out. As punishment God now promised through Micah's words (2:4) that foreigners would confiscate the land, imposing the same treatment on the wealthy that they had put their poorer brothers through.

How had the affluent circumvented the original law God had commanded? Likely, they had instituted statutes that made their actions appear proper and businesslike. However, just because something is legal does not make it right in God's sight. Christians today should take careful inventory of their business practices. There are no loopholes in God's laws. His laws are permanent, no matter what the prevailing legal establishments sanction.

B. The Results of Corruption (3:9-11)

9. Hear this, I pray you, ye

heads of the house of Jacob, and princes of the house of Israel, that abhor judgment, and pervert all equity.

10. They build up Zion with blood, and Jerusalem with iniquity.

11. The heads thereof judge for reward, and the priests thereof teach for hire, and the prophets thereof divine for money: yet will they lean upon the Lord, and say, Is not the Lord among us? none evil can come upon us.

The judges, the priests, and the false prophets of Micah's day were motivated purely by greed. Everything in the society was defined in terms of money. The services of the nation's leadership were for sale to those who could afford it. "The issue was not that they were being paid; obviously they needed to earn a living. But they had corrupted their offices by allowing money to distort their leadership. Rather than saying what was true, right, and just, they said whatever they were paid to say. They grew wealthy from their positions, but their integrity went bankrupt" (*The Word in Life Study Bible.*)

These people had forgotten God's commandments; nevertheless, they still felt that God was pleased with them and would continue to bless them in their hypocrisy. Because they saw themselves as God's chosen, they told themselves nothing could hurt them—including impending invasions, which Micah and other true prophets were predicting.

Micah's diagnosis of the nation's problems was not really new. God had made clear what was right and

wrong when He gave the law. The word *abhor* in verse 9 means "despise." God gave His people a similar message in Leviticus 26:15, 16: "And if you reject my decrees and abhor my laws and fail to carry out all my commands and so violate my covenant, then I will do this to you: I will bring upon you sudden terror, wasting diseases and fever that will destroy your sight and drain away your life. You will plant seed in vain, because your enemies will eat it" (*NIV*). Micah was now echoing punishment that God had much earlier promised. The Lord was not going to allow those who claim to be His own get away with violating His law and still expect peace and prosperity.

Does anyone ever get away with sin? Can you ever mistreat another individual without repercussions? Explain.

II. DIVINE INDICTMENT
(Micah 6:9-16)

A. A Sentence of Judgment
(vv. 9-12)

9. The Lord's voice crieth unto the city, and the man of wisdom shall see thy name: hear ye the rod, and who hath appointed it.

10. Are there yet the treasures of wickedness in the house of the wicked, and the scant measure that is abominable?

11. Shall I count them pure with the wicked balances, and with the bag of deceitful weights?

12. For the rich men thereof are full of violence, and the

inhabitants thereof have spoken lies, and their tongue is deceitful in their mouth.

It is not enough to act as though we are spiritual; it is necessary to live it. In the verse prior to this passage (v. 8), Micah laid out a three-point summary of how God's people should live: (1) treat everyone with justice; (2) be merciful in every situation; (3) walk humbly before God. These are indeed noble goals, but they can easily be forgotten in a dog-eat-dog world. Micah's words condemned Israel for forgetting godly values and using instead dishonest weights, measures, audits and wages, and other unethical practices. The rod is the punishment the people would have to endure for its sins. There would be an invasion by a foreign power, which God would allow. Micah's words reiterate those of another prophet—Amos: "Seek good, not evil, that you may live. Then the Lord God Almighty will be with you, just as you say he is. Hate evil, love good; maintain justice in the courts" (Amos 5:14, 15, NIV).

Micah pointed out that Israel had failed to live up to God's plan. "God had delivered the Israelites from Egypt and established them as a nation. He called them to be a model society that would attract other nations to him (Deuteronomy 4:5, 6). Instead they exploited the poor, selfishly pursuing their own interests. They rebelled against God's authority and rejected his prophets" (*The Quest Study Bible*).

Micah's emphasis was on social sins much more so than the sins of idolatry—although the two are closely linked. God is interested in every facet of our lives. Though we are saved by faith, not works, it is imperative that this faith pervade every area of daily existence. Paul presented a balanced picture of a living faith when he said, "For it is by grace you have been saved, through faith—and this not from yourselves, it is the gift of God—not by works, so that no one can boast. For we are God's workmanship, created in Christ Jesus to do good works, which God prepared in advance for us to do" (Ephesians 2:8-10, NIV). God's people are to mirror His character. We must treat others fairly, justly, and with compassion. We cannot separate our spiritual and secular lives.

B. Results of Sins Against the Poor (6:13-16)

(Micah 6:16 is not included in the printed text.)

13. Therefore also will I make thee sick in smiting thee, in making thee desolate because of thy sins.

14. Thou shalt eat, but not be satisfied; and thy casting down shall be in the midst of thee; and thou shalt take hold, but shalt not deliver; and that which thou deliverest will I give up to the sword.

15. Thou shalt sow, but thou shalt not reap; thou shalt tread the olives, but thou shalt not anoint thee with oil; and sweet wine, but shalt not drink wine.

God's prophets generally did not say anything really new but rather echoed words the Lord had already said. Micah did this in this passage as he reiterated what Moses spoke centuries earlier when the Israelites prepared to enter Canaan. The consequences for disobeying God had not changed: "You will sow much seed in the field but you will harvest little, because locusts will devour it. You will plant vineyards and cultivate them but you will not drink the wine or gather the grapes, because worms will eat them. You will have olive trees throughout your country but you will not use the oil, because the olives will drop off. You will have sons and daughters but you will not keep them, because they will go into captivity. Swarms of locusts will take over all your trees and the crops of your land" (Deuteronomy 28:38-42, *NIV*).

Men have short memories. If there is one thing that history teaches, it is that humanity too seldom learns from or remembers the lessons of history. Micah repeated here the curses God had already ordained if the people forgot His commandments. The people had not only forgotten them but actually believed their lives were pleasing to God. Their empty rituals and sacrifices had replaced real integrity.

The reference to Omri in verse 16 was a reminder to the people of how one of Israel's most wicked kings had perverted God's legal system. He had been famous for abusing the poor and leading the people into idol worship. If the people were going to follow such an example of hypocrisy, they were truly in bad shape.

We are saved by faith and not by works. However, can we claim salvation if we continue sinful practices in our daily lives?

III. GOD'S COMPASSION
(Micah 7:18-20)

(Micah 7:20 is not included in the printed text.)

A. Victory Assured (vv. 18, 19)

18. Who is a God like unto thee, that pardoneth iniquity, and passeth by the transgression of the remnant of his heritage? he retaineth not his anger for ever, because he delighteth in mercy.

19. He will turn again, he will have compassion upon us; he will subdue our iniquities; and thou wilt cast all their sins into the depths of the sea.

Micah looked into the future as he came to the close in his prophecy. He saw a time when God would gather Israel as a shepherd gathers his sheep (v. 14). The ruined city of Jerusalem would again rise from the ashes. The people would have to endure God's punishment, but His mercy and compassion would eventually restore them. The wonder of God's grace is extolled in the rhetorical question "Who is a God like unto thee?" Only the one true God would grant such mercy to an undeserving people.

God still longs to restore people today. He invites us to come as we are and repent of the sins we have committed. He is, as always, the Lord of mercy, compassion, and justice. He wants us to enjoy peace, prosperity, and an unbroken relationship with Him.

B. God's Faithfulness to the Covenant With Abraham (v. 20)

(Micah 7:20 is not included in the printed text.)

Centuries before, God had sworn a covenant with Abraham. He would bless the seed of the patriarch and shower them with His affections. Despite the disciplines now being laid out, this promise would still hold true. God's justice demands that His people live righteously. If they turn away from God into sin, then discipline is required to bring them back. Just as loving parents use "tough love" to train their children, so does God. To allow sin to continue would actually be a breach of the covenant made with Abraham.

God's anger had been kindled toward his wayward people, but it would not continue forever. There would be a believing remnant who would see an end of the humiliation. There was reason for optimism. God would be faithful to Abraham's seed.

Can we avoid having to go through God's discipline? Can we learn from the painful lessons that others have had to endure so that we can dodge those same pitfalls?

REVIEW QUESTIONS

1. In a society that is so caught up with greed and personal gain, how can we as Christians avoid letting these sins invade our lives?

2. Which is the easiest for believers to handle spiritually—blessing or adversity? Explain your answer.

3. How willing are we to listen to God's servants who have a negative message? Have we so emphasized God's love that we have forgotten His justice?

4. What are some business practices today that are legal but do not meet God's high standards of ethics?

GOLDEN TEXT HOMILY

"IT IS OF THE LORD'S MERCIES THAT WE ARE NOT CONSUMED, BECAUSE HIS COMPASSIONS FAIL NOT" (Lamentations 3:22).

In the beginning of the chapter, Jeremiah referred to his calamities, which were numerous. However, in verse 22, our Golden Text for this lesson, he acknowledged that were it not for the Lord's mercies and unfailing compassions, he and others would have been consumed or destroyed.

What is God's *mercy*? It is "a blessing that is an act of divine favor."

What is *compassion*? It is the "sympathetic consciousness of others' distress together with a desire to alleviate it."

In Lamentations we find one of the most beautiful and meaningful confessions of faith in the goodness of God. It is a remarkable testimony to the extent and force of divine grace.

None of us deserve the mercies of God, and we would have no right to complain if suddenly they all stopped. However, we can be thankful God's mercies will never stop. His mercies are constantly renewed, and He adapts His graces to the immediate needs of the hour.

God faithfully gives to each of us new mercies (v. 23). He is living and acting in our midst every day and at each moment. Whatever mercy is needed, He provides it.

As God keeps this old world green by renewing it every spring, likewise He refreshes and invigorates His people by springtimes of His graces.

The fact that God's mercies never stop is proof of His faithfulness. This confirms His promise that He will never leave nor forsake His people.

The daily mercies we receive from God are recurrent reminders of His faithfulness. They are new every morning and are like light after darkness and strength after sleep.

God has not forgotten, nor will He ever forget, to be gracious. His mercies and His compassions are among His gracious attributes.

Like the children of Israel were on numerous occasions, many people today are ungrateful for the blessings of God and are rebellious. By our ingratitude and rebellion we test the Lord's compassion, but He is greater and better than our highest and purest thoughts of Him. "His compassions fail not."

God's mercies are the only guarantee we have that we will not be consumed. The only adequate defense against the destroying powers we experience in this life is found in God. The wisest action we can take is to put ourselves into the hands of our kind and compassionate heavenly Father.—**O.W. Polen, D.D., Coordinator of Special Projects, Pathway Press, Cleveland, Tennessee**

SENTENCE SERMONS

GOD IS COMPASSIONATE despite human sinfulness.
—Selected

MAN MAY DISMISS compassion from his heart, but God will never.
—William Cowper

THE DEW of compassion is a tear.

—Lord Byron

EVIL CAN NEVER BE undone, but only purged and redeemed.
—Dorothy L. Sayers

ILLUMINATING THE LESSON

The plans for a new highway system had just been unveiled in a particular community. They called for a thoroughfare going through a riverfront area that had always been remote, and thus never seen as valuable. It turns out, however, that several local businessmen—prominent church leaders among them—had already heard about this plan and had bought up most of the land from the unsuspecting poor blacks living in that area. Suddenly, these were the hottest properties in the county. All the affluent wanted riverfront homes and were willing to pay astronomical prices for lots there.

The businessmen were praised by most for having been so astute. When others criticized them for taking advantage of the poor, they defended themselves by saying that this was simply good business—capitalism at work. And besides, they were taking a risk themselves.

We are a part of a society that looks for inside information, the right tip, the way to get to the marketplace first. But how does this fit with what Micah had to say about the way we treat others? If our business successes come at the expense of those less fortunate (or by means of unethical inside information), aren't we just as guilty as the people of Judah and Israel? How will God judge us?

DAILY BIBLE READINGS

M. Rebellion.
1 Kings 21:1-4
T. Idolatry.
1 Kings 21:5-16
W. God's Grace.
2 Chronicles 30:6-9
T. God Is Just.
Nehemiah 9:26-33
F. Forgive Others.
Matthew 18:21-33
S. God Is Merciful.
Romans 9:14-18

Faith During Troubled Times

Study Text: Habakkuk 1:1 through 3:19

Objective: To recognize that God is with us in adversity and call on Him with faith.

Time: The Book of Habakkuk was written between 609 and 589 B.C.

Place: The Book of Habakkuk was written in Judah (southern kingdom).

Golden Text: "In the day of my trouble I will call upon thee: for thou wilt answer me" (Psalm 86:7).

Central Truth: Faith in God enables us to persevere in difficult times.

Evangelism Emphasis: Times of distress present opportunities to lead the lost to Christ.

PRINTED TEXT

Habakkuk 1:1. The burden which Habakkuk the prophet did see.

2. O Lord, how long shall I cry, and thou wilt not hear! even cry out unto thee of violence, and thou wilt not save!

3. Why dost thou shew me iniquity, and cause me to behold grievance? for spoiling and violence are before me: and there are that raise up strife and contention.

4.   Therefore the law is slacked, and judgment doth never go forth: for the wicked doth compass about the righteous; therefore wrong judgment proceedeth.

2:1. I will stand upon my watch, and set me upon the tower, and will watch to see what he will say unto me, and what I shall answer when I am reproved.

2. And the Lord answered me, and said, Write the vision, and make it plain upon tables, that he may run that readeth it.

3. For the vision is yet for an appointed time, but at the end it shall speak, and not lie: though it tarry, wait for it; because it will surely come, it will not tarry.

4. Behold, his soul which is lifted up is not upright in him: but the just shall live by his faith.

20. But the Lord is in his holy temple: let all the earth keep silence before him.

3:16. When I heard, my belly trembled; my lips quivered at the voice: rottenness entered into my bones, and I trembled in myself, that I might rest in the day of trouble: when he cometh up unto the people, he will invade them with his troops.

17. Although the fig tree shall

not blossom, neither shall fruit be in the vines; the labour of the olive shall fail, and the fields shall yield no meat; the flock shall be cut off from the fold, and there shall be no herd in the stalls:

18. Yet I will rejoice in the Lord, I will joy in the God of my salvation.

19. The Lord God is my strength, and he will make my feet like hinds' feet, and he will make me to walk upon mine high places. To the chief singer on my stringed instruments.

DICTIONARY

Habakkuk (ha-BAK-uk)—Habakkuk 1:1—A prophet who served God and wrote at about the same time as Jeremiah.

LESSON OUTLINE
  I. PERPLEXING QUESTIONS
     A. The Prophet's Identity
     B. The Prophet's Lament
     C. The Justice System Paralyzed
 II. GOD'S ANSWERS
     A. The Prophet's Resolve
     B. The Lord Speaks
     C. The Just Shall Live by Faith
     D. God's Holiness Prevails
III. TRIUMPHANT FAITH

LESSON EXPOSITION

INTRODUCTION

Habakkuk looked with dismay at his native Judah and saw violence, injustice, hypocrisy, and hard-heartedness everywhere. The country sat on the precipice of destruction, yet the people refused to change their sinful ways. Society was hopelessly out of control as men drifted further into apostasy. The greater tragedy in Habakkuk's mind, however, was that God had somehow forgotten, had turned His back on the world's affairs, and was doing nothing to change the situation. In his frustration, Habakkuk cried out to God with perplexing questions: "Where are you, God? Why are the wicked prospering at the expense of the poor? Why are righteous people beaten down? Don't you care about what your people are doing?"

Without thought as to whether or not it was blasphemy to question God, Habakkuk poured out an honest heart to God. He freely expressed his concerns, his frustrations, and his doubts to God. The issues that concerned him are the same as those that have disturbed believers down through the centuries: Why are evil and suffering so rampant? Why do goodness and justice fail? If God is good, why does He let these things happen? Why is God so slow to act?

Habakkuk's prophecies were spoken against the dramatic background of the decline and fall of Judah. He watched the great power of the previous century, Assyria, crumble as mighty Babylon established itself. When Nebuchadnezzar's armies destroyed Nineveh in 612 B.C., the stage was set for a new archenemy to sweep into Palestine and dominate everything.

The last glimmer of prosperity in Judah was under Josiah during the next three years, but the godly monarch was killed in battle in 609 B.C. From that point on, life progressively degenerated. The first invasion took place, and captives were taken in 605 B.C. Habakkuk, therefore, saw it all—the decline from relative abundance and the possibility of revival under Josiah to the destruction of the nation.

Nothing is known about Habakkuk himself except his name. *Chabaqquwq* is a rare Hebrew name derived from the verb *chabaq*, meaning "to embrace." This became appropriate for the prophet at the end of the book, for he chose to trust and embrace the Lord, regardless of what happened. Habakkuk may have been a priest connected with Temple worship in Jerusalem. This is suggested by the reference "to the chief musician" at the end of the book.

Habakkuk was apparently a bold prophet. It took strong resolution to speak God's words to a rebellious people, but it took even greater courage to wrestle openly and honestly with God himself over problems and issues that tested his faith. Habakkuk directed hard questions to the Lord in two rounds of dialogue. He was not afraid to complain about things he did not understand. Instead of forsaking God for not immediately answering the perplexing questions of life, he poured His questions out to the only One who could answer them. This is a wonderful lesson for every believer. "If I bring the doubts and the questions to God and seek his face about them, I will come up with an answer of some kind. But if I turn from him, if I isolate myself, if I throw the Scriptures away, if I reject the church and its people, then I'm in trouble" (Briscoe).

I. PERPLEXING QUESTIONS (Habakkuk 1:1-4)

A. The Prophet's Identity (v. 1)

1. The burden which Habakkuk the prophet did see.

Habakkuk prophesied in Judah primarily during the 11-year reign of Jehoiakim (see 2 Kings 23:36—24:5). He watched Assyria fall and Babylon rise as the nemesis of the small kingdom. While other Old Testament prophets generally acted as God's mouthpiece to the people, Habakkuk brought men's questions to God. In the midst of the crises he was watching develop around him, Habakkuk wanted to know the big picture. He wanted to know what were God's long-range plans for taking control of a world rampant with sin.

Habakkuk began by identifying himself as a prophet. Thus, from the beginning he showed himself to be an insider asking questions. He never denied the existence of God or his loyalties to Him. He was simply concerned about why things were the way they were. He was not afraid to petition God. Although some would see this as arrogance, all believers have to agree that they too have times when they cannot understand God's ways. "Any Christian who is worth his salt will have some degree of distress of soul. He or she will be constantly dealing with the issue of who God is in the light of what is going on in his world. If we are not struggling with this, either we are not taking

God seriously or we are not really taking a long, hard look at the world in which we live" (Briscoe). Even though there was the chance that God would not give him a full answer, Habakkuk posed his questions—but never with a mind to forsake God. While he had his doubts, he never doubted who controlled the universe. He simply wanted a better understanding.

B. The Prophet's Lament (vv. 2, 3)

2. O Lord, how long shall I cry, and thou wilt not hear! even cry out unto thee of violence, and thou wilt not save!

3. Why dost thou shew me iniquity, and cause me to behold grievance? for spoiling and violence are before me: and there are that raise up strife and contention.

Habakkuk asked God how long He would allow the wickedness of Judah to go unnoticed and unpunished. Judah's citizens had perverted justice and were committing sins without remorse. The people openly worshiped idols, sacrificed their children to pagan gods, and ignored the prophets Jehovah sent them. King Jehoiakim even burned the writings of Jeremiah as a defiant act against God's warnings. In light of the fact that just a few years earlier there had been renewed hope for revival under Josiah, Habakkuk must have been especially brokenhearted. How quickly even the righteous citizens had succumbed to the onslaught of sin. Was no one else concerned for the condition of the nation?

If left unchecked, sin has always had a gradual numbing effect on people. The late 20th century provides vivid evidence of this. Evil and horrible events that a few years ago would have brought outrage barely raise an eyebrow. As sin increases, Christians can easily feel overwhelmed by the enormity of the burden and become discouraged in their attempts to fight it. Most good people eventually avert their eyes from the wickedness around them. This lack of reaction to sin is much of what brought out the burning frustration in Habakkuk.

In verse 2, Habakkuk asked the question "How long?" In a casual reading of his book, one might think that God immediately answered his question. More likely, however, the prophet cried out to the Lord for as long as 12 years before he received a response from the Lord. Was God ignoring his prayers during this time? No. Rather, events and kingdoms were being moved into place so that answers would be totally clear.

The word *violence* in verses 2 and 3 indicates "the use of physical force, usually with an intent to violate or destroy" (*Nelson's Illustrated Bible Dictionary*). It denotes ethical wrong and brutality, one person injuring another. The corruption surrounding Habakkuk had become so flagrant that he could not help but cry out to God. What was the horror that brought such a reaction from the prophet? No one knows for sure, but the child sacrifice rituals that went with paganism was a strong possible culprit.

C. The Justice System Paralyzed (v. 4)

4. Therefore the law is slacked, and judgment doth never go forth: for the wicked doth compass about the righteous; therefore wrong judgment proceedeth.

442 Faith During Troubled Times

When the systems of law and justice become corrupted in a nation, the disintegration of that society cannot be far behind. The wealthy controlled the courts to their own advantage in Judah. No real justice could be found. Habakkuk lamented the fact that there was no fairness in the land. Corruption prevailed.

We are experiencing much the same today. Wealth, power, and influence are still peddled in the name of the law. Lenient sentences, legal loopholes, and overturned convictions are allowing criminals to go free and repeat the same crimes over and over, while religious groups are becoming the targets of ridiculous lawsuits. Believers are being forced to do just as Habakkuk did—cry out to the Lord.

At what point do the sins around us disturb us so much that we cry out passionately to God as Habakkuk did?

II. GOD'S ANSWERS
(Habakkuk 2:1-4, 20)

A. The Prophet's Resolve (v. 1)

1. I will stand upon my watch, and set me upon the tower, and will watch to see what he will say unto me, and what I shall answer when I am reproved.

Just how Habakkuk heard God's answer to his first lament is not known, but the Lord did speak clearly to him. What he received was hardly the solution the prophet had anticipated. God would use the rising power of the day, the Babylonians, to punish the nation of Judah. These were extremely wicked people, as declared by God's

own words—"ruthless and impetuous" (Habakkuk 1:6, *NIV*). Babylon was northwest of the Persian Gulf, in what is now modern Iraq. Nebuchadnezzar had conquered both the Assyrian and Egyptian empires in his rise to world dominance.

Habakkuk was well aware of the Babylonians' reputation. Stories of their cruelties were flying throughout Palestine—horsemen and chariots trampling people, armies laying siege to cities and starving the inhabitants to death, women and children being tortured. And now, this frightening machine of death was focusing in on Judah. The only god these ruthless warriors worshiped was their own military strength (1:11, 16).

If Habakkuk had been disturbed by the sin he saw within Judah, he was now absolutely appalled that God would consider using the cruel Babylonians as an instrument of discipline for His own people. But this was exactly what God was setting in motion. In essence the Lord was saying, "I will work something ultimately good from something that is terrible indeed. I will bring justice through those who are absolutely unjust. I will punish my own people through a people who are even more pagan than my people are. I have chosen to do this. Nothing will stop it."

Habakkuk was aghast, but at the same time he knew that Judah had been warned. This was not the whim of a capricious god. The Lord had pleaded with the people to repent. They had seen the example of Israel when it fell to the Assyrians. Despondent at what was happening, Habakkuk again questioned God. He did not curse

God—or forsake Him—but, rather, he honestly questioned Him. The *New International Version* of the verse above reads, "I will stand at my watch and station myself on the ramparts." Habakkuk was committed to waiting until God answered. "Around-the-clock watchmen stood in watchtowers to guard against possible invasion or to watch for messengers. Ramparts, embankments of earth beyond the city walls, were the first lines of defense. Habakkuk, like a watchman, was waiting and ready to hear God's answer to his question" (*The Quest Study Bible*).

B. The Lord Speaks (vv. 2, 3)

2. And the Lord answered me, and said, Write the vision, and make it plain upon tables, that he may run that readeth it.

3. For the vision is yet for an appointed time, but at the end it shall speak, and not lie: though it tarry, wait for it; because it will surely come, it will not tarry.

God gave a clear answer to Habakkuk. Evil would not always prevail, and the wicked Babylonians would receive their just punishment in due time. Surely and steadily, God was working the big picture to fit His eternal plans. "It will not tarry" (v. 3) does not denote a time frame, but rather a surety that God would act. God's workings are certain, though they may not be immediate.

C. The Just Shall Live by Faith (v. 4)

4. Behold, his soul which is lifted up is not upright in him: but the just shall live by his faith.

"The just shall live by his faith" is one of the most familiar statements in the entire Bible. It is a clear declaration of a great spiritual truth, and few statements have had such far-reaching implications. Habakkuk, however, probably had no idea just how powerful these words really were. It took the apostle Paul to deepen the vision and understanding of what God had said centuries earlier through the prophet. Through the life and ministry of Jesus, Paul was able to see further into the larger plan that God had for mankind. Living a life of faith was never meant to be an outward observation of the law, as most would have assumed, but rather a heart commitment to God and a recognition that Jesus Christ is the only means of righteousness before God. There is still the need for faithfulness, that is, godly living, but a means of accomplishing such has now been provided through Jesus' shed blood.

The New Testament references for this declaration include Romans 1:17, Galatians 3:11, and Hebrews 10:37, 38. The entire Protestant Reformation hinged on Martin Luther's discovery of its reality. By the 16th century, much of the concept of faith, faithfulness, and obedience to God had been lost to the church. The illumination that came to Luther cut through the legalism that had developed and once again shed the light of the powerful truth Habakkuk had stated so long ago: "The just shall live by faith."

The actual Hebrew word used by Habakkuk, *emuwnah*, carries the connotation of both faith and faithfulness. This is an important aspect that we have somehow missed in recent years. "If you have genuine faith, it will be exhibited by faithfulness. In other words, if I have faith in a faithful God, others will know it by the way that I live. The God in whom I claim to have faith will be so real to me that I will make him real to you" (Briscoe).

D. God's Holiness Prevails (v. 20)

20. But the Lord is in his holy temple: let all the earth keep silence before him.

Habakkuk was not the only person in the Bible to honestly express his complaints and questions before God. Moses, Gideon, Elijah, and Job all argued with the Lord. All of them discovered in the long run, however, that God seldom fully explains Himself. Even if He did, they would not have the mental capacity to understand His ways. In the end, each of these great Biblical figures came to realize that God is still God, His power and love are consistent, He is still on the throne, and though we may not know the answers to life's questions, we can trust Him completely with the future.

Was God angry with Habakkuk for asking his perplexing questions? On what do you base your answer?

III. TRIUMPHANT FAITH
(Habakkuk 3:16-19)

16. When I heard, my belly trembled; my lips quivered at the voice: rottenness entered into my bones, and I trembled in myself, that I might rest in the day of trouble: when he cometh up unto the people, he will invade them with his troops.

17. Although the fig tree shall not blossom, neither shall fruit be in the vines; the labour of the olive shall fail, and the fields shall yield no meat; the flock shall be cut off from the fold, and there shall be no herd in the stalls:

18. Yet I will rejoice in the Lord, I will joy in the God of my salvation.

19. The Lord God is my strength, and he will make my feet like hinds' feet, and he will make me to walk upon mine high places. To the chief singer on my stringed instruments.

In the end Habakkuk was like a terminally ill patient who resigns himself to the inevitability of the outcome of the killing disease. He accepts it as unavoidable, but at the same time he learns to trust the Lord in his pain. Habakkuk in essence prayed, "I understand that Your judgment is coming, O God. You have made this known to me. I cannot change Your mind. Yet I will trust You completely." He then went on to affirm his faith in God's sovereignty. Briscoe sums up Habakkuk's attitude with a paraphrase of verses 17-19: "Though my job goes and my health fails and the forces of evil seem to have things their own way; and even though the economy doesn't work the way I want it to, and the election doesn't work out the way I hope, and I'm not appreciated among my friends, and everything goes wrong, I won't pull the plug on you, Lord. I won't resent you, Lord. I will have my doubts and questions about how you are working. I won't stop questioning—but there is one other thing that I won't stop doing either. I won't stop rejoicing in you. For you are my rock and you are my strength" (Briscoe, *Hearing God's Voice Above the Noise*).

With no buds or blossoms on the fig tree (v. 17), there was no hope for a harvest. Figuratively, there was thus no expectation of better times to come. Figs were such a valuable commodity in the ancient Middle East as a food source that a crop failure meant devastation to the economy. Nevertheless, even in the face of such grim prospects, Habakkuk determined not to give up hope in God. That hope could come only through trusting God. He looked beyond the present circumstances and saw that God would eventually bring restoration.

Paul was apparently a well-trained student of the writings of Habakkuk. The statement in verse 18, "Yet I will rejoice in the Lord," was echoed by the great apostle in Philippians 4:4: "Rejoice in the Lord always. I will say it again: Rejoice!" (*NIV*). He found himself in circumstances just as vile as Habakkuk had experienced. He was in prison, yet he was telling the church to rejoice. He knew that whatever happened, Jesus Christ would be with him. The Lord was still in charge of all events and circumstances. His faithfulness could be trusted.

Explain how that after Habakkuk examined God's ways, he found Him to be faithful.

REVIEW QUESTIONS

1. Does God use only righteous people to execute His will?

2. Does the fact that God uses unjust men to accomplish His will justify the sins they commit?

3. Why should not be afraid to question God's ways? Why must we never doubt His wisdom?

4. How can we deal with our own impatience in wanting God to rectify situations?

GOLDEN TEXT HOMILY

"IN THE DAY OF MY TROUBLE I WILL CALL UPON THEE: FOR THOU WILT ANSWER ME" (Psalm 86:7).

When should we call to the Lord for help? How often can we call on Him for assistance?

Most of us never even consider either of these two questions. But occasionally we encounter a person whose views on this topic cause us to do some serious reflecting. For example, during a study on prayer, a sincere lady stated she never bothered God about the little needs. She reserved her pleas for help for the big problems rather than "being a bother." On the other hand, however, by so doing she missed out on the fullness of what it means to be a child of God.

This verse reveals both the psalmist's practice and the pattern we too should follow. God cares about us! He wants to aid us in our troubles on a daily basis, if that's how often trouble comes our way. The size of the trouble doesn't matter. The point for consideration is whether or not we need help. Some small problems can be very painful and also temporarily disabling. They can affect us like a stubbed toe, an aching tooth, or a blinding headache.

We have the opportunity to call on the Lord. Jesus taught that we are to ask if we want to receive. God does know our needs before we ask. He could, and often does, intervene without our ever saying a word. However, He both wants and expects us as dependent children who love our Father to turn to Him in our need.

After calling to Him, we can expect an answer. He doesn't disregard us. It's easy to assume that silence is no answer. But if we're honest, we know that God may be saying "No!" very clearly.

God also answers yes. In doing so, we find Him assisting us in a variety of ways. Sometimes there is a dramatic rescue. At other times we experience unusual provision. And not to be forgotten are those times when He infuses us with divine strength to bear an unchanged circumstance.

God is listening! Let's call on Him in our time of trouble!—**Jerald Daffe, D.Min., Chairman, Bible and Christian Ministries, Lee College, Cleveland, Tennessee**

SENTENCE SERMONS

FAITH IN GOD enables us to persevere in difficult times.
—Selected

IT IS NOT our trust that keeps us, but the God in whom we trust who keeps us.
—Oswald Chambers

TROUBLE IS OFTEN the lever in God's hands to raise us up to heaven.
—Draper's Book of Quotations for the Christian World

NEVER PUT a question mark where God has put a period.
—John R. Rice

ILLUMINATING THE LESSON

The headlines in the paper read: "Mother Kills Three-Year Old Son On His Birthday. No Apparent Motive!" The details of the story reveal a sordid, horrible situation. What is worse, this is the third case in the same city in the last week where a parent murdered his own child!

Did these terrible crimes happen in some distant metropolis? No. They occurred in the relatively small town where this writer lives. While studying the Book of Habakkuk, one startling fact becomes clear: Nothing is really any different today from the time in Judah just before its fall. Idolatry is just as rampant. Child sacrifice is also common; it has just taken a different form. The idol god, however, is self. People are so caught up in their own personal wants and happiness that they will destroy anything that gets in their way. Children are an inconvenience, therefore they are deemed expendable. Many are sacrificed before they are born.

Just as in Habakkuk's day, this has a numbing effect on the people. The frequency with which these actions occur leads even Christians to say, "After all, these things happen all the time, and there's nothing anyone can do!" How frightening!

We need to be more like Habakkuk! We must never let ourselves become desensitized to the evil around us. We must pour our hearts out to God to intervene. If we allow ourselves to become complacent, we soon resemble the people of Judah and our destruction cannot be far off.

DAILY BIBLE READINGS

M. God Provides for Our Needs.
   Exodus 16:9-15
T. Trusting in God.
   2 Chronicles 32:2-8
W. Our Help Is From God.
   Psalm 124:1-8
T. Faith in God Brings Results.
   Matthew 9:18-25
F. God's Cure for Anxiety.
   John 14:1-14
S. Standing Firm in Faith.
   Acts 27:21-25

Give God First Place

Study Text: Haggai 1:1-15; Malachi 3:16 through 4:3

Objective: To understand that God honors those who give Him first place and exalt Him in our lives.

Time: The Book of Haggai was probably written around 520 B.C. The Book of Malachi was written between 450 and 400 B.C.

Place: Both of the books, Haggai and Malachi, were written at Jerusalem.

Golden Text: "Thou shalt have no other gods before me" (Exodus 20:3).

Central Truth: Giving God first place is demonstrated in a life of righteousness.

Evangelism Emphasis: Christians who give God first place are effective witnesses to the lost.

PRINTED TEXT

Haggai 1:2. Thus speaketh the Lord of hosts, saying, This people say, The time is not come, the time that the Lord's house should be built.

3. Then came the word of the Lord by Haggai the prophet, saying,

4. Is it time for you, O ye, to dwell in your cieled houses, and this house lie waste?

5. Now therefore thus saith the Lord of hosts; Consider your ways.

6. Ye have sown much, and bring in little; ye eat, but ye have not enough; ye drink, but ye are not filled with drink; ye clothe you, but there is none warm; and he that earneth wages earneth wages to put it into a bag with holes.

7. Thus saith the Lord of hosts; Consider your ways.

8. Go up to the mountain, and bring wood, and build the house; and I will take pleasure in it, and I will be glorified, saith the Lord.

9. Ye looked for much, and, lo, it came to little; and when ye brought it home, I did blow upon it. Why? saith the Lord of hosts. Because of mine house that is waste, and ye run every man unto his own house.

Malachi 3:16. Then they that feared the Lord spake often one to another: and the Lord hearkened, and heard it, and a book of remembrance was written before him for them that feared the Lord, and that thought upon his name.

17. And they shall be mine, saith the Lord of hosts, in that day when I make up my jewels; and I will spare them, as a man spareth his own son that serveth him.

18. Then shall ye return, and discern between the righteous and the wicked, between him that serveth God and him that serveth him not.

4:1. For, behold, the day cometh, that shall burn as an oven; and all the proud, yea, and all that do wickedly, shall be stubble: and the day that cometh shall burn them up, saith the Lord of hosts, that it shall leave them neither root nor branch.

2. But unto you that fear my name shall the Sun of righteousness arise with healing in his wings; and ye shall go forth, and grow up as calves of the stall.

3. And ye shall tread down the wicked; for they shall be ashes under the soles of your feet in the day that I shall do this, saith the Lord of hosts.

DICTIONARY

Haggai (HAG-ay-eye)—Haggai 1:3—A prophet in Jerusalem when the Israelites came back from Babylonian captivity.

LESSON OUTLINE

I. MISPLACED PRIORITIES

   A. Haggai the Prophet

   B. Reluctance to Build the Temple

   C. Results of Misplaced Priorities

II. CORRECT PRIORITIES

   A. Finish the Task

   B. A Positive Response

III. RIGHTEOUSNESS REWARDED

LESSON EXPOSITION

INTRODUCTION

In 538 B.C., the Persian King Cyrus issued a decree allowing Jewish captives to return to their homeland. There they could rebuild their temple and reinstate the public worship of Jehovah. The first band of returnees were led by Zerubbabel soon afterward.

The Babylonian captivity was now finally history—a bad memory, a difficult learning experience. The Jews were back in the Promised Land, though what they faced bore little resemblance to the days of its glorious past. Jerusalem had been totally destroyed in 586 B.C., with the great temple of Solomon left in absolute ruin. Nevertheless, the determined pilgrims put themselves to the task of rebuilding it for the glory of God.

Sixteen years later the picture had changed. Somewhere along the way the people became discouraged and put their personal needs and comforts ahead of the Lord's work. The rebuilding project stopped completely. One source of difficulty for the pilgrims was the Samaritans, a mixed race that had resulted from intermarriage between Assyrians and Jews who had been left in Palestine. At first these people tried to join the Jews in the rebuilding project but were refused. A strong animosity developed between the two groups, one that has lasted through Biblical times and down to the present.

The Samaritans began to terrorize the pilgrims, causing them to concentrate on their own safety and well-being and to postpone the work of rebuilding the Temple.

To the frightened remnant Haggai spoke his message. He saw that fear controlled the people. Though they were surrounded by hostile neighbors, his words were uncompromising: They needed to fear God instead of men.

Malachi's writings mark the close of the Old Testament and the beginning of 400 years of silence before the coming of Christ and the New Testament era. Speaking in Jerusalem around 430 B.C., Malachi dealt with a populace who had been back in the homeland for nearly a century. He rebuked them for neglecting the worship of God and failing to live according to the law. He singled out the priests; for if the religious leaders were off track, how could the people be expected to follow the Lord's commandments? They knew what the Lord required, but their sacrifices and services were casual, insincere, and without conviction. In a question and answer format, Malachi pointed out Judah's hardness and pronounced a curse on all who practiced false and profane worship.

But there was hope! Malachi would conclude with a promise that another prophet like Elijah would offer God's forgiveness through repentance and faith. He predicted this messenger would clear the way before the Lord (3:1). John the Baptist fulfilled the role some 400 years later (see Matthew 11:7-15).

I. MISPLACED PRIORITIES
(Haggai 1:1-6)

A. Haggai the Prophet (v. 1)

(Haggai 1:1 is not included in the printed text.)

The prophet himself is not well-known to Bible readers. Outside the book that bears his name, Haggai is mentioned in only two isolated references, in Ezra 5:1 and 6:14, and possibly in Zechariah 8:9. He may have been born in Babylon and returned to Jerusalem in 538 with the first wave of returnees under Zerubbabel, although there is the possibility that he was at least 70 years old and may have seen Solomon's temple before the fall of Jerusalem. Some think this is most likely the case because of his heartening words to the older pilgrims who compared the meager new temple under construction with the earlier grand one (2:3).

Haggai stands out as unique among the prophets of the Bible, for the people listened to his words and obeyed. Only four years elapsed from the time he first encouraged the resumption of work on the new Temple until it was completed. Jonah had immediate results from his preaching to the Ninevites, but in that particular book the larger focus is on Jonah's reluctance to carry God's message to the heathen city. Haggai apparently heard God speak and immediately relayed His message to the people. His obedience brought positive results quickly.

B. Reluctance to Build the Temple (v. 2)

2. Thus speaketh the Lord of hosts, saying, This people say, The time is not come, the time that the Lord's house should be built.

Upon their arrival in Jerusalem, the people had eagerly begun work on the Temple. Opposition soon arose from the hostile Samaritan population, and a spirit of discouragement pervaded the people. The work was suspended as they concentrated on their homes and crops. Discouragement turned into apathy, complacency, and procrastination.

This verse quotes what the people were saying. Perhaps they had come to feel that the time was not right for building the Temple because there was difficulty and opposition. In any case, they had rationalized that God must not be ready for them to complete the project, that they should wait for better circumstances.

Haggai let it be known that rarely is there a time when all the circumstances fall perfectly into place. He mirrored Solomon's thoughts in Ecclesiastes 11:4: "Whoever watches the wind will not plant; whoever looks at the clouds will not reap" (*NIV*). *The Living Bible* has an interesting paraphrase of this verse: "If you wait for perfect conditions, you will never get anything done."

C. Results of Misplaced Priorities
   (vv. 3-6)
   3. Then came the word of the Lord by Haggai the prophet, saying,
   4. Is it time for you, O ye, to dwell in your cieled houses, and this house lie waste?
   5. Now therefore thus saith the Lord of hosts; Consider your ways.
   6. Ye have sown much, and bring in little; ye eat, but ye have not enough; ye drink, but ye are not filled with drink; ye clothe you, but there is none warm; and he that earneth wages earneth wages to put it into a bag with holes.

God's message to the people through Haggai began with a rhetorical question (v. 4). The obvious spiritual answer to this query was a resounding "No!" But the returnees had put their own needs and comforts ahead of the Temple's. The word *cieled* refers to some type of overlay— wood, plaster, or another material or substance. It indicates a measure of added luxury, which at the same time seemed unaffordable in the Temple.

Haggai presents an indictment to God's people of all ages who lavish themselves while shortchanging what they owe to the Lord's work. Most believers would be fooling themselves to say that they put the Kingdom's needs ahead of their own. Paul pointed this out by showing how Timothy was an exception in the early church: "For everyone looks out for his own interests, not those of Jesus Christ" (Philippians 2:19-21, *NIV*). When David recognized this imbalance in his own life, he felt prompted to begin preparations for the building of the original temple. He admitted of himself to Nathan the prophet, "Here I am, living in a palace of cedar, while the ark of God remains in a tent" (2 Samuel 7:2, *NIV*).

Jesus addressed this subject by saying, "Seek first his kingdom and his righteousness, and all these things will be given to you as well" (Matthew 6:33, *NIV*). It is certainly commendable that the people in Jerusalem were taking care of their houses and families; but when they put them ahead of rebuilding the Temple, it showed they had misplaced their priorities. Had they kept the building project as the first order of business, their personal needs would also have been met.

The point was made that their homes were completed, while the Temple was not.

Haggai emphasized the predicament that had resulted from these misplaced priorities: lean harvests, personal suffering from not enough of the right foods for good health, watered-down wine, clothes insufficiently heavy to keep out the winter chill, and not enough income to meet expenses. "It is possible that inflation was working against solvency, as in our day." (Zondervan *NIV Bible Commentary*). All of this speaks to us today. Problems are often the result of our having become too preoccupied with our own interests and wants.

Most American Christians live on a higher standard than the rest of the world. How do we distinguish between what are truly physical needs in our lives and those things that are merely luxuries?

II. CORRECT PRIORITIES
(Haggai 1:7-15)

A. Finish the Task (vv. 7-11)

(Haggai 1:10, 11 is not included in the printed text.)

7. Thus saith the Lord of hosts; Consider your ways.

8. Go up to the mountain, and bring wood, and build the house; and I will take pleasure in it, and I will be glorified, saith the Lord.

9. Ye looked for much, and, lo, it came to little; and when ye brought it home, I did blow upon it. Why? saith the Lord of hosts. Because of mine house that is waste, and ye run every man unto his own house.

The message Haggai delivered to the people began with four commands:

1. *Consider your ways.* The Lord asked the people to think about their living conditions. Their economic problems and agricultural failures were a signal that God was displeased with their selfishness. Their harvests were poor because they had put themselves first. This is a message we need to hear today. In an age of materialism marked by an advertising onslaught that creates false needs, we must each constantly examine ourselves to make sure we keep the Lord's work in proper balance with our own whims and wants.

2. *Go up to the mountain.* The old adage "A journey of a thousand miles begins with the first step" holds true here. God not only asked the people to consider their ways, but He also told them to move! Spiritual growth always requires action. A simple definition of repentance is a *change of directions*. However, this implies not only a turning around but also a motion in that new direction. The people needed to get to work. It is not certain whether the mountains spoken of meant those farther north or simply the rugged hills surrounding Jerusalem. Because of the limited resources of the people, the intended location was probably the local forests.

3. *Bring wood.* The fact that only wood was required may indicate that just the interior work of the Temple needed finishing. Had the people become discouraged when the job was actually near completion? What a shame for us to come so close to spiritual victory and then be sidetracked by discouragement and personal needs!

4. *Build the house.* Haggai's message didn't dwell on the fact the people had failed in complete their task. There was still time. The people simply had to make a decision to get to work. Often, people continue in defeat because they think failure is a permanent condition. However, God's grace always allows the opportunity for humankind to start again. The Lord takes pleasure in the fruit of our labors when we put ourselves to the task of completing the job we have started for Him.

B. A Positive Response (vv. 12-15)

Haggai 1:12-15 is not included in the printed text.)

The leaders, both political (Zerubbabel) and religious (Joshua the high priest), responded positively to Haggai's message from the Lord. They recognized that the prophet was anointed by God. "Some charisma or ring of authority must have prompted this obedience and fear. A people who had been driven to their knees by the days of drought and famine would be all the more receptive to a word from God." (Zondervan *NIV Bible Commentary*).

The actual rebuilding began just 23 days after Haggai's first message. The people responded to the anointed word from the Lord. What a message for us today. It does no good to hear a wonderful sermon or experience a great worship service if there is no response on our part. Action is always the logical result of the moving of God's Spirit. May we never be guilty of failing to follow the Holy Spirit's leading.

Think back to the last time God spoke to your heart—either through a sermon, a teaching, or an illumination from the Word. Have you responded to that message He spoke to you?

III. RIGHTEOUSNESS REWARD-
    ED (Malachi 3:16—4:3)

3:16. Then they that feared the Lord spake often one to another: and the Lord hearkened, and heard it, and a book of remembrance was written before him for them that feared the Lord, and that thought upon his name.
17. And they shall be mine, saith the Lord of hosts, in that day when I make up my jewels; and I will spare them, as a man spareth his own son that serveth him.
18. Then shall ye return, and discern between the righteous and the wicked, between him that serveth God and him that serveth him not.
4:1. For, behold, the day cometh, that shall burn as an oven; and all the proud, yea, and all that do wickedly, shall be stubble: and the day that cometh shall burn them up, saith the Lord of hosts, that it shall leave them neither root nor branch.
2. But unto you that fear my name shall the Sun of righteousness arise with healing in his wings; and ye shall go forth, and grow up as calves of the stall.
3. And ye shall tread down the wicked; for they shall be ashes under the soles of your feet in the day that I shall do this, saith the Lord of hosts.

A full century passed between the time the Jerusalem pilgrims responded positively to Haggai's message and the day of Malachi, the final prophet of the Old Testament. One is reminded that Nahum prophesied against Nineveh 150 years after that city had responded with repentance to the preaching of Jonah. Just as the Ninevites "repented of their repentance" and returned to their terrible sins, so the people of Judah forgot how God had brought them back from captivity and helped them rebuild their temple. The freshness of their experience was gone, and worship was nothing but a meaningless routine.

Why this laxity? Possibly because the prosperity the people had thought would come after the Captivity never materialized. Life was a drudgery in Palestine, and the prevailing attitude was that it simply was not worth the effort to serve the Lord. The message of Malachi, however, is not one of imminent destruction, as had been the case with Nahum's prophecy against Nineveh. Instead, he appealed to the people to break through their barriers of disbelief, disappointment, and discouragement.

Using a question and answer format, the Book of Malachi begins with God speaking to His children. His words to them were a reaffirmation of His continuing love in spite of the people's lethargy. He begged them (especially the priests) to realize that their lack of blessing was not due to indifference on God's part, but rather to their own compromise and sin. He also appealed to them to bring the tithes and offering due the Lord into the storehouse. The nation had robbed God, and this had brought the people great pain and much suffering.

Some of Malachi's hearers did heed the message, and they would be remembered in a "book of remembrance" (3:16). Their sincere love and respect for God would not be forgotten. They were even called "jewels" (v. 17). The time, heat, pressure, shaping, and polishing that it takes to turn a jewel in the rough into a gemstone is similar to the process that this faithful remnant would have to endure. However, the Lord promised His people that a time will come when the wicked will be judged and those who fear and serve Him will be blessed and rewarded. The day of the Lord will finally reveal that it is not "vain to serve God" (v. 14).

Do you sometimes become weary in your worship of the Lord because the freshness of your experience has been lost among life's difficulties?

REVIEW QUESTIONS

1. Haggai's message was anointed by the Lord, and it received a positive response. But does the *anointing* automatically ensure that people will listen?

2. Zerrubbabel and Joshua, the high priest, heeded Haggai's plea. Do you think the people would have resumed work on the Temple if these leaders had not done so? How important is it for spiritual leaders to respond to the Lord's voice?

3. Should we ever give up on the Lord just because He seems to be slow in answering our prayers?

4. Does our laxity in giving of tithes and offerings indicate a complacency in our relationship with the Lord? Explain your answer.

GOLDEN TEXT HOMILY

"THOU SHALT HAVE NO OTHER GODS BEFORE ME" (Exodus 20:3).

In the Decalogue, direct commands are issued. There is no room for adjustment. God has spoken. It's a sure word.

The first commandment, "Thou shalt have no other gods before me," prohibits all substitutes. This includes every variety of mental idolatry and all inordinate attachment to earthly things.

What does this first commandment say to us today? We have little problem with "golden calves," groves to Baal, or statues and images. Could it be that this directive is a prohibition on giving any creature or human creation the honor or devotion which belongs to God alone?

"What means it," asked Martin Luther, "to have a god?" He replied, "Whatever thy heart clings to and relies upon, that is properly thy god." A god is someone or something to which we give inordinate attention or precedence over Jehovah God. "No other gods" strikes at the strong possibility that daily within our lives many altars smoke with sacrifice to many gods.

Joshua tested the stance of the people toward other gods. The challenge was issued, "Choose you this day whom ye will serve; whether the gods which your fathers served that were on the other side of the flood, or the gods of the Amorites, in whose land ye dwell." Joshua was decisive, as every child of God should be: "But as for me and my house, we will serve the Lord" (Joshua 24:15).—
Joel Harris, M.Div., Pastor, Mobile, Alabama

SENTENCE SERMONS

GIVING GOD FIRST PLACE is demonstrated in a life of righteousness.
—Selected

OUR LORD had only one desire, and that was to do the will of His Father, and to have that desire is a characteristic of a disciple.
—Oswald Chambers

A MAN'S HEART has only enough life in it to pursue one object fully.
—Charles W. Spurgeon

THE FIRST PRIORITY is to keep the first priority the first priority.
—H. Bert Ames

EVANGELISM APPLICATION

CHRISTIANS WHO GIVE GOD FIRST PLACE ARE EFFECTIVE WITNESSES TO THE LOST.

Someone has said that the "greatest enemies of a new move of God in any generation are the leaders of the last move of God." Haggai had to deal with a number of people who had seen Solomon's temple, experienced its grandeur, and had institutionalized its memory. Haggai himself may have been old enough to be a part of this group. Yet he wisely realized that what was in the past was only a memory. It would not return.

The same trap that those older pilgrims fell into has occurred over and over down through the years. Many people today in historic church congregations get caught up in their heritage and refuse to allow God to move as He pleases for the present generation. Also, those who were part of great revivals in years past easily fall into the trap of thinking that their experience is the prescribed way God will move again.

Haggai wisely did not rebuke those who revered the former glories of Jerusalem. He did, however, exhort them to open their eyes to what could be done now. They should remember the past but not ignore the reality of present needs. God is at work in every generation, and every generation needs its own revival. If we keep our hearts and minds open, He may do even greater things than our parents and grandparents ever saw.

ILLUMINATING THE LESSON

The line "The darkest hour is just before the dawn" may well have described the situation Haggai dealt with in Jerusalem. Since only wood was required to finish the Temple, it would appear that the project was actually nearly finished when the people got discouraged. Isn't this true of all things spiritual? Satan will fight to frustrate us the most when we are actually closest to victory.

Do you have unfinished business in your spiritual life? Have you let yourself stop growing because you hit a snag along the way? Could it be that you gave up just at the point when victory was in sight?

If your spiritual walk toward maturity has been sidetracked, stop and consider your ways. There are things you can do to get back on track. Repent of the long-term sins and bad habits that have hindered you. Get back into fellowship with other believers who will encourage you. Find a brother or sister to whom you can be accountable. Establish a discipline of Bible reading and prayer.

Remember this, too: In order to get the wood needed to finish the Temple, the people had to go up to the mountain. This meant climbing, and thus it meant *work*. All spiritual growth requires action and discipline. We will never get anywhere in terms of growth if we are lazy! So, consider your ways—and get back to work!

DAILY BIBLE READINGS

M. Tested by Trials.
   Genesis 39:7-16, 21-23
T. Blessings Promised.
   Psalm 128:1-6
W Standing True to God. Daniel 3:8-18
T. Self-Denial Required.
   Matthew 16:21-27
F. Sacrificial Worship.
   John 12:1-8
S. Excel in Giving to God.
   2 Corinthians 8:1-7

Christian Values and Morality

Study Text: Isaiah 5:20-23; Matthew 22:36-40; Luke 6:31; Romans 1:28-32; 13:8-10; Ephesians 5:1-10

Objective: To understand the relationship between values and morality and live by Christian values.

Golden Text: "Be not wise in thine own eyes: fear the Lord, and depart from evil" (Proverbs 3:7).

Central Truth: Christian values are essential for morality that pleases God.

Evangelism Emphasis: Living by Christian values is necessary for being true witnesses of Christ.

PRINTED TEXT

Isaiah 5:20. Woe unto them that call evil good, and good evil; that put darkness for light, and light for darkness; that put bitter for sweet, and sweet for bitter!

21. Woe unto them that are wise in their own eyes, and prudent in their own sight!

22. Woe unto them that are mighty to drink wine, and men of strength to mingle strong drink:

23. Which justify the wicked for reward, and take away the righteousness of the righteous from him!

Romans 1:28. And even as they did not like to retain God in their knowledge, God gave them over to a reprobate mind, to do those things which are not convenient;

29. Being filled with all unrighteousness, fornication, wickedness, covetousness, maliciousness; full of envy, murder, debate, deceit, malignity; whisperers,

30. Backbiters, haters of God, despiteful, proud, boasters, inventors of evil things, disobedient to parents,

31. Without understanding, covenantbreakers, without natural affection, implacable, unmerciful:

32. Who knowing the judgment of God, that they which commit such things are worthy of death, not only do the same, but have pleasure in them that do them.

Matthew 22:36. Master, which is the great commandment in the law?

37. Jesus said unto him, Thou shalt love the Lord thy God with all thy heart, and with all thy soul, and with all thy mind.

38. This is the first and great commandment.

39. And the second is like unto it, Thou shalt love thy neighbour as thyself.

40. On these two commandments hang all the law and the prophets.

Luke 6:31. And as ye would that men should do to you, do ye also to them likewise.

Romans 13:8. Owe no man any thing, but to love one another: for he that loveth another hath fulfilled the law.

10. Love worketh no ill to his neighbour: therefore love is the fulfilling of the law.

Ephesians 5:1. Be ye therefore followers of God, as dear children;

8. For ye were sometimes darkness, but now are ye light in the Lord: walk as children of light:

9. (For the fruit of the Spirit is in all goodness and righteousness and truth;)

10. Proving what is acceptable unto the Lord.

LESSON OUTLINE

I. WRONG VALUES CORRUPT MORALS
   A. Woe to Those Who Confuse Evil and Good
   B. God's Judgment Against Sin

II. CHRISTIAN VALUES NEEDED
   A. The Two Greatest Commandments
   B. Loving One's Neighbor
   C. The Debt of Love

III. CHRISTIAN VALUES PRODUCE MORALITY
   A. Followers of God Walking in Love
   B. Children of Light

LESSON EXPOSITION

INTRODUCTION

What we believe and how we think determines to a great extent the kind of person we become. How we act and carry out our daily lives is a direct reflection of what we think inside. The daily choices we make about what's right and what's wrong, true and false, absolute and situational are a representation of our character—and those choices shape the future we making for ourselves. Eternity is awaiting us, and how we live this temporary life on earth dictates where we will spend the coming millennia.

Unfortunately, the real problem of the 1990s is that powerful forces from many directions and social agendas have replaced the once-held values of the Bible. No longer is God's Word held in absolute reverence, nor is it the dominant force in shaping what society believes. We are in danger of raising a generation of people that is to a large degree ignorant of the difference between right and wrong. Then they would have no real basis for making solid moral judgments. The prophet Hosea lamented, "My people are destroyed from lack of knowledge" (Hosea 4:6, NIV). What a sobering thought! Do we have a generation headed toward destruction because of sheer ignorance?

While it is true that life's foundational values have generally been known by man innately since Creation, the rebellion we are seeing has all but vilified man's conscience, allowing him to believe that what is wrong is really right. True wisdom can only be found in recognizing God as God and then seeking in His Word the standards for establishing what we should believe. Any other direction man goes leads to anarchy and then total destruction.

Daniel and the three Hebrew children are fine examples of men who stood for honorable convictions in the midst of a degenerate society. But how were they able to summon courage to do what was right? It was only by having already settled the issue in the hearts—based on an upbringing that had taught them clearly what God commanded. They did not have to struggle to discern the right way from the wrong. That had already been established. "Daniel and his friends settled in their hearts what they needed to do and not do, based on biblical principles. As a result, they were able to carry out a plan with tough-minded resolve. In other words, they showed moral backbone." (*The Word in Life Study Bible*).

Values has become a popular topic these days. But whose values? Are they godly mores, or are they based on faulty premises? As Christians, we face ethical choices on every hand. Before we can summon the fortitude to stand for our ideals, we must establish a basis for forming that standard of conduct. There is a direct link between knowledge of God's Word and strong Christian character. We must first learn God's values and then make them our own.

I. WRONG VALUES CORRUPT MORALS (Isaiah 5:20-23; Romans 1:28-32)

A. Woe to Those Who Confuse Evil and Good (Isaiah 5:20-23)

20. Woe unto them that call evil good, and good evil; that put darkness for light, and light for darkness; that put bitter for sweet, and sweet for bitter!

21. Woe unto them that are wise in their own eyes, and prudent in their own sight!

22. Woe unto them that are mighty to drink wine, and men of strength to mingle strong drink:

23. Which justify the wicked for reward, and take away the righteousness of the righteous from him!

Four kinds of fools are described in the Bible, especially in Proverbs. The first is the *simpleton*. Proverbs 1:22 says, "How long will you simple ones love your simple ways?" (*NIV*). The Hebrew word translated "simple" in Proverbs generally denotes one without moral direction and inclined to evil. The *simpleton* doesn't know the difference between truth and falsehood. He has no personal principles and thus is easily swayed in any direction. Therefore he is quite likely to confuse evil and good. The second kind of fool is found in the same verse: "How long will mockers delight in mockery and fools hate knowledge?" (*NIV*). The *mocker* laughs at wisdom and toys with evil, thinking all the while that nothing will harm him. A third type of fool is the *proud*. Proverbs 10:23 describes him: "A fool finds pleasure in evil conduct, but a man of understanding delights in wisdom" (*NIV*). This person knows what is right and wrong, but chooses to live purely for his own selfish interests. The fourth type of fool is the *rebel*. Proverbs 1:7 says that "The fear of the LORD is the beginning of knowledge, but fools despise wisdom and discipline" (*NIV*). The rebel knows what is right but hates it. He fights the truth with all his might.

Isaiah was probably referring to all four types of fools in the above verses. These people are misled because they have not learned the truth of God's Word. They see themselves, however, as wise, educated, and discriminating—but this "wisdom" is based instead on ignorance. They do not understand that true wisdom comes only from God.

Just a few verses earlier in the same chapter, Isaiah identified one great culprit that creates such fools: "Woe to those who join house to house, who add field to field, till there is no place where they may dwell alone in the midst of the land!" (Isaiah 5:8, *NKJV*). There is a tremendous danger that comes with riches and success. If not kept in check, these things corrupt morals and values. Isaiah was warning the wealthy people of Judah of what was happening to them as a result of their affluence. They were buying more houses and lands, but forgetting their morals and ethics along the way. Are not the same things true today? The richest nation in the world is also one of the most morally corrupt. One needs only to look at the lives of movie stars, sports figures, and business tycoons to find the most degenerate behavior.

Isaiah constantly warned of the potential dangers that affluence brings: unethical practices (1:23), robbing the poor (3:14, 15), making gods out of accomplishments and possessions (2:8; 5:21), and abusing people (3:15). The results of such corrupting of morals include spoiled children (3:5), a breakdown of the family and society (3:6, 7), and the loss of a work ethic (5:11-13). Certainly God intends for His people to prosper, but every believer needs to pause frequently to take stock of his blessings, making sure they are not turning into fatal snares.

The punishment Isaiah declared for all these things is expressed in the word *woe*. *Nelson's Bible Dictionary* defines this as "deep sorrow, grief, or affliction." In the Bible the word *woe* was often used, particularly by the Old Testament prophets, as an exclamation expressing dismay or misfortune. To express woe was to indicate that major problems were on the way!

B. God's Judgment Against Sin
   (Romans 1:28-32)

28. And even as they did not like to retain God in their knowledge, God gave them over to a reprobate mind, to do those things which are not convenient;
29. Being filled with all unrighteousness, fornication, wickedness, covetousness, maliciousness; full of envy, murder, debate, deceit, malignity; whisperers,
30. Backbiters, haters of God, despiteful, proud, boasters, inventors of evil things, disobedient to parents,
31. Without understanding, covenantbreakers, without natural affection, implacable, unmerciful:
32. Who knowing the judgment of God, that they which commit such things are worthy of death, not only do the same, but have pleasure in them that do them.

Just prior to these verses, Paul indicated that God has definitely revealed His presence to all men through His creation (1:18-20). Evidence is everywhere that there is a God. The beauty and complexity of the earth and its creatures all point to a Master Designer. To deny this is foolish. Yet the verses above indicate that this is precisely what man has done. Though man was created as pure and noble, he has become wicked and hurtful toward others. Paul describes this condition as sin (Romans 3:23). Because of man's rebellion, God gave him up totally to the fruition of his vile behavior. The results make up the list Paul gave—sexual immorality, perverted vile passions, and debased minds. Paul then went on in the remainder of the Book of Romans to show the implications of this rebellion, warning that sin is very real. "It is not just bad feelings or an overly sensitive conscience. We have alienated ourselves from a righteous and holy God, and there is a penalty to pay— the penalty of eternal death, of everlasting separation from him" (*The Word in Life Study Bible*).

How can God clearly be seen in this world? How can man step over his inner knowledge of God's presence to carry out vile behavior?

II. CHRISTIAN VALUES NEEDED
    (Matthew 22:36-40; Luke 6:31; Romans 13:8-10)

A. The Two Greatest Commandments
   (Matthew 22:36-40)

36. Master, which is the great commandment in the law?

37. Jesus said unto him, Thou shalt love the Lord thy God with all thy heart, and with all thy soul, and with all thy mind.

38. This is the first and great commandment.

39. And the second is like unto it, Thou shalt love thy neighbour as thyself.

40. On these two commandments hang all the law and the prophets.

The Pharisees were trying to trap Jesus by asking what in their minds was a technical question. They had classified over 600 laws, outlining minute details for every area of behavior. Thus they were anxious to trap Jesus by asking him to identify the most important law. Likely they thought he would respond with some rigid command. However, Jesus answered them by quoting from Deuteronomy 6:5 and Leviticus 19:18. If a person kept these two commandments, all others would fall into place. The love He was calling for was *agape* love, a conscious and sustained choice of the will to serve and glorify God and one's fellowman, expecting nothing in return. It is the kind of love that can be expressed only as men accept God's love toward them. This is impossible for man to achieve on his own merits. As we respond to God's love, He then empowers us to live the same way toward others (see 1 John 3:11-24).

B. Loving One's Neighbor
   (Luke 6:31)

31. And as ye would that men should do to you, do ye also to them likewise.

This statement reiterates and summarizes what Jesus had just said to the multitudes. Certainly he had shocked them when He said "Love your enemies, do good to those who hate you, bless those who curse you, and pray for those who spitefully use you" (vv. 27, 28, NKJV). His listeners, already very familiar with the law, knew the commandments to love their neighbor (Leviticus 19:18), but to go so far as loving one's enemies was shocking. How could they possibly love the Roman overlords who kept them impoverished, or the pagan peoples around them who practiced idolatry? This had to sound foreign to their ears.

Yet this is exactly what the Lord was demanding. Interestingly,

Jesus spoke these words to those who could probably come closest to understanding such a truth—the poor multitudes. Poverty brings everyone down to an even playing field and causes people to realize they must depend on one another to survive. During the Great Depression years of the 20th century, millions of Americans survived not because of an independent spirit but rather because they were all in the same financial straits and had to help one another. The poor of Palestine were likewise familiar with the need for community effort. Obviously, it would still appear impossible to love one's enemies, but the necessity of depending on others might at least have made this a little more palatable.

Today, with the collapse of moral principles and integrity, another view prevails. Financial prosperity and an untamed independent spirit have skewed the sense of need to love others, especially one's enemies. "Modern society lives by the rules of survival of the fittest. 'The one who dies with the most toys wins,' reads one bumper sticker. So does the nation with the best weapons and the largest gross national product." (Philip Yancey, *The Jesus I Never Knew*).

Jesus' words left many confused and enraged because His sense of morality went against everything that seemed natural. However, that which seems natural is often the result of a fallen nature. To live as we should, we have to move contrary to what an unbelieving society says and take a different road—one that cares for others as much as for self.

C. The Debt of Love
   (Romans 13:8-10)

   (Romans 13:9 is not included in the printed text.)

8. Owe no man any thing, but to love one another: for he that loveth another hath fulfilled the law.

10. Love worketh no ill to his neighbour: therefore love is the fulfilling of the law.

The key word in this entire passage is *owe*. We are to owe nothing to anyone but love. God apparently hates unpaid debts. However, this passage is not confined to financial accountability. In the seven verses prior to this one, Paul brought into focus a larger view of debt (beyond taxes, customs, tariffs, and fees) to include *fear* (the respect we owe those in authority over us) and *honor* (the respect due those in high positions—whether we personally like those individuals or not).

This does not mean that there will not be times when we should do all within our means to fight wrong laws or corrupt governments and officials. All through the history of the church, there have been times when Christians have had to obey God rather than man and resist evil governments and regimes. However, the principle that government is basically good and in our best interest prevails in Scripture. To be moral and show integrity before God, we must do all we can to pay our debts—including those to the government.

We are to be permanently in the debt of love. This is because Christ lavished such love on us with His divine sacrifice. The only possible way we can repay Him is to always be sharing that same love He poured on us with others. We never finish paying this debt.

What are ways we can work to change corrupt laws and governments and yet still be respectful of those in authority?

III. CHRISTIAN VALUES PRO-
DUCE MORALITY
(Ephesians 5:1-10)

A. Followers of God Walking in
Love (vv. 1-7)

(Ephesians 5:2-7 is not included
in the printed text.)
**1. Be ye therefore followers of
God, as dear children.**
Christ is our example, and we
are to emulate Him. Just as a loving parent sets a behavioral model
for his children, so likewise Jesus
has given us a perfect model by
which we can set a standard for
wise actions and lifestyle. That
pattern includes (1) sacrificial giving of ourselves for others (v. 2); (2)
resisting temptations toward
immoral, impure behavior (vv. 3, 5);
(3) replacing crude communication
with positive affirmation of others
and thanksgiving to God (v. 4); (4)
realization that vile behavior has no
place in the kingdom of Christ (v.
5); (5) recognizing that God's wrath
ultimately comes upon those will
willfully disobey His commandments (v. 6); (6) learning to avoid
those who will corrupt our standards (v. 7).
The world is constantly looking
for heros to look up to. Sports
stars, politicians, and movie actors
are too often extremely poor examples to copy, yet these are the models our society sets before us.
Christians should be very careful
not to let any other than Christ
himself be our model for determining our behavior and lifestyle.

B. Children of Light (vv. 8-10)

**8. For ye were sometimes
darkness, but now are ye light in
the Lord: walk as children of
light:**
**9. (For the fruit of the Spirit
is in all goodness and righteous-**
ness and truth;)
**10. Proving what is acceptable
unto the Lord.**
If we are children of light, then
we certainly need to make sure our
actions reflect our faith. Unless we
are consistently following Christ
daily, no one will see Him in us or
want to adopt our faith. The
church is often accused of being
irrelevant because it has become
too much like the world itself.
Newsweek magazine carried an
article a few years ago that pointed
this out: "Who makes the rules
these days that determine how our
society is going to work—the code
of ethics behind the laws that
determines our values and decides
how we are going to live together in
community? It isn't the churches.
It's not so much that their moral
leadership is being ignored as that,
to a great extent, they've abdicated
the role. Collectively they seem to
exude the same relativism and
insecurity about right and wrong as
the rest of us" (Nicols Fox, "What
Are Our Real Values?" *Newsweek*,
February 13, 1989).
Christ must be our model. If our
lives reflect anyone else, we will fail
in carrying out the task He left us
to do. We should live like Him so
that we can truly reflect His goodness to others.

---

*Who are the heroes your chil-
dren look up to? What kind of
behavior models do they follow?*

REVIEW QUESTIONS

1. A true knowledge of God's
value system and morality must be
taught. What can we do to make
sure our children are learning the
truth and not the relativism of the
world?

2. How can we best demonstrate our faith to a lost world?

3. How much should believers get involved in trying to change the corruption around us in business and government?

4. How can we be a witness to the sinners around us without letting their behavior and lifestyles affect us?

GOLDEN TEXT HOMILY

"BE NOT WISE IN THINE OWN EYES: FEAR THE LORD, AND DEPART FROM EVIL" (Proverbs 3:7).

True wisdom is not mere knowledge or learning or wisdom of a theoretical kind; rather, it is wisdom of a practical nature, imbuing and controlling every area of human life. Louis Goldberg defines it as "godly cleaverness and skill which results in practical action." Solomon's early reign exhibited this quality. It is a quality much needed in our homes, our churches, and our nation.

The text makes three short, sharp points, each of which is a part of this godly wisdom.

"Be not wise in thine own eyes." What Spurgeon said of humility is true of wisdom: "When it says, 'I am here,' it is gone." This is a perpetual danger. The pursuit of wisdom is like climbing a high precipice; take care or you will fall to your death. Solomon himself is the classic case. The wisest of all men when he was a youth fell to abysmal folly in later years.

"Fear the Lord." This is not fear in the sense of terror but in the sense of trust—a godly, reverential fear—the fear of God which Jesus had (Isaiah 11:3; Hebrews 5:7) and which Noah also had (Hebrews 11:7). This "fear of the Lord" keeps wisdom under control, holding it back from the danger described in the previous clause. He who truly fears the Lord will not become wise in his own eyes.

"Depart from evil." This too is a concomitance and consequence of fearing the Lord. Reverence for God will control both mind and morals. It will save from both intellectual conceit and moral downfall. "How then can I do this great wickedness, and sin against God?" (Genesis 39:9). Solomon could have learned much from Joseph!**—Noel Brooks, D.D., Bath, England, Writer (Retired),** *Adult Sunday School Teacher Quarterly,* **International Pentecostal Holiness Church, Oklahoma City, Oklahoma**

SENTENCE SERMONS

CHRISTIAN VALUES are essential for morality that pleases God.

—Selected

THE HUMAN VALUE is not the ultimate, but only the penultimate value; the last, the highest ultimate is God the Father.

—Karl Adam

LEARN TO HOLD loosely all that is not eternal.

—Agnes Maude Royden

MORALITY does not make a Christian, yet no man can be a Christian without it.

—Daniel Wilson

EVANGELISM APPLICATION

LIVING BY CHRISTIAN VALUES IS NECESSARY FOR BEING TRUE WITNESSES OF CHRIST.

A passage from Romans in this lesson speaks of owing nothing to anyone else except the debt of love. We are also told in a verse of the same passage (Romans 13:9) to love our neighbor as we love ourselves.

There has been much written in recent years about loving oneself. So many people walk around with a terrible self-image, low esteem, and a sense of worthlessness. The breakdown of the family and traditional values have left thousands wounded. There is a certain truth, then, that we should love ourselves.

The primary meaning of Paul's words, however, is that we should love others as much as ourselves. No matter how little we think of our own lives, we are still quite willing to make sure we are clothed, fed, and sheltered. Even the person with the lowest self-esteem still generally looks out for number one. He gets angry when someone else comes against him and is quite willing to protect himself from harm or injury.

Isn't this then the same kind of love Paul is saying we should have for others? We should want to see our neighbors fed, clothed, sheltered, and protected—just as much as we do ourselves. Loving others means reaching out to see that their needs are met just as our own are.

Let us never get so captivated by an overly conscious need for self-love that we forget the greater meaning of God's command. Only as we reach out to others in love, exhibiting concern for their well-being, can we convince them of the love of Christ for them.

ILLUMINATING THE LESSON

The adage "You are known by the company you keep" is well rooted in Scripture. Paul warned the Ephesian believers about their association with sinners: "Be not ye therefore partakers with them"

(Ephesians 5:7). He didn't mean, however, that we should totally avoid people of the world. What good would we be to anyone if we even tried such? Also, Jesus constantly befriended sinners during His earthly ministry. He seemed more comfortable around those who knew they were fallen than He was with self-righteous religious people. However, His purposes were always to lead them out of their sin, not to be entrapped by it.

We are never to condone or join in the lifestyles of those who trample over the laws of God, and we must guard our own heart to make sure we aren't led into the same vices that have lured these people. We need to show our best Christian behavior when around those who are immoral, evil, or opposed to godly standards. At the point we find ourselves picking up their language or rationalizing that what they do is "not so bad after all" is the time we should walk away. Then we need to take a hard look at our own motives for mixing with sinners. Are we being influenced more toward evil than we are influencing them toward good?

DAILY BIBLE READINGS

M. God's Moral Law.
    Deuteronomy 5:16-21
T. Honesty in Business.
    Deuteronomy 25:13-16
W. God Defines Morality.
    Isaiah 33:13-16
T. Honesty in Relationships.
    Colossians 3:9-15
F. Morality Commanded.
    2 Timothy 2:19-22
S. Right Living Rewarded.
    Revelation 22:12-15

Maintaining Personal Integrity

Study Text: Job 27:4-6; Psalm 24:3-5; Proverbs 4:23-27; Romans 12:17-21; 2 Corinthians 6:4- 10; 1 Peter 3:10-13

Objective: To recognize that loyalty to God is the basis for integrity and be a person of integrity.

Golden Text: "The integrity of the upright shall guide them: but the perverseness of transgressors shall destroy them" (Proverbs 11:3).

Central Truth: Obedience to God results in personal integrity.

Evangelism Emphasis: Christians, as persons of integrity, can be powerful witnesses for Christ.

PRINTED TEXT

Job 27:4. My lips shall not speak wickedness, nor my tongue utter deceit.

5. God forbid that I should justify you: till I die I will not remove mine integrity from me.

6. My righteousness I hold fast, and will not let it go: my heart shall not reproach me so long as I live.

2 Corinthians 6:4. But in all things approving ourselves as the ministers of God, in much patience, in afflictions, in necessities, in distresses,

5. In stripes, in imprisonments, in tumults, in labours, in watchings, in fastings;

6. By pureness, by knowledge, by longsuffering, by kindness, by the Holy Ghost, by love unfeigned.

Proverbs 4:23. Keep thy heart with all diligence; for out of it are the issues of life.

24. Put away from thee a froward mouth, and perverse lips put far from thee.

25. Let thine eyes look right on, and let thine eyelids look straight before thee.

26. Ponder the path of thy feet, and let all thy ways be established.

27. Turn not to the right hand nor to the left: remove thy foot from evil.

Romans 12:17. Recompense to no man evil for evil. Provide things honest in the sight of all men.

18. If it be possible, as much as lieth in you, live peaceably with all men.

19. Dearly beloved, avenge not yourselves, but rather give place unto wrath: for it is written, Vengeance is mine; I will repay, saith the Lord.

20. Therefore if thine enemy hunger, feed him; if he thirst, give him drink: for in so doing thou shalt heap coals of fire on his head.

21. Be not overcome of evil, but overcome evil with good.

Psalm 24:3. Who shall ascend into the hill of the Lord? or who shall stand in his holy place?

4. He that hath clean hands, and a pure heart; who hath not lifted up his soul unto vanity, nor sworn deceitfully.

5. He shall receive the blessing from the Lord, and righteousness from the God of his salvation.

1 Peter 3:10. For he that will love life, and see good days, let him refrain his tongue from evil, and his lips that they speak no guile:

11. Let him eschew evil, and do good; let him seek peace, and ensue it.

12. For the eyes of the Lord are over the righteous, and his ears are open unto their prayers: but the face of the Lord is against them that do evil.

LESSON OUTLINE

LESSON EXPOSITION

INTRODUCTION

All of us have probably heard the following statement: "I'm not sure what I'm looking for, but I'll know it when I see it." There are certain things that are difficult to define, although we know what they are. We have a clear picture in mind but just don't know how to describe what we are seeing. The same is true for integrity. It's not always easy to define, but we definitely know a person of integrity when we encounter one. Just to mention the word probably brings to mind certain individuals whom we see as examples of this wonderful attribute.

The word *integrity* is defined by *Nelson's Illustrated Bible Dictionary* as "honesty, sincerity, singleness of purpose." Noah, Abraham, Jacob, David, and Job are listed in the Old Testament as people of integrity. Interestingly, Jesus never used the word, but He did call for purity of heart (Matthew 5:8), singleness of purpose (Matthew 6:22), and pure motives (Matthew 6:1-6). All of these things are a part of a life of integrity.

The Pharisees, despite their hatred of all that Jesus stood for, still recognized His integrity: "They sent their disciples to him along with the Herodians. 'Teacher,' they said, 'we know you are a man of integrity and that you teach the way of God in accordance with the truth. You aren't swayed by men, because you pay no attention to who they are. Tell us then, what is your opinion? Is it right to pay taxes to Caesar or not?'" (Matthew 22:16, 17, *NIV*). These men were trying to trick Jesus into making a dangerous statement; still, they saw something in Him that they recognized as genuine integrity.

Paul encouraged Titus to show integrity in his ministry: "In everything set them an example by doing what is good. n your teaching show integrity, seriousness and soundness of speech that cannot be condemned, so that those who oppose you may be ashamed because they have nothing bad to say about us" (Titus 2:7, 8, NIV). To Paul integrity was the sum total of all that can be good and right in an individual.

Someone has said that reputation is what others think of you, while character is what you really are. Integrity involves both of these. Paul included a good reputation as a qualification for overseers: "He must also have a good reputation with outsiders, so that he will not fall into disgrace and into the devil's trap" (1 Timothy 3:7, NIV). Reputation is most often a public reflection of what an individual really is. Good reputation and strong Christian character produce a life of integrity.

I. INTEGRITY EXEMPLIFIED
(Job 27:4-6; 2 Corinthians 6:4-10)

A. An Old Testament Model of Integrity (Job 27:4-6)

4. My lips shall not speak wickedness, nor my tongue utter deceit.

5. God forbid that I should justify you: till I die I will not remove mine integrity from me.

6. My righteousness I hold fast, and will not let it go: my heart shall not reproach me so long as I live.

Job was a perfect example of a man who maintained absolute adherence to his life principles. God pointed this out to Satan when he came with other angels to present themselves before the Lord: "Have you considered my servant Job? There is no one on earth like him; he is blameless and upright, a man who fears God and shuns evil. And he still maintains his integrity, though you incited me against him to ruin him without any reason" (Job 2:3, NIV). Like so many others have done to people of integrity over the centuries, Satan misjudged Job. He assumed that his relationship with God was based on the Lord's buying Job's loyalty by giving him great success, wealth, and favor. Satan was right in recognizing that devotion which comes purely from rewards is suspect. Many people are interested in a relationship with the Lord purely for what He can do for them. "In effect, their walk with God operates on the basis of reciprocity: He gives to them, and in exchange they follow Him" (The Word in Life Study Bible).

Job was not like other men, however. He knew the only real thing of value he had was his integrity. Interestingly, even the Lord was impressed with this man's determination to live righteously. Job had been a fabulously wealthy man before the first disasters struck him. The chances of his affluence corrupting him were extremely great, yet he kept his possessions in proper perspective. He knew that these were all volatile and could dissipate without a moment's notice: "The Lord gave, and the Lord has taken away; blessed be the name of the Lord" (Job 1:21, NKJV).

Job apparently had let it be known that his integrity was his most important asset. His sermons were not always understood, even by those closest to him. This is shown by what his wife said to him after his wealth and children were taken away and he was struck with boils. She had seen enough and in exasperation cried out, "Are you still holding on to your integrity? Curse God and die!" (Job 2:9, *NIV*). Job's loss of possessions and children had been her loss as well, but she apparently did not possess the determined faith that her husband clung to.

Job knew, however, that there was little security in this world. The dangers of Job's day included diseases to livestock and people; famines; crop failures; destructive pests and predators; natural disasters such as hail, wind, earthquakes, and drought; robbers; thieves; and health calamities such as deadly children's diseases, and childbirth complications. All these were rampart 3,000 years ago. But has anything really changed that much today? Job lost his wealth, his family, and his health to the same perils that we still face. In every generation men live on the edge of ruin, the next breath a possible disaster. There is never a complete shield from ruin—except our trust in the Lord. Job recognized that everything is a vapor but the Lord's graciousness and kindness toward us. Therefore, to maintain integrity before the Lord was the greatest goal he could possibly pursue.

B. Integrity in Ministry—A New
   Testament Model
   (2 Corinthians 6:4-10)

   (2 Corinthians 6:7-10 is not included in the printed text.)

   4. But in all things approving ourselves as the ministers of God,

in much patience, in afflictions, in necessities, in distresses,

5. In stripes, in imprisonments, in tumults, in labours, in watchings, in fastings;

6. By pureness, by knowledge, by longsuffering, by kindness, by the Holy Ghost, by love unfeigned.

Paul was defending his integrity and ministry against the false teachers of his day. He wanted the Corinthian church to know that he had suffered greatly for the gospel, but none of this was for personal gain. Instead, he described his years of effort as full of tribulation, tumult, distress, a hungry stomach, and many sleepless nights. He had not accumulated any wealth for his faithfulness, but he had reaped other rewards that were far more lasting and real. These included a good report, joy, and peace of mind. All others treasures were laid up in heaven. He could honestly testify that his motives were always for the sake of the gospel. The sum total of his efforts was a life of integrity. He had not done anything to hurt his witness for the gospel.

Paul also here gave a synopsis of the difficulties that come with Christian living. Many come to the Lord expecting freedom from tension, conflict, and suffering. They mistakenly think that faith in Jesus Christ will produce a stress-free existence on earth and automatically bring prosperity, health, and bliss. This is not an accurate picture. There will always be trouble, dissension, and difficulty. In actuality, these are the things that provide for us the opportunity for integrity to build, for character to grow, and maturity to develop. James encouraged the church to rejoice in trials: "Consider it pure joy, my brothers, whenever you face trials of many kinds, because you know that the testing of your faith develops perseverance. Perseverance must finish its work so that you may be mature and complete, not lacking anything" (James 1:2-4, *NIV*). The writer of Hebrews indicated that troubles are a sign for us that we are really God's children: "If you are not disciplined (and everyone undergoes discipline), then you are illegitimate children and not true sons" (Hebrews 12:8, *NIV*).

Peter suggested that if we are to share in Christ's glory, we must experience at least a portion of trials and suffering like He endured: "But rejoice that you participate in the sufferings of Christ, so that you may be overjoyed when his glory is revealed" (1 Peter 4:13, *NIV*). We are to expect testings and pressures on our faith. This gives our integrity a chance to shine. Maintaining principle under stress is the only way to find out what we really believe in and stand for. The wonderful thing is that we are being prepared for future glory. Although Job in the Old Testament had all his wealth restored after extreme testings, the New Testament heroes of faith had to wait until heaven to receive their rewards. Virtually all these men and women experienced great personal loss (including a martyr's death) for their stand. Yet they considered this no great sacrifice. Their integrity was their most prized possession, and even death could not take it away.

How important is it for us to guard our integrity? What effect does loss of integrity have on our ability to witness for the Lord Jesus?

II. INTEGRITY COMMANDED (Proverbs 4:23-27; Romans 12:17-21)

A. Maintaining Self-Control (Proverbs 4:23, 24)

23. Keep thy heart with all diligence; for out of it are the issues of life.
24. Put away from thee a froward mouth, and perverse lips put far from thee.

The *New International Version* of verse 23 reads: "Above all else, guard your heart, for it is the wellspring of life." A literal wellspring is a source of water. If it gets polluted, habitation becomes difficult or impossible. In a figurative sense, our hearts are our source of intelligence, emotion, and affections. If they are not kept pure, then the life they sustain becomes contaminated. We are to guard our hearts, making sure that we dwell on those things that are good and useful and that push us in the right direction. We are to avoid the things that would trip us up. We should always carefully consider our choices, ever watchful that they be consistent with God's Word.

Jesus expressed the conflict between our hearts and our tongues when He said, "The good man brings good things out of the good stored up in him, and the evil man brings evil things out of the evil stored up in him" (Matthew 12:35, *NIV*). The unredeemed heart is a constant source of evil: "For out of the heart come evil thoughts, murder, adultery, sexual immorality, theft, false testimony, slander" (Matthew 15:19, *NIV*). Even the most disciplined tongue cannot change what the heart is thinking. We are to guard our words, but first we have to let the Holy Spirit work in us to give us the right attitudes and motives. Our speech and actions will then reflect the inner cleansing that has taken place in our hearts. Discipline of the tongue and actions is still necessary, but the heart is no longer polluted.

B. Checking One's Course
   (vv. 25-27)

25. Let thine eyes look right on, and let thine eyelids look straight before thee.

26. Ponder the path of thy feet, and let all thy ways be established.

27. Turn not to the right hand nor to the left: remove thy foot from evil.

Humans are the only creatures God made with the capacity for reflection, self-evaluation, and goal setting. We can look back on past decisions, judge what they accomplished and how they affected our integrity, and then set a new course. These verses encourage us to make those reflections wisely. If we make decisions based on personal wants, desires, and temptations, we will stray from the righteous path and set a disastrous course. The result will be a loss of integrity. We must keep our eyes focused on the right goal—heaven and dwelling eternally in God's presence.

C. Regard for Others (Romans
   12:17-21)

17. Recompense to no man evil for evil. Provide things honest in the sight of all men.

18. If it be possible, as much as lieth in you, live peaceably with all men.

19. Dearly beloved, avenge not yourselves, but rather give place unto wrath: for it is written, Vengeance is mine; I will repay, saith the Lord.

20 Therefore if thine enemy hunger, feed him; if he thirst, give him drink: for in so doing thou shalt heap coals of fire on his head.

21. Be not overcome of evil, but overcome evil with good.

These verses put in a nutshell the heart of Christian living. If we express to others the love that Christ has loved us with, we will treat them just as He would. Paul here was summarizing what Jesus had earlier said. In the Sermon on the Mount (Matthew 5—7), Jesus presented a revolutionary concept— that we treat those who hurt us with love and mercy: "But I tell you, Do not resist an evil person. If someone strikes you on the right cheek, turn to him the other also. . . . You have heard that it was said, 'Love your neighbor and hate your enemy.' But I tell you: Love your enemies and pray for those who persecute you, that you may be sons of your Father in heaven" (Matthew 5:39, 43-45, *NIV*).

These were difficult words to understand or accept. They probably left Jesus' listeners aghast. How can one love his enemy? It can only be accomplished, of course, through grace. Having experienced God's undeserved favor, the believer then has the capacity to give an enemy a drink, forgive his evil, and love him into the Kingdom. However, this still does not come naturally. It must be a conscious decision of attitude and will. By reaching out to those who harm us, we break the cycle of "eye for eye," "evil for evil." Even if that person who has hurt us never actually changes, at least we are free from bitterness and the harm it can do in our own hearts.

Is it possible to maintain Christian integrity while at the same time holding a grudge against or ill will toward another person?

III. INTEGRITY REWARDED (Psalm 24:3-5; 1 Peter 3:10-13)

A. The Necessity of Integrity (Psalm 24:3-5)

3. Who shall ascend into the hill of the Lord? or who shall stand in his holy place?

4. He that hath clean hands, and a pure heart; who hath not lifted up his soul unto vanity, nor sworn deceitfully.

5. He shall receive the blessing from the Lord, and righteousness from the God of his salvation.

The psalmist makes it very clear who can enter God's presence. In a literal sense he was talking about climbing the hill of Mount Zion, then going into the consecrated rooms of the temple. In a broader sense the writer was speaking of anyone trying to please the Lord. We can only do so as we purify our motives. "We must sincerely desire God's mercy and forgiveness; otherwise we cannot approach him. In fact, the only way to have a pure heart is through the grace of God, granted in response to our faith

and obedience" *(The Quest Study Bible)*.

Such pure motives require an honest heart. We deceive only ourselves when we think we can hold on to bitterness, sin, or wrong attitudes and still draw near to God. There is no way to fool Him! He knows every thought we think even before we think it. Honesty before God is the beginning of integrity.

B. Controlling the Tongue—A Sign of Integrity (1 Peter 3:10-13)

(1 Peter 3:13 is not included in the printed text.)

10. For he that will love life, and see good days, let him refrain his tongue from evil, and his lips that they speak no guile:

11. Let him eschew evil, and do good; let him seek peace, and ensue it.

12. For the eyes of the Lord are over the righteous, and his ears are open unto their prayers: but the face of the Lord is against them that do evil.

Both Peter and James had much to say about the importance of controlling our tongues. Possibly, evil is done by words ill spoken than by deeds actually carried out—especially if considered by their volume. Also, what we don't say is just as important as what we do say. Holding backing from speaking harsh words when we are provoked will certainly help us avoid great problems. We are to avoid harmful words (such as gossip, bragging, putting others down, exaggeration, complaining, etc.), but we are also admonished to positively lift others with good words of commendation. This extends to our enemies as well. By reaching out to those who hurt us, speaking positively to them, we open the door to reconciliation. Harsh words put a scar on our spirits, affect how others see us, and damage our integrity.

Is there a person in your life that needs to hear positive words from you?

REVIEW QUESTIONS

1. How long does it take to build integrity? Is this an instant gift or a lifetime process?

2. What are some Biblical examples of people of integrity? What was the most important attribute that these people possessed?

3. Why is integrity so important to church leadership?

4. Why is the tongue so hard to tame, and why are our words so crucial to developing integrity?

GOLDEN TEXT HOMILY

"THE INTEGRITY OF THE UPRIGHT SHALL GUIDE THEM: BUT THE PERVERSENESS OF TRANSGRESSORS SHALL DESTROY THEM" (Proverbs 11:3).

The word *integrity* may be defined as "the quality or state of being of sound moral principle." A good synonym for *integrity* is *sincerity*.

The upright man is guided in his behavior, then, by his sound moral principle or sincerity. "His principles are fixed, his rule is certain, and therefore his way is plain; his sincerity keeps him steady, and he need not tack about every time the wind turns, having no other end to drive at than to keep a good conscience" (Matthew Henry).

Once an upright man knows the right thing to do in a situation, he moves in that direction. This is not to say that it is always easy for him to do the right thing. He is human, and he may dislike going against other people's desires or feelings if they conflict with what he perceives to be the right course of action. But because the upright man is sincere, because he has a solid basis for his conduct, he proceeds along the path of righteousness. He does the right thing, He does so in his home, on his job, in his social life, and at his church. Needless to say, in all walks of life, we need more upright men and women—those who will always conduct themselves in accordance with sound principles and will always be sincere.— **Excerpts from the** *Evangelical Commentary*, **Vol. 27**

SENTENCE SERMONS

OBEDIENCE TO GOD results in personal integrity.
—Selected

IF ONE CAN be sure that his principles are right, he need not worry about the consequences.
—Robert Elliott Speer

A GOOD NAME keeps its brightness even in dark days.
—Latin Proverb

WHEN A CHRISTIAN jealously guards his secret life with God, his public life will take care of itself.
—Oswald Chambers

EVANGELISM APPLICATION

CHRISTIANS, AS PERSONS OF INTEGRITY, CAN BE POWERFUL WITNESSES FOR CHRIST.

Integrity is the best attribute we can take with us to our graves. There is no finer obituary one can read than that of a life lived by solid principle. How is such a noble goal accomplished? In Proverbs we are told, "Let your eyes look straight ahead, fix your gaze directly before you" (4:25, *NIV*). Obviously we have to know where we are going. If our goal is heaven and eternity with the Lord, we have to keep a clear focus and steady aim at that target to make it.

How do we do this? One way is to make frequent evaluations of where we are—assessing our attitudes, behavior, and accomplishments. Several questions we should ask ourselves include these:

1. Is our purpose for living clear, or are we merely wandering through our days with no goal in mind?

2. Are we influencing the lost for Christ by our daily walk with Him?

3. Where are we on our journey in comparison to five years ago? Have we grown in Christian character? Are we struggling with the same pitfalls? In what areas have we seen victory?

4. How does our daily routine honor the Lord? Can others see Christ exemplified in all that we do?

5. How are we dealing with evil? With temptation?

Looking back to see what God has accomplished should be a regular exercise for every Christian. Paul looked back at the end of his ministry and saw that his goal had been realized. He could say of his life and ministry, "I have fought the good fight, I have finished the race, I have kept the faith" (2 Timothy 4:7, *NIV*).

A life of integrity convinces the lost that the life of a sincere Christian has a quality they do not possess.

ILLUMINATING THE LESSON

I grew up on a small farm. As a young boy I had to do all our plowing in the fields with an old two-wheel garden tractor. It did the same job as the modern garden tiller but was much bulkier and more difficult to control. The hardest part of working with it was "laying off the rows." Every good farmer prides himself in plowing a straight furrow. This was not an easy accomplishment with "Betsy" the garden tractor.

I did eventually learn a secret, however. When getting ready to plow a row, I would look straight ahead to the end of the field. I set my eyes on some object that was exactly the target of where I wanted the row to finish. Then I put the tractor in gear and never looked down, but rather kept my eyes on the object in the distance. After the first row was completed, I looked back to make sure it was straight, and then set another object in sight, figuring before I ever started exactly where I wanted to go.

This is what we must do in life. We set goals toward heaven, never veering from the planned course. No matter how bumpy the journey or how rough the ground, we look straight ahead to where we have focused our eyes. This is the real meaning of *integrity*—a consistent focus on a righteous goal.

DAILY BIBLE READINGS

M. Integrity of Abraham.
  Genesis 18:16-19
T. Integrity of Joseph.
  Genesis 50:14-21
W. Integrity of Samuel.
  1 Samuel 12:1-5
T. Integrity of Job. Job 2:7-10
F. Integrity of Paul.
  1 Thessalonians 2:1-6
S. Integrity of Peter.
  2 Peter 1:12-16

God's Plan for Human Sexuality

Study Text: Genesis 1:27; 2:21-24; Exodus 20:14; 1 Corinthians 6:9, 10, 13-20; 7:1-5; Ephesians 5:28-33; Hebrews 13:4

Objective: To acknowledge that marriage is the framework for human sexuality and obey God's laws in all relationships.

Golden Text: "But fornication, and all uncleanness . . . let it not be once named among you, as becometh saints" (Ephesians 5:3).

Central Truth: God commands His people to be sexually moral.

Evangelism Emphasis: Moral purity in all relationships helps us point people to Christ.

PRINTED TEXT

Genesis 1:27. So God created man in his own image, in the image of God created he him; male and female created he them.

2:21. And the Lord God caused a deep sleep to fall upon Adam, and he slept: and he took one of his ribs, and closed up the flesh instead thereof;

22. And the rib, which the Lord God had taken from man, made he a woman, and brought her unto the man.

23. And Adam said, This is now bone of my bones, and flesh of my flesh: she shall be called Woman, because she was taken out of Man.

24. Therefore shall a man leave his father and his mother, and shall cleave unto his wife: and they shall be one flesh.

Exodus 20:14. Thou shalt not commit adultery.

1 Corinthians 6:9. Know ye not that the unrighteous shall not inherit the kingdom of God? Be not deceived: neither fornicators, nor idolaters, nor adulterers, nor effeminate, nor abusers of themselves with mankind,

10. Nor thieves, nor covetous, nor drunkards, nor revilers, nor extortioners, shall inherit the kingdom of God.

18. Flee fornication. Every sin that a man doeth is without the body; but he that committeth fornication sinneth against his own body.

19. What? know ye not that your body is the temple of the Holy Ghost which is in you, which ye have of God, and ye are not your own?

20. For ye are bought with a price: therefore glorify God in your body, and in your spirit, which are God's.

Hebrews 13:4. Marriage is honourable in all, and the bed undefiled: but whoremongers and adulterers God will judge.

1 Corinthians 7:1. Now concerning the things whereof ye wrote unto me: It is good for a man not to touch a woman.

2. Nevertheless, to avoid for-

nication, let every man have his own wife, and let every woman have her own husband.

3. Let the husband render unto the wife due benevolence: and likewise also the wife unto the husband.

4. **The wife hath not power of her own body, but the husband: and likewise also the husband hath not power of his own body, but the wife.**

5. Defraud ye not one the other, except it be with consent for a time, that ye may give yourselves to fasting and prayer; and come together again, that Satan tempt you not for your incontinency.

LESSON OUTLINE

I. MARRIAGE ORDAINED OF GOD
   A. Created for Marriage
   B. The Two as One Flesh

II. SEXUAL IMMORALITY FORBIDDEN
   A. The Sin of Adultery
   B. Sexual Sins Not Allowed in the Kingdom
   C. Members of Christ's Body
   D. Marriage—An Honorable Institution

III. FIDELITY IN MARRIAGE
   A. The Husband and Wife
   B. Loving One's Spouse

LESSON EXPOSITION

INTRODUCTION

The spirit of the age is "I can do exactly as I please." This self-proclaimed freedom is nowhere more pronounced than in the area of sexuality. Every possible illicit behavior is now practiced and to a great extent accepted in our society. Sexual deviancy has become so commonplace that marriage is often portrayed as boring, confining, and joyless, and purity, loyalty, and faithfulness are scorned.

Many people say they should be allowed to use their bodies in any way they please. They maintain it is their "right" and their desires should be respected. They see this as an expression of their freedom. But is it? Isn't this instead just another form of slavery—slavery to one's own desires? Real freedom is found in Christ. This is freedom from sin and the guilt that comes with immoral lifestyles.

God's Word is absolutely clear in its position on sexuality. God created sex to be a beautiful and joyful privilege of marriage. Anything else is an expression of self-will and rebellion. Yet Christians are not free from temptation. Allurements are everywhere and can trap even the most dedicated in an unguarded moment. We must constantly guard our hearts and keep focused on what is right. The consequences of sexual sins are so devastating that, even though they are not beyond God's grace and forgiveness, they leave scars on our character, integrity, and reputation.

I. MARRIAGE ORDAINED OF GOD (Genesis 1:27; 2:21-24)

A. Created for Marriage (1:27)

27. So God created man in his own image, in the image of God

created he him; male and female created he them.

What is obviously clear in this verse is that God made man and woman equally in His image. They were both at the top of His creation, and neither was considered superior to the other. Yet the myth propagated today is that woman must fight against man because she has not been treated as his equal over the centuries. Modern feminism has concocted the idea that if woman can gain freedom from man, and in many cases mastery over him, she will achieve some sense of well-being hithertofore unknown to her. Interestingly enough, however, the vast majority of people still want to be married. Although the sexual revolution has made mockery of traditional values, something deep inside the human spirit still longs for the sense of family, human companionship, and well-being that comes with lifelong commitment.

In order to restore the moral fiber and integrity of the family, people must once again realize that man and woman are already equal in God's sight. Their roles are different, but neither is depreciated in God's view of how His creation should function.

The word *image* does not carry the idea of a physical resemblance but rather a spiritual one. Like God, we have a conscience, a sense of individual will, and a distinct personality. We can also take on other features that resemble those of God. As new creatures in Christ, we are to "put on the new self, created to be like God in true righteousness and holiness" (Ephesians 4:24, *NIV*).

B. The Two as One Flesh (2:21-24)

21. And the Lord God caused a deep sleep to fall upon Adam, and he slept: and he took one of his ribs, and closed up the flesh instead thereof;

22. And the rib, which the Lord God had taken from man, made he a woman, and brought her unto the man.

23. And Adam said, This is now bone of my bones, and flesh of my flesh: she shall be called Woman, because she was taken out of Man.

24. Therefore shall a man leave his father and his mother, and shall cleave unto his wife: and they shall be one flesh.

In the original creation God had made every living thing in pairs, male and female—all except for man. Did God really plan for man to live alone, thus viewing the creation of woman as only an afterthought? No. "The Lord allowed Adam to come to the self-realization that he needed fellowship, friendship, and intimacy from a creature corresponding to himself" (*The Quest Study Bible*). Because God viewed the union of man and woman in marriage so highly, man needed to understand his own utter need of a companion. Thus, marriage would be more sacred to him, and would carry a commitment that was unknown to the rest of creation. God knew that Adam was lonely, and even an intimate relationship with Himself would not satisfy that need.

God's choice to make woman from the man's rib instead of from the dust of the ground was symbolic of His plan for the two to become one flesh. Marriage is a mystical union of two individuals coming together to create one heart and life. Anyone approaching marriage should be ready to make a commitment that goes far beyond friendship, sexual need, or desire for children. Oneness must be the highest goal if a marriage is to succeed as God planned.

God made woman to be a helper. By no means does this relegate her to a lower status. The word *helper* actually carries a connotation of *strength* or *power.* Scripture often views God as our helper, and there is certainly no devaluation of His character in such a usage: "We wait in hope for the Lord; he is our help and our shield" (Psalm 33:20, *NIV*; see also Psalm 115:9-12). Neither did God mean for woman to be viewed in a lower sense by giving her such a role. Woman is man's equal and partner for life. Both are to view each other in this light. Each are to honor God in their roles. "Man gives life to woman; woman gives life to the world. Each role carries exclusive privileges that should eliminate any attitudes about an inferior or superior sex" (*Life Application Bible*).

Verse 24 indicates that there are three aspects of the marriage relationship that distinguishes it from all others: (1) Man leaves his parents and promises himself to a new relationship; (2) the man and woman are joined together to form a new covenant, thus taking on the responsibility of each other's needs; (3) the man and woman intimately become a new family, or new "flesh." If any of these three are missing, the marriage will be in trouble. Reluctance to leave parents, refusal to take on the spouse's needs as one's own, or lack of intimacy (or betrayal of that intimacy through adultery) will result in major problems for the marriage. Every couple approaching marriage should make sure they are committed to all three of God's marriage principles.

Can any marriage prosper if either the husband or wife does not fully commit to making it work?

II. SEXUAL IMMORALITY FORBIDDEN (Exodus 20:14; 1 Corinthians 6:9, 10, 13-20; Hebrews 13:4)

A. The Sin of Adultery (Exodus 20:14)

14. Thou shalt not commit adultery.

Adultery can be defined as sexual relations with anyone other than one's husband or wife. Jesus went even further to say that *lust* in itself constitutes adultery: "But I tell you that anyone who looks at a woman lustfully has already committed adultery with her in his heart" (Matthew 5:28, *NIV*). Many of the Jews of Jesus' day had perverted the law through the teachings and traditions passed down by rabbis. For instance, a writ of divorce had become a simple document to obtain. Those who followed the teachings of Rabbi Hillel could use almost any reason to divorce their wives, including such a minor thing as poor cooking. Jesus saw that a mockery had been made of God's commandment against adultery. He knew that hypocrisy was being paraded as "living by the law," and He insisted on purity of heart among those who would follow Him. Thus He proclaimed that God's intent in the original commandment is that man should abstain from anything that causes him to lust.

The verse in the text above is from the Ten Commandments, a summary of all the law God gave the Israelites. These were recorded on stone tablets and placed in the ark of the covenant (see Exodus 25:16). In the original Mosaic Law, any couple caught in the act of adultery would both be subject to execution (Deuteronomy 22:22). The severity of the punishment indicates how much God hates this sin—and also how much it plays havoc with lives. The classic case is David's liaison with

Bathsheba. What started as a lust of the eye led to adultery and murder and ultimately brought a heritage of disaster and bloodshed on David's household. The prophet Nathan declared to David, 'The sword will never depart from your house, because you despised me and took the wife of Uriah the Hittite to be your own'" (2 Samuel 12:10, *NIV*). All sin brings undesired consequences, but this is especially true of sexual ones, as seen in David's life.

David's sin also shows how evil is often exposed, no matter how well hidden it might seem. David had so hardened himself that he could not see through the parable that Nathan told him (2 Samuel 12:1-6). It was only when the prophet pointed to him directly that conviction struck his heart for disobeying God's commandment. A sense of guilt, alienation from the Lord, and sheer misery immediately flooded his heart.

Sadly, this misery is never limited to the guilty individuals. When adultery is exposed in a marriage, it brings with it hurt, frustration, and a sense of betrayal to the marriage partner as well. It sets up a barrier that only God's grace can overcome. Thus, God gave the commandment against the sin of adultery for the protection of the entire family. Marriage is sacred in God's sight, and those things that harm this institution must be avoided.

B. Sexual Sins Not Allowed in the Kingdom (1 Corinthians 6:9, 10)

9. Know ye not that the unrighteous shall not inherit the kingdom of God? Be not deceived: neither fornicators, nor idolaters, nor adulterers, nor effeminate, nor abusers of themselves with mankind,

10. Nor thieves, nor covetous, nor drunkards, nor revilers, nor extortioners, shall inherit the kingdom of God.

Paul here cataloged a series of sins that exclude a person from the kingdom of God. None of these, however, is beyond God's grace and forgiveness. Notice also that these sexual sins are listed among other harmful and damaging sins—greed, drunkenness, slander, and theft. All sin is wrong. Paul was describing the characteristics of the unrighteous as a group. One is not immediately excluded from the Kingdom just because he struggles with evil desires, however. God's grace extends even to those who have committed the most vile acts. But to persist in such evil after experiencing Christ's saving power is totally inconsistent with the redeemed life.

The perfect example of this principle is the story of the woman taken in adultery (John 8:3-9). According to the law of Moses, she should have been stoned to death. Jesus, however, extended forgiveness. He never excused her sin, but rather He forgave her. He then commanded her, "Sin no more" (John 8:11). She could not continue in sin and expect continued grace.

C. Members of Christ's Body (vv. 13-20)

(1 Corinthians 6:13-17 is not included in the printed text.)

18. Flee fornication. Every sin that a man doeth is without the body; but he that committeth fornication sinneth against his own body.

19. What? know ye not that your body is the temple of the Holy Ghost which is in you, which ye have of God, and ye are not your own?

20. For ye are bought with a price: therefore glorify God in your body, and in your spirit, which are God's.

We do not belong to ourselves. We are members of Christ's body.

As members of His body we have been given certain freedoms. The enjoyment of food is one of those freedoms. However, we are not to abuse this privilege by becoming gluttonous. One responsibility of belonging to the Kingdom is balance, and balance requires restraint. We use restraint to manage those things that would control us.

For our own good, God put parameters to our freedom relating to sexual matters. He intends this area of life to be enjoyed fully, but only within the boundaries of marriage. He put restraints on sexuality to protect us from the devastating results sexual sin produces. "It hurts God because it shows we prefer following our own desires instead of the leading of the Holy Spirit. It hurts others because it violates the commitment so necessary to a relationship. It often brings disease to our bodies, and it deeply affects our personalities, which respond in anguish when we harm ourselves physically and spiritually" (*Life Application Bible*).

D. Marriage—An Honorable Institution (Hebrews 13:4)

4. Marriage is honourable in all, and the bed undefiled: but whoremongers and adulterers God will judge.

This exhortation is prefaced with the all-consuming appeal to "keep on loving each other as brothers" (Hebrews 13:1, *NIV*). This is a simple rewording of the Golden Rule that Jesus gave (see Matthew 7:12). When we live with the goal of treating others just as we would like to be treated, we will avoid sexual sins completely. Sexual behavior outside of marriage harms others and is thus a violation of this principle for living.

The connotation of Hebrews 13:4 is "Let marriage be held in honor by all, and let the bed be undefiled, for God will judge the adulterer and the

sexually immoral." The precept is leveled against impurity, against the easy-divorce practice, and against the false asceticism of those "forbidding to marry" (1 Timothy 4:3). "Marriage is honorable," the writer was saying. "Keep it that way!"

Can anyone please God and at the same time be involved in any form of sexual misconduct?

III. FIDELITY IN MARRIAGE (1 Corinthians 7:1-5; Ephesians 5:28-33)

A. The Husband and Wife (1 Corinthians 7:1-5)

1. Now concerning the things whereof ye wrote unto me: It is good for a man not to touch a woman.

2. Nevertheless, to avoid fornication, let every man have his own wife, and let every woman have her own husband.

3. Let the husband render unto the wife due benevolence: and likewise also the wife unto the husband.

4. The wife hath not power of her own body, but the husband: and likewise also the husband hath not power of his own body, but the wife.

5. Defraud ye not one the other, except it be with consent for a time, that ye may give yourselves to fasting and prayer; and come together again, that Satan tempt you not for your incontinency.

Paul was in a sense elevating the status of women with this passage. In an age when women had few rights and could be abused by men without penalty, the apostle urged Christian husbands to treat their wives lovingly—never taking advantage of them either physically, sexually, or emotionally. He also insisted that neither spouse use sex as a means of controlling the other, but rather enjoy this part of their relationship with a total sense of giving. In doing so, both partners would be strengthened to overcome temptation in the immoral society where they lived.

Paul's first response to the Corinthians' letter of inquiry concerned marriage. His view that it is good for a man not to marry has been variously interpreted. Bear in mind, however, that he was responding to the conditions that existed at that time in Corinth. By remaining single, men could give themselves more fully to God's service without the responsibilities and burdens of a family. Nevertheless, Paul also recognized an inherent danger of singleness in Corinth. Verse 2 is better rendered, "because of the [prevalent] fornication." It was such a general practice in Corinth and so infrequently regarded as sin that the unmarried were more likely to be led into it than those who had their own marriage partner. Then there were those who were so strongly opposed to the great sexual immorality in the Corinthian culture that these believers thought all sex was wrong, even within marriage. So Paul had to set the record straight for them as well: "Do not deprive each other except by mutual consent and for a time . . ." (v. 5, *NIV*).

B. Loving One's Spouse
   (Ephesians 5:28-33)

(Ephesians 5:28-33 is not included in the printed text.)

Marriage is a mystical union in which two individuals become one flesh. What affects one then will also affect the other. Individual personalities are not lost, but responsibility and concern for the other's good becomes just as important as consideration for one's own self.

Notice that Paul devoted much more time to how the husband treats the wife than how the wife acts toward her husband. Those in the modern world who say that Christianity has deprived women have not read the words of either Paul or Jesus. The Christian man should be willing to sacrifice for his wife, make her his primary concern, and care for her just as if her body were his own body. No woman has ever been mistreated by a husband who lives up to these commands.

Why is it good for some men not to marry? Did God ordain that every person marry?

REVIEW QUESTIONS

1. Why does Satan come at Christians so hard with sexual temptations?

2. What does it take to restore trust in a marriage after one spouse has betrayed the other sexually?

3. Why are sexual sins so devastating?

4. In what ways do sexual sins harm others (family and friends especially)?

GOLDEN TEXT HOMILY

"BUT FORNICATION, AND ALL UNCLEANNESS . . . LET IT NOT BE ONCE NAMED AMONG YOU, AS BECOMETH SAINTS" (Ephesians 5:3).

The apostle Paul used the term *saint* when he referred to the people to whom he was writing. This reference is at the beginning or at the end of his letters. For example, the letter to the Ephesians began: "Paul an apostle of Jesus Christ by the will of God, to the saints who are in Ephesus, and faithful to Christ Jesus" (*NKJV*).

We do not often use this term *saint* today when we refer to fellow Christians unless those people have lived for Christ many years and have died in the faith. At their funeral you may hear the minister refer to them as "a great saint of God." And yet there is nothing wrong with referring to fellow Christians as "saints" while they are alive. That is exactly what Paul did!

What is special about a saint? A saint is a believer and follower of Jesus Christ. That person has chosen a certain lifestyle that sets him apart from others. Paul described this in Ephesians 5:1-3: "Therefore be followers of God dear children. And walk in love, as Christ also has loved us and given Himself for us, an offering and a sacrifice to God for a sweet-smelling aroma. But fornication and all uncleanness or covetousness, let it not even be named among you, as is fitting for saints; neither filthiness, nor foolish talking, nor coarse jesting, which are not fitting" (*NKJV*). Paul further explained in this chapter the lifestyles of saints as compared to the lifestyles of sinners. He was saying that sin separates us from God and cannot exist in a saint's lifestyle. Paul listed different types of sin and made it clear that no sin is fitting for a "saint."—**Levy E. Moore, Mayor, City of Franklin Springs, Franklin Springs, Georgia**

SENTENCE SERMONS

GOD COMMANDS HIS PEOPLE to be sexually moral.

—Selected

IT IS with our passions as it is with fire and water. They are good servants, but bad masters.

—Sir Roger L'Estrange

THERE IS no getting away from it: the old Christian rule is "Either marriage with complete faithfulness to your partner, or else total abstinence."

—C.S. Lewis

ILLUMINATING THE LESSON

In Galatians 5:18, Paul said, "But if you are led by the Spirit, you are not under the law" (*NIV*). Many people have interpreted this statement as giving them freedom from the restraints of the Ten Commandments. Did he really mean that believers no longer have to obey the Old Testament law? After all, Jesus himself had said, "The Law and the Prophets were proclaimed until John. Since that time, the good news of the kingdom of God is being preached, and everyone is forcing his way into it" (Luke 16:16, *NIV*). Jesus, however, was not speaking of canceling the ceremonial law of the Old Testament but rather of fulfilling it. As to the moral law, He came to give new depth, meaning, and understanding to the Ten Commandments. Paul's intent was that we recognize that true freedom comes by the Spirit. Only those who are walking by the Spirit have the ability to obey the moral law. The Spirit provides the power and motivation to avoid the temptations that would lead us into sin.

Instead of seeing the Ten Commandments as negative, we should view them as positive opportunities for the Holy Spirit to operate in us. It is in doing this that we experience the real freedom that God intends for us.

DAILY BIBLE READINGS

M. Respect for a Virtuous Woman. Ruth 3:1-11

T. Wise Counsel for Moral Purity. Proverbs 6:23-33

W. Jesus' Teaching on Adultery. Matthew 5:27-32

T. Jesus' Teaching on Marriage. Mark 10:2-9

F. Abstain From Sexual Sins. 1 Thessalonians 4:1-7

S. The Way to Overcome Lust. 1 John 2:12-17

Protecting Human Life

Study Text: Genesis 2:7; 9:5, 6; Exodus 1:15-17, 20; 20:13; Job 33:4; Psalm 139:13-16; John 10:10; Acts 16:27-30

Objective: To respect the sacredness of human life and commit to protecting it.

Golden Text: "Thou shalt not kill" (Exodus 20:13).

Central Truth: Human life is a precious gift of the Creator.

Evangelism Emphasis: God demonstrated His love for human life by providing salvation through His Son.

PRINTED TEXT

Genesis 2:7. And the Lord God formed man of the dust of the ground, and breathed into his nostrils the breath of life; and man became a living soul.

Job 33:4. The spirit of God hath made me, and the breath of the Almighty hath given me life.

Psalm 139:13. For thou hast possessed my reins: thou hast covered me in my mother's womb.

14. I will praise thee; for I am fearfully and wonderfully made: marvellous are thy works; and that my soul knoweth right well.

15. My substance was not hid from thee, when I was made in secret, and curiously wrought in the lowest parts of the earth.

16. Thine eyes did see my substance, yet being unperfect; and in thy book all my members were written, which in continuance were fashioned, when as yet there was none of them.

Genesis 9:5. And surely your blood of your lives will I require; at the hand of every beast will I require it, and at the hand of man; at the hand of every man's brother will I require the life of man.

6. Whoso sheddeth man's blood, by man shall his blood be shed: for in the image of God made he man.

Exodus 20:13. Thou shalt not kill.

John 10:10. The thief cometh not, but for to steal, and to kill, and to destroy: I am come that they might have life, and that they might have it more abundantly.

Exodus 1:15. And the king of Egypt spake to the Hebrew midwives, of which the name of the one was Shiphrah, and the name of the other Puah:

16. And he said, When ye do the office of a midwife to the Hebrew women, and see them upon the stools; if it be a son, then ye shall kill him: but if it be a daughter, then she shall live.

17. But the midwives feared God, and did not as the king of Egypt commanded them, but saved the men children alive.

20. Therefore God dealt well with the midwives: and the people multiplied, and waxed very mighty.

Acts 16:27. And the keeper of the prison awaking out of his sleep, and seeing the prison doors open, he drew out his sword, and would have killed himself, supposing that the prisoners had been fled.

28. But Paul cried with a loud voice, saying, Do thyself no harm: for we are all here.

DICTIONARY

Shiphrah (SHIF-rah) and Puah (PU-ah)—Exodus 1:15—Midwives who risked their lives to save the Hebrew babies from death by the Egyptians.

LESSON OUTLINE

I.   HUMAN LIFE IS SACRED
   A.   The Soul of Man
   B.   Man's Recognition of God
   C.   Fearfully and Wonderfully Made

II. HUMAN LIFE IS PRECIOUS
   A.   Blood for Blood
   B.   Murder Is Wrong
   C.   The Good Shepherd's Role

III. CHOOSE LIFE
   A.   Disobeying Authority to Protect Life
   B.   God Rewards Obedience
   C.   Suicide Is Wrong

LESSON EXPOSITION

INTRODUCTION

We live in an age in which many attempt to put all life forms on the same level. In this contemporary thought, man is assigned no higher value than any other living creature. In fact, according to this reasoning, man has abused his position of higher intellect and should be punished. It is true that God did not give man permission to abuse His creatures or creation. However, extremists have even gone so far as to value animal life above human life.

If man views himself as nothing but a walking animal with a little higher intelligence, then he is also likely to see no reason to live nobly, honestly, purely, or with any measure of integrity. He can simply follow his instincts and do as he pleases.

However, this is not the story of mankind according to the Bible. Man is the pinnacle of God's creation. God made this one special species to have dominion over all others, to have a conscience, and also to have fellowship with his Creator. In light of this, human life becomes very valuable, even sacred.

Many of the great debates of our day revolve around issues of man's worth—right to life, fetal research, abortion on demand, the death penalty, assisted suicide, the right to end one's own life. In this lesson we will look at Scripture passages that deal with the sacredness of life and seek to find a godly perspective for living through these difficult times.

I. HUMAN LIFE IS SACRED (Genesis 2:7; Job 33:4; Psalm 139:13-16)

A. The Soul of Man (Genesis 2:7)

7. And the Lord God formed man of the dust of the ground, and breathed into his nostrils the breath of life; and man became a living soul.

God thought so much of the grand pinnacle of His creation that a second description of man's origin is given (for the first, see Genesis 1:26-29). The first account emphasizes that man is made in God's image. This second one speaks of man's becoming a living soul.

Man was given more than simply a greater degree of intellect over other living creatures. He has the potential for a knowledge of God that goes beyond the objective to a personal knowledge of and relationship to Him. The apostle John said, "Now this is eternal life: that they may know you, the only true God, and Jesus Christ, whom you have sent" (John 17:3, NIV). Man is also blessed with a drive to find purpose and meaning in life. The psalmist declared, "Blessed are those who have learned to acclaim you, who walk in the light of your presence, O Lord" (Psalm 89:15, NIV), and Paul exhorted believers, "Put on the new self, which is being renewed in knowledge in the image of its Creator" (Colossians 3:10, NIV).

That man is a moral being with the capacity to decide what is right and wrong puts him on a different plane from the rest of creation. God's express will is innately imbedded in his heart, "since what may be known about God is plain to them, because God has made it plain to them. For since the creation of the world God's invisible qualities—his eternal power and divine nature—have been clearly seen, being understood from what has been made" (Romans 1:19, NIV). Because of this infusion, man has the capability to separate himself from evil, worship God, and be holy in His sight: "His divine power has given us everything we need for life and godliness through our knowledge of him who called us by his own glory and goodness" (2 Peter 1:3, NIV).

B. Man's Recognition of God (Job 33:4)

4. The spirit of God hath made me, and the breath of the Almighty hath given me life.

These words were spoken by Elihu, the youngest of Job's comforters. After Eliphaz, Bildad, and Zophar had gone to great lengths to identify the cause of Job's woes, this fourth counselor brought a different perspective to the argument by recognizing that God was refining Job through the fires of difficulty for his own greater good and maturity. The very fact that the four men spent so much time searching for answers to Job's condition illustrates that man is on a higher plane than all other creatures. These men all observed Job's pitiful situation, perhaps even empathized with him, sought abstract answers to the reason for his condition, and in their misguided reasoning showed a measure of compassion for his plight. Man's reasoning ability, as well as his recognition of a creator, puts him in a class apart from God's lower creation.

C. Fearfully and Wonderfully Made (Psalm 139:13-16)

13. For thou hast possessed my reins: thou has covered me in my mother's womb.

14. I will praise thee; for I am fearfully and wonderfully made: marvellous are thy works; and that my soul knoweth right well.

15. My substance was not hid from thee, when I was made in secret, and curiously wrought in the lowest parts of the earth.

16. Thine eyes did see my substance, yet being unperfect; and in thy book all my members were written, which in continuance were fashioned, when as yet there was none of them.

The 139th psalm, and especially these verses, epitomizes the Bible view concerning the sanctity of human life. God exercises a role in every detail of our lives, including our formation in the womb. He molds us with distinctive plans for our life spans. The Hebrew word for "hast possessed" is *qanah* (kaw-naw). This means "to erect, that is, create; by extension, to procure, especially by purchase; by implication, to own" (*Strong's Hebrew/Greek Dictionary*). The key meaning is ownership. God knows us so well because He owns us. "He is like the inventor who carefully designs and builds a device and then becomes the owner of its patent" (*Word in Life Study Bible*).

The word for "covered" in the figurative sense means "to protect." However, the literal meaning carries the connotations of knitting something together, crafting, or entwining. Job recognized this aspect of God's sovereignty: "Remember that you molded me like clay. Will you now turn me to dust again? Did you not pour me out like milk and curdle me like cheese, clothe me with skin and flesh and knit me together with bones and sinews? You gave me life and showed me kindness, and in your providence watched over my spirit" (Job 10:9-12, *NIV*). Humans are not the hap-

hazard result of millions of years of evolution. We are God's masterpiece of creation, made with specific plan and purpose of design.

There are many difficult dilemmas in life to resolve. Psalm 139 is the place to begin in building a Biblical foundation for dealing with traumatic events such as birth defects and miscarriages. Recognizing that God cares and is involved helps to ease the pain that accompanies these tragedies. The psalm also helps establish an ethical guideline for viewing the pre-birth issues of abortion, artificial insemination, in vitro fertilization, surrogate birth, and fetal tissue research. Knowing that God has a special interest in what takes place in the womb should make anyone hesitant to misuse this sacred place where a life is formed.

David was amazed at the complexity of the human life and expressed his awe in the words "I am fearfully and wonderfully made" (v. 14). He responded with thanksgiving and saw that God had a purpose for his life, even from the embryo stage. All his days had been prenumbered and written down in the book of life: "All the days ordained for me were written in your book before one of them came to be" (v. 16, *NIV*).

Those who argue that life does not begin in the womb would say that this entire psalm was written only in a figurative sense and was never meant to be taken literally. However, the fact that God is involved in every aspect of life is the overwhelming theme, and tampering with that sovereignty in any way is certainly dangerous territory.

Can anyone sincerely deny God's existence, or must he override his own conscience to do so?

II. HUMAN LIFE IS PRECIOUS
(Genesis 9:5, 6; Exodus 20:13; John 10:10)

A. Blood for Blood (Genesis 9:5, 6)

5. And surely your blood of your lives will I require; at the hand of every beast will I require it, and at the hand of man; at the hand of every man's brother will I require the life of man.

6. Whoso sheddeth man's blood, by man shall his blood be shed: for in the image of God made he man.

After the Flood, God made a covenant with Noah and his family, promising never to destroy the human race again by water. Also, as long as the earth and human history should last, there would be regular seasons, day and night, planting time and harvesttime (Genesis 8:22). This in itself shows God's concern for man's well-being. Despite man's sinful condition, there would be constants he could depend on for making life easier.

God then commanded that human life be held sacred. Even the animals would be to a certain degree responsible if they killed a human (see Exodus 21:28, 29). God explained that murder is wrong. Killing another person destroys someone else who is also made in His image. God then instituted capital punishment, a requirement of the life of the murderer for the life he had taken. Without such a stiff punishment, human life is cheapened and society becomes threatened. In Deuteronomy 19:13 a further explanation is given for the need of such penalty: "You must purge from Israel the guilt of shedding innocent blood, so that it may go well with you" (NIV). The land had to be cleansed of guilt because an innocent life had been taken, and the general society would suffer if the guilty party was left unpunished and allowed to go free.

Many say that the New Testament's emphasis on grace and forgiveness does away with the need for capital punishment. These words of Jesus are used in this argument: "If any one of you is without sin, let him be the first to throw a stone at her" (John 8:7, NIV). Others disagree, insisting that an upright society must not let those who refuse to live by the law go unpunished. They maintain that even though individuals may find forgiveness for their sins through the blood of Christ, they must still pay for their crimes.

The apostle Paul seems to have accepted the idea of capital punishment as a given factor of society: "If, however, I am guilty of doing anything deserving death, I do not refuse to die. But if the charges brought against me by these Jews are not true, no one has the right to hand me over to them. I appeal to Caesar!" (Acts 25:11, NIV). He voiced his objection not to the death penalty itself but rather to the false accusation and trumped-up charges leveled against him.

Taking another life as a punishment for a criminal offense should never be approached lightly. The idea of "innocent until proven guilty" is probably the best deterrent to using such a sentence recklessly.

B. Murder Is Wrong (Exodus 20:13)

13. Thou shalt not kill.

The sixth commandment is more aptly worded in the New King James Version: "You shall not murder." There are seven Hebrew words for kill, but a different word is used here (ratsach). This word specifically means "to murder."

God wants man to respect all other human life, but obviously there are times when defending oneself or one's family can lead to killing someone. Also, accidental killings, execution of murderers (see Genesis 9:6), and certain wartime military actions require some exemption. Even in these cases, the taking of another life should be viewed with extreme gravity.

C. The Good Shepherd's Role (John 10:10)

10. The thief cometh not, but for to steal, and to kill, and to destroy: I am come that they might have life, and that they might have it more abundantly.

This verse is part of Jesus' comparison of Himself to a good shepherd. Whereas Psalm 23 presents a beautiful metaphor of a sheep admiring his shepherd, John 10:1-15 is a verbal picture of a shepherd's role among his flock. A good shepherd is committed to his sheep, even willing to lay down his life for them. He values his sheep and wants them to have healthy, contented lives. A thief, however, has no respect for the life of the sheep. He sees only the profit he can make for himself. He is reckless and willing to kill.

Is there ever a circumstance in which murder can be justified? What is the difference between murder and self-defense?

III. CHOOSE LIFE (Exodus 1:15-17, 20; Acts 16:27-30)

A. Disobeying Authority to Protect Life (Exodus 1:15-17)

15. And the king of Egypt spake to the Hebrew midwives, of which the name of the one was Shiphrah, and the name of the other Puah:

16. And he said, When ye do the office of a midwife to the Hebrew women, and see them upon the stools; if it be a son, then ye shall kill him: but if it be a daughter, then she shall live.

17. But the midwives feared God, and did not as the king of Egypt commanded them, but saved the men children alive.

While there are situations when the sixth commandment is exempted during wartime service for one's nation, there are also times when civil disobedience to horrendous laws of a nation becomes necessary. The Hebrew midwives in Egypt were ordered by Pharaoh to kill all the Hebrew baby boys at birth. Yet they risked their lives and refused to obey such a terrible edict. No doubt, the midwives were friends, neighbors, and blood kin to the women they served, but the reason the Bible gives for their disobedience to such an evil command was that they feared God. "When we are ordered to act in disobedience to God's Word, we must take a stand to obey God rather than man." (*Life Application Bible*).

It is easy to see why the midwives chose to do what was right and disobey the Pharaoh. However, it is not always a simple matter to make such a decision. We must pray for both the courage and discernment in knowing how to deal with difficult ethical questions.

B. God Rewards Obedience (Exodus 1:20)

20. Therefore God dealt well with the midwives: and the people multiplied, and waxed very mighty.

The midwives lied to Pharaoh or, at best, told him a half-truth. They explained that the Hebrew mothers were so quick to birth their babies that the midwives could not get to them in time to intervene (Exodus 1:19). Some believe that they should have told the complete truth and trusted God for the outcome. Others justify what they did by reasoning that murder is a much more wicked sin than lying. In spite of the midwives' lack of courage to stand up to the Pharaoh and tell him they honored and feared God above the king, God rewarded their obedience to Him in refusing to take the lives of the newborn baby boys.

C. Suicide Is Wrong (Acts 16:27-30)

(Acts 16:29, 30 is not included in the printed text.)

27. And the keeper of the prison awaking out of his sleep, and seeing the prison doors open, he drew out his sword, and would have killed himself, supposing that the prisoners had been fled.

28. But Paul cried with a loud voice, saying, Do thyself no harm: for we are all here.

Fearing that his prisoners had fled after an earthquake, the Philippian jailer thought all hope was lost for himself and prepared to commit suicide. The Roman officials had given him a strict command to carefully guard Paul and Silas and to prevent their escape (Acts 16:23). Paul intervened quickly to stop the man from hurting himself. He was then able to lead the jailer and his entire household to Christ. This story is a perfect example of the desperation that causes most suicides to take place. What those who take their own lives fail to realize is that there is always hope. A ray of light is available to them in Christ Jesus.

The word *suicide* does not occur in either the Old or New Testament. Probably the two most famous Bible characters to kill themselves were Saul and Judas Iscariot. Saul was mentally deranged by the time of his death, and Judas hanged himself out of shame and guilt for betraying Christ. There is little commentary made in either situation, yet the Bible overall is very clear that only God should control one's life—including whether it continues or ceases. Job, even in all his misery, trusted God with the outcome of his existence and made no move to end his own life: "Naked I came from my mother's womb, and naked I will depart. The Lord gave and the Lord has taken away; may the name of the Lord be praised" (Job 1:21, *NIV*).

Suicide is most certainly not God's plan for His creation. We do know, however, that there are mental diseases that make people sick just as there are physical ones. Some people simply cannot be held responsible for their actions. When Saul went to the witch of Endor and asked her conjure up Samuel's spirit, the Lord let the demented king speak with the old prophet. These were Samuel's prophetic words to Saul: "The Lord will hand over both Israel and you to the Philistines, and tomorrow you and your sons will be with me" (1 Samuel 28:19, *NIV*). Did Samuel mean that Saul would be in sheol with the righteous dead? It appears so. Also, David had always refused to harm Saul because he was special in God's sight: "Who can stretch forth his hand against the Lord's anointed, and be guiltless?" (1 Samuel 26:9). Only God can be the judge in situations like this. We are not the arbiters of God's justice. At the same time we should constantly remind those who are troubled and depressed that there is hope in Jesus. There is never a time that God's children are without hope.

Why should we never allow ourselves to even consider suicide as an answer to life's troubles?

REVIEW QUESTIONS

1. In view of Psalm 139, when does life begin—at birth or in the womb?

2. Does the New Testament emphasis on grace and forgiveness negate the necessity of punishment for sins committed?

3. As Christians, how should we view wartime combat situations where death is common? Should we consider this as murder?

4. How should we counsel someone who appears to be contemplating suicide?

GOLDEN TEXT HOMILY

"THOU SHALT NOT KILL" (Exodus 20:13).

The basic foundation for mankind's lifestyle is within the framework of the Ten Commandments. This document was prepared by Jehovah himself and delivered to the children of Israel for the purpose of shaping their community lifestyle.

The Ten Commandments leave no room for debate. God originated them, God wrote them, and God delivered them to the people. They are applicable to both the Jewish and Gentile population. The Commandments cover our responsibilities to God, our parents, and our fellowman.

The sixth Commandment, "Thou shalt not kill," is emphatic concerning a man's responsibility toward his fellowman. It is to respect the God-given life of every person. The fact is, God gives life and God expects to withdraw life. This leaves no room for a man to take another man's life.

Although this commandment was originally given by God to the children of Israel to ensure the protection of human life within the community of Israel, we now recognize it to include not just the Israelites but all mankind. We now clearly understand through the teachings of Christ that God's laws are universal. They must be considered every man's duty to his fellowman, as a part of his responsibility to his Maker. As each individual is God's creature, created in God's image, we are commanded to respect his person, his family, and his possessions.—**Wayne S. Proctor (Retired), Former Pastor, Lexington, Kentucky**

SENTENCE SERMONS

HUMAN LIFE is a precious gift of the Creator.

—Selected

THERE IS NOT ONE LIFE which the Life-giver ever loses out of His sight, not one which sins so that He casts it away, not one which is not so near to Him that whatever touches it touches Him with sorrow or with joy.

—Phillips Brooks

EVERY PERSON'S LIFE is a plan of God.

—Horace Bushnell

NO PERSON is living at his best who is not living at his best spiritually.

—W. Marshall Craig

EVANGELISM APPLICATION

GOD DEMONSTRATED HIS LOVE FOR HUMAN LIFE BY PROVIDING SALVATION THROUGH HIS SON.

A major controversy arose when First Lady Hillary Clinton's book, *It Takes a Village*, was published. Many conservative people were disturbed that this was a thinly disguised promotion for government interference in the raising of children. Their view was that child rearing should be the sole responsibility of parents. Anything else is a threat to the family as God ordained it. The book was viewed as a dangerous omen for parents having authority over what their children should be taught, especially about religion.

In one sense, however, it does "take a village" for children to be raised properly. A society must have law and order, punishment for crimes, and respect for the sacredness of human life in order to survive. And the government is the agent that should enforce this! Otherwise, the children in a society will be the first to suffer. Government intervention in the lives of families to control how they raise their children is senseless if at the same time the general society loses its sense of respect for human life.

ILLUMINATING THE LESSON

Perhaps the greatest Scriptural argument for human life is the 139th psalm. Here David acknowledged that God knew everything about him in intimate detail—his thoughts, his hopes, his fears, his loves—even before he was born.

An interesting aspect of this beautiful psalm is often missed, however. At one point David's train of thought was suddenly interrupted by anger: "If only you would slay the wicked, O God! Away from me, you bloodthirsty men! They speak of you with evil intent; your adversaries misuse your name. Do I not hate those who hate you, O Lord,

and abhor those who rise up against you? I have nothing but hatred for them; I count them my enemies" (Psalm 119:19-22, *NIV*). As if then catching himself, David quickly reverted back to a humble plea: "Search me, O God, and know my heart: try me, and know my thoughts: and see if there be any wicked way in me, and lead me in the way everlasting" (vv. 23, 24).

For a moment David had let himself burn with anger against those who were evil but then quickly realized that only God could judge them. Perhaps he remembered, too, that God had made all these other people and knew them just as intimately as He knew David. The psalmist humbled his heart upon that realization. Should we not do the same? As we struggle to win the fight for sanctity of life, we cannot make progress by hating. To kill an abortionist is taking a life as surely as is abortion. More people will recognize God's divine plan for human life if we demonstrate that plan with humility, prayer, anguish for the loss of innocent lives, and love for all people—even those who perpetrate the slaughter of the unborn. We must pray that God will open their eyes to the truth, for only He can redeem them and turn them from their evil practice.

DAILY BIBLE READINGS

M. Power Over Life and Death.
   Deuteronomy 32:35-43
T. Prayer for Life. Psalm 13:1-6
W. God Values Human Life.
   Jonah 4:1-11
T. God Cares for Human Life.
   Matthew 6:25-34
F. Christ Gives Abundant Life.
   John 10:7-11
S. Eternal Life Is God's Gift.
   1 John 5:9-12

Greed and Excessive Comsumption

Study Text: Matthew 6:19-21; 13:22; Mark 8:34-37; Luke 12:15-21; 1 Timothy 6:17-19

Objective: To see that greed and excessive consumption are selfish and destructive and live free of these evils.

Golden Text: "Take heed, and beware of covetousness: for a man's life consisteth not in the abundance of the things which he possesseth" (Luke 12:15).

Central Truth: The example and teachings of Christ are a rebuke to materialism.

Evangelism Emphasis: A Christlike attitude regarding material possessions will enhance our witness for Christ.

PRINTED TEXT

Luke 12:15. And he said unto them, Take heed, and beware of covetousness: for a man's life consistent not in the abundance of the things which he possesseth.

16. And he spake a parable unto them, saying, The ground of a certain rich man brought forth plentifully:

17. And he thought within himself, saying, What shall I do, because I have no room where to bestow my fruits?

18. And he said, This will I do: I will pull down my barns, and build greater; and there will I bestow all my fruits and my goods.

19. And I will say to my soul, Soul, thou hast much goods laid up for many years; take thine ease, eat, drink, and be merry.

20. But God said unto him, Thou fool, this night thy soul shall be required of thee: then whose shall those things be, which thou hast provided?

21. So is he that layeth up treasure for himself, and is not rich toward God.

Matthew 13:22. He also that received seed among the thorns is he that heareth the word; and the care of this world, and the deceitfulness of riches, choke the word, and he becometh unfruitful.

Mark 8:34. And when he had called the people unto him with his disciples also, he said unto them, Whosoever will come after me, let him deny himself, and take up his cross, and follow me.

35. For whosoever will save his life shall lose it; but whosoever shall lose his life for my sake and the gospel's, the same shall save it.

36. For what shall it profit a man, if he shall gain the whole world, and lose his own soul?

37. Or what shall a man give in exchange for his soul?

Matthew 6:19. Lay not up for yourselves treasures upon earth, where moth and rust doth corrupt, and where thieves break through and steal:

20. But lay up for yourselves treasures in heaven, where neither moth nor rust doth corrupt, and where thieves do not break through nor steal:

21. For where your treasure is, there will your heart be also.

1 Timothy 6:17. Charge them that are rich in this world, that they be not highminded, nor trust in uncertain riches, but in the living God, who giveth us richly all things to enjoy;

18. That they do good, that they be rich in good works, ready to distribute, willing to communicate;

19. Laying up in store for themselves a good foundation against the time to come, that they may lay hold on eternal life.

LESSON OUTLINE

LESSON EXPOSITION

INTRODUCTION

As we come to the close of this millennium, we find that greed is probably the greatest sin overtaking Western society. Never before has there been such luxury and wealth available to the average citizen. Many of the poorest in the United States actually enjoy more amenities than the overwhelming majority of people who ever lived before us. Why? Because so many things we take for granted were not available even to the rich in the past. Until this century no one knew the comforts of central heating and air-conditioning systems or the convenience of electric appliances, air travel, mass communication, and automobiles. Even those of us who judge ourselves to be poor are really quite rich compared to the millions before us who struggled just to survive.

Interestingly, none of these wonderful inventions have brought satisfaction. They have simply created an insatiable desire for more. Greed is nothing but a search in the wrong direction for something that will satisfy. The longings of the human heart cannot be fulfilled with things, yet greed deceives us into thinking they can. "It is precisely when life treats us best that the deepest dissatisfaction arises. As long as we lack worldly happiness, we can deceive ourselves with the 'if only' syndrome: If only I had this or that, I would be happy. But once we have our this and that and are still unhappy, the deception is exposed" (Peter Kreeft, *Heaven, the Heart's Deepest Longing*).

What we are really looking for is God himself. Our hearts long to know Him intimately. The problem is that we lose sight of this and let the things of the world deceive us. We fall prey to temporal values and forget that we are strangers passing through this life. "The only ultimate disaster that can befall us, I have come to realize, is to feel ourselves to be at home on earth. As long as we are aliens, we cannot forget our true homeland" (Malcolm Muggeridge, *Jesus Rediscovered*). It's when we begin to enjoy the pleasures of this life too much that greed then slips in unawares. Soon we are caught in its vicious trap. In this lesson we will examine what God's Word says about earthly possessions and how we should view them. We must remember that God desires to bless us bountifully, but only as we keep a proper balance in our lives.

I. FOOLISHNESS OF GREED (Luke 12:15-21)

A. Watch Out for Greed (Luke 12:15)

15. And he said unto them, Take heed, and beware of covetousness: for a man's life consisteth not in the abundance of the things which he possesseth.

In the verses just prior to verse 15, someone in the crowd had called out to Jesus. He wanted Him to persuade his brother to share the family inheritance. It was not unusual for individuals to make similar requests of a recognized teacher or leader. Problems were frequently brought to teachers and rabbis of the day for a judicial decision. Jesus did not directly answer the man's request. Instead, He used the opportunity to comment on a greater issue—greed. Life is far more important than how much wealth one acquires. The implications go far beyond wealth, however. Possessions can include, power, influence, intelligence, beauty, family heritage, and social class. None

of these in themselves can bring contentment. Only God can satisfy the spiritual longing in every human being.

The man's question about inheritance, however, is not to be taken lightly. The Old Testament spent much time dealing with family estates and the succession of land and property. God is very much concerned about our material needs. Property and wealth are blessings He gives us to manage. We are God's stewards; everything we have belongs to the Lord. We should never put our trust in possessions; we are to trust the Giver, not the gifts.

To love and serve the Lord in poverty is ultimately much better than to have possessions and go the way of the world: "Better the little that the righteous have than the wealth of many wicked" (Psalm 37:16, *NIV*). To acquire the wisdom of the Lord is a much higher goal than riches: "How much better to get wisdom than gold, to choose understanding rather than silver!" (Proverbs 16:16, *NIV*).

B. Parable of the Rich Fool (vv. 16-20)

16. And he spake a parable unto them, saying, The ground of a certain rich man brought forth plentifully:

17. And he thought within himself, saying, What shall I do, because I have no room where to bestow my fruits?

18. And he said, This will I do: I will pull down my barns, and build greater; and there will I bestow all my fruits and my goods.

19. And I will say to my soul, Soul, thou hast much goods laid up for many years; take thine ease, eat, drink, and be merry.

20. But God said unto him, Thou fool, this night thy soul

shall be required of thee: then whose shall those things be, which thou hast provided?

The fact that the man in this story suddenly found himself to be exceedingly wealthy is apparently not the real problem—but that he planned to use it totally for his own selfish pleasure, with complete disregard for others less fortunate than himself. Also he gave no recognition that it was God who so bountifully supplied the increase in the yield of his land. This is also a major problem in our materialistic society today. We are bombarded from every side with advertising pushing us to buy the newer, the bigger, the better. With the creation of these false needs comes the misery of dissatisfaction with the blessings we already have.

The deeper aspect of greed, of course, is that it causes us to forget God. When we take our eyes off Christ, the law of diminishing returns sets in—the more we become absorbed with our possessions, the less time we spend in the Word and seeking to know and do God's will. Material wealth can never satisfy the spiritual longing of the soul. Only as we focus on Christ can we keep a proper perspective concerning wealth and material blessings and find real contentment.

The man in the parable died before he could enjoy the "retirement" funds he was laying up for himself. It is certainly wise for every believer to plan for his later earthly years. This is good stewardship. However, neglecting to provide for one's eternal future and simply accumulating wealth for this life is disastrous. We should always view the blessings of wealth as a means of helping others.

C. Selfish Treasures (Luke 12:21)

21. So is he that layeth up treasure for himself, and is not rich toward God.

Our treasure, of course, is whatever we view as having great worth or value, something we esteem as precious. Some people's treasure is their bank account or an expensive collection of jewels. But for others it is their relationship with God and the salvation of their loved ones. Paul used the term to declare that in Jesus "are hidden all the treasures of wisdom and knowledge" (Colossians 2:3, NIV). Building integrity, honesty, wisdom, and knowledge of God are certainly treasures that will have everlasting value to us. On the other hand, if we put our attentions only on earthly material wealth, we will enter eternity empty-handed. Building godly priorities as our treasures should far outpace our efforts to store up earthly goods.

In a materialistic society what can we do to keep greed from slipping into our lives?

II. DANGER OF MATERIALISM (Matthew 13:22; Mark 8:34-37)

A. Seeds Among Thorns (Matthew 13:22)

22. He also that received seed among the thorns is he that heareth the word; and the care of this world, and the deceitfulness of riches, choke the word, and he becometh unfruitful.

The parable of the four soils illustrates the various conditions people are in when the gospel is presented to them. All three synoptic writers record this story (Matthew 13:3-23; Mark 4:3-20; and Luke 8:4-15). The farmer can do nothing to change the soil he is seeding. The same is true for the gospel sower, but he can nurture any faith that might germinate where the seed falls. In the parable, the first seeds mentioned did not sprout at all but were eaten by birds. The second sprouted quickly on rocky soil but soon died in the hot sun. The third fell among thorns and were eventually choked out by the overwhelming strength of the weeds and thistles that already occupied that portion of ground. Only the seeds that fell on good, fertile soil were able to bring an abundant harvest.

The "seed among thorns" is a simple analogy to understand. Many people willingly receive the gospel but never surrender the things that keep them from fully serving Christ. They see Him as their *Savior* but not as their *Lord*. Pleasures, riches, and concerns for this life "choke out" the real commitment that is required to produce fruit.

Does true Christian commitment require a certain degree of literal poverty? Jesus indicated such when He said, "I tell you the truth, it is hard for a rich man to enter the kingdom of heaven. Again I tell you, it is easier for a camel to go through the eye of a needle than for a rich man to enter the kingdom of God" (Matthew 19:23, 24, *NIV*). Notice that He emphasized His point by repeating and expanding it. However, just a little later in the same discussion with His disciples, He qualified this comment by adding, "With God all things are possible" (Matthew 19:26). Obviously, the deception of wealth can keep a person from putting his priorities on the Kingdom. We must constantly strive to keep our earthly possessions in proper perspective. They are blessings from God to be used for His kingdom, and we must guard against putting our trust in them.

Wealth also often brings a loss of focus on heaven. Those who are poor are often most likely to see their real rewards in the future, while those who are wealthy have a tendency to want to enjoy the benefits of the present. The poor Christian sings, "This world is not my home; I'm just a-passing through," while the affluent may be so attuned to the "pleasures of this life" (Luke 8:14) that their vision becomes "nearsighted," and they may lose their ability to envision the blessings of our eternal home. Jesus proclaimed in the Beatitudes, "Blessed are the poor in spirit, for theirs is the kingdom of heaven" (Matthew 5:3, *NIV*). Philip Yancey, in his book *The Jesus I Never Knew*, delves into this matter with tremendous clarity. He issues a great wake-up call, especially to the American church that languishes in its prosperity.

B. The Cost of Discipleship
 (Mark 8:34-37)

34. And when he had called the people unto him with his disciples also, he said unto them, Whosoever will come after me, let him deny himself, and take up his cross, and follow me.

35. For whosoever will save his life shall lose it; but whosoever shall lose his life for my sake and the gospel's, the same shall save it.

36. For what shall it profit a man, if he shall gain the whole world, and lose his own soul?

37. Or what shall a man give in exchange for his soul?

Jesus said in the Beatitudes, "Blessed are the poor in spirit" (Matthew 5:3). The great cost of discipleship is to forsake all that we have in this life and follow Christ. This does not necessarily mean that we have to give away everything we own to others—but we do have to give it all to Christ. We must be constantly aware that nothing we possess can come close to the value of allowing Christ to live in us. We must also be willing to use all our material possessions to further the Kingdom. We cannot live for self-satisfaction; rather, our goal must be to let Him use us for His glory.

Mark's Gospel was written primarily to an audience that would understand the symbolism of the Roman cross. Anyone hearing the words "take up his cross" would know exactly what was meant. Crucifixion was the cruelest form of execution and was reserved for the most serious criminal offenders. To take up one's cross would certainly mean marching to one's death. In following Christ, then, we must die to our own desires. We may be allowed to enjoy some material success, but we may also have to endure suffering. In either case, we see ourselves as dead to our own wishes and alive to do His will.

What possessions do you have that would be difficult to give up? Have these things been given fully to Christ?

III. TREASURE IN HEAVEN
     (Matthew 6:19-21; 1 Timothy
     6:17-19)

A. Treasures on Earth
   (Matthew 6:19)

19. Lay not up for yourselves treasures upon earth, where moth and rust doth corrupt, and where thieves break through and steal.

Augustine said, "Thou has made us for thyself, and [therefore] our hearts are restless until they find rest in thee" (*Confessions*). He recognized that man's ultimate hunger is for God himself, and nothing else will satisfy that quest. It has frequently been said that there is a "God-shaped vacuum" in the heart of every man, a part of him that longs for fel-

lowship with his Creator. The problem with most people is that they don't understand what their heart really wants, and thus they go after earthly treasures as an ignorant substitute for the real thing.

Earthly treasures—whether material goods, position, power, or influence—will never provide anything but temporary respite in the search for God. There is an interesting mind game one can play that helps prove this: "First imagine what you want. Then imagine getting it all. Finally, imagine having it for eternity. How soon do you think you would grow bored or restless?" (Peter Kreeft, *Heaven, the Heart's Deepest Longing*). Ultimately, having everything this life can provide still leaves the heart empty, searching, and frustrated.

When two of the disciples of John the Baptist came to follow Jesus, He turned and asked them, "What seek ye?" (John 1:38). The *New International Version* of this question is phrased, "What do you want?" What did these men see in Jesus that they had to have? A political savior to rid themselves of the Romans? A superhuman who would provide for their physical needs? A charismatic superstar to hang out with? These were certainly reasons many in the crowds came, but these reasons do not explain these men. The fact that they had already been following John indicates they were searching. They knew there was something eternal and totally satisfying in Jesus. They caught a glimpse of what their hearts were really seeking.

God is the only answer for man's longing. If we try to find satisfaction in anything else, we are doomed to disappointment. Another thought experiment that exemplifies this was described by Augustine: "Imagine God appeared to you and said, 'I'll make a deal with you if you wish. I'll give you anything and everything you ask: pleasure, power, honor, wealth, freedom, even peace of mind and a good conscience. Nothing will be a sin; nothing will be forbidden; and nothing will be impossible for you. You will never be bored and you will never die. Only . . . you shall never see my face." Never seeing God's face makes everything we could accomplish be compared to "chasing after the wind" (Ecclesiastes 6:9, *NIV*).

B. Your Heart Will Be Where Your Treasure Is (Matthew 6:20, 21)

20. But lay up for yourselves treasures in heaven, where neither moth nor rust doth corrupt, and where thieves do not break through nor steal:

21. For where your treasure is, there will your heart be also.

Jesus explained that our first priority should be put on those things that are permanent, cannot be stolen or used up, and can never wear out. We should always be careful to keep a check on our material desires, lest they take control of us. Three verses later in this same text (v. 24) Jesus explained that "No one can serve two masters" (*NIV*). We live in a materialistic world where wealth has become the chief god of the people. They spend all their time trying to collect and store more of it. We should daily check our hearts to make sure we aren't getting caught in this trap. Whatever occupies our thoughts and time is the thing we serve. If Christ and His kingdom are not central to our daily existence, then very quickly we will find ourselves headed for trouble.

Anything that we allow to become a substitute for seeking God ultimately proves to be a "chasing after the wind." We were designed for worship. Either we will worship God with our whole hearts or we will be trapped into worshiping some part of His creation. We are born to feed on God. If we seek nourishment anywhere else, we starve.

C. Commands for Wealthy Christians (1 Timothy 6:17-19)

17. Charge them that are rich in this world, that they be not highminded, nor trust in uncertain riches, but in the living God, who giveth us richly all things to enjoy;

18. That they do good, that they be rich in good works, ready to distribute, willing to communicate;

19. Laying up in store for themselves a good foundation against the time to come, that they may lay hold on eternal life.

There are several potential pitfalls that come with affluence: First, wealth can cause people to view themselves as a power unto themselves. Some apparently forget that they are subject to the same laws that govern everyone else. Second, wealth has a tendency to cause people to want to control others. Third, wealth can give one a false sense of security. Finally, wealth has too frequently caused people to exclude God from their lives.

In his writings to Timothy, Paul gave him advice for some of the problems in the church at Ephesus. Apparently there were well-to-do believers among its membership who had lost their focus on what Christ had done for them. Ephesus was a very prosperous city. Paul did not condemn these Christians for being wealthy; rather he taught them that great responsibilities come with affluence. They must be generous and never arrogant. They must be careful not to trust in their possessions, and they must realize that the only security is in God himself.

What are ways that we can be generous with the prosperity God has given us?

REVIEW QUESTIONS

1. What are the pressures in contemporary life that cause greed to be such a great temptation?

2. In view of the fact that people are living so much longer today, how should Christians prepare financially for their future? Should they put their trust in their retirement savings?

3. American Christians live in unprecedented affluence. How much is this wealth a threat to our dedication to the Lord?

4. How can we learn to "be content" and not let greed overtake us?

GOLDEN TEXT HOMILY

"TAKE HEED, AND BEWARE OF COVETOUSNESS: FOR A MAN'S LIFE CONSISTETH NOT IN THE ABUNDANCE OF THE THINGS WHICH HE POSSESSETH" (Luke 12:15).

The Greek word rendered *covetousness* (*plenoexia*) describes a moral characteristic which is extremely ugly. Perhaps the word *greediness* most nearly expresses its meaning. It is used 10 times in the New Testament in a variety of ways. Christ's warning seems to have these various expressions in view. The Greek text, followed by modern versions, reads, "Be on your guard against greed of every kind" (*New English Bible*).

However, it is clear that, in con-text, Jesus was thinking specifically of greed for money and material things. He was replying to a man in His audience who interrupted the sermon with a request that Jesus would intervene in his quarrel with his brother over the family inheritance. Jesus discerned that this man was so eaten up with greed for more that he could not wait until the conclusion of the service to seek His assistance.

Instead of opening his heart and mind to the pearls of wisdom which were falling from Christ's lips this man was probably thinking, *How can I use this great man for my own material prosperity?*

What are we really thinking about when we settle down in a church service to listen to the preacher? How often and easily our dominant desires and interests will surface during these moments. If we have enthroned the modern gods of pleasure and money in our hearts, we may actually be quietly and secretly worshiping them even in the stillness of the church service.

Jesus warns us that when we enthrone the god of money, we miss out on our true life. In the words of Jeremiah, we "have forsaken . . . the fountain of living waters, and hewed . . . out cisterns, broken cisterns, that can hold no water" (Jeremiah 2:13).—**Noel Brooks, D.D. (Retired), Writer,** *Adult Sunday School Teacher Quarterly,* **International Pentecostal Holiness Church, Bath, England**

SENTENCE SERMONS

THE EXAMPLE and teachings of Christ are a rebuke to materialism.
—**Selected**

NO GAIN satisfies a greedy mind.
—Latin Proverb

EVANGELISM APPLICATION

A CHRISTLIKE ATTITUDE REGARDING MATERIAL POSSESSIONS WILL ENHANCE OUR WITNESS FOR CHRIST.

Every good homemaker knows you should never go into a grocery store hungry. The average food bill skyrockets when we walk down the aisles of the supermarket after not eating for hours. The stores are more than willing to take advantage of impulsive shoppers! End-aisle displays and register counters are set up intentionally to entice customers to purchase. Nonessential items glare at us, while staples are scattered in less conspicuous places throughout the store. However, if you go into the market with a specific list of items—and your present hunger satisfied—the "extras" are not nearly so tempting.

That's the way it is with material possessions. To avoid the lure of materialism, we must sit at Christ's table and fill ourselves with Him. The contentment He brings will help us avoid the greed that consumerism promotes, and it will be obvious in our lives when we tell others that Christ satisfies the inner longings of individuals.

ILLUMINATING THE LESSON

Our lesson teaches that we should avoid covetousness. We should seek contentment by putting our greater attention to our relationship with Christ. An ideal picture of this can be found in Paul's letter to the Philippians: "But I rejoiced in the Lord greatly that now at last your care for me has flourished again; though you surely did care, but you lacked opportunity. Not that I speak in regard to need, for I have learned in whatever state I am, to be content: I know how to be abased, and I know how to abound. Everywhere and in all things I have leaned both to be full and to be hungry; both to abound and to suffer need. I can do all things through Christ who strengthens me" (Philippians 4:10-13, *NKJV*).

Several key points help explain Paul's contentment: (1) He rejoiced in the Christian friends he had. Fellowship with other believers gives us a wonderful sense of brotherhood and well-being. (2) He had seen both prosperity and poverty and found them both to have no real bearing on inner security. Neither one made him any more content. (3) He realized that both wealth and poverty were transitory conditions, much like the weather. He saw his various circumstances as having little effect on his purpose in life. (4) He looked to Christ to satisfy his needs—physical, material, and spiritual. Everything he was and had was centered in this relationship. With that in mind, nothing could shake him, and he could be content wherever he was. Greed could not take hold of him.

DAILY BIBLE READINGS

M. Acknowledge God's Blessings. Deuteronomy 8:10-20

T. Righteousness Is Better Than Wealth. Psalm 37:16-25

W. Generosity and Greed Contrasted. Proverbs 28:20-27

T. God Honors Liberality. Acts 10:1-6

F. God Loves a Cheerful Giver. 2 Corinthians 9:6-11

S. False and True Riches. Revelation 3:17-22

God's Love in Race Relations

Study Text: Genesis 5:1, 2; 10:1, 31, 32; Acts 10:34-36; 17:24-31; 1 John 2:9-11; 4:20, 21

Objective: To understand that God created and loves all people, and reject racial prejudice.

Golden Text: "If a man say, I love God, and hateth his brother, he is a liar: for he that loveth not his brother whom he hath seen, how can he love God whom he hath not seen?" (1 John 4:20).

Central Truth: God's love will cause us to love all people.

Evangelism Emphasis: We should love and seek to bring all people to Christ.

PRINTED TEXT

Genesis 5:1. This is the book of the generations of Adam. In the day that God created man, in the likeness of God made he him;

2. Male and female created he them; and blessed them, and called their name Adam, in the day when they were created.

10:1. Now these are the generations of the sons of Noah, Shem, Ham, and Japheth: and unto them were sons born after the flood.

31. These are the sons of Shem, after their families, after their tongues, in their lands, after their nations.

32. These are the families of the sons of Noah, after their generations, in their nations: and by these were the nations divided in the earth after the flood.

Acts 17:24. God that made the world and all things therein, seeing that he is Lord of heaven and earth, dwelleth not in temples made with hands;

25. Neither is worshipped with men's hands, as though he needed any thing, seeing he giveth to all life, and breath, and all things;

26. And hath made of one blood all nations of men for to dwell on all the face of the earth, and hath determined the times before appointed, and the bounds of their habitation;

27. That they should seek the Lord, if haply they might feel after him, and find him, though he be not far from every one of us:

28. For in him we live, and move, and have our being; as certain also of your own poets have said, For we are also his offspring.

29. Forasmuch then as we are the offspring of God, we ought not to think that the Godhead is like unto gold, or silver, or stone, graven by art and man's device.

1 John 2:9. He that saith he is in the light, and hateth his brother, is in darkness even until now.

10. He that loveth his brother

abideth in the light, and there is none occasion of stumbling in him.

11. But he that hateth his brother is in darkness, and walketh in darkness, and knoweth not whither he goeth, because that darkness hath blinded his eyes.

4:20. If a man say, I love God, and hateth his brother, he is a liar: for he that loveth not his brother whom he hath seen, how can he love God whom he hath not seen?

21. And this commandment have we from him, That he who loveth God love his brother also.

DICTIONARY

Shem, Ham and Japheth (Jay-fith)—Genesis 10:1—Sons of Noah

LESSON OUTLINE

I. UNITY OF THE HUMAN RACE
   A. Man's Genealogy
   B. The Generations of Noah
II. GOD'S RELATIONSHIP TO ALL PEOPLE
   A. The Unknown God
   B. Mankind's Role on Earth
III. LOVE FOR ALL COMMANDED
   A. God Does Not Discriminate
   B. Hatred Brings Self-Imposed Blindness
   C. Commanded to Love One's Brother

LESSON EXPOSITION

INTRODUCTION

Our lesson deals first with recognizing that God loves all people and then with realizing that we should put away prejudice. There is really no room in Christ's kingdom for bias of any kind—racial, social, economic, religious, or intellectual.

It is imperative that we understand that all people are the same in the Creator's sight.

God must certainly grieve at the bigotry that can be found on earth but especially that within the church. It should never be among the ranks of the redeemed. The recognition that we are all followers of Christ should be the beginning point for establishing unity. "We are one in having Christ as our Leader and Redeemer. There is no distinction important enough to eclipse that overriding reality in our lives. Whether rich or poor, big or little, pretty or not-too-pretty, president or potwasher, the true sense of our identity in Christ as followers of Him makes us inseperably one" (Joseph M. Stowell, *Following Christ*).

It would be fruitless—and dishonest—to deny that prejudice exists even among Christians. We are prone to think of ourselves as somehow a little better than certain other groups that are somewhat different from ourselves. The body of Christ is a diverse group, comprised of many races, nationalities, cultures, and socio-economic mixes. There is one overriding commonality, however: We are followers of the

Lord Jesus Christ. And when we make Him our central focus, most of our petty prejudices dissipate. The mix of peoples found in the early church often had little in common other than their belief in Christ. Two things in particular made them powerful. First, they recognized that Christ was more important to them than their differences. "As long as they perceived themselves, their direction, and their destiny in terms of following Christ, they perceived themselves on equal footing with each other" (Stowell). They shared the privilege of knowing Him as their Savior. Second, they recognized their need for each other. The persecution they suffered from outside forced them to unity among themselves. The cause of Christ was compelling enough to keep them from fighting each other.

Many of the problems within the contemporary church society might well be the result of its members not loving one another as Christ commanded. We must change our hearts and respect all individuals the same. Otherwise, we will continue to see infighting, prejudice, and ill-will among the people who claim to love God and profess to be followers of Christ.

I. UNITY OF THE HUMAN RACE
(Genesis 5:1, 2; 10:1, 31, 32)

A. Man's Genealogy (5:1, 2)

1. This is the book of the generations of Adam. In the day that God created man, in the likeness of God made he him;

2. Male and female created he them; and blessed them, and called their name Adam, in the day when they were created.

The Bible is replete with genealogies. This one traces Adam's descendants to Noah. Several things come clear here: First, man

was given the name Adam, and from him all races descended, sharing one flesh and one blood. Second, the naming of the man casts God in a father role. The concept that man was created in the likeness of God is reiterated. Third, both male and female were called *Adam* (Genesis 5:2), indicating a sense of equality. God showed no prejudice in His creation. All descendants were and are loved by Him. There is no difference in the importance of individuals by race or gender in His sight.

Since every race of man has this common heritage, we should make sure that we follow the precept that no one is better that anyone else. Some are born with better opportunities culturally, socially, and economically; but we are all made in the likeness to our Creator.

B. The Generations of Noah
(10:1, 31, 32)

10:1. Now these are the generations of the sons of Noah, Shem, Ham, and Japheth: and unto them were sons born after the flood.

31. These are the sons of Shem, after their families, after their tongues, in their lands, after their nations.

32. These are the families of the sons of Noah, after their generations, in their nations: and by these were the nations divided in the earth after the flood.

After the flood the world's population consisted of only one family. Noah, his wife, his three sons, and their wives faced a "brave new world" with God's command to start over. Genesis 10 gives a listing of the peoples that came out of this plan. The nations seen here, if read by their modern names, would be very familiar to us. The descendants of Shem are primarily the Semitic peoples. Those of Ham are generally thought to be the inhabitants of Egypt, Ethiopia, North Africa, and much of the Middle East. Those with Indo-European roots are believed to be descendants of Japheth.

God's judgment of the Flood covered all the world, but so did His blessing after the Flood. God had told Noah and his sons to repopulate the earth (Genesis 9:1), and this is what they did. God is concerned with all peoples; after all, they all come from the same root family. Jesus declared this thought in John 3:16, 17. Just as the Flood was a starting point for re-building the human race, so was Christ's work another starting point for building a new kingdom. This kingdom would not consist of one people group but rather would draw from all peoples and nations.

Do we ever have the right to be selective toward whom we will share the gospel with?

II. GOD'S RELATIONSHIP TO ALL PEOPLE (Acts 17:24-29)

A. The Unknown God (vv. 24, 25)

24. God that made the world and all things therein, seeing that he is Lord of heaven and earth, dwelleth not in temples made with hands;

25. Neither is worshipped with men's hands, as though he needed any thing, seeing he giveth to all life, and breath, and all things.

Paul had come to Athens and was deeply disturbed at the various idols the people were serving there. Likely, what bothered him even more was the fact that this was supposedly a culture of the most educated, the most philosophical, the most intellectual—and yet they were some of the most ignorant. Those who should have been quick to recognize the real God of the universe had closed their eyes to the evidence. Adding to their superstitious ignorance was the fact that they even included an idol to the unknown god—just to be on the safe side.

The incognizance of the Athenian intellectuals was exemplified some six centuries later when the people tried to avoid a terrible epidemic sweeping their way. They took a flock of sheep to the Areopagus and let them wander freely. "Wherever a wandering sheep lay down, it was sacrificed on the nearest altar to appease that god. If no altar was nearby, the people built an altar to an unknown god and sacrificed the sheep on it" (*The Quest Study Bible*).

Paul attempted to witness to the Greek philosophers of the one true God by showing His hand in creation. Athens was described as a city given over to idols (Acts 17:16). These people paid homage to many idols but failed to understand that there truly is only one eternal master creator. They were satisfied with their ignorance, preferring to appease the gods of their own making with sacrifices rather than to come to an understanding of the real Divinity. They fit the description Paul later wrote to Timothy: ". . . always learning but never able to acknowledge the truth" (2 Timothy 3:7, *NIV*).

B. Mankind's Role on Earth (vv. 26-29)

26. And hath made of one blood all nations of men for to dwell on all the face of the earth, and hath determined the times before appointed, and the bounds of their habitation;

27. That they should seek the Lord, if haply they might feel after him, and find him, though he be

not far from every one of us:

28. For in him we live, and move, and have our being; as certain also of your own poets have said, For we are also his offspring.

29. Forasmuch then as we are the offspring of God, we ought not to think that the Godhead is like unto gold, or silver, or stone, graven by art and man's device.

Paul proclaimed that the one true God had made all nations and people from one common ancestor. Most readers overlook what Paul was saying here, showing more interest in the fact that he was carrying on an intellectual exercise with the Athenian elite. In reality he was describing the role of mankind on this earth. Man was created for fellowship and communion with his maker. Unlike any of the other creatures God created, man has a likeness to God. He is created in God's image. It is God's plan to draw men into fellowship with Himself. What Paul intended to show was that a redeemer—Jesus—had been sent to bring this about. Man is not only to have fellowship with God, but he is also to glorify God with all he does.

If we are all descendants of one man, Adam, do we have any reason for seeing one of our "kindred" as less than ourselves?

III. LOVE FOR ALL COMMAND-
    ED (Acts 10:34-36; 1 John 2:9-
    11; 4:20, 21)

A. God Does Not Discriminate
    (Acts 10:34-36)

(Acts 10:34-36 is not included in the printed text.)

The story of Cornelius, a Roman centurion, coming into the church is a turning point in the Book of Acts. It was also a breakthrough in

race relations. If ever a people had discriminated against other races, the Jews had. Their position as God's chosen people had brought on a pride that caused them to look at everyone else as beneath them.

Gentile is a term the Jews used to refer to all other people not of the Jewish race. It was not a word used in a complimentary sense. In early Jewish history non-Jews had been treated well by the Israelites. Marriages to Gentile women were frequent—including Rahab, Ruth, and Bathsheba. However, after captivity in Babylon intermarriage with other races was vigorously discouraged, and an extreme hostility developed toward Gentiles. Anyone outside of Judaism was despised, and contact with foreigners was avoided completely if possible.

Obedient to his heavenly vision, Peter accompanied the three men sent by Cornelius back to Cornelius' house, where a group of Gentiles awaited his arrival to hear him preach the gospel message. When the Holy Spirit was poured out on them, the apostle saw for the first time how much God also loved other peoples. He came to realize this also because of the extraordinary circumstances by which he and Cornelius were brought together. A reading of Acts 10 makes it absolutely clear that God was using these two men to establish a oneness of races in His church.

It is interesting to note that God used Peter to bring about this fusion of peoples. A look at the personalities in the early church would perhaps lead us to conclude that a more likely choice would have been Philip. The story of his sharing the gospel with the Samaritans and with the Ethiopian eunuch (Acts 8) portrays him as having no problems at all with race relations. God chose to use Peter, however. Apparently a wall had to be broken in Peter's heart for the church to go forward. We can speculate that Peter would probably have been one of the first to oppose bringing Gentiles into the church if he had not had to confront the issue firsthand.

Many centuries earlier God had charged the Jews to stay away from the heathen practices of other peoples, especially idolatry. His concern for moral purity was later turned into a racial hatred by the people. We must be careful to avoid the same pitfall today. We are certainly charged to maintain the integrity of the gospel, but we must not turn this into an attitude of spiritual elitism.

God saw Cornelius in a totally different light from how the Jews viewed him. Cornelius was devout, generous, a man of prayer whose prayers were heard by God, declared as "clean" by God (Acts 10:2, 4, 15), and worthy of a visit from Peter. God wanted the early church leaders to recognize that when Jesus had said "whosoever believeth" (John 3:16), He had meant just that.

B. Hatred Brings Self-Imposed Blindness (1 John 2:9-11)

9. He that saith he is in the light, and hateth his brother, is in darkness even until now.

10. He that loveth his brother abideth in the light, and there is none occasion of stumbling in him.

11. But he that hateth his brother is in darkness, and walketh in darkness, and knoweth not whither he goeth, because that darkness hath blinded his eyes.

The apostle John was writing to a second generation of believers. He wanted to give them confidence and assurance of their faith in Christ. However, along the way he presented several hard truths to make sure his readers knew the real meaning of following Christ.

One such truth is that a person is only fooling himself if he thinks he can harbor hatred against someone else and still be in God's will.

How do we deal then with people who annoy us? Who hurt us? How do we love those whose personalities grate on us? Obviously there will always be individuals we do not personally like. However, love is not a matter of what we feel but rather how we choose to act. We must choose to treat them well, show them respect, be concerned for their needs—even if we do not feel any affection toward them.

C. Commanded to Love One's Brother (1 John 4:20, 21)

20. If a man say, I love God, and hateth his brother, he is a liar: for he that loveth not his brother whom he hath seen, how can he love God whom he hath not seen?

21. And this commandment have we from him, That he who loveth God love his brother also.

It is easy to say we love God. It is much harder to prove we love Him by loving those around us. Yet this is the way we must show our affection toward Him. As Christians we are a part of a large family of believers. God himself determines who is in His family. We cannot afford to pick those we would prefer to be a part of God's family and love only them. We must accept our family members, whoever they are, and love them as God commanded.

Can we disagree with others and still love them? Is there truth to the admonition to "love the sinner but hate the sin"?

REVIEW QUESTIONS

1. How can the church lead the

way in healing the wounds of racism? Does your church show prejudice? Do you harbor prejudice?

2. Why did God choose Peter as the catalyst for removing racial barriers in the early church?

3. How well do you treat other members of the Christian family whom you do not personally like?

4. Is it possible to harbor hatred toward another person and still be a follower of Christ?

GOLDEN TEXT HOMILY

"IF A MAN SAY, I LOVE GOD, AND HATETH HIS BROTHER, HE IS A LIAR: FOR HE THAT LOVETH NOT HIS BROTHER WHOM HE HATH SEEN, HOW CAN HE LOVE GOD WHOM HE HATH NOT SEEN?" (1 John 4:20).

God's Word does not pull any punches. He tells it like it is. We must remember that here He is speaking of *agape* love, that spiritual love that is not based on human feelings or emotions, that does not take into account the words or actions, the race or color, the education or the ignorance of the one loved. It has to be God-imparted and become an innate part of our being.

It is impossible for a person to love God and hate his brother. The two are just not compatible. I have worked for five decades with four races in over 20 countries and found that racial prejudice is not limited to one race or geographical boundary. We all live and breathe an atmosphere permeated with racial prejudice. To yield ourselves to God and let Him saturate our soul with His divine love is the only escape.

First John 4:20 must go hand in hand with verses 18 and 19. If we do not have this pure love in our heart, we will have a fear of the judgment. Only the love of God can impart this pure love for others.

There is prejudice in all unregenerate people, and the only cure for any person is that divine love which God can impart to the yielded soul.

How can we really love God whom we have not seen? We love Him because of what we know of Him through His Word, by what others tell us about Him, and by the way we have experienced Him in our own life. His Word is His love letter to us.

If you really wish to experience this liberating, exhilarating love of God, just yield yourself without reservation to Him. You will find the greatest freedom imaginable. Do it today.— **William R. McCall, Missionary, Church of God, Cleveland, Tennessee**

SENTENCE SERMONS

GOD'S LOVE will cause us to love all people.

—Selected

PREJUDICE IS the child of ignorance.

—William Hazlitt

GOD PROVED His love on the cross. When Christ hung and bled and died, it was God saying to the world, "I love you."

—Billy Graham

IF MY HEART is right with God, every human being is my neighbor.

—Oswald Chambers

EVANGELISM APPLICATION

WE SHOULD LOVE AND SEEK TO BRING ALL PEOPLE TO CHRIST.

This century has produced many great leaders. Without the MacArthurs, Eisenhowers, Pattons, Roosevelts, and Churchills, the shape of our world might be frightfully different today. These strong men unified their people and armies around a cause. If the soldiers in an army are fighting among themselves, they will soon be destroyed by the enemy. However, if their cause (life, freedom, survival of their nation) is great enough, they will find themselves working together with the others in the army. They will see their common cause more than their differences.

Racial problems dissipate when everyone realizes what their cause is—and who their common enemy is. Our cause is the gospel of Jesus Christ. Our great enemy is Satan and all the wickedness he stands for. A great concern of Jesus just before His death was that we be unified. He prayed, "That all of them may be one, Father, just as you are in me and I am in you. May they also be in us so that the world may believe that you have sent me" (John 17:21, *NIV*). Let's begin today to care for one another, regardless of race or position, and make the cause of Christ more important than any differences between us. "This is not to say that we are not free to discuss, express our opinions, and even disagree. But at the end of the day, nothing of lesser value should divide us; in the context of truth and righteousness, we prize more than anything else the advancement of the gospel, our love for one another, and the unity of the church" (Stowell, *Following Christ*).

ILLUMINATING THE LESSON

Arbitrators are individuals who are skilled at bringing compromise between disagreeing parties. In recent years such individuals have been called in frequently to mediate in strikes between large corporations and their labor unions. Sometimes the arbitrator can be successful in forging contracts that no one would have thought possible, with both sides giving ground where they might never have otherwise.

A similar phenomenon takes place in science. Chemists frequently use a third chemical to combine two others that are otherwise incompatible. This is called a *catalyst*. It causes the two chemicals to become one but never lose their individual makeup. Interestingly, the catalyst never loses its properties either.

Our unity in the church is just like this. We can become one because Christ is our catalyst (and frequently has to be our arbitrator). Many of us would never come together if it were not for Him. We still possess our individual character, personalities, talents, styles, and so forth; yet we can join with others who are not just like ourselves. In the process, Christ remains the same. He bonds us together in unity and oneness.

DAILY BIBLE READINGS

M. Prejudice Punished.
   Numbers 12:1-10
T. Risking Life for Another.
   Jeremiah 38:7-13
W. Share the Gospel With All.
   John 4:1-13
T. Put Away Prejudice.
   Acts 11:1-18
F. Prejudicial Behavior Rebuked.
   Galatians 2:11-14
S. Redeemed From All Nations.
   Revelation 7:9-12